Critical Acclaim for *Sarah Morgan*

"Sarah Morgan's diary will henceforth be linked in value with the diary of Mary B. Chesnut. . . . Miss Morgan's personal feelings and intimate thoughts eclipse even [Chesnut's]. . . . Always, throughout this work, are the inner thoughts, dreams, and conflicts with reality that daily consumed a young lady who, in so many respects, was above the intellect of her times. . . . It is deserving of all the praise, and of all the use, that it will receive."

—*Richmond News Leader*

"The diary of Sarah Morgan, at last available in its complete form, is both a delightful read and an invaluable source for southern, women's, and Civil War history."

—Drew Gilpin Faust,
Annenberg Professor of History,
University of Pennsylvania

"A remarkable diary. . . . As she writes of her hopes, fears, and sadness, Sarah Morgan emerges as an extraordinary person forced to grow up fast in the crucible of the Civil War."

—*The Orlando Sentinel*

"Morgan's diary should rank alongside Mary Chesnut's famous wartime journal as one of the most important personal records of the Civil War. Highly recommended."

—*Library Journal*

"Adds immeasurably to an accurate portrait of life on the Confederate homefront. . . . Intelligent, sensitive, and well educated, [Sarah Morgan] could put into words what her eyes saw and her heart felt. . . . An extraordinary account of how one family responded to the war and suffered the consequences of its decision."

—*The Charleston Post and Courier*

"Sarah's diary evokes the city and the deprivations of war with remarkable clarity and detail."

—*The Memphis Commercial Appeal*

"A remarkable portrait of a family caught in the turmoil of war . . . [but] also, a fascinating portrait of one woman's clear observations on what was happening and why."

—*Richmond Times-Dispatch*

Sarah Morgan:

The Civil War Diary of a Southern Woman

Edited by Charles East

A TOUCHSTONE BOOK
Published by Simon & Schuster
New York   London   Toronto   Sydney   Tokyo   Singapore

TOUCHSTONE
Simon & Schuster Building
Rockefeller Center
1230 Avenue of the Americas
New York, New York 10020

1   3   5   7   9   10   8   6   4   2

Library of Congress Cataloging-in-Publication Data
Dawson, Sarah Morgan, 1842–1909.
[Civil War diary of Sarah Morgan]
Sarah Morgan : the Civil War diary of a southern woman /
edited by Charles East.—1st Touchstone ed.
p.   cm.
Originally published: The Civil War diary of Sarah
Morgan. Athens : University of Georgia Press, © 1991.
"A Touchstone book."
Includes bibliographical references and index.
1. Dawson, Sarah Morgan, 1842–1909—
Diaries.   2. Louisiana—History—Civil War, 1861–1865
—Personal narratives.   3. United States—History—Civil
War, 1861–1865—Personal narratives,
Confederate.   4. Women—Louisiana—Diaries.   I. East,
Charles.   II. Title.
[E605.D28   1992]
973.7'82—dc20   92-21798
[B]   CIP

ISBN 0-671-78503-6

The editor was the recipient of a grant from the Louisiana
Endowment for the Humanities, the state affiliate of the
National Endowment for the Humanities.

Originally published under the title *The Civil War Diary of
Sarah Morgan*.

For Sarah—
and for Rachel and Katie

CONTENTS

Preface | ix

Introduction | xv

Maps and Family Tree | xiii

THE DIARY

Book One | 3

Book Two | 119

Book Three | 187

Book Four | 395

Book Five | 535

Index | 613

PREFACE

MY ACQUAINTANCE with Sarah Morgan goes back more than thirty years, to 1958, when James I. Robertson, Jr., approached me about identifying people and places in the diary he was editing—a Civil War diary kept by a Baton Rouge girl and long out of print in its 1913 edition. Robertson, a student of historian Bell I. Wiley, was teaching at Emory University in Atlanta while completing work on his doctorate and would shortly become editor of *Civil War History*. At the time he wrote me, he was researching the notes for the new Civil War Centennial Edition of *A Confederate Girl's Diary* that Indiana University Press would publish in 1960.

Over the next several months, as I responded to Bud Robertson's queries, I came to know Sarah Morgan and the people who figured in the diary. But I wanted to know more about Sarah, and from the beginning I was intrigued by the fact that the diary had undergone substantial cutting—cuts that were not restored in the Indiana University Press edition, though the editor did briefly quote from some of those passages in his notes to the new edition. Indeed, except for the foreword and the notes, the 1960 edition was a facsimile of the earlier. It retained the introduction written by the first editor, the diarist's son Warrington Dawson, in which he explained that he had "taken no liberties, have made no alterations, but have strictly adhered to my task of transcription, merely omitting here and there passages which deal with matters too personal to merit the interest of the public."

It was not until I sat down with a microfilm copy of the diary provided me by the Duke University Library, first in 1975, when I obtained a copy of the first of the books in which Sarah Morgan kept her diary, then with more concentration in 1987, with the entire diary on the microfilm reader in front of me, that I realized the problems with the

text presented to us by Warrington Dawson. Aside from frequent and
sometimes serious misreadings (in the entry of April 12, 1862, for example, Sarah says that the man who killed her brother Harry in a duel
"is a wanderer now," but the editor reads it "is a murderer now"), I
found a great many passages where the editing crossed the line into
rewriting.

And there was the cutting. Sometimes words or phrases are missing; sometimes sentences; frequently whole entries, or parts of them,
involving several pages of the diary. In a few instances an entry, or
what appears as an entry under a single date, is in fact a composite of
passages from two of Sarah's entries. Here and there throughout the
diary the editor has used the ellipsis to signal an omission, but for every
ellipsis there are perhaps ten, or even twenty, places where a cut has
occurred with nothing to mark it.

When I completed my transcription I discovered that the published
diary amounted to approximately half, a little less than half, of the
original. The editing done by Sarah Morgan's son was not altogether
misguided, though there can be no doubt that the diary suffered at his
hands and that a definitive edition was badly needed. On the other
hand, we should be grateful to Warrington Dawson for recognizing the
importance of the diary and for persuading his mother not to destroy it.

Even in its edited version *A Confederate Girl's Diary* (the title given
it by Dawson or his publisher) was recognized as an important wartime diary. Douglas Southall Freeman, the biographer of Lee, praised
it in his book *The South to Posterity*, and historian E. Merton Coulter
called it "one of the best war diaries relating to the Confederacy." Other
historians—among them Francis Butler Simkins and Mary Elizabeth
Massey, and more recently Anne Firor Scott, George C. Rable, and
Randall C. Jimerson—used the diary in their studies.

Nor did the praise come entirely from historians. In 1955 literary
critic and man of letters Edmund Wilson focused his attention on three
Confederate women and their diaries in an essay for the *New Yorker*,
and Sarah Morgan was one of them. (The other two were Kate Stone,
another Louisiana diarist, and Mary Boykin Chesnut, the most famous
of the women Civil War diarists.) In the essay, which Wilson subsequently brought into his book *Patriotic Gore: Studies in the Literature
of the American Civil War* (1962), he called Sarah "unquestionably a

girl of unusual intelligence and character," and her diary, one "distinguished not only by naturalness and vivacity but by something of a sense of style."

I believe this new edition of the diary, revealing as it does more of her thinking and her thought processes, enhances that perception of her. My own research has confirmed what an extraordinarily good observer she was and how much we may rely on her, not only for an understanding of wartime events in her part of the world, but for a grasp of the life of the times.

I would know less about Sarah Morgan than I do had I not been given access to a number of unpublished sources, among them memoirs written by Sarah's nephew Howell Morgan. Fortunately I kept copies of my correspondence with Professor Robertson in 1958–59 and my research notes dating back to that period. I might also mention that an otherwise insignificant fact of my early life enabled me to visualize life in the Morgan home on Church Street (today Fourth) in Baton Rouge in 1862: as a college student in the mid-1940s I lived for a year in the house that had once stood next to the Morgan home and that had been, before he went away to war, the home of Sarah's brother Gibbes and his wife Lydia Carter Morgan. The two houses—and a third, all in a row—were built at the same time by the same family and were virtually identical.

I have also had the good fortune to become acquainted with Judge Cecil Morgan, dean emeritus of the Tulane University Law School, whose father was a son of Gibbes Morgan and a nephew of Sarah—indeed the nephew who for a time made his home with her. I am deeply grateful for my conversations with Judge Morgan and for the access he gave me to the materials in his collection. It has seemed to me little short of incredible that the gentleman with whom I was talking, still sharp of mind and quick of tongue at ninety-one, was the boy who in 1913 took the photograph of the Morgan home that his cousin Warrington Dawson used in the first edition of *A Confederate Girl's Diary*. Such is the continuity of history!

I am of course grateful to James I. Robertson, Jr., for the opportunity that he gave me to get to know Sarah Morgan. And I am grateful to those who early helped me with my research, especially to Fred G. Benton, Jr., whose foresight and efforts over a period of many years resulted in the preservation of the battlefield at Port Hudson. He shared his knowledge of the Confederate defense of Port Hudson as well as the manuscripts and other documents in his collection, including the useful Halbert E. Paine memoir.

Much of my research was done in the Louisiana and Lower Mississippi Valley Collections in the library at Louisiana State University, and I would like to express my thanks to Faye Phillips, Stone Miller, and Judy Bolton on the staff there. I would also like to acknowledge the assistance of Florence M. Jumonville at the Historic New Orleans Collection, and that of Virginia Smith and Judy Smith in the Louisiana section of the Louisiana State Library. I cannot overpraise the help given me by Gary Ferguson in the reference section of the State Library.

Over the time I was transcribing the diary at the Centroplex Library in Baton Rouge I received a great deal of assistance and—as important—friendly encouragement from the librarians on the staff there, among them Sylvia Walker and Clark Sudduth.

I am grateful to Robert Byrd, curator of manuscripts at Duke University, for making a microfilm copy of the diary available to me over a much longer period than I at first anticipated, and to Linda McCurdy, Pat Webb, and other members of the staff who were so helpful when I visited the Duke campus in the spring of 1990 to complete my research on the diary.

Lewis P. Simpson, who was for many years coeditor of the *Southern Review* and who continues to serve as editor of the Louisiana State University Press's Library of Southern Civilization, was as always helpful and encouraging. Author David Madden kindly gave me access to a group of Morgan papers which were at that time in his possession. Michael F. Howell was helpful in identifying some of the East Feliciana people mentioned in the diary, and Barbara Howell gave me much-needed assistance in reading Sarah Morgan's occasional excursions into French. Historian Arthur W. Bergeron, Jr., was generous with his knowledge of the Civil War in Louisiana, and his *Guide to Louisiana Confederate Military Units* proved to be an invaluable source for me.

I would like to thank H. Parrott Bacot, director of the Anglo-American Art Museum at Louisiana State University, for allowing me to use two of the Adrien Persac paintings from the museum's collections. One of these appears on the dust jacket.

And there are others whose help I gratefully acknowledge: Gregg Potts at the Port Hudson Commemorative Area, Harriet Callahan, Virginia Lobdell Jennings, Irene Reid Morris, Malcolm Cain, H. H. Forrester, Jr., the late John W. Loucks, Evelyn M. Lambert, Eugene Groves, Karen McCaskill, John B. Nolan, Scott Duchein Barton, Todd Valois, Tony Jenkins, Lynn Roundtree, Jean D. Streeter at the Missouri Historical Society, Dr. Norwood Kerr at the Alabama Department of Archives and History, Emily M. Clack, great-granddaughter of Eliza Ann Morgan LaNoue, and Jo Ann and Ed Hackenberg, the present owners of Linwood.

The Louisiana Endowment for the Humanities provided grant funds that enabled me to do research at Duke, and I am most appreciative of their support. I am also grateful to the University of Georgia Press, especially to Malcolm Call, Karen Orchard, Sandra Hudson, and Madelaine Cooke, for their enthusiastic response to the new edition.

Most of all I am grateful to my wife Sarah, whose interest in Sarah Morgan equalled my own, and without whom I would not have been able to complete the project. If it was I who sometimes labored over Sarah Morgan's words as I transcribed her diary, it was the other Sarah who labored over my handwriting as she put the diary on the computer. Indeed, my wife's contribution to this new edition of the diary from beginning to end was substantial.

INTRODUCTION

WHEN SARAH MORGAN BEGAN HER DIARY in the first days of 1862, she was nineteen—she would be twenty at the end of February. The year that had just passed into history had been an eventful one. Early in January of 1861 state troops ordered to Baton Rouge by the governor had seized the United States military post and arsenal. By the end of the month Louisiana, following the lead of South Carolina and other Southern states, had broken away from the Union. The break came after a lopsided vote of the secession convention that met in the House chamber of the State House, only five blocks from the Morgan home.[1] Three months later the two parts of a divided country were at war with each other.

Baton Rouge, like other towns and cities across the South, was swept up in the spirit and passion of the times. Even before the first shot was fired in Charleston harbor, the sounds of fife and drum were heard in the streets of Louisiana's capital as military companies began forming. In the spring and summer of 1861 the young men of the town, among them three of Sarah's brothers, went off to fight in a war that no one foresaw would last four years and take such a dreadful toll in casualties.

But Sarah Morgan, although she was herself caught up in the fever of war, would remember 1861 most of all for the deaths of the two people perhaps closest to her. Sarah's first entry, that of January 10, 1862, in fact looks back at the tragedy that had come to the family in April of the previous year when her brother Harry, about to begin his medical practice, was killed by another young man of the town in a duel that took place in New Orleans. In her second entry, that of January 26,

1. The convention met on January 23 and cast its ballots on January 26. The vote was 113 to 17 in favor of secession.

1862, she recalls the illness and death of her father, Thomas Gibbes Morgan. Judge Morgan, a prominent Baton Rouge attorney who had served as both district judge and district attorney—and in the decade of the 1840s as collector of customs for the port of New Orleans—died on November 14, 1861, in the Morgan home on Church Street where Sarah now sat down with her diary.

Again and again over the next three years she would come back to these two events, one of which—the death of her brother—no doubt reinforced the questions she appears to have already had about Southern society and its code of honor. Clearly her relationship with Harry Morgan was a special one. He was, she says, "the one I loved best of all." It was Harry who encouraged her to read, and Sarah wrote that he "had read every thing, and could converse so well, no wonder every one called him intelligent." As to her father, he was a man of "clear judgement and understanding that has placed him above other men."

The culture that shaped Sarah Morgan's adolescent years was very much the culture described by Bertram Wyatt-Brown in his book *Southern Honor*.[2] In the typical upper-class Southern household the father was the patriarch whose authority embraced his wife and children no less than his servants. The mother's role was a subordinate one: she was expected to be loving and properly submissive to her husband, to raise the children and look after their early education, to occupy the domestic sphere. As Wyatt-Brown observes, Southern women were exalted in part to offset the disadvantages of their secondary status.

Southern fathers loved their daughters (Sarah believed she was her father's favorite) and were very protective of them, but expected them to play the role assigned them. Fathers assumed that their daughters were virgins and that until marriage they would remain so. They would marry and have children; they would define themselves in their mothers' images, which meant they would sacrifice their interests to the good of the men of the household. The sons were encouraged to take their fathers as role models. Manliness was a prime virtue, and the South's code—with its emphasis on courage—decreed that a man defend his honor by dueling to the death if necessary. Long after the

2. *Southern Honor: Ethics and Behavior in the Old South* (New York, 1982), 117–48. See also Anne Firor Scott, *The Southern Lady: From Pedestal to Politics, 1830–1930* (Chicago, 1970), 4–44.

practice was challenged, it was defended by many Southerners as the preferred way of settling arguments that might otherwise result in street fighting.[3]

It was a society that aspired to gentility and that prized those things—wealth was one—that gave it power and status. The sons of upper-class Southern families were educated, not infrequently in Northern schools. If they were to be lawyers, they studied the law in their fathers' law offices, as the younger Gibbes Morgan did.[4] Since there was no role for the daughters beyond that of wife and mother, formal schooling for them was not a matter of the same priority, though by the middle of the century voices were being heard in favor of education for women.[5] More often than not, however, education of the daughters was left to the mother or to older sisters.

This was the world into which Sarah was born and which her diary reveals she had already begun to question. If we look for an explanation for her questioning spirit, beyond the vagaries of personality itself, we should not overlook the fact that her father was not born into Southern society but came to it in his young manhood. A native of New Jersey, born at Prospect, his grandfather's estate near Princeton, Thomas Gibbes Morgan grew up in Pennsylvania. He and his brother Morris Morgan settled in Baton Rouge sometime in the 1820s. The brother's marriage to one of the daughters of Colonel Philip Hicky would give him a place in the planter society,[6] and Thomas Gibbes Morgan earned for himself a high standing in the community with his law practice and his successful pursuit of public office.

After the death of his first wife, Eliza Ann McKennan, he married in 1830 Sarah Hunt Fowler, also Northern-born, daughter of a former

3. In Bertram Wyatt-Brown's discussion of dueling he cites the case of James Stith, a Baton Rouge duelist. *Southern Honor*, 360. Stith is mentioned several times in the diary.

4. See document dated March 28, 1857, in Thomas Gibbes Morgan Sr. and Jr. Papers, Manuscript Department, Duke University Library, Durham, N.C. Judge Morgan certifies that Thomas Gibbes Morgan, Jr., "has studied in my office and under my direction upwards of two years."

5. Scott, *The Southern Lady*, 67–71.

6. For the genealogy of the Hicky family, giving dates of birth of Colonel Philip Hicky (1778–1859), his children, and his Morgan and Fowler grandchildren, see Philip Hicky and Family Papers, Louisiana and Lower Mississippi Valley Collections, LSU Libraries. The name is sometimes spelled Hickey. See also Morgan Family Papers, LSU Collections.

officer in the British army, but orphaned at an early age and reared on a Louisiana plantation by her kinsman and guardian George Mather, who was connected to the Hickys by marriage.[7] Thus, the diarist's father, not of the planter class himself, was nevertheless allied with it and moved within its circles. He and his second wife were married at Belle Alliance, the Mather plantation in St. James Parish, and several of their children were born in the old "Hicky house," a home that the Morgans had acquired on a square overlooking the river, the future site of the State House.[8]

The years that Sarah's father lived in New Orleans may also have shaped the character of the family and have had an important influence on Sarah herself. Judge Morgan's job as collector of customs brought him into contact with the mercantile elite of New Orleans. It is no coincidence that many of the New Orleans people Sarah mentions were members of those families: wives or daughters of cotton brokers or commission merchants, if not lawyers. As one of the largest ports in the country, New Orleans looked beyond the South, to the world, and life in the Southern metropolis could only have been broadening.

In trying to explain Sarah's independence and her breadth of vision we must also not overlook her contact with the Baton Rouge arsenal. Insulated as the city was—and it was little more than a small town then— the United States military post and arsenal loomed large in the life of the community, and had since the 1820s. The military post brought Baton Rouge citizens into contact with men from other parts of the country, some of whom married into the community. Judge Morgan's sister Ann, for example, had met and married Captain Thomas Barker at the arsenal. And Sarah's oldest sister, Lavinia, had married Captain Richard C. Drum during the time he was stationed there. Many of the married officers had brought their wives with them. It is clear that a great deal of Baton Rouge's social life in the years before the war centered on the arsenal.[9]

7. Colonel Hicky married George Mather's sister Anna.

8. See Cecil Morgan, "A Profile of My Father, Howell Morgan, 1863–1952," unpublished manuscript in collection of Cecil Morgan. Also see East Baton Rouge Parish land conveyance records.

9. Among the officers who served at the military post was Zachary Taylor. Taylor left Baton Rouge for Washington early in 1849 to assume the presidency.

Undoubtedly Judge Morgan was a major force—perhaps the major force—in Sarah's intellectual development. But in the end the combination of mind and spirit and personality that we see in the diary likely came from within her. "Of my opinions," she wrote, "some I gained from father, some I formed for myself."

Sarah Ida Fowler Morgan, the seventh child and the youngest of four daughters, was born at the Morgan home on Esplanade Avenue on February 28, 1842, during the time that her father was collector for the port of New Orleans.[10] She was eight when the Morgans returned to Baton Rouge in 1850. In that year the legislature met for the first time in the new capital—in the new State House—and Judge Morgan's return was very likely motivated by the prospects of a successful law practice.[11] In any event, the judge seems to have been prosperous if not wealthy—or at least not wealthy in the manner of Colonel Philip Hicky, later described by the judge's youngest son as "a man of great wealth and unbounded hospitality."[12]

The Morgan home in Baton Rouge was a two-story frame house with upstairs and downstairs galleries—not the mansion it has sometimes been referred to as being, but a comfortably large mid-nineteenth century dwelling with outbuildings to accommodate the servants. When the 1860 census was taken, Sarah's father owned eight slaves, all of whom lived on the Church Street property.[13] All of his neighbors on the block were also slaveholders.

In the debate over secession Judge Morgan favored a course that would preserve the Union, and Sarah, who shared that view, would later write in her diary that "there never was a more unnecessary war than this in the beginning." But when the war came the Morgans cast their lot with the majority of their neighbors and became loyal, if not always unquestioning, Confederates. Not long before his death Sarah's

10. The Morgans lived at 191 Esplanade. Miriam was the first of the Morgan children to be born there, in 1840. See Morgan Papers, Duke University.

11. One project that engaged his attention in the 1850s was the annotation of the *Civil Code of Louisiana* and the *Code of Practice in Civil Cases*.

12. James Morris Morgan, *Recollections of a Rebel Reefer* (Boston and New York, 1917), 11.

13. By 1862 there appear to have been nine slaves. See entries of June 1 and August 29, 1862.

father wrote a friend that he regretted not being able to fight alongside his three sons who were serving the Confederacy. "What ever may have been my feelings six months ago—I now feel that we are struggling for existance [*sic*]." [14]

As was frequently the case in this war, there was a division of loyalties within the family. One of Judge Morgan's sons-in-law, Major Richard C. Drum, was a U.S. Army officer now on wartime duty in California. [15] Philip Hicky Morgan, the judge's son by his first marriage, would remain a Unionist and sit out the war in occupied New Orleans.

At the time Sarah began her diary, she and her mother and her sister Miriam occupied the Morgan home on Church Street, together with another sister, Eliza, or Lilly as she was called, Lilly's husband Charles LaNoue, and their five children. The LaNoues had closed their own home and moved into the Morgan home after the death of Judge Morgan. Sarah's brothers Gibbes and George were serving in the army in Virginia. Young Jimmy Morgan, whose career at the United States Naval Academy had been interrupted by the war, was serving as a midshipman in the Confederate Navy.

Sarah had no intimation at the time that within a matter of months the war would come to her doorsteps. The early optimism following the Confederate victory at Manassas had not yet been tempered by the news of those wounded or killed at Shiloh, and there was still talk that the war would be a short one. Sarah and her friends still occupied themselves with buggy rides and strolls on the terraced grounds of the State House. Then came late April and word that a Union fleet under Flag Officer David Farragut had entered the river and had passed the forts guarding the approaches to New Orleans—that New Orleans, the Confederacy's largest city and the key to the Mississippi, had fallen— that Sarah Morgan's town would be next.

The mood of the diary changes as Sarah describes the panic that seized the capital as her brother-in-law and others set fire to the cotton to keep it out of the hands of the Yankees. The first of the Union gunboats to anchor off Baton Rouge reached there on May 7. Farragut himself arrived two days later. Union sailors came ashore and

14. Letter to Henry Marston, June 14, 1861, in Henry Marston and Family Papers, LSU Collections.

15. Drum would later become adjutant general of the United States.

pulled down the Confederate flag that flew over the arsenal. In the same month Union troops under the command of General Thomas Williams occupied the city. From then until the end of the war, except for a period of a few months toward the latter part of 1862 when the Federals evacuated the capital, Baton Rouge was under the control of military authorities. The state itself would remain divided—part Union, part Confederate—with a dual government, one functioning first in Opelousas and then in Shreveport, the other in New Orleans.

In Union-held Baton Rouge, the Morgans came under the shells from the gunboats and more than once fled their home, taking refuge in the nearby countryside or in the building that housed the State Asylum for the Deaf and Blind. In early August, warned that a Confederate army was marching on the city, they crossed the river and sought refuge with their friends among the West Baton Rouge planters. There Sarah witnessed the end of the *Arkansas*, the ironclad ram that had blazed its way past the Federal fleet at Vicksburg and that had been sent to engage the gunboats at Baton Rouge while the Confederate army was attacking.

General Williams was killed in the battle of August 5, 1862, but the Union army remained in control of the city. After a few days the Morgans made their way to Linwood, the Carter plantation in East Feliciana Parish, twenty miles to the north of Baton Rouge and only five miles from Port Hudson, where the Confederates would soon fortify the bluffs overlooking the river. The siege of Port Hudson in the spring and summer of 1863 would in fact be one of the most important military operations of the war in Louisiana.[16]

Much of the diary covers the months Sarah and Miriam spent at Linwood, largely happy ones for the diarist despite the fears and uncertainties that hung over them and the injuries she suffered in an accident that temporarily left her an invalid. Meanwhile, her mother and her sister Lilly, with Lilly's five children and some of the Morgan servants, endured privation and hardships in the nearby town of Clinton. But as a Union army under General Nathaniel P. Banks converged on Port Hudson in the spring of 1863, Sarah, her mother, and Miriam

16. See Lawrence Lee Hewitt, *Port Hudson, Confederate Bastion on the Mississippi* (Baton Rouge, 1987), and David C. Edmonds, *The Guns of Port Hudson*, 2 vols. (Lafayette, La., 1983, 1984).

fled once again—this time to the north shore of Lake Pontchartrain, and from there into New Orleans, which, like Baton Rouge, was an occupied city. There they came to light finally in the home of Sarah's oldest brother—her half brother, Judge Philip Hicky Morgan.

Sarah was in New Orleans when the news came of the death of her brothers Gibbes and George. She was there when the war ended, and there the fifth book of her diary ends, in June of 1865. (In July she began another, the last of the six books in which she wrote, but it does not seem to belong with the wartime diary, as I will explain.)

THE WAR that Sarah Morgan sees and enables us to see is in a far corner of the Confederacy. Baton Rouge, though the state's capital, with a population in 1860 of less than 6,000 (about the size of Fredericksburg, Virginia), is no Richmond. Her cast of characters will include, not Jefferson Davis or Lee or the Davis cabinet, but the future wartime governor, the men of the *Arkansas*, the general in command of the Confederate stronghold at Port Hudson, the captains, colonels, and privates who while away their evenings at Linwood in the weeks before the coming battle. And of course planters and their wives—and the refugees who had fled their homes in Baton Rouge and New Orleans in order to live within the Confederacy. But what we also see is Sarah herself: one woman's spirit and courage, and occasional despair, as she lives through a time of turbulence and crisis.

There can be no doubt that Sarah Morgan's diary is one of the important diaries of a war that produced a great many of the genre, and I believe its significance first of all lies in the character and force of personality of the diarist. Sarah Morgan compels our attention. In some respects she is exactly who we expected her to be—the young girl wearing the Confederate flag on her bosom, lamenting (as many Southern women did) her inability to take an active part in the fighting. But in many others she is her own person: intelligent, proud, sure of her *place* but unsure of her *self*, fiercely independent. Above all, she is blessed with an observant eye and that most wonderful and indispensable thing for a diarist, a questioning nature.

Meeting Colonel Henry Watkins Allen for the first time—Allen is a war hero and will shortly become governor of Confederate Louisiana— she thinks: "My friend, I know nothing of your history or tastes; but if you are not vicious, then I shall no longer believe in intuitive aversion."

When others in the family are reluctant to send food and bandages to a wounded Union officer for fear of reprisals from the townspeople, she stands squarely for an act of kindness. "Mob shall never govern my opinions, or tell me how much I may be allowed to do. I will do what Conscience alone dictates." She soon learns that it is not so simple; there are others—for instance, her brother-in-law Charles LaNoue— to consider. Meanwhile, Northern soldiers lie dying in a hospital within a block of her. "If I could help these dying men! Yet it is as impossible as though I was a chained bear. I cant put out my hand. . . . Die, poor men, without a woman's hand to close your eyes! We women are too *patriotic* to help you!"

In the early entries of the diary at least, she can find as much to praise about the men of the occupying army as she can about her own people, and the humanity with which she embraces the women of the North, mothers and sisters and daughters of the men fighting her brothers, is remarkable. But as the war drags on, and especially after she sees for herself the damage done to the Morgan home, she thinks of Union soldiers only as enemies. "This is a dreadful war," she writes, "to make even the hearts of women so bitter!"

Later she says: "I confess my self a rebel, body and soul. *Confess?* I glory in it!" On one level she is identifying herself as a loyal Southerner—not, to be sure, one of the noisy "Patriot women" she despises— but her diary makes unmistakably clear that she was a rebel in other ways that mattered.

It is what she was rebelling against that makes her so interesting and so important: for one thing, the hypocrisies and tyranny of the society she had grown up in; the restraints imposed on her as a woman; in general, ignorance and stupidity, and—yes—bad manners. Again and again she voices her contempt for the role she is expected to play: the adoring and submissive wife, the loving and attentive mother. At one point she dreams of living out her life far away in a quiet cottage with a sign over the door that says "No gentlemen or children admitted." Her words seem to resound all the more when we recall her age when she wrote them.

"Abandon your past!" she advises women. She wants no man for her "lord and master."

It is not only the war that has caused her to question the inequities and injustices of a society that says it is the men who will go into battle, though the cry "If I was only a man—!" runs like a refrain through the entries. If there were a few Southern women in the ranks, she says, "they could set the men an example."

What we are observing are the first stirrings of the feminism we will see later in Sarah's postwar newspaper pieces. "Women who look to marriage as the sole end and object of life," she says, "are those who think less of its duties; while those who see its responsibilities, and feel its solemnity, are those who consider it by no means the only aim and purpose."

"O how I hate to be like other women! To talk in the same dull, empty, simpering round that thousands have trod before!" She regrets having no room "to expand in," "no new part to play." What she wants above all is to redefine herself: "I wish there was a new school for women—I dont exactly know what I want, except that it is something new."

Nowhere does she seem to feel the burden of her womanhood more than in the passage in which she raises questions about why she was denied the education that would have enabled her "to be the equal" of the men whom she most admires for their knowledge and intelligence. "Why was I denied that education? Who is to blame? . . . Have I done myself injustice in my self taught ignorance or has injustice been done to me? Whose is the fault? I cried."

The desire to know is in fact a passion with her. Although Sarah Morgan belonged to the privileged class, by her account she received only ten months of formal education, probably in one of the local girls' academies. She was early taught at home by her mother, but by and large she seems to have educated herself, with a rigorous program of study and reading that is, even as she writes, continuing. Her literary allusions and frequent references to authors or titles suggest that she had read widely, as many other Southern women of her class had: Shakespeare, Cowper, Boswell, Dryden, Moore, Tennyson, Byron, Scott, Dickens, Dumas, Thackeray, Poe, Longfellow, Addison and Pope, Macaulay—the Bible.

She also read some of the popular women writers of the day—for instance, Maria Cummins, one of the "literary domestics" who are the subject of Mary Kelley's study.[17] "It sounds wofully little," Sarah writes,

17. *Private Woman, Public Stage: Literary Domesticity in Nineteenth-Century America* (New York, 1984), 24, 128–29, 313–14.

"but my list of books grows to quite a respectable size, in the course of a year." She seems to have kept a French grammar near her. Like many young women of her class in the antebellum South, particularly in Louisiana, she was fluent in French as well as in English.

Although Sarah chafes under the restraints of a society dominated by men, and at one point writes, "Bondage, woman that I am, I can never stand," she appears to have no serious questions about slavery. She has of course grown up in a family in which black servants are a part of the household, there to light the fires and cook the meals and nurse the children and rouse you from sleep to tell you your father is dying. At the level of children themselves, as Sarah sees them. "Children and servants like me, even if big people dont!"

On the one hand she can praise the blacks for their conduct, while on the other writing: "Wicked as it may seem, I would rather have all I own burned, than in the possession of the negroes." When Anna Badger slaps her black maid Malvina during Sarah's stay at Linwood, the diarist makes a note of it and by inference disapproves of it, but she quickly passes over the incident with the remark that "Mal and I should have sympathized;—only we didn't."

"If Lincoln could spend the grinding season on a plantation," she says in another entry, "he would recall his proclamation." She scoffs at the idea of white cruelty to slaves, and evokes an idyllic picture of smiling black faces. "Poor oppressed devils! . . . Really, some good old Abolitionist is needed here, to tell them how miserable they are."

Only at moments do we perhaps see a countercurrent in Sarah's thinking, as when she makes a passing reference to "the bitterness of slavery" and writes of Tiche's (Tiche is one of the slaves) "burdens." The nightly Bible classes that she holds for some of the Morgan slaves demonstrate only her interest in their salvation, not her doubts about the institution of slavery or her wish to free them. Indeed she records with pride the fact that the Morgan slaves chose to remain with them while five thousand other blacks from the town and neighborhood "followed their Yankee brothers." [18]

Sarah Morgan's racial attitudes should not surprise us—they were very much those of other women of her class across the South. As Eliza-

18. Entry of September 3, 1862. Later at least one of the Morgan slaves, Liddy, left to claim her freedom. See entry of March 14, 1863.

beth Fox-Genovese has pointed out, for slaveholding women slavery "constituted the fabric of their beloved country—the warp and woof of their social position, their personal relations, their very identities."[19] "Our servants too," Sarah writes, "we are loath to part with."

One reason why scholars and others have responded to the diary as they have is obviously that Sarah Morgan has succeeded in evoking the world around her. The story that she has to tell is the oldest ever: the human drama of a family swept up in the turmoil and danger of war, responding to events that are almost beyond their enduring. How will it end? Will the Morgans return to Baton Rouge? Will they make it across the lake to safety in New Orleans? Will Sarah's brothers return safely? As C. Vann Woodward has observed, the appeal of the diary form itself, the genre, is "the freshness and shock of experience immediately recorded, the 'real-life' actuality of subject matter, the spontaneity of perceptions denied knowledge of the future."[20] These the Morgan diary of course has to offer.

One other reason why readers have responded as they have to the diary and why I believe it will continue to be an enduring part of our literature is the writing itself, the way in which Sarah tells her story— the sense of style that Edmund Wilson noted.[21] Unlike Mary Chesnut's wartime entries, which are often quite brief and written in haste—a name here, an observation there, the essentials[22]—Sarah Morgan's are full, many of them running on for pages. This gives her the space to develop the narrative—as she does, for instance, in the scene at Linwood when Will Carter comes riding up to claim his intended bride, who has no intention of marrying him. A scene, by the way, that I think must owe a great deal (in the way it is told) to Sarah's reading.

19. *Within the Plantation Household: Black and White Women of the Old South* (Chapel Hill, 1988), 334.

20. Introduction to *Mary Chesnut's Civil War*, edited by C. Vann Woodward (New Haven, 1981), xvi.

21. *Patriotic Gore: Studies in the Literature of the American Civil War* (New York, 1962), 267.

22. With Mrs. Chesnut, the elaboration and reflection came later. See C. Vann Woodward and Elisabeth Muhlenfeld, *The Private Mary Chesnut: The Unpublished Civil War Diaries* (New York, 1984). I am not trying to disparage Mary Chesnut, merely making a point of comparison. Obviously Mrs. Chesnut's work deserves an important place in our literature.

In other passages, and there are many of them, it is the power of the language as much as the power of the intellect and the humanity of the diary that moves us. Sarah's evocation of the scene as the little party of women rides out into the dark night of Lake Pontchartrain on a schooner bound for New Orleans is one such passage. In other times this would be a midnight excursion, a boat ride. Now, she and the others are saying goodbye to the Confederacy. "We sang Farewell dear land with a slight quaver in our voices, looked at the beautiful starlight shining on the last boundary of our glorious land, and fervently and silently praying, passed out of sight.

"God bless you, all you dear ones we have left in our beloved country! God bless and prosper you, and grant you the victory in the name of Jesus Christ."

Sarah Morgan and Mary Chesnut have a great deal in common other than the fact that both kept wartime diaries. Both were widely read; both had wit and intelligence. Like Mrs. Chesnut, Sarah could be critical of those she encountered—and indeed felt superior to most of them. Two things Sarah lacked were Mary Chesnut's ambition and her love of politics. "What a consolation it is to remember there are no 'Politics' in heaven!" Sarah wrote. She of course moved in a more limited circle than Mrs. Chesnut, and she lacked Mrs. Chesnut's maturity (Mary Chesnut was almost nineteen years older). But Sarah's youth gives her a point of view that is nevertheless refreshing, and her diary is in some respects superior to Mrs. Chesnut's. The book that brought the older woman fame turned out not to be a diary at all, but an elaboration and revision of the much briefer one she had kept, the novelist joining hands with the diarist, as it were.[23]

Drew Gilpin Faust, in her perceptive critique of the new edition of Mary Chesnut's book and the original diary, noted that Mrs. Chesnut "was a woman who criticized, yet remained part of, her world, and her writing therefore reveals both the strengths and weaknesses of her society."[24] The same thing can be said of Sarah Morgan. The manner

23. *A Diary from Dixie, as Written by Mary Boykin Chesnut,* edited by Isabella D. Martin and Myrta Lockett Avary (New York, 1905). The 1949 edition edited by Ben Ames Williams brought Mrs. Chesnut even more attention.

24. "In Search of the Real Mary Chesnut," *Reviews in American History* 10 (March 1982): 57.

of Harry Morgan's death—the duel, that most violent of male ritu-
als—must surely have caused his sister to reexamine the doubts she
seems to have already had about the Southern code of honor if not the
patriarchy. Yet she can still, many entries later, insist that the man she
marries "must be brave as man can be; brave to madness, even."

If Sarah Morgan's diary is an important part of the literature of
the Civil War, one of the most interesting examples of its genre, as I
think it is, it is also important as a look into the mind of a nineteenth-
century woman intellectual. The diary is in fact the story of a young
woman's emotional development—her passage from her first experience of death, the loss of a beloved brother, through adolescent intro-
spection and self-examination to a self-reliance she is not herself aware
of, and finally to a more mature view of life and the realization that
tragedy and grief are the lot of humankind. It is a life's lesson learned
in the most terrible way—compressed into the span of a war instead of
a lifetime.

On one occasion Sarah refers to her diary, perhaps facetiously, as
"this precious autobiography I am at present compiling." The truth is,
the diary did serve an important purpose for her at the time she was
writing it. For one thing, it occupied her time while she waited for the
next turn in the road, the next rumor of an advancing army, the next
letter from her brothers—and, after a while, simply for the war to be
over. As she comes to the end of the first book in which she kept the
diary, she says that it has "proved such a resource to me in these dark
days of trouble that I feel as though I were saying goodbye to an old
and tried friend." Later, at Linwood, she writes: "I would die with out
some means of expressing my feelings in the stirring hour so rapidly
approaching."

Keeping the diary is also, Sarah at one point confesses, an act of defiance, proof "to my own satisfaction that I am no coward." Crossing
the Mississippi River to safety on the eve of the Confederate attack on
Baton Rouge, she writes: "I cross with this book full of Treason." The
diary in fact becomes a part of the story, as real as any character, as
she slips it into her "running bag" or takes it with her on the flight to
Greenwell or leaves the book she has just completed with her sister in
Clinton while she begins another. It is impossible to hold the books of
the diary in one's hands without feeling a sense of history.

I HAD NOT advanced very far into the editing of Sarah Morgan's diary before I discovered that several choices had to be made. One of these was how far to go in maintaining the integrity of the original—whether, for instance, to regularize spelling or punctuation in the interest of readability. The choice I made, and it is one I have felt comfortable with, was to take as few liberties as possible, but to make certain compromises when there seemed to be compelling reasons for doing so. I have, for instance, held to her spelling and spacing of words, even when there are inconsistencies. *Without* alternates with *with out*, *upstairs* with *up stairs*, *every body* with *everybody*, *gunboats* with *gun boats*, to mention only a few examples. Indeed, it was not always easy to tell whether she intended a space or whether the break between letters was a peculiarity of her handwriting.

In a few cases, inconsistencies were introduced by Sarah later when she came back to the diary and corrected some of her spelling—changing *ernest* to *earnest*, for instance, and *sugar cain* to *sugar cane*. I have noted inconsistencies in her spelling of names (*McClelland* for *McClellan*, *Gardener* or *Gardiner* for *Gardner*, *Steadman* alternating with *Steedman*), but have left them as she wrote them.

My principal compromise—and it was made only after I had transcribed much of the diary and seen how it looked, and *read*—was to introduce paragraph indentions. I discovered, or rather rediscovered, for I had encountered this early in my career as an editor, that paragraphs which go on for two or three or more pages bother the reader's eye and dull his senses. On the other hand, many of the paragraph breaks in this new edition are Sarah's, as nearly as I was able to determine them: sometimes she used an indention at the left margin of the page, sometimes she left space in the middle of the line between sentences, occasionally she left space in the line following a sentence, then dropped down to the line below without an indention. All of these signaled to me her sense of a break, and so I used the standard indention, adding indentions of my own when I felt the need for them.

I have also occasionally introduced a comma or removed one, or added some other mark where one was missing, when I felt that the punctuation was needed for the sense of it. Otherwise, the diary appears just as Sarah wrote it. Words that she underlined in the longhand diary are printed in italics; words and phrases in French were not underlined and are not in italics. I have in some cases used [*sic*] to indicate eccentric or incorrect spellings, usually only on the first instance of the spelling. The asides of the editor are also in brackets, as are the page numbers (by book) of the manuscript diary. The page numbers are not Sarah's, but were written in by archivists at Duke University when the diary was accessioned (with the exception of the numbers in Book 5, which were already printed in the ledger when Sarah used it).

Sarah wrote entirely in ink, and in some cases I was able to determine whether her notations between the lines or in the margins of the page were contemporaneous by comparing them with the ink in the original entry. In the places where it seemed clear she had gone back later—perhaps only days or weeks later, but in other cases many years later—to comment or to elaborate, I have placed her afterthought in a footnote. I have not indicated strike-throughs where it seemed obvious to me that the diarist was merely correcting herself as she wrote, rather than going back to reconsider and occasionally to conceal what she had written.

What strikes one first in sitting down with the diary is the economy of the diarist: the small size of the handwriting and the number of words she manages to get onto even the smallest of the pages.[25] But if the writing is small, it is also surprisingly legible, and this, together with Sarah's generally good sense of punctuation—and I might say her use of the period to end a sentence—made the editor's job much easier. Only in the passages toward the back of Book 4, where she attempted to extend the life of the book by resorting to tiny letters over the space of several pages, did the task of transcription become difficult.

I have attempted to identify all of the people and places mentioned in the diary as well as the source of quotations, and to provide information concerning such things as missing pages and excisions (fortunately there are few of either). Where the first reference to a person is not footnoted, I was unable to come up with an identification. I have tried to clarify, and occasionally elaborate on, wartime events referred to by Sarah, especially events that occurred in Louisiana, but I have not attempted to correct all of the false rumors and misinformation which came her way as a natural consequence of her isolated circumstances.

25. The first two books are the smallest, Book 2 being 5 × 8 inches and Book 1 slightly larger. Books 3, 4, and 5 are approximately the same size, ranging from 7½ × 12¼ to 7¾ × 12¾ inches. Book 6 is 6½ × 7¾ inches.

In many cases she eventually corrects these herself, or at least raises a question about them—for instance, in reports of battles fought and victories won in Virginia.

The most difficult of the choices I had to make was whether to include all six of the books in which Sarah kept her diary or the five that cover the wartime years, as Warrington Dawson did in the 1913 edition. As I weighed the arguments for and against each, I was determined to set aside the question of length and space, and I can say in good conscience that I did so. What persuaded me finally was, I suspect, what must have persuaded Warrington Dawson, and that was the wholeness of the first five books and the break that I felt each time I went from the fifth book into the sixth. Only three weeks have passed between entries, but something has happened in those three weeks: Sarah has begun to put the war—or perhaps it is only the weariness and despair of the previous book—behind her.

The sixth book begins with the entry of July 4, 1865. Sarah and her younger brother are at sea on their way to South Carolina, by way of New York, for Jimmy Morgan's wedding to Helen Trenholm, whose father served in the Confederate cabinet.[26] The sixth book of the diary is in fact in many respects a travel book. Sarah tells of the voyage from New Orleans aboard the *Evening Star,* of the several days spent in New York, of the stormy voyage from New York to Charleston, the trip by train and carriage to Columbia, the return trip to Charleston, the wedding, yet another voyage to New York, this time with Jimmy and Helen, and finally a train trip west from New York to Pittsburgh and Chicago, and south, as Sarah, her brother, and her brother's wife make their way to New Orleans. In the third-to-last entry of the book that has survived, that of December 7, 1865, they have boarded a steamboat on the Ohio River at Cairo.

The next entry was written a little over three years later, January 8, 1869. Sarah was then in Philadelphia. It begins by picking up where the diary left off: "What followed?—The gayest winter of my life. I think it was about the 13th [of December, 1865], Wednesday, that Jimmy, Helen and I arrived in New Orleans." The last entry was written in

26. Their older brother Philip Hicky Morgan went with them as far as New York, but did not accompany them to South Carolina. At that time there were no passenger steamers operating between New Orleans and Charleston. Helen's father, George A. Trenholm, was secretary of the treasury.

1871, and is not so much an entry as a brief notation at the bottom of the page on which she had last written two years earlier: "Left Mrs Davidsons yesterday, 19th June, Bay of St. Louis Miss. June 20th 1871."[27]

We know from a notation at the back of the book that there were other entries which were later destroyed. Sarah says the diary continued on to the end of January 1873, when she and her mother were living at Hampton, Wade Hampton's former plantation on the Congaree River near Columbia. We also know from her notations that the sixth book was the one she had the most doubts about keeping—that she in fact left instructions that it be destroyed: "This book must be burned unread. June 9th 1873." But in the year of her death, her son tells us in a note of his own, he persuaded her to countermand the order.

Even with the excisions, the sixth book is interesting, especially so for what it tells us about the Trenholms, about South Carolina in the wake of Sherman, and about rail and ship travel in the 1860s, but in neither spirit nor fact is it a part of the wartime diary that ends in occupied New Orleans.

There was one final choice to be made and that was what to do about the presence, at the end of the fifth book, of four entries which were written there out of sequence. Sarah had already put the book aside and begun another. She had returned from her 1865 travels. Then in the summer and fall of 1866, instead of picking up where she had left off in the sixth of the journals (as she would do in 1869), she went back to the blank pages at the back of the earlier one. There are two short entries: that for June 2 records her concern over the approaching marriage of her sister Miriam to Alcée Louis Dupré—a marriage which we know in retrospect ended unhappily—and that for September 6, in which she is uncharacteristically despondent. "What I have sufferred [sic] since Miriam pledged herself to this," she says in the first of these, "is indescribable."

The third and fourth of the 1866 entries are dated October 16 and October 17 and tell of her fear that another of her brothers—this time Jimmy—will be killed in a duel with a friend, a Colonel Hill,[28] to satisfy

27. Wealthy New Orleanians had summer homes on the bay, which is on the Mississippi Gulf Coast east of New Orleans.

28. Colonel James D. Hill of New Orleans. See biographical sketch in John Smith Kendall, *History of New Orleans* (Chicago and New York, 1922), 3:1117–18.

the South's code of honor. Her brother is determined on satisfaction. "Satisfaction!" Sarah writes. "What a mockery!" In an effort to resolve the matter, she goes to the other man's father. The outcome is in question, but in a note appended thirty years later she reveals that "the duel was never fought." This entry is dated July 25, 1896, and is followed by one written February 3, 1904, and another—the last of the entries in Book 5—dated January 27, 1906.

I have allowed the wartime diary to end where she first ended it, with the entry of June 15, 1865, a few sentences beyond the point where Warrington Dawson ended the 1913 edition of *A Confederate Girl's Diary*. In his introduction Dawson tells us that his mother put the diary away and did not return to it until 1896, when she took the books out of the linen wrapping in which she had kept them, a wrapping made secure by her stitches. The 1896 entry appears to have been written after she finished her reading. "I never knew until a moment ago that this journal ended just here," she says. ". . . I do not know why this volume was laid aside.[29] There is another, which I shall not have the courage to read, I have so cried my heart out to-day for my dead brothers. Thirty two years and a half have passed, and still I can recall the agony . . ."

Presumably it was at this point, or not long after this, that she made some of the alterations that we find—marginal comments, excisions, an occasional correction of spelling.[30] The book that she did not, at that moment, have the courage to read was of course the sixth book, from which she would remove a number of pages. The notation in her handwriting at the back of that book is dated 1896. "I regret having destroyed these half glimpses of the most awful period of my life," she says. "Nothing else would have accounted for the blessedness of my married life, and my adoration of my husband."

29. Above the line, she later added: "Because I was going to South Carolina, for Jimmy's marriage, & wanted a new book."

30. In his introduction to the 1913 edition Warrington Dawson tells of his mother's chance encounter with an unnamed Philadelphian to whom she sent a transcription of portions of the manuscript diary: "It was in due course returned, with cold regrets that the temptation to rearrange it had not been resisted. No Southerner at that time [the Philadelphian said] could possibly have had opinions so just or foresight so clear as those here attributed to a young girl." Dawson says that his mother was "keenly wounded and profoundly discouraged." The manuscript diary vindicates Sarah. No correspondence has been found that confirms the story.

Without more evidence it would be futile to speculate on why those were bad years for her and what it was that brought her to the point of destroying some of the pages of the diary. Possibly it was the economic hard times of those postwar years, the condition of her health (never good), the burden of attending her aging mother, the reality of spinsterhood, or her obvious distress over the marriage of her sister Miriam. Perhaps there was an unhappy romance. But none of these things can be documented.[31] What we know is that the young woman who wrote this extraordinary diary never returned to Baton Rouge to live,[32] but instead stayed on in New Orleans for a time after the war and then made a new life for herself in South Carolina.

JAMES MORGAN'S WIFE Helen died in childbirth in 1866, less than a year after their marriage. Briefly he joined his mother and Sarah in New Orleans before returning to South Carolina. In the spring of 1872 the two women went to live with him at Hampton plantation after his tour of duty in Egypt as one of a small group of American officers in the Khedive's army. Sarah took her young nephew Howell Morgan, Gibbes's son, with her, planning to educate him and adopt him—plans that were to materialize only partially, though he remained with her for more than three years.[33]

---

31. Sarah's future husband does mention in an 1873 letter that he has been told there was a "quasi-engagement" between her and a Colonel Hill, obviously the same Colonel Hill who was a friend of her brother Jimmy. See F. W. Dawson to Sarah Morgan, January 19, 1873, F. W. Dawson Papers, Duke University. And in the 1866 entry in Book 5 of the diary, Sarah says that Colonel Hill was the man her family wished her to marry. But there is nothing that connects him to the period of unhappiness she mentions.

32. After James Morgan's return to Baton Rouge in 1874 for his mother's funeral, he wrote F. W. Dawson that the Morgan home "is in a general state of delapidation and will not bring more that [sic] $1000 to $1200—the town is perfectly dead." Letter dated March 31, 1874, Dawson Papers, Duke University.

33. Later, after the death of her husband, Sarah asked her nephew to come back and make his home with her while he completed his education, and he returned for a period of a year or more. Howell Morgan's deep affection for his aunt is apparent in an unpublished memoir written in the last years of his life. "Young as I was . . . I realized that I was in contact with the most brilliant mind I had met," he wrote, "and she was certainly the best read woman of her age I have known even to this day." Manuscript in Sarah Morgan Dawson and Family Papers, LSU Collections.

It was while Sarah was living at Hampton that she met Francis Warrington Dawson, who had come up from Charleston to visit her brother.
Dawson, born Austin John Reeks, was in the process of becoming one
of the most important of the late nineteenth-century Southern editors,
a commanding figure in South Carolina.[34] A native of England, he had
come to America to fight for the Confederacy (it was at this point that
he changed his name, in order not to disgrace his family), and in the
years after the war had become editor and co-owner of the Charleston *News*. In 1873 he and his partner B. R. Riordan would acquire the
Courier and merge it with their paper to found the *News and Courier*.
Frank Dawson was obviously the kind of man Sarah had in mind
years earlier when she speculated on who she might marry.[35] He must
be intelligent—"I place that first." He must be a gentleman and a "man
of the world," he must have "a sense of honor," and he should have a
profession. Dawson met all of those qualifications. More than that, he
seems to have been deeply in love with her. The letters dispatched from
the editor in Charleston to Sarah Morgan on the plantation or at White
Sulphur Springs over the spring, summer, and fall of 1873—and there
are a great many of them—testify to his determination to win her.[36]
Dawson's first wife had died only the December before, and the propriety of a marriage so soon after appears to have been at least part,
though not all, of Sarah's reluctance to make a commitment. It is likely
that the old response to male attention that we see again and again in
the diary—the impulse to withdraw when pressed—was still with her.
At one point she wrote him that his love was a "misfortune" for her,
that he only loved her because of the "insuperable difficulty" of winning her.[37] However, Dawson persisted, and on January 27, 1874, they
were married at the Gadsden home in Charleston where Sarah and her
mother had been living since James Morgan's second marriage.

34. See E. Culpepper Clark, *Francis Warrington Dawson and the Politics of Restoration,
1874–1889* (University, Ala., 1980). There are brief biographies of Dawson in the *Dictionary of American Biography* and *The National Cyclopaedia of American Biography*. A
biographical sketch of Sarah appears in the latter source (vol. 23, pp. 300–301).

35. See entry of May 6, 1862.

36. See Dawson Papers, Duke University.

37. Letter dated June 25, 1873, Dawson Papers.

The year before her marriáge marked an important turn for Sarah. Over that time, at Frank Dawson's invitation and encouragement, she wrote a number of pieces for the *News* and later for the *News and Courier* for which the newspapers paid her. The income her writing would provide was very likely not the only motive for pursuing a career in writing, but it appears to have been a major one. "You know, 'no song, no supper!' " she replied when Dawson wrote that he feared she would stop writing.[38]

Sarah's fears about how she might earn a living for herself surface more than once in the wartime diary. The death of her father and one of her brothers and the absence of her other brothers forced her to think about the future, to be less dependent. It is doubtful, however, that the thought of writing for a newspaper would have then occurred to her. Journalism, along with almost everything else except teaching, was a man's profession. The woman's place was in the home. *Her* profession, as she was so often reminded, was wife and mother.

That Sarah began to write for his newspaper at Dawson's insistence and over her own strong doubts is suggested by the surviving correspondence. The first of these pieces, "The New Andromeda," appeared on the editorial page of the *News* in its March 5, 1873, issue. In it she compared the suffering of Louisiana under Reconstruction to the fate of the legendary Andromeda. "The Use and Abuse of Widows," the first of the pieces in which she commented on social customs and relationships, was published a few days later.[39] "Your paper on Widows is the best article from an inexperienced writer which has passed through my hands," Dawson wrote her. "I pledge my word, as a gentlemen, that my judgment is not biased by any feeling for you."[40]

There then followed "editorials" on old maids, on mothers-in-law, on bachelors and widowers, criticism disguised as humorous comment on the hypocrisy inherent in societal relationships and customs. Old maidhood (and here Sarah of course wrote from personal experience) was "the dreaded limbo" of women. "An infinite number of foolish virgins," she said, "prefer marrying men unworthy of a good woman's

38. Letter dated August 8, 1873, Dawson Papers.

39. March 10, 1873.

40. Letter quoted by S. Frank Logan in "Francis W. Dawson, 1840–1889: South Carolina Editor" (M.A. thesis, Duke University, 1947), 101.

respect to facing the jibes and sneers of their mating and mated asso-
ciates."[41] In another of the pieces she suggested that a tax be imposed
"on derelict Bachelors and Widowers, to be devoted to the support of
Old Maids and unenterprising Widows."[42]

In the early weeks some of the topics apparently were suggested by
Dawson or his partner, though it is clear that Sarah was shortly given
the freedom to write what pleased her. In "Young Couples," the piece
written for the March 29 issue, she turned her attention to the role
and status of women. "Man is unquestionably a tyrant," she wrote, an
attack on the patriarchy that she softened by adding, "but woman was
made for him. Consequently reasonable submission is a duty." And
she challenged the "article of belief" that marriage is the sole end for
which woman was created: "Marriage is *not* the end of woman!" In
another of the pieces she praised the North for its efforts to open a
wider field of work for women, and wrote that "the most modest and
retiring may hail the promise of a day when the equality of the sexes
will be established on the true basis of equal remuneration for equal
services."[43]

Her access to the editorial columns of a major Southern newspaper
was highly unusual for that time, and the series that she wrote over the
spring and summer of 1873 even more so. By fall she had gotten even
bolder. "There is good reason," she wrote, "for the prejudice against
learned women. Man was by nature intended for her sovereign. What
becomes of a sovereign when his subjects not only suspect, but know,
that he is unfit to dictate to them?" Mental equality, she added, "or
perhaps a shade of superiority, is a crime never pardoned."[44]

The series leaves no doubt that Sarah Morgan Dawson, despite her
strongly voiced antipathy to the women's righters and their cries for
the right to vote[45]—something she was not ready to accept—was one
of the nineteenth-century feminists. On the other hand, Sarah never
reached the point of abandoning the society of which she was a part,
or the system she was criticizing. It never occurred to her that she was

41. "Old Maids," Charleston *Daily News*, March 15, 1873, p. 2.
42. "Bachelors and Widowers," Charleston *Daily News*, March 22, 1873, p. 2.
43. "Work for Women," *News and Courier*, April 15, 1873, p. 2.
44. "The Natural History of Women," *News and Courier*, September 20, 1873, p. 2.
45. "Suffrage-Shrieking," *News and Courier*, May 20, 1873, p. 2.

anything but one of "The Aristocrats," "The Proud Morgans," or that there were not—and ought not to be—such distinctions.

The author of one scholarly study sees her as an example of the Southern woman who combined Southernism and feminism to make the transition into the new order. "She joined the forces trying to improve woman's lot while maintaining her home and family as the center of her life."[46] I would argue that notwithstanding the strong feminist impulses within her, Sarah never joined the forces of the women's rights movement, but remained the independent she always was. The conflict between her feminism and her commitment to the old order was never resolved.

Even in the year that she was speaking out for a new role and new opportunities for women (pieces which were published anonymously), she was also writing columns from White Sulphur Springs—the lady reporting on the latest fashions and the new arrivals at the springs while partaking of the waters, and the society, herself.[47] She continued to write book reviews, and occasionally editorials, for her husband's newspaper after their marriage, but her career as a professional journalist had essentially ended. From 1874 on, certainly from 1875 on, she devoted most of her energies to being a wife and mother.

As a matter of fact, the choice was made once she decided to marry the Roman Catholic Frank Dawson. Their first child, Ethel, was born late in 1874, ten months after their marriage, and much of their married life was marked by a series of births and miscarriages. Warrington was born in 1878, and their second son, Philip Hicky Dawson, three years later. The baby's death at five months deeply grieved the family.

Warrington Dawson wrote that his father "rarely if ever took a decisive step in his public career without first requesting her opinion,"[48] and Sarah does appear to have been a force in her husband's thinking and his editorship of the newspaper. An editorial that he wrote in 1879, in which he argued that equal pay for equal work was "simple

46. Charlotte Telford Breed, "Sarah Morgan Dawson: From Confederate Girl to New Woman" (M.A. thesis, Duke University, 1981), 86.

47. These pieces, the first of them published June 26, 1873, were signed *Feu Follet* (Will-o'-the-wisp).

48. Warrington Dawson transcription, Dawson Papers, quoted in Mary Katherine Davis, "Sarah Morgan Dawson: A Renunciation of Southern Society" (M.A. thesis, University of North Carolina, Chapel Hill, 1970), 54.

justice,"[49] echoes the views she had expressed earlier on the same subject, and although he appears to have been independently opposed to dueling (he was twice challenged himself, but refused both challenges), his wife's feelings on the subject must surely have influenced him in the campaign against the practice that he launched in the 1880s. The result was a law that brought an end to the duel in South Carolina.

In his career as editor of the *News and Courier* Frank Dawson proved himself a man of courage and conviction, like Henry Grady an outspoken advocate of a forward-looking New South, and a foe of corruption in government. In his sketch of Dawson written for the *Library of Southern Literature*, his friend J. C. Hemphill wrote: "For years he was the controlling spirit in the political life of South Carolina."[50]

Marriage to the Charleston editor apparently provided the intellectual stimulation that Sarah required, and gave her the opportunity to travel abroad as well as in her own country. At home in Charleston, she entertained in the mansion they occupied at 99 Bull Street. But the marriage was to end tragically when Dawson was shot to death on March 12, 1889, in an encounter with a Charleston physician—an encounter provoked by the complaint of the Dawsons' governess that the doctor was pressing his attentions on her.[51] At the age of forty-seven Sarah Morgan Dawson found herself a widow with two children.

Acquittal of her husband's murderer embittered her, as did the long struggle over finances with General Rudolph Siegling, the banker who had been Dawson's partner. She did not feel that she was being treated equitably in the settlement of his estate, and in an angry barrage of letters to friends and stockholders she struck out at South Carolina in general and Charleston in particular as well as the ungentlemanly—and dishonest, she thought—partner.[52]

In researching his 1947 study on Dawson, Frank Logan interviewed

49. See Clark, *Dawson and the Politics of Restoration*, 103.

50. Vol. 3, p. 1372.

51. Dawson went to the doctor's home to take the matter up with him. In a note appended to Book 6 of her diary, Sarah wrote that her husband died "in the defense of a helpless woman." The trial of Dr. Thomas B. McDow for murder ended in his acquittal—a verdict widely condemned in the press. For an account of the murder and the trial that followed, see Clark, *Dawson and the Politics of Restoration*, 215–29.

52. Clark, *Dawson and the Politics of Restoration*, 229–30.

a Charleston woman who remembered Sarah Morgan Dawson from this period. She recalled Sarah as "a delicate, charming, and very intellectual person with a distinctive 'air' about her."[53] The writer Grace King has given us an even more vivid picture of her. She recalled seeing her for the first time on a mountaintop in North Carolina, walking with her son, "a lady clad in the long, clinging skirts of black then in fashion." Sarah was in mourning. "She knew no one, no one spoke to her; the men raised their hats, she bowed graciously and passed on, pale, silent. . . . She had been sent to the mountains in search of health, and she did not seem to care if she lost or found it."[54]

Sarah's mother had died in 1874, not long after her marriage to Frank Dawson, and in 1898 she suffered a painful loss with the death of her sister Miriam. In the same year Ethel Dawson, Sarah's oldest child, married the prominent New York lawyer Herbert Barry and left her mother's home in Charleston, and her son Warrington went to live in Paris. The following year his mother joined him.

After Frank Dawson's death Sarah had written several fiction pieces, one of them published in *Cosmopolitan*, and in Paris she resumed her writing. In 1903 she published *Les Aventures de Jeannot Lap*, a French version of the Brer Rabbit stories, and she undertook at least two other translations. Meanwhile her son pursued his career as a foreign correspondent, diplomat, and writer.[55]

Paris was an exile for her—the distance she needed to put the Charleston tragedy in perspective. Grace King, who came to know her after their meeting on the mountain, visited her in Paris and wrote that she had gone there "to leave a country that had become loathsome to her." Always "cold and reserved," Miss King wrote, "she had, nevertheless, surrounded herself with a group of friends that kept off isolation."[56]

53. "Francis W. Dawson," 87.

54. *Memories of a Southern Woman of Letters* (New York, 1932), 206–7.

55. Warrington Dawson wrote several novels, among them a Reconstruction novel, *The Scar* (1906), and *The Gift of Paul Clermont* (1921). An invalid for most of his life, confined to his apartment at Versailles, he died in 1962. See Dale B. J. Randall, *Joseph Conrad and Warrington Dawson: The Record of a Friendship* (Durham, N.C., 1968).

56. *Memories of a Southern Woman of Letters*, 208–9.

Sarah corresponded with her family and with friends and publishers. In 1904 and again in 1906 she went back to the wartime diary and wrote brief notations in the book where there were pages left to write on. She liked to walk the boulevards and to accompany Warrington to the opera. Her letters leave no doubt that her son and his successes as a journalist and writer were the things that brought the most joy to her. "Keep an eye on that boy!" she wrote. Dale B. J. Randall has written that "Objectivity and the passage of time make it clear that Sarah Dawson loved more intensely than wisely, and that she wanted too much from her son."[57]

Sarah Morgan Dawson died in Paris, May 5, 1909. Her son was in Africa. In America her son-in-law Herbert Barry cabled Harry Hays Morgan, serving at a diplomatic post in Europe, to hurry to her. Her nephew did so, but reached Paris only in time to make the necessary arrangements. A few months later her body was taken back to Charleston and buried next to that of her husband in St. Lawrence Cemetery.[58]

In his introduction to the 1913 edition of *A Confederate Girl's Diary* Warrington Dawson wrote that he most loved to remember her in the broad tree-shaded avenues of Versailles, "dreaming of a tragic distant past." She was, he said, "destined to outlive not only her husband, but all save three of her eight brothers and sisters, and most of the relatives and friends mentioned in the pages which follow."[59]

Five years before her death she had written in the back of one of the books in which she kept her diary: "It is not far to the end, now . . . . I shall die here, far from all I once clung to more than life. So be it! I need no Home, no friends, no old associations. The Peace of God supplies all deficiencies."

The diary she began as a girl of nineteen and kept through a lifetime, the "old and tried friend," survived her.

---

57. *Joseph Conrad and Warrington Dawson*, 18.

58. On October 7, 1909, James Morgan wrote his cousin Henry Gibbes Morgan, Jr., that the train carrying Sarah's body to Charleston passed through Washington the Saturday before (October 2) and that she was buried the following day. Letter in Morgan Family Papers, LSU Collections. Harry Hays Morgan was the grandfather of Gloria Vanderbilt.

59. Sarah Morgan Dawson, *A Confederate Girl's Diary*, with an introduction by Warrington Dawson (Boston and New York, 1913), xviii-xix. In the same year a British edition was published by William Heinemann.

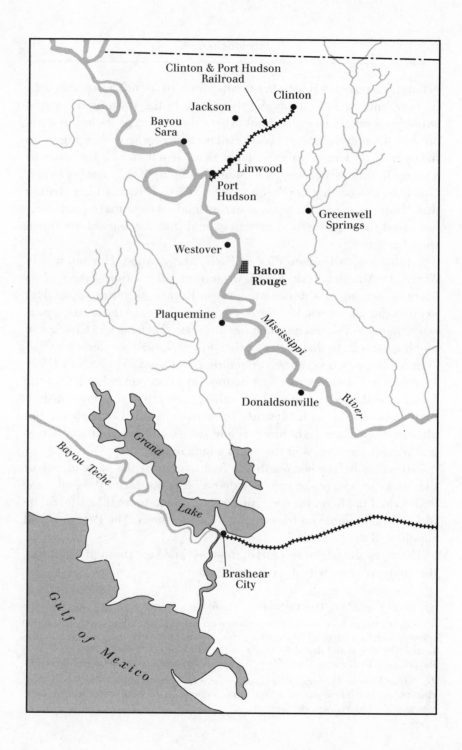

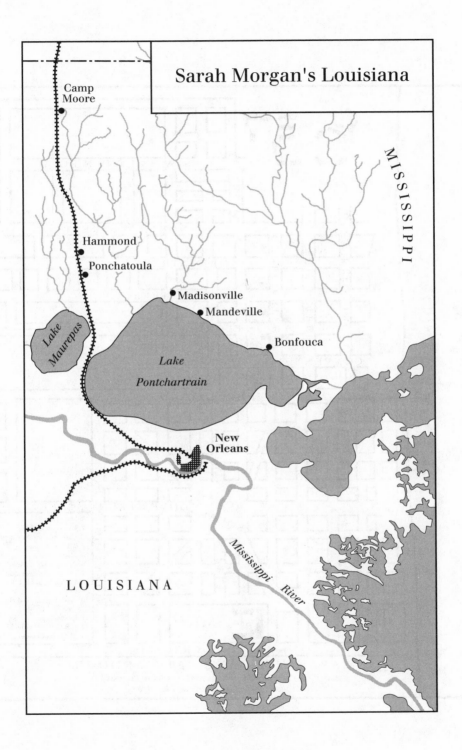

Sarah Morgan's Louisiana

Camp
Moore

MISSISSIPPI

Hammond

Ponchatoula

Madisonville

Mandeville

Bonfouca

Lake
Maurepas

Lake

Pontchartrain

New
Orleans

Mississippi River

LOUISIANA

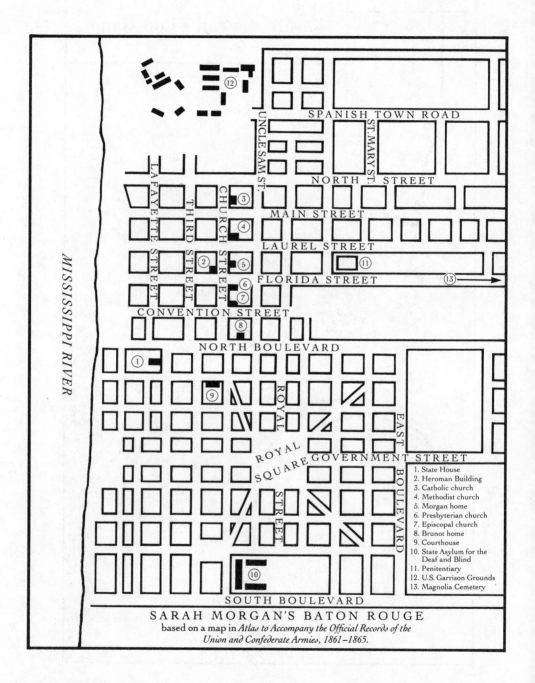

MISSISSIPPI RIVER

SPANISH TOWN ROAD

NORTH STREET

MAIN STREET

LAUREL STREET

FLORIDA STREET

CONVENTION STREET

NORTH BOULEVARD

GOVERNMENT STREET

SOUTH BOULEVARD

LAFAYETTE STREET

THIRD STREET

CHURCH STREET

UNCLE SAM ST.

ST. MARY ST.

ROYAL STREET

ROYAL SQUARE

EAST BOULEVARD

1. State House
2. Heroman Building
3. Catholic church
4. Methodist church
5. Morgan home
6. Presbyterian church
7. Episcopal church
8. Brunot home
9. Courthouse
10. State Asylum for the
    Deaf and Blind
11. Penitentiary
12. U.S. Garrison Grounds
13. Magnolia Cemetery

SARAH MORGAN'S BATON ROUGE
based on a map in *Atlas to Accompany the Official Records of the
Union and Confederate Armies, 1861–1865.*

The Morgan Family

Eliza Ann McKennan d. July 16, 1828 — m. — Thomas Gibbes Morgan b. June 12, 1799 d. Nov. 14, 1861 — m. — Sarah Hunt Fowler b. 1807

Beatrice Ford — m. — Philip Hicky Morgan (Sister) (Brother) b. Nov. 9, 1825

Lavinia (Sis) b. Jan. 4, 1832 — m. — Richard C. Drum

- Charlotte b. 1853
- Nellie b. 1855
- Lavinia b. 1857
- Hicky Hunt b. 1858
- Harry Hays b. 1860
- Miriam b. 1861
- Elizabeth b. 1863
- Beatrice b. 1864

John — m. — Eliza Ann (Lilly) b. Mar. 21, 1835, Charles LaNoue (Charlie) b. Jan. 8, 1833, died a prisoner of war Jan. 21, 1864

- Susie
- Emily b. 1850
- Henrietta b. 1862

Thomas Gibbes, Jr. — m. — Lydia Carter Waller

- Adele Lavinia (Delie) b. 1853
- Gibbes Morgan (Morgan) b. 1855
- Sarah Morgan b. 1857
- Hipolite b. 1860
- Louis b. 1861
- Beatrice b. 1864
- George Morgan b. 1864
- Albert Thomas Carter, died in infancy b. 1860
- Gibbes b. 1863
- Howell Carter, III died in 1861, Apr. 30

Thomas Gibbes, Jr. b. Oct. 24, 1836, Confederate service killed in a duel Jan. 12, 1864

Henry Waller Fowler b. July 12, 1838, died in Confederate service Jan. 12, 1864

George Mather b. 1836, killed in a duel Jan. 12, 1864

Miriam Antoinette b. Mar. 18, 1840, married Alcée Louis Dupré Sept. 29, 1866

Sarah Ida Fowler b. Feb. 28, 1842 the diarist

James Morris (Jimmy) b. Mar. 10, 1845, married Helen Trenholm Nov. 16, 1865

Note: This chart gives only births, deaths, and marriages that occurred before or roughly during the period covered by the diary.

The Diary

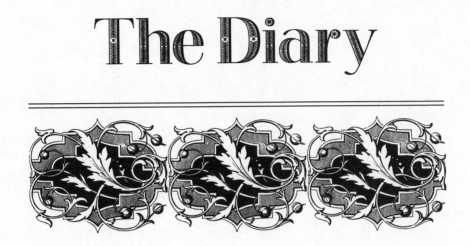

Book One

(This was an old book Brother[1] had in Paris, before I was born. He gave it to me for my 2d Journal, though I call it my First. The other was begun when I was Eleven years old.)

[p. 1] 1862. Jan 10th   B.R. [Baton Rouge]

A new year has opened to me while my thoughts are still wrapped up in the last; Heaven send it may be a happier one than 1861. And yet there were many pleasant days in that year, as well as many bitter ones. Remember the bright sunny days of last winter; the guests at home, the visits abroad; the buggy rides, the walks, the dances every night; the merry, kind voices that came from laughing lips, the bright eyes that then sparkled with pleasure? Is there nothing to remember with gratitude in all that?

What if grief came afterwards; long days and nights of heart breaking grief that only God knows of, [when I was] so heart broken that even God seemed so far off that prayers could not reach him; all the days of my life had been unclouded happiness, without pain or sadness until that awful night when I looked at mother's stony, horror struck face as she lay on the floor with father kneeling over her, and heard her cry out to me with that unnatural voice "Harry is dead![2] You loved him Sarah!" And my soul seemed to expand in one vast world of agony and then I laughed and said "Father, it is not true! tell her so!" Then

1. When Sarah refers to Brother, she means her half brother, Philip Hicky Morgan, an attorney and a judge of the district court in New Orleans. He was 36 at the time she began her diary.

2. Another of her brothers. Dr. Henry Waller Fowler Morgan died April 30, 1861, after being wounded in a duel at "the Oaks," the dueling ground in New Orleans. Harry was five years older than Sarah.

5

as he lifted up his face all tearstained [p. 2]—my dear old father!—and said—"It *is* true, dear" my heart fairly stopped beating—and I knew or saw nothing more until I heard his voice saying "My child, for God's sake control yourself!"

It called me back from I know not where; some place that I remember now as being void of everything except awful darkness; and when I saw his face dimly through the veil that seemed wrapped around me, and remembered what he was suffering, with one gasp I conquered something that was dragging me into that dark nothing again, and crept close to mother to help father to hold her. Then, for the first time I knew what grief was. But I had always been so happy until then! "Shall we receive good at the hand of the Lord, and shall we not receive evil also?" [3]

O that dreary night! Presently I found myself in the street. A crowd was gathered at the gate, but I passed through and ran on to where I knew I would find Miriam. [4] I remember putting my arms around her and saying "Miriam, my Harry is dead!" and then we were in the street again, I dont know how—and presently some one's hand was on my arm and some one said "Hush!"—I know not why—but I threw off the hand and ran away; they had no right to hold me; it was *my* brother that was dead, the one I loved best of all.

People were in the house gathering around mother; they took Miriam too; but I shook them off, for one [p. 3] word or one touch would unnerve me, and I must be brave for father's sake. They said I must go to Lilly [5] and some one took me there where people were standing around her too, and when I saw her come to, only to faint again, I thought she too would die. It was hard to keep from crying then, so every two or three minutes I would run away and hide until I could come back quiet.

That night seemed to last forever. Again I was home; the same scene was there. Mother's dull cry of misery never ceased or varied, Miriam helpless and without self control could do nothing for herself or her.

---

3. Job 2:10. Sarah's quotations are from memory. I will not note deviations from the original.

4. Miriam Antoinette Morgan, the sister closest in age to Sarah. Miriam was two years older.

5. Nickname of Sarah's sister Eliza Ann, married to John Charles LaNoue. Lilly was eight years older than Sarah.

Father had all to do. I tried to help him; I dont know whether I did though. My thoughts were so busy elsewhere. How did he die? the question haunted me where ever I turned, but I dared not ask; I felt what it was. It must have been very late when I asked Mrs Day,[6] and I felt as though it was stamped in red hot iron on my brain; Mr Sparks had killed him[7]—she need not have told me. I must have known it centuries before, and through all those ages it had been burning in my very soul.

Had he ever lived? It must have been a dream, all those pleasant days, where Harry was mingled with all happy thoughts. Was it years ago, or only a week past that very night that he was laughing at me while I dragged mother around in a dance, that he joined his violin to my guitar, and called on Miriam and Lydia[8] to sing with us? That last supper where we were so [p. 4] happy, where I drew from him stories of London and Paris,[9] and complained that he did not tell me enough, and promised myself that one day, when I should be his little house-keeper, he should tell me all—was that real? O no! it had never been. "Harry" was a name, a fancy of my own brain—he had never lived.

And yet in the same breath, I cried "He was so good!" *Was!* and I did not believe that he had ever existed—*was* I said, when the next instant I could not realize that he could possibly be no more! Those were strange thoughts that took possession of me then, and though now it seems to me that I was little short of insane, at the time I fairly hugged myself with the satisfaction of knowing that outwardly at least, I was calm, and that no one would guess what I suffered. I who felt that self control, when there was real anguish, was impossible!

After a while, one by one every one left; Miriam was to stay all night with Lilly, and I was left alone with father and mother. Mother would

6. Lavinia Day, wife of Dr. Richard H. Day. The Days lived in the same block of Church Street (today Fourth Street) immediately to the south of the Morgans.

7. James Sparks had shot Harry Morgan in the duel in New Orleans. According to the *Daily Picayune*, May 1, 1861, the duel was fought with "shot guns, loaded with balls, and fired at a distance of thirty paces."

8. Lydia Morgan, wife of Thomas Gibbes Morgan, Jr., and sister-in-law of Sarah. She was 25 when this was written.

9. In his *Recollections of a Rebel Reefer* (p. 41) James Morgan says that his brother Harry "had recently returned from Europe where he had been for the purpose of taking a post-graduate course in his medical studies."

cry out "What will you do without him, Sarah? you loved each other so! You will miss him, for he loved you best of all!" Poor mother! she forgot her loss in thinking of mine. I believe it was that consciousness of his love for me that was sustaining me through all that. I thought of his life, where we two had been thrown more together than any of the others, and recalling all the past, could thank God that I had never said or thought a harsh word about him.

The day he left home, he had taken [p. 5] off a shirt which mother wanted to use as a pattern for the set she was making him. It was lying at the foot of the bed, where she had been sewing on the others until sunset that evening, with nothing to show it had been worn save the crease in the collar and cuffs. But she cried out when she saw it, and said to take it away. Father wanted to take it; he thought I would be afraid. Afraid of dear, dead Harry who had been so good to me all his life! I could not feel so, and I carried it away my self.

That long night as I lay awake in bed, I held his daguerreotype[10] in my hand, and thought of him lying cold and stiff in the coffin so far away. I could see the gas light shining on his white face, I could see all as though I were present. I thought how fortunate it was that Lydia, Gibbes and I had not gone to Linwood[11] that morning as we intended; how strange it was that when I awoke at five, and heard the rain, I checked my feeling of disappointment with "I'll have to be thankful I cannot go yet" and when I went down to breakfast with a feeling of vague misery that I could not shake off, all laughed at me for my first attack of blues, they said, and declared it was because I did not get off. Father said "This is the first time I ever knew you to give way to a feeling of disappointment; I must say I thought you more reasonable." I felt the reproach, but could only declare that I was not sorry we did not go, I was sure it was for the best, and in return got laughed at again.

Even Lydia wondered at me, and all the morning over at her house[12]

10. Early photograph on a thin sheet of copper plated with silver. Daguerreotypes usually came in small leather-bound cases.

11. The plantation home of General Albert G. Carter some twenty miles north of Baton Rouge, in East Feliciana Parish. Lydia Morgan, married to Sarah's brother Gibbes, was the daughter of General Carter.

12. In 1860 Gibbes Morgan and his wife Lydia purchased the almost identical house next door to and to the north of his father's home. Early in 1862, a little over two months

with [p. 6] Miriam, I was weighed down with the load I felt on my heart. In going over to dinner, I felt that I must try to be myself again, and commenced singing Harry's "Partant pour la Syrie" to prove my resolution; but I could not finish. At last, while at table I said to Miriam "I *will* conquer! What o'clock is it?" "Just three." "Good! from this hour, Richard is himself again!" [13] and from that time, I was as gay as I had before been depressed. Laughing still, I went to Mrs Brunot's,[14] and I shall never forget the horror struck face, as she fell back against the wall, looking at me with out a word. I thought she must have heard bad news of Felix,[15] and entered the parlor without staying to ask. The girls [16] met me so singularly, I felt as though I was an unwelcome guest. They were talking of something strange I knew, but the instant I entered all was still.

Three or four gentlemen were there, and all eyed me until I was ill at ease. I tried to talk, but every time I mentioned Harry they seemed unwilling to speak of him, until I really felt piqued about it. Presently, we went to walk in the State House grounds, I with Mr Walsh.[17] I could not help speaking of Harry still. He remarked Gibbes looked very handsome with his hair cut short. I said "That's because he looks like Hal. Hal is the handsomest, as well as the best man God ever made. I know people do not think so, but, Bah! nobody can appreciate him as I do!" He looked so curiously at me, that I was half angry with him; but he

---

after Sarah wrote this, they sold it to Mrs. Mary C. Daigre, widow of Gilbert Daigre and daughter of the wealthy planter Abraham Bird.

13. An expression drawn from Shakespeare's *Richard III*, act 5, scene 3, the Colley Cibber adaptation (1700).

14. Mrs. Sophia (Sophie) Brunot, widow of James M. Brunot and a close friend of the Morgans. The Brunot home was on North Boulevard in the block just east of Church Street.

15. Not long afterwards, Mrs. Brunot's son Felix, a young lawyer serving as a lieutenant in the 3rd Louisiana Infantry, died in Arkansas while on the march to Corinth, Mississippi. See W. H. Tunnard, *A Southern Record: The History of the Third Regiment Louisiana Infantry* (Baton Rouge, 1866), 161. See also diary entry of May 31, 1862.

16. Mrs. Brunot's daughters Eugenia (Dena), Annette (Nettie), and Sophia (Sophie), 18, 17, and 14 in the 1860 census.

17. Henry Walsh, whose mother was one of the daughters of Colonel Philip Hicky. Another of the Hicky daughters married Sarah's paternal uncle, Morris Morgan, and a third married her maternal uncle, Henry Waller Fowler. The State House, a Gothic Revival structure built in the late 1840s, stood on the site of the former Morgan home.

said nothing. At last I came home, and taking my guitar sang alone [p. 7] in the parlor until first Lydia, then father and mother came in. Then came that scream from mother, who had gone up for her keys with father; and then remembering how sick he looked as he came in, I thought he must be dying, and ran up too. But I dared not see him die, and ran out in the street calling Gibbes. Lydia caught me, and said "Wait! I'll tell you!" but I could only say Father! and dragged her up stairs with me, while she was trying to tell me, but she never did; mother told it.

O that never ending night! What a relief to see daylight at last, and to be able to get up from the place I had never moved from all night, without thinking of sleep! I dressed in a hurry, and came to this room— his then—where all his clothes were lying, as though he would be back in a little while, and folded them and put them away. The brown cap— the one he said he would save for this winter!—which he wore until he left, was lying there too. He said he loved it, it had been so serviceable to him; so I took it to keep for him. My task was finished, and the sun was rising on the first of May.

They said Jimmy[18] had come, and running down, I met him in the entry. It was the first time in a year, for he had just come from Annapolis. It was such a sad time to welcome the dear little fellow home; may I never witness such another scene, as his meeting with mother! It was then, for the first time, that we knew how he [Hal] died, fully. Every body knew it, but ourselves, less than an hour after, but we did not know even of his death, until four hours after it occured. Jimmy said he looked [p. 8] so grand lying so still and pale, there was such a holy light shining on his face, and all pain and sorrow had passed away, and Hal's soul was before God, trusting in His mercy. Gone in his brightest days! Gone when all on earth seemed to promise only pleasure, and merited happiness for the rest of his days! Gone, with his heart full of the beauty and goodness of the whole world—gone to dust and ashes!

O Hal! Was I right in saying when you came home, that you would not be with us long, that Death was shining in your eyes? Mother and Miriam would not believe me, and laughed, but I knew you must go.

18. James Morris Morgan, Sarah's younger brother, was 17 when he resigned from the U.S. Naval Academy at the beginning of the war. He had stopped off in New Orleans on his way home, and was there when the duel occurred.

Those eyes looked too holy to stay here; they did not belong to this world. God sent that light there to show me that he would take you from the harm to come; there is no disappointment in the tomb, Hal; and it was written in the book of Fate that you were not to prosper in this world; your aim was too high, and disappointment would have crushed your soul to the earth. Better be laying in your grave, Hal, with all your noble longings unsatisfied, than to have your heart filled with bitterness as it would have been, for your motto, as I always said when you spoke of future success, was that ominous "Never!" Those glorious eyes, with God's truth sparkling in them, are now dimmed forever, Hal. Yet, *not* forever; I shall see them at the Last Day; bury me where I may see them again. O please God, let me die as calmly as he. And let Hal be the first to welcome me, and lead me before Thee, in the name of Jesus Christ!

[p. 9] Jan 26th 1862

Three months ago today, how hard it would have been to believe, if any one had fortold what my situation was to be in three short weeks from then! Even as late as the eighth of November, what would have been my horror if I had known that in six days more, father would be laid by Harry's side! That evening he looked so well and was so cheerful, and felt better than he had been for two weeks; I little thought of what was coming. How well I remember that same day, at our reading club at Mrs Brunot's, I stopped reading to tell the girls of the desk father had that morning given me, and I went on to talk of his care and love, for my comfort and me, until—I don't know why, unless it was the premonition of his coming death—I lost all control, and burst out crying, though I tried to laugh it off. At that hour, one week after, I was standing at the head of his grave, looking down at his coffin with dry eyes.

When we came home from reading, we found father with a severe attack of Asthma, but he had it so often, that we thought this too would pass off in a little while; but it was not to be; he never again drew a free breath. At night, he grew so much worse, that Dr Woods was sent for at his request, as Dr Enders could not be found.[19] O how hard I

19. Dr. A. V. Woods was a physician, age 27 and unmarried in the 1860 census. Dr. Peter M. Enders lived in the same block with the Morgans.

prayed God that he might be relieved! It seemed as though my prayer was answered, and for an hour and a half, he seemed to suffer less. At the end of that time, about nine at night, he told me to go to Lilly, and let Charlie[20] stay with him all night. I kissed him good night as he sat in his arm [p. 10] chair under the chandelier in the parlor, and went away confident that I would find him well in the morning.

I woke at [*sic*] early the 9th, but dreaded to move for fear that something, which I vaguely felt hovering over me should be true, but Lilly called to me to dress quickly and go home with her, for father had been insensible ever since I had left. At the corner, as we were hurrying here, we met Dr Enders, who laid his hand on Lilly's arm and said "If you go to see your father, you must be prepared for what ever may happen." I waited long enough to hear her ask if he was dying, and his answer "I believe so" and then I was off, and never knew how I reached the parlor.

Father was lying on matresses [*sic*] on the left of the mantle as I entered, or rather he was sitting up, propped with pillows, for he was too sick to be carried up stairs. His hands were moving as though he were writing, and his eyes, though staring, had not a ray of light in them. Dr Woods, Miriam and mother were supporting him, and someone told me he had not an hour to live. I went to my room then, and asked God to spare him a little while longer; it was dreadful to have him go without a goodbye, our dear father we all loved so. When I came down, I felt he would not die just yet. He was still the same, and until two, we watched for some change. Then he began to expectorate, and Dr Woods told me if he could throw off the phlegm from his lungs, his reason would return.

It was a sad way of keeping Brother's birthday, sitting by what was to be father's death bed. But he grew better towards evening, and they said [p. 11] he was perfectly conscious, and almost out of danger. Mother did not believe them; she said if he was conscious he would want to know what he was doing on the floor in the parlor instead of being in his bed. He seemed to know that he had not full possession of his reason for once when I was sitting by him he asked for his spectacles; I brought

20. Sarah's brother-in-law John Charles LaNoue, age 33 in the 1860 census.

them and he said "Where is my paper, dear?" I told him he had not been reading, and he gave me back his spectacles saying "Take them, darling; my mind wanders."

That was Saturday; but Sunday, he was much better, and perfectly himself, as I knew the moment I entered the room, for he put out his hand and said "How is my little daughter today?" We thought him out of danger now, for he talked with every one, and seemed almost well. About twelve, Brother and Jimmy came from New Orleans, for we had telegraphed the day before for them. Jimmy had a violent chill a few moments after he came in, and as I was the least fatigued, I undertook to nurse him. After I got him to lie down on our bed, I had to sit by him the greater part of the time and soothe his head when the fever came on, and hold his hand. He is the most affectionate boy I ever saw. All the time he was sick, he could not rest unless he had his arms around somebody's neck, or somebody's hand in his. I sat by him until night, only looking in the parlor every hour or so to see how father was, and then Miriam and I changed patients; she laid down by Jimmy and went asleep, and I went down to sit up all night with [p. 12] father.

I found him still better, and talking of law business with Brother, so I read until Brother went over to Gibbes' house, where his bed had been prepared. As soon as he had gone, father was seized with Pleurisy, and suffered dreadfully until the next morning. Dr Woods, mother and I sat up with him, the former trying every thing to relieve him. He was very kind to father; as tender with him as though he was a woman; and half the time, would anticipate me when I would get up to put a wet cloth on father's head, and lay it as tenderly on his forehead as though he were his son. I shall always remember him gratefully for that. Father would beg me to go to bed; he was afraid it would make me sick he said; he was always so uneasy about me, my dear father! O father! how your little daughter misses you now! It was almost four when I at last consented to lie down in the dining room but I soon fell asleep, and knew nothing more until sunrise when they told me that father had suffered a great deal after I left.

It seems to be an invariable rule, that whenever I spend a sleepless night, there is a trunk to pack in the morning and this morning I had to pack the children's trunk, for when the Dr pronounced father out of danger, Brother decided to go home, and take the children. I was sorry to see them go, for Charlotte, Nellie and Lavinia [21] had been with us since the 1st of August; but I felt it was for the best. I think they were sorry to leave; they kissed father again and again, and Charlotte actually cried. Brother's good bye was "The Doctor says you will be all right in a day or two; good bye, Pa," as he leaned [p. 13] over him. Father followed him with his eyes to the door, and he never saw him again.

The greater part of the day I was busy with Jimmy who was still unable to leave his bed, but now and then I would steal down and comb father's head with his little comb—the one I gave him when I was eleven years old, that he ever after used. Better and stronger he still grew, and O how happy I felt. Tuesday he was well enough to sit up in his large chair, and read Sword and Gown [22] through while I combed his silver hair. How little I realized what was so soon to happen! The next day I was sitting by Jimmy rubbing his hands, when Dr Woods came up to see him. He sat there a long while laughing with me, and I went down to see father with him. Charlie was hastily putting up a bedstead where the matresses had laid, to my great surprise, for I had hoped they would have been able to take father upstairs that day, he was so well. Instead of making any remark, I turned to father and told him some joke Dr Woods and I had just been laughing about. He smiled at me, but the gastly [sic], wan look startled me; there was something in his face which had not been there an hour ago.

A sick, deathly sensation crept over me. I heard him whisper—for he could never talk above a whisper after that Monday—I heard him whisper to Charlie to help Dr Woods lift him in his bed, and I could hear no more. I ran out of the room with that heart sick feeling. One week or ten days before when I expressed my fear that with his attack of Rheumatism he could not walk up stairs without pain, and had better have a bed brought down, he said to me "My dear, if they [p. 14] ever again make me a bed in the parlor, I shall give myself up for lost. I shall expect never to leave it again." They were putting him in it then; what if his prediction should be realized?

21. Sarah's nieces, children of her brother Philip Hicky Morgan. At the time she is recalling, November 1861, Charlotte was 8, Nellie 6, and Lavinia 4.

22. *Sword and Gown,* a popular novel by George Alfred Lawrence first published in 1859.

I fought against the idea, and tried to talk cheerfully to Jimmy, and had almost succeeded in persuading myself that I was foolishly uneasy when Miriam passed by and put a piece of paper in my hands. On it was "I do not think there is vitality sufficient to recover from this attack." The words stamped themselves on my memory; they meant that we were soon to be fatherless; Dr Woods' name was signed; he wanted us to be prepared. It was kindly meant, but how cold. They chilled me, those icy words.

I heard Jimmy ask what was the matter, but I could not speak with that choking [*sic*] ball in my throat, and that stiff tongue. I felt my way into the little end room, I could not see. And then I knelt and prayed the dear Lord to spare our father, if it might be, if he could be the same that he had always been. But if he was ever to suffer this worse than death again—if his great noble soul was to be weakened, or deprived of its strength on which we so much relied—for I remembered how terribly he had suffered—then, I said, let God take him now, that he may never know this pain again; father would not wish to live without that clear judgement and understanding that has placed him above other men. If God will spare him to us with renewed health, and unimpaired faculties, Well! If not—God grant us strength to bear it. But I could not bear it patiently; my heart failed me when I thought of father's leaving me here; until then, I had hoped to die first. I gave away in [p. 15] spite of my endeavor to be quiet, so I promised myself that this would be my day, since I could not conquer, but tomorrow should be Miriam's and mother's; I would be calm for their sake. And I kept that promise.

Poor mother! she did not expect father would die, until late in the afternoon, and wonderfully she bore up, never showing what she felt until he lay dying before her. Jimmy guessed what was to happen, and dressed himself and lay down on the sofa, where he could be near father in the parlor, and Miriam took turns in sitting on the bed near him, with me, brushing away the flies and combing his head. It was about four o'clock in the evening. Lilly and I were alone in the room with him, when he whispered something to us that we could not understand. He cast such an imploring look first at one, then the other, but Lilly put her ear to his lips, and said we had not heard. This time he whispered "Have I committed any mortal sin? I believe in the Resurrection and the Life." Then he looked at each again for an answer, but

Lilly cried and kissed him. Since he had been taken sick, every one had been coming to inquire about him, and even now they were still sending, and I had to leave the room to answer the same sad thing to each one—"very low." And then I would have to stay away until I could wipe my eyes and be quiet enough to stand by him.

Sunset came; all without was so quiet and calm; not a breath stirring. I walked up and down the balcony, where I could see him through the open windows. Within, it was more deathly calm than without. Though [p. 16] there were so many there, not a word was spoken, not a hand moved, and the gas, just lighted, was shining on the white coverlid that rose and fell at every painful breath, and father's pale face and silvery hair looked so deathlike that [I thought] my heart would fail me. Several times during the day, I had caught sight of my self in the mirror, and hardly knowing the face that stared so despairingly back at mine, I would whisper "Hush!" to the quivering lips I saw, as though it were a living creature, and would say to the shadow reflected there "It means that tomorrow you will be an orphan," and would vaguely wonder why it trembled so. I felt as sorry for that shadow as though it were living— and yet, I was not sorry for myself; I tried to forget my own identity.

O how still that room was, with the single sound of that dreadful breathing! It made the silence more intense. Among all those living souls, the noblest there was going: floating out to the Great Beyond. Our hearts sickened and turned cold, his never failed; he knew God was just, and he "Believed in the Resurrection and the Life." It was about eight at night, when he beckoned to Jimmy, and drawing him near, he kissed him repeatedly and said "God bless you my boy! Good-night." Poor little Jimmy burst into tears and ran out of the room. He watched him out, and after waiting awhile, and unable to talk, he put his arms around mother and kissed her good bye, then me, then Miriam. O dear father! can I ever forget that last good bye? It said everything that a last kiss can say; and when I turned [p. 17] away, I felt as though my last and best friend was gone.

How kind Charlie was! All those days he never left his side for more than a moment or two, and only for one or two nights, when Cousin Will[23] or Dr Woods sat up with father did he leave him. No son could

23. Her cousin William G. Waller.

have been more devoted. I do not know what would have become of us, without Charlie.

I had determined to sit up all night by father, but half an hour after he had kissed me good bye, they said I must go out while they changed his blisters.[24] I waited with aunt Caro and aunt Adèle[25] in the dining room, but after a while Mr McMain[26] and Charlie said I must go to bed; Lilly was lonesome up stairs, and the Doctors found father much better, they would call me if he needed me. I do not know how it happened, but presently I found myself lying on the bed near Lilly, and slept for some time, when Miriam woke me to say father was still better, and I must take my clothes off and go back to bed. I had not the energy to resist, and did as I was told, though every half hour I would wake up, to hear Charlie tell Lilly how father was, and directly fall asleep again. It was always "His pulse has gained" "He is stronger" "Dr Enders finds him much better," until I persuaded myself that he would get well. I kept repeating "O live father! live for your children!" and would fall asleep praying that father might be spared.

The last thing I heard, was that he was still better; it was then half past four. I fell into a heavy sleep, and did not wake until I felt someone trying to raise me up, and kissing me, to wake me. It must have been a few moments [p. 18] after seven then. I half way opened my eyes, and saw it was Tiche,[27] but had not the energy to say anything, though I had not seen her for several weeks, she having come up from New Orleans while I was asleep. I heard her say "Run to Master," and then she was gone.

Half way dreaming, I got up, and slowly put on my shoes and stockings. Then I deliberately commenced to comb my hair, but just then, Margret[28] came in and said "Never mind your hair; Master is dying; run!" In another instant, I was standing by him. I remember to have

24. A common medical treatment of the day was to blister the skin by applying wrappings containing irritants. Sarah herself was subjected to blistering later in the diary.

25. Aunt Caroline Morgan and Aunt Adèle Fowler, both widows.

26. Probably James W. McMain, a Baton Rouge merchant.

27. Catiche, a slave, enjoyed senior rank among the family servants. In his book of reminiscences James Morgan wrote that Katish (his spelling) "nursed and bossed" all of the Morgan children. *Recollections of a Rebel Reefer*, 5.

28. A slave, one of the Morgan servants.

heard them carry Lilly out of the room, while she was crying; but I saw nothing until I reached his bed. Someone was holding mother, as she stood at the head, wringing her hands and afraid of touching him. Poor mother! how she was crying! Miriam had thrown herself by his side, on the other side of the bed, with her face buried in one of his pillows sobbing aloud, but no one was touching him. So I went to him as he lay on the edge of the bed, and put my left hand in his, while I laid my right on his fore head. The hand of death would not have been colder than mine; but I remembered my promise "To day is mine, tomorrow, Miriam's and mother's," and did not shed a tear.

Father lay motionless, save for that deep drawn breath, each of which seemed to be the last, with his eyes perfectly blue and unclouded fixed on the parlor door, as though waiting for some one to enter. Only four times can I distinctly remember having seen him breathe after I came in the room. What a long, long interval there was between [p. 19] each! It may have been only a few moments that I stood there, but to me it seemed hours. Presently I bent over him to see him breathe again, but mother cried "Shut his eyes!" and closed them with her own hands. I kissed him as he lay so motionless, and turned away, for I knew father was dead. Jimmy was crying aloud in a chair at the foot of the bed, but I dared not go to him; one word, one touch would have unnerved me, and I had my promise to keep. So I went to my room, and hurried on my clothes, for all this while I had been standing in my nightgown.

I looked at the watch as I went out—quarter past seven, it said. When I came back, every one had disappeared, except aunt Adèle who was brushing away the flies. I took her place, and she left me alone with dead father. It seemed impossible that he should be dead, he looked so warm and lifelike, and then I held my breath to hear him breathe again. From that hour, the idea that he would presently come to, never forsook me until I saw his coffin lid screwed. People wondered at my self control, but I could never have kept my promise so faithfully, if it had not been for that wild thought.

I dont know how long I sat there alone, but presently the men came to dress him, and Charlie took me away. The slippers I worked for him his last birthday were at the foot of the bed, where he had them put when he took them off the day before; the little comb was lying on his pillow, so I took them away with me. [p. 20] When I had brought his grave clothes, and the men had finished, Miriam and I sat down on each side of him, and remained there except for a moment or so at a time, all day. People came in in crowds, but I wanted them to be quiet; I felt I would give away if I spoke.

About ten, it must have been, Lydia came; she knew he was very sick, and the crape at the door told her the rest. She held on to me as she looked at his dead face; they all seemed to think poor weak me the strongest. Father had been so kind and tender to her; no wonder she cried so bitterly! I could not stand it; but I remembered what father said when Hal died—that I had more fortitude than any woman he had ever seen[29]—and I determined to make his words come true. But it was a relief when Lydia went up to mother; I could be quiet then.

People might come and go; I neither saw or cared for them; my hand was on father's head, I was watching for the eyes to open, I was thinking of those away. Poor Sis![30] this will break her heart! California is such a long way off, and even now she does not know what has fallen on our home! George was at Norfolk;[31] he left New Orleans the day before Harry died. Gibbes was at Centreville;[32] Brother should have been there at daylight, and father had died waiting for him, and though the day was wearing on he had not come.

Sunset came, then the early twilight, and only Mattie[33] was left with us. I still kept my place with my hand on his forehead, watching. I could see the moon [p. 21] shining on the white fence over the way, and the blue sky through the open windows. Then the gas was lighted, and

29. "Sarah has been the stay of the household—I never saw such fortitude," Thomas Gibbes Morgan wrote his son George, then in Virginia. Letter dated May 8, 1861, in Thomas Gibbes Morgan Sr. and Jr. Papers, Manuscript Department, Duke University Library.

30. Sarah's oldest sister, Lavinia, married to Major Richard C. Drum and living in California. Lavinia was ten years older than Sarah.

31. Sarah's brother George Mather Morgan, a captain in the 1st Louisiana Volunteers, was 23 at the time she wrote this.

32. In Virginia. Gibbes had enlisted as a second lieutenant in Company C, 7th Louisiana Infantry, on June 7, 1861; at the time his father died, he had been promoted to captain and the regiment was in Virginia.

33. Mattie Stith, two years older than Sarah, was the wife of James H. Stith and daughter of Thomas Castleton, who operated the Castleton Seminary. Dr. Castleton had served earlier as pastor of the Presbyterian church.

shone just as it did last night full on his quiet face and silver hair. But last night those lips called me and kissed me, and to night—O it was so sad!

Then those who were to watch, came in, but I did not look at them; I heard them while I was watching. Later, Charlie put his arm around me, and carried me in the dining room to get my supper; it was hard to eat, but I tried to please him, and when I wanted to go back and wait, he would not let me. Then I promised, if he would let me kiss father good night, I would do whatever he pleased. So I kissed him for Sis too, and went back as I said I would, and Charlie made me go to bed with Lilly. I kept quiet; I hardly dared breathe for fear I should cry; but I grew so cold and numb, I thought my blood was frozen. We were lying in father's bed, and directly below, he was lying so stiff and cold! I could see him as though I were standing by him, where ever I turned even with my eyes shut I could still see him; and that awful hush seemed to pervade the whole world. Then a step broke the stillness, and I knew Brother had come; he could not have known it until he reached the door, and he was standing by our dead father at that moment. I grew colder and colder, until I crept closer to Lilly, and I knew that at one touch I would give away, for I cried my self asleep in Lilly's arms.

Then the next morning before sunrise, I was sitting [p. 22] by father again, looking at his grand head. It looked so magnificent, there was some thing so majestic in the form, that I could not cover it up. Brother came and stood by me; he too was trying to control himself; but I knew all he was suffering, by what I suffered myself. Presently came the men with an iron coffin, and set it down almost at my feet, with a dull, hollow clang, that went to my very heart; and they said Miriam and I must go out; but we would not, and stayed by, and saw him put in it. When they brought the lid, we kissed him good bye—poor Sis! I kissed him for her too—and Brother cried, but did not touch him; and even I had to turn to the window, for the tears would come. And we watched them cement the iron lid, and screw it down, and then I took my old place at his head, and held the handle nearest me, though I could no longer see his dear face again.

I took no notice of time, but I must have been there a long while, when I was roused by footsteps, and saw two or three strange faces looking at me. I knew it must be ten, so I put on my bonnet and cloak, and came back to him, and layed my hand on his coffin. Some one made me go to the other side of the room, I dont know who, for when I tried to see, there was only an indistinct sea of faces before me, and I did not even know whether I had ever seen them before. I knew nothing except that father was lying dead in that coffin before me.

When [p. 23] Mr Gierlow[34] said "I am the resurrection and the Life" I looked up, and saw him standing by the side of the coffin, and only Brother at the foot, who put out his hand for me. I got up, and groped my way towards him, for all save those three in the centre was indistinct to me, and he caught me and held me tight while Mr Gierlow read the service, until the prayers, when I knelt alone by father, with my face on his cold coffin. Presently there was a deep hush, and then, looking up from the chair brother had placed me in, I saw them preparing to carry father away. Then Brother put my hand on his arm, and slowly made his way through a crowd that suffocated me, as far as the front door, and there Gen Carter[35] took me away from him and passed through a still greater crowd, until he put me in the carriage with Miriam and Lydia, and Howell[36] got in with me, and we slowly drove off.

Then came the dreary drive to the graveyard,[37] following in the very steps of the horses that were carrying father away from us; and then, we stopped at the gate, and Howell gave me his arm, and took me to the enclosure where Hal was burried [sic], and stood with me at the head of an open grave, where I knew father was to be put. Brother, Lydia, and Miriam stood at the side, and then they brought father, and lowered him into his last home. I tried so hard to keep my promise, that God gave me [p. 24] the strength, and I watched him down in his grave without a tear, only holding tighter still to Howell to save myself from falling. "Earth to earth, dust to dust, ashes to ashes," the earth rattled on the coffin lid, the last prayer was said, I looked for the last time at

34. Rev. John Gierlow, rector of St. James Episcopal Church and the Morgans' pastor.

35. Lydia's father.

36. Lydia's brother Howell Carter, two years younger than Sarah. A few months after she wrote this, Carter joined one of the companies that would become a part of the 1st Louisiana Cavalry. He wrote *A Cavalryman's Reminiscences of the Civil War* (New Orleans, n.d.).

37. Magnolia Cemetery, on the eastern outskirts of the town, about a mile from the Morgan home.

what held all that remained of our dear father, and Howell was once more putting me in the carriage, and I was going home.

Home! What a dreary, desolate place it was! How forsaken every thing looked! There was such a strange echo in the deserted rooms, such a forlorn look in every place! All that made our home happy, or secured it to us, was gone; a sad life lay before us. My heart failed me when I remembered what a home we had lost, but I could thank God that I had loved and valued it while I had it, for few have loved home as I. Sis, Hal, and I, it is all we lived for. How it would have pained Hal to see that day! I was thankful he had gone before. It would have broken his heart if any of us had died. And O Hal my darling, how I miss you now! How I long for you, wait for you, pray for you, and you never come! Do you no longer love your little sister? Father is with him now; both lying so close together, yet so far apart; side by side, and they speak not, though they once loved one another so much!

Once more alone, and all control was thrown to the wind; it would have killed me to be calm then. And after [p. 25] dinner, when Brother made Miriam and me sit on his lap, when the others had gone, and talked so kindly to us, when he laid his head on the table and cried until his whole frame trembled, at the mere mention of father's name, I felt marble again and could pity and soothe him as though he were the weak woman, I the strong man. Where did I get that strength?

He talked so nobly and kindly to us, and said he would be our father, and love us and care for us as the dear dead one did, that we no longer felt hopeless and forsaken. Are kind words recompensed in Heaven? Then surely God will bless Brother for the words he spoke that evening. And it was decided then, that until George could come from the wars and take care of us, Lilly and Charlie would stay here with us, until something else could be done. After all, we would not be utterly helpless; with God in heaven, our brothers on earth, should we not be thankful? And this is the simple story of how my poor mother was made a widow, and we were left orphans on that sad fourteenth of November, 1861.

March 1st. 1862.
[No entry; p. 26 blank]

[p. 27] March 9th, 1862.

Here I am, at your service, Madame Idleness, waiting for any suggestion it may please you to put in my weary brain, as a means to pass this dull, cloudy Sunday afternoon; for the great Pike clock over the way[38] has this instant struck only half past three; and if a rain is added to the high wind that has been blowing ever since the month commenced, and prevents my going to Mrs Brunots before dark, I fear I shall fall victim to "the blues" for the first time in my life. Indeed it is dull. Miriam went to Linwood with Lydia yesterday, and I miss them beyond all expression. Miriam is *so* funny! she says she cannot live without me, and yet, she can go away, and stay for months without missing me in the slightest degree! Extremely funny! And I—well it is absurd to fancy myself alive without Miriam. She would rather not visit with me, and yet, be it for an hour or a month, I never half way enjoy myself without her, away from home. Miriam is my "Rock ahead" in life; I'll founder on her yet. It's a grand sight for people out of reach, who will not come in contact with the breakers, but it is quite another thing to me, perpetually dancing on those sharp points in my little cockle shell that forms so ludicrous a contrast to the grand scene around. I am sure to founder!

I hold that every family has at least one genius, in some line, no matter what—except in our family, where each is a genius, in his own way. Hem! And Miriam has [p. 28] a genius for the Piano. Now I never could bear to compete with anyone, knowing that it is the law of my being to be inferior to others, consequently, to fail, and failure is humiliating

38. Clock on the bank of William S. Pike. The Baton Rouge Branch of the Louisiana State Bank was on Third Street (today Riverside Mall), one block west of Church Street.

to me. So it is, that people may force me to abandon any pursuit, by competing with me; for knowing that failure is inevitable, rather than fight against destiny, I give up de bonne grace.[39] Originally, I was said to have a talent for the piano, as well as Miriam. Sister[40] and Miss Isabella said I would make a better musician than she, having more patience and perseverance. However I took hardly six months lessons, to her ever so many years, heard how well she played, got disgusted with myself, and gave up the piano at fourteen, with spasmodic fits of playing every year or so.

At sixteen, Harry gave me a guitar. Here was a new field where I would have no competitors, I knew no one who played on it, so I set to work, and taught myself to manage it, mother only teaching me how to tune it. But Miriam took a fancy to it, and I taught her all I knew; but as she gained, I lost my relish, and if she had not soon abandoned it, I would know nothing of it now. I know now that she does not know half that I do about it, they tell me I play much better than she, yet, let her play on it in company before me, and I cannot pretend to play after. Why is it? It is *not* vanity, or I would play, confident of exceling her. It is not jealousy, for I love to see her show her talents. It is not selfishness; I love her too much to be [p. 29] selfish to her. What is it then? "Simply lack of self esteem" I would say if there was no phrenologist near to correct me, and point out that well developed bump at the extreme southern, and heavenward portion of my Morgan head.

Self esteem, or not, Mr Phrenologist, the result is, that Miriam is by far the best performer in Baton Rouge, and I would rank forty third even in the delectable village of Jackson.[41] And yet, I must have some ear for music. To "Know as many songs as Sarah" is a family proverb; not very difficult songs, or very beautiful ones, to be sure, besides being very indifferently sung; but the tunes *will* run in my head, and it must take *some* ear to catch them. People say to me "Of course you play?" to which I invariably respond "O no! but Miriam plays *beautifully*!" "You sing, I believe?" "Not at all!—except for father" (that is what *I*

---

39. With good grace.

40. When Sarah refers to Sister, she means her sister-in-law Beatrice Ford Morgan, wife of Philip Hicky Morgan. References to Sis are to her sister Lavinia.

41. Jackson, Louisiana, in East Feliciana Parish, then the home of Centenary College.

used to say)—"and the children. But *Miriam* sings." "You are fond of dancing?" "Very; but I cannot dance as well as Miriam." "Of course you are fond of society?" "No indeed! Miriam is, and she goes to all the parties and returns all the visits for me." The consequence is, that if the person who questions is a stranger, he goes off satisfied that "That Miriam must be a great girl, but that little sister of hers—! Well! a *prig* to say the least!" So it is Miriam catches all my fish—and so it is too, that it is not raining, and I'm off.

[p. 30] March 11th.

I was right in saying strangers did not like me. Is it a compliment, or the reverse, that none but my own family, and those who have known me long, like me? I consider it a compliment. Let me make home happy, and myself beloved in it, and a fig for the rest of creation! And I *think* I am loved at home. Father—I may say it here without vanity—father was *very* proud of me. They *used* to say I was his favorite daughter. Sis is more intelligent, Lilly more amiable and womanly, Miriam more accomplished and outside, a greater favorite than I; but I alone was father's "Little daughter."

One compliment father paid me—how well I remember what I felt! My first thought was humiliating; I did not deserve it; my next was resolve; I said "With God's help I will try to merit it." I need not say that I deserve it as little now, as then; but the words were these "She comes nearer perfection than any woman I ever knew." I must remember that, and strive harder to make his words come true, in the few years I have still probably to live. Brother's favorite, I decidedly am; Sis idolizes the whole family; Miriam loves me better than she does the rest, I am satisfied, though I do not know why she should: you know you are not a nice girl, Sarah.

And the one who loved me best of all, Harry—he is gone. Hal, my darling, God only knows how I loved you! "Hal," that is my name; no one called him so but me, except Sis and Miriam, occasionally. It *belonged* to me, and that is all I have left. [p. 31] He was proud of me. Why, I wonder? He loved me more than anybody did. If I went out of the room, it was always "Where is Sarah?" A day or two before he went away for ever, I was coming down late to breakfast, and heard him say "Pshaw! Where is Sarah? *She* can 'take' a pun. Send for her. I shant waste my wit on you dull people." And I ran in, and made some re-parti [*sic*] to his puns, and our breakfast passed off in laughter, as they always did.

If Hal was in trouble, he came to me to tell it; if he was gay, he came to make me laugh too; if he had a pleasant book, he would read aloud that I might enjoy it too; when he had a buggy, he would drive out with me; and so those happy days went by. Hal thought me pretty, I believe. He used to say "These people cannot appreciate you; when I get rich, I [will] take you to France; you'll pass for a beauty there," and when I would laugh and say that would be nothing, if all french women were as ugly as he thought them, he said "No matter; *I* think you the best looking here," as though that made me so.

Once, a few days after he came from Paris, I asked what kind of a man Mr Guibourd was, and if he really loved him so much. He laughed as he said "*Love* him? I told him once that if he would come to Louisiana, he might marry my little sister; judge *now* if I loved him!" When he repeated the description he had given his friend of me, I was glad that he would not see me for many a long day, to destroy the illusion.

[p. 32] March 12th.

I know few things that have caused me as much useless wonder as that senseless question I sometimes put to myself—"How can anyone ever think me even [?] presentable?" It often occurs to me when anyone flatters me. Dont imagine I am vain in saying this; the ugliest people have someone uglier still to admire then, and why not I? "Every body is beautiful to somebody else." Sometimes, I will not deny, I am pleased with myself; I believe it is when I have on an unusually neat dress, and feel very happy, for seeing my self unexpectedly in a mirror, I have felt satisfied, if nothing else. But the next instant, seeing mother's pretty face, or Lilly's, or Miriam's handsome one, or Sophie Brunot, I shrink from myself and cry "Hide your face Sarah before them; you know you are ugly!" And somehow ugliness seems to creep out of my pores, and I feel it taking root all over, until I am so ashamed to find anyone looking at me! Half the time, I feel that it is meant as an insult.

I wonder if pretty people feel perfectly satisfied with themselves? Not *pretty* people either, but beautiful ones; every one is pretty according to public opinion—Me! Pshaw! looks are nothing! I have seen the most unfortunately ugly people show heavenly traits of character that one would hardly believe could be found except in angels, while others pretty as wax dolls could show Satan a few tricks he had until then ignored. Witness Phillie Nolan and Mollie Castleton.[42] Was there ever as true, noble, and christianly a Woman as Phillie? [p. 33] And the other? Well, I must pray God to teach me to forgive and forget her too.

Revenons à nos moutons.[43] I was about to say that I had once had an impartial view of myself, but as that was the most prepossessing part of me, and was seen through a mistaken medium, I retract. It happened that I was going over to call on Medora Renshaw,[44] just about two years ago, dressed very nicely as I thought, nothing more. The house was the double cottage style, two rooms on each side of a wide hall, and I turned to the left, as I entered, to reach the parlor. As I stood on the threshold for an instant, my eye caught sight (in the mirror over the mantle) of Medora, as I thought, walking toward the chimney in her mother's room, opposite.

"How elegantly she is dressed!" was my first thought. "What a pretty silk, and how beautifully it fits!" was my second. I am ashamed to record that my next was "I wish I had such a pretty figure, and such a tiny waist." I looked higher and exclaimed "What a quantity of hair! Why—!" here I turned crimson with shame, having suddenly discovered that I was praising myself. The mirror over Mrs Renshaw's mantle corresponded exactly with the one in the parlor. Walking very slowly towards the latter, I did not observe that the young lady so stylishly attired was—myself, from a back view as reflected in the former. The pretty silk, which looked ashes of roses through that medium, was nothing but my pale blue checked silk, with little flounces—the handsomest dress I ever had. And if it had not been for the sudden thought that I knew nobody [p. 34] in New Orleans with such a quantity of tawny hair, there is no knowing what else I might have said about Dora.

That is *once* that I was pleased with myself. Such is the power of

42. Philadelphia Nolan McDowell, daughter of Dr. John T. Nolan, a West Baton Rouge planter; and Mollie Castleton, younger daughter of Thomas Castleton. Phillie Nolan, age 18 in the 1860 census, married Edward McDowell the following year.

43. But let us return to the subject.

44. Medora Renshaw, daughter of the New Orleans commission merchant Henry Renshaw.

prejudice, and mantua makers![45] But the next instant, all feeling of satisfaction had flown; instead of the stylish—no, she is not stylish—*well dressed,* graceful, selfpossessed Medora, I beheld Miss Sarah, whom I had until then overlooked in my admiration of her friend, now looking remarkably foolish and embarrassed, though no one was in the room to witness her mistake.

I am half way inclined to believe that "Handsome is what Handsome"—chooses to think of its self. If I chose to say to my friends and acquaintances, "I think I am really *very* good looking; have I not a Grecian nose, rather than a snub, and is not my mouth rather pleasing than otherwise?" If, I say, I should throw out such hints as these, occasionally, in a very short time, people would begin to believe there *was* something in me after all. Those who had no idea of beauty, would take my word for it, I would have the majority on my side, and when public opinion is on my side, who would not cry "Hurrah?" These people who are not praised and lauded by the world, have only to blame their lack of self appreciation. Let a woman know her own worth and attractions, and there is not a knee that will not bow to the power of her—self esteem.

Even in such a trifle as a foot, think well of it, and [p. 35] all the world will agree. There is Medora, five inches smaller than I, as proud of her No. 1 as though it was extraordinary; Miriam, a quarter of an inch shorter than I, prides herself on her No. 3, and thinks she has a very pretty foot,—ergo, every one says "What a beautiful foot Miss Morgan has!" "What tiny feet Miss Renshaw has!" I am five feet, four and a half inches; this day I have on number ones; who shouts "what an extraordinary foot has Sarah?" Bah! it is only because I dont say "Look at *that* foot! Aint it a beauty?" I have the misfortune of thinking every one has a nicer one, or quite as nice, that is all!

March 31st 1862.

For a young woman who pretends to such a feeling of contempt for all egotism, and self conceit, it strikes me, on looking back a page or two, that I my self have displayed an inordinate amount of it. The question is where did it all come from? for really "public opinion" says I am

45. Dressmakers.

not *very* egotistical, and of course no one would dispute the point, in consequence of that decree being infallible. Fact is, I am trying myself. I want to see how it feels to play "Ego sum" constantly, as well as occassionally [*sic*]. I would become a perfect bore [p. 36] if I talked of myself any more than I do, so I take refuge in writing all that is too preposterous to say aloud. Besides, one's diary is surely private property, and there is no more fitting place for talking about the only inexhaustible subject in the world, the only one of which we never tire, namely— yourself. I assume the right then, of talking about myself as much as I please, satisfied that no one will take the trouble of saying for me, what I do not first say for myself. I mean to record some few of my fancies now, that I may have the pleasure of contrasting them with those of a few years hence, to see whether I have become a better girl, or a worse.

I was as old at six, as most people are at sixty; so old, that I took a turn, and grew younger every year, [words lined through] I do not believe there existed a more perfect child than myself. [Word lined through] now, I am making up for an infancy spent in old age, with a perfect trust in something that God has in store for me, some where, and a baby's contentment in the present, with a promise, and hints it brings of the future towards which I only allow my thoughts to wander, vaguely, just as the rest of the babies "open their mouths and shut their eyes" while waiting for that extraordinary something that is to "make them wise."[46] My turn has not yet come, but I [end of p. 36; four pages of the diary that followed (two pages front and back) have been excised]

[p. 37, top of page excised] my happy life! I love to think of it now. Until that dreary 1861, I had no idea of sorrow or grief. "Sorrow may endure for a night, but joy cometh in the morning;"[47] let me believe that my sunshine is only obscured by a passing cloud, and that presently it will gild my life as brightly as ever. I danced my [words excised] and I danced it out. I sang, I laughed, I felt how supremely happy I was, and believed every one the same. When I came from the city,[48] one pleasure succeeded another, we received many visitors, and every thing went on as merry as a feast of pleasure could. Then during the six

46. Children's rhyme.
47. Psalms 30:5.
48. New Orleans.

weeks of Mattie Castleton's engagement, she and Mollie stayed here the greater part of the time, and it was one whirl of excitement and preparation, until she was married, the 2d August.[49]

The day after, or night after, rather, Miriam, Mr Pinkney,[50] Howell and I went up [p. 38, top of page excised] mischief *"Only* ten—only *nine* miles to Baton Rouge!" it was ludicrous to see how he would gasp as though choking. The moon rose on us while we were yet four miles away from home, before the flush of sunset had died away; but the other two who had sung with us the whole way, grew very silent, and no word or sound reached us two seated in front, except an occasional sigh from the backseat, which sounded like [?] a [words excised] of Vesuvius on the eve of an irruption—and they were redoubled, as though put out at compound interest, for every mile we drew nearer home. But *we* laughed, and sat full in the moonlight, singing together, and making Time, and the horses feet, fly.

We landed at Gibbes' house, for mother had moved there while this was being repaired.[51] Neither she or father were home, but we made the bare walls ring with the sound of our voices, until they came in, so glad to see us home again, the first time, I believe, as well as the last, we had left them entirely alone; though [p. 39] to be sure Lydia & Gibbes had been with them most of the time. The young midshipman's spirits were falling below zero; during supper, though I tried my best to enliven him, I only implanted pins and needles in his sensitive heart, and got only the most desperate, heart rending ghost of an occasional smile.

After supper, all walking on the pavement in the moonlight, poor Will came to Howell, and said he must speak to me, where upon, the other drew back, and the latter informed me he was going to ask father—no matter what! I argued, entreated; said father had the gout,

49. 1860. Mattie's husband, James H. Stith, enlisted in the 1st Louisiana Heavy Artillery the following year.

50. William Elder Pinkney was a midshipman at the U.S. Naval Academy before the war. At the time Sarah wrote this, he was a lieutenant colonel in the 8th Louisiana Infantry Battalion. When Louisiana military records are cited, the sources are *Records of Louisiana Confederate Soldiers and Louisiana Confederate Commands*, compiled by Andrew B. Booth (New Orleans, 1920), and Compiled Service Records of Confederate Soldiers Who Served in Organizations from the State of Louisiana (Microcopy 320).

51. Evidently the Morgans had lived in the house for some time before June 2, 1860, when Sarah's father purchased the property from the succession of James N. Brown.

please wait for a more auspicious moment, *do* now! but to no purpose. He *would* go right off, only—only—he didn't mind telling me that he was *awfully* afraid! and his heart—was beating like—like—just feel it! And to my infinite astonishment, with one jerk, he placed my hand on the organ aforesaid, before I could protest that my curiosity was not at all excited on the subject. Now, never having had much experience concerning the pulsation of the human heart of the masculine gender, I cannot say whether it was actually a heart that was carrying on in the style of a cheval fringant,[52] or whether it was a foot ball so long tossed about by boys that it had discovered the secret of perpetual motion, by a series of short jerks; but if it had been in the dark, and I, unaware of my locality, I should always have believed that I had stumbled over a mouse trap [p. 40] containing half a dozen freshly caught inmates, each of which was endeavoring to make off in opposite directions, bearing all the others together with the trap. It was laughable—only I was too— I cant say what—to laugh; though since I have enjoyed it beyond all expression—the laugh I was cheated out of then. It was so naive!

The next thing I knew, Howell and I were walking alone on the pavement; it seems to me the moon was brighter in 1860 that [*sic*] it has been since. Passing the parlor windows which were always wide open in summer, I beheld the prettiest tableau I ever yet have seen. Seated in the centre of the room, under the chandelier, sat father, with the crutch he was at that time obliged to use, leaning against the arm of his large rocking chair. He was alone in the room reading. Through the open parlor door came two figures, hand in hand. The one nearest us was a tall, strongly made young man, who looked as firm and honest as any one who has made up his mind to a desperate venture, could look; there was actually something noble in the manly air he assumed, as he walked towards father (who had dropped his book now) grasping the front of his coat with his left hand. The other was a girl, [words lined through]; Her eyes cast down on the floor, quiet and calm as a marble statue, and yet there was that in her air, that told of a heart beating [p. 41] wildly under that handsome, still face.

Still hand in hand, they stopped in front of father, who was evidently waiting, though perfectly calm, to hear more. The young man's lips

52. Frisky horse.

moved; I caught the first word, "Judge," and the proud manly look, with the head thrown back, and yet the air of humility, told the rest. I read, from his looks the story of his love, his hopes, his fears, as plainly as though I stood by him. Father looked up to answer, and Miriam sprang to his side and put her arms around his neck, and I heard her say "Yes, father." Her young, girlish face lying on his bluish grey hair, her beautiful arms clasped around his neck, the tears sparkling on her cheek; he talking so ernestly to the young man who now stood alone, with his arms folded over his breast, formed the most touching picture I had ever seen.

I felt it sacrilege to stay, though the whole had scarcely occupied a minute, so Howell and I passed on, with only this comment which I made silently to myself "It must be *awful* to 'ask pa!'" As we passed back, father was alone in the room; I saw him draw a deep breath and shade his eyes with his hand, and my heart was full, thinking of my dear old father. Here Will came running out of the house and told me all about it, and how nobly father had spoken to him; as though he ever spoke otherwise! The other [p. 42] part of the story I heard from Miriam when we were alone in our room. It was brief, and consisted in "O Sarah never 'ask pa' unless you want to feel desperately uneasy!" as we threw our arms around each other, she laughing, I half crying.

It was that year that we all dressed with such care, and vied with each other in our pretty muslins, and lace capes, for every evening the two Castletons, three Brunots, Miriam and I, who formed a clique by ourselves, who walked in the State House garden, and made it "fashionable," for it speedily became the rendezvous of all the young men, who joined us in our walks, and of the rest of the town. Every evening crowds would assemble above, watching the younger ones below walking on the terraces, or running in the lower ground, or sitting around the pond in knots of twos, and threes.

Those days passed merrily by! One day though, I was no longer numbered among those who danced in the twilight on the terrace. It was toward the beginning of November, when this house was finished, and mother preparing to move over, that I undertook to give her a charming surprise, and ended in surprising myself. I decided it would be a new, and agreeable experience to lay down a carpet in our room, without telling any one about it. Every one would be so astonished to find it only waiting for the furniture! So I provided myself with every thing, came over to the deserted house, and commenced. [p. 43] There was a very heavy mahogany armoir, and a bed in the room, so I called Margret to help me. Knowing she was weak, I made her only pass the carpet under the former, whilst I, Hercules the second, lifted it up. Then I dismissed her, and got on nicely with the bed by raising it up with my shoulders, while pulling the carpet under the legs. Behold me driving the last tack in, author of all the industry I surveyed! I threw open the doors, and called all in to admire and applaud.

While relating my exploit to father in great glee at table, I suddenly gave three groans, in answer to three raps I thought I had received from the abused hammer up stairs, each so firmly struck on my temple, as to cause the water to stream from my eyes. The next moment I laughed it off, but father looked very anxious and uneasy, while mother talked of rush of blood to the head. For two weeks after, I was unable to walk at all, and then, I began to doubt whether my carpet exploit was worth the pain it cost me, when people threatened me with spine disease. A trip to Linwood restored me, and I only felt an occasional weakness and fatigue, and many a dreary December evening I walked slowly up and down the parlor waiting to hear of Hal's return from Europe, thinking of him at sea, and always singing "When through the torn sail the wild tempest is streaming." New Year evening of 61, I went to a party at Mrs [p. 44] Brunot's, and inaugurated my return to health, by dancing enough to lay me up forever.

April 5th 1862.

One year ago to day, Harry came home. I was up stairs sewing alone, when Dophy[53] cried "Here is Marse Harry" and throwing down every thing that stood in my way, I rushed down stairs, and met him near the parlor door. I could say nothing but "O Hal! I am so glad!" And he did not speak, but throwing his arms around me, carried me the length of the hall to the back door, where mother was seeing Tiche draw off a cask of wine. Then we sent to Lilly's house for her and Miriam, who had just gone there, and to the office for father, and O what a happy meeting it was!

53. One of the Morgan servants.

Hal made me a promise an hour or two after, which we often talked about during the few, happy days that followed. We were both looking in his trunk for a book he had brought me, when he told me of Sallie Maynadier,[54] and what a nice girl she was, and added "I came *very* near falling in love with her, I can tell you!" I felt jealous of her; I could not help saying "Did you love her *more* than me, Hal?" "No! I loved both her, and her sister because they reminded me so much of you and Miriam," he said, and then went on to say they were *very* nice girls, laughing at me all the time.

I asked one more question; I was growing jealous of the [p. 45] girl he could even like; so I asked if he could love her enough to marry her, and leave me. He was kneeling on one knee near the trunk, and in his odd, abrupt way, he looked up quickly at me, and said "Come! let us make a bargain! Promise me you will never marry, and I promise you *I* will not; and I'll grow rich for both, and you shall take care of me, and be my little housekeeper; will you?" I laughed and said "Yes!" And we ran in the dining room, and told father of our "bargain" and how we meant to keep it.

One year ago to day, one year ago to day! Ah me! and I am alone up here, as I was one year ago, and he, he is lying in his last home, alone and desolate, with no little sister to stay by him, and tell him how much he is loved, and missed; and he will never come again, as he did at this hour a year ago to day, and put his arms around me, and promise to take care of me always; for the feet that ran to meet me are dust and ashes, the arms that were thrown around me lie helpless by his side, one pierced five times by that cruel bullet that took away his life. I sat by his grave yesterday while I decked it with flowers, thinking of my darling who lay beneath so still, who would never, never lay his hand on my head again, or look at me with those deep grey eyes so loving and kind, and I thought my heart would break. Hal! God only knows how sad it is here with out you, and yet, Thank God you are at rest!

---

54. Probably the daughter of Captain (later Colonel) William Maynadier, the U.S. Army's assistant chief of ordnance, who lived in Washington. The families were connected by marriage. Harry Morgan may have seen Sallie Maynadier on his return from Europe.

[p. 46] April 7th

[Words lined through] how I love to think of myself at that time! Not as *myself*, but as some happy, careless child who danced through life, loving God's whole world too much to love any particular one, outside of her own family. She was more childish than [words lined through], yet I like her, for all her folly; I can say it now, for she is as dead as though she was lying under ground.

Now, do not imagine that Sarah has become an aged lady, in the fifteen months that have elapsed since, for it is no such thing; her heart does ache occasionally, but that is a secret between her and this little rosewood furnished room; and when she gets over it, there is no one more fond of making wheelbarrows of the children, or of catching Charlie or mother by the foot and making them play lame chicken. Nor do I know any one more fond of sitting on poor Lydia's head and alternately tickling and pounding her, until I have forced her to confess that she is an old green dog with a red tail and blue eyes, a lame young monkey, or a good for nothing wretch—all of which she acknowledges with the greatest complacency, and usually is rewarded by being pulled out of bed by one foot. Now all this done by a young lady who re-members eighteen months ago with so much regret that she has lost so much of her high spirits, might argue that her spirits were before tremendous; and yet they [p. 47] were not. That other Sarah was lady-like, I am sure, in her wildest moments, but there is something hurried and boisterous in this one's tricks, that reminds me of some one who is making a merit of being jolly under depressing circumstances. No! this is not a nice Sarah now, to *my* taste.

The commencement of 61 promised much pleasure for the rest of the year, and though secession was talked about, I do not believe any one anticipated the war that has been desolating our country ever since, with no prospect of terminating for some time to come. True the garri-son was taken,[55] but then several pleasant officers of the Louisiana Army were stationed there, and made quite an agreeable addition to our small parties, and we did not think for a moment that trouble would

55. The U.S. Army military post at the northern end of the city, also referred to as the Arsenal. State troops had seized the Arsenal early in January of 1861, even before the secession convention met.

grow out of it—at least we girls did not. Next Louisiana seceeded [*sic*],[56] but still we did not trouble ourselves with gloomy anticipations, for many strangers visited the town, and our parties, rides, and walks grew gayer and more frequent.

One little party—shall I ever forget it? was on the 9th of March, I think; such an odd, funny little party! Such queer things happened! What a fool Mr McGimsey[57] made of himself! Even more so than usual. But hush! It is not fair to laugh at a lady—under peculiar circumstances. And he tried so hard to make himself agreeable, poor fellow, that I ought to like him for being so obedient to my commands. "Say something new; something funny," I said, tired of a subject on which he had been expatiating all the evening; [p. 48] for I had taken a long ride with him before sunset, he had escorted me to Mrs Brunot's, and here he was still at my side, and his conversation did not interest me.

To hear, with him, was to obey. "Something funny? Well—!" here he commenced telling something about somebody, the fun of which seemed to consist in the somebody's having "knocked his *shins*" against something else. I only listened to the latter part; I was bored, and showed it. "Shins!" Was I to laugh at such a story? I turned slightly, and looked at him; I felt the contempt in my heart, curl my lip, for an instant, I knew he would read what I thought in my eye, so I looked at him. If one fold of my dress had touched him then, I *know* I should have hated him! Wither, wither, wilt! He caught the expression, and how he did shrink! He knew he had forfeited my good opinion, and stopped with an embarrassed laugh. My vengeance stopped at the instant he felt it, and I tried to make him like himself again, and his gratitude rewarded me. Only—

What in the world made me think of that little episode—that little drama that was so quietly acted that evening with every one for audience, and none in [on] the secret save Miriam, Mr Trezevant,[58] & Lydia who thought themselves so wondrous wise? It was mean to write it; I

56. The Ordinance of Secession that split the state away from the Union was adopted January 26, 1861.

57. William C. McGimsey, age 21 in the 1860 census, son of a Baton Rouge physician, Dr. J. W. P. McGimsey.

58. James H. Trezevant, who would shortly join the 1st Louisiana Regulars as a first lieutenant.

was just talking to mother about feeling such contempt for some people, and some things, when that little pantomine flashed before me, said "Write!" and I wrote, I am sorry to say, for I should forget it. Of those [end of entry]

[p. 49] April 12th

Day before yesterday, just about this time of the evening, as I came home from the graveyard, Jimmy unexpectedly came in. Ever since the 12th of February he has been waiting on the Yankees' pleasure, in the Mississippi, at all places below Columbus, and having been under fire for thirteen days at Tiptonville, Island No. 10 having surrendered Monday night, and Commodore Hollins[59] thinking it high time to take possession of the iron clad ram at New Orleans, and give them a small party below the forts, he carried off his little aid[e] from the McRae[60] Tuesday morning, and left him here Thursday evening, to our infinite delight, for we felt as though we would never again see our dear little Jimmy. He has grown so tall, and stout, that it is really astonishing, considering the short time he has been away. As to handsome!—well! perhaps that is only a weakness of the family. (!)

What a dear little rascal it is! Such affectionate, winning ways! Such a baby to mother and his sisters, such a noble little man to all the world besides! Ah! there are no boys like the Morgan boys: why are not the rest of the men as good, noble and true as they? Our boys look like— like themselves; nothing else can express it. See Brother, for instance. With his six feet three and a half of mortality, and that tremendous frame; his talents, manners, and education, what a magnificent Czar he would make! He looks like an emperor even now.[61] Then see Gibbes, the Prince of Good Fellows. Short, and almost stout, with his fine [p. 50]

59. Commodore George N. Hollins of the Confederate Navy. Hollins had taken a squadron of ships upriver as far as Columbus, Kentucky, in an unsuccessful attempt to halt the downward progress of the Union's Western flotilla.

60. In 1861 and the early months of 1862 the *McRae* was Commodore Hollins's flagship. The ironclad ram that Sarah mentions was no doubt the *Louisiana*, one of two Confederate fighting ships nearing completion in New Orleans.

61. For a vivid description of Sarah's oldest brother, see James A. Renshaw, "Recollections of Yesterday," *Louisiana Historical Quarterly* 8 (1925): 429–32. After the war Philip Hicky Morgan served on the state supreme court, and in 1880 was appointed U.S. minister to Mexico.

massive head, handsome intelligent face, let him nod his head at you, and you will be convinced that he is "the best fellow in the world," and would instantly clap him on the shoulder, and say "Hello, Tom!"

Harry—my Harry—words will not do for him now. What a mild, benevolent face, yet how full of character and determination! What beautiful, laughing eyes, and what a noble head! No one called him handsome, except Lilly and I, but it was always "what an intelligent face!" "Rather good looking" that was said of him abroad. Then he had carefully studied his profession, and he had read every thing, and could converse so well, no wonder every one called him intelligent. Ah! he was diffident, and awkward among strangers, but his home character was so beautiful! Nothing that could give pleasure, was too trifling for him to do; just about this time last year, he spent half an hour pasting together a picture Louis had torn from my Eclectic,[62] which he knew I valued. A few days since, I picked up the book, but the pieces had fallen apart, as well as the hands that had joined them. Who but one of *our* brothers would think of doing such a trifle? Any man would do it for his sweetheart; but for his sister—?

Hal thought I had a soul; that is what I liked, rather than be treated like a baby, as the other boys treat me. I like the petting, but I want them to believe that I am to be relied on, and have a soul above a new dress or a beau. When a man of understanding converses with you as though you were rational, and had a soul to save, it unconsciously gives [p. 51] you a better opinion of yourself. You think, surely so wise a man cannot be mistaken, and there must be something in you after all; and it is such a delicious sensation! So it was, when Hal read, or talked to me, I liked myself better for appreciating him, and liked him better for believing I would understand what he said.

Courage is what women admire above all things and that he possessed in the most eminent degree, in common with all his brothers. It was stamped in every line of his face, and all might see that he was a man who did not know fear. Months after he died, passing a group of gentlemen in New Orleans, Jimmy heard them mention Harry's name, and one said "I saw him when he stood up, and I saw him fall, and I

62. A school book, probably one of the *McGuffey Eclectic Readers*, although there were also *Eclectic Spellers, Eclectic Histories*, and so forth. Sarah is referring to her nephew Louis LaNoue, age 2.

never saw as brave a man." "That is the way with all the men of that family; they are as brave as can be, and those girls are not an inch behind them" returned another. No! there never was a braver man than Harry. New Orleans rung with the story of his death. Men talked of his coolness, and applauded his bravery, while his broken hearted mother and sisters wept over him at home. Ah! men admire everything that ends in breaking a woman's heart!

[p. 52] April 13th 1862. Sunday.

How can I describe George? By leaving his actions to speak for him, I expect, for I certainly cannot do him justice. As to personal appearance, Monseigneur is just of a nice size, and perfectly in proportion. A head that might serve as a model for an Apollo; hair of a beautiful chesnut, or brown, that *will* curl up in the most extraordinary shapes; blue eyes of a most wonderful size, which do terrific execution among the girls; a handsome nose that says "Character" as plainly as though it were a posted bill; the prettiest mouth ever seen on man, [words lined through], these all serve to make up the "personnel" of my amiable brother, who is certainly the most amiable, easy going, fiery, determined and patient man I ever knew.

Jimmy, every one's pet at home and abroad, will be handsomer than he, I think, for George's features are too perfect for a man, to my taste, though I'm glad he does not hear me, for it enrages him to be called effeminate. Jimmy is everything that a boy should be, and fit for nothing in the world but an officer. He is such a brave devil-may-care, generous boy; likes fun, frolic and danger so well that he would make a jolly old tar. As it is, he is a perfect duck of a Midshipman. Yesterday to our great distress, he jumped up from dinner, and declared he must go to the city on the very next boat. Commodore Hollins would need him, he must be at his post, etc. and in twenty minutes he was off, the rascal, before we could believe he had been here at all. There is something in his eye that reminds me of Harry, and tells me that like Hal, he will die young.

[p. 53] And these days that are going by, remind me of Hal, too. I am walking in our footsteps of last year. The eighth, was the day we gave him a party, on his return home. I see him so distinctly standing near the pier table talking to Mr Sparks whom he had only met that morning, and who, three weeks after, had Harry's blood upon his hands. He is a wanderer now, without aim or object in life, as before; with only one desire—to die—and death still flees from him, and he Dares not rid himself of life. All those dancing there that night have undergone trial and affliction since. Father is dead, and Harry. Mr Trezevant lies at Corinth with his skull fractured by a bullet; every young man there has been in at least one battle since, and every woman has cried over her son, brother or sweetheart, going away to the wars, or lying sick and wounded. And yet we danced that night, and never thought of bloodshed! The week before Louisiana seceeded, Jack Wheat[63] stayed with us, and we all liked him so much, and he thought so much of us— and last week—a week ago to day, he was killed on the battle field of Shiloh.

April 16th

Among the many who visited us in the beginning of 1861, was that horrid Mr. Bradford.[64] I took a dislike to him the first time I ever saw him, and being accustomed to say just what I pleased to all the other gentlemen, tried it with him. It was at dinner, and for a long while I had the advantage, and though father would sometimes look grave, Gibbes, and all at my [p. 54] end of the table would scream with laughter. At last Mr Bradford commenced to retaliate, and my dislike changed into respect for a man who could make an excellent reparti with perfect good breeding, and after dinner, when the others took their leave, and he asked permission to remain, during his visit which lasted until ten o'clock, he had gone over such a variety of subjects, conversing so well upon all, that Miriam and I were so much interested—that we forgot to have the gas lit!

Here was an intelligent man, I thought, so I liked him for about a week. But after that, how he grated upon my nerves! We would talk for an hour, and if I would say anything inconsistent with my first proposition—which was frequently—he would say in that up and down voice,

63. Captain J. T. Wheat commanded a company in the 1st Louisiana Regulars.

64. J. B. (Buck) Bradford, one of three brothers who appear in the diary. See entry of November 2, 1862. Also see J. B. Bradford to J. L. Bradford, January 18, 1860, James L. Bradford Papers, LSU Collections.

"Now Miss Sarah let me tell you what you said at first," [65] and no matter how long or stupid my speech had been, this torturer would repeat it word for word, and set my nerves and teeth on edge. There is *nothing* I hate more than these people who *will* repeat all [of] a stupid conversation, to prove any Fact. I hate facts! What is the use of *proving* that I am inconsistent? It is proving an axion; dont I know I am inconsistent? What is the use of forcing it constantly on my notice, then? So I used to plead "Be merciful, and spare me the repetition! I agree to any, every, and all things, only spare me!" But no! he must go on, and so, though I thought him very intelligent, he grated so on my sensibilities that I grew to hating the sight of him, and always felt more Christianly if I heard him talk in the dark, where I could not be irritated by looking at that disagreeable mouth of his. And the last time I saw him, I am convinced he disliked me as much as I did him.

[p. 55] April 17th.

And another was silly little Mr Butler,[66] my little golden calf. What a—dont call names! I owe him a grudge for "cold hands," and the other day when I heard of his being wounded at Shiloh, I could not help laughing at little Tom Butler's being hurt. What was the use of throwing a nice, big cannon ball, that might have knocked a man down, away on that poor little fellow, when a pea from a pop gun would have made the same impression? Not but what he is brave, but little Mr Butler is so soft.

Then there was rattle brain Mr Trezevant who, commencing one subject, never ceased speaking until he had touched on all. One evening he came in talking, and never paused even for a reply until he bowed himself out, talking still, when Mr Bradford, who had been forced to silence as well as the rest, threw himself back with a sigh of relief and exclaimed "This man talks like a woman!" I thought it the best description of Mr Trezevant's conversation I had ever heard. It was all on the surface, no pretentions to anything except to put the greatest possible number of words of no meaning in one sentence, while speaking of the most trivial thing.

65. Sarah tilted some of the words to indicate the ups and downs.
66. Thomas Butler, a captain in the 1st Louisiana Regulars.

Night or day, Mr Trezevant never passed home without crying out to me "Ces jolies yeux bleus!"[67] and if the parlor was brightly lighted so that all from the street might see us, and be invisible to us themselves, I always nodded my head to the outer darkness and laughed, no matter who was present, though it sometimes created remark. You see I knew the joke. Coming [p. 56] from a party escorted by Mr Butler, Miriam by Mr Trezevant,[68] we had to wait a long while before Rose[69] opened the door, which interval I employed in dancing up and down the gallery— followed by my cavalier—singing "Mes jolies yeux bleu, Bleu comme les cieux, Mes jolies yeux bleu on ravi son âme,"[70] etc. Which naïve remark, Mr Butler not speaking French, lost entirely, and Mr Trezevant endorsed it with his approbation and belief in it, and ever afterwards called me "Ces jolies yeux bleu."

Mr Trezevant was good, doubtless, and I liked him well enough—as the companion of an evening; but as the companion of the Evening of Life—Que le ciel m'en préserve![71] He would be invaluable at a fishing party; but if he was an angler in the stream of Matrimony—heaven help the poor little fish that is caught by that "loud" bait, it must have been suffering from famine in its own land!

He is good; but—"he talks like a woman!" He judged me so strangely. The day after Hal came home, Mr Trezevant said to me "You have been raving about Harry, and now he is here you are not glad to see him." Hal laughed, while I looked defiance at anyone who could say such a preposterous thing. He went on "No, you dont care for him. Last night I passed here during the storm, and only you, he, and your father were in the room. He was telling your father a story, and you, instead of listening as anyone else who loved a brother would, you had your back turned to him, and were reading." I said nothing. He did not know I

---

67. "Those pretty blue eyes!"

68. In a note written in later, Sarah adds: "O propriety! Gibbes and Lydia were with us too!" A few of the notes of this kind are dated 1896, the year she says she got out the diary and read it for the first time in more than thirty years. Others must have been written in the years when she was keeping the diary, some of them not long after she wrote the original entry.

69. One of the servants.

70. "My pretty blue eyes, Blue as the skies, My pretty blue eyes have delighted his soul."

71. Heaven protect me from that!

was leaning over the book to hide what I felt when Hal was telling how the poor Irishwoman—whose life I know he saved on the ship—waved her old sunbonnet and cried "God bless the doctor!" as she was carried ashore. So we are judged! Of we three, I only am alive now.

[p. 57] April 19th 1862.

Another date, in Hal's short history! I see myself walking home with Mr McGimsey just after sundown, meeting Miriam and Dr Woods at the gate; only that was a Friday, instead of Saturday, as this. From the other side, Mr Sparks comes up, and joins us. We stand talking in the bright moon light which makes Miriam look so white and statue like. I am holding roses in my hand, in return for which one little pensé has been begged from my garden, and is now figuring as a shirt stud. I turn to speak to that man of whom I said to Dr Woods, before I even knew the name, "Who is this man who passes here so constantly? I feel that I shall hate him to my dying day." He told me his name was Sparks, a good, harmless fellow, etc. And afterwards, when I did know him, [Dr. Woods] would ask every time we met "Well! do you hate Sparks yet?" I could not really hate any one in my heart, so I always answered "He is a good natured fool, but I will hate him yet." But even now I cannot; my only feeling is intense pity for the man who has dealt us so severe a blow; who made my dear father bow his grey head, and shed such bitter tears.

The moon is rising still higher now, and people are hurrying to the grand Meeting, where the state of the country is to be discussed,[72] and the three young men bow, and hurry off too.

Later, at eleven o'clock, Miriam and I are up at Lydia's, waiting (until the boat comes) with Miss Comstock[73] who is going away. As usual, I am teasing and romping by turns. Harry suddenly stands in the parlor door, looking very grave, [p. 58] and very quiet. He is holding

72. Probably the meeting announced for the evening of Friday, April 19, 1861: "The citizens of Baton Rouge and vicinity, are requested to meet to-night at Academy Hall, for the purpose of making the necessary arrangements for raising a volunteer company to go to Fort Pickens, or wherever else their services may be demanded." Baton Rouge *Daily Advocate*, April 19, 1861.

73. Isadora Comstock, daughter of George C. Comstock, agent for the Clinton and Port Hudson Railroad. Her brother, Midshipman John H. Comstock, had served on the *McRae* with Jimmy Morgan. The Comstocks lived in Clinton.

father's stick in his hand, and says he has come to take us over home. I was laughing still, so I said "Wait" while I prepared for some last piece of folly, but he smiled for the first time, and throwing his arm around me said "Come home, you rogue!" and laughing still, I followed him. He left us in the hall, saying he must go to Charlie's a moment, but to leave the door open for him. So we went up, and I ran in his room, and lighted his gas for him, as I did every night when we went up together. In a little while I heard him come in, and go to his room.

I knew nothing then; but next day, going into mother's room, I saw him standing before the glass door of her armoir, looking at a black coat he had on. Involuntarily I cried out "O dont, Hal!" "Dont what? isn't it a nice coat?" he asked. "Yes, but it is buttoned up to the throat, and I dont like to see it! It looks—" here I went out as abruptly as I came in; that black coat so tightly buttoned troubled me. He came to our room after a while, and said he was going ten miles out in the country for a few days. I begged him to stay, and reproached him for going away so soon after he had come home. But he said he must, adding "Perhaps I am tired of you, and want to see something new! I'll be so glad to get back in a few days." Father said yes, he must go, so he went, without any further explanation.

Walking out to Mrs Davidson's[74] that evening, Lydia and I sat down on a fallen rail beyond the Catholic graveyard,[75] and there she told me what had happened. The night before, sitting on [p. 59] Dr Woods gallery with six or eight others who had been singing, Hal called on Mr Henderson[76] to sing. He complied by singing one that was not nice.[77] Old Mr Sparks[78] got up to leave, and Hal said "I hope we are not dis-

74. The home of Thomas Green Davidson, a widower despite Sarah's habit of calling it Mrs. Davidson's. She and Lydia would have been going to visit his daughters. Tom Green Davidson had returned to Baton Rouge to practice law after leaving the U.S. House of Representatives in which he had served since 1855. In her book *Social Life in Old New Orleans* (New York and London, 1912), Eliza Ripley gives several vivid glimpses of him in her recollections of Baton Rouge. See pp. 254, 264–70.

75. The Catholic Cemetery was on Main Street between Main and North, almost a mile east and north of the Morgan home.

76. Probably George Henderson, age 30 in the 1860 census, who lived near the Morgans.

77. In a note written in later, Sarah identifies the song as "Annie Laurie."

78. William H. Sparks, who would later write *The Memories of Fifty Years* (Philadelphia, 1870). He makes no mention of his son or the duel in the book. In the 1850s Sparks owned a plantation near Baton Rouge in partnership with Judah P. Benjamin.

turbing you?" No, he said; he was tired, and would go home. As soon as he was gone, his son, who I have since *heard* was under the influence of opium—though Hal always maintained that he was not—said it was a shame to disturb his poor old father. Hal answered "You heard what he said. We did *not* disturb him." "You are a liar" the other cried.

That is a name that none of our family have either merited or borne with; and quick as thought Hal sprang to his feet, and struck him across the face with the walking stick he held. The blow sent the lower part across the banquet[te], in the street, as the spring was loosened by it, while the upper part, to which was fastened the sword—for it was father's sword cane—remained in his hand. I doubt that he ever before knew the cane could come apart. Certainly he did not perceive it, until the other whined piteously, he was taking advantage over an unarmed man; when, cursing him, he [Harry] threw it after the body of the cane, and said "*Now* we are equal." The other's answer was to draw a knife,[79] and [he] was about to plunge it in Harry who disdained to flinch, when Mr Henderson threw himself on Mr Sparks and dragged him off. It was a little while after, that Harry came for us.

The consequence of this was a challenge from Mr Sparks in the morning, which was accepted by Harry's friends, who appointed Monday, at Greenwell,[80] to meet. [p. 60] Lydia did not tell me that; she said she thought it had been settled peaceably, so I was not uneasy, and only wanted Harry to come back from Seth David's[81] soon. The possibility of his fighting never occured to me.

Sunday evening I was on the front steps with Miriam and Dr Woods, talking of Harry and wishing he would come. "You want Harry!" the Dr repeated after me. "You had better learn to live without him." "What an absurdity!" I said, and wondered when he would come. Still later, Miriam, father and I were in the parlor, when there was a tap on the window, just above his head, and I saw a hand, for an instant. Father hurried out, and we heard several voices, and then steps going away.

79. Later note by Sarah: "Bowie-knife."

80. Greenwell Springs, a rustic resort on the Amite River about fifteen miles northeast of Baton Rouge. It became a popular watering place after a hotel and cottages were built there in the mid-1850s.

81. In an unpublished memoir written in the 1930s, Howell Morgan, Sarah's nephew, states that it was at Seth David's home that Harry Morgan practiced for the duel that would cost him his life.

Mother came down and asked who had been there, but we only knew, that whoever it was, father had afterward gone with them. Mother went on "There is something going on, which is to be kept from me. Every one seems to know it, and to make a secret of it." I said nothing, for I had promised Lydia not to tell; and even I, did not know all.

When Father came back, Harry was with him. I saw by his nod, and "How are you, girls" how he wished us to take it, so neither moved from our chairs, while he sat down on the sofa, and asked what kind of a sermon we had had. And we talked of anything except what we were thinking of, until we went up stairs. Hal afterwards told me that he had been arrested there, and father went with him to give bail; and that the sheriff had gone out to Greenwell after Mr Sparks. He told me all about it, next morning, saying he was glad it was all over, but sorry for Mr Sparks; for he had [p. 61] a blow on his face that nothing would wash out. I said "Hal, if you *had* fought, much as I love you, I would rather he had killed you, than that you should have killed him. I love you too much to be willing to see blood on your hands." First he laughed at me, then said "If I had killed him, I never would have seen you again."

We thought it was all over; so did he. But Baton Rouge was wild about it. Mr Sparks was the bully of the town, having nothing else to do, and whenever he got angry or drunk, would knock down anybody he chose. That same night, before Harry met him, he had slapped one man, and dragged another over the room by the hair; but these coolly went home, and waited for a *voluntary apology*. So the mothers, sisters, and intimate friends of those who had patiently borne the blows, and being "woolled," vaunted the example of their heroes, and asked why Dr Morgan had not acted as *they* had, and waited for an apology? Then there was another faction who cried only blood could wash out that blow, and make a gentleman of Mr Sparks again, as though he ever *had* been one! So knots assembled at street corners, and discussed it, until father said to us that Monday night "These people are so excited, and are trying so hard to make this affair worse, that I would not be surprised if they shot each other down in the streets," speaking of Harry, and the other.

Hal seemed to think of it no more though, and Wednesday said he must go to the city, and consult Brother as to where he should permanently establish himself. I was sorry; yet glad that he would then get away from all this trouble. I dont [p. 62] know that I ever saw him in higher spirits than he was that day, and evening, the 24th. Lilly and Charlie were here until late, and he laughed and talked so incessantly that we called him crazy. We might have guessed by his extravagant spirits, that he was trying to conceal something from us.

After Lilly had gone, I was sitting in the window talking to Hal who had now thrown himself in father's rocking chair, of the unpleasant feeling that had been created, by my having yielded to his wish, and Mr McGimsey's importunities, and having gone with the latter to our picnic. He said I must not mind it. "Never let anything come between you and the Brunots, Sarah. They will be your friends when all others turn against you. I would rather have you with them, than any girls I know. Remember what I say, and promise me." I said I would try.

It was growing very late, and I was standing behind his chair, with my hands playing with his hair, when Miriam came to tell him good-bye. He burst out laughing as she bent over, and asked if *she* was going away. She turned away saying "I shall not kiss you, I dont believe you are sorry to go." He sprang forward saying "O Miriam come tell me good bye!" He looked so earnest that I laughed while she bent over and just touched his lip before she passed out. I stayed longer, with my hands still on his head, and laying my cheek on his head said "O Hal come back soon to me." He turned suddenly and kissed me, saying "I will." At the door, I half way paused and saw him still lying back in the arm chair. That was my last look. He went away before daylight, and I never saw him again.

[p. 63] April 26th 1862.

There is no word in the English language which can express the state in which we are all now, and have been for the last three days. Day before yesterday news came early in the morning of three of the enemy's boats passing the forts, and then the excitement commenced,

and increased so rapidly on hearing of the sinking of eight of our gunboats in the engagement, the capture of the forts, and last night, of the
burning of the warves [sic] and cotton in the city,[82] while the Yankees
were taking possession, that to day the excitement has reached almost
the crazy point. I believe that I am one of the most self possessed in
my small circle of acquaintance, and yet, I feel such a craving for news
from Miriam, and mother and Jimmy, who are in the city, such patriotic and enthusiastic sentiments, etc, that I believe I am as crazy as the
rest, and it is all humbug when they tell me I am cool.

Nothing can be heard positively, for every report *except that our gunboats were sunk, and theirs coming up to the city,* has been contradicted,
until we do not really know whether it is in their possession or not. We
only know we had best be prepared for anything, so day before yesterday Lilly and I secured what little jewelry we had, that may yet be of
value to us if we *must* run. I vow I will not move one step, unless forced
away! I remain here, come what will.

We went this morning to see the cotton [p. 64] burning, a sight which
was never before presented to our view, and probably never will be
again. Wagons and drays, and everything that could be driven, or rolled
along were to be seen in every direction loaded with the bales, and
taking them a few squares back, to burn on the commons. Negroes
were running around cutting them open, piling them up, and setting
fire to them, all as busy as though they hoped to obtain their salvation
by fooling the Yankees. Later, Charlie sent for us to come to the river,
and see him fire a flatboat loaded with the precious material for which
the Yankees are risking their bodies and souls to obtain. Up and down
the levee, as far as we could see, negroes were rolling it down to the
brink of the river, where they would set them afire, and push them in,
to float burning down the tide, each sending up its wreath of smoke
and looking like so many little steamers puffing away—only I doubt
that there are as many boats from the source, to the mouth of the river.

The flat boat was piled with as many bales as it could possibly hold
without sinking, most of them cut open, while negroes staved in the

82. New Orleans. Once the Union fleet managed to pass Fort Jackson and Fort St. Philip,
which guarded the river approach to New Orleans, the city's fate was decided. The Confederate river defense forces were no match for David G. Farragut's flotilla of sloops,
gunboats, and mortar vessels. On April 29 the Federals occupied the city.

heads of barrels of Alcohol, whisky, etc. and dashed buckets of it over the cotton, while others built up little chimneys of wood every few feet, lined with pine knots and loose cotton, to set it afire. There, piled the length of the whole levee, or burning in the [p. 65] river, lay the work of thousands of negroes for more than a year gone by. It had come from all directions, but many men stood by who could claim an interest in the cotton that was burning, or was waiting to be burned, and either looked on, or helped with cheerfulness. Charlie only owned some sixteen bales—a matter of some fifteen hundred dollars, but he was head man of the whole affair, and burned other people's as well as his own. A single barrel of the whisky that was thrown on the cotton cost the man who gave it one hundred and twenty-five. It shows what a nation in earnest is capable of doing.

Only two men got on the flat boat with Charlie when it was ready, when it was towed into the middle of the river set on fire in every direction, and then they jumped into a little skiff fastened in front, and rowed back to land, leaving the cotton floating down the Mississippi one sheet of living flame, even in the strong sunlight. It would have been a glorious sight at night; but we will have fun watching it this evening anyway, for they cannot get through to day, though no time is to be lost. Hundreds of bales remain still untouched, and they are all to go with the others. An incredible amount of property has been destroyed to day, but nobody begrudges it. Every grog shop has been emptied, and gutters and pavements [are] floating with liquors of all [p. 66] kinds, so that if the Yankees are fond of strong drink, I fear they will fare ill.

Yesterday, Mr Hutchinson and a Dr Moffat[83] stopped here to see me, but as I was not in, and they had but a moment to stay, they told their errand to Lilly. They wanted to tell me Jimmy was safe, that though

83. S. W. Hutchinson had served with Jimmy Morgan on the *McRae*. Muster rolls for 1861 list him as captain's clerk. Subsequent to his stop-off in Baton Rouge, Hutchinson appears on the rolls of officers at the Confederate naval station at Jackson, Mississippi, together with Charles M. Morfit, assistant surgeon. In July 1862 Dr. Morfit was assistant surgeon on the *Arkansas* on its run through the Union fleet, but apparently he left the ram at Vicksburg. See *Official Records of the Union and Confederate Navies*, ser. I, 19:132, and ser. II, 1:290, 320, hereafter cited as *ORN*. Also see Dr. Charles M. Morfit to Joseph Jones, July 6, 1890, in Joseph Jones Collection, Howard-Tilton Memorial Library, Tulane University.

sick in bed he had sprung up, and rushed to the warf [*sic*] at the first tap of the alarm bell in the city; but as nothing was to be done, he would probably be home with Mother and Miriam today—I have seen or heard nothing of them since, though. The McRae, he said went to the bottom, with the others; he did not know if any one had escaped. God be praised that Jimmy was not on her! The boat he was appointed to,[84] is not yet finished, so he is saved. I was distressed about Capt Huger,[85] and could not help dropping just one tear; but then I remembered Miss Cammack[86] might forget it was because I was grateful for his kindness to Jimmy, and might think it *too* tender, so I stopped. O I hope he escaped! I can tell him how frightened we were then, and have a laugh.

Mr Hutchinson was on his way above, on some ship, going to join the others where the final battle on the Mississippi is to be fought, and had not time to sit down even; and I felt doubly thankful to him for his kindness, remembering that this was the very man Jimmy thrashed not a month ago, on the McRae, and was sorry I could not see him to thank him in person. Lilly was so excited, that she gave him a letter [p. 67] I had written to George just before going out, and begged of him to address it for me, and mail it at Vicksburg, or somewhere else, for no mail will ever leave *here* for Norfolk for some time to come. The fun of it is he does not know George, though he gladly undertook the charge, and promised to remember the address which, Lilly told him, was *Richmond*!

Well! if the Yankees *do* get it, they will find only a crazy scrawl, for I was so intensely excited that though I wanted to calm his anxiety about us, I could write nothing but "dont mind us; we are safe; fight, George fight!" until the repetition was perfectly ludicrous. I hardly knew *what*

84. The Confederate ironclad *Mississippi*. Sarah wrote "Mississippi" above the line, followed by several words that she lined through.

85. Lieutenant Thomas B. Huger, in command of the *McRae*, was mortally wounded when ships of the Confederate river defense force engaged the Union fleet on the river below New Orleans. He died May 11, 1862. In the entry of May 23, 1862, Sarah recalls a meeting with Huger, which probably occurred when the *McRae* was at Baton Rouge being fitted out with guns in 1861.

86. Possibly Fanny Cammack, daughter of the New Orleans banker Charles W. Cammack. The name given one of her brothers, Morgan, suggests a connection between the two families.

I said, I was so anxious for him to remain where he is, and defend us. Ah Mr Yankee! if you had nothing in the world but your brothers, and their lives hanging on a thread, *you* would write crazy letters too! And if you want to know what an excited girl is capable of, call around, and I will show you the use of a small seven shooter, and large carving knife which vibrate between my belt, and pocket, always ready for use.

April 27th.

What a day! Last night came a dispatch that New Orleans was under British protection (!) and that as it could not consequently be bombarded, the enemy's gun boats would probably pay us a visit this morning—those few (from nine to fifteen) which had succeeded in [p. 68] passing the Forts which have *not* surrendered (?). I went to church, sans m'inquietée,[87] but grew wonderfully anxious to get away before it was through, with the feeling that I was needed at home. When I at last got back, I found Lilly wild with excitement, picking up hastily what articles of clothing were necessary, and preparing for instant flight. The Yankees were in sight, the town was to be burned, we were to run to the woods, etc.

If the house had to burn, I had to make up my mind to run. So my treasure bag being tied around my waist as a bustle, a sack on my arm with a few necessary trifles and a few *un*necessary ones—I had not the heart to leave the prayer books father gave us—carving knife and pistol safe, I stood ready for instant flight. My papers I piled on the bed, ready to burn, with matches lying on them. I may here say, after all alarm was over, I found I had still on my desk all the letters I had ever received, almost, except the four I had hidden on me, and a bundle of odd things I had scratched off for my own amusement, besides this precious autobiography I am at present compiling, all of which would have afforded vast amusement to the Yankees. My pile still lies there though there may yet be reason to burn them, if not the house also. People fortunately changed their minds about the auto-da-fé, and the Yankees have not come at this hour, sundown, so the excitement abated somewhat, and Lilly tumbled in bed with a high fever as a consequence of her terror and exertions. [The page that followed is missing.]

87. Without worrying.

[p. 69] I was right, in my prophecy, for this is not the Will Pinkney I parted with. So woe begone, subdued, care worn, and sad! Where is devil-may-care, hearty, laughing mischief loving Will? He is good looking now, which he never was before, but I could not help saying "O Will, I would rather never have seen you, than find you so changed!" His old smile lighted his face for an instant as he said "Now quit, Sarah," and reproached me for not being glad to see him; but the next moment it died away, and here I sat talking to Will's ghost.

His was a sad story. He held one side of the river as the Yankees passed, until forced to retreat with his men as their cartridges gave out and Gen. Lovell[88] omitted sending them more, when they had to pass through the swamps, wading seven miles and a half, up to their waists in water, to escape. He gained the edge of the swamp, saw he was out, and tumbled over senseless. Two of his men got him some milk, and "woke him up" he says, so I suppose he must have fainted. His men fell down with exhaustion, got lost, or died in the swamp, until out of five hundred, one hundred reached here with him. All this he told in a quiet, sad way, leaving me to guess half, looking so heartbroken that it made my heart swell to look at him. He showed me his feet, with their thick clumsy shoes, and said an old negro had pulled them off to give him, for he came out of the swamp barefooted. They reached Lafourche river,[89] I believe, seized a boat, and landed here last night.

His wife and her child were on board with him—Heaven only knows how they got there; I did not [p. 70] understand. Theodore[90] went up with the rest of the troops to Port Hudson,[91] while he stopped here. I wanted to go for his wife, but he said she could not stay, and was not

88. Confederate General Mansfield Lovell, in command in New Orleans until he evacuated his troops before the arrival of Federal forces.

89. Bayou Lafourche, a distributary of the Mississippi River which runs in a southeasterly direction from the west-bank town of Donaldsonville through Ascension, Assumption, and Lafourche parishes.

90. Theodore Pinkney, younger brother of Will Pinkney, later served in the 4th Louisiana Infantry. While census and military records spell the name Pinkney, court records in East Feliciana Parish spell it Pinckney. The brothers were sons of Dr. Charles E. Pinckney and his wife Ellen Elder.

91. Town on the Mississippi River north of Baton Rouge. The Confederates fortified positions on the bluffs there late in 1862 and early in 1863 in an attempt to restrict Union control of the river, but surrendered the garrison after a siege that ended July 9, 1863.

in a state to be seen, for she had run off just as she then was. He was going for a carriage, would leave in half an hour, and take her to his grandfather's [92] without delay. He would rejoin his men there, on the railroad, and march from Clinton to the Jackson railroad,[93] and on to Corinth. A long journey for men so dispirited, but they will conquer in the end. Beauregard's army [94] will increase rapidly at this rate; the whole country is aroused, and every man who owns a gun, and many who do not, are on the road to Corinth. We will conquer yet.

Ah! Will! Will Pinkney! how I wish I could have seen the same merry, good old face I looked goodbye at, a year ago, instead of this sad, care-worn one! I'll never see my Will Pinkney again—Will that I liked, and who liked me so much; this is his ghost, for mine is dead. There was nothing to recall him, except the frank, cordial way in which he met me, and a shadow of a smile that died in an instant. What made him change? he was so nice before, he could not have been better; so what was the use of altering at all? I almost wish I had not seen him; it makes me sad. Bah! I expect a man who has narrowly escaped death, and who is now running for his life to be jolly, and look extremely happy! When he comes back, and the war is over, I will see the same old Will again— only we will not meet again, I fear!

[p. 71] April 30th

I have but one thought to day—one that must ever be connected with that date—Harry. I see him standing before that gun, the flash, his fall. The rain pouring down on his prostrate body, see him borne to the carriage, and hear his moan of "To Brother's! For God's sake, quick to Brother's!" From that early hour until the clock struck three, his suffering and patience, while Sister sat near and waited on him or held his hand, God bless her for her tenderness and love!

92. William Elder, in whose household William and Theodore Pinkney were enumerated in the 1860 census. Elder, age 71 in that census, and his wife Mary, 60, operated a hotel in the vicinity of Linwood.

93. The New Orleans, Jackson & Great Northern Railroad. The Clinton and Port Hudson Railroad would take them as far as Clinton.

94. Confederate General P. G. T. Beauregard, a hero after Fort Sumter and First Manassas, had pulled his army back to Corinth, Mississippi, following a performance at Shiloh that brought him criticism. At the end of May he abandoned Corinth.

She told me all afterwards; how he would groan and say "What a fool I have been!" (O Hal!) so often through the day, and said he was glad they had sent for mother. Then his restlessness after all the doctors had left him, though they said it was nothing and he would soon be well, asking if they were not coming, yet; but begging her at the same time not to go away to find out. "For God's sake, dear Sister, dont leave me, or I shall die!" and as she hurried away in spite of his prayer, to bring the doctor, she met him at the door, and brought him back. The doctor looked, saw the change that had taken place, and went to prepare Brother. As he came back, and stood in the door, Hal called him and said there was something the matter with his throat. The doctor said no, there was nothing; but he never moving—he never moved of himself after they laid him there, said "Yes there is; I am dying, Sister." She sprang forward, so did the doctor, but he lay dead before them. Not a gasp, not a [p. 72] moan.

Brother had been told he would live through the night; as he came to the door, Sister met him, and her face told him all was over. Her hands closed his eyes, and she sat by our dead Harry until the men came to dress him. Jimmy had left him sleeping; as he came in again, Sister was sitting by his white, cold form which looked sleeping still. And God wiped all care and sorrow from his brow, and shed over his face the look they say I will wear when I too am dead. All night, from her room opposite the parlor where he lay, Sister watched him, and so much did he resemble me, that it was only by leaning over his coffin she could satisfy herself it was not I. It was good of God to let him look like me then; I love him so much for it!

What an awful hush there must have been in that house! Death is dreadful any where; but the first in so large a family—O it was awful! I dont suppose I will ever again feel what I did then; it was [my] first experience of a great misery, and I will hardly feel it so intensely again. I was with father when he died, had heard him say he looked to it as a release from his sufferings, saw how fearlessly he waited for it, and how willingly he died; so it was not so hard to bear as this, for we had not recovered from Harry's death, and a blow that might otherwise have crushed us, was not so severe as it might have been before, for we were too stunned to realize what had happened for many a day after. But this, so sudden and unexpected, he to go so young[95] and with his life just opening before him, in [p. 73] so short a time—it was indeed hard to bear! Perhaps it would have been easier, if I could have kissed his dead face as I did father's; but that was not to be, for he was buried the next morning in New Orleans. But it was too sad to have him sleeping where we could never carry flowers to his grave, so father sent for his dead body.

Friday the 3d, I lay down for an hour, when father woke me to stay with mother; the boat had come, and Miriam was staying with Lilly; so I got up just as the clock struck midnight, to wait. I shall never forget the dreadful sensation of waiting for his coffin to come. The whistle of the boat, the ringing of the bells, the motion of the paddles, had never seemed so loud, or so unearthly before; and I buried my face in my hands leaning on Harry's bed, and listened and waited, before I went to mother. Then we two were left alone, waiting together, until father brought Sister, and went out again. She took mother's hand, and sat by her while I sat at her feet, looking at one and the other, hardly seeing either. Not a word was spoken; I believe she bent down and kissed me, but we sat silent and motionless for a long hour, with no sound from the whole world around reaching us, but the puffing of that boat which had brought them to us, and the jingling of the bells.

At last father came, and mother spoke to ask if he had brought Harry; no: they were carrying him to his grave even now. That was the first we knew of never even seeing his coffin again; she gave a loud cry, and Sister took me out on the gallery where she laid my head in her lap and [p. 74] told me of his last few days, and how he died. The boat had gone then, and there was an awful hush in that dim light, where every star seemed looking at me with a deeper meaning than I had ever before seen in their eyes. Here we sat until Brother came in at four, with Gibbes, Charlie, and Cousin Will, the few who had followed him to his grave that night. Sister went home again in the morning, and took Miriam with her, so Jimmy and I were alone at home with father & mother. I went alone to his grave that evening, and jumped the high fence to get to him, for the gate was locked. Jimmy came for me in the

95. Later Sarah added a note: "24 yrs & 6 mos."

buggy and took me away, driving far out on another road with me.

I did not know of my weakness until Sunday, when walking a few squares back of home with Lydia, after sunset, I felt my strength going. We got within half a square of home, when I felt I was losing all control over my limbs, and would presently fall, but I said nothing. I knew the footstep that was following behind us, and that to show my inability to proceed would be to chalenge [*sic*] his assistance; I would have moved on if it had cost me my life. Would he keep just behind us always, and never pass? I forgot everything in my effort to keep up until he should pass before. At last he did, stopping an instant, as though he wanted to speak; my head dropped; he passed on, on ten steps, I knew I was safe, and dropped heavily on Lydia's shoulder, managed to say I could no longer walk. She held me up, and half way dragged me home, and for three weeks I lay still on my sofa.

At first father and Jimmy would drive out with me in the evening, such nice, long rides; but the Dr stopped them in a [p. 75] week or two, and kept me quiet on my sofa. They said it was the long walk, the jump over the fence; I did not know, or care until I looked at father's anxious distressed face as he would bend over me and ask how his little daughter was, and then felt the pain I suffered was nothing to what he felt on seeing me in that state, and I tried to get strong for his sake. At the end of three weeks I said I would get well at Linwood, so I stayed there ten days, and then coming home, renounced all claims to invalidism, only father did not believe I was well, and still looked so unhappy about me that I pretended to be much stronger than I was. The sick, tired feeling never left me. So tired, that it seemed as if only Death could rest me; yet I acted a lie almost daily in the six months following, and would get up and walk around the parlor when hardly able to stand, to show him how well I was.

I could not walk more than a few squares, so he and Jimmy would take me to the graveyard in the buggy when ever I wanted to go, until the horse died, a few months later, when I announced myself strong enough to walk there, and able or not, have done it ever since. Some days, when I felt really strong, father would look so happy to see me going about as usual; but those days were not as numerous as I pretended. And yet, I blame myself for not trying harder to keep up, though I hardly know how I could; I am sure I did my best. And yet father died believing me doomed to die young, saying his only regret was that he could not live to take care of me, that I needed it more than the rest. I wish he could see how strong I am now! Though here comes the old wearied, tired feeling which I shall never be rid of, warning me to cease.

[p. 76] May 4th Sunday.

Howell and Lydia drove down yesterday, and spent the day with us, so our "goodbye" remained to be said over again, positively the last, this time, for we are assured the Yankees will be here before night closes, and then I would like to see either of them venture down here! Shortly after they came in, Capt Davis and Mr Hughes entered with Charlie, for they were to be his guests for a day or two. I never saw, or heard of them before, and have not an idea of who they are, beyond that they are friends of Charlie's, and live in Texas, but I liked them.

I cannot give up my childish habit of judging of people at first sight; I rather believe in it; so while they were making their bow (they came in while Howell was making me promise solemnly to write, if I should ever have an opportunity of evading Yankee watchfulness, which promise I mean to keep, so help me my mother wit and native cunning) while they were bowing, I say, I made up my mind that the tall one, with so much white to his eye, must be called Adolphe, or something still more sentimental, and that I would not like him as much as the smaller one, who looked so good, nice, and clean, that his name must be George. (Mem. I have since discovered it is *Sam*! Horrid, but still, he *is* nice!) So having made up my mind I would like them, I next made up my mind to be agreeable—whether I succeeded or not, is of no importance—I did not ask. But I liked them both, and was sorry to see them go, when half an hour ago they said good bye, for they are getting [p. 77] out of the way of the Yankees, too.

I noticed about them something which, within the last year, I have begun to notice about others also; and that was a look of halfway wonder, and then a quiet, though hearty laugh, at the end of one of my stupid remarks, just as though it were something original or witty. I dont halfway like it; it makes me wonder too, what they laugh at, and as I do not see the fun, it is not altogether comfortable to think they are laughing at something I am ignorant of. I would never have noticed it, if it had not been for one person, or mother saying "Did you see how shocked Miss So and So was at what you said? or how Mr Such a one was laughing?"

All such remarks repeated any time these last four years, has [*sic*] at last had the effect of making me distrust myself; when I hear anyone laugh at me, and wonder what gaucherie I can have committed unconsciously. If the laugh was an impertinent, or obtrusive one, I should be the first to take offense, for I have the reputation at least, of being sensitive; but when I look quickly at the guilty one, I am satisfied that he— it is almost invariably a gentleman—is wondering while he laughs, at something he does not half comprehend, just as I am, so I cannot ask what it is, or get angry. I should like to know what it is too. Do you know, Sarah, that I am sometimes inclined to believe what mother has often told me, that you sometimes say dreadful things in speaking to gentlemen? But it cannot be that, because you would feel it the next instant, if you did; besides, gentlemen [p. 78] would not laugh at it.

Dear me! what a position mine is. All really vulgar, low minded people turn up their noses at me and cry "What a prude!" and all prudes roll their saintly eyes heavenward, and shriek "How improper!" When I venture to say the truth, the whole truth, and nothing but the truth. I hang between heaven and hell, as it were, and am fit for neither. Prudes are afraid of me, and I'll have nothing to do with the vulgar. For I can *feel* a vulgar mind, before I know it. There is a taint in the moral atmosphere around them that strikes me instantly, and I can trace it in the lip, in the eye, never allowing myself to judge them, or give it a name, but feeling that such are not friends for me, gathering the while the spiritual robes of my soul, that they may not come in contact. Not that I consider myself more pure, for we are children of one Father, but to use a homely, though to *me* forcible illustration, my friendship, and bucket, are alike sacred objects in my eye, and no one is invited to share either, who is not particularly clean and nice.

And all this tirade is àpropos of what? It was first suggested by one of those looks before alluded to, which I *felt* was exchanged between the two gentlemen who have just gone, and afterwards, my fancy rushed off in a strain it has charted many times before, to its self, and had its own way. Now it is exhausted, let us return. Yes; I liked those two gentlemen; enough to give them up my pretty little room, at all events.

[p. 79] I wonder if they thought it pretty too? They probably know all about it, for I know they played with my dumb bells, examined my pet books, and undoubtedly saw Miriam's old corset I afterwards discovered on top of my desk. Pleasant, is it not? I wonder if my Cologne was nice, and what they thought of the toilet table? Ugh! Just think of a couple of pair of boots reposing on my snow white spread! Away with the monstrous thought!

And what do I care what that look meant? Whether it meant I was cracked, crazy, fool, idiot, or wicked? As though it mattered, so long as they love me at home! Let it mean what they will, so long as they were anything but impudent to me. Charlie has just stopped me to tell me a sentence I shall put down here to prove whether I was right in my opinion of the one I called "Adolphe." His friend said to him "You have completely upset poor Hughes by bringing him here; you should not have done it." In answer to Charlie's why? he said something about "having been obliged to give him a good lecture last night, and tried to impress him with the idea that these were not 'marrying' times."

Bah! I have devoted more time and space than I have yet bestowed on my best friend, to two utter strangers I'll never see, or care to see again! So here ends the last word of them, or thought, which will ever trouble my brains.

May 5th.
Vile old Yankee boats, four in number, passed up this morning without stopping![96] After all our excitement, this "silent contempt" annihilates me! What in the world do they mean? The river was covered with burning cotton; perhaps they want to see where it came from.

[p. 80] May 6th.
Gibbes once said of me "I believe she agrees with me, that there is no man on earth good enough, or smart enough, for her." It gave me a thrill of delight to hear that *he* thought that, but as to the idea ever entering *my* brain, never, Gibbes, never! Once, about eighteen month[s], or two years ago, it flashed over my mind that Hal, and father

96. The *Brooklyn*, the *Itasca*, the *Sciota*, and the *Winona*. See ship's logs in *ORN*, ser. I, vol. 18.

thought I was—not *smart*, but that I was—reasonable. I hate even to write it here, it looks so conceited, but the idea did present its self an instant, so I must tell the truth; I remember feeling a vague wonder for an instant, when I checked it with a laugh at my presumption. It came again, and again, though. I gathered it from the way Hal spoke to me, the pride father took in me, and the way Miriam, whom I considered so wise and independent, consulted me, and defered to my judgement (?) How could I help it?

To be sure I was conscious that it was all a mistake, and that I was sailing under false colors, as it were; but I could not help feeling an occasional sensation of pleasure at the mere thought of being considered something better than a fool, though I myself was satisfied I was not, in reality. It may be very pleasant to humbug the whole world; but what gratification is it, when you are behind the scenes, and know it is all make believe? Give me the unpretending, solid ore, and I'll leave you all the tinsel it would require to blind the world's eyes with.

No, Gibbes. I have just sense enough to know I am a fool; so it is not because I consider myself wiser than others, that I dont tumble in love and get married [p. 81] immediately; nor is it because I think myself so good that I can afford to feel a superiority over others, either. I know my wicked, sinful heart too well. Hal used to say he did not believed [*sic*] I had ever sinned; but he did not know. It is pleasant to have one's brothers talk that way of you; but it is also mortifying, when you consider how little it is deserved.

Shall I say here, if not aloud, why it is I have never yet fallen in love? Simply because I have yet to meet the man I would be willing to acknowledge as my lord and master. For unconfessed to myself, until very recently, I have dressed up an image in my heart, and have unconsciously worshipped it under the name of Beau Ideal. Not a very impossible one, for doubtless there are many such, though the genus is not to be found in Baton Rouge; but still I am ashamed to acknowledge such a schoolgirl weakness, even to myself; for I know if any moonstruck girl described her beau ideal to me, the only sympathy she would get would be a slight elevation of the nose. I hate sentimentality; but way down in my heart, I am afraid I rather like *sentiment*.

Do you remember the distinction? Well, my lord and master must be some one I shall never have to blush for, or be ashamed to acknowledge; the one that, after God, I shall most venerate and respect; and as I cannot respect a fool, he must be intelligent. I place that first, for I consider it the chief qualification in man, just as I believe a pure heart is the chief beauty of a woman. Yes, and he [p. 82] must be smart enough for two; his brains must do duty for both, and supply all my deficiencies.[97] Now that is settled, I hardly know what comes next; I place all other qualifications on a single level. Oh! I forgot amiability! That ranks immediately after intelligence; sometimes I am inclined to give it the precedence, for I am satisfied that no home is a happy one where it is not an inmate. He must be amiable enough to set me a good example, and philosophical enough to teach me to laugh at the petty annoyance of this life. I could be forever cheerful where I had a kind smile to meet mine; loving hearts and kind words are as necessary as the air I breath[e], so my Master must be amiable. He must be brave as man can be; brave to madness, even. I would hate him if I saw him flinch for an instant while standing at the mouth of a loaded cannon. Let him die, if necessary; but as to a coward—! Merci! je n'en veux pas![98] I am no coward; it does not run in our blood; so how could I respect a man who was one? O what unspeakable contempt I would feel for him!

He must be a man of the world. I have mixed so little in society, have so great a distaste for it, and so much mauvaise honte,[99] that I am by no means calculated to shine there; but I would wish him to do so. Of course he must be entitled to it by birth and education; I could marry no other than a gentleman. I do not mean gentleman in the vulgar sense— handsome young fellow with well oiled [p. 83] hair, and even more impudence than pomatum; *such* a beauty, and *so* rich! (although he may have been a shoe black when very young)—, no; I mean gentleman in my signification of the term, which, to the qualities mentioned a while ago, adds principle as firm and immoveable—as the rock of Gibralta [*sic*], a sense of honor as nice and delicate as a woman's, and a noble,

97. In the space at the top of the page she later wrote: "*Wonderful!* 1896."

98. Thanks! I don't want any of it!

99. Self-consciousness.

generous, pure heart. That is what I call a gentleman; how many of my present friends answer to the description? There are many such in this world, though.

He may be as ugly as mud, and I will never think of it; the more ugly he is, the more intelligent he will be. Who ever saw a perfect face on man or woman that showed a spark of intelect [*sic*]? Then, the uglier he is, the better he will be; your handsome men care much more for their beauty than they do for their morals. I never saw a blackleg,[100] that I know of, but from what I have heard, am inclined to believe they are all good looking.

I would not wish him to be rich; "poor and content is rich enough:"[101] I would like him to be just what I have been all my life, neither rich nor poor. I am satisfied that is the true secret of happiness. As I said before, he must be au-fait in the ways of the world. There is a nameless something in the air, or manner of a perfect gentleman which has a perfect fascination for me, though I cannot give it a name. I always look for it though, and feel as [p. 84] though something was missing when I do not find it, which means ninty nine cases out of every hundred. Above all, he must have—a Profession! If he is rich, smash! go the Banks some fine morning, and Master is turned adrift on the tender mercies of the world, without the means to turn an honest penny, even if he had the inclination or energy, which most rich men do not. "He cannot work, to beg he is ashamed,"[102] so he quietly settles down, and goes to the dogs, not forgetting you, but insisting on your company for the first time in your married life. If he is poor, the Banks may fail without hurting him; his profession gives him a position until he can claim and sustain it by his own exertions; success crowns his efforts at last. Poverty, with such a person as I have described, is infinitely better than wealth in abundance, with a fool of a parvenue. I am satisfied that it is the life for me.

Woe be to me, if I could feel superior to him for an instant! Black misery would drape the rest of my young days, and settled despair grace my old ones. I need some one I would delight to acknowledge as the

---

100. A professional gambler or sharper.
101. Shakespeare, *Othello*.
102. Luke 16:3.

model of all goodness and intelect on earth; some one to look up to, and admire unfeignedly, some one to lead me upward, and teach me to be worthy of his regard. From what I have said, one of these days, looking back when I am an old maid, I will turn up my nose and say "Why did you not say marry a teacher at once? better marry a *man* and engage a teacher afterwards." Merci, my old maid! let me have my talk out while I am young! In a dozen years from now, perhaps it will be only [p. 85] reasonable for me to turn up my nose at all such folly, fancy sketches, etc. Mais en attendant,[103] let me have my fun out, will you?

I have described such a man as I firmly believe exists, such a one as I believe I should marry, if I expect to be happy. One that I could respect above all others; one, whose children (I may here say I have the greatest penchant for widowers and lawyers) I could bring up in the belief my mother taught hers, that their father was the greatest and best man in the world. *When* I meet such a man, then, O Gibbes! I will tumble heels over head in love, and get married forthwith, even if I had to do the courting! Until then, Cupid spare my heart! I will need it *all* for him, and am inclined to believe that hearts and eggs are much the same: they keep fresh enough if you let them alone, but get wofully addled by being tossed about. Cupid spare my heart, I say! I prefer an omlette of fresh eggs, and perhaps *he* does too! "Go thy way; when I have a more convenient season, I will send for thee!"[104]

May 9th

Our lawful (?) owners have at last arrived. About sunset day before yesterday, the Iroquois anchored here, and a graceful young Federal stepped ashore, carrying a Yankee flag over his shoulder, and asked the way to the Mayor's office.[105] I like the style! If we girls of B.R. had

103. But in the meantime.

104. Acts 24:25.

105. The officer had been sent by Captain James S. Palmer, commanding the *Iroquois*.

been at the landing instead of the men, that Yankee should never have insulted us by flying his flag in our faces! *We* would have opposed his landing except under a flag of truce; but [p. 86] the men let him alone, and he even found a poor Dutchman willing to show him the road! He did not accomplish much; said a formal demand would be made next day, and asked if it was safe for the men to come ashore and buy a few necessaries, when he was assured the air of B.R. was very unhealthy for Federal soldiers at night. He promised very magnanimously not [to] shell us out, if we did not molest him; but I notice none of them dare set their feet on terra-firma, except the officer who has now called three times on the Mayor,[106] and who is said to tremble visibly as he walks the streets.

Last evening came the demand: the town must [be] surrendered immediately; the federal flag Must be raised, they would grant us the same terms they granted to New Orleans. Jolly terms those were! The answer was worthy of a Southerner. It was "the town was defenseless, if we had cannon, there were not men enough to resist; but if forty vessels lay at the landing,—it was intimated that we were in their power, and more ships coming up—we would not surrender; if they wanted, they might come Take us; if they wished the Federal flag hoisted over the Arsenal, they might put it up for themselves, the town had no control over Government property." Glorious! What a pity they did not shell the town! But they are taking us at our word, and this morning they are landing at the Garrison, and presently the Bloody banner will be floating over our heads. "Better days are coming, we'll all go right."

"All devices, signs, and flags of the confederacy [p. 87] shall be suppressed." So says Picayune Butler.[107] Good. I devote all my red, white, and blue silk to the manufacture of Confederate flags. As soon as one is confiscated, I make another, until my ribbon is exhausted, when I will sport a duster emblazoned in high colors, "Hurra! for the Bonny blue flag!" Henceforth, I wear one pinned to my bosom—not a duster, but a little flag—the man who says take it off, will have to pull it off for

---

106. The mayor was Benjamin F. Bryan.

107. One of the nicknames given General Benjamin F. Butler, from a minstrel song of that name. The picayune was a small coin and Butler was a small man, or at least a short one. He was better known as Beast Butler for his iron-fisted military rule in New Orleans.

himself; the man who dares attempt it—well! a pistol in my pocket will fill up the gap. I am capable, too.

This is a dreadful war to make even the hearts of women so bitter! I hardly know myself these last few weeks. I, who have such a horror of bloodshed, consider even killing in self defense murder, who cannot wish them the slightest evil, whose only prayer is to have them sent back in peace to their own country, *I* talk of killing them! for what else do I wear a pistol and carving knife? I am afraid I *will* try them on the first one who says an insolent word to me. Yes, and repent for ever after in sack cloth and ashes! O if I was only a man! Then I could don the breeches, and slay them with a will! If some few Southern women were in the ranks, they could set the men an example they would not blush to follow. Pshaw! there are *no* women here! We are *all* men!

May 10th.

Last night about one o'clock, I was wakened, and told mother and Miriam had come. Oh how glad I was! I tumbled out of bed half asleep and hugged Miriam in a dream, but waked [p. 88] up when I got to mother. They came up under a flag of truce, on a boat going up for provisions, which, by the way, was brought to by half a dozen Yankee ships in succession, with a threat to send a broadside into her if she did not stop—the wretches knew it *must* be under a flag of truce; no boats leave, except by special order to procure provisions.

What tales they had to tell! They were on the warf, and saw the Yankee ships sailing up the river, saw the broadside fired into Will Pinkney's regiment,[108] the boats we set afire—our gunboats—floating down to meet them wrapped in flame, twenty thousand bales of cotton blazing in a single pile, molasses and sugar spread over everything, and stood there opposite to where one of the ships landed, expecting a broadside every instant, and resolute not to be shot in the back. How I wish I had been there!

And Capt. Huger is *not* dead! They had hopes of his life for the first time day before yesterday. Miriam saw the ball that had just been taken from his wound, and which will probably leave him lame for the rest of his life. It will be an ornament, a glory to him, for even Yankee officers

108. The 8th Louisiana Infantry Battalion.

say, that never in their lives, did they see so gallant a little ship, or one who fought so desperately as the McRae! Men and officers fought like devils. Think of all those great leviathans after the poor little Widow Mickey! One came bearing down on her side ways, while the Brooklyn[109] fired on her from the other side, when brave Captain Warley[110] put the nose of the Manassas under the first, and tilted her over so that the whole broadside passed over, instead of through the McRae, who spit back its poor little [p. 89] fire at both, and after all was lost, carried the wounded and prisoners to New Orleans, and was scuttled by its own sailors in port. Glorious Capt. Huger! and think of his sending word to Jimmy, sick as he is, that "his little brass cannon was 'game' to the last!" O good Capt Huger! How I hope he will get well!

Brave Capt. Warley, that dare devil, is prisoner, on his way to Fort Warren,[111] the home of all brave and patriotic men. We'll have him out. I wish I could fight for him! And Jimmy, my poor little brother! If I have not mentioned him, it is not because he has been an instant out of my thoughts. The day the McRae went down, he got out of his sick bed, resolved to go on her as the Mississippi was not ready. He got as far as the St. Charles[112] when he fell so very sick, that he had to be carried back to brother's. Only his desperate sickness saved him from being among the killed or wounded on that gallant little ship. A few days after, they told him the fate of the ship and that Capt Huger was dead; and the dear little fellow burst out crying when he told mother of it. No wonder! Capt Huger has been as tender and kind to him as his own father was, God bless him for it! I shall love him for ever for it, and all those who are kind to my dear little brother.

The enemy ships were sailing up, and throwing a few articles in a carpet sack he kissed them good bye and started off on the railroad for Richmond, Corinth, anywhere to fight. Sick, weak, staggering, hardly able to stand, he went off two weeks ago yesterday, we know not where,

109. The *Brooklyn*, a steam-driven sloop, was a sister ship of Farragut's flagship, the *Hartford*.

110. Lieutenant Alexander F. Warley was in command of the ironclad ram *Manassas*, one of the vessels in the Confederates' Mississippi River fleet.

111. Union prison in Boston harbor.

112. The St. Charles Hotel in New Orleans, where Commodore Hollins and General Mansfield Lovell (and later General Butler) had their headquarters.

and have never since heard of him. Whether he has succumbed [p. 90] to his Jaundice, and the dreadful dysentery he has been suffering, and lies sick or dead on the road, God only knows. We can only wait and pray; and O please God take care of him and send my dear little Jimmy home in safety.

And this is war! Heaven save me from like scenes and experiences again. I was wild with excitement last night when Miriam described how the soldiers marching to the depot,[113] waved their hats to the crowds of women and children shouting "God bless you ladies! We'll fight for you!" And they, waving their handkerchieves, sobbed with one voice "God bless you soldiers! Fight for us!" What a scene! How I wish I had been in the ranks!

We too are having our fun. Early in the evening, four more boats sailed up before the town.[114] We saw them from the corner, though three squares off, crowded with men even up the riggings. The American Flag was flying from every peak, and received in profound silence, from the hundreds gathered together. I could hardly refrain from a groan. Much as I once loved that flag, I *hate* it now! I came back, made myself a Confederate one about five inches long, put the stem in my belt, pinned the flag to my shoulder, and walked down town, creating great excitement among women & children. One old negro cried "My young missus has got *her* flag a flying anyhow!" Nettie had a modest little one of two inches hidden almost in the folds of her dress, but we were the only two who ventured. Now that *we* have set the example, I suppose the rest will follow.

We went to the State House grounds, took a good look at the Brooklyn, which was crowded [p. 91] with people who took a look at us too. [Sentence lined through] The picket stationed at the Garrison took alarm at half a dozen men on horse back, and ran saying the citizens were attacking them; when the kind officers sent us word again that if they were molested, the town would be shelled. Let them! Wretches! Does it take thirty thousand men, and millions of dollars to murder defenseless women and children? O the great nation! Bravo!

113. The railroad station in New Orleans, before Miriam and her mother's return to Baton Rouge.

114. These appear to have been the *Brooklyn*, which had left and then returned; the *Hartford*, with Farragut aboard; the *Richmond*; and gunboat No. 4, the *Wissahickon*.

May 11th

I—I am disgusted with myself. No unusual thing but I am *peculiarly* disgusted this time. Last evening I went to Mrs Brunots, with not an idea of going beyond, with my flag again flying. They were all going to the State House, so I went with them; to my great distress, some fifteen or twenty Federal officers were standing on the first terrace, stared at like wild beasts by the curious crowd. I had not expected to meet them, and felt a painful conviction that I was unnecessarily attracting attention by an unladylike display of defiance, from the crowd gathered there. But what was I to do? I felt humiliated, conspicuous, everything that is painful and disagreeable; but—strike my colors in the face of an enemy? Never! Nettie and Sophie had them too, but that was no consolation for the shame I suffered by such a display so totally distasteful to me. How I wished myself away, and chafed at my folly, and hated myself for being there, and every one for seeing me! I hope it will be [p. 92] a lesson to me always to remember a lady can gain nothing by such displays.

I was not ashamed of the flag of my country—I proved that by never attempting to remove it in spite of my mortification—but I was ashamed of my position, for these are evidently gentlemen, not the Billy Wilson's crew [115] we were threatened with. Fine, noble looking men they were, showing refinement and gentlemanly bearing in every motion; one cannot help but admire such foes. They set us an example worthy of our imitation, & one we would be benefitted by following. They come as victors, without either pretentions to superiority, or the insolence of conquerors; they walk quietly their way, offering no annoyance to the citizens, though they themselves are stared at most unmercifully, and pursued by crowds of ragged little boys, while even men gape at them with open mouths. They prove themselves gentlemen, while many of our citizens have proved themselves boors, and I admire them for their conduct. With a conviction that I had allowed myself to be influenced by bigoted narrow minded people, in believing them to be unworthy of respect or regard, I came home wonderfully changed in all my newly acquired sentiments, resolved never more to

115. The 6th New York Zouaves commanded by Colonel William Wilson had a reputation for toughness. They were assigned to the defense of Santa Rosa Island, near Pensacola, Florida.

wound their feelings, who were so careful of ours, by such unnecessary
display, and hung my flag on the parlor mantle there to wave, if it will,
in the shades of private life; but to make a show, make me conspicuous
and ill at ease, as I was yesterday—Never again!

[p. 93] There was a dozen officers in church[116] this morning, and the
Psalm for the 11th day seemed so singularly appropriate to the feelings of the people, that I felt uncomfortable for them. They answered
with us, though; drew out their prayerbooks, found the places, knelt
and stood at the right time, so I was satisfied they were brought up in
that religion. I could not help noticing the three directly in front of us,
though I did not examine the others. Just before we sat down for the
sermon, I put my prayer book on the back of their pew, where it always
lays. I put it too far out on my side, for as I turned to sit down, my dress
caught it, and my hoops gently slipped it over into their pew before
I could catch it. I sat down dreadfully mortified. I was afraid if they
noticed it they would believe I did it purposely to attract their attention,
or make them pick it up, and between my agony for fear they should,
and my hope that they would not, I lost the first part of the sermon
entirely, and only by the greatest effort compelled myself to listen to
the latter. I hated myself worse than ever.

What if they should believe I was contemptible enough to do it purposely? Not that I cared particularly for them, but for all those I knew
back of me would *they* believe it too? Those capable of such things,
would gladly include me in their list, so I dare not raise my eyes, from
shame at the mere suspicion. As we stood up to go, one turned for his
hat—the book was on it—I waited to see no more, but hurried out of
the pew with Miriam, leaving them still standing, and left the book
there to be recovered at some future time; it would have been *too* much
to get it then. My name printed in full, too! O it is dreadful! What can
they believe?

[p. 94] May 14th.

I am begining [sic] to believe we are even of more importance in
Baton Rouge than we thought we were. It is laughable to hear the
things a certain set of people who know they cant visit us, say about the

116. The Morgans worshipped at St. James Episcopal Church in the next block south on
Church Street.

whole family. Of course we cannot notice any remarks made by such a class, and the consequence is that indifference to their opinions redoubles their rage and spite, until they exhaust themselves in venting their petty jealousy in loud words which occasionally reach our ears—and have a wonderful effect on our conduct, of course! When father was alive, they dared not talk about us aloud, beyond calling us the "Proud Morgans" and the "Aristocrats of Baton Rouge" which titles, far from annihilating us, we only received as our due, conscious of deserving them, and by no means ashamed of it. But now father is gone, these people imagine we are public property to be criticised, vilified and abused to their hearts' content, and occasionally find themselves mistaken.

There was our beloved friend Mollie who put her arms around my neck and cried with me saying she knew how I worshipped home and father, and knew what a blow his death was to me, and was *so* sorry for me! I believed her, and loved her for speaking so of father. How could I know she was a liar or a hypocrite? I am not enough of either to be able to find her out alone, and gave her credit for as much truth and sincerity as I myself possessed. The Innocent went down town two days after father was buried, said she had never in her life seen people act as shockingly [p. 95] as we had the day after father was buried, and as to Sarah—her "carrying on" and laughing was perfectly disgraceful! She and a "parcel of young men" went there to condole with the poor people, but bless your soul! she found there was no condolence needed *there*! Was there ever a more useless—lie?

That evening, Miriam and I had just come in from the graveyard at dark, and after supper, we, mother, and Charlie sat down in the parlor, each sick at heart, not exchanging a word. We heard a rustle at the folding doors, and then saw Miss Castleton peeping at us through the opening. Of course we asked her in. O dear no! she couldn't; she heard we were going to New Orleans, and came to find out if it was true. She sat down though, saying Mr Enders [117] was waiting for her at the front door—a person we knew by sight, but had never met. Charlie said ask him in, and in he came. Failing in finding out all she wished, after sus-

117. Probably Frank H. Enders, who appears in Sarah's diary frequently over the months she and Miriam were at Linwood. He was not a son of Dr. Peter M. Enders, though he may have been a nephew or a cousin.

taining half an hour's conversation by her own conversational powers, she took her leave, and this most indelicate, unfeeling visit came to an end. It was an outrage on decency; and mother said at the time she had only come to find out how we behaved. I could not believe in such depravity, and gave her credit for the most charitable motives. I flatter myself that we made no unnecessary display of our feelings before a heartless woman, and strange man; if I had choaked, I would not have shown the border of my handkerchief.

The story she told on all occasions, to our friends, as well as foes, originated from that. Only she had a thousand variations [p. 96] and additional particulars. One story was that she did not mean to come in with "her young man," but Miriam, laughing and talking on the gallery (by herself?) called them and *insisted* on their coming in, instead of passing, and they passed a charming evening! That girl came here for six weeks after; shed her crocodile tears over me, spoke of what father was to us, and how she had wept to hear me speak of his dying—she went on with her same old lies all the time. We gave a semblance to the tale by being seen in her company, and no one had the Christian charity to tell us of these lies, until Mrs Carter[118] took pity on me, for fighting that girl's battles and believing her to be what the whole world said she was not, and told me this story.

When it was known it had reached me, the whole town was ready to rush in and corroborate it; many who had heard her tell it were among them. I asked no confidence. I was cut to the heart. If it had been true, I would not have suffered so; but a lie is harder to refute than the truth, and this came near making me very sick. For three days at Linwood I could not hold up my head, or even talk, except when I made an effort to be cheerful before the General. But once alone, down went my head, and I shed more tears over my first lesson in human depravity than I ever expect to shed again. I prayed God to forgive her, and teach me to, harder than I have prayed for myself, I fear. But once let the thought of *my* rejoicing at my dear father's death, or the rest of us acting so shockingly cross my mind, and down my head would drop again, and many a night I cried myself asleep in my bed.

118. It is difficult to tell whether Sarah's references to "Mrs Carter" are to General Carter's wife, Frances Priscilla Howell Carter, or his daughter-in-law, Helen Carter. Most seem to be to Helen. Frances Carter was a first cousin of Varina Howell Davis.

When I came home, she [p. 97] ran up to me with open arms, and wanted to kiss me. This was my revenge; I flatter myself it is peculiar: I put out my arm, and motioned her not to kiss me. "Not going to kiss me?" she asked in amazement, and came nearer. I put my hand on her shoulder, and pushed her off gently saying "No; dont dare kiss me" as quietly as though I was in fun. She knew how earnest it was though, for she sat down, and after a while said she would not call again, until she had an explanation. "Certainly not" I answered. "I shall not expect you again; but am ready to give you my explanation at any time or place you name." She never asked for it though; a guilty conscience needs no accuser.

The next time I met, I bowed. It is a civility I bestow on every negro I meet in the street, and I would not willingly place her below negroes in my estimation. Besides, it is so dreadfully low to "cut" people, that I knew she could do it better than I could, as I very seldom practice vulgarities of any kind, and remembered she was an adept in the art. As I expected, she cut me dead. So much the better. It is *something* to cut one of the Miss Morgans, and she can boast of it for the rest of her life; where as it would have been no honor to me to cut *her*. That was my sole revenge. We have never contradicted her story; our most intimate friends have never received any information from us on the subject; while she goes about talking of us constantly, and asking what we say about her as though we took the trouble to mention her!

That was the first lie brought up against us. It throve so well, that others have been tempted to try their hands, too, 'till [p. 98] their number is amazing. The town bothers its self about our concerns much more than we do. They went wild on the subject of our not going in mourning; their tender feelings were outraged at such a breech [sic] of propriety and decency, and of *course* we were not grieved at father's or Harry's death, if we did not wear black! I went to church the Sunday after each died; they were shocked. Propriety required that I should not appear for several weeks; as though I cared for Propriety! I went to church because I needed the consolation I felt it would afford, and did not see an object in the whole house except the minister, so that if virtuous indignation had been stamped on every face, I would not have seen it. Bah! let them attend to their own affairs! If they regulate their own conduct, they will be doing well.

And now, because they find absurdities dont succeed, they try improbabilities. So yesterday the town was in a foment because it was reported the Federal officers had called on the Miss Morgans, and all the gentlemen [were] anxious to hear how they had been received. One had the grace to say "If they did, they received the best lesson there that they could get in town; those young ladies would meet them with the true Southern spirit." The rest did not know; they would like to find out. I suppose the story originated from the fact that we were unwilling to blackguard—yes, that is the word—the Federal officers here, and would not agree with many of our friends in saying they were liars, thieves, murderers, scoundrels, the scum of the [p. 99] earth, etc. Such epithets are unworthy of ladies, I say, and do harm, rather than advance our cause. Let them be what they will, it shall not make me less the lady; I say it is unworthy of anything except low newspaper war, such abuse, and will not join in.

I have a brother-in-law in the Federal army that I love and respect as much as anyone in the world, and shall not readily agree that his being a Northerner would give him an irresistible desire to pick my pockets, and take from him all power of telling the truth. No! There are few men I admire more than Major Drum, and I honor him for his independence in doing what he believes Right. Let us have liberty of speech, and action in our land, I say, but not gross abuse and calumny. Shall I acknowledge that the people we so recently called our brothers are unworthy of consideration, and are liars, cowards, dogs? Not I! *If* they conquer us, I acknowledge them as a superior race; I will not say we were conquered by cowards, for where would that place us? It will take a brave people to gain us, and that the Northerners undoubtedly are. I would scorn to have an inferior foe; I fight only my equals. These women may acknowledge that *cowards* have won battles in which their brothers were engaged, but I, I will ever say *mine* fought against brave men, and won the day. Which is most honorable? To the glory of our nation be it said, that it is only the women who talk that way. The men are all fighting, and these poor weak females sit over their knitting and pour [p. 100] out a weak, spiteful, pitiful stream of deluted [*sic*] rage against Cowards (?) their husbands and brothers think it worth while to fight against!

I hate to hear women on political subjects; they invariably make fools of themselves, and it sickens me to see half a dozen talking at once of what *they* would do, and what ought to be done; it gives me the greatest disgust, so I generally contrive to absent myself from such gatherings, as I seldom participate. But in this cause, it is necessary for me to express my opinion, sometimes, so I give it here, that I may not believe in after years I am quite a weathercock. I was never a secessionist, for I quietly adopted father's views on political subjects, with out meddling with them; but even father went over with his state,[119] and when so many outrages were committed by the fanatical leaders of the North, though he regretted the Union, said "Fight to the death for our liberty." I say so too. I would want to fight until we win the cause so many have died for. I dont believe in Secession, but I do in Liberty. I want the South to conquer, dictate its own terms, and go back to the Union[120] for I believe that apart, inevitable ruin awaits both.

It is a rope of sand, this Confederacy founded on the doctrine of Secession, and will not last many years—not five. The North Cannot subdue us. We are too determined to be free. They have no right to confiscate our property to pay debts they themselves have incurred. Death as a nation, rather than Union on such terms! We will have our Rights secured on so firm a [p. 101] basis, that it can never be shaken. If by power of overwhelming numbers they conquer us, it will be a barren victory over a desolate land. We, the natives of this loved soil will be beggars in [a] foreign land; we will not submit to despotism under the garb of Liberty. The north will find herself burdened with an unparalelled [sic] debt, with nothing to show for it, except deserted towns, and burning homes, a standing army which will govern with no small caprice, and an impoverished land. England will then be ready to step in, and Crash! the American Commonwealth will disappear in the British Monarchy.

Therefore I say, let us conquer, make our *own* terms, and be a band

119. A Unionist, Thomas Gibbes Morgan opposed secession, but remained loyal to his state after it seceded. "While I regret the existance [sic] of war," he wrote not long before his death, "I regret also that my advanced age and physical debility prevents me from taking the field with my sons, all of whom are in the service." Letter to Henry Marston, June 14, 1861, in Henry Marston and Family Papers, LSU Collections.

120. Here, between the lines, Sarah later wrote in "(Death and extermination first!)" and dated it "June," probably the same year. Two lines down she wrote: "(Death in the confederacy, rather than bliss in the Union!)."

of brothers in deed, and in truth; and so I pray daily "God bless our Southern Nation, and grant us peace in the name of Jesus Christ!" If that be treason, make the most of it!

May 17th

One of these days, when we are at peace, and all quietly settled in some corner of this wide world without anything particularly exciting to alarm us every few moments, and with the knowledge of what is the Future to us now, and will be the Past to us then, seeing it has all come right in the end, and has been for the best, we will wonder how we could ever have been foolish enough to await each day and hour with such anxiety, and if it were really possible that half the time as we lay down to sleep, we did not know but that we might be homeless and beggars in the morning. It will look unreal then; we will say it was imagination; but it is bitterly true now.

[p. 102] The Yankees left us some four days ago, to attack Vicksburg, leaving their flag flying in the Garrison, without a man to protect it, with the understanding that the town would be held responsible for it. It was meant for a trap, and the bait took, for night before last it was pulled down, and torn to pieces. Now, unless Will will have the kindness to sink a dozen of their ships up there—I hear he has command of the lower batteries—they will be back in a few days, and will execute their threat of shelling the town. If they do, what will become of us? All we expect, in the way of earthly property, is as yet mere paper; which will be so much trash if the South is ruined, as it consists of debts due father by many planters for professional services rendered, who, of course, will be ruined too, so all money is gone.

That is nothing; we will not be ashamed to earn our bread, so let it go. But this house, is really something to us, a shelter from the weather at least, if all associations and pecuniary values were put aside, and our servants too, we are loath to part with. Here the Yankees are on the side of the river, longing for an opportunity of "giving us a lesson," and a band of guerillas now organizing just back of us who will soon number over two thousand, are generally eager to have a "brush" with the enemy. With fire front and rear what chance is there for poor Baton Rouge? We will be burnt up in a few hours, with these people fighting over our heads, as it were.

The men say all women and children must be removed. Where to? Charlie suggests Greenwell for us. If we go, even if the town is spared the ordeal of fire, our house will be broken open by the soldiers and pillaged, for Butler has decreed that no [p. 103] unoccupied house will be respected. If we stay and witness the fight, if *they* are victorious, we are subject to hourly insult, for I understand that the officers who were here said "if the people did not treat them decently, they would know what it was, when Billy Wilson's crew got here. *They* would give them a lesson!" That select crowd is now in the city. Heaven help us when they will reach here! It is these small cities which suffer the greatest outrages. What are we to do?

A new proclamation from Butler has just come. It seems that the ladies have an ugly way of gathering their skirts when the Federals pass, to prevent contact, and some even turn up their noses—unlady-like to say the least, but which may be owing to the odor they have, which is said to be unbearable even at this early season of year. Butler says, whereas the so called *ladies* of New Orleans insult his men and officers, he gives one and all, permission to insult *any* or all who so treat them, then and there, with the assurance that the women will not receive the slightest protection from the government, and the men will all be justified.[121] I did not have time to read it, but repeat it as it was told me by mother who is in perfect despair at the brutality of the thing.

These are our brothers? None for me! Let us hope for the honor of this nation that Butler is not counted among the *gentlemen* of the land. And so, if any man takes a fancy to kiss me, or put his arm around me, he will be upheld in the outrage if he only says I pulled my dress from under his feet? That will justify them! And [p. 104] if we decline receiving their visits, it is another excuse to insult us, on the plea of prior insult to them!

O my brothers, George, Gibbes and Jimmy, never did we more need protection! where are you? If Charlie must go, we are defenseless.

121. Butler's infamous General Orders No. 28, issued May 15, 1862, stated that "here-after when any female shall by word, gesture, or movement insult or show contempt for any officer or soldier of the United States she shall be regarded and held liable to be treated as a woman of the town plying her avocation." *The War of the Rebellion: A Compilation of the Official Records of the Union and Confederate Armies* (Washington, 1880–1901), ser. I, 15:426, hereafter cited as *OR*.

Come to my bosom O my discarded carving knife, laid aside under the impression (fate it seems) that these were *gentlemen* sent to conquer us. Come, I say, and though sheathless now, I will find you a sheath in the body of the first man who attempts to Butlerize—or brutalize—(the terms are synonymous) me! I didn't kiss *my* sweetheart even! shall I let some northern beggar take the first? With the blessing of Heaven, no! It is a hard case to kiss someone's [sic] else, if you cant kiss your own sweetheart. If I was only a man! I dont know a woman here who does not groan over her misfortune in being clothed in petticoats; why cant we fight as well as the men?

Still not a word from the boys; we hear Norfolk has been evacuated but no particulars, and George was there. Gibbes is where ever Johnston[122] is, supposed to be on the Rappahannock, but we have not heard from either for more than six weeks, and all communication is now cut off. And Jimmy—I groan in spirit every time I think of him. Suppose he is lying sick, or perhaps dying, on the road? I wont think of it. I shut my eyes tightly and say please God take care of him. O if He will only send back the boys in safety how thankful we shall be! I know our fate though; the men of our family who are worth something, will die off in their prime; while [p. 105] we worthless women, of no value or importance to ourselves or the rest of the world, will live on, useless trash in creation. Pleasant, is it not?

O for Peace! If it were not for the idea that it must dawn on us before many months were over, I would lie down and die at once. Hope alone sustains me. Yet I do not say give up; let us all die first. But Peace—! what a blessing it would be! No one who has not passed through such times can appreciate it. Think of meeting your brothers and friends again—such as are spared! Think of the blessing of lying down in quiet at night, and waking in safety in the morning, with no thought of bomb shells breaking the silence of the night, or of thieving lawless soldiers searching for plunder. Think of settling quietly into the life Heaven has appointed for you, whether in comfort or poverty, content because He sends it, and because either will be rest, and quiet at last!

O Peace! how it will be appreciated by those who have suffered in

122. General Joseph E. Johnston, then in command of the Army of Northern Virginia, was on the Peninsula, pulling his army back toward Richmond.

this struggle! I fore warn all not to consider me a responsible creature when it is once declared. I shall be insane with delight I know. I have a bad habit of hugging people when I am very happy, so every one who does not wish to be embraced had better keep away. I remember we were all standing at Mrs Brunot's gate, in a crowd of some three hundred people watching the militia drill, last October, when father joined us and told us of the battle of the Passes.[123] Jimmy was there, and I knew every officer engaged; we had won, and I was so wild with delight that I came near killing Dena by hugging, and laughed with tears streaming down my face, and father said he must never tell me news in the streets again.

[p. 106] May 21st

I have had such a search for shoes this week, that I am disgusted with shopping. I am triumphant now, for after traversing the town in every direction and finding nothing, I finally discovered a pair of *boots* just made for a little negro to go fishing with, and only an inch and a half too long for me, besides being unbendable; but I seized them with avidity, and the little negro would have been outbid if I had not soon after discovered a pair more seemly, if not more serviceable, which I took without further difficulty. Behold my tender feet cased in crocodile skin, patent leather tipped, low quarter Boy's shoes, No. 2! "What a fall was there, my country!"[124] from my pretty English glove kid to sabots made of some animal closely connected with the hippopotamus! A dernier resort, vraiment,[125] for my choice was that, or cooling my feet on the burning pavement au naturel; I who have such a terror of any one seeing my naked foot! And this is thanks to war and blockade! Not a decent shoe in the whole community! N'importe![126] "Better days are coming, we'll all"—have shoes—after a while—perhaps!

123. The Federal blockade of the port of New Orleans provoked this naval action. On the morning of October 12, 1861, a small fleet of Confederate vessels attacked ships of the Union Navy at the head of the Passes, near the mouths of the Mississippi River, and forced them to withdraw into the Gulf.

124. Shakespeare, *Julius Caesar.*

125. A last resort, really.

126. Never mind!

Why did not Mark Taply[127] leave me a song calculated to keep the spirits up, under depressing circumstances? I need one very much, and have nothing more suggestive than the Old Methodist hymn "Better days are coming, we'll all go right" which I shout so constantly as our prospects darken, that it begins to sound stale. Now if I only had a really enlivening one, something "real jolly," what a capital of good humor I could realize with it! Who will write me one? I wish I had genius enough to do it for myself. I know dozens of comic ones, but they hardly apply to the present state of affairs. Perhaps there is more credit in being "jolly" with out any incentive, [p. 107] though; I certainly have a fine opportunity of exercising my talent.

Apropos of talent, which would you rather be: a most amiable fool, or a vicious wonderous smart-man—woman rather. I am almost ready to say I prefer being a *thundering* big fool, for the longer I live, the more I see that amiability is the most necessary thing in the world— the only thing that can make life endurable under some circumstances. It is a virtue I long to possess; with it, I could conquer all things. Why am I not? I cant say, really. Father used to call me his amiable little daughter; that was in the days that I had no cause to be bad and cross— though I am sorry to say I was both frequently—but now that the trials have come, I wonder if Lilly or Miriam could call me their amiable sister? Come! that is an excellent joke—only I do not enjoy it! For I *do* want to be amiable, and I hate to make such a lamentable failure.

I am too intensely sympathetic; that is the secret. I make up my mind to be very good & amiable, and the next minute let anyone, big or little, child or servant say any thing crass or disagreeable, and my spirits ooze out, until my only safety lies in flight, and if I want to regain my equanimity of temper I have to run away and sing Dixie, or Keep your Ark a-moving, before I make another sortie. Miriam says her head aches— I may be in splendid spirits, but "thump!" goes mine at that instant, and it takes a strong effort to restore me to health. It is a misfortune, but cant be avoided.

We are a row of bricks, and in point of amiability, at least, it is impossible for one to fall, without bringing down another after him. Where-

127. Character in Charles Dickens's novel *The Life and Adventures of Martin Chuzzlewit* whose name is synonymous with cheerfulness and relentless good humor.

fore, considering how much the [p. 108] happiness of those around us depends on our loving words, and kind feelings towards them, how whole days may be made miserable by one cross word or thoughtless deed, how a dozen merry faces can be clouded by one ill tempered or angry one—considering how we are responsible to God for every evil influence which may cause others to sin, cultivate amiability, Sarah, as you would the rarest talent bestowed on you, prize it above all things. No one has a right to cast a gloom over the hearts of others; I hold all should make an effort to be gay and lively under all circumstances, even if I *dont* practice it.

If ill humor must have a vent, make faces at your looking glass; but when you enter the family circle, do as our dear father did; throw all care and annoyance to the winds, have a pleasant word for all, for you enter the Holy of Holies—Home—the least and lowest can add a new pleasure, or a new disturbance, the duty of contributing to the common happiness is encumbent on all. Let the home circle be the place for the exchange of pleasant thoughts, let all disagreeable ones be put away. Ours was a happy home; father's example should influence his children. O Sarah my dear! if you are ever inflicted with a large and interesting family—which Kind Heaven forbid!—teach them to cultivate amiability as the only safeguard of happiness. Teach it, preach it, incessantly. Yes! and by the time my "interesting family" is brought up in the way it should go, I will not have amiability enough myself to make a respectable appearance! So much for theory without practice!

[p. 109] May 23d

The train of thought that carried me off the other day suggests another that has pursued me constantly for several years past, which is, of the millions of wives and mothers in the world, how many are fit to be either? It annoys me constantly; I hate to see a state God intended to be so holy and beautiful, degenerate into indifference, bickering and tears in the first, weak nerves and children governed by temper in the second. Of the first, I must say my experience is but very slight, for I have seen but few cases, though I am told many such exist. I wish I had not been told; I hardly believe it. I want to think all marriages as happy, all husbands as indulgent and kind, all wives as mild and submissive as father and mother. I look for no more beautiful model.

Theirs must have been the picture of married life the prophet thought of when he said in the eyes of God, the most beautiful thing was a man and his wife who agree. Why cannot the rest of the world be like them? I believe there are many such, but they tell me there aren't; I hope my belief will never be shaken, and that I will die in my delusion.

Of the second, sorry am I to say many instances have come under my observation. Instead of [the] mild, uniform firmness [that] Theory would suggest, considering their temptations, but insisting on your own rights, how many mothers you see bear acts of disobedience and wrong through a mistaken idea of amiability until forbearance ceases to be a virtue, when with one burst of unexpected temper, the offender has all the concentrated rage of hours vented on [p. 110] his devoted head, when one firm word at first, would have obviated all necessity for such display of unreasoning passion! I know some people who never punish their children unless they are in a temper; I call that brute reasoning. Yet how all theories vanish away, and how all rules are inefficient, where children are concerned!

Do what you will, there is always some one to find fault. If you are firm, the world calls you harsh; if you are indulgent, they say you are ruining your children. Every one takes the liberty of condemning yours, and advancing their own theory, and what woman ever brought up her family according to the ideas of her next door neighbor! Ah me! what a martyrdom! Any woman who has brought up her children in the way they should go, and has not in the meanwhile become a shrew, or lunatic, deserves a seat in Heaven, and no questions asked! I talk as though I had had some experience? Well! I have had. Did I not bring myself up—and didn't I have my hands full too? Have I not noticed the thousands of young mothers around me, and wondered if they ever for a moment thought of the dreadful responsibility resting on them? Have I not seen women who were ignorant that they had souls to save, undertake the charge of innocent young spirits fresh from Heaven, without a thought of the consequences, or a qualm of conscience? Such things chafe me; I have thought much of such lives, I am not ashamed to say; more than most young girls have, and it confirms my old experience, that women who look to marriage [p. 111] as the sole end and object of life are those who think less of its duties; while those who see its responsibilities, and feel its solemnity, are those who consider it by no means the only aim and purpose of life.[128] The first think their destiny is fulfilled, they have nothing to do in future but to kill time; the second, feel that the real trial of life has now commenced, and take up their burden with an humble, self-mistrusting heart, looking above for help. How few they number!

Last summer I was talking to Capt Huger on this subject—only I could express my views much more clearly in speaking, than I have in this cramped space—and being convinced of what I said, and not afraid of saying it, I gave full flow to all my opinions. Concluding my peroration with "if women only considered for one minute all the awful responsibilities that hang on that solemn 'I will!' and then could resolve to bear them come what will, there would be fewer unhappy marriages in the world." He gave me one of those curious looks I have elsewhere mentioned as being frequently bestowed on me by strangers, and then looking steadily into my eyes said "You are the most innocent girl I ever saw! I wish there were more like you!" It had the effect of silencing me for five minutes on all subjects, and for ever on that one. I did not know but what he was ridiculing me, and laughing at me under his quiet face; and besides I thought I must have said something I had better not have said, as mother says I do, from that curious look he gave me. I am sure I do not know what it could have been. If he did not want my real opinion why did he commence the subject?

I give myself too [p. 112] much concern about the affairs of the world in general. What does it matter to me whether women are reasoning animals or not? True I belong to the sex, but what right have I, the least among them, to condemn others around me? Dont I know that if I had half a dozen children to take care of, who depended on me for every thing, that I could no more do my duty than I could become an angel, and that in less than a year I would be a nervous peevish ill tempered vixen?

There is nothing more lovable and interesting than a child that begins to understand, and notice; I love them dearly then; but before that, the days and nights of shrieking and squealing, the months of long misery during which all babies take a fancy to sit up all night

128. A theme that Sarah returned to later, after the war, in some of the pieces she wrote for the Charleston *News* and the *News and Courier.*

and admire the moon—Merci je n'en veux pas! [129] I repeat, all mothers who survive their thankless task, should be canonized. After all, those who are not brought up at all, get on just as well as those who have most pains taken with them. There seems to be some provision made by nature for such little unfortunates. They knock around the world until they get all the rough points rubbed off, and turn out as polished after a while, as those who have been undergoing the grinding process all their lives. Nature is a wise mother. Perhaps I had better trouble myself as little as she; I would get on just as well as the rest of the world.

I see so many dear, sweet little women in the world, who slept their early youth away and eat [sic] sugar plums; who passed through the ordeal of boarding schools, certainly no wiser, perhaps [p. 113] worse than when they entered; who spent the days of their girlhood as they did their money—on useless objects, taking no account of either—who had had fortunes spent on their education, and were yet in the most heavenly state of ignorance, with out one developed talent or idea except that of dancing la valse à deux temps; [130] women who lounge through life, between the sofa and rocking chair with dear little dimpled hands that are never raised except to brush away a fly, who never think of touching anything more solid than a yellow covered novel [131]—many such I see, who are loved and adored by the world, much more than I, who so unworthily judge them; for who on earth, except those at home, and my few friends, ever cared for me?

It takes long acquaintance for me to gain new friends; those who become so, do it from their own kindness, not because the attraction lies in me; and I love such, Pharisee that I am, because they love me. I do not pretend to be better than such women; they occupy a place in public opinion which I could never attain, even if I aspired to it; but I look at them and wonder if God thought it worth while to give them souls to be crushed in that narrow little casket of the brain, which seems to die, and yet leave them living; and wonder too, if He accepts those who never try to please Him, and if such as these are fit for Eternity? For if our enjoyment in Heaven consists in understanding, feeling,

129. Thanks! I don't want any of it!

130. The quick waltz.

131. Popular novels published in cheap editions were known as yellow backs.

and appreciating the wisdom of God, and worshiping Him, can these enjoy it?

What becomes of souls capable of no exalted deeds or thoughts on earth? Let us hope there is some wise provision made for such by Nature; for as they consist of the majority of [p. 114] people on earth, surely God did not make so many souls for no purpose, earthly or heavenly. And yet—Bah! who, what, am *I* that I should judge? Leave it to my own doom to decide what becomes of souls who neither do their duty to God, nor serve man on earth!

May 25th

Yet I try to be good, even though I do not succeed. I try to fill up each moment of time that I may not be idle, but what is that? Each night as I lie down I ask myself "What have you done this day to please God or your neighbor?" and the answer is invariably "Nothing!" I see hundreds of little deeds and words that if performed or spoken, would have made some one more happy; as many, which, had I refrained from them, would have pleased God more. Little acts of selfishness—big ones too—hasty words which were not even meant, impatient looks and gestures, irritations of temper which might have been controled—all these rise up before me when I close my eyes and I cry "O thou that judgest thy brother, judge now thy self! 'Thou that sayest man should not sin, dost *thou* sin?'" I am humbled and cast down when I compare what I am, with what I should be. Ah! who is perfect on earth? Not I, certainly! But if God would only look in my heart and make and pronounce it good and pure, what would I care what Man thinks of me then? I can dispense with the love of the world so long as I have our home hearts around me; but if I pleased God in all things, I wonder if the world would love me too? Can any one please both Him and man? [end of p. 114 and end of entry; four pages of the diary that followed (two pages front and back) are missing]

[p. 115] May 27th.

The cry is Ho! for Greenwell! Very probably this day next week will see us there. I dont want to go. If we were at peace, and were to spend a few months of the warmest season out there, no one would be more eager and delighted than I: but to leave our comfortable home and all it contains for a rough pine cottage seventeen miles away even from this scanty civilization, is sad. It must be. We are hourly expecting two regiments of Yankees to occupy the Garrison, and some fifteen hundred of our men are awaiting them a little way off, so the fight seems inevitable. And we must go, leaving what little has already been spared us, to the tender mercies of Northern volunteers, who from the specimen of plundering they gave us two weeks ago, will hardly leave us even the shelter of our roof.

O my dear Home! How can I help but cry at leaving you forever? For if this fight occurs, never again shall I pass the threshold of this house where we have been so happy and sad, the scene of joyous meeting and mournful partings, the place where we greeted each other with glad shouts after ever so short a parting, the place where Harry and Father kissed us good bye and never came back again!

I know what Sis has suffered this long year, by what we have suffered these last six weeks. Poor Sis so far away! How much easier poverty if it must come, would be if we could bear it together! I wonder if the real fate of the boys, if we ever hear, can be so dreadful as this suspense? Still no news of them. My poor little Jimmy! And think how desperate Gibbes and George will be when they read Butler's proclamation, and they not able to defend us! Gibbes was in our late victory of Fredericksburg I know; what if he fell? And George? [p. 116] and Jimmy—? who knows if they still live? No! I will not think of it. Soon to be houseless, with the loss of those most dear to us threatened, famine, fever, desolation staring us in the face, I yet laugh and sing as gayly as though I had not heart to feel these afflictions, or reason to see them, defying the world to judge me, and saying in my heart "God will provide." So long as that belief is left in my heart, Lincolndom, I defy you, Fate, and the rest of the world! "Blow winds, and crack your cheeks!" [132] you cant harm me.

If the wish is not blasphemous, I would pray that if one of the boys must die, God would take me in his place, not that I want to die, but if one must go, I could be much better spared than any of the others. If Death wanted one, I could not say which to take, they are all so dear. Brother, with his large family, Gibbes with his young wife and

132. Shakespeare, *King Lear.*

child, George upon whom we have set all our hopes of future protection, Jimmy who is loved by all—not one can be spared. I cant give my sisters—I cant live without Miriam—so please Lord, I who am the least worthy among them, I who do the least for thy glory, who am so unfitted to battle through the world, take me, and spare them to comfort mother's few remaining days on earth! It will break her heart to lose another son.

In other days, going to Greenwell was the signal for general noise and confusion. All the boys gathered their guns and fishing tackle, and thousand and one amusements, father sent out provisions, we helped mother pack, Hal and I tumbled over the libraries to lay in a supply of reading material, and all was bustle until the carriage drove to the door at daylight one morning, and swept us off. It is not so gay this time. I wandered around this morning selecting books alone. We can take only what [p. 117] is necessary, the rest being left to the care of the Northern militia in general. I never before knew how many articles were perfectly "indispensable" to me before. This or that little token or keepsake, piles of letters I hate to burn, many dresses, etc. I cannot take conveniently, lay around me, and I hardly know which to choose among them, yet half must be sacrificed; I can only take one trunk.

May 30th Greenwell.

After all our trials and tribulations, here we are at last, and no limbs lost! How many weeks ago was it since I wrote here? It seems very long after all these events; let me try to recal[l] them. Wednesday the 28th— a day to be for ever remembered—as luck would have it, we rose very early, and had breakfast sooner than usual, it would seem for the express design of becoming famished before dinner. I picked up some of my letters and papers, and set them where I could find them whenever we were ready to go to Greenwell, burning a pile of trash, and leaving a quantity equally worthless, which were of no value even to myself, except from association. I was packing up my traveling desk with all

Harry's little articles that were left me, and other things, and saying (to myself) that my affairs were in such confusion, that if obliged to run unexpectedly I would not know what to save, when I heard Lilly's voice down stairs crying as she ran in—she had been out shopping— "Mr Castle has killed a Federal officer on a ship, and they are going to shell—" [133] Bang! went a cannon at the word, and that was all our warning.

Mother had just come in, and was lying down, but sprang to her feet and [p. 118] added her screams to the general confusion. Miriam who had been searching the libraries ran up to quiet her, Lilly gathered her children crying hysterically all the time, and ran to the front door with them as they were; Lucy saved the baby,[134] naked as she took her from her bath, only throwing a quilt over her. I bethought me of my "running" bag which I had used on a former case, and in a moment my few precious articles were secured under my hoops, and with a sunbonnet on, [I] stood ready for any thing.

The firing still continued; they must have fired half a dozen times before we could coax mother off. What awful screams! I had hoped never to hear them again, after Harry died. Charlie had gone to Greenwell before daybreak, to prepare the house, so we four women, with all these children and servants, were left to save ourselves. I did not forget my poor little Jimmy; (by the way, I always thought it a he-bird until she surprised me by laying ten eggs in rapid succession.) I caught up his cage, and ran down, just at this moment mother recovered enough to insist on saving father's papers—which was impossible, as she had not an idea of where the important ones were—I heard Miriam plead, argue, insist, command her to run, Lilly shriek, and cry she should go, the children screaming within, women running by without, crying and moaning, but I could not join in. I was going I knew not where; it was impossible to take my bird, for even if I could carry him, he would

133. A group of guerrillas on horseback had fired on a boat coming ashore from the *Hartford*, wounding the first engineer and two of his men. Henry Castle, Jr., age 16 in the 1860 census and presumably 17 or 18 when the incident occurred, was subsequently arrested by military authorities and might have been executed but for the intervention of Confederate General Daniel Ruggles. See Ruggles to General Butler, July 15, 1862, in *Private and Official Correspondence of Gen. Benjamin F. Butler* (Norwood, Mass., 1917), 2:67–69, hereafter cited as *Butler Correspondence*.

134. Beatrice LaNoue, born December 30, 1861. Lucy was one of the servants.

starve. So I took him out of his cage, kissed his little yellow head, and tossed him up. He gave one feeble little chirp as if uncertain where to go, and then for the first and last time I cried, laying my head against [p. 119] the gate post, and with my eyes too dim to see him. O how it hurt me to lose my little bird, one Jimmy had given me, too!

But the next minute we were all off, in safety. A square from home, I discovered that boy shoes were not the most comfortable things to run in, so ran back, in spite of cannonading, entreaties, etc, to get another pair. I got home, found an old pair that were by no means respectable which I seized without hesitation, and being perfectly at ease, thought it would be so nice to save at least Miriam's, and my toothbrushes, so slipped them in my corsets. These in, of course we must have a comb— that was added—then how could we stand the sun without starch to cool our faces? This included the powder bag, then I must save that beautiful lace collar, and my hair was tumbling down, so in went the tucking comb and hair pins with the rest, until, if there had been any one to speculate, they would have wondered a long while at the sin- gular appearance of a girl who is considered as very slight, usually. By this time, Miriam, alarmed for me, returned to find me, though urged by Dr Castleton[135] not to risk her life by attempting it, and we started off together. We had hardly gone a square, when we decided to return a second time, and get at least a few articles for the children and our- selves, who had nothing except what we happened to have on when the shelling commenced. She picked up any little thing and threw them to me, while I filled a pillow-case jerked from the bed, and placed my powder and brushes in it with the rest. Before we could leave, mother, alarmed for both, came to find us, with Tiche. All this time they had been shelling, but there was quite a lull when she got there, and she commenced picking up father's papers, vowing all the time she would not leave.

Every [p. 120] argument we could use, was of no avail, and we were desperate as to what course to pursue, when the shelling recommenced in a few minutes. Then mother recommenced her screams and was ready to fly any where, and holding her box of papers, with a faint idea

135. Sarah could be referring to either Dr. Thomas Castleton, the former Presbyterian minister, or his son, Dr. Henry Castleton, a physician, age 27 in the 1860 census.

of saving something, she picked up two dirty underskirts and an old cloak, and by dint of Miriam's vehement appeals, aided by a great deal of pulling, we got her down to the back door. We had given our pillow case to Tiche, who added another bundle, and all our silver to it, and had already departed.

As we stood in the door, four or five shells sailed over our heads at the same time, seeming to make a perfect corkscrew of the air—for it sounded as though it went in circles. Miriam cried never mind the door! Mother screamed anew, and I staid behind to lock the door, with this new music in my ears. We [had] reached the back gate, that was on the street,[136] when another shell passed us, and Miriam jumped behind the fence for protection. We had only gone half a square when Dr Castleton begged of us to take another street, as they were firing up that one. We took his advice, but found our new street worse than the old, for the shells seemed to whistle their strange songs with redoubled vigor. The height of my ambition was now attained. I had heard Jimmy laugh about the singular sensation produced by the rifled balls spinning around one's head, and hear [*sic*] I heard the same peculiar sound, ran the same risk, and was equal to the rest of the boys, for was I not in the midst of flying shells, in the middle of a bombardment? I think I was rather proud of it.

We were alone on the road; all had run away before, so I thought it was for our especial entertainment, this little affair. I cannot remember how long it lasted; I am positive that the clock struck ten before I left home, but [p. 121] I had been up so long, I know not what time it began, though I am told it was between eight and nine. We passed the graveyard; we did not even stop, and about a mile and a half from home, when mother was perfectly exhausted with fatigue and unable to proceed farther, we met a gentleman in a buggy who kindly took charge of her and our bundles. We could have walked miles beyond, then, for as soon as she was safe we felt as though a load had been removed from our shoulders; and after exhorting her not to be uneasy about us, and reminding her we had a pistol and a dagger—I had secured a "for true" one the day before, fortunately—she drove off, and we trudged on

136. The Morgans' property was L-shaped and had a narrow access on Laurel Street as well as the frontage on Church. The back gate was on Laurel.

alone, the only people in sight, on foot, though occasionally carriages and buggies would pass, going towards town.

One party of gentlemen put their heads out and one said "There are Judge Morgan's daughters sitting by the road!" but I observed he did not offer them the slightest assistance. However others were very kind, and one I never heard of, volunteered to go for us, and bring us to mother, when she was uneasy about our staying so long, when we went home to get clothes. We heard him ring and knock, but thinking it must be next door, paid no attention so he went back, and mother came herself.

We were two miles away when we sat down by the road to rest, and have a laugh. Here were two women married, and able to take care of themselves, flying for their lives and leaving two lorn girls alone on the road, to protect each other! To be sure, neither could help us, and one was not able to walk, and the other had helpless children to save, but it was so funny when we talked about it, and thought how sorry both would be when they regained their reason! While we were yet resting, we saw a cart coming, and giving up all idea of our walking to Greenwell, called the people to stop. To our great delight, it proved [p. 122] to be a cart loaded with Mrs Brunots affairs, driven by two of her negroes, who kindly took us up with them, on the top of their baggage, and we drove off in state, as much pleased at riding in that novel place, as though we were accustomed to ride in wheelbarrows. Miriam was in a hollow between a flour barrel and a mattress, and I at the end, astride, I am afraid, of a tremendous bundle; for my face was turned down the road, and each foot was resting very near the sides of the cart. I tried to make a better arrangement though, after a while. These servants were good enough to lend us their umbrella, with out which I am afraid we would have suffered severely, for the day was intensely warm.

Three miles from town we began to overtake the fugitives. Hundreds of women and children were walking along, some bare headed, and in all costumes. Little girls of twelve and fourteen were wandering on alone. I called to one I knew, and asked where her mother was; she didn't know; she would walk on until she found out. It seems her mother lost a nursing baby too, which was not found until ten that night. White and black were all mixed together, and were as confidential as though related. All called to us and asked where we were going, and many we knew, laughed at us for riding on a cart; but as they had walked only five miles, I imagined they would like even these poor accommodations, if they were in their reach.

The negroes deserve the greatest praise for their conduct. Hundreds were walking with babies, or bundles; ask them what they had saved, it was invariably "My mistress's clothes, or silver, or baby." Ask what they had for themselves, it was "Bless your heart honey, I was glad to get away with mistress things; I didn't think 'bout mine."

It was a heartrending scene. Women [p. 123] searching for their babies along the road, where they had been lost, others sitting in the dust crying and wringing their hands, for by this time, we had not an idea but what Baton Rouge was either in ashes, or being plundered, and we had saved nothing. I had one dress, Miriam two, but Tiche had them, and we had lost her, before we left home.

Presently we came on a Guerilla camp. Men and horses were resting on each side of the road, some sick, some moving about carrying water to the women and children, and all looking like a monster Barbecue, for as far as the eye could see through the woods, was the same repetition of men and horses. They would ask us the news, and one, drunk with [words excised] excitement or whisky informed us that it was our own fault if we had saved nothing, the people must have been —— fools not to know trouble would come before long, and that it was the fault of the men who were aware of it, that the women were thus forced to fly. In vain we pleaded that there was no warning, no means of forseeing this; he cried "*You* are ruined; so am I, and my brothers too! And by —— there is nothing left but to die now, and I'll die!" "Good!" I said. "But die fighting for us!" He waved his hand black with powder and shouted "That I will!" after us, and that was the only swearing guerilla we met; the others seemed to have too much respect for us to talk aloud.

Lucy had met us before this; early in the action, Lilly had sent her back to get some baby clothes, but a shell exploding within a few feet of her, she took alarm, and ran up another road for three miles, when she cut across the plantations and regained the Greenwell route. It is fortunate that without consultation, the idea of running here should have seized us all.

[p. 124] May 31st

I was interrupted so frequently yesterday, that I know not how I contrived to write so much. First, I was sent for to go to Mrs Brunot who
had just heard of her son's death, and who was alone with Dena, and
some hours after, I was sent for to see Fanny, now Mrs Trezevant[137]
who had just come with her husband to bring us news of George. A Mrs
Montgomery who saw him every day at Norfolk, said Jimmy was with
him, and though very sick at first, was now in good health. The first
news in all this long time! When the city was evacuated, George went
with his regiment seven miles from Richmond, Jimmy to the city its
self, as aid[e] to Com. Hollins.[138] This lady brought George's opal ring,
and diamond pin for [words excised]. Howell and Mr Badger, who had
just joined the guerillas as independants,[139] spent the day with me. We
were all in such confusion, that I felt ashamed. Every one as dirty as
possible; I had on the same dress I had escaped in, which though then
perfectly clean, was now rather—dirty. But they knew what a time we
had had.

To return to my journal.[140] Lucy met mother some long way ahead
of us, whose conscience was already reproaching her for leaving us,
and in answer to her "What has become of my poor girls?" ran down
the road to find us, for Lucy thinks the world cant keep on moving
without us. When she met us, she walked by the cart, and it was with
difficulty we persuaded her to ride a mile; she said she felt "used" to
walking now. About five miles from home, we overtook mother. The

137. Fanny Davidson, daughter of Tom Green Davidson, had married James H. Trezevant the month before. He was on leave, recuperating from a head wound. For a humorous account of the wedding and the subsequent flight from Baton Rouge, see Eliza Ripley,
Social Life, 264–72. She describes Trezevant as "a strikingly handsome man, even with
a bandaged head."

138. Commodore George N. Hollins had been ordered to Richmond not long before the
passage of the forts below New Orleans and the naval action in which he would have
participated as commander of the Confederate river defense fleet.

139. Later Howell Carter joined the 1st Louisiana Cavalry. In his reminiscences published more than thirty years after the war, he wrote: "Some regularly enlisted and others
joined as independents ('peacocks' the boys called them), that is, they were willing to
fight with us and do guard duty, but would not be sworn in; they wanted to reserve the
right to leave when they felt so disposed." See pp. 24–25. Mr. Badger was Howell Carter's
cousin, Francis Edmond (Ned) Badger, age 18 in the 1860 census and then living in New
Orleans in the household of his father, Wallace Badger.

140. Sarah means: To return to the events of May 28.

gentleman had been obliged to go for his wife, so Mary[141] gave her her seat on the cart, and walked with Lucy three miles beyond, where we heard that Lilly and the children had arrived in a cart, early in the day. All the talk by the road side was of burning homes, houses knocked to pieces by balls, famine, murder, [p. 125] desolation; so I comforted myself singing "Better days are coming" and "I hope to die shouting the Lord will provide;" while Lucy toiled through the sun and dust, and answered with a chorus of "I'm a runnin', a runnin' up to Glor-y."

It was three o'clock when we reached Mr Davids, and found Lilly. How warm and tired we were! A hasty meal, which tasted like a feast after our fatigue, gave us fresh strength, and Lilly and Miriam got in an old cart with the children to drive out here, leaving me with mother and Dellie[142] to follow next day. About sunset, Charlie came flying down the road, on his way to town. I decided to go, and after an obstinate debate with mother, in which I am afraid I showed more determination than amiability, I wrung a reluctant consent from her, and promising not to enter if it was being fired or plundered, drove off in triumph. It was a desperate enterprise for a young girl, to enter a town full of soldiers on such an expedition at night; but I knew Charlie could take care of me, and if he was killed I could take care of myself; so I went.

It was long after nine when we got there, and my first act was to look around the deserted house. What a scene of confusion! Armoirs spread open, with clothes tumbled in every direction, inside, and out, ribbons, laces on floors, chairs overturned, my desk wide open covered with letters, trinkets, etc; bureau drawers half out, the bed filled with odds and ends of everything. I no longer recognized my little room. On the bolster was a little box, at the sight of which I burst out laughing. Five minutes before the alarm, Miriam had been selecting those articles she meant to take to Greenwell, and holding up her box, said "If we were forced to run for our lives with out a moment's warning, I'd risk my life to save this, rather than leave it!" Yet here lay the box, and she was safe at Greenwell! It took me [p. 129][143] two hours to pack

141. Probably one of the Brunot servants.

142. Nickname of Adèle Lavinia LaNoue, Lilly's oldest child. Dellie was 8, almost 9, at the time.

143. The diary continues from the bottom of p. 125 to the top of p. 129. There is poetry on pp. 126–27; p. 128 is blank.

father's papers, then I packed Miriam's trunk, then some of mother's, and mine, listening all the while for the report of a cannon; for men were constantly tramping past the house, and only on condition our guerrillas did not disturb them, had they promised not to recommence the shelling. Charlie went out to hear the news, and I packed alone.

It seems the only thing that saved the town, was two gentlemen who rowed out to the ships, and informed the illustrious commander that there were no men there to be hurt, and he was only killing women and children.[144] The answer was "he was sorry he had hurt them; he thought of course the town had been evacuated before the men were fools enough to fire on them, and had only shelled the principal streets to intimidate the people!" Those streets, were the very ones crowded with flying women and children, which they must have seen with their own eyes, for those lying parallel to the river led to the garrison at the end, the crevasse at the other, which cut off all the lower roads,[145] so that the streets he shelled were the only ones that the women could follow, unless they wished to be drowned. As to the firing, four guerillas were rash enough to fire on a yawl which was about to land, with out a flag of truce, killing one, wounding three, one of whom afterwards died.[146] They were the only ones in town, there was not a cannon in our hands, even if a dozen men could be collected, and this cannonading was kept up in return for half a dozen shots from as many rifles, with out even a show of resistance after!

So ended the momentous shelling of Baton Rouge, during which

144. The illustrious commander was Farragut. The log of the *Kennebec*, actually the first of the Union ships to open fire, reports the arrival, under a flag of truce, of three men. In his report to the secretary of the navy, Farragut wrote: "The citizens came on board and denounced the act as a most cowardly act on the part of the guerillas, but confessed that they had not the power to control them, and appeared grateful to me for not injuring the city more." *ORN*, ser. I, 18:520.

145. The break in the levee had occurred two weeks earlier, on the morning of May 18. The crevasse was on the plantation of J. M. Williams about two miles below the city. See diary of John A. Dougherty, May 18, 1862, in John A. Dougherty Papers, LSU Collections.

146. No other source has been found that confirms Sarah's figures. The *Hartford*'s chief engineer, James B. Kimball, was wounded in the face, head, and shoulder by buckshot, but recovered. One of the other two men who were wounded is also known to have recovered, and there is no evidence in ship's logs that the third man died.

the valliant Faragut[147] killed one whole woman, wounded three, struck some twenty houses several times a piece,[148] and indirectly caused the [p. 130] death of two little children who were drowned in their flight, one poor little baby that was born in the woods, and several case[s] of the same kind, besides those who will yet die from the fatigue, as Mrs W. D. Phillips who had not left her room since January, who was carried out in her night gown, and is now supposed to be in a dying condition.[149] The man who took mother told us he had taken a dying woman—in the act of expiring—in his buggy, from her bed, and had left her a little way off, where she had probably breathed her last a few moments after. There were many similar cases. Hurrah for the illustrious Farragut, the "Woman Killer!!!"

It was three o'clock before I left off packing, and took refuge in a tub of cold water, from the dust and heat of the morning. Tiche was thoughtful enough to provide it; I forgot to say we found her safe at home, having lost all trace of us, preparing to start on foot to Greenwell in the morning. What a luxury the water was! and when I changed my underclothes, I felt like a new being. To be sure I pulled off the skin of my heel entirely, where it had been blistered by the walk, dust, sun, etc, but that was a trifle, though [it is] still quite sore now. For three hours I dreamed of rifled shells and battles, and at half past six, I was up and at work again. Mother came soon after, and after hard work, we got safely off at three, saving nothing but our clothes and silver. All else is gone. It cost me a pang to leave my guitar, and Miriam's piano, but it seems there was no help for it, so I had to submit.

It was dark night when we reached here. A bright fire was blazing in front, but the house looked so desolate, that I wanted to cry. Miriam cried when I told her her piano was left behind. [p. 131] Supper was a new sensation, after having been without any thing except a *glass* of clabber (no saucers) and a piece of bread since half past six. I laid down on the hard floor to rest my weary bones, thankful that I was so fortunate as to be able to lie down at all. In my dozing state, I heard

147. Flag Officer David G. Farragut.

148. Sarah wrote in later: "(some)."

149. Mrs. Caroline Phillips, wife of a local merchant. Mrs. Phillips survived and two weeks later gave birth to "a fine boy." See Dougherty diary, June 13, 1862.

the wagon come, and Miriam ordering a mattress to be put in the room for me. I could make out "Very well! you may take that one to Miss Eliza,[150] but the next one shall be brought to Miss Sarah!"

Poor Miriam! she is always fighting my battles! She and the servants are always taking my part against the rest of the world. I dont think [word erased] likes it. [Word erased] said sometime ago Miriam always swore to what I said, even if she didn't know what it was, or did not believe it; it sufficed for it to be "Sarah's word" and she was willing to take an oath to it. I remarked it was very flattering to me, but [word erased] did not like it. If Miriam and I did not fight for each other, I wonder if any one would do it for us. She and Lucy made a bed and rolled me in it with no more questions, and left me with damp eyes at the thought of how good and tender everyone is to me. Poor Lucy picked me a dish of blackberries to await my arrival, and I was just as grateful for it, though they were eaten by some one else before I came.

Early yesterday morning, Miriam, Nettie, and Sophie, who did not then know of their brother's death, went to town in a cart, determined to save some things, Miriam to save her piano. As soon as they were half way, news reached us that any one was allowed to enter, but none allowed to leave the town, and all vehicles confiscated as soon as they reached there. Alarmed for their safety, mother [p. 132] started off to find them, and we have heard of none of them since. What will happen next? I am not uneasy. They dare not harm them. It is glorious to shell a town full of women, but to kill four lone ones, is not exciting enough. They do not belong to the retail business, these "Woman Exterminators."

June 1st. Sunday.

From the news brought by one or two persons who managed to reach here yesterday, I am more uneasy about mother and the girls. A gentleman tells me that no one is permitted to leave with out a pass, and of these, only such as are separated from their families who may have left before. All families are prohibited to leave, and furniture, and other valuables also. Here is an agreeable arrangement! I saw the "pass" just

150. Lilly.

such as we give our negroes, signed by a Wisconsin Colonel.[151] Think of being obliged to ask permission from some low ploughman, to go in or out of our own homes!

Cannon are planted as far out as Col. Davidson's, six of them at our graveyard, and one or more on all the other roads. If the guerillas do not attempt their capture, I shall take it upon myself to suggest it to the very next one I see. Even if they cannot use them, it will frighten the Yankees, who are in a constant state of alarm about them. Their reason for keeping people in town is that they hope they will not be attacked so long as our own friends remain; thereby placing us above themselves in the scale of humanity since they acknowledge we are not brute enough to kill women and children, as they did not hesitate [p. 133] to do. Farragut pleads that he could not restrain his men, they were so enraged when the order was once given to fire, and says they *would* strike a few houses, though he ordered them to fire solely at horses, and the clouds of dust in the street, where guerillas were supposed to be. The dust was by no means thick enough to conceal that these "guerillas" were women, carrying babies instead of guns, and the horses were drawing buggies in which many a sick woman was lying.

A young lady who applied to the Yankee General for a pass to come out here, having doubtless spoken of the number of women here who had fled, and the position of the place, was advised to remain in town, and write to the ladies to return immediately, and assure them that they would be respected and protected, etc. but that it was madness to remain at Greenwell, for a terrific battle would be fought there in a few days, and they would be exposed to the greatest danger. The girl wrote the letter; but, Mr Fox, we are not quite such fools as to return there to afford you the protection our petticoats would secure to you, thereby preventing you from receiving condign punishment for the injuries and loss of property already inflicted upon us by you! No! we remain *here*; and if you are not laid low before you pass the Comite Bridge,[152] we can take to the woods again, and camp out, as many a

151. The only Wisconsin regiment in Baton Rouge at this time was the 4th Wisconsin, Lieutenant Colonel Sidney A. Bean commanding.

152. Bridge across the Comite River on the Greenwell Springs Road northeast of Baton Rouge.

poor woman is doing now, a few miles from town. Many citizens have been arrested, and after being confined awhile, and closely questioned, have been released, if the information is satisfactory. A negro man is [p. 134] informing on all cotton burners, violent Secessionists, etc.

I was so much amused at an annecdote [sic] told about me, and universally believed, because "It is just like Sarah Morgan." Every body, it seems, manifests the greatest desire to hear of the safety of "Judge Morgan's wife and daughters"; the other day a man I dont know rode up to me and asked if I knew if they were safe. Well! Someone asked someone else if they knew what had become of the Morgans, who answered "They are all safe, except Sarah, who walked a mile back, in the midst of the cannonading, facing all those shells, to get her veil which she has lost, and I dont know what became of her afterwards." Who could have told it, I cant imagine; for I held my veil in my hand all the time, until we ran out of the back gate the last time, when I found I had dropped it, and ran half a square for it. The way it is told, with my supreme contempt for Yankee shells, is vastly amusing. Didn't they whistle past our ears down the Penitentiary road![153] One passed a foot above Sophie Brunot's head. A Mr Mitchell, a guerilla, told mother that he felt more alarm for her and her two daughters than for anyone else, for he saw the shells flying around us, and knew we were in the greatest danger.

Well, our home is deserted, Miriam's piano and my guitar lost beyond hope of recovery, I am afraid, and here we are in this rough pine house which is in the most delapidated [sic] condition, threatening to go over at any moment. Last night a violent wind storm came up, and Lilly was so alarmed that she moved children, servants [p. 135] and all, into the office, for safety; but as I could not quite reconcile myself to the idea of sleeping in a room with seventeen people, nine of whom were negroes (among them a few who are not endurable in the open air, even), I walked to Mrs Brunots[154] in my night gown, and slept there with Dena.

Sunday night. The girls have just got back, riding in a mule team,

153. The continuation of Florida Street, which ran east past the State Penitentiary.
154. Mrs. Brunot's cottage at Greenwell Springs.

on top of baggage, but without either mother, or any of our affairs. Our condition is perfectly desperate. Miriam had an interview with Gen. Williams,[155] which was by no means satisfactory. He gave her a pass to leave, and bring us back, for he says there is no safety here for us; he will restrain his men in town, and protect the women, but once outside, he will answer neither for his men, or the women and children. As soon as he gets horses enough, he passes this road, going to Camp Moore[156] with his cavalry, and then we are in greater danger than ever. Any house shut up, shall be occupied by soldiers. Five thousand are there now, five more expected. What shall we do?

Mother remained, sending Miriam for me, determined to keep us there, rather than sacrifice both our lives and property by remaining here. But then—two weeks from now the Yellow fever will break out; mother has the greatest horror of it, and we have never had it; dying is not much in the present state of our affairs, but the survivor will suffer even more than we do now. If we stay, how shall we live? I have seventeen hundred dollars in Confederate notes now in my "running" bag, and three or four in silver. The former will not be received there, the latter might last two days. If we save our house and furniture, it is at the price of starving.

I am of [the] opinion we should send for mother, and [p. 136] with what money we have, make our way somewhere in the interior, to some city where we can communicate with the boys, and be advised by them; this is not living. Home is lost beyond all hope of recovery; if we wait, what we have already saved will go too; so we had better leave at once, with what clothing we have, which will certainly establish us on the footing of ladies, if we chance to fall among vulgar people who never look beyond. I fear the guerillas will attack the town to night; if they do, God help mother!

Gen. Williams offered Miriam an escort, when he found she was

155. General Thomas Williams, in command of the Union troops occupying Baton Rouge. See biographical sketch in Ezra J. Warner, *Generals in Blue* (Baton Rouge, 1964), 563–64.

156. Confederate camp about sixty miles northeast of Baton Rouge. The camp was on the New Orleans, Jackson & Great Northern Railroad between Jackson, Mississippi, and New Orleans.

without a protector, in the most fatherly way; he must be a good man. She thanked him, but said "she felt perfectly safe on *that* road." [157] He bit his lip, understanding the allusion, and did not insist. She was to deliver a message from parties in town to the first guerillas they met, concerning the safest roads, and presently six met them, and entered into conversation. She told them of the proffered escort, when one sprang forward crying "Why didn't you accept, miss? The next time, *ask* for one, and if it is at all disagreeable to you, *I* am the very man to rid you of such an inconvenience! I'll see that you are not annoyed long!" I am glad it was not sent; she would have reproached herself with murder for ever after. I wonder whether the General would have risked it?

Baton Rouge June 3d.

Well! Day before yesterday, I almost vowed not to return, and last evening I reached here! Verily consistency thou art a jewel! I determined to get to town and lay both sides of the question before mother; saving home, and property, [p. 137] by remaining, thereby cutting ourselves off for ever from the boys, and dying of yellow fever; or flying to Mississippi, losing all save our lives. So as Mrs Brunot was panic stricken, and determined to die in town rather than be starved at Greenwell, and was going in on the same wagon load that came out the night before, I got up with her and Nettie, and left Greenwell at ten yesterday morning, bringing nothing except this old book, which I would rather not lose, as it has been an old and kind friend during these days of trouble. At first, I avoided all mention of political affairs, but now, there is nothing else to be thought of; if it is not burnt for treason, I will like to look it over one of these days—if I live.

I left Greenwell, with out ever looking around it, beyond one walk to the hotel, so I may say I hardly know what it looks like. Miriam stayed

157. Meaning that the road was under the control of the Confederates.

much against her will, I fear, to bring in our trunks, if I could send a wagon. A guerilla picket stopped us before we had gone a mile, and seemed disposed to turn us back. We said we must pass; our all was at stake. They then entreated us not to enter, saying it was not safe. I asked if they meant to burn it; "We will help try it" was the answer. I begged them to delay the experiment until we could get away. One waved his hat to me and said he would fight for me. Hope he will—at a distance.

They asked if we had no protectors; "None" we said. "Dont go then," and they all looked so sorry for us. We said we must; starvation, and another panic awaited us out there, our brothers were fighting, our fathers dead; we had only our own judgement to rely on, and that told us home was the best place for us; if the town must burn, let us burn in our [p. 138] houses, rather than be murdered in the woods. They looked still more sorry, but still begged us not to remain. We would, though, and one young boy called out as we drove off, "What's the name of that young lady who refused the escort?" I told him, and they too expressed the greatest regret that she had not accepted. We met many on the road, nearly all of whom talked to us, and as they were most respectful in their manner (though they saw us in a mule team!), we gave them all the information we could, which was all news to them, though very little.

Such a ride in the hot sun perched up in the air! One of the servants remarked "Miss Sarah aint ashamed to ride in a wagon!" With truth I replied "No; I never was so high before." Two miles from home we met the first Federal Pickets, and then they grew more numerous, until we came on a large camp near our graveyard, filled with soldiers and cannon. From first to last, none refrained from laughing at us; not aloud, but they would grin and be inwardly convulsed with laughter as we passed. One laughed so comically that I dropped my veil hastily for fear he should see me smile. I could not help it; if any one smiled at me while I was dying, I believe I would return it.

We passed crowds, for it was now five o'clock, and all seemed to be promenading. There were several officers standing at the corner, near our house, who were very much amused at our vehicle. I did not feel like smiling then. After reducing us to riding in a mule team, they were heartless enough to laugh! I forgot them presently, and gave my whole attention to getting out respectably. Now getting *in* a wagon is bad enough; but getting out—! I hardly know how I managed it.

I had fully three feet to step down before reaching [p. 139] the wheel; once there, the driver picked me up and set me on the pavement. The net I had gathered my hair in fell in my descent, and my hair swept down half way between my knee and ankle in one stream. As I turned to get my little bundle, the officers had moved their position to one directly opposite to me, where they could examine me at leisure. Queens used to ride drawn by oxen hundreds of years ago, so I played this was old times, the mules were oxen, I a queen, and stalked off in a style I am satisfied would have imposed on Juno herself. When I saw them as I turned, they were perfectly quiet; but Nettie says up to that moment they had been in convulsions of laughter, with their handkerchiefs to their faces. It was not polite!

I found mother safe, but the house was in the most horrible confusion. Jimmy's empty cage stood by the door; it had the same effect on me that empty coffins produce on others. Oh my birdie! At six, I could no longer stand my hunger. I had fasted for twelve hours, with the exception of a mouthful of hoe cake at eleven; I that never fasted in my life!—except last Ash Wednesday when Lydia and I tried it for breakfast, and got so sick we were glad to atone for it at dinner. So I got a little piece of bread and corn beef from Mrs Daigre's servant,[158] for there was not a morsel here, and I did not know where, or what to buy.

Presently some kind friend sent me a great short cake, a dish of strawberry preserves, and some butter which I was grateful for, for the fact that the old negro was giving me part of her supper made me rather sparing, though she cried "Eat it all honey! I get plenty more!" Mother went to Cousin Will's, and I went to Mrs Brunot's to sleep, and so ended my first day's ride on a mule [p. 140] team. Bah! A lady can make anything respectable by the way she does it! What do I care if I had been driving the mules? Better that than walk seventeen miles.

I met Dr Du Chêne[159] and Dr Castleton twice each, this morning.

158. Mrs. Mary Daigre, the Morgans' next-door neighbor, kept one black house servant at her home in Baton Rouge. The rest of her slaves—and she had more than one hundred—were on her plantation. See Joseph Karl Menn, *The Large Slaveholders of Louisiana—1860* (New Orleans, 1964), 139–40.

159. Dr. Jean Bertrand Duchein, a young physician, married Eugenia (Dena) Brunot in 1866.

They were as kind to me, as they were to the girls the other day. The latter saved them a disagreeable visit, while here. He, and those three, were packing some things in the hall, when two officers passed, and prepared to come in, seeing three good looking girls seemingly alone, for Miriam's dress hid Dr Castleton as he leaned over the box. Just then she moved, the Dr raised his head, and the officers started back with an "Ah!" of surprise. The Dr called them as they turned away, and asked for a pass for the young ladies. They came back bowing and smiling, said they would write one in the house, but they were told very dryly that there was [sic] no writing accommodations there. They tried the fascinating, and were much mortified by the coolness they met. Dear me! "Why wasn't I born old and ugly?" Suppose I should unconsciously entrap some magnificent Yankee? What an awful thing it would be!!

Sentinels are stationed at every corner; Dr C. piloted me safely through on one expedition; but on the next, we had to part company, and I passed through a crowd of at least fifty, alone. They were playing cards in the ditch, and swearing dreadfully, these pious Yankees; many were marching up and down, some sleeping on the pavement, others— picking odious bugs out of each others heads! I thought of the guerillas, Yellow fever, and all, and wished they were all safe at home with their mothers and sisters, and we at peace again.

What a day I have had! Here mother and I are alone, not a servant on the lot. [p. 141] We will sleep here tonight, and I know she will be too nervous to let me sleep. The dirt and confusion was extraordinary in the house. I could not stand it, so I applied myself to making it better. I actually swept two whole rooms! I ruined my hands at gardening, so it made no difference. I replaced piles of books, crockery, china, that Miriam had left packed for Greenwell; I discovered I could empty a dirty hearth, dust, move heavy weights, make myself generally useful and dirty, and all this is thanks to the Yankees!

Poor me! this time last year I thought I would never walk again! If I am not laid up for ever after the fatigue of this last week, I shall always maintain I have a Constitution. But it all seems nothing in this confusion; every thing is almost as bad as ever. Besides that, I have been flying around to get Miriam a wagon. I know she is half distracted at being there alone. Mother chose staying with all its evils. Charlie's life would pay the penalty of a cotton burner if he returned, so Lilly remains at Greenwell with him. We three will get on as best we can here.

I wrote to the country to get a wagon, sent a pass from Head Quarters, but I will never know if it reached her, until I see her in town. I hope it will; I would be better satisfied with Miriam.

June 4th

Miriam and Mattie drove in, in the little buggy last evening after sunset, to find out what we were to do. Our condition is desperate. Beauregard is about attacking these Federals. They say he is coming from Corinth, and the fight will be in town.[160] If true, we are lost again. Starvation at Greenwell, fever and [p. 142] bullets here, will put an end to us soon enough. There is no refuge for us, no one to consult. Brother, whose judgement we rely on as implicitly as we did on father's, we hear has gone to New York; there is no one to advise or direct us, for if he is gone, there is no man in Louisiana whose decision I would blindly abide by. Let us stay and die. We can only die once; we can suffer a thousand deaths with suspense and uncertainty; the shortest is the best.

Do you think the few words here can give an idea of our agony and despair? Nothing can express it. I feel a thousand years old to day. I have shed the bitterest tears to day that have fallen from my eyes since father died. I cant stand it much longer; I'll give way presently, and I know my heart will break. Shame! Where is God? A fig for your religion, if it only lasts while the sun shines! "Better days are coming"—I cant [sentence incomplete]

Troops are constantly passing and repassing. They have scoured the country for ten miles out, in search of guerillas. We are here without servants, clothing, or the bare necessaries of life; suppose they should seize them on the way! I procured a pass for the wagon, but it now seems doubtfull if I can get the latter—a very faint chance. Well! let them go; our home [will be] next, then we can die sure enough. With God's help, I can stand any thing yet in store for me. "I hope to die shouting the Lord will provide!" Poor Sis! if she could only see us! I am glad she does not know our condition.

5, P.M. What a day of agony, doubt, uncertainty and despair! Heaven save me from another such! Every hour, fresh difficulties arose, until

160. A false rumor. Beauregard had retreated from Corinth to Tupelo and would shortly be removed from field command.

I believe we were almost crazy, every one of us. As Miriam was about stepping in the buggy to go to [p. 143] Greenwell to bring in our trunks, mother's heart misgave her, and she decided to sacrifice her property rather than remain in this state any longer. After a desperate discussion which proved that each argument was death, she decided to go back to Greenwell and give up the keys of the house to Gen. Williams, and let him do as he pleased, rather than have it broken open during her absence.

Mattie and Mr Tunnard[161] were present at the discussion, which ended by the latter stepping in the buggy and driving Miriam to the garrison. Gen. Williams called her by name, and asked about Major Drum. It seems all these people, native and foreign, know us, while we know no one. Miriam told him our condition; how our brothers were away, father dead, and mother afraid to remain, yet unwilling to lose her property by going away; how we three were alone and unprotected here, but would remain rather than have our home confiscated. He assured her the house should not be touched, that it would be respected in our absence as though we were in it, and [he] would place a sentinel at the door to guard it against his own men who might be disposed to enter. The latter she declined, but he said he would send his aid[e] to mark the house, that it might be known.

A moment after they got back, the Aid[e], Mr Biddle[162] (I have his name to so many passes that I know it now), came to the door. Mr Tunnard left him there uncertain how we would receive a Christian, and I went out, and asked him in. He looked uncertain of his reception too, when we put an end to his doubts by treating him as we invariably treat gentlemen who appear such. He behaved remarkably well under the trying circumstance, and insisted on a sentinel; for, he said, though they would respect the property, there were many [p. 144] bad characters among the soldiers who might attempt to rob it, and the sentinel would protect it. After a visit of ten minutes, devoted exclusively to the affair, he arose and took his leave, leaving me under the impression

161. Carriage maker William F. Tunnard or, more likely, one of his sons. Tunnard had recently returned home after giving up his commission as major in the 3rd Louisiana Infantry. All three of his sons also served in the Confederate army, but the youngest, Alexander, seems to have been in Baton Rouge at the time Sarah describes.

162. Lieutenant James C. Biddle, aide to General Williams.

that he was a gentleman wherever he came from, even if there were a few grammatical errors in the pass he wrote me yesterday; but "thou that judgest another, dost thou sin?"

Well, now we say, fly to Greenwell. Yes! and by to night, a most exaggerated account of the whole affair will be spread over the whole country, and we will be equally suspected by our own people. Those who spread useless falsehoods about us, will gladly have a foundation for a monstrous one. Didnt Camp Moore ring with the story of our entertaining the Federal Officers? didn't they spread the report that Miriam danced with one to the tune of Yankee Doodle in the State House garden? What will they stop at now? O if I was only a man, and knew what to do!

Night. We were so distressed by the false position in which we would be placed by a Federal sentinel, that we did not know what course to pursue. As all our friends shook their heads and said it was dangerous, we knew full well what our enemies would say. If we win B.R. as I pray we will, they will say we asked protection from Yankees against our own men, are consequently traitors, and our property will be confiscated by our own government. To decline Gen. Williams kind offer, exposes the house to being plundered. In our dilemna, we made up our minds to stay, so we could say the sentinel was unnecessary.

Presently a file of six soldiers marched to the gate, an officer came to the steps and introduced himself as Col. McMillan, of 21st [p. 145] Indian[a] Vol[s].[163] He asked if this was Mrs Morgan's; the General had ordered a guard placed around the house; he would suggest placing them in different parts of the yard. "Madam, the pickets await your orders." Miriam in a desperate fright undertook to speak for mother, and asked if he thought there was any necessity. No, but it was an additional security, he said. "Then, if no actual necessity, we will relieve you of the disagreeable duty, as we expect to remain in town," she said. He was very kind, and discussed the whole affair with us, saying when we made up our minds to leave—we told him after we could not decide— to write him word, and he would place a guard around to prevent his men and the negroes from breaking in. It was a singular situation: our

163. Colonel James W. McMillan, later promoted to general. See sketch in Warner, *Generals in Blue*, 305–6.

brothers off fighting them, while these Federal soldiers leaned over our fence, and an officer standing on our steps offered to protect us.

These people are certainly very kind to us. Gen. Williams especially must be a dear old gentleman; he is so good. How many good and how many mean people these troubles have showed us! I am beginning to see my true friends now; there is a large number of them, too. Everybody from whom we least expected attention, has agreeably surprised us. Here is Mr Tunnard, whom I have seen every day since I have been in B.R., and yet never thought of speaking to him all these years. Last evening he was talking with Mattie on the pavement, I made some remark to him—because I felt like it, not because I know him—he heard us say we could not turn on the gas, offered his services, sat down after, and spent the evening, and all [p. 146] day he has been either here, or running after passes, etc for us. Gen. Williams will believe we are insane from our changing so often.[164]

June 5th.

Last night, determined to stay, Miriam went after our trunks at daylight. A few hours after, Lilly wrote we must go back. McClellan's army was cut to pieces and driven back to Maryland, by Jackson, the Federals were being driven into the swamps from Richmond too. Beauregard is undoubtedly coming to attack Baton Rouge; his fire would burn the town, if the gunboats do not; the Yankees will shell it at all events if forced to retire. It cannot stand. We cant go to New Orleans. Butler says he will lay it in ashes if he is forced to evacuate it from yellow fever or other causes. Both must be burned. Greenwell is not worth the powder it would cost, so we must stand the chance of murder and starvation there, rather than the certainty of being placed between two fires here. Oh my home, my home! must I lose you for ever? Well, I see nothing but bloodshed and beggary staring us in the face. Let it come. "I hope to die shouting the Lord will provide."

June 6th

We dined at Mrs Brunots yesterday, and sitting on the gallery later,

164. A short sentence on the last line of the entry appears to have been written in later: "His guard [we] positively refused."

had the full benefit of a Yankee drill. They stopped in front of the house and went through some very curious manoeuvres, and then marched out to their drill ground beyond. In returning, the whole regiment drew up directly before us, and were dreadfully quiet for [p. 147] five minutes, the most uncomfortable I have experienced for some time. For it was absurd to look at the sky, and I looked in vain for one man with downcast eyes where on I might rest mine; but from the officers down to the last private, they were all looking at us. I believe I would have cried with embarrassment if the command had not been given at that moment. They drilled splendidly, and knew it, too, so went through it as though they had not been at it for an hour before. One conceited, red headed lieutenant smiled at us in the most fascinating way; perhaps he smiled to think how fine he was, and what an impression he was making.

We got back to our solitary house before twilight, and were sitting alone on the balcony, when Mr Biddle entered. He came to ask if the guard had been placed here last night. It seems to me it would have saved him such a long walk if he had asked Col. McMillan. He sat down though, and got [to] talking in the moonlight, and people passing, some citizens, some officers, looked wondering at this unheard of occurrence. I wont be rude to any one in my own house, Yankee or Southern, say what they will. He talked a great deal, and was very entertaining; what tempted him, I cannot imagine. It was two hours before he thought of leaving. He was certainly very kind. He spoke of the scarcity of flour in town; said they had quantities at the garrison, and asked permission to send us a barrel, which we of course refused. It showed a very good heart though. He offered to take charge [p. 148] of any letters I would write, said he had heard Gen Williams speak of Harry; and when he at last left, I was still more pleased with him for his kindness to us. He says Capt Huger is dead. I am very, very much distressed. They are related, he says. He talked so reasonably of the war, that it was quite a novelty after reading the abusive newspapers of both sides. I like him, and was sorry I could not ask him to repeat his visit. We are not accustomed to treat gentlemen that way; but it wont do in the present state to act as we please. Mob governs.

Mother kept me awake all night to listen to the mice in the garret. Every time I would doze she would ask "what's that?" and insist that the mice were men. I had to get up and look around for an imaginary host, so I am tired enough this morning.

Miriam has just got in with all the servants, our baggage is on the way, so we will be obliged to stay, whether we will or no. I dont care; it is all the same, starve or burn.

Oh! I forgot. Mr Biddle did *not* write that pass! It was his clerk. He *speaks very* gramatically, so far as I can judge!!!

June 8th. Sunday.

These people mean to kill us with kindness. There is such a thing as being too kind. Yesterday General Williams sent a barrel of flour to mother accompanied by a note begging her to accept it "in consideration of the present condition of the circulating currency," and the intention was so kind, the way it was done so delicate, that there was no refusing it. I had to write her thanks, and got in a violent fit of the "trembles" at the idea of writing to a stranger. One [p. 149] consolation is, that I am not a very big fool, for it took only three lines to prove myself one. If I had been a thundering big one, I would have occupied two pages to show myself fully. And to think that it is out of our power to prove them our appreciation of the kindness we have universally met with!

Many officers were in church this morning, and as they passed us while we waited for the door to be opened, Genl. Williams bowed profoundly; another followed his example; we returned the salute of course. But by tomorrow, those he did not bow to will cry treason against us. Let them howl. I am tired of lies, scandal and deceit. All the loudest gossips have been frightened into the country, but enough remain to keep them well supplied with town talk. I wish people would find some family equally worthy of their attention, besides ours. We neither listen to nor tell tales on them, and keep aloof from their slanderous circles; that draws down vengeance, and there is always someone ready to tell unpleasant things. I do not believe there is a family on earth more looked up to by the lower class, more envied and abused by the vulgar, more admired and respected by our equals, than ours. Let some of these low gossips, finding no flaw in our characters or pretentions after turning us inside out like the heel of some old stocking, content themselves with flying in a rage because we dont admire them, and call us "The Proud Morgans," "The Aristocrats." That is the acme of their spleen; they commence by lying. Let them rave. Who so worthy of the appelations as we? We do not object to the distinction.

[p. 150] It is such a consolation to turn to the dear good people of the world after coming in contact with such cattle. Here, for instance is Mr Bonnecase[165] on whom we have not the slightest claims. Every day since we have been here, he has sent a great pitcher of milk, knowing our cow is out; one day he sent rice, the next sardines, yesterday two bottles of Port and Madeira which cannot be purchased in the whole South. What a duck of an old man! That is only one instance.

June 10th

This morning while attending to my flowers, I was very much startled by a little bird alighting on my shoulder and pecking most affectionately at my neck. It was my little Jimmy! He flew off when I recognized him, ungrateful Jimmy; it seemed as though he merely tapped to see if I was at home. Such a dirty little fellow! When he stayed with me he had bright yellow feathers; now, they are sadly dingy. I set his cage open to invite him back, but he did not notice it. O Jimmy! I am sure I took better care of you than you take care of yourself! Come back, birdy; I cannot live with out something to pet.

While I was still at work, several soldiers stopped in front of me, and holding on the fence, commenced to talk about some brave Colonel, and a shooting affair last night. When all had gone except one who was watching me attentively, as he seemed to wish to tell me, I let him go ahead. The story was that Col. McMillan was shot through the shoulder, breast, and liver by three guerillas while four miles from town last night on a scout. He was a quarter of a mile from his own men at the time, killed one who shot him,[166] took the other two prisoners and fell from [p. 151] his horse, himself, when he got within the lines. The sol-

---

165. Leon Bonnecaze, a well-to-do Baton Rouge merchant, a native of France, age 59 in the 1860 census.

166. Lieutenant Josiah Roberts. Colonel McMillan was wounded by the lieutenant's father, Stephen Roberts, who was subsequently imprisoned at Fort Jackson and Ship Island. An account of the incident that appeared in a Baton Rouge newspaper three years later says the son "was pursued whilst at home on a furlough" and that the father, "in gallantly striving to defend him and revenge his death, which occurred at his threshold, shot and wounded Col. McMillan." *Tri-Weekly Advocate*, October 27, 1865, p. 2.

dier said these two guerillas would probably be hanged, while the six we saw pass captives Sunday, would probably be sent to F. Jackson for life. I think this guerilla affair mere murder, I confess; but what a dreadful fate for these young men! One who passed Sunday, was Jimmy's schoolmate, a boy of sixteen; another Willie Garig,[167] the pet of a whole family of good, honest country people. Suppose Howell, or his father should be among those of last night? I believe I would go crazy if either suffered such a doom. I hope Howell has rejoined his regiment, as he told me he would, when at Greenwell. This is a dreadful affair.

These soldiers will get in the habit of talking to me after a while, through my own fault. Yesterday I could not resist the temptation to ask the fate of the six guerillas, and stopped two volunteers who were going by, to ask them. They discussed the state of the country, told me F. Pillow and Vicksburg were evacuated, the Mississippi opened from source to mouth; I told them of Banks' and McClellan's defeat;[168] they assured me it would all be over in a month—which I fervently pray may be so—told me they were from Michigan (one was Mr Bee, he said, cousin of our general),[169] and would probably have talked all day if I had not bowed myself away with thanks for their information.

It made me ashamed to contrast the quiet, gentlemanly, liberal way these volunteers spoke of us, and our cause, with the rabid, fanatical, abusive violence of our female Secession declaimers. Thank Heaven, I have never yet made my appearance as a Billingsgate orator on these occasions. All my violent feelings, which in moments of intense excitement were really violent, I have recorded in this book; I am [p. 152] happy to say only the reasonable dislike to seeing my country subjugated has been confided to the public ear, when necessary; and that even now, I confess that nothing but the reign of terror, and gross prejudice by which I was surrounded at that time, could justify many

167. William Garig, age 21 in the 1860 census, the son of George and Mary Kleinpeter Garig. In the years after the war he would become a wealthy businessman and banker. See sketch in *Biographical and Historical Memoirs of Louisiana* (Chicago, 1892), 1:430–31.

168. General Nathaniel P. Banks, a former governor of Massachusetts and speaker of the House of Representatives, had been put to flight by Stonewall Jackson in Virginia. However, George B. McClellan, at this time the Union Army's ranking general, was still a threat to Richmond.

169. Brigadier General Hamilton P. Bee, a Texan.

expressions I have here applied to them. Fact is, these people have disarmed me by their kindness. I expected to be in a crowd of ruffian
soldiers who would think nothing of cutting your throat, or doing anything they felt like; and I find among all these thousands, not one who
offers the slightest annoyance, or disrespect. The former is the thing as
it is believed by the whole country, the latter the true state of affairs.

I admire foes who show so much consideration for our feelings. Contrast these, with our volunteers from New O.—all gentlemen—who
came to take the garrison from Major Haskins.[170] Several of them passing our gate where we were standing with the Brunots, one exclaimed
"What pretty girls!" It was a stage "aside" that we were supposed not
to hear. "Yes" said another, "Beautiful! but they look as though they
could be fast!" Fast, and we were not even speaking! not even looking
at them!

Sophy and I were walking presently, and met half a dozen. We had to
stop to let them pass the crossing; they did not think of making way for
us; No. 1 sighed. Such a sigh! No. 2 followed, and so on, when they all
sighed in a chorus for our edification, while we dared not raise our eyes
from the ground. That is the time I would have made use of a dagger!
Two passed in a buggy, and trusting to our not recognising them from
the rapidity of their vehicle, kissed their hands to us until they were out
of sight! All went back to N.O. vowing B.R. had the prettiest girls in
the world. These were our own people, the élite [p. 153] of N.O., loyal
Southerners and gentlemen. These Northerners pass us satisfied with
a simple glance, some take off their hats, for all these officers know our
name, though we may not know theirs; how, I can't say.

When I heard of Col. McMillan's misfortune, mother conspired with
me to send over some bandages, and something Tiche manufactured
of flour, under the name of "nourishment," for he is across the street
at Heroman's.[171] Miriam objected on account of what "our people" will

---

170. Major Joseph A. Haskin, the one-armed officer who was in command of the U.S.
Arsenal at Baton Rouge when it was seized by state troops early in 1861. For an account
of the incident, see John D. Winters, *The Civil War in Louisiana* (Baton Rouge, 1963),
9–10.

171. The three-story brick building at the northwest corner of Church and Florida
streets, built by George M. Heroman in the 1850s. Union officers may have been quar-

say, and what we will suffer for it if the guerillas reach town, but we persuaded her we were right. Public opinion, I say, is nothing to me when counterbalanced by what I believe to be the foundation stone of our religion, "Do unto others as you would they should do unto you."[172] I never hated man or beast in my life, no matter what they might say or do to me; why should I hate this wounded man?[173] If I thought he had killed George last night, I would offer to help him this morning. I would do it for Mr Sparks, I am sure; and God knows he came near breaking my heart. "Love your enemies" Christ said. Are we to keep his commandment only on certain occasions?

You can imagine our condition at present, many years hence, Sarah, when you reflect that it is the brave, noble hearted, generous Miriam who is afraid to do this deed on account of "public opinion," which indeed is "down" on us. At Greenwell they are frantic about our returning to town, and call us traitors, Yankees, and vow vengeance. Our friends forsake us, we are too proud to seek the protection of our enemies, and we stand between two fires of two "public opinions," besides the "for true" fire of the gun boats and our own soldiers. A lady said to me "The guerillas have a black list containing the names of those remaining in [p. 154] town. All the men are to be hanged, their houses burned, and all the women are to be tarred and feathered." I said "Madam, If I believed them capable of such a vile *threat*, even, much less the execution, I would see them cut down without a feeling of compassion," (which is not true) "and swear I was a Yankee rather than claim being a native of the same country with such brutes." She has a long tongue; when I next hear of it, it will be that *I* told the story, and called them brutes and hoped they would be shot, etc. And so goes the world. No one will think of saying I did not believe they were guilty of the thought, even.

Our three brothers may be sick or wounded at this minute; what I do for this man, God will send some one to do for them, and with that

---

tered in the building, but it seems more likely that at least some part of it was being used as a military hospital.

172. The Golden Rule, from Matthew 7:12 and Luke 6:31.

173. What Sarah may also have known is that Sparks had been given a general court-martial and discharged from the army four months after enrolling in the Pelican Rifles.

belief, I do it. So Tiche carried the "nourishment" and linen rags, and if I can do anything on earth for that man, I'll do it if I die for it! Let our "friends" burn our home for it. I would be proud to sacrifice myself for the sake of God and Religion. Mob shall never govern my opinions, or tell me how much I may be allowed to do. I will do what Conscience alone dictates. Of my opinions, some I gained from father, some I formed for myself; I obtrude them on no one, I am satisfied to be alone. Toleration, I say, is all that can keep the world afloat; think as you please, my friend, I do not ask for your approbation. Go your way, and I defy you to cross mine. If you place yourself in my path, ten chances to one I'll step over you without seeing you, in a fit of abstraction. I dare say I have crushed many a worm without seeing it.

[p. 155] June 11th

Last evening mother and Miriam went to the Arsenal to see if they would be allowed to do any thing for the prisoners. General Williams received them, and fascinated Miriam by his manners, as usual. Poor Miriam is always being fascinated, according to her own account. He sent for little Nathan Castle,[174] and Willie Garig, and left them alone in the room with them, showing his confidence, and delicacy by walking quietly away. The poor young men were very grateful to be remembered; one had his eyes too full of tears to speak. Mr Garig told Miriam that when the story of her refusing the escort was told in Camp, the woods rang with shouts of "Three cheers for Miss Morgan!" They said they were treated very well, and had no want, except clean clothes, and to let their mothers know they were well and content.

Miriam came home vowing she was Yankee, and afraid to say it; I tell her I am a Southerner, and not ashamed to say I admire our foes. Consequence is, she passes for "Secesh," I for Yankee, among the rabid. News has reached us from Clinton that we have all gone over to the Northerner, and that our house is thronged with Federal officers daily. To think we have the reputation of receiving them, when we were forced to act like ill bred curs in order to avoid giving occasion for scandal! Miriam says what is the use of denying ourselves their society, when it

---

174. Nathan Castle, age 14 in the 1860 census, the younger brother of Henry Castle, Jr. Obviously he is the "boy of sixteen" mentioned in the entry before.

is universally believed they visit us? She would rather be called guilty with justice, than unjustly accused. I would not; "Conscious Integrity" is enough for me.

I wish we had acted differently though. These gentlemen know us to be ladies; but have we proved it? Mr Biddle evidently wished the privilege of visiting here; were we not obliged to pass it over in perfect silence? [p. 156] I cant forgive myself for the rudeness; I wish I could have extended the same courtesy to him which other gentlemen have been in the habit of receiving here. "Public Opinion"—I mean that of these long tongued slandering women—what an unspeakable contempt I have for you! [Sentence lined through] But—, there is always a But—in such cases.

I have been hard at work mending three or four suits of the boys' clothing for those poor young men. Some needed thread and needle very much, but it was the best we could do. So I packed them all up—not forgetting a row of pins—and sent Tiche off with the bundle perched real Congo fashion on her many colored head handkerchief, which was tied in the most superb Creole style in honor of the occasion.

June 12th.

Father's birthday. Aged 63 this day. It is wofully different from other aniversaries [*sic*]. It used always to bring a great dinner, except last year, when there was only the family. It was then I brought him the slippers I had embroidered, and he kissed me, and was so proud of them. And he wore them every evening, until the day he took them off for the last time and put them by his bed. It was that evening that he called me to bring my guitar and sing,—he had not had a concert [in] so long—and we sang in the moonlight for the first time since Harry died, in honor of his birthday. And this time—

[p. 157] June 13th

I enjoy this débonnaire way of life, just we three women to do, say, think, as we please, and no questions asked. I feel Roger Bontemps![175] Hurra for Independence! We get up when we please, breakfast from

175. Expression meaning carefree and contented, from the song "Roger Bontemps" by Pierre-Jean de Béranger.

half past eight, to half past nine; dinner after three, supper when we feel like it, to bed when we are sleepy, do what we will all day, sing and play all the evening. Guitar goes finely on the balcony these moonlight nights, and I feel wonderfully content and happy, considering the depressing state of affairs around.

Evening. Lilly and the children came in town at two o'clock to day, to our great surprise. One universal desertion at Greenwell one would imagine, from the scarcity of provisions. Whole place evacuated in an hour. There must be more "Traitors" in town than the Morgans, just now!

June 14th

I try not to cry when I think of father, but I cannot help it to night. All are in bed save I, and alone in my solitary little room, the remembrance of what I lost when father died has proved to[o] strong for me. That last night, which is ever before me, comes more awfully before me now. I see his calm face, his noble head shaded by his silver hair, his eyes turned so lovingly on each by turns; that ghastly gas light streaming on his death bed. O how solemn it was! And I see that grand, sublime old man lying there so calm and holy, feeling death creep inch by inch towards his heart, knowing better than we how few hours he had to live—he, while we trembled with a vague awe, waited quietly for the end, watched it drawing near, and nearer, felt its approach without terror, looked at it without fear—went to God with that sublime look on his face which said "Thou [p. 158] art just" while over his whole person there was a look of magnificent trust in His mercy as though the soul had fulfilled its mission here on earth, and waited patiently for a merited reward. O dear father! was there ever such a beautiful death as yours? was there ever a life more noble? O father! how could you die and leave me? And yet, I would not call you back. No! thank God you are sleeping!

June 16th Monday

My poor old diary comes to a very abrupt end, to my great distress. The hardest thing in the world is to break off journalizing when you are once accustomed to it, and mine has proved such a resource to me in these dark days of trouble that I feel as though I were saying goodbye to an old and tried friend. Thanks to my liberal supply of pens, ink, and paper, how many inexpressibly dreary days I have filled up to my own satisfaction, if not to that of others! How many disagreeable affairs it has caused me to pass over without another thought, how ma[n]y times it has proved a relief to me where my tongue was forced to remain quiet! Without the blessed materials, I would have fallen victim to despair and "the Blues" long since; but they have kept my eyes fixed on "Better days a coming" while slightly alluding to present woes, kept me from making a fool of myself many a day, acted as lightning rod to my mental thunder, and have made me happy generally. For all of which I cry "Vive pen, ink, and paper!" and add with regret "Adieu my mental Conductor! I fear this unchained lightning will strike somewhere, in your absence!"

Book Two

[p. 1] "I hope to die shouting the Lord will provide!"[1]
Monday June 16th 1862.

There is no use in trying to break off journalizing, particularly in "these trying times." It has become a necessity to me. I believe I would go off in a rapid decline if Butler took it in his head to prohibit that, among other things. I get nervous and unhappy in thinking of the sad condition of the country and of the misery all prophesy [h]as in store for us, get desperate to think I am fit for nothing in the world, could not earn my daily bread, even, and just before I reach the lowest ebb, I seize my pen, dash off half a dozen lines, sing "Better days are coming" and Presto! Richard is himself again! O what a resource that and my books have been to me!

But to day I believe I am tired of life. I am weary of every thing. I wish I could find some "lodge in some vast wilderness"[2] where I could be in peace and quiet; where I would never hear of war, or rumors of war, of lying, slandering, and all uncharitableness; where I could eat my bread in thanksgiving and trust God alone in all things; a place where I would never hear a woman talk politics or lay down the law— Bah! how it disgusts me! What paradise that would be, if such a place is to be found on earth! I am afraid it is not. What a consolation it [p. 2] is to remember there are no "Politics" in heaven! I reserve to myself the privilege of writing my opinions, since I trouble no one with the expression of them; the disgust I have experienced from listening to others, I hope will forever prevent me from becoming a "Patriotic woman."

1. Line from the hymn "Confidence" by the English hymnist John Newton (1725–1807). Sarah substitutes "I" for "We." Lines from other hymns appear on the unnumbered page facing this one in the diary.

2. The quotation is from William Cowper, *The Task*.

121

In my opinion, the Southern women, and some few of the men, have disgraced themselves by their rude, ill mannered behavior in many instances. I insist, that if the valor and chivalry of our men cannot save our country, I would rather have it conquered by a brave race, than owe its liberty to the Billingsgate oratory and demonstrations of some of these "ladies." If the women have the upper hand then, as they have now, I would not like to live in a country governed by such tongues.

Do I consider the female who could spit in a gentleman's face merely because he wore United States buttons, as a fit associate for me? Lieut. Biddle assured me he did not pass a street in New Orleans without being most grossly insulted by *ladies*. It was a friend of his into whose face a lady *spit*[3] as he walked quietly by without looking at her. (Wonder if she did it to attract his attention?) He had the sense to apply to her husband[4] and give him two minutes to [p. 3] apologize or die, and of course he chose the former. Such things are enough to disgust anyone. "Loud" women, what a contempt I have for you! How I despise your vulgarity!

Some of these Ultra Secessionists evidently very recently from "down East" who think themselves obliged to "kick up their heels over the Bonny blue flag" as Brother describes female patriotism, shriek out "What! see those vile Northerners pass patiently? No true Southerner could see it without rage! I could kill them! I hate them with all my soul, the murderers, liars, thieves, rascals! You are no Southerner if you do not hate them as much as I!" Ah ça! a true blue Yankee tell me that I, born and bred here, am no Southerner! I always think "It is well for you, my friend, to save your credit, else you might be suspected by some people, though your violence is enough for me." I always say "*You* may do as you please; my brothers are fighting for me, and doing their duty, so this excess of patriotism is unnecessary for me as my position is too well known to make any demonstrations requisite." I flatter myself that "tells."

This war has brought out wicked, malignant feelings that I did not believe could dwell in woman's heart. I see some with the holiest [p. 4] eyes, so holy one would think the very spirit of Charity lived in them

3. Above "friend of his" Sarah later wrote "Farragut"; above "lady" she wrote "Alas, I know her!"

4. Later note by Sarah: "She had none!"

and all Christian meekness, go off in a mad tirade of abuse and say with the holy eyes wonderously changed "I hope God will send down plague, Yellow fever, famine, on these vile Yankees, and that not one will escape death."[5] O what unutterable horror that remark causes me as often as I hear it! I think of the many mothers, wives and sisters who wait as anxiously, pray as fervently in their far away lonesome homes for their dear ones, as we do here; I fancy them waiting day after day for the footsteps that will never come, growing more sad, lonely, and heartbroken as the days wear on; I think of how awful it would be to me if one would say "your brothers are dead," how it would crush all life and happiness out of me; and I say "God forgive these poor women! They know not what they say!" O woman! into what loathsome violence you have debased your holy mission! God will punish us for our hardheartedness.

Not a square off, in the new theater,[6] lie more than a hundred sick soldiers. What woman has stretched out her hand to save them, to give them a cup of cold water? Where is the charity which should ignore nations and [p. 5] creeds, and administer help to the Indian or Heathen indifferently? Gone! all gone in Union versus Secession! *That* is what the American War has brought us. If I was independent, if I could work my own will without causing others to suffer for my deeds, I would not be poring over this stupid page, I would not be idly reading or sewing. I would put aside woman's trash, take up Woman's duty, and I would stand by some forsaken man and bid him God speed as he closes his dying eyes. *That* is Woman's mission! and not Preaching and Politics. I say I would, yet here I sit! O for liberty! the liberty that *dares* do what conscience dictates, and scorns all smaller rules!

If I could help these dying men! Yet it is as impossible as though I was a chained bear. I cant put out my hand. I am threatened with Coventry[7] because I sent a custard to a sick man who is in the army, and with the anathema of society because I said if I could possibly do anything for

5. "Such venom one must see to believe," General Thomas Williams wrote at about the same time. ". . . I look at them and think of fallen angels." Letter dated June 13, "Letters of General Thomas Williams, 1862," *American Historical Review* 14 (January 1909): 320.

6. Theater built in 1861 by the Baton Rouge banker and entrepreneur William S. Pike. Later it was called Pike's Hall. The theater fronted on Third Street and extended back toward Church in the block south and west of the Morgan home.

7. Popular euphemism for ostracism.

Mr Biddle—at a distance—(he is sick) I would like to very much. [Sentence lined through][8] [Word erased] thinks we have acted shockingly in helping Col. McMillan, and [p. 6] that we will suffer for it when the Federals leave. I would like to see the *man* who *dared* harm my father's daughter! But as he seems to think our conduct reflects on him, there is no alternative. Die, poor men, without a woman's hand to close your eyes! We women are too *patriotic* to help you! I look eagerly on, cry in my soul "I wish—"; you die, God judges me. Behold the woman who dares not risk private ties for God's glory and her professed religion! Coward, helpless woman that I am! If I was free!—

[p. 7] June 17th 1862.

Yesterday, and day before, boats were constantly arriving, and troops embarking from here, destined for Vicksburg.[9] There will be another fight, and of course it will fall. I wish Will was out of it; I dont want him to die. I got the kindest, sweetest, letter from Will when Miriam came from Greenwell—! It was given to her by a guerilla on the road who asked if she was not Miss Sarah Morgan. I was glad to see that I was not forgotten; but there is no danger of his forgetting me. After his wife, I flatter myself there is no one on earth he loves more than Miriam and me. Mother does not believe in Platonic affection, she says, but here is a specimen of it. I would not have been any more willing to see Miriam marry him, than I would have been willing to—marry him myself! There now! Is that satisfactory enough? I had my own reasons for it; but I do believe that a more noble, generous heart than Will's, does not beat on earth. Indeed I like him! Perhaps it is because he was so connected with what was on the whole the happiest year of my happy life, 1860.

I remember well the first time I saw him. The week before Mattie was married[10] Miriam went to Linwood for her health. She came back the

8. In the 1913 edition Warrington Dawson transcribed this as "Charlie," which appears to have been the first word.

9. The Confederates held the city itself, which was situated on bluffs above the Mississippi River. The Union plan was not to take Vicksburg by assault, but rather to dig a cutoff canal across a neck of land opposite the city in an attempt to divert the river and bypass the fortifications there.

10. Mattie Castleton married James H. Stith on August 2, 1860.

Monday before the wedding, and [p. 8] told me of what a fine young man she had met twice there, a midshipman on a visit home. The next evening we were in the parlor with some young lady, when looking up, I saw a young man in citizen's dress just passing by Lydia's gate. "Here is Mr Pinkney" I said to Miriam. She would not mind, but went on talking. He passed the window, still not even looking at the house. I told her again it was he. Presently I heard a step on the balcony, and said "It *is* he; if you dont go out and meet him, I will!" She went out still incredulous, for she knew I had never seen him, and could not know him, and in another moment I was introduced to Mr Pinkney. How did I know him, I wonder? If he had been in uniform, I might have guessed; but he was in plain citizen's dress, as I said before. That was the last day of July; and from that day, to the first of September, there was hardly an hour of the day in which we did not see him, besides the occasional visits he and Howell used to pay us after, until one went to Annapolis, and the other to college.

That August at Linwood—! were we not happy? I wish we were all back again to 1860, that this war had never broken out, that Will was as merry and gay as he was then, and we [p. 9] were all back at Linwood dancing to the tunes from Lydia's, or Helen Carter's[11] fingers, which would have made a puritan dance. I wish we could all be together for one day again! Ah me! I have not danced since the 29th of April 1861, I that danced forever, even while combing my hair! Howell and Will taught me to waltz then, and we danced at all times after, morning, noon, and night, just as we pleased. What rides we took! what walks! And moonlight nights walking around the circle and sitting on the balcony singing in the moonlight or dancing in the parlor! That was real pleasure; I only hope we will be as happy again.

Will played so beautifully on the violin, too. I never hear "[words lined through]" with out thinking of him; it is a sad air to me. Do you remember that warm breathless evening when after stifling us with the intense heat, the sun suddenly disappeared behind a great black cloud and with a sudden rush the wind swept over the sugar cane bending the tops to the ground, and blew for an hour with the greatest violence?

11. Wife of Eugene Carter and daughter-in-law of General Albert G. Carter. Helen was 23 at the time this was written.

Do you remember how, like a great baby, shaking with your terror of storms, wind especially, you sat in Helen Carter's lap speechless with fear while she rocked you in her arms in silent [p. 10] sympathy? and how Howell reasoned and coaxed, and Theodore[12] stood silently by holding a glass of water and looking very miserable, and Wallace Badger[13] cried aloud because you looked frightened, and Miriam laughed " '*Aint*' you ashamed?" While Will struck up "[words lined through]" and danced to his own music in illustration of the tune while exhorting, begging, insisting that you would laugh just once, there was no danger?

Ah! it was very pleasant to be made so much of; I am afraid I was a spoilt child then, and made some suffer for my whims, though none ever complained. I always got double share of every thing, even of fruits. Will used to send peaches and grapes to Miriam; The [Theodore] and Howell sent them to me. "Fedo" 's,[14] I was at liberty to give away; but Howell's—? that was treason! I must eat every one myself (which was frequently more than I could accomplish) and he would peel the peaches, and help me eat them, too. What babies we were! every time we would go out walking, Howell would fill his pockets with almonds, gingerbread and raisins, and we would walk down the road laughing, singing, and eating our nuts like any other children.

Both "Fedo" and Howell used Moore frequently for my benefit, and I am afraid wasted many pencils. [p. 11] Sometimes I would call for a truce to nonsense and settle my self comfortably to read in a great arm chair, and the next minute, Howell would be by me teasing me to put the book down and talk. I would insist I had nothing to say, he must be quiet for an hour or two and let me read a little before my eyes got rusty; but he would only promise on condition he could sit there and watch me; and sitting on a stool at my feet, would never move until I did, save [?] to touch my hand, never take his eyes off of mine. Miriam and Will used to laugh and ask him if he never got tired of the inter-

12. Theodore Pinkney, age 17 in the 1860 census. Theodore and his brother William, 20, were then residing with their grandfather William Elder.

13. The younger son of Wallace and Mary Badger, age 11 in the 1860 census. Mrs. Badger was the sister of General Carter.

14. Nickname of, or possibly a child's name for, Theodore Pinkney. Sarah sometimes refers to him as The.

esting game; but he always strenuously denied the possibility of such a thing.

Bah! children! children that we were!—and I the greatest baby of the two, for I had not sense enough to know it was not right to let the boy like me so much! It amused me, so I did not mind. When we came home mother spoke to me about it; I did not really believe it until then; I thought it was fun. "Bah! ça se passera"[15] I said. Mother said—no matter what, for time will prove I was right, and she wrong. [p. 12 blank]

[p. 13] June 18th

How long, O how long is it since I have laid down in peace, thinking "this night I will rest in safety?" Certainly not since the fall of Fort Jackson. If left to myself, I would not anticipate evil, but would quietly await the issue of all these dreadful events; but when I hear men who certainly should know better than I, express their belief that in twenty four hours the town will be laid in ashes, I begin to grow uneasy, and think it must be so, since they say it. These last few days, since the news arrived of the intervention of the English and French, I have alternately risen and fallen from the depth of despair to the height of delight and expectation, as the probability of another Exodus diminishes and peace appears more probable. If these men would not prophesy the burning of the city, I would be perfectly satisfied; what is the use of making women and children unnecessarily unhappy? I am very much afraid it will produce a very unpleasant effect on me, making me believe after a while only a small proportion of what they say, and think that perhaps I myself know as much as they, after all—which will look dreadfully conceited.

Annoyed by these constantly expressed beliefs, this morning I put [p. 14] several changes of clothes in a large bag to await the final issue; so if I must run, I will have a change of clean linen *this* time, for the next time it is shelled B.R will certainly disappear from the face of creation. My better sense tells me there is very little probability of such an event; the sensation mongers cry it is inevitable; can I be wiser than the rest? Of course they must know. All loyal patriots, who own no property here, cry loudly "Burn the town down! I'll help!" Thanks, Messieurs.

15. "Bah! that will pass."

But which of you will charitably provide us with a home when you have destroyed ours? If burning our house would be of any benefit to the Nation, take us one step farther, or bring peace a day nearer, let it burn! But "patriots" even acknowledge that it would be nothing "except depriving the Yankees of what we cannot ourselves enjoy." That is a piece of spite unworthy even of a jealous woman, much less men.

Mes amies,[16] out of all the thousands of square miles in the Southern Confederacy, Baton Rouge occupies but one; cant you leave that little spot to hundreds of unprotected women and children? In all [the] vast extent of woods and open country lying around us is there not space enough to fight without coming into [p. 15] this cramped little place? Must the misery of women always be combined with victory to make it sweet? Spare our towns, I say, and fight like Kilkenny cats in the open plains, if you will, until Heaven in mercy sends us peace. O for blessed Peace! I can only think, pray, for that and the boys.

Well! I packed up a few articles to satisfy my conscience, since these men insist that another run is inevitable, though against my own conviction. I am afraid I was partly influenced by my dream last night of being shelled out unexpectedly and flying without saving an article. It was the same dream I had a night or two before we fled so ingloriously from Baton Rouge, when I dreamed of meeting Will Pinkney suddenly, who greeted me in the most extraordinarily affectionate manner, and told me that Vicksburg had fallen. He said he had been chiefly to blame, and the Southerners were so incensed at his losing, the Northerners at his defending, that both were determined to hang him, he was running for his life. He took me to a hill from which I could see the Garrison, and the American flag flying over it. I looked, and saw we were standing in blood up to our knees, while here and there ghastly white bones shone [p. 16] above the red surface. Just then below me I saw crowds of people running. "What is it?" I asked. "It means that in another instant they will commence to shell the town. Save yourself." "But Will— I must save some clothes, too! How can I go among strangers with a single dress? I *will* get some!" I cried. He smiled and said "You will run with only what articles you may happen to have on." Bang! went the first shell, the people rushed by with screams, and I awaked to tell Miriam what an absurd dream I had had.

16. My friends.

It happened as Will had said, either that same day, or the day after; for the change of clothes we saved apiece were given to Tiche, who lost sight of us and quietly came home when all was over, and the two dirty skirts and old cloak mother saved, after carrying them a mile and a half, I put in the buggy that took her up; so I saved nothing, except the bag that was tied under my hoops. Will was right. I saved not even my powder bag.[17] My handkerchief I gave mother before we had walked three squares, and through that long fearfully warm day riding and walking through the fiery sunshine and stifling dust, I had neither to cool or comfort me.

[p. 17] June 19th

Miriam and I have disgraced ourselves! This morning I was quietly hearing Dellie's lessons, when I was startled by mother's shrieks of "Send for a guard! they've murdered him!" and Lilly presently joined in the chorus of horror. I saw through the window a soldier sitting in the dusty road just opposite, with blood streaming from his hand in a great pool in the dust. I was down stairs in three bounds, and snatching up some water, ran to where he sat alone, not a creature near, though all the inhabitants of our side of the street were looking on from the balconies, all crying Murder! and help! without moving themselves. I poured some water on the man's bloody hand, as he held it streaming with gore up to me saying "The man in there did it" meaning the one who keeps the little grog shop, though it puzzled me at the time to see that all the doors were closed and not a face visible.

I had hardly time to speak when Tiche called loudly to me to come away—she was safe at the front gate—and looking up, I found myself in a knot of a dozen soldiers, and took her advice and retreated home. It proved to be the guard Miriam had roused. She ran out as I did, and seeing a seeming gentleman, begged him to call [p. 18] the guard for that murdered man. The individual—he must have been a "patriot"—said he didn't know where to find one. She cried out they were at Heroman's, and he said he didn't believe they were. "Go! I tell you!" she screamed at last; but the brave man said he didn't like to, so she ran to the corner and called the soldiers herself. O most brave man! Before

17. Sarah added above the line: "(Tiche had it in the bundle)."

we got back from our several expeditions we heard mother, Lilly, Mrs Day, all shouting "Bring in the children! lock the doors!" etc, all for a poor wounded soldier!

We after discovered that the man was drunk, and had cursed the woman of the grog shop, whereupon her husband had pitched him out in the streets where we found him. They say he hurt his hand against a post; but wood could never have cut deep enough to shed all that gore. I dont care if he was drunk or sober, soldier or officer, Federal or Confederate! If he had been Satan himself lying helpless and bleeding in the street, I would have gone to him! I cant believe it was as criminal as though I had watched quietly from a distance, believing him dying and contenting myself with looking on. Yet it seems it was dreadfully indecorous; Miriam and I [p. 19] did very wrong; we should have shouted murder with the rest of the women and servants. Whereas the man who declined committing himself by calling one soldier to the rescue of another supposed to be dying, acted most discreetly, and showed his wisdom in the most striking manner.

May I never be discreet, or wise, if this is Christian conduct or a sample of either! I would rather be a rash, impulsive fool! Charlie says he would not open his mouth to save a dozen from being murdered, I say I am not Stoic enough for that. Lilly agrees with him, Miriam with me, so here we two culprits stand alone before the tribunal of patriotism. Madame Roland, I take the liber[t]y of altering your words and cry "O *Patriotism*! how many base deeds are sanctioned by your name!"[18] Dont I wish I was a heathen! In twenty four hours the whole country will be down on us.

> O for a pen to paint the slaves
> Whose "Country" like a deadly blight
> Closes all hearts when Pity craves
> And turns God's spirit to darkest night!
> [p. 20] May life's patriotic cup for such
> Be filled with glory overmuch;
> And when at last their spirits go above in their pride,
> Spirit of Patriotism let these valiant abide

18. The words attributed to the French revolutionary on her way to the guillotine were "O liberty! O liberty! What crimes are committed in thy name!"

Full in the sight of grand mass meeting—I don't
  want you to cuss them
But put them where they can hear politics,
  and yet cant discuss them! [19]

June 21st

Miriam and I have been discussing for an hour, a subject on which we cannot agree. That is, whether it is best to let misfortunes and grief bear you down and crush all the sunshine out of your heart, turning you to cold unfeeling marble, or to laugh at all things, and be happy with Destiny's hand stretched out to darken your life. She holds the former, I the latter. She says she wants all the "Champagne" taken off from her heart, wants to be calm, cold, reserved, silent, not easily affected, etc— enfin, une femme incomprise,[20] I say. I cry Heaven preserve me from being such a piece of stone! She objects to my singing "Better days are coming;" she says it is a mockery, where I really feel anything; I say "Let me fool myself into being merry, if I cant [p. 21] believe it with reason." We totally differ here.

Far from wishing myself melancholy or sad, the whole aim of my life has been to look at the bright side of affairs, to be as happy under troubles as I would be with out—the greater the difficulty, the greater the credit. Not that I always succeed, though, I humbly confess; for there are troubles where a merry face would indeed be a mockery; I alude only to the little trials, and unpleasant anticipations in life. I believe it to be a sacred duty incumbent on all—even little children can contribute their mite—though again I confess I myself fail but too frequently. My ambition has ever been to show my nature as God made it, rather than hide it under a thousand folds of transparent muslin. I have passed my life among those who knew my disposition and fancies perfectly; who fairly read my thoughts, so I grew up to believe my heart was pinned to my sleeve where all could see that there was nothing hid or dissembled, and believe I was rather proud of being so perfectly plain and honest.

That was Sarah as father knew her, and as I gathered from him, I believe there are some few who are not very intimate with me who

19. Note added later: "(I cant say worse than that!)."
20. In short, a misunderstood woman.

think me [p. 22] very different: those for instance who, being deep and designing themselves, think me doubly so, because by one plain word I obtain what would cost them a month's manoeuvering,—of course I must be more skilled than they to accomplish things so much sooner. But those are nasty people; let them pass. It was very well to be forever cheerful and happy in the pleasant days gone by; but now that trouble has come, I find I have two hearts: one open and exposed as ever to public inspection, laughing at coming events with "sufficient unto the day is the evil thereof,"[21] ready to laugh with the merry or cry with the sad, professing "all for the best" and loving all people and all things and fighting against fancied or real woes; the other is labeled "Private" and is best undescribed. It is the one sacred spot where no one has a right to look; it is my Holy of Holies where I myself seldom dare enter.

When I talk of father and Harry, it is with the first; I speak of them as though in the next room, repeat some jest, some laughable incident in which they were concerned, and even smile, while stranger eyes look at me in wonder, think me [p. 23] heartless, unfeeling, I know not what. But I never flinch or falter while all the time another deeper heart is beating so loud, so painfully, and cries—but I say "No!" I stifle it, smother it. These people shall not hear its voice; it is sacred; wait 'til I am alone, and I will listen to what it says, and bow my head; but here, before these people? Never! Crush it, first! So I cover it up until then, and when I am secure from all eyes I say "Tell me your tale" and listen to what it says while on my knees, hear it beat, beat, so dull and heavy, and cry "God help me bear this cheerfully!" When I come out, I am ready to laugh again, to say all the world is happy, and I among the happiest; it is shut up then, I wont listen to what it has been telling me.

Each of us have our burdens; little Louisa[22] as well as mother, Tiche, as well as any of us. Suppose we each took a fancy to consider ourselves the most miserable of mortals, and acted accordingly, going about with our eyes streaming, groaning over our troubles, and never cease to mourn. What a jolly world it would be!—And wouldn't my white dress that Tiche is ironing for me to wear to church tomorrow [p. 24] get

21. Matthew 6:34.

22. Probably a slave child. The 1860 census gives the age of the youngest Morgan slave as six months.

wofully damp!—Ah no! let us all learn to laugh and be happy, and sing "Better days are coming;" even if we dont believe it, it will make those around us happy. I know I feel the unhappiness of the merest child; how much more then that of a grown person? Who would not be willing to undertake that most awful, thankless of responsibilities—a baby with strong lungs—if it could be taught to laugh its wants, rather than cry them? What a delightful novelty it would be! So then, let us laugh and be happy while the sun still shines, for "the night approacheth."

Come Miriam! you no more fancy la femme incomprise than I. Why then profess a taste for the grand, melancholy, stern, morose female who carries about in her breast a petrified heart? As to me, so long as I have the strength, I shall battle against Melancholy. I am not philosopher enough to reason it away, so I'll be content with singing it off. Let me feel what I will, within, a laugh shall satisfy those without; none have a right to look beyond. I shall keep the Champagne of my life carefully in its ice bucket. It shall not be roughly or madly shaken, for fear that [p. 25] bursting all restraints it rushes wildly out in foam, and is lost in one frantic ebulition which dies in a moment; no; I take it in small bottles, opening each as the dregs begin to show in the other, and my motto shall be "a large supply constantly on hand." I'll laugh so long as there is a fancy to laugh at, I'll sing so long as there is a particle of tune in my throat, and I'll dance, maybe, one of these days, when better days come for true. Until then, all ye advocates of dark Melancholy, stand from before me out of my sunlight! In secret I may moan; but in public?—so long as God loves me, and there is a piece of blue sky shining through the clouds, I am happy!

June 23d.

I wish I could see Lydia. I want her ever so much. Such a dear little body! So convenient to pet, kiss, hug, slap or pinch! Suits my humor, provided it is an amiable one. Such a charitable little soul! has something good to say for every body, and is as true a Christian as ever lived. O my "gear Lygia"![23] dont I wish I had you this evening to tease you some! Miriam loves her dear Sarah better than [p. 26] anything in the world, but she is not of the playful kind—she wont let me "fool"

23. Child's rendering of "dear Lydia."

around her; her Majesty is too stately for such nonsense. But Lygia—in spite of her [words lined through], I can do what I please with her tiny little body, and she won't fight me for it. And dont I long to see Sis—! It wont do to talk about it even; I want to see her more than I could say. I want to see every body. There is Gibbes—ah! and George—Oh! and Jimmy—O me! Which would I rather see? All three at once! I dreamed of their coming home the other night and the recollection of it made me happy for a whole day. O that awful battle! What if— Hush! Dont think of it again.

I dont get petting enough to keep a flea alive! I am satisfied that they all love me, and that mother would sacrifice anything for me, and Lilly would turn herself wrong side out to please me, and Miriam sleep on the floor to accommodate me, but that only makes me selfish. I would rather have the petting and that is not in any of their natures; they are not demonstrative, whatever they may feel. I believe I was born to pet. My life [p. 27] should have passed away in our old home; I should have died when I was so sick last summer, before father went. All I am fit for, is to be spoiled. I was made only for sunshine. Made for father to call me "darling" and "little daughter" and be proud of poor little worthless me; for Sis to pet me and call me "Sis names;" for Harry to talk to, and care for; for Miriam to make a fuss over, and fight my battles for me, and spoil me generally; and for the rest to be loving and kind as they have ever been. That is the life I was made for. But all this dreary 1862 I have had no one to pet, myself, beyond tumbling mother occasionally with a bear hug, ever since Lydia and Jimmy went away.[24]

Jimmy used to lay his head in my lap, the lazy rascal, and tell me some of his laughable yarns in the evening, or we would walk around the parlor with our arms about each other's shoulders singing "Joe Bowers" to Miriam's great annoyance, when she wanted quiet, or playing any prank which would suggest its self at the time. Lazy Jimmy! he is not satisfied with one holding his head; he likes somebody to hold his feet besides; often Miriam and I are engaged in the arduous [p. 28] task. And like his sister Sarah, he has the greatest fancy for holding somebody's hand; to his credit be it said, his sisters have the preference.

24. With Captain Gibbes Morgan away in the war, Lydia had gone back to her family at Linwood, but she would soon go to Richmond to be near her husband. Jimmy Morgan was presumably still in Virginia.

It is only recently that I have been able to break myself of the habit of holding to some one. I am never so perfectly at ease, or happy as when I have some one's hand; only within the last few months have Sophy Brunot and I ceased, by mutual consent, the extraordinary practice of for ever holding each other's hands walking or sitting, in private or public. It grew to be a proverb; and even in company, seated side by side, invariably her left and my right hand would disappear under the folds of our two dresses, while the others remained in their natural position as though we had but one pair between us—which was literally the fact. This Human Contact, how I have clung to it! It must be put away with all childish things though; [words lined through]!

Yes, I was made for nothing in the world but warm sunshine; I am not fitted for the winter of Adversity. [p. 29] They say dreadful things are yet in store for us; I dont believe it; "the darkest hour is just before day." They say the town is going to be shelled, tell dreadful tales of fire and desolation the Yankees are spreading out side of the limits, burning sugar houses, the homes of rich and poor; confiscated property—it would be too much to tell of the horrors that reach our ears even though we are almost entirely cut off from communication with the rest of the world in this little place, but I dont want to believe it all. It cant be perfectly reliable in every particular as the only authority is "They say." Who, I wonder, since we are neither permitted to leave or enter the town? In one week more "they say" (I could give authority *this* time) that starvation will be upon us; we will perish by famine. Do I believe it? Not a bit! God will not suffer it. He will provide food for us, someway; Elijah had his ravens, the widow her cruise of oil; why should I be uneasy? "God will help us, and that right early." Come! grim "next week"! I dare say "something will turn up" before then, and you will find me as content as I am now! I am not afraid. "I hope to die shouting the Lord will provide!"

[p. 30] June 26th

Yesterday morning just as I stepped out of bed I heard the report of four canon [*sic*] fired in rapid succession, and every body ask every body else "Did you hear that?" so significantly, that I must say my heart beat very rapidly for a few moments, at the thought of another stampede. At half past six this morning I was wakened by another report, followed by seven others, and heard again the question "Did you hear *that?*" on a higher key than yesterday.—It did not take me many minutes to get out of bed, and to slip on a few articles, I confess. My chief desire was to wash my face before running, if they were actually shelling us again. It appears that they were only practicing, however, and no harm intended. But we are living on such a volcano, that not knowing what to expect, we are rather nervous.

I am afraid this close confinement will prove too much for me; my long walks are cut off, on account of the soldiers. One month to-morrow since my last visit to the graveyard! That haunts me always; it must be so dreary out there!

[p. 31] Here is a sketch of my daily life, enough to finish me off forever, if much longer persisted in. First, get up a little before seven. After breakfast, which is generally within a few minutes after I get down (it used to be *just* as I got ready, and sometimes before, last winter), I attend to my garden, which consists of two strips of ground the length of the house, in front, where I can find an hour's work in examining and admiring my flowers, replanting those that the cows and horses occasionally (once a day) pull up for me, and in turning the soil over and over again to see which side grows best. Ah my garden! abode of rare delights! how many pleasant hours I have passed in you, armed with scissors, knife, hoe or rake, only pausing when Mr This or Mr That leaned over the fence to have a talk!—last spring, that was; ever so many are dead now, for all I know, and all off at the war. Now I work for the edification of proper young women, who look in astonishment at me, as they would consider themselves degraded by the pursuit. A delicate pair of hands my flower mania will leave me!

Then I hear Dellie's, and Morgan's [25] lessons, after which I open my [p. 32] desk, and am lost in the mysteries of Arithmetic, Geography, Blair's Lectures, Noël et Chapsal, Ollendorff, and reading aloud in french and english, besides writing occasionally in each, and sometimes a peep at Lavoisne, [26] until very nearly dinner. The day is not half

25. Gibbes Morgan LaNoue, Lilly's oldest son, born August 2, 1855.

26. The books Sarah mentions appear to have been Hugh Blair's *Lectures on Rhetoric;* Noel and Chapsal's book of selections of French literature, or perhaps their French grammar; a French grammar by Heinrich Ollendorff; and *A Complete Genealogical, Historical, Chronological, and Geographical Atlas* by C. V. Lavoisne.

long enough for me. Many things I would like to study I am forced to give up, for want of leisure to devote to them. But one of these days, I will make up for present deficiencies. I study only what I absolute[ly] love, now, but then, if I can, I will study what I am at present ignorant of, and cultivate a taste for something new.

The few moments before dinner, and all the time after, I devote to writing, sewing, knitting, etc. and if I included darning, repairs, alterations, etc, my list would be tremendous, for I get through with a great deal of sewing. Somewhere in the day, I find half hour, or more, to spend at the piano. Before sunset I dress, and am free to spend the evening at home, or else walk to Mrs Brunot's, for it is not safe to go farther than those three squares, away from home. From early twilight until supper, Miriam and I sing with the guitar, generally, and after, [p. 33] sit comfortably under the chandelier and read until about ten. What little reading I do, is almost exclusively done at that time. It sounds wofully little, but my list of books grows to quite a respectable size, in the course of a year.

At ten comes my bible class for the servants. Lucy, Rose and Nancy & Dophy assemble in my room, and hear me read the bible, or stories from the bible for a while. Then one by one say their prayers—they cannot be persuaded to say them together; Dophy says "she cant say with Rose, 'cause she aint got no brothers and sisters to pray for," and Lucy has no father or mother, and so they go. All difficulties and grievances during they [*sic*] day are laid before me, and I sit like Moses judging the children of Israel, until I can appease the discord. Sometimes it is not so easy. For instance that memorable night when I had to work Rose's stubborn heart to a proper pitch of repentance for having stabbed a carving fork in Lucy's arm in a fit of temper. I dont know that I was ever as much astonished as I was at seeing the dogged, sullen girl throw herself on the floor in a burst of tears, and say if God would forgive her she would never do it again. [p. 34] I was lashing myself internally, for not being able to speak as I should, furious at myself for talking so weakly, and lo! here the girl tumbles over wailing and weeping!

And Dophy, overcome by her feelings, sobs "Lucy I scratched you last week! please forgive me this once!" and amazed and bewildered I look at the touching tableau before me of kissing and reconcilliation, for Lucy can bear malice towards no one, and is ready to forgive before others repent, and I look from one to the other, wondering what it was that upset them so completely, for certainly no words of mine caused it. Sometimes Lucy sings a wild hymn "Did you ever hear the heaven bells ring," "Come my loving brothers," "When I put on my starry crown," etc, and after some such scene as that just described, it is pleasant to hear them going out of the room saying "Good night Miss Sarah" "God bless Miss Sarah!" and all that.

Ah me! children and servants like me, even if big people dont! I believe I prefer it. Passing a crowd of negroes day before yesterday, I heard them discussing my merits, and really felt pleased, I am sorry to say; but flattery from these humble creatures [p. 35] does not seem fulsome to me. There is one woman, I dont know who she is, who always has something to say to me. One evening walking with Miriam and Lydia, she met us, and cried out seeing Miriam who was in advance "Here comes my queen!" and seeing me just behind cried again "No! *here* comes my pretty thing!" All such little traits of affection in their nature pleases me, I confess. I prefer their honest devotion to the hollow profusions of many fine people I know of. Here I am discussing the affection all servants have for me, à-pro-pos of nothing! It is time to conclude before running off in another strain as little to the purpose.

June 27th 1862

A proclamation of Van Dorn[27] has just been smuggled in town, which advises all persons living within eight miles of the Mississippi to remove into the interior, as he is determined to defend his department at all hazards to the last extremity. Does not look like the Peace I have been deluding myself with, does it? That means another Exodus. How are we to leave, when we are not allowed to pass the limits of the corporation [p. 36] by the Federals? Where are we to go? We are between the two armies, and here we must remain patiently awaiting the result. Some of these dark nights, bang! we will hear the cannon, and then it will be sauve qui peut[28] in a shower of shells. Bah! I dont believe God will suffer that we should be murdered in such a dreadful way! I dont believe He will suffer us to be turned homeless and naked on the

27. In the summer of 1862 Confederate General Earl Van Dorn was put in command of the Department of Mississippi and East Louisiana, with headquarters in Jackson.

28. Every man for himself.

world! "Something will turn up" before we are attacked, and we will be spared, I am certain.

We cant look forward more than an hour at a time now, sometimes not a minute ahead (witness the shelling frolic) so I must resume my old habit of laying a clean dress on my bed before going to sleep, which I did every night for six weeks before the shelling of B.R, in order to run respectably as muslin cross bar night gowns are not suitable for day dresses. When will all this end?

[p. 37] June 28th

I am afraid I shall be nervous when the moment of the bombardment actually arrives. This suspense is not calculated to soothe one's nerves. A few moments since, a salute was fired in honor of General Butler's arrival, when women, children and servants rushed to the front of the houses, confident of a repitition [*sic*] of the shelling which occured a month ago today. The children have not forgotten the scene, for they all actually howled with fear. Poor little Sarah[29] stopped her screams to say "Mother, dont you wish we was dogs 'stead o' white folks?" in such piteous accents that we had to laugh.

Dont I wish I was a dog! Sarah is right. I dont know that I showed my uneasiness a while ago, but certainly my heart has hardly yet ceased beating rather rapidly. If I knew what moment to expect the stampede, I would not mind; but this way—to expect it every instant, it is too much! Again, if I knew where we could go, for refuge from the shells! To tell the truth, I would not care for an asylum for myself, if I could save some few things I value, such as the guitar Harry gave me, some of his articles, and [p. 38] many letters I prize very much. This time, there is no trunk packing; I'll not get back as I did the last, to save anything.

Sometimes I fancy how all will burn, until it makes me sick to think of it. Fancy a great shell in this little room! Crash! the bed posts will fall with the tester, the marble slab of the toilet table, and its ornaments will disappear in fine dust, long flames will creep in my desk and lick my letters and papers, and will turn over the pages of my books with their long red tongues quicker than my fingers can. They will swallow the washstand at one mouthful, together with all I keep in it; they will break in the armoir—they have no more respect for rosewood than

29. Sarah LaNoue, Sarah Morgan's niece and namesake, age 4.

pine—they will take up my dresses one by one and turn them over as though to taste them (some *are* sweet enough to eat), they will roll down the skirts and up the sleeves, eat all the lace and trimming, these wicked flames!

Nettie said yesterday "I cannot help thinking of what a pity it will be to lose all yours and Miriam's beautiful clothes! cant you save them?" Save them, when I dont know that I will save [p. 39] myself! Yet it is distressing to lose them; I will never have such a wardrobe again, for after the shelling we will be beggars. I would like to have a few respectable suites to commence life in, though, I confess! I am not quite equal, however, to the young lady, who when told she must leave New Orleans instantly as it was to be shelled, said if her trunks could not go too, she would remain and share their fate. No; I say "O my blue flounce! 'Ah my magenta muslin! Ouf my pretty barège! And O my lovely white! What a pity to burn that mull with all that Valencienne!" and so I go on through the whole list, wishing it could be otherwise, but knowing I will be thankful to save a calico, even.

Two muslins, the prettiest imaginable, lie as yet untouched, for I have not had the energy to cut them out; it is useless to sew for fire. All that would be in this one room, and I did not include Miriam's treasures. Then fancy them rolling through mother's and Lilly's rooms! and down stairs! how they will crunch father's and mother's pictures, and sweep over Miriam's piano and my guitar! and how they will leave all things we love and value beyond expression, [p. 40] one heap of smouldering ashes!

Why then do I write this, since it is to burn with the rest? Ah! there is a proof of my hopeful disposition! They tell me these things must be, before many days, but I am willing to believe "Better days are coming, we'll all go right!"—a window banging unexpectedly just then, gave me a curious twinge; not that I believed it was the signal, O dear no! I just thought—what, I wonder?

Pshaw! "Picayune Butler's coming, coming"[30] has upset my nervous system. He interrupted me in the middle of my Arithmetic, and I have not the energy to resume my studies. I shall try what effect an hour's

30. Line from the song "Picayune Butler." See *Louisiana Historical Quarterly* 27 (1944):495.

practice will have on my spirits, and will see that I have a pair of clean stockings in my stampede sack, and that the fastenings of my "running bag" are safe. Though if I expect to take either, I should keep in harness constantly. How long, O Lord! how long?

[p. 41] June 29th Sunday.

"Any more, Mr Lincoln, any more?" cant you leave our racked homes in repose? We are all wild. Last night, five citizens were arrested, on no charge at all, and carried down to Picayune Butler's ship.[31] What a thrill of terror ran through the whole community! we all feel so help-less, so powerless under the hand of our tyrant, the man who swore to uphold the Constitution and the laws, who is professedly only fight-ing to give us all Liberty, the birthright of every American, and who, neverless [*sic*] has ground us down to a state where we would not re-duce our negroes, who tortures and sneers at us, and rules us with an iron hand! Ah Liberty! what a humbug!

I would rather belong to England or France, than to the North! Bond-age, woman that I am, I can never stand! Even now, the northern papers distributed among us, taunt us with our subjection, and tell us "how coolly Butler will grind them down, paying no regard to their writhing and torture beyond tightening the bands still more!" Ah truly! this is the bitterness of slavery, to be insulted and reviled by cowards who are safe at [p. 42] home, and enjoy the protection of the laws, while we, captive and overpowered, dare not raise our voices to throw back the insult, and are governed by the despotism of one man, whose word is our law! And that man, they tell us, "Is the right man in the right place. *He* will develope a union sentiment among the people, if the thing can be done!"

31. Butler arrived on the steamer *McClellan*, an army transport. Another Baton Rouge diarist wrote: "Several prominent citizens are arrested and taken on board the 'McClel-land' [*sic*] and at midnight are released upon parole" on condition that they appear the following morning. See John A. Dougherty diary, June 28, 1862.

Come and see if he can! Hear the curse that arises from thousands of hearts at that man's name, and say if he will "speedily bring us to our senses." Will he accomplish it by love, tenderness, mercy, compassion? He might have done it; but did he try? When he came, he assumed his natural rôle of Tyrant, and bravely has he acted it through, never once turning aside for Justice or Mercy. If this is American Liberty, Despotism in a foreign land, I accept you in preference. Dearly as I love Louisiana, it can never be my home, under such a sway. I feel that we have lost all things, honor included; we are serfs; we have forfeited the respect of foreign nations by submitting patiently to our yoke of iron; we are bondsmen, no longer free citizens. [p. 43] We are to be governed by men imported from Northern states, who are prejudiced, and taught to hold us in contempt from their birth; our laws are to be made by them, with out suffering us to raise our voice in our own cause; we are required only to submit blindly.

Can we so submit? God have mercy on us and deliver us from the hands of our enemies! This degradation is worse than the bitterness of death! I see no salvation [on] either side. No glory awaits the Southern Confederacy if it does achieve its independence; it will be a mere speck in the world, with no weight or authority. The North confesses its self lost with out us, and has paid an unheard of ransom to regain us. On the other hand, conquered, what hope is there in this world for us? Broken in health and fortune, reviled, contemned, abused by those who claim already to have subdued us, with out a prospect of future support for those few of our brothers who return; outcasts without home or honor, would not death or exile be preferable? O let us abandon our loved home to these implacable enemies, and find refuge elsewhere! Take from us property, [p. 44] every thing, only grant us liberty!

Is this rather frantic, considering I abhor politics, and women who meddle with them, above all? My opinion has not yet changed; I still feel the same contempt for a woman who would talk at the top of her voice for the edification of Federal officers, as though anxious to receive an invitation requesting her presence at the garrison. I have too much respect for my father's memory to adopt so pitiful a warfare. "I can suffer and be still" as far as outward signs are concerned; but as no word of this has passed my lips, I give it vent in writing, which is more lasting than words, partly to relieve my heart, partly to prove to my own satisfaction that I am no coward; for one line of this, surrounded as we are by soldiers, and liable to have our houses searched at any instant, would be a sufficient indictment for high treason.

Under Gen William's rule, I was perfectly satisfied that whatever was done, was done through necessity, and under orders from head-quarters, beyond his control; we all liked him.[32] But now, since Butler's arrival, I believe [p. 45] I am as frantic in secret as the others are openly. I know that war sanctions many hard things, and that both sides prac-tice them; but now we are so completely lost in Louisiana, is it fair to gibe and taunt us with our humiliation? I could stand any thing save the cowardly ridicule and triumph of their papers. Honestly, I believe if all vile abusive papers on both sides were suppressed, and some of the fire eating editors who make a living by lying were soundly cowhided or had their ears clipped, it would do more towards establishing peace, than all the bloodshedding either side can afford. I hope to live to see it, too. Seems to me, more liberty is allowed to the press, than would be tolerated in speech. Let us speak as freely as any paper, and see if tomorrow we do not sleep at Fort Jackson![33]

This morning the excitement is rare; fifteen more citizens were ar-rested and carried off,[34] and all the rest grew wild with expectation.

32. Others agree. For instance, William Watson wrote that General Williams was "a brave, upright, and strict officer, and did not allow any insult or outrage to be committed on the inhabitants." *Life in the Confederate Army* (New York, 1888), 394. But some of the officers and men who served under Williams were not so kindly disposed to him. "What a sad thing it is," Colonel Halbert E. Paine wrote his wife on August 3, 1862, "that all the high hopes of gallant military service cherished by the officers of the 4th Wisconsin 6th Michigan & 21st Indiana regiments have been dashed to earth by the absurd blunder of government which placed us under an imbecile puerile drunken malignant shallow cowardly traitorous incompetent blockhead." Letter in collection of Fred G. Benton, Jr.

33. After occupying New Orleans, Butler used Fort Jackson as a prison where disloyal or recalcitrant citizens were sent, including the mayor of New Orleans.

34. On his return to New Orleans, Butler wrote Secretary of War Edwin M. Stanton: "I brought away with me, and now have under arrest, five of those who had used threats toward the men who had shown themselves favorable to the Union." *OR*, ser. I, 15:503. In his diary entry for June 29, John A. Dougherty says: "Some 20 persons were notified to meet Gen Butler this morning . . . and after having a talk with him were dismissed. Cravens, Hyams, Magruder, McKitrick, Shoe [?] Jones & Roberts were taken away in the ship." Of these, the first three can be identified with certainty: N. A. Cravens, the Methodist minister; Henry J. Hyams, editor of the West Baton Rouge *Sugar Planter;* and Professor William H. N. Magruder of the Magruder Collegiate Institute, a boys' school.

So great a martyrdom is it considered, that I am sure those who are not arrested will be wofully disappointed. It is ludicrous to see how each man thinks he is the very one they are in search of! [p. 46] We asked a two penny lawyer, of no more importance in the community than Dophy is, if it was possible he was not arrested. "Not yet," was the modest reply; "But I am expecting to be, every instant!" So much for modest self assurance! Those arrested have some been quietly released (those are so smiling and mysterious that I suspect them), some been obliged to take the oath, some sent to Fort Jackson. "Ah Liberty! What a blessing it is to enjoy thy privileges!" If some of these poor men are not taken prisoners, they will die of mortification at the slight.

Our valiant governor, the brave Moore, has by order of the real governor, Moïse,[35] made himself visible at some far distant point, and issued a proclamation saying, whereas we of Baton Rouge were held forcibly in town, he therefore considered men, women, and children prisoners of war, and as such, the Yankees are bound to supply us with all necessaries, and consequently, anyone sending us aid or comfort, or provisions from the country will be severely punished.[36] Only Moore is fool enough for such an order. Held down by the Federals, our paper money so much trash, with hardly any other [p. 47] to buy food, and no way of earning it; threatened with starvation and utter ruin, our own friends by way of making our burden lighter, forbid our receiving the means of prolonging life, and after generously warning us to leave town, which they know is perfectly impossible, prepare to burn it over our heads, and let the women run the same risk as the men.

Penned in one little square mile, here we await our fate like sheep

35. Thomas Overton Moore was governor at the start of the war and served until January of 1864. With the state's capital occupied, Moore moved the seat of government to Opelousas, and later to Shreveport. A native of Charleston, E. Warren Moise had been influential as speaker of the House and as attorney general. With the coming of the war he served first as circuit judge in New Orleans and later as judge of the Confederate district court at Natchitoches.

36. Sarah must be referring to Moore's "Address to the People of Louisiana," issued on June 18, 1862. See *OR*, ser. I, 15:504–10. Although it does not say precisely what she says it does, Moore did cut off all communication and commerce with Louisianians in those parts of the state occupied by the Federals. It was a bellicose document. "Let every citizen be an armed sentinel," he wrote. "Let all our river-banks swarm with armed patriots to teach the hated invader that the rifle will be his only welcome on his errands of plunder and destruction."

in the slaughter pen. Our hour may be at hand now, it may be tonight; we have only to wait; the booming of the cannon will announce it to us soon enough.

Of the six sentenced to Fort Jackson, one is the Methodist minister Mr Craven.[37] The only charge is, that he was heard to pray for the Confederate States by some officers who passed his house during his family prayers. According to that, which of us would escape unhung? I do not believe there is a woman in the land who closes her eyes before praying for God's blessing on the side on which her brothers are engaged. Are we all to cease? Show me the dungeon deep enough to keep me from praying for them! The man represented [p. 48] that he had a large family totally dependent on him, who must starve. "Let them get up a subscription" was Gen Butler's humane answer. "I will head it my self." It is useless to say the generous offer was declined.

June 30th

As a specimen of the humanity of Gen Butler, let me record a threat of his, uttered with all the force and meaning language can convey, and certainly enough to strike terror in the hearts of frail women, since all these men believe him fully equal to carry it in execution, and some even believe it will be done. In speaking to Mr Benjamin[38] of foreign intervention in our favor, he said "Let England or France try it, and I'll be d—— if I dont arm every negro in the South, and make them cut the throat of every man, woman and child in it! I'll make them lay the whole country waste with fire and sword, and leave it desolate!" Draw me a finer picture of Coward, Brute, and Bully, than that one sentence portrays! O men of the North! you do your noble [p. 49] hearts wrong in sending such ruffians among us as the representatives of a great people.

Was ever a more brutal thought uttered in a more brutal way? Mother, like many another, is crazy to go away from here, even to

37. N. A. Cravens. The Methodist parsonage was at the southeast corner of Church and Laurel streets, two doors from the Morgan home.

38. Sarah later wrote in "Solomon," his given name. A local merchant, Benjamin was the brother of Confederate Secretary of State Judah P. Benjamin. In the letter to Secretary of War Stanton written following his visit to Baton Rouge, Butler tells how he persuaded Solomon Benjamin and Mayor Benjamin F. Bryan to take the oath of allegiance.

New O., but like the rest, will be obliged to stand and await her fate. I dont believe Butler would *dare* execute his threat, for at the first attempt, thousands who are passive now would cut the brutal heart from his inhuman breast, but is it brave, or manly to employ such means? It looks wonderously like a bully, to me. Did he come here to slaughter women? if he did, we would gladly accept death by a volley from his soldiers; but leave us to the butchery of unreasoning animals who would stop at no cruelty when once incited to revolt—? Ah no! death at the hands of our *once* brothers, first! O degraded Southerners! Where now is your boasted freedom and pride? Fallen, fallen below the level of your meanest slave! And *this* is the Glorious American *Union*!

[p. 50] Tuesday July 1st

I heard such a good joke last night! If I had belonged to the female declaming [*sic*] club, I fear me I would have resigned instantly through mere terror. (Thank heaven I dont!) These officers say the women talk too much, which is undeniable. They then said, they meant to get up a sewing society, and place in it every woman who makes herself conspicuous by her loud talking about them. Fancy what a refinement of torture! But only a few would suffer; the majority would be only too happy to enjoy the usual privilege of Sewing Societies, Slander, abuse, and insinuations. How some would revel in it!

The mere threat makes me quake! *If* I could so far forget my dignity and my father's name as to court the notice of gentlemen by contemptible insult, etc, and *if* I should be ordered to take my seat at the sewing society—!!! I would never hold my head up again! Member of a select Sewing circle! Fancy me! (I know "there is never any *gossip* in *our* society, though the one over the way gets up dreadful reports"; I have heard all that, but would rather try neither.) O how I would beg [p. 51] and plead! Fifty years at Fort Jackson, good, kind Genl Butler, rather than half an hour in your sewing society! Gentle, humane ruler, spare me and I [will] split my throat in shouting Yankee Doodle and hurrah for Lincoln! Any, every, thing / so I am not disgraced! Deliver me from your sewing society, and I'll say and do what you please!

Butler told some of these gentlemen that he had a detective watching almost every house in town, and he knew everything. True or not, it looks suspicious. We are certainly watched. Every evening two men may be seen in the shadow on the other side of the street, standing there until ever so late, sometimes until after we have gone to bed. It may be, that far from home, they are attracted by the bright lights and singing, and watch us for their own amusement. A few nights ago, so many officers passed and repassed while we were singing on the balcony that I felt as though our habit of long standing had suddenly become improper. Saturday night, having procured a paper, we were all crowding around, Lilly and I reading every now and then a piece of news from [p. 52] opposite ends of the paper; Charlie, walking on the balcony, found five officers leaning over the fence watching us as we stood under the light, through the open window. Hope that wont elect me to the sewing society!

July 2d

Last evening by some unknown means, a report was started that the town was either to be shelled last night, or this morning. I hardly think any of us really believed it, but we were all uneasy until Charlie had traced the report to its original nothing at all, and it was more than an hour before we were undeceived. Mean time Lilly grew desperate at the idea of taking Dellie out of her bed, for she had fever all day; and besides a rain was coming up, the first in a whole month, which we supposed would be a hard one. It was not pleasant for any of us. I wont mind running in our weather, or daylight, but at night, it will be too much, and if in a storm, I would die at once of fright.

I must really overcome my terror of storms; it is too childish. For weeks, months even, before hand, I anticipate them with such fear, that [p. 53] frequently the anticipation is worse than the reallity. I have been looking forward for one for several months now, in consequence of the prophecy of the clairevoyante, uttered last summer in N.O. It was that Louisiana would suffer first through war, then from crevasses, next a severe storm, after which she would return to the Union. The first two have come to pass, and I am anxiously awaiting the third which is to usher in the fourth. Suppose it should be a repitition of the 2d October 1860! What an awful storm that was! How well I remember my shudder of horror when at sunset the second day Gibbes called to father to make the servants leave the kitchens for the other house, as they would certainly go over in the coming blast! Lydia on one side, I on the other threw our arms around his neck in alarm and clung to him while it struck the house and twisted down the trees in every direction. My first impulse is to hold to someone, no matter who, [just] so it is a human being.

That evening Mattie told me of her engagement, after we had parted, I was standing at the gate talking to father in the hot, breathless air, so close was it that [p. 54] breathing was really a labor, when suddenly without the slightest warning there swept from the north a tremendous wind that whirled me completely around and threw the dust up in clouds which obscured everything. I remember rushing in, and recollecting father, running out again in the furious gale, and begging him to come in; but the moment I put my hand on his shoulder, I burst into tears, and I remember his carrying me to the sofa, and telling me how wrong it was to give way so foolishly, and talking so wisely and kindly, that I made up my mind to conquer. But as long as he lived, never did a storm come up, that I did not run to him and stay there until it was over.

Only since his death, now that I have him no longer to depend upon, have I learned to be quiet about it. And such control! Let the sky grow black, and every employment becomes impossible; so I walk, (sitting is out of the question) look out of the windows, and without saying a word, grow desperately sick at my stomach (an effect fear frequently has upon me) until I see a piece of blue sky somewhere. And O how I love God when I see a tiny blue [p. 55] speck! The rapture is worth the previous terror I have endured. I feel as though God were really every thing, and every where, that I could worship him beyond the power of word, madly adore him, live, die for him, and believe it bliss! Ah! I cant express what a piece of blue sky does for me! I always want to go up and kiss it, and lay my cheek on it.

Well, I hope the clairevoyante's storm at least will come to naught. As to the other, if we could whip the northerners so in every battle, as to force them to acknowledge our equallity, then make our own terms and go voluntarily back to the Union, à la bonheur![39] I would accept the storm if it would bring about such a happy result. But if on the other hand we are to be whipped in and have all we own wrested from us, and the best blood of the land flow on some scaffold, Merci! Je m'en

39. *A la bonne heure:* Fine!

passe[40] as well of the storm, as of the Union on such terms. Gallant little Vicksburg still holds out; I pray we may win the day. O this dreary bloodshed makes me sick! And so many of these poor soldiers are dying here—! I wish they were safe at home. When will we be at Peace?

[p. 56] Thursday night July 3d

Another day of sickening suspense. This evening, about three, came the rumor that there was to be an attack on the town tonight, or early in the morning,[41] and we had best be prepared for any thing. I cant say I believe it, but in spite of my mistrust, I made my preparations. First of all I made a charming improvement in my knapsack, alias pillow case, by sewing a strong black band down each side of the centre from the bottom to the top, when it is carried back and fastened below again, allowing me to pass my arms through and thus present the appearance of an old peddlar. Miriam's I secured also, and tied all our laces in a handkerchief ready to lay it in the last thing.

But the interior of my bag! what a medley it is! First, I believe, I have secured four underskirts, three chemises, as many pair of stockings, two underbodies, the prayer book father gave me, Tennyson that Harry gave me when I was fourteen, two unmade muslins, a white mull, english grenadine trimmed with lilac, and a purple linen, and night gown. Then, I must have Sis' daguerreotype, and how could I leave Will's, when perhaps he was dead? Besides, Howell's [p. 57] and Will Carter's were with him, and one single case did not matter. But there was Tom Barker's I would like to keep, and O! let's take Mr Stone's! and I cant slight Mr Dunnington,[42] for these two have been too kind to Jimmy for me to forget; and poor Capt. Huger is dead, and I *will* keep his, so they all went together. A box of pens too, was indispensible, and a case of french notepaper, and a bundle of Harry's letters were added. Miriam insisted on the old diary that preceded this, and found [a] place for it,

40. Thanks! I pass [I will do without].

41. Sarah means an attack by Confederate forces against the Union troops occupying the city.

42. Tom Barker was Sarah's cousin, the son of her father's sister Ann, who married Captain Thomas Barker. Midshipman S. G. Stone and Lieutenant John W. Dunnington were officers on the *McRae* in the early months of the war. See *ORN*, ser. II, 1:290.

though I am afraid if she knew what trash she was to carry, she would retract before going farther.

It makes me heart sick to see the utter ruin we will be plunged in if forced to run to night. Not a hundredth part of what I most value can be saved—if I counted my letters and papers, not a thousandth. But I cannot believe we will run tonight. The soldiers tell whoever questions them that there will be a fight before morning, but I believe it must be to alarm them. Though what looks suspicious is, that the officers said— to whom is not stated—that the ladies must not be uneasy if they heard cannon to night, as they would [p. 58] probably commence to celebrate the fourth of July about twelve o'clock. What does it mean? I repeat, I dont believe a word of it; yet I have not yet met the woman or child who is not prepared to fly.

Rose knocked at the door just now to show her preparations. Her only thought seems to be mother's silver, so she has quietly taken pos- session of our shoe bag which is a long sack for odds and ends with cases for shoes outside, and has filled it with all the contents of the silver box; this hung over her arm, and carrying Louis and Sarah, this young Sampson [sic] says she will be ready to fly.

I dont believe it, yet here I sit, my knapsack serving me for a desk, my seat the chair on which I have carefully spread my clothes in order; at my elbow lies my running, or treasure bag surmounted by my cabas filled with hairpins, starch, and a band I am embroidering, etc, near it lie our combs, etc, and the whole is crowned by my dagger—by the way I must add Miriam's pistol which she has forgotten, though over there lies her knapsack ready too, with our bonnets and veils. It is long past eleven, and no sound of the cannon. Bah! I do not expect it. "I'll lay me [p. 59] down and sleep in peace, for thou only Lord makest me to dwell in safety."[43] Good night! I will wake up to morrow the same as usual, and be disappointed that my trouble was unnecessary.

July 4th

Here I am, and still alive, having wakened but once in the night, and that only in consequence of Louis and Morgan crying; nothing more alarming than that. I ought to feel foolish, but I do not. I am glad I was

43. Psalms 4:8.

prepared, even though there was no occasion for it. While I was taking my early bath, Lilly came to the bath house and told me through the weatherboarding of another battle. Stonewall Jackson has surrounded McClelland[44] completely, and victory is again ours. This is said to be the sixth battle he has fought in twenty days, and they *say* he has won them all. And the Seventh Regiment distinguished its self, and was presented with four cannon on the battlefield in acknowledgement of its gallant conduct! Gibbes belongs to the "ragged howling regiment that rushed in the field yelling like unchained devils and spread [p. 60] a panic through the army" as the northern papers said, describing the battle of Manassas. O how I hope he has escaped! And "they say" Palmerston[45] has urged the recognition of the Confederacy, and an armed intervention on our side. Would it not be glorious? O for peace, blessed peace, and our brothers once more!

Palmerston is said to have painted Butler as the vilest oppressor, and having added he was ashamed to acknowledge him of Anglo-Saxon origin. Perhaps, knowing the opinion entertained of him by foreign nations, caused Butler to turn such a somerset. For a few days before his arrival here, we saw a leading article in the leading Union paper of N.O. threatening us with the arming of the slaves for our extermination if England interfered, in the same language almost as Butler used when here, and three days ago the same paper ridiculed the idea, and said such a brutal, inhuman thing was never for a moment even thought of, it was too absurd. And so the world goes! We all turn somersaults occasionally.

And yet, I would rather we [p. 61] would achieve our independence alone, if possible. It would be so much more glorious! And then I would hate to see England conquer the North, even if for our sake; my love for the old Union is still too great to be willing to see it so humiliated. If England would just make Lincoln come to his senses, and put an end to all this confiscation which is sweeping over everything, make him agree to let us alone and behave himself, that will be quite enough. But what a task! If it were put to the vote tomorrow to return free and

44. Union General George B. McClellan. The news of the war in Virginia that Sarah receives is sketchy and frequently, as it is here, in error.

45. The British prime minister, Lord Palmerston.

unmolested to the Union, or stay out, I am sure Union would have the majority; but this way, to think we are to be sent to Fort Jackson and all the other prisons for expressing our ideas, however harmless, to have our houses burned over our heads, and all the prominent men hanged, who would be eager for it?—unless indeed it was to escape even the greater horrors of a war of extermination.

[p. 62] July 5th

I am so tired, that I feel it is too great an exertion even to live. I hardly know what is the matter, and care still less. This life is killing me; I'll die in a month unless some brighter prospect opens. What is the use of looking forward? I dare not; all is too uncertain for anticipation. What is the use of looking for a settled home once more, when George, on whom all our future prospects depend, may never come to us again? O my home, my home! I could have borne all thing[s] in my old happy home; but this way, it is killing me! I miss father and Harry more and more as the days go on; what a trifle all this would be if they were here! O my home! if it were not blasphemous, I would wish I had died before I lost you! It is the one thing on earth I madly crave for, it is the one thing I will never again possess. My heart was wrapped up in Home, it was all I lived for; and I thank God I knew its value before it was lost to me for ever.

Sometimes, when all are asleep, and I alone here with the door shut, I cry, I rave for what I can never have again. Father, Harry, Home, all lost in six short months! O if I could have [p. 63] died in Harry's place! I was not made for this life; I am not strong enough to fight its battles. Cowards to the rear! I am not worthy of the strife! Have I the right to murmur even here, when the thousands suffer more than I? O I wish I was brave and strong, that I might fight to the death.

Sophy and I laid a novel wager; it is that I will, or will not die before the first of August. I bet her her wedding dress against a bouquet on my tombstone that I would. Nous verrons.[46] Think, that since the 28th of May, I have not walked three squares at a time, for my only walks are to Mrs Brunots! It is enough to kill any one; I might as well be at Ship

46. We will see.

Island,[47] where Butler has sentenced Mrs Phillips for laughing while the corpse of a Federal officer[48] was passing—at least, that is to be the principle [*sic*] charge, though I hope for the sake of Butler's soul that he had better reasons. Shocking as her conduct was, she hardly deserved two years' close confinement in such a dreadful place as that, because she happened to have no sense of delicacy, and no feeling.

[p. 64] "The darkest hour is just before day;" we have had the blackest night for almost three months, and I dont see the light yet. "Better days are coming"—I am getting skeptical, I fear me. I look forward to my future life with a shudder. This one shall not last long; I will be "up and doing" before many months are past. Doing what? Why, if all father has left us is lost forever, if we are to be pennyless, as well as homeless, I'll work for my living. How I wonder? I will teach! I know I am not capable, but I can do my best. I would rather die than be dependent, I would rather die than teach. There now, you know what I feel! Teaching, before dependence, death before teaching. My soul revolts from the drudgery.

I never see a governess that my heart does not ache for her. I think of the nameless, numberless, insults and trials she is forced to submit to; of the hopeless, thankless task that is imposed on her, to which she is expected to submit with out a murmur; of all her griefs and agony [p. 65] shut up in her heart, and I cry Heaven help a governess! my heart bleeds for them and—1 o'clock P.M. Thus far had I reached when news came that our forces were attacking the town, and had already driven the pickets in! I am well now! We all rushed to make preparations instantly. I had just finished washing my hair, before I commenced writing, and had it all streaming around me; but it did not take a minute to thrust it into a loose net. Then we each put on a fresh dress, except myself, as I preferred to save a linen cambric worn several times before, to a clean one not quite so nice, for this can do good service when washed. The excitement is intense; mother is securing a few of

47. Island off the Mississippi coast, used by Union forces as a staging area for the attack on New Orleans in the spring of 1862, and also used from time to time to hold prisoners.

48. In a note written in later Sarah identifies the officer as "De Kay—our relative." Lieutenant George C. DeKay, aide to General Thomas Williams, was wounded at Grand Gulf, Mississippi, and died later in New Orleans. On orders from Butler, the wife of Philip Phillips was imprisoned for her disrespectful behavior.

father's most valuable papers, Lilly running around after the children, and waiting for Charlie who cannot be found; Miriam after securing all things needful has gone down stairs to wait the issue, and I, dressed for instant flight, with my running bag tied to my waist, and knapsack, bonnet, veil, etc on the bed, occupy my last few moments at home in this profitable way.

[p. 66] Nobody knows what it is. A regiment has been marched out to meet our troops, some say commanded by Van Dorn / which I doubt. The gun boats are preparing to second them, we hear the garrison drum, and see people running, that is all. We dont know what is coming. I believe it will prove nothing after all. But—! The gun boat is drawn up so as to command our street here; the guns aimed up the street just below; and if a house falls, ours will be about the first. Well! this time next year, we will know all of which we are now ignorant. That is one consolation! The house will either be down or standing, then.

6 P.M. We have once more subsided; how foolish all this seems! Miriam and I laughed while preparing, and laughed while unpacking; it is the only way to take such things, and we agree on that, as on most other subjects. "They say" the affair originated from half a dozen shots fired by some Federal soldiers through idleness, whereupon the pickets rushed in screaming Van Dorn was after them at the [p. 67] head of six thousand men. I have my reasons for doubting the story; it must have been something more than that, to spread such a panic; for they certainly had time to ascertain the truth of the attack before they beat the long roll and sent out their troops, for if it had been Van Dorn, he would have been on them before that. Whatever it was, I am glad of the excitement, for it gave me new life for several hours; I was really sick before.

O this life! when will it end? Evermore and for Evermore shall we live in this suspense? I wish we were in the Sandwich Islands.

July 6th Sunday.

Is this to be my life for ever? I have such an insatiable craving for a better one! I so desire something nobler, purer, higher! will I ever attain it? "I have immortal longings within me;"[49] are they too to perish in

49. Shakespeare, *Antony and Cleopatra*.

this stagnation? I know not what the desire is; but sometimes when it sweeps over me, half defined, though still too vague to express, I seize it with avidity, and think I almost understand it, when at the [p. 68] instant it has passed away. What is it? Sometimes it comes in a wave, as it were, and I feel floating out, out, I know not where, except that it is to a higher Something; sometimes it steals over me, and I feel that Time has taken me back a thousand years, and I am no longer myself, but something greater, something—I know not what. Then again it sweeps suddenly over me, and I feel that I have lived ages before, and felt these same things, and will feel them again a thousand years hence. It is the same, and yet not the same sensation; there are a thousand shades to this secret that perplexes me.

Sometimes it comes on in awe, as of Eternity; then in I cant say what; for sometimes, standing before a mirror where I could perfectly see myself, the thought has suddenly occurred to me "What, or who am I?" and it is so abrupt, so unanswerable, that a feeling of dreadful awe creeps over me at the sight of this curious, mysterious figure, so familiar, yet so unknown, and while vainly endeavoring to reassure myself, and prove that it [p. 69] is only Myself, the dread, unspeakable mystery grows darker and darker, and though seeing myself, I loose [*sic*] all sense of my personal identity, and feel as though I stood face to face with the ghost of one who perished centuries and centuries ago. What is it? But that is not the feeling I mean. That must be a baser one, founded on—I cant say what; fear, perhaps.

But the one that so constantly possesses me, which for a week has made me restless and given me a craving for something beyond this present life until I am sick of it because it holds me down in this cramped place, has pursued me ever since I was twelve, though it never kept possession of me for so long a time before. It commenced in an intense desire to Know, which made me read anything that would take me nearer my object, with avidity, and yet the more I craved, the less I accomplished, until it seemed that I had not advanced a step. And so it has pursued me, now making me hungry to know more, now seeming to leave me in quiet, until this day. What ever the desire is, it is not compatible with [p. 70] my present life. If I read poetry any length of time, Tennyson or Longfellow especially, it brings the desire more irresistably before me; a desire, as I said before, for something nobler, better, something which I feel to be my right, which is so near me, yet so far off; something I could so easily obtain—If—! Ah me! how many blanks in our lives are filled up by a But, or an If!

It comes frequently in a longing for new scenes, and travel in foreign lands, and I sometimes think that is my chief desire, if so vague a feeling can be called a wish. To visit England, France, Italy, Germany, Palestine, Egypt, ah! that would be happiness! And yet, so inconsistant am I, that if I had my wish, in the Louvre, I would picture home, and cry for it; in foggy England I would mourn for my Louisiana sunsets; in looking at St Peter's I would recall the State House; floating down the Rhine I would long for the muddy Mississippi;[50] at Christ's tomb I would recall that of those he died to save, and would rove to kneel by them again. No; there is no [p. 71] such thing as perfect happiness in the world. No matter how happy we are, the Past clings to us, and so long as we remember it, we are forced to contrast it with the present, and its beauty is always enhanced, for like dead friends, the Past looses [*sic*] all defects in our eyes, and retains its pleasures only.

It is the Past that is killing me now; contrasting what Ought to be, with what Is. It is wearing me out, drinking the very life from my heart. And yet, I dare say, in after years, looking back I will say "Why was I not satisfied then? I should have been happy." Happy! yes, I *should* be; but Am I? Can I be? Ah no! there is another life somewhere, for me; in the next world if not in this; this one does not satisfy. Am I to die with these nameless longings unfulfilled? I cannot define them, but God can. It seems to me it would occupy an Eternity to fulfill our desires. I am *not* satisfied! I am *not* content! Something better, something Beyond! Shall I never, never attain it?

[p. 72] July 7th.

As we have no longer a minister—Mr Gierlow having gone to Europe, and no papers, I am in danger of forgetting the days of the week, as well as those of the month; but I am positive that yesterday was Sunday because I heard the Sunday school bells, and Friday I am sure was the

50. This passage suggests that Sarah had read H. W. Allen, *The Travels of a Sugar Planter* (New York, 1861), a book drawn from Allen's letters from Europe published in the *Weekly Advocate* in 1859. See entry of November 2, 1862, for her reaction to the future governor upon meeting him for the first time.

fourth, because I heard the national salute fired. I must remember that to find my dates by.

Well, last night being Sunday, a son of Capt. Hooper who died in the Fort Jackson fight,[51] having just come from New Orleans, stopped here on his way to Jackson to tell us the news, or rather to see Charlie, and told us afterwards. He says a boat from Mobile reached the city Saturday evening, and the Captain told Mr La Noue[52] that he brought an extra from the former place, containing news of McClelland's surrender with his entire army, his being mortally wounded, and the instant departure of a French and English man of war, from Hampton Roads, with the news. That revived my spirits considerably—all except McClelland's being wounded; I could dispense with that. But *if* it were true, and *if* peace would follow, and the boys come home—! [p. 73] what bliss! I would die of joy as rapidly as I am pining away with suspense now, I am afraid!

About ten o'clock, as we came up, mother went to the window in the entry to tell the news to Mrs Day, and while speaking, saw a man creeping by under the window, in the narrow little alley on the side of the house, evidently listening, for he had previously been standing in the shadow of a tree, and left the street to be nearer. When mother ran to give the alarm to Charlie, I looked down, and there the man was, looking up, as I could dimly see, for he crouched down in the shadow of the fence. Presently, stooping still, he ran fast towards the front of the house, making quite a noise in the long tangled grass. When he got near the pepper bush, he drew himself up to his full height, paused a moment as though listening, and then walked quietly towards the front gate. By that time Charlie reached the front gallery above, and called to him asking what he wanted; without answering, the man walked steadily out, closed the gate deliberately, then suddenly remembering drunkeness would be the best excuse, gave a lurch [p. 74] towards the house, walked off perfectly straight in the moonlight, until seeing Dr Day fastening his gate, he reeled again.

That man was not drunk! Drunken men cannot run crouching, do

51. Eugene Hooper, whose father, Captain Isaac Hooper, was in command of the *Resolute*, one of the ships in the Confederate fleet.

52. Charlie LaNoue's brother Eugene, a steamboat captain and very likely captain of the boat that brought Hooper's son to Baton Rouge.

not shut gates carefully after them, would have no inclination to creep in a dim little alley, merely to creep out again. It may have been one of our detectives. Standing in the full moonlight, which was very bright, he certainly looked like a gentleman, for he was dressed in a handsome suit of black. He was no citizen; form your own conclusions. Well! after all he heard no treason! let him play eaves dropper if he finds it consistent with his character as a gentleman.

The Captain who brought the extra from Mobile wished to have it reprinted, but it was instantly seized by a Federal officer, who carried it to Butler, who monopolized it; so *that* will never be heard of again; we must wait for other means of information. The young boy who told us, reminds me very much of Jimmy; he is by no means so handsome, but yet there is something that recalls him, and his voice, though more childish, sounds like Jimmy's too. I had an opportunity of writing to [p. 75] Lydia by him, of which I gladly availed myself, and have just finished a really tremendous epistle.

Wednesday 9th July.

Poor Miriam! Poor Sarah! they are disgraced again! Last night we were all sitting on the balcony in the moonlight, singing as usual with our guitar. I have been so accustomed to hear father say in the evening "Come girls! where is my concert," and he took so much pleasure in listening, that I could not think singing on the balcony was so very dreadful, since he encouraged us in it. But last night changed all my ideas. We noticed Federals, both officers and soldiers, pass singly, or by twos and threes at different times, but as we were not singing for their benefit, and they were evidently attending to their own affairs, there was no necessity of noticing them at all. But about half past nine, after we had sung two or three dozen others, we commenced Mary of Argyle. As the last word died away, while the chords [p. 76] were still vibrating, came a sound of—clapping hands, in short!

Down went every string of the guitar; Charlie cried "I told you so!" and ordered an immediate retreat; Miriam objected, as undignified, but renounced the guitar; Mother sprang to her feet, and closed the front windows in an instant, where upon, dignified or not, we all evacuated the gallery, and fell back in the house. All this was done in a few moments, and as quietly as possible; and while the gas was being turned off down stairs, Miriam and I flew up stairs—I confess I was mortified to death; very, very much ashamed, but we wanted to see the guilty party, for from below they were invisible. We stole out on the front balcony above, and in front of the house that used to be Gibbes', we beheld one of the culprits.

At the sight of the creature, my mortification vanished in intense compassion for his. He was standing under the tree, half in the moonlight, his hands in his pocket, looking at the extinction of light below, with the true state of affairs dawning on his astonished mind, [p. 77] and looking by no means satisfied with himself. Such an abashed creature! He looked just as though he had received a kick, that, conscious of deserving, he dared not return! While he yet gazed on the house in silent amazement and consternation, hands still forlornly searching his pockets, as though for a reason for our behavior, from under the dark shadow of the tree, another slowly picked himself up from the ground— hope he was not knocked down by surprise—and joined the first. His hands sought his pockets too, and if possible, he looked more mortified than the other. After looking for some time at the house, satisfied that they had put an end to future singing from the gallery, they walked slowly away, turning back every now and then to be certain that it was a fact.

If ever I saw two mortified, hang-dog looking men, they were those two as they took their way home. Was it not shocking? But they could not have meant it merely to be insulting, or they would have placed themselves in full view of us, rather than [p. 78] out of sight, under the trees. Perhaps they were thinking of their own homes, instead of us. Perhaps they came from Main[e], or Vermont, or some uncivilized people, and thought it a delicate manner of expressing their appreciation of our songs. Perhaps they just did it without thinking at all, and I really hope they are sorry for such a breech of decorum. But I can forget my mortification when I remember their exit from the scene of their exploit! Such crest fallen people!

O Yankees! Yankees! why did you do such a thoughtless thing! it will prevent us from ever indulging in moonlight singing again. Yet if we sing in the parlor, they always stop in front of the house to listen, while if we are on the balcony, they always have the delicacy to stop just above or below, concealed under the shadows. What's the difference?

Must we give up music entirely, because some poor people debarred of female society by the state of affairs like to listen to old songs they may have heard their mothers sing when they were babies?

[p. 79] July 10th

A proclamation is out announcing that any one talking about the war, or present state of affairs, will be "summarily" dealt with. Now, seems to me "summary" is not exactly the word they mean, but still it has an imposing effect. What a sad state their political affairs must be in, if they cant bear comment! An officer arrived day before yesterday bringing the surprising intelligence that McClelland [*sic*] had captured Richmond and fifty thousand prisoners; that is the time *they* talked. But when we yesterday received confirmation of his being finally defeated by our troops, and the capture of his railroad train twelve miles in length, they forbid farther mention of the subject. I wonder if they expect to be obeyed? What a stretch of tyranny!

O Free America! You who uphold free people, free speech, free everything, what a foul blot of despotism rests on a once spotless name! A nation of brave men, who wage war on women, and lock them up in prisons for using their woman weapon, the tongue; a nation of Free people who advocate despotism; a nation of Brothers who bind the weaker ones hand and foot, and scourge them with [p. 80] military tyrants and other Free, Brotherly institutions; what a picture! Who would not be an American? One consolation is, that this proclamation, and the extraordinary care they take to suppress all news except what they themselves manufacture, proves [to] me our cause is prospering more than they like us to know. I do believe day is about to break!

If our own troops are determined to burn our houses over our heads to spite the Yankees, I wish they would hurry and have it over at once. Ten regiments of Infantry are stationed at C. Moore, and Scott's Cavalry[53] was expected at Greenwell yesterday, both preparing for an attack on B.R. If we must be beggars, let it come at once; I cant endure this suspense.

Sunset. This cool, misty evening, made fresh and spring like by little showers, I spend on the upper balcony, as I am decidedly too unwell to

53. The 1st Louisiana Cavalry, commanded by Colonel John S. Scott. There was no truth to the rumor that Scott's Cavalry was in the vicinity of Baton Rouge at this time.

venture out even as far as Mrs Brunots; so the "Fascinating" Sophy will look in vain for me this evening. She is the "Fascinating," Dena, the "Erudite," Nettie the "Sarcastic," Miriam the "Majestic," I, the "Gushing." What cognomens! Some of them [p. 81] are not so unappropriate, either. Well, what am I thinking of? A thousand things, truly! I am looking down at the officers as they pass, and wishing they were safe in their own homes, and would leave us to enjoy ours; I am wishing for peace, and the boys, more and more ernestly as the hours wear on—heart sick for both; I am wishing this beautiful town might be spared; I am wishing this book was not drawing so very near its close as to force me to leave out many an incident I would like to mention, and a hundred things besides, with still less connection. What do I not wish? My whole life for the last eight months can only be expressed by a great "I wish—!" If peace was once more established, and the boys home, I believe I would be *almost* as content as I was when father was alive, though.

July 11th

A letter from George this morning! It was written on the 20th June, and he speaks of being on crutches, in consequence of his horse having fallen with him, and injured his knee. Perhaps then he was not in the first battle of the 25th! But bah! I [p. 82] know George too well to imagine he would keep quiet at such a moment, if he could possibly stand! I am sure he was there with the rest of the Louisiana regiment. The papers say "the conduct of the 1st La. is beyond all praise;" of course George was there! And Jimmy is with him at Richmond; but whether in the army, or navy, or what rank if in the first, he does not say; he only says he is looking remarkably well. Gibbes he had heard from in a letter dated the sixteenth, and up to then he was in perfect health. His last letter here was dated 10th of March, so we are thankful enough now. I was so delighted to read the accounts of the "gallant Seventh" in some paper we fortunately procured. At Jackson's address, and presentation of the battery they had so bravely won,[54] I was beside myself with delight; I was thinking that Gibbes of course was "The" Regiment, had

54. Jackson's presentation of a battery of artillery pieces is first mentioned by Sarah in the entry of July 3, 1862. Presumably these were the guns captured in the fighting at Port Republic the previous month (June 9).

taken the battery with his single sword, and I know not what besides. Strange to say, I have not an idea of the names of the half dozen battles he was in, in June, but believe that one to be Port Republic.

[p. 83] June [July] 12th

Brother writes that rumors of the capture of B.R. by our troops, has [*sic*] made him very uneasy about us; and he wishes us to go down to N.O. if possible. I wish we could. The impression here, is that an attack is inevitable, and the city papers found it necessary to contradict the rumor of Ruggles'[55] having occupied it alread[y]. I wish mother would go. I can see no difference there or here, except that there, we will be safe, for a while at least. This life is killing me; Sophy will lose her bet if I stay here much longer. If it were not so shockingly selfish, I would go there myself, for a few weeks to see what a change of scene would do for my drooping health and spirits. But I know Miriam could not get along without me! I dont pretend to say I am very pleasant or agreeable as a companion just now, but still, I think that what ever we have to endure, we would stand it better together. O this war, this war! it is killing me!

I grow desperate when I read these Northern papers reviling and abusing us, reproaching us for being broken and dispersed, taunting us with their victories, sparing no humiliating name in speaking of us, and laughing as to what "we'll see" when we vile rebels are [p. 84] crushed out of Virginia, and the glorious Union firmly established. I cant bear these taunts! I grow sick to read these vile, insulting papers that seem written expressly to goad us into madness! I cannot live in such a country; let peace come, and on these terms, I leave home for ever. Conquered by a people who have the magnanimity of cats, I could stand it; but by such mean spirited caitif[f]s—! There must be many humane, reasonable men in the North; can they not teach their Editors decency in this their hour of triumph?

July 13th. Sunday.

A profitable way to spend such a day! Being forced to dispense with

55. Brigadier General Daniel Ruggles would command one of two divisions when Confederate forces under John C. Breckinridge attacked the Union army at Baton Rouge the following month.

church going, I have occupied myself reading a great deal, and writing a little, which latter duty is a favorite task of mine after church on Sundays. But this evening the mosquitoes are so savage that writing became impossible, until Miriam and I instituted a grand Extermination process, which we partly accomplished by extraordinary efforts. She lay on the bed with the bar half drawn over her, and half looped up, while I was commissioned to fan the wretches from all corners into the pen. It was rather fatiguing, and in spite of the number slain, hardly recompensed me for the trouble of hunting them around the room; but still, [p. 85][56] Miriam says exercise is good for me, and she ought to know.

I have been reading that old disguster, Boswell. Bah! I have no patience with the toady! I suppose "my mind is not yet thoroughly impregnated with the Johnsonian ether," and that is the reason why I cannot appreciate him, or his work. I admire him for his patience and minuteness in compiling such trivial details. He must have been an amiable man to bear Johnson's brutal, ill humored remarks; but seems to me if I had not spirit enough to resent the indignity, I would at least not publish it to the world! Briefly, my opinion which this book has only tended to confirm, is that Boswell was a vain, conceited prig, a fool of a jack-a-nape, an insufferable sycophant, a—whatever mean thing you please; there is no word small enough to suit him. As to Johnson, he is a surly old bear; in short, an old brute of a tyrant. All his knowledge and attainments could not have made me tolerate him, I am sure. I [p. 86] could have no respect for a man who was so coarse in speech and manners, and who eat [*sic*] like an animal.

Fact is, I am not a Boswellian, or a Johnsonian, either. I do not think him such an extraordinary man. I have heard many conversations as worthy of being recorded as nineteen twentieths of his. In spite of his learning, he was narrow-minded and biggoted which I despise above all earthly failings. Witness his tirades against Americans, calling us Rascals, Robbers, Pirates, and saying he would like to burn us! Now I have railed at many of these ordinary women here, for using like epithets for the Yankees, and have felt the greatest contempt for their absurd abuse. These poor women do not aspire to Johnsonian wisdom, and their ignorance may serve as an excuse for their narrowminded-

56. The top of p. 85 (and its reverse, p. 86) is missing, but appears to have been removed before Sarah wrote the entry.

ness; but the wondrous Johnson to rave and bellow like any Billingsgate nymph! Bah! He is an old disguster!

[p. 87] July 14th. 3 P.M.

Another pleasant excitement. News has just arrived that Scott's cavalry was having a hard fight with the Yankees eight miles from town.[57] Every body immediately commenced to pick up stray articles, and get ready to fly, in spite of the intense heat. I am resigned, as I hardly expect a shelling. Another report places the fight fourteen miles from here. A man on horseback came in for reinforcements. Heaven help poor Howell, if it is true. I am beginning to doubt half I hear. People tell me the most extravagant things, and if I am fool enough to believe, and repeat them, I suddenly discover that it is not half so true as it might be, and as they themselves frequently deny having told it, all the odium of "manufacturing" rests on my shoulders, which have not been accustomed to bear lies of any kind. I mean to cease believing anything, unless it rest on the word of some responsible person.

By the way—the order I so confidently believed, concerning the proclamation, turns out not quite so bad. I was told women were included, and it extended to private houses as well as public ones, though I [p. 88] fortunately omitted that when I recorded it. When I read it, it said "all discussions concerning the war, is [*sic*] prohibited in bar rooms, public assemblies, and street corners." As women do not frequent such places, and private houses are not mentioned, I cannot imagine how my informant made the mistake, unless, like me, it was through hearing it repeated. Odious as I thought it then, I think it wise now; for more than one man has lost his life through discussions of the kind.

July 17th, Thursday.

It is decided that I am to go to New Orleans next week. I hardly know which I dislike most; going, or staying. I know I shall be dreadfully homesick; but—Remember—and keep quiet, Sarah, I beg of you. Every thing points to an early attack here. Some say this week. The Federals are cutting down all our beautiful woods near the Peneten-

---

57. Again, a rumor unsupported by fact. Any fighting at this time would have involved guerillas or units such as the Partisan Rangers.

tiary,[58] to throw up breastworks some say. Cannon are to be planted on the foundation of Mr Pike's new house;[59] every body is in a state of expectation. Honestly, if B.R. *has* to be shelled, I shall hate to miss the fun. It will be worth seeing, and I would like to [be] present, even at the risk of losing my big toe by a shell. But then by going, I can save many of my clothes, and then Miriam and I can divide when [p. 89] every thing is burnt—that is one advantage, besides being benefited by the change of air. *They say* the town is to be attacked to night. I dont believe a word of it.

O I was so distressed this evening! They tell me Mr Biddle was killed at Vicksburg. I hope it is not true.[60] Suppose it was a shot from Will's battery?

July 20th. Sunday.

Last night the town was in a dreadful state of excitement. Before sunset a regiment that had been camped out of town, came in, and pitched their tents around the new theater, in front of our church.[61] All was commotion and bustle; and as the pickets had been drawn in, and the soldiers talked freely of expecting an attack, every body believed it, and was consequently in rather an unpleasant state of anticipation. Their cannon were on the commons back of the church, the artillery horses tied to the wheels; while some dozen tents were placed around, filled with men who were ready to harness them at the first alarm.[62]

58. The State Penitentiary was on Florida Street three blocks east of the Morgan home. The Federal Building and United States Courthouse today occupies part of the site.

59. The war interrupted the building of William S. Pike's house. According to Eliza Ripley, the banker and his family, "as was the custom, lived 'over the bank.'" *Social Life,* 321. Mrs. Ripley was married to James A. McHatton and living on a plantation near Baton Rouge in the early years of the war.

60. Lieutenant Biddle was not killed at Vicksburg. On July 20, 1862, General Thomas Williams wrote his wife from the vicinity of Vicksburg that Biddle "left me yesterday to go up the river and home with a fever on him." "Letters of General Williams," 324.

61. An 1863 photograph by McPherson & Oliver shows tents to the rear of Mr. Pike's new theater and across Church Street from the Episcopal church. When photographer W. D. McPherson arrived in Baton Rouge in December 1862, he at first operated out of a tent set up across from the church. See Baton Rouge *Weekly Gazette and Comet,* December 31, 1862, p. 3.

62. The guns and horses were those of the 6th Massachusetts (Everett's Battery), the

With all these preparations in full view, we went to bed as usual. I did not even take the trouble of gather[ing] my things which I had removed from my "pedler sack;" and slept, satisfied that if forced to fly, I would lose almost every thing in spite of my precaution of making a bag.

Well! night passed, and here is morning, [p. 90] and nothing is heard yet. The attack is delayed until this evening, or tomorrow, they say. Woman though I am, I am by no means as frightened as some of these men are. I cant get excited about it. Perhaps it is because they know the danger, and I do not. But I hate to see *men* uneasy! I have been so accustomed to brave, fearless ones, who would beard the devil himself, that it gives me a great disgust to see anyone less daring than father and the boys.

I have been so busy preparing to go to the city,[63] that I think if the frolic should intervene, and prevent my departure, I would be disappointed, though I do not want to go. It would be unpleasant, for instance, to pack all I own in my trunk, and just as I place the key in my pocket to hear the shriek of "Van Dorn!" raised again. This time it is to be Ruggles, though. I would not mind if he came before I was packed. Besides, even if I miss the fun here, they say the boats are fired into from Plaquemine;[64] and then I [would] have the pleasure of being in a fight anyhow. Mother is alarmed about that part of my voyage, but Miriam and I persuade her it is nothing.

If I was a man—! O wouldn't I be in Richmond with the boys! Poor little Jimmy! Suppose he is wounded! He would die if he had not somebody to hold his hand [p. 91] and rub his head, and kiss him occasionally. I hope God will send some dear kind woman, with sons of her own, who will take our place. O my brothers! if God will spare you, what more do we want?

Why was I not a man? what is the use of all these worthless women, in war times? If they attack, I shall don the breeches, and join the assailants, and fight, though I think they would be hopeless fools to attempt to capture a town they could not hold for ten minutes under the gun

section left in Baton Rouge when General Williams took most of his men upriver to work on the canal being dug opposite Vicksburg.

63. New Orleans.

64. Town on the west bank of the Mississippi River a few miles south of Baton Rouge.

boats. How do breeches and coats feel, I wonder? I am actually afraid of them. I kept a suit of Jimmy's hanging in the armoir for six weeks waiting for the Yankees to come, thinking fright would give me courage to try it, (what a seeming paradox!) but I never succeeded. Lilly one day insisted on my trying it, and I advanced so far as to lay it on the bed, and then carried my bird out—I was ashamed to let even my canary see me—but when I took a second look, my courage deserted me, and there ended my first and last attempt at disguise. I have heard so many girls boast of having worn men's clothes; I wonder where they get the courage.

To think half the men in town sat up all night in expectation of a stampede, while we poor women slept serenely! [p. 92] Every body is digging pits to hide in when the ball opens. The Days have dug a tremendous one; the Wolfs, Sheppers,[65] and some fifty others have taken the same precaution. They may as well dig their graves at once; what if a tremendous shell should burst over them, and bury in the dirt those who were not killed? O no! let me see all the danger, and the way it is coming, at once. To morrow—or day after—in case no unexpected little incident occurs in the interval, I purpose going to N.O., taking father's papers, and part of Miriam's, and mother's valuables for safe keeping. I hate to go, but they all think I should, as it will be one less to look after *if* we are shelled—which I doubt. I dont know that I require *much* protection, but I might as well be agreeable and go. Ouf! how I will grow homesick, before I am out of sight!

Midnight. Here we go, sure enough. At precisely eleven o'clock, while we were enjoying our first dreams, we were startled by the long roll which was beat half a square below us. At first I only repeated "The roll of the drum" without an idea connected with it; but hearing the soldiers running, in another instant I was up, and was putting on my stockings when Miriam ran in in her night gown. The children were roused and dressed [p. 93] quickly, and it did not take us many instants to prepare—the report of two shots, and the tramp of soldiers, cries of "Double quick" and sound as of cannon moving, rather hastening our movements. Armoirs, bureaus, and everything else were thrown open,

65. John L. Wolff, the cabinet maker (or possibly Henry L. Wolfe, the tax collector), and Louis Sheppers.

and Miriam and I hastily packed our sacks with any articles that came to hand, having previously taken the precaution to put on everything fresh from the armoir. We have saved what we can; but I find myself obliged to leave one of my new muslins I had just finished, as it occupies more room than I can afford, the body of my lovely lilac, and my beauteous white mull. But then, I have saved eight half made linen chemises! that will be better than the outward show.

Here comes an alarm of fire—at least a dreadful odor of burning cotton which has set every body wild with fear that conflagration is to be added to these horrors. The Cavalry swept past on their way to the river ten minutes ago, and here comes the news that the gunboats are drawing up their anchors and making ready. Well! here an hour has passed; suppose they do not come after all? I have been watching two sentinels at the corner, who are singing and dancing in the gayest way. One reminds me of Gibbes; I have seen him dance that way often. I was glad to see a good humored man again. I wish I was in bed. I am only sitting up to satisfy my conscience, for I have long since ceased to expect a [p. 94] *real* bombardment. If it must come, let it be now; I am tired of waiting.

A crowd of women have sought the protection of the gunboats. I am distressed about the Brunots; suppose they did not hear the noise? O girls! if I was a man, I wonder what would induce me to leave you four, lone, unprotected women sleeping in that house, unconscious of all this? Is manhood a dream that is past? Is humanity an idle name? Fatherless, brotherless girls, if I was honored with the title of Man, I do believe I would be fool enough to run around and wake you, at least! Not another word though. I shall go mad with rage and disgust. I am going to bed. This must be a humbug.

Morgan comes running in, once more in his night gear, begging Lilly to hear his prayers. In answer to her "Why? you have said them to night!" he says "Yes! but I've been getting up so often!" Poor child! no wonder he is perplexed! One hour and a half of this nonsense, and no result known. We are told the firing commenced, and the pickets were driven in, twenty minutes before the long roll beat.

July 21st

It is impossible to discover the true story of last night's alarm. Some say it was a gang of negroes who attacked the picketts in revenge for having been turned out of the garrison; others say it was a number of our soldiers who fired from the bushes; and [p. 95] the most amusing story is that they took alarm at an old white horse, which they killed mistaking him for the Confederates. One regiment has refused to do pickett duty; and the story runs among these poor soldiers that our army, which is within a mile, is perfectly overwhelming. The excitement still continues.

I have been writing to the Brunots the news confirming the death of McClellan, the surrender of his army, and the good tidings of our Ram's recent exploits above Vicksburg, and her arriving safely under the guns there.[66] If we could keep all the dispatches that have passed between us since the battle of the forts, what a collection of absurdity and contradiction it would be! "Forts have been taken." "Their ships have passed; forts safe; Yankees at our mercy." "Ships at N.O. City to be bombarded in twelve hours." "Forts surrendered." "City under British protection." "No it isn't." "City surrendered." "Mistake." "B.R. to be burned when Yankee ships come." And so on, sometimes three times a day, each dispatch contradicting the other, and all equally ridiculous.

The crowd here seems to increase. The streets are thronged with the military, and it will soon be impossible to go even to Mrs Brunot's, which will be a great privation to me. I was so mortified this evening! [p. 96] in going there, just as I got to Dr. Enders' corner,[67] a gust of wind exposed my feet fully to the gaze of a party of officers who were contemplating me from Heroman's balcony. I hardly know which I hated most; the men for seeing, or myself for exposing my feet. Some of these officers dont mind staring a bit. Two passed Mrs B.'s as we sat on the steps, and examined each one of us as though they meant to know us again, never pretending to turn their heads the other way. I had no sooner got home, than the same ones passed as I was sitting on the balcony, and evidently recognized me. After having satisfied themselves of my identity, and the position of the house, they went as far as the

66. While suffering heavy damage and severe casualties itself, the *Arkansas* dealt a humiliating blow to the Union Navy when it blazed its way past the Union fleet above Vicksburg on July 15. The rumors of McClellan's death and the surrender of his army are of course false.

67. The two-story home of Dr. Peter M. Enders was at the northeast corner of Church and Florida. In the early months of 1863 it was used by General C. C. Augur as his headquarters.

corner, and turning back again, walked leisurely along and looked at me again until out of sight.

If I had had on a white dress, I might have thought it was because they thought white unusual for evening costume, and stared for impertinence; for some time ago I happened to be standing dressed in white on the balcony, with not an ornament or flower even, nothing but a tiny blue ribbon at my collar, when two naval officers passed. As I never look at the people after the first glance, I did not think of them until mother made some remark about their staring, and on looking up from the sock I was knitting for some [p. 97] soldier, I saw them coming again. Mother insisted that they thought I was dressed to attract their attention, and wished to gratify me, and Lilly declared I must go in if they passed again. Back they came at the instant, and after a promenade of three or four times the length of the fence, they finally disappeared. Mother voted white dresses an abomination, in war times; and if I had not been satisfied that it had been my favorite costume long before the civil war was heard of, I might have been persuaded that it was a shocking taste too. But it is a little too much to dress to please the Yankees; I would rather please myself. Five thousand are to come next week, and then it will really be impossible to go in the streets, dressed, or not dressed.

July 22d Tuesday.

Another such day, and there is the end of me! Charlie decided to send Lilly and the children in the country early to-morrow morning, and get them safely out of this doomed town. Mother, Miriam and I were to remain here alone. Take the children away, and I can stand whatever is to come; but this constant alarm, with five babies in the house, is too much for any of us. So we gladly packed their trunks and got them ready, and then news came pouring in. First a negro man just from the country [p. 98] told Lilly that our soldiers were swarming out there—that he had never seen so many men. Then Dena wrote us that a Mrs Bryan had received a letter from her son, praying her not to be in B.R. after Wednesday morning, as they were to attack to-morrow. Then a man came to Charlie, and told him that though he was on parole, yet as a Mason he must beg him not to let his wife sleep in town to night; to get her away before sunset. But it is impossible for her to start before morning.

Hearing so many rumors, all pointing to the same time, we began to believe there might be some danger; so I packed all necessary clothing that could be dispensed with now in a large trunk for mother, Miriam and me, and got it ready to send out in the country to Mrs Williams.[68] All told, I have but eight dresses left; so I'll have to be particular. I am wealthy compared to what I would have been Sunday night, for then I had but two in my sack, and now I have my best in the trunk. If the attack comes before the trunk gets off, or if the trunk is lost, we will verily be beggars; for I pack well, and it contains every thing of any value in clothing. The excitement is on the increase, I think. Every body crazy to leave town.

[p. 99] Thursday July 24th.

Yes! that must be the date, for one and two nights have passed since I was writing here. Where shall I begin the story of my wanderings? I dont know that it has a beginning, it is all so hurried and confused. But it was Tuesday evening that the Federals were seized with a panic which threw the whole town in alarm. They said our troops were within eight miles, ten thousand in number. The report was even started that the advance guard was skirmishing with the Federals; the shots were heard distinctly, a dozen people were ready to swear. The Yankees struck their tents, galloped with their cannon through the street[s] with the most terrific din, troops passed at double quick on their way to the garrison, every thing was confusion.

Mr Tunnard told us yesterday he was present when part of them reached the gate of the garrison, and saw one of the officers spring forward waving his sword and heard him cry "Trot, men! Gallop, I say! Damn you! *run* in!" with a perfect yell at the close; whereupon all lookers on raised a shout of laughter, for the man was frightened out of his wits. A Federal officer told him that their fright was really a dis-

---

68. Probably Anna Williams, wife of J. M. Williams. The campus of Louisiana State University today occupies what was then the Williams plantation.

grace; and if one thousand of our men had come in town, the [p. 100] whole thirty five hundred[69] would have been at their mercy. Even the naval officers denounce it as a most arrant piece of cowardice; for instead of marching their troops out to meet ours, and fight them on open ground, they all rushed in the garrison where if attacked their only retreat would have been in the river.

The gunboats were ordered in the middle of the stream, in front of the garrison, and cooped up their [*sic*], these valiant men awaited the assault in such trepidation, that yesterday they freely said the whole force could be purchased for fifty cents, they are so ashamed of their panic.

Imagine what effect all this had on the inhabitants! Soon, an Exodus took place, in the direction of the Asylum,[70] and we needs must follow the general example and run too. In haste we packed a trunk with our remaining clothes—what we could get in—, and the greatest confusion prevailed for an hour. Beatrice[71] had commenced to cry early in the evening, and redoubled her screams when she saw the preparations; and Louis joining in, they cried in concert until eight o'clock, when we finally got off.

What a din! Lilly looked perfectly exhausted; that look on her face made me heart sick. Miriam flew around everywhere; mother always had one more article to find, and the noise was dreadful, when white and black assembled in the hall ready at last. Charlie placed half [p. 101] the trunks on the dray, leaving the rest for another trip, and we at last started off.

Besides the inevitable running bag tied to my waist (which invariably throws me in a violent perspiration) on this stifling night I had my sunbonnet, veil, comb, tooth brush, cabas filled with dozens of small articles, & dagger to carry; and then my heart failed me when I thought of my guitar; so I caught it up in the case, and remembering father's

69. General Williams left two regiments of infantry in Baton Rouge, the 6th Michigan and the 21st Indiana, in addition to one section of the 6th Massachusetts Artillery and a company of cavalry (Magee's). On the eve of his departure he wrote that he was leaving "about 1200 men, and 5 guns." "Letters," 322.

70. The State Asylum for the Deaf and Blind on the southern edge of the city, a Gothic Revival structure built in the 1850s. Later the Union army used it as a general hospital.

71. Beatrice LaNoue, Lilly's baby.

heavy inkstand, I seized that too, with two fans. If I was asked what I did with all these things, I could not answer. Certain it is I had every one in my hand; and was not *very* ridiculous to behold.

Seventeen in number counting white and black,[72] our procession started off, each loaded in their own way. The soldiers did not scruple to laugh at us. Those who were still waiting in front of the churches[73] to be removed laughed heartily, and cried "Hello! where are you going? Running? Good bye!" Fortunately they could not see our faces, for it was very dark. One stopped us under a lamp post and wanted us to go back. He said he knew we were to be attacked, for the Confederate[s] were within five miles; but we were as safe at home as at the asylum. He was a very handsome, respectable looking man, though dirty as Yankee soldiers always are, and in his shirt sleeves besides. We thanked him for his kindness, and went on.

All stopped at the Brunot's, to see that they were ready to fly, but the two parties were so tremendous [p. 102] that we gladly divided, and Miriam and I remained with them until they could get ready, while our detachment went on. Wagons, carts, every vehicle imaginable passed on to places of safety, loaded with valuables, while women and children hurried on, on foot. It took the Brunots as long to prepare as it did us. I had to drag Sophy out of her bed, where she threw herself vowing she would not run, and after an interminable length of time, we were at last ready and started with the addition of Mrs Loucks and her sons[74] in our train. The volunteer whose sole duty seems to be to watch the Brunots, met us as we got out. He stopped as he met the first, looked

72. Presumably seven of the seventeen were blacks. In an earlier entry (June 1) Sarah mentions that there were nine with the family in the flight to Greenwell Springs. In one place or another the diary provides the names of eight who appear to have been Morgan slaves: Tiche (Catiche), Margret, Dophy, Rose, Nancy, Lucy, Louisa, and Liddy. The slave schedule of the 1860 census lists eight slaves owned by Sarah's father, all females except one male, age 4.

73. The procession would have passed first the Presbyterian church and then St. James Episcopal, both in the same block.

74. Mary Loucks remained in Baton Rouge and taught school to make a living for herself and her children after her husband Richard H. Loucks, an attorney, returned to New York. Her sons were Richard Newcomb Loucks and Francis Henry Loucks, ages 12 and 9 in the 1860 census. See correspondence with John W. Loucks in Charles East Papers, LSU Collections.

in silence until Sophy and I passed, and then burst out laughing. No wonder!

What a walk it was! Nobody hesitated to laugh, even though they meant to run themselves, and we made fun of each other too, so our walk was merry enough. When we reached there, the Asylum was already crowded—at least it would have been a crowd in any other place, though a mere handful in such a building. The whole house was illuminated, up to the fifth story, and we were most graciously received by the director, who had thrown the whole house open to who ever chose to come, and exerted himself to be accommodating. It looked like a tremendous hotel where every one is at home; not a servant or one of the deaf and dumb children was to be seen; we had [p. 103] all the lower story to ourselves.

Wasn't it pleasant to unload, and deposit all things in a place of safety! It was a great relief. Then we five girls walked on the splendid balcony which goes around the house until we could no longer walk, when I amused myself by keeping poor Sophy standing, since she would not sit down like a Christian, but insisted on going to bed like a lazy girl, as she is. When I finally let her go, it did not take her many minutes to undress, and soon we were all ready for bed.

The Brunots had beds on the parlor floor; across the wide hall, we had a room opposite, and next to ours, Lilly and the children were all sleeping soundly. I ran the blockade of the hall in my nightgown, and had a splendid romp with the girls after rolling out of bed, and jerking Netty up. Mother and Mrs Brunot cried "Order," laughing, but they came in for their share of the sport, until an admiring crowd of females at the door told us by their amused faces they were enjoying it too, so I ran the gauntlet again, and got safely through the hall, and after a few more inroads in one of which Miriam accompanied me, and on which occasion I am sure we were seen in our nightgowns, we finally went to bed. I wont say went to sleep, for I did not pretend to doze.

All our side of the house had bars, except me; and the mosquitoes were unendurable; so I watched mother and Miriam in their downy slumbers and lay [p. 104] on my hard bed for hours fighting the torments with bare arms. Every now and then I heard a stir among the females above, indicating that some few were anticipating a panic. Once they took a rush from the fourth story, and cried they heard the cannon; twenty guns had been fired, etc. I lay still, determined not to believe it; and presently all subsided. I lay there for hours longer it seemed, when Nettie at last wandered in disconsolate to find if we were asleep; for with the exception of Sophy, they too had been awake all night. I went to the parlor with her, when she, Dena, and I decided to dress at once and sit on the balcony since sleep was hopeless. Behold me in a blue muslin flounced to the waist, with a cape, too! What a running costume! Miriam only had time to take off her white dress before starting.

All dressed, we went to the north west corner, as far as possible from the rest of the household, and sat in a splendid breeze for hours. It was better than fighting insatiable mosquitoes; so there we sat talking through the greater part of a night which seemed to have borrowed a few additional hours for our benefit. We'll have no Leap year in '64; the twenty four extra hours were crowded in, on that occasion I think. We discussed our favorite books, characters, authors, repeated scraps here and there of the mock sentimental, talked of how we would one day like to travel, and where we would go; discussed love and marriage, and [p. 105] came to the conclusion neither was the jest it was thought to be. (O wise young women!)

Dena says marriage is awful, but to be an old maid more awful still. I wont agree. I mean to be an old maid myself, and show the world what such a life can be. It shocks me to hear a woman say she would hate to die unmarried. I have heard girls say they would rather be wretched, married, than happy as old maids.[75] Is it not revolting? If I had my choice of wretchedness on either hand, I would take it alone; for then I only would be to blame, while married, *he* would be the iron that would pierce my very soul. I can fancy no greater hell—if I may use the only word that can express it—than to be tied to a man you could not respect and love perfectly. Heaven help me, and my husband too, if he for an instant lets me see I am the better man of the two! Wouldn't I despise him!

Poor Nettie retired in despair, and we two watched alone for hours longer. The sun must have been arrested by some Joshua on the road;

75. This foreshadows a newspaper piece that Sarah would write eleven years later, the year before her marriage to Francis Warrington Dawson. See "Old Maids," Charleston *News*, March 15, 1873, p. 2.

couldn't make me believe it was doing its duty as usual. We wandered around the balconies, through the grounds in the dim starlight (for it was cloudy), and finally beholding a faint promise of morning, sat still and waited for the coming of the lazy sun. What was still more aggravating was that every time we looked in at the others showed them sleeping peacefully. Miriam lay her full length with outstretched arms, the picture of repose, looking *so* comfortable! When the sun finally made his appearance (he was out on a [p. 106] spree, I found, for his eyes were not half opened, and he looked dull and heavy as he peeped from behind his bed curtains) others began to stir, and in an hour more, we were ready to leave. Those who had slept, came out with swelled eyes, and drowsy looks; while we three who had been up all night were perfectly calm, though *rather* pale; but I am seldom otherwise.

Were we not thankful to see home still standing! I did not feel tired *much*, but some how, when it struck half past six, and I found myself alone here (Miriam having stopped at Mrs Days), I suddenly found myself divested of my flounces, and most other articles; and involuntarily going towards the bed. I could not sleep, wasn't thinking of such a thing; meant to—there was an end of my soliloquy! Where I went, I dont know. As the clock struck eight, I got up as unaccountably, and discovered I had lost all idea of time in sleep. If it had not been for the clock, I should have said I had slept a day and night, and it was now Thursday morning. A giant refreshed, I rose from my slumbers, took a hasty cup of coffee and set to work packing Lilly's trunk, for I was crazy to see the children off as soon as possible. It was no short work, but we all hurried, said good bye, and saw them go with a feeling of relief. By the experience of the night before, we knew that when the real moment came, it would be impossible to get them off in time to escape danger.

Poor Lilly! we miss her sadly; but are [p. 107] thankful to know that she is out of danger with her poor little children. She looked heart broken at the idea of leaving us alone; but then when one weak woman has five small babies to take care of, is it fair to impose three big ones on her? I'd never stay here, if she sacrificed her children to take care of us [words lined through] need no protection. I was very lazy after they left, and sat reading until a note was brought from Charlie saying they were safe beyond the lines.

Last night came another alarm. Some fifty cannon were fired some-

where above, reports came that a body of our troops were a few miles
out, so a thousand of these men took courage and went out to recon-
noitre. Mrs Brunot and mother insisted on going again to the Asylum
for protection against the coming attack, though we at first begged and
pleaded to stay at home. But we had to follow, and I dont think any of
us were in the best of humors, as we were all conscious of doing a foolish thing. I was in a fit of disgust. I had just heard the most astounding
lies about us. Some ladies from here, said at Dr Nolan's [76] table that
Miriam and I daily paraded the streets with these officers; we were
met at every corner with them. Liars! is there no punishment for such?
Another story is that when I was informed Mr Biddle was in the parlor,
I rushed in, and throwing my arms over my head, with a great deal of
annimation cried to him "Hurrah for Lincoln" three times. O how can
people stain their souls with such vile, base, calumny! [p. 108] What
did they gain by it?

Only those who never saw me would believe it. Those who know me
will recognize the fabrication, for it is the last thing that would be believed of a girl who passes for such a cold, reserved creature as I am
called abroad. Mattie Stith was the mother of that lie, whether inten-
tionally or not. After Mr Biddle left the house, she and Miriam were
talking of how kind it was in Gen. Williams to offer us every assurance
that the house should be respected, when I said to her "If all Yankees
are like him, hurrah for Lincoln, then." Not a word more or less. O I
am so disgusted with liars! I hope I will never meet another.

Then, to crown all, some low little Accadian from W.B.R.[77] (that I
never heard of, though mother has) who goes by the name of Lévéque, hearing these stories of the devotion of the Federals to the Miss
Morgans, mistook the two families, and in order to show his contempt
and disapprobation, cut poor Bena and Mary[78] dead! So much for mistaking names. I dont know the puppy,[79] but I should like one of the boys

76. Dr. John T. Nolan.

77. What Sarah must mean is an Acadian—a Cajun, descendant of the French who
were expelled from Nova Scotia and migrated to Louisiana in the eighteenth century.
W.B.R. is West Baton Rouge.

78. Sarah's cousins, daughters of her Aunt Caro (Caroline Hicky Morgan) at Hope
Estate. Bena was a nickname for Aurore Hortense Morgan.

79. In Sarah's usage, a term of contempt. "A vain, empty-headed, impertinent man":
Oxford English Dictionary.

to thrash him for his impertinence that merely reflects on us. Trouble will grow out of these malicious falsehoods, circulated by people who surely *know* they are lying. It crazes me. I wish they would not tell me of such things. I wont stoop to deny such low slander; let it eat its own head. But it is maddening to hear such things. Let the women lie until the[y] exhaust themselves; I am beginning to believe it is only their way of telling the truth; but the first *man* who dares [p. 109] take up their lies, if the boys do not cut the word Liar on his face with a cowhide, I am mistaken in them, that is all. Somebody will be hurt yet.

As I am angry about it still, I was surely not pleased about it last night; but Sophy and I talked each other in a good humor walking on the balcony at the asylum, where we were cordially received again, and got quite gay. Sleeping accommodations [were] no better than before, as far as I was concerned. Soph, Miriam, and I, had but one bar between us, so we placed two matresses side by side, and by dint of chairs and strings stretched the net as far as possible over them. Those two were well enough; but to my share fell a baby matress two feet by four, placed between the wall and the other great bed, with the end of the bar a foot above my face, and one sheet to do the duty of two— however, they had only one, also. Well! I believe I am tall, so my bed did not fit me. As it was two inches higher than theirs, there was no sharing. In spite of a heavy rain that was now pouring, my warm place was intolerable, and the perspiration streamed from my face so as to be disagreeable, to say the least. It drove me to walk in my sleep, I am afraid, for I have an indistinct recollection of finding myself standing at the window trying to breathe.

It was a very, very, little piece of sleep I got after all, and that little by no means refreshing. Up at sun rise again, but it took some time to get ready, for I had to get some clothes out of the trunks, to send home. Well, ever since I reached here I have been writing, [p. 110] and I am ashamed to say how long it is. As the time grows more exciting, my book grows shorter, to my distress. What will I do? We all vowed this would be the last time we would run until we heard the cannon, or had some better reason than a Yankee panic to believe the Confederates were coming, though if we listened to mother, she would go there every night if this lasted for a whole year.

Kind Phillie Nolan wrote insisting on our staying with them on the plantation until it was over, but we cannot do it; the time is too uncertain; if we *knew* it was to come this week, we might stay that long with her; but to go for an indefinite period, Miriam and I wont hear of. This comes from a stranger; and our relations five miles down the coast have never even offered to take charge of a bundle to keep in safety for us, though aunt Adèle did have the conscience to send a negro last week to ask if we were *frightened*.

I have kept for the last a piece of news I received with thankfulness, when I finally heard it; for though known to the whole family and all the town on Tuesday night, no one thought it worth while to tell me until I heard it by accident last evening. It was that a Mr Bell, writing to his wife, says Gibbes asked him to send word to mother that he, George, and Jimmy were in the fight of the 10, & 11th, and all safe. God be praised!

[p. 111] July 25th.

An old gentleman stopped here just now in a carriage and asked to see me. Such a sad, sick, old man! He said his name was Caldwell, and that passing through E. Feliciana, Mrs Flynn[80] had asked him to deliver a message to us. Had we heard from our brothers? I told him the message from Mr Bell. He commenced crying. There was one of them, he said, who got hurt. I held my breath and looked at him. He cried more still, and said yes, it was Gibbes—in the hand—not dangerous— but— Here I thought he meant to tell me worse; perhaps he was dead; but I could not speak, so he went on saying Lydia and the General had gone on to Richmond instantly, and had probably reached there before to day. He took so long to tell it, and he cried so, that I was alarmed, until I thought perhaps he had lost one of his own sons; but I dared not ask him.

Just then one of the horses fell down with sunstroke, and I begged the old gentleman to come in and rest until they could raise the horse; but he said no; he must go on to the river. He looked so sick that I could not help saying he looked too unwell to go beyond, and I wished he would come in. But he burst into tears saying "Yes, my child, I am

80. Probably Ellen E. Flynn, enumerated in the household of William and Mary Elder in the 1860 census. Mrs. Flynn was the Elders' daughter and the mother of William and Theodore Pinkney.

very, very, sick, but I must go on." Poor old man, with his snow white beard! I thought of my own father, and felt so sorry for him! He knew father and all the boys, he said, and cried as he said it. Poor man! He must be very, very sick to cry so!

[p. 112] And Gibbes? Well! I am afraid hope amounts to presumption in me. I cannot believe God will take any of our brothers from us yet. We are so helpless without them! He has been so merciful to us, that I am willing to leave this in His hands, satisfied that He will hear our prayers as He always does. Shall I ever forget how awfully one prayer of mine was answered last year? I was thinking how noble and good Hal was, what a glorious soul he had, until it seemed sinful to think a mere mortal so great; I was afraid I might think more of him than I did of God; I would not say it anywhere except here, but I just knelt down and asked God not to let me love him so much; not to let me make an earthly idol of him; I was afraid I would believe him, rather than my own conscience. In ten days came a dreadful answer to a dreadful prayer, for I could not have loved Hal as much as he deserved; yet in the ten short days, God had taken him suddenly and unexpectedly away from me. My prayer was heard; I could no longer make an earthly idol of Harry; I would never again hear his voice, or see his face on earth. God answers all my prayers.

July 27th

I have my bird back! As I waked this morning I heard a well known chirp in the streets, and called to mother I knew it was Jimmy. Sure [p. 113] enough it *is* my bird. Lucy Daigre[81] has had him ever since the shelling, as a negro caught it that day and gave it to her. She told me of it soon after, but never returned it until now. I was so glad to see him! and he knew me, too. It must have been some other bird that perched on my shoulder when I came home. Dear little birdie! I was *very* glad to get him again.

Day before yesterday, I heard something about my sack, that if it had not been for the impertinence of the man, I might have thought a rough compliment to my ingenuity. Dophy was dragging it from the Asylum in a little cart, with some other articles of clothing which had been left

81. Daughter of Mrs. Mary Daigre, who lived next door to the Morgans.

there, when a gentleman, she says, stopped her and asked who made that knapsack. On her answering, he said "If I had a wife, she should make one like it! Tell Miss Morgan, when she runs, I'll carry the knapsack and run with her." The latter part might well be dispensed with; but I was pleased to hear some one besides myself say it was worth making.

July 29th

This town, with its ten thousand soldiers, is more quiet than it was with its old population of seven thousand citizens.[82] With this tremendous addition, it is like a graveyard, in its quiet, at times. These poor soldiers are dying awfully. Thirteen went yesterday. On Sunday the boats discharged hundreds of sick at our landing.[83] Some lay there all the afternoon in the hot sun, waiting for the wagons to carry them to the hospital, which task [p. 114] occupied the whole evening. In the meantime these poor wretches lay uncovered on the ground, in every stage of sickness. Cousin Will saw one lying dead without a creature by to notice when he died. Another was dying, and muttering to himself as he lay too far gone to brush the flies out of his eyes and mouth, while no one was able to do it for him. Cousin Will helped him though. Another, a mere skeleton, lay in the agonies of death too; but he evidently had kind friends, for several were gathered around holding him up, and fanning him, while his son leaned over him crying aloud. Tiche says it was dreadful to hear the poor boy's sobs.

All day our vis-a-vis Baumstark[84] with his several aids plies his hammer; all day Sunday he made coffins, and says he cant make them fast enough. Think, too, he is by no means the only undertaker here! O I

82. The population of Baton Rouge in 1860 was 5,428. It is doubtful that the figure had reached 7,000 two years later. The breakdown by race was 3,693 whites and 1,735 blacks; 1,247 of the blacks were slaves and the rest were free. See *Population of the United States in 1860* (Washington, 1864).

83. Malaria and other diseases took a heavy toll of the occupying army. The boats Sarah mentions were steamers used as transports to bring General Williams and his men back to Baton Rouge from the swamps near Vicksburg where many had suffered from heat and exhaustion.

84. Ambrose Baumstark, a cabinetmaker and undertaker whose place of business was at the corner of Church and Laurel, across the street from and just to the north of the Morgan home.

wish these poor men were safe in their own land! It is heart breaking to see them die here like dogs, with no one to say Godspeed. The Catholic priest went to see some, some time ago, and going near one who lay in bed, said some kind thing, when the man burst into tears and cried "Thank God I have heard *one* kind word before I die!" In a few minutes, the poor wretch was dead.

July 31st

I believe I forgot to mention one little circumstance, in my account of that first night at the Deaf and Dumb Asylum, which at the time struck me with extreme disgust. [p. 115] That was seeing more than one man who had no females or babies to look after, who sought there a refuge from the coming attack. At daylight, one dapper young man, in fashionable array, came stepping lightly on the gallery, carrying a neat carpet bag in his hand. I hardly think he expected to meet two young ladies at that hour; I shall always believe he meant to creep away before any one was up; for he certainly looked embarrassed when we looked up, though he assumed an air of indifference, and passed by bravely swinging his sack—but I think he wanted us to believe he was not ashamed. I dare say it was some little clerk in his holiday attire; but I cant say what contempt I felt for the creature.

Honestly, I believe the women of the South are as brave as the men who are fighting, and certainly braver than the "Home Guard." I have not yet been able to coax myself into being as alarmed as many I could name are. They say it is because I do not know the danger. Soit![85] I prefer being brave through ignorance, to being afraid in consequence of my knowledge of coming events. Thank Heaven my brothers are the bravest of the brave! I would despise them if they shrunk back, though Lucifer should dispute the path with them. Well! *all* men are not Morgan boys!

They tell me cowards actually exist, though [p. 116] I hope I never met [*sic*] one. The poor men that went to the Asylum for safety might not have what Sis calls "a moral backbone." No wonder then they tumbled in there! Besides, I am told half the town spent the night on the banks of

85. Agreed!

the river on that occasion; and perhaps these unfortunates were subject to colds, and prefered the shelter of a good roof.

Poor little fellows! How I longed to give them my hoops, corsets, and pretty blue organdie in exchange for their boots and breeches!— Only I thought it was dangerous; for suppose the boots had been so used to running, that they should prance off with me, too? Why it would ruin my reputation! Miss Morgan in petticoats is thought to be "as brave as any other man;" but these borrowed articles might make her fly as fast "as any other man," too, if panic is contagious, as the Yankees here have proved it is. One consolation is, that all who could go with any propriety, and all who were worthy of fighting, among those who believed in the South, are off at the seat of war; it is only trash, and those who are obliged to remain for private reasons, who still remain.[86] Let us count those young individuals as trash, and step over them. Only ask Heaven why you were made with a man's heart, and a female form, and those creatures with beards were made so bewitchingly nervous?

[p. 117] Aug 2d Saturday.

I had thought my running days were over; so little did I anticipate another stampede, that I did not notice the report of the attack that was prophesied for night before last, and went to bed without gathering my clothes. But to day comes a hasty note from Charlie, telling us to leave instantly as Genl. Breckenrige[87] is advancing with ten thousand men to attack us, and at 12 M, yesterday was within 34 miles. He begged us to leave to day; there would be trouble before to morrow night. It was so ernest, and he asserted all so positively, that we are going to Philly's this evening, to stay a week, as they say eight days will decide it.

Ah me! our beautiful town! Still I am skeptical. If it *must be,* pray Heaven that the blow comes now! Nothing can be equal to suspense. These poor men! Are they not dying fast enough? Will Baumstark have orders for an unlimited supply of coffins next week? Only Charlie's

86. Eliza Ripley wrote that "the few able-bodied men lingering outside the rank of fighters . . . were facetiously called 'Druthers,' because they'd druther not fight, or in other words, would druther stay at home." *Social Life,* 266.

87. Confederate General John C. Breckinridge, the former vice president of the United States and a presidential candidate in the 1860 election.

family, ours, and the Brunots know it. He enjoined the strictest secrecy, though the Bs. sent to swear Mrs Loucks in, as she, like ourselves has no protector. I would like to tell everybody; but it will warn the Federals. I almost wish we too, had been left in ignorance; it is cruel to keep it to ourselves. I believe the Yankees expect something. "They say" they have armed fifteen [p. 118] hundred negroes. Foes and insurrection in town, assailing friends outside. Nice time!

Our cavalry has passed the Amite.[88] Poor Charlie has come all the way to the ferry landing on the other side to warn us. If we do not take advantage, it will not be for want of knowing what is to come. How considerate it was in him to come such a long way! I am charmingly excited! If I only had a pair of pants, my happiness would be complete. Let it come! I lose all, but in Heaven's name let us have it over at once! My heart fails when I look around, but "Spit fire!" and have an end to this at once! Liberty for ever, though death be the penalty.

Treason! here lies my pass at my elbow in which has been gratuitously inserted that "Parties holding it are considered to give their Parole not to give information, countenance, aid or support to the So called Confed. S." As I did not apply for it, agree to the stipulation, or think it by any means proper, I dont consider it binding. I could not give my word for doing what my conscience tells me is Right. I cross with this book full of Treason. It "countenances" the C.S.; shall I burn it? That is a stupid ruse; they are too wise to *ask* you to subscribe to it; they just append it. If mother only would not groan and cry every time they [p. 119] whisper "attack," I protest I could honestly say I am enjoying myself. But what pleases me sets her lamenting aloud—and it is not calculated to raise the spirits to hear such dreadful moans and groans and exclamations when each should try to make the other comfortable. Mother is *so* nervous!

88. The Amite River, east of Baton Rouge.

Aug. 3d 1862 Westover.[89]

Enfin nous sommes arrivées![90] And after what a trip! As we reached the ferry, I discovered I had lost the pass, and had to walk back and search for it, aided by Mr Tunnard who met me in my distress, as it has always been his luck to do. But some body had already adopted the valuable trifle, so I had to rejoin mother and Miriam without. The guard resolutely refused to let us pass until we got another, so off flew Mr Tunnard to procure a second—which was vastly agreeable as I knew he would have to pay twenty five cents for it—Yankees having come down as low as that, to procure money. But he had gone before we could say anything, and soon returned with the two bits' worth of leave of absence. Then we crossed the river in a little skiff after sundown, in a most unpleasant state of uncertainty as to whether the carriage was waiting at the landing for us, for I did not know if Philly had received my note, and there was no place to go if she had not sent for us. However we found it waiting, and leaving mother and Miriam to pay the ferry, [p. 120] I walked on to put our bundles in the carriage.

A man stepped forward, calling me by name and giving me a note from Charlie before I reached it; and as I placed my foot on the step, another came up and told me he had left a letter at home for me at one o'clock. I bowed yes; (it was from Howell; must answer to-morrow.) He asked me not to mention it was him; a little servant had asked his name but he told her it was none of her business. I laughed at the refined remark, and said I had not known who it was—he would hardly have been flattered to hear I had not even inquired. He modestly said he was afraid I had seen him through the window. O no! I assured him. Well, please, *any* how dont say it's me! he pleaded most grammatically. I an-

89. The Nolan plantation in West Baton Rouge Parish, across the river from Baton Rouge.

90. Finally we have arrived.

swered smiling "I did not know who it was then, I know no more now, and if you choose, I shall always remain in ignorance of your identity." He burst out laughing, and went off with "O do Miss Morgan, forget all about me!" as though it was a difficult matter! Who can he be?

We had a delightful drive in the moonlight, though it was rather long; and it was quite late when we drove up to the house, and were most cordially welcomed by the family. We sat up late on the balcony listening for the report of cannon, which however did not come. B.R. is to be attacked to-morrow, "*they say*." Pray Heaven it will all be over by that time! Nobody seems to doubt it, over here. A while ago a long procession of guerillas passed a short distance from the house, looking for a party of Yankees they heard of, in the neighborhood, and waved their hats, for lack of handkerchiefs, to us as we stood on the balcony.

I call this writing under difficulties! Here I am employing my knee as a desk, a position that is not very natural to me, and by no means comfortable. I feel so stupid from want of sleep last night, that no wonder I am not even respectably bright. I think I shall lay aside this diary with my pen. I have procured a nicer one, so I no longer regret its close. What a stupid thing it is! As I look back, how faintly have I expressed things that produced the greatest impression on me at the time, and how completely have I omitted the very things I should have recorded! Bah! it is all the same trash! And here is an end of it—for *this* volume, whose stupidity can only be equaled by the one that precedes, and the one that is to follow it. But who expects to be interesting in war times? If I kept a diary of events, it would be one tissue of lies. Think! There was *no* battle on the 10th or 11th, McClellan is *not* dead, and Gibbes was never wounded! After that, who believes in "reliable" information. Not I!

Book Three

[p. 1] Monday. August 4th. 1862. Westover.

A fresh volume! Where shall I be at the end of it? Will I be once more seated at my old desk in my dear little room, comfortably settled at home? Or will I have no home then, and be what to me is worse than death—a wanderer who has no spot that may be called "home"? Will the blank pages record the burning of Baton Rouge, and the loss of our all? Will the close of it find me still running, or at last settled in what is to be our future dwelling in New Orleans? Will they leave us at Peace, or in war? Who knows? Leave it to Destiny. Write page after page, day after day, and mark the final event. It takes many days to bring about such a result; make them fly past, and thank Heaven that is one day nearer the end. Wait patiently, I say. This war cannot last for ever; and then comes blessed Peace! Will I be able to appreciate it?

Here we are at Dr Nolan's plantation, with Baton Rouge lying just seven miles from us to the east.[1] We can surely hear the cannon from here. They are all so kind to us, that I ought to be contented; but still I wish I was once more at home. I suppose it is very unreasonable in me, but I cannot help it. I miss my old desk very much; it is so awkward to write on my knee that I cannot get used to it. Mine is a nice little room up stairs, detached from all the rest, for it is formed by a large dormer window looking to the north, from which I have seen a large number of guerillas passing and repassing in their rough costumes, constantly. I enjoy the fresh air, and all that, but pleasant as it is, I wish I was at home, and all the fuss was over. Virginia Nolan[2] and Miriam are

1. Actually, east and south. The Mississippi River flows north to south in a series of turns and bends. Just above Baton Rouge it takes a turn to the east for several miles before bending back south.

2. Phillie's sister, also referred to as Ginnie, one of the four daughters of Dr. John T. Nolan. She was 14 at the time this was written.

already equiped in their riding costumes, so I must lay this down, and get ready to join them in a scamper across the fields. How delighted I will be to get on a horse again.

August 5th.

This morning we three girls were up before sunrise, determined to have a second edition of last evening's ride in the cool of the morning. And a glorious ride it was, following the river up for several miles above, and getting back long before the late breakfast. I spoiled the pleasant impression mine left on me, by taking a shocking fall after I had dismounted. I was getting down on a stepladder about four feet high, and somehow, when I had only got half way to the bottom I found myself unexpectedly on the ground, with not even the energy to get up. Presently—it seemed a long while after—I dimly saw the above mentioned ladder leaning gracefully towards me, when I perceived [p. 2] that if not arrested it might injure the ground by dashing my brains over it, so I mechanically caught it before it hurt its self, and restored it to its balance, though it was some moments before I recovered mine. I believe I was hurt. But about half past nine, as we got up from the breakfast table, I forgot all about it, when a guerilla told us the ram Arkansas was lying a few miles below, on her way to co-operate with Breckenridge, whose advance guard had already driven the picketts [sic] into Baton Rouge.³ Then we all grew wild with excitement.

Such exclamations! such delight that the dreadful moment had at last arrived! and yet you could see each stop as we rejoiced, to offer up a prayer for the preservation of those who were risking their lifes [sic] at that moment. Reason, and all else was thrown aside, and we determined to participate in the danger, if there was any to be incurred. Mother threatened us with shot and shell and bloody murder, but the loud report of half a dozen cannon in slow succession, only made us more determined to see the fun, so Lilly Nolan and Miss Walters⁴ got on horseback, and Phillie, Ginnie, Miriam and I started off in the broiling sun, leaving word for the carriage to overtake us.

3. The plan was for the *Arkansas* to engage the *Essex* and the other Union gunboats in the river at Baton Rouge while Breckinridge's army attacked from the east.

4. Mary Elizabeth (Lilly) Nolan, the youngest of Dr. Nolan's daughters, and Margaret Walter, or possibly her sister Fanny, daughters of Mrs. Leocadie Walter. Like the Morgans, the Walters had left Baton Rouge on the eve of the battle.

When we once got in, the driver being as crazy as we, fairly made his horses run along the road, to catch a glimpse of our Ram. When, miles below, she came in sight, we could no longer remain in the carriage, but mounted the levee, and ran along on foot until we reached her, when we crossed to the outer levee, and there she lay at our feet. And nothing in her after all! There lay a heavy, clumsy, rusty, ugly flat-boat with a great square box in the centre, while great cannon put their noses out at the sides, and in front. The decks were crowded with men, rough and dirty, jabbering and hastily eating their breakfast. That was the great Arkansas! God bless and protect her, and the brave men she carries.[5]

While there a young man came up and in answer to Phillie's inquiries about her father, who having gone to town yesterday to report, being paroled, had written last night to say no passes were granted to leave town, the young fellow informed her *so* pleasantly that her father was prisoner, held as hostage for Mr Castle.[6] Poor Phillie had to cry, so, to be still more agreeable he told her yes, he had been sent to a boat [p. 3] lying at the landing, and ran the greatest risk, as the ram would probably sink the said boat in a few hours. How I hated the fool for his relish of evil tidings!

But never mind our wild expedition, or what came of it. Am I not patient, ever since I commenced to write, the sound of a furious bombardment has been ringing in my ears; and beyond an occasional run to see the shells fly through the air (their white smoke, rather) I have not said a word of it! The girls have all crowded on the little balcony up here, towards town, and their shrieks of "There it goes!" "Listen!" "Look at them!" rise above the sound of the cannon, and occasionally draw me out, too. But I sit here listening, and wonder which report preceeds the knocking [?] down of our home; which shell is killing some one I know or love. Poor Teach[7] and Dophy! where are they? And O I hope they did not leave my birdie Jimmy to die in his cage! I charged them to let him loose if they could not carry him. Dophy will be so

5. Crippled by engine trouble just as she was about to turn the point, the ram was unable to join the battle. The next morning her engines failed once more, and the crew set fire to her when she came under attack from the *Essex*. See J. Thomas Scharf, *History of the Confederate States Navy* (Atlanta, 1887), 332–38.

6. Probably Henry Castle, Jr. It is not clear whether he had escaped or was paroled.

7. Sarah's variant spelling of Tiche.

frightened. I hope they are out of danger. O my dear home! shall I ever see you again? And the Brunots! O how I hope they are safe.

These loud cannon make me heart sick, and yet I am so excited! How rapidly they answer each other! I am told the attack commenced at five this morning, and lasted three hours. Those girls are shouting that B.R. must be on fire, from the volume of smoke in that direction. How they scream as the balls go up, to show it to each other! Think I'll take a look too.—

We are all going four or five miles through this warm sun to be nearer the scene of action. Any one might know there was no white man on the premises. There is the carriage! O I am *so* sea sick! What will I be before we get back?

August 6th.

We six madcaps got in the carriage and buggy, and rode off in search of news.[8] We took a quantity of old linen rags along, and during the whole drive, our fingers were busy making lint.[9] Once we stopped at a neighbor's to gather the news, but that did not interfere with our labors at all. Four miles from here we met a crowd of women flying, and among them recognized Mrs La Noue and Noémie.[10] A good deal of loud shouting brought them to the carriage in great surprise to see us there. They were running from the plantation where they had taken refuge, as it was not safe from the shells, as the gunboats had proved [to] them. The reports we had heard in the morning were from shots fired on this [p. 4] side of the river by them, in hopes of hurting a guerilla or two. Noémie told us that two western regiments had laid down their arms, and Genl Williams had been killed by his own men.[11] She looked so delighted, and yet it made me sick to think of his having been butchered so. Phillie leaned out, and asked her, as she asked every

8. Sarah picks up the story where she left off the day before; consequently, the entry of August 6 covers some of the events of August 5.

9. Lint made by scraping cotton cloth or linen was used in dressing wounds. For the women of the South, this was a way of participating in the war effort.

10. Charlie LaNoue's widowed mother, Mrs. Adelaide LaNoue, and his sister Noemie.

11. General Thomas Williams had been killed, but not by his own men. The rumor that two of the Union regiments had laid down their arms was also false. The Confederate attack had failed. Breckinridge withdrew his army.

body, if she knew anything about her father. Noémie in her rapture over that poor man's death, exclaimed "Dont know a word about him! know Williams was cut to pieces, though," and that is all that we could learn from her.

We went on until we came in sight of Baton Rouge. There it stood, looking so beautiful against the black, lowering sky that I could not but regret its fate. We could see the garrison, State House, Asylum, and all that; but the object of the greatest interest to me was the steeple of the Methodist Church, for to the right of it lay home.[12] While [I was] looking at it, a negro passed who was riding up and down the coast collecting lint, so I gave him all we had made, and commenced some more. Presently we met Mr Philips,[13] to whom Phillie put the same question. "He is on the Laurel Hill [14] a prisoner—confound that negro! where did she go?" And so on, each answer as far as concerned her, seeming a labor, but the part relating to the servant very hearty. Poor Phillie complained that everybody was selfish—thought only of their own affairs, and did not sympathise with her. "Yes, my dear" I silently assented; for it was *very* true; every one seemed to think of their own interests alone. It was late before we got home, and then we had great fun in watching shells which we could dimly trace against the clouds, falling in what must have been the garrison. Then came a tremendous fire, above, which *may* have been a boat—I dont know.

I hear a tremendous firing again, and from the two volumes of smoke, should judge it was the Arkansas and Essex [15] trying their strength at a distance. We are going down to see what's the fun. It would be absurd to record all the rumors that have reached us, since we can rely on none. They say we fought up to nine last night, and occupied the garrison for five minutes, when the shells forced us to abandon it. Also that *four* regiments laid down their arms, that the Federals were pursued by our men to the river, driven to the gunboats, [p. 5] and pushed off to

12. The Methodist church faced Church Street at the northeast corner of Church and Laurel, two houses and the width of a street away from the Morgan home.

13. Probably William D. Phillips, the Baton Rouge merchant.

14. The steamer *Laurel Hill* was used as a Union troop transport.

15. The most formidable of the Union gunboats at Baton Rouge was the ironclad *Essex*, commanded by William D. Porter. Porter would later refute other accounts and claim credit for the destruction of the *Arkansas. OR*, ser. I, 53:531–32.

prevent the Western men from coming aboard. An eye witness, from this side, reports that. Genl Williams "They say" was forcibly held before a cannon and blown to pieces. For the sake of humanity, I hope this is false.

O what a sad day this is for our country! Mother disapproved so of our going to the levee to see the fight, that we consented to remain, though Miriam and Ginnie jumped in the buggy and went off alone. Presently came tidings that all the planter[s] near Baton R. were removing their families and negroes, and that the Yankees were to shell this whole coast, from there up to here. Then Phillie, Lilly [Nolan], and I jumped in the carriage that was still waiting, and ran after the others to bring them back before they got in danger; but when we reached the end of the long lane, we saw them standing on the high levee, wringing their hands and crying. We sprang out and joined them, and there, way at the bend, lay the Arkansas on fire!

All except myself burst into tears and lamentations, and prayed aloud between their sobs. I had no words or tears; I could only look at our sole hope burning, going, and pray silently. O it was so sad! Think it was our sole dependence! And we five girls looked at her as the smoke rolled over her, watched the flames burst from her decks, and the shells as they exploded one by one beneath the water, coming up in jets of steam. And we watched until down the road we saw crowds of men toiling along towards us. Then we knew they were those who had escaped, and the girls sent up a shriek of pity.

On they came, dirty, half dressed, some with only their guns, a few with bundles and knapsacks on their backs, grimy and tired, but still laughing. We called to the first, and asked if the boat were really afire; they shouted yes, and went on, talking still. Presently one ran up and told us the story. How yesterday their engine had broken, and how they had labored all day to repair it; how they had succeeded, and had sat by their guns all night; and this morning, as they started to meet the Essex, the other engine had broken; how each officer wrote his opinion that it was impossible to fight her with any hope of success under such circumstances, and advised the Captain to abandon her; how they had resolved to do so, had exchanged shots with the Essex across the point, and the first of the latter (only one, also) had set ours afire, when the men were ordered to take their side arms. They thought it was to

board the Essex, assembled together, when the order was given to fire
the Arkansas and go ashore, which was [p. 6] done in a few minutes.
Several of the crew were around us then, and up and down the road
they were scattered still in crowds.

Miriam must have asked the name of some of the officers; for just
then she called to me "He says that is Mr Read!"[16] I looked at the
foot of the levee, and saw two walking together. I hardly recognized
the gentleman I was introduced to on the McRae, in the one that now
stood below me in rough sailor pants, a pair of boots, and a *very* thin
and slazy lisle undershirt. That was all he had on, except an old straw
hat, and—yes! he held a primer! I did not think it would be embarrassing to him to meet me under such circumstances; I only thought of
Jimmy's friend as escaping from a sad fate; so I rushed down a levee
twenty feet high, saying "O Mr Read! You wont recognize me, but I
am Jimmy's sister!" He blushed modestly, shook my hand as though
we were old friends, and assured me he remembered me, was glad to
meet me, etc. Then Miriam came down, and talked to him, and then
we went to the top of the levee where the rest were, and watched the
poor Arkansas burn.

By that time, the crowd that had gone up the road came back, and
we found ourselves in the centre of two hundred men, just we five girls,
talking with the officers who stood around us as though they were old
friends. You could only *guess* they were officers, for a dirtier, more forlorn set I never saw. Not *dirty* either; they looked clean, considering
the work they had been doing. Nobody introduced anybody else; we
all felt like brothers and sisters in our common calamity. There was
one handsome Kentuckian, whose name I soon found to be Talbot,[17]
who looked charmingly picturesque in his coarse cotonade [*sic*] pants,
white shirt, straw hat, black hair, beard and eyes, with rosy cheeks. He
was a graduate of the Naval Academy some years ago. Then another
jolly faced young man from the same Academy, pleased me too. He,

16. Lieutenant Charles W. Read had served on the *McRae* in 1861 and the early months
of 1862. See his account of the *Arkansas*'s encounter with the Union fleet at Vicksburg
and its ill-fated run to Baton Rouge in *Southern Historical Society Papers* 1:331–62,
hereafter cited as *SHSP*. See also biographical sketch in *Confederate Military History*
(Atlanta, 1899; Extended Edition, 1987–89), 9:458–61.

17. Midshipman Daniel B. Talbott. The ram's officers are listed in *ORN*, ser. I, 19:132.

the doctor and the Captain, were the only ones who possessed a coat in the whole crowd, the few who saved theirs, carrying them over their arms. Mr Read more than once blushingly remarked that they were prepared to fight, and hardly expected to meet us; but we pretended to think there was nothing unusual in his dress. I can understand though, that he should feel rather awkward; I would [p. 7] not like to meet *him*, if I was in the same costume.

They all talked over their loss cheerfully, as far as the loss of money, watches, clothes, were concerned; but they were disheartened about their boat. One threw himself down near my feet saying "Me voilà.[18] I have saved my gun, et puis[19] the clothes that I stand in!" and laughed as though it were an excellent joke. One who had been on the Merrimac[20] chiefly regretted the loss of the commission appointing him there, though he had not saved a single article. The one with the jolly face told me Will Pinkney was among those attacking Baton Rouge, and assured him he expected to take supper there last night. He thought it would be with us, I know! I hope he is safe!

After a while the men were ordered to march up the lane, to some resting spot it is best not to mention here, and straggled off; but there was many sick among them, one wounded at Vicksburg, and we instantly voted to walk the mile and three quarters home, and give them the carriage and buggy. But long after they left, we stood with our new friends on the levee watching the last of the Arkansas, and saw the Essex, and two gunboats crowded with men,[21] cautiously turn the point, and watch her burn. What made me furious was the thought of the glowing accounts they would give of their "capture of the Arkansas!!!" Capture, and they fired a shot a piece! for all the firing we heard was the discharge of her guns by the flames. We saw them go back as

18. Here I am.

19. And only.

20. The famous armored warship rebuilt by the Confederates after being scuttled early in the war. Renamed the *Virginia*, it survived an encounter with the *Monitor*, but was later destroyed to keep it out of Union hands.

21. The two Union gunboats that accompanied the *Essex* were the *Cayuga* and the *Sumter*. See *ORN*, ser. I, 19:118. The *Kineo* and the *Katahdin* remained on station off Baton Rouge.

cautiously, and I was furious, knowing the accounts they would publish of what we ourselves had destroyed. We had seen many shells explode, and one magazine, and would have waited for the other, if the clouds had not threatened rain speedily. But we had to leave her a mere wreck, still burning, and started off on our long walk.

In our hurry, I had brought neither handkerchief or gloves, but hardly missed either, I was so excited. Mr Talbot walked home with me, and each of the others with some one else. He had a small bundle and a sword, and the latter I insisted on carrying. It was something, to shoulder a sword made for use, rather than ornament! So *I would* carry it. He said "he would remember who had carried it, and the recollection would give it a new value in his eyes, and I might rest assured it should never be disgraced after *that*," and all that sort of thing, of *course*, as it is usual to say it on such occasions. But I shouldered the sword bravely, determined to show my appreciation of the sacrifice they had made for us, in coming to our rescue on a boat [p. 8] they had every reason to believe was unsafe.

I liked Mr Talbot! He made himself very agreeable in that long walk. He asked permission to send me a trophy from the first action in which he used "that" sword, and *didn't* I say yes! He thought Southern men had every encouragement in the world, from the fact that the ladies welcomed them with equal kindness in victory or defeat, insinuating he thought they hardly deserved our compassion after their failure on the Arkansas. But I stoutly denied that it *was* a failure. Had they not done their best? was it their fault the machinery broke? and in defeat or victory, were they not still fighting for us? Were we the less grateful when they met with reverse? O didn't I laud the Southern men with my whole heart!—and I think he felt better, for it, too! Yes! I like him.

We all met at the steps, and water was given to our cavaliers who certainly enjoyed it. We could not ask them in, as Dr Nolan is on his parole; but Phillie intimated that if they chose to order, they might do as they pleased, as women could not resist armed men! So they took possession of the sugar house, and helped themselves to something to eat, and were welcome to do it, since no one could prevent! But they first stood talking on the balcony, gaily, and we parted with many warm wishes on both sides, insisting that if they assisted at a second attack on B.R., that they must remember our house was at their service, wounded, or in health. And they all shook hands with us, and looked pleased, and said God bless you, and good bye.

Evening. I heard a while ago, the doctor of the Ram who brought back the buggy, say the Arkansas' crew were about leaving; so remembering poor Mr Read had lost everything, mother suggesting he might need money, gave me twenty dollars to put in his hands, as some slight help towards reaching his destination. Besides, coming from Jimmy's mother, he could not have been hurt. But when I got down, he was far up the lane, walking too fast for me to overtake him; then I tried to catch Mr Stephenson,[22] to give it to him for me, but failed. Presently we saw I am afraid to say how many wagons loaded with them, coming from the sugar house, so Phillie, Lilly [Nolan] and I [p. 9] snatched up some five bottles of Gin, between us, and ran out to give it to them. A rough old sailor received mine with a flood of thanks, and the others gave theirs to those behind. An officer rode up saying "Ladies, there is no help for it! The Yankee cavalry are after us, and we must fight them in the corn. Take care of yourselves!" We shouted yes! told them to bring us the wounded and we would nurse them. Then the men cried God bless you, and we cried hurrah for the Arkansas' crew! and fight for us! altogether it was a most affecting scene.

Phillie seeing how poorly armed they were, suggested a gun, which I flew after and delivered to a rough old tar. When I got out, the cart then passing held Mr Talbot who smiled benignly and waved his hat, like the rest. He looked still better in his black coat, but the carts reminded me of what the guilliotine [sic] days must have been in France. He shouted Good bye, we shouted "come to us, if you are wounded;" he smiled and bowed, and I cried "Use 'that' sword!" whereupon he sprang to his feet and grasped the hilt as though about to commence. Then came other officers; Mr Scales, Mr Barblaud, etc.,[23] who smiled recognition, stopped the wagon as Philly handed up a plate of bread and meat, and talked gaily as they divided it, until the captain rode up. "On, gentlemen! not a moment to lose!" then the cart started off,

22. Sarah is apparently referring to Lieutenant Henry K. Stephens, the executive officer of the *Arkansas*, who took over command at Vicksburg in the absence of the ram's captain, Isaac N. Brown.

23. Midshipman Dabney M. Scales and Lieutenant Alphonse Barbot.

the empty plate was flung over board, and they rode of[f] waving hats, and crying "God bless you, ladies!" in answer to our repeated offers of taking care of them, if they were hurt. And they have gone to meet the Yankees, and I hope they *wont,* for they have worked enough to-day, and from my heart I pray God prosper those brave men!

August 7th.

Last night, shortly after we got in bed, we were roused by loud cannonading towards Baton Rouge, and running out on the small balcony up here, saw the light of a great fire in that direction. From the constant reports, and the explosion of what seemed to be several powder magazines, we imagined it to be either the garrison or a gunboat. What ever it was, it was certainly a great fire. We all ran out in our nightgowns, and watched for an hour in the damp air, I, without even shoes. But presently Ginnie had me in a chair, with a cloak around me, and a thick rug between the wet planks and my bare feet. She is so good to me! What makes her take such care of me? But everybody is tender and kind to me. We listened to the fight a long while, until the sound ceased, and we went back to bed.

Evening. I am so disheartened! I have been listening with the others, to [p. 10] a man who was telling us about Baton Rouge, until I am heartsick. He says the Yankees have been largely reinforced, and are prepared for another attack which will probably take place to-morrow; that the fight was a dreadful one, we driving them in, and losing 12 hundred, to their fifteen hundred.[24] It must have been awful! And that our troops have resolved to burn the town down, since they cannot hold it under the fire of the gunboats. Must this be? Is there no help for this, and are we really beggars? O my home! I cannot live without you! Think of wandering around houseless and homeless, with not even the chance of making one for myself, for nothing is to be done! Beggared! How shall I endure it? If I had only had the sense to carry something away! But I never believed in the burning of the town. I thought we would surely be back in three days; and now—!

Well! what have we left? Comparatively, nothing at all. Miriam's piano, my guitar, given by those who can never give us anything again,

24. The figures are exaggerated. Sarah corrects them in the entry of August 9.

all our furniture, all our winter clothes, and thousands of articles that can never be replaced, fathers valuable law library, all our books that were more to us than I can say, everything is lost! O how each little article gives me a pang as I recall it, and how I wish I had brought some few here! Then the house, with its associations, that is gone forever too! O my home! Shall I never see you again?

Aug 8th. Friday.

Again last night, about nine, we heard cannon in B.R., and watched the flashes which preceded the reports by a minute, at least, for a long time. We must have seen our own firing; perhaps we wanted to find out the batteries of the enemy. It was not the most delightful thing imaginable to watch what might be the downfall of our only home! And then to think each ball might bring death to some one we love! Ah no! it was not pleasant!

Miriam and I have many friends in Breckenridge's division, I expect, if we could only hear the names of the regiments. The fourth[25] is certainly there. And poor Will! I wonder if he has had his supper yet? I have been thinking of him ever since Mr Scales told me he was there, and praying myself sick for his safety and that of the rest. I shut my eyes at every report and say "O please! poor Will!—and the others too!" And when I *dont* hear the cannon, I pray, to be in advance of the next. I wonder if Will knows I am watching his [p. 11] cannon, and praying for him so ernestly? I am sure I would cry if he was hurt. Phillie said yesterday when I spoke of it "Why you seem as fond of him as his wife is!" Not *quite*! But I knew him first, and he has been a good friend to me, and I expect to like him until he proves himself unworthy of my regard—which is not likely to take place.

It is now mid day, and again we hear firing; but have yet to learn the true story of the first day's fight. Preserve me from the country in such stirring days! We might as well be in Europe, as to have the Mississippi between us and town. *Cant* our homes be spared?

By unanimous consent, the little lane in front of the house has been christened Guerilla lane, and the long one leading to the river, Arkan-

25. The 4th Louisiana Infantry, which included companies from East and West Baton Rouge as well as from other parishes.

sas. What an episode that was, in our lives! The officers go by the name of Miriam's, Ginnie's, Sarah's, as though they belonged to each! Those girls did me the meanest [?] thing imaginable. Mr Talbot and I were planning a grand combined attack on Baton Rouge, in which he was to command a fleet and attack the town by the river, while I promised to get up a battalion of girls and attack them in the rear. We had settled it all, except the time, when just then all the others stopped talking. I went on "And now, it is only necessary for you to name the day—" here the girls commenced to giggle, and the young men tried to suppress a smile; I felt annoyed, but it did not strike me until after they had left, that I had said anything absurd. What evil imaginations they must have, if they could have fancied I meant anything except the battle!

Aug 9th.

To our great surprise, Charlie came in this morning from the other side. He was in the battle, and Genl Carter, and dozens of others that we did not think of. See the mountain reduced to a mole hill! He says though the fight was desperate, we lost only eighty five killed, and less than a hundred and fifty wounded! And we had only twenty five hundred, against the Yankees' four thousand five hundred.[26] There is no truth in our having held the garrison even for a moment, though we drove them down to the river in a panic. The majority ran like fine fellows, but a Main[e] regiment fought like devils. He says Will [Pinkney] and Thompson Bird[27] set fire to the Yankee camp with the greatest alacrity, as though it were rare fun. Genl Williams was killed as he passed Piper's,[28] by a shot from a window, supposed to have been

26. Confederate casualties in the Battle of Baton Rouge totaled 456, including 84 killed, 315 wounded, and 57 captured or missing. The Union loss was 383, including 84 killed. General Williams may have had as many as 5,000 men under his command, including the 1,200 he left in Baton Rouge and the 3,200–3,300 he refers to in his letters from near Vicksburg. However, on July 21, five days before he returned to Baton Rouge, 1,200 of the men he had taken upriver were on the sick list, and many of those he left behind were unfit for combat. See "Letters of General Williams," 325–26.

27. Thompson J. Bird, a wealthy planter, commanded a company in the 11th Louisiana until the regiment was disbanded. Later he held the rank of major in the 1st Battalion Trans-Mississippi Cavalry.

28. The business establishment of Jacob Piper (house furnishers and cabinetmakers) on Main Street.

fired by a citizen. Some one from town told him that the Federals were breaking [p. 12] in the houses, destroying the furniture, and tearing the clothes of the women and children in shreds, like maniacs. O my home! I wonder if they have entered ours? What a jolly time they would have over all the letters I left in my desk!

Butler has ordered them to burn B.R. if forced to evacuate it.[29] Looks as though he was not so sure of holding it. Miss Turner told Miriam that her mother attempted to enter town after the fight to save some things, when the gallant Col. Dudley[30] put a pistol to her head, called her an old she devil, and told her he would blow her d—— brains out if she moved a step; that anyhow, none but we d—— women had put the men up to fighting, and we were the ones who were to blame for the fuss. There is no name he did not call us. What a brute of a man he is! Among all those who have done their best to disgrace their cause and country, Col. Dudley's name has the honor of standing first on the list of infamy.

Well, Baton Rouge is to be laid in ashes, and I am heartbroken. I might as well die as to be homeless. I cannot be a wanderer much longer. To add to my distress, Miriam went to Linwood with Charlie at one o'clock, and left me desolate. I feel as though my last hope were taken away. Indeed it was not fair to go away, from me; I would not have left her, I am sure, at such a time.

Aug 10th. Sunday.

Is this really Sunday? Never felt less pious, or less seriously disposed! Listen to my story, and though I will, of course, fall far short of the actual terror that reigned, yet it will show it in a luke warm light, that can at least recall the excitement to me. To begin, then, last evening, about six o'clock, as we sat reading, sewing, and making lint in the parlor, we heard a tremendous shell whizzing past, which those who watched, said passed not five feet above the house. Of course there was a slight stir among the unsophisticated; though we who had passed through bombardments, sieges, & alarms of all kinds, coolly remarked

29. If Butler's orders had been allowed to stand, the city would have been burned. Colonel Halbert E. Paine, in command at Baton Rouge following the death of General Williams, persuaded Butler to reverse himself. See *OR*, ser. I, 15:552–53.

30. Colonel N. A. M. Dudley of the 30th Massachusetts.

"a shell," and kept quiet. (The latter class was not very numerous.) It was from one of the three Yankee boats that lay in the river close by (the Essex and two gunboats) which were sweeping teams, provisions, and negroes from all the plantations [p. 13] they stopped at from B.R. up.[31] The negroes, it is stated, are to be armed against us as in town, where all those who manned the cannon on Tuesday, were, for the most part, killed, and served them right!

Another shell was fired at a carriage containing Mrs Durald[32] and several children, under pretense of discovering if she was a guerilla, doubtless. Fortunately she was not hurt, however. By the time the little émeute[33] had subsided, determined to have a frolic, Miss Walters, Ginnie and I got on our horses, and rode off down the Arkansas lane, to have a gallop and a peep at the gunboats from the levee. But mother's entreaties prevented us from going that near, as she cried that it was well known they fired at every horse or vehicle they saw in the road, seeing a thousand guerillas in every puff of dust, and we were sure to be killed, murdered, and all sorts of bloody deaths awaited us; so to satisfy her, we took the road about a mile from the river, in full view, however.

We had not gone very far before we met a Mr Watson,[34] a plain farmer of the neighborhood, who begged us to go back. "You'll be fired on, ladies, sure! you dont know the danger! Take my advice and go home as quick as possible before they shell you! They shoot buggies and carriages, and of course they wont mind *horses* with women! Please go home!" But Ginnie, who had taken a fancy to go on, acted as spokeswoman, and determined to go on in spite of his advice, so, nothing loth to follow her example, we thanked him, and rode on. Another met us; looked doubtful, said it was not so dangerous if the Yankees did not see the dust; but if they did, we would be pretty apt to see a shell soon after. Here was frolic! so we rode on some mile or two beyond, but failing to see anything startling, turned back again.

About two miles from here, we met Mr Watson coming at full speed.

31. Three months later Sarah came back and wrote a note at the top of this page. See entry of November 21, 1862.

32. Victorine Duralde, wife of Joseph V. Duralde of West Baton Rouge Parish.

33. Disturbance.

34. George Washington Watson.

The ladies he said, had sent him after us in all haste; there was a report that the whole coast was to be shelled; a lady had passed flying with her children; the carriage was ordered out; they were only waiting for us, to run too. We did not believe a word of it, and were indignant at their credulity, as well as determined to persuade them to remain where they were, if possible. When told their plan was to run to the house formerly used as a guerilla camp, we laughed heartily. Suppose the Yankees fired a shell in it to discover its inhabitants? The idea [p. 14] of choosing a spot so well known! And what fun in running to a miserable hole, when we might sleep comfortably here? I am afraid rebellion was in the air. Indeed, an impudent little negro who threw open the gate for us, interrupted Ginnie in the midst of a tirade with a sly "Here's the beginning of a little fuss!"

We found them all crazy with fear. I did not say much; I was too provoked to trust myself to argue with so many frightened women. I only said I saw no necessity. Ginnie resisted, but finally succumbed. Mr Watson, whom we had enlisted on our side also, said it was by no means necessary, but if we were determined, we might go to his house about four miles away, and stay there. It was very small, but we were welcome. We had in the mean time thrown off our riding skirts, and stood just in our plain dresses, though the others were freshly dressed for an Exodus. Before the man left, the carriage came, though by that time we had drawn half the party on our side; we said we would take supper, and decide after, so he went off.

In a few moments, a rocket went up from one of the boats, which attracted our attention. Five minutes after, we saw a flash directly before us. "See it? Lightning, I expect," said Phillie. The others all agreed; but I kept quiet, knowing that some, at least, knew what it was as well as I, and determined not to give the alarm—for I was beginning to feel foolish. Before half a minute more came a tearing, hissing sound, a sky rocket whose music I had heard before. Instantly I remembered my running bag, and flew up stairs to get it, escaping just in time from the scene which followed on the gallery which was afterwards most humorously described to me. But I was out of hearing of the screams of each (and yet I must have heard them), neither saw Miss Walters tumble against the wall, or mother turn over her chair, or the general mêlée that followed, in which Mrs Walters, trying to scale the carriage, was pulled out by uncle Will[35] who shouted to his plunging horses first, then to the other unreasoning creatures "Woa, there! 'taint safe! take to the fields! take to the woods! run to the sugar house! take to your heels!" in a frenzy of excitement.

I escaped all that, and was putting on my [p. 15] hoops and hastily catching up any article that presented itself to me in my speed, when the shell burst over the roof, and went rattling down on the gallery, according to the account of those then below. Two went far over the house, out of sight. All three were seen by Mr Watson, who came galloping up in a few moments, crying "Ladies, for God's sake leave the house!" Then I heard mother calling "Sarah! you will be killed! leave your clothes and run!" and a hundred ejaculations that came too fast for me to answer except by an occasional "Coming, if you will send me a candle." Candle was the same as though I had demanded a hand grenade, in mother's opinion, for she was sure it would be the signal for a bombardment of my exposed room; so I tossed down my bundles, swept comb and hairpins in my bosom (all points up), and ravished a candle from some one. How quickly I got on, then! I saved the most useless of articles with the greatest zeal, and probably left the most serviceable ones. One single dress did my running bag contain—a white linen cambric with a tiny pink flower—the one I wore when I told Hal good bye for the last time. The others I left. When I got down with my knapsack, mother, Phillie and Mrs Walters were

At Randallson's Landing.[36] Aug 11th

I dont mean those ladies were, but that I am at present. I'll account for it after I have disposed of the stampede. Imagine no interruption and continue—in the carriage urging uncle Will to hurry on, and I had barely time to thrust my sack under their feet before they were off. Lilly [Nolan] and Miss Walters were already in the buggy, leaving Ginnie and me to follow on horseback. I ran up after my riding skirt, which I was surprised to find behind a trunk, and rolled up in it, was my running bag, with all my treasures! I was very much provoked at

35. The Nolans' black driver.

36. A crossing point on the east bank of the Mississippi River not far below Port Hudson. The name was Ronaldson.

my carelessness; indeed I cannot imagine how it got there, for it was the first thing I thought of. When I got back, there was no one to be seen except Ginnie and two negroes who held our horses, and who disappeared the instant we were mounted; so with the exception of two women who were running to the woods, we were the only ones on the lot, until Mr Watson galloped up to urge us on.

Again I had to notice this peculiarity about women—that the married ones are invariably the first to fly, in time of danger, and always leave the young ones to take care of themselves. Here were our three matrons, prophesying that the house would be burnt, the Yankees upon us, and all murdered in ten minutes, flying down the guerilla lane, [p. 16] and leaving us to encounter the horrors they foretold, alone.

It was a splendid gallop in the bright moonlight, over the fields, only it was made uncomfortable by the jerking of my running bag, until I happily thought of turning it before. A hard ride of four miles in about twenty minutes brought us to the house of the man who so kindly offered his hospitality. It was a little hut, about as large as our parlor, and already crowded to overflowing, as he was entertaining three families from B.R. Cant imagine where he put them, either. But it seems to me the poorer the man, and the smaller the house, the greater the hospitality you meet with. There was [sic] so many of us, that there was not room on the balcony to turn. The man wanted to prepare supper, but we declined, as Phillie had sent back for ours which we had missed.

I saw another instance of the pleasure the vulgar take in the horrible. A Mr Hill, speaking of Dr Nolan, told Phillie he had no doubt he had been sent to New Orleans on the Whiteman,[37] that carried Genl Williams body; and that every soul had gone down on her. Fortunately, just then the overseer brought a letter from him saying he had gone on another boat, or the man's relish of the distressing, might have been gratified.

It was so crowded there, that we soon suggested going a short distance beyond, to Mr Lobdell's,[38] and staying there for the night, as all

37. The *Whiteman* sank on the morning of August 7, 1862, after colliding with the USS *Oneida*.

38. The plantation of Abraham Lobdell. Though Sarah does not mention seeing Mrs. Caroline Frémaux and her children at the Lobdell home, Céline Frémaux would later make a note of having met the Morgans there. See Céline Frémaux Garcia, *Celine: Remembering Louisiana, 1858–1871*, edited by Patrick J. Geary (Athens, Ga., 1987), 255.

strenuously objected to our returning home, as there was danger from prowling Yankees. So we mounted again, and after a short ride, we reached the house, where all were evidently asleep. But necessity knows no rules; and the driver soon aroused an old gentleman who came out and invited us in. A middle aged lady met us, and made us perfectly at home by leaving us to take care of ourselves; most people would have thought it indifference; but I knew it was manque de savoir faire,[39] merely, and prefered doing as I pleased. If she had been officious, I would have been embarrassed.

So we walked in the moonlight, Ginnie and I, while the rest sat in the shade, and all discussed the fun of the evening, those who had been most alarmed laughing loudest. The old gentleman insisted that we girls had been the cause of it all; that our white bodice (I wore a russian shirt) and black skirts could easily have caused us to be mistaken for men. That at all events, three or four people on horseback would be a sufficient pretext for firing a shell or two. "In short, young ladies," he said, "there is no [p. 17] doubt in my mind that you were mistaken for guerillas, and that they only waited to give you time to reach the woods where they hear they have a camp, before shooting at you. In short, take my advice, and never mount a horse again when there is a Yankee in sight."

We were highly gratified at being mistaken for them, and pretended to believe it was true. I hardly think he was right, though; it is too preposterous. Pourtant,[40] Sunday morning the Yankees told a negro they did not mean to touch the house, but were shooting at some guerillas at a camp just beyond. We know the last guerilla left the parish five days ago.

Our host insisted on giving us supper, though Phillie represented that ours was on the road; and by eleven o'clock, tired alike of moonlight and fasting, we gladly accepted, and rapidly made the preserves and batter cakes fly. Ours was a garret room, well finished, abounding in odd closets and corners, with curious dormer windows that were reached by long little corridors. I should have slept well; but I lay awake all night. Mother and I occupied a narrow single bed, with a bar of the thickest, heaviest material imaginable. Suffocation awaited me inside,

39. Lack of savoir faire.
40. However.

gnats and mosquitoes out. In order to be strictly impartial, I lay awake to divide my time equally between the two attractions, and think I succeeded pretty well. So I spent the night on the extreme edge of the bed, never turning over, but fanning mother constantly.

I was not sorry when day break appeared, but dressed and ascended the observatory to get a breath of air. Below me, I beheld four wagons loaded with the young Mrs Lobdell's [41] baggage. The Yankees had visited them in the evening, swept off every thing they could lay their hands on, and with a sick child she was obliged to leave her house in the night, and fly to her father in law. I wondered at their allowing her four wagons of trunks and bundles; it was very kind. If I was a Federal, I think it would kill me to hear the whisper of "Hide the silver" where ever I came. Their having frequently relieved families of such trifles, along with negroes, teams, etc,[42] has put others on their guard now.

As I sat in the parlor in the early morning, Mrs Walters en blouse volante and all échevelée,[43] came in to tell me of Mr Lobdell['s] misfortunes. "They took his negroes; (right hand up) his teams; (left hand up) his preserves; (both hands clutching her hair); they swept off everything, except four old women who could not walk! they told him if he didn't come report himself, they'd come fetch him in three days! they beggared him!" (both eyes rolling like a ship in a storm.) I could not help laughing. Mr Bird sat on the gallery, and had been served in [p. 18] the same way, with the addition of a pair of handcuffs for a little while. It was not a laughing matter; but the old lady made it comical by her gestures.

When we suggested returning [to the Nolan home], there was another difficulty. All said it was madness; that they [sic] Yankees would sack the house and burn it over our heads; we would be insulted, etc. I said no one yet had ever said an impudent thing to me, and Yankees cer-

41. Angelina Bird Lobdell, wife of James L. Lobdell and daughter-in-law of Abraham Lobdell.

42. Fearing another attack by the Confederates, Colonel Paine sent detachments into the countryside to round up blacks to work on the fortifications. He ordered his men to bring in as many field hands as possible, but none who had families of children. "If men have wives, who are field hands, and willing to work on fortifications, both will be brought if they desire it." Order dated August 9, 1862, quoted in "Manu Scripta Minora," Paine's unpublished memoir in the collection of Fred G. Benton, Jr.

43. In flying blouse and all disheveled.

tainly would not attempt it; but the old gentleman told me I did not know what I was talking about; so I hushed, but determined to return, Ginnie and I sat an hour on horseback waiting for the others to settle what they would do, and after having half roasted ourselves in the sun, they finally agreed to go too, and we set off in a gallop which we never broke until we reached the house which to our great delight we found standing, and not infested with Yankees.

Linwood. Aug. 12th

Another resting place! Out of reach of shells for the first time since last April! For how long, I wonder? for where ever we go, we bring shells and Yankees. Would not be surprised at a visit from them out here, now!

Let me take up the thread of that never ending story, and account for my present position. It all seems tame now; but it was very exciting at the time. As soon as I threw down bonnet and gloves, I commenced writing; but before I had halfway finished, mother who had been holding a consultation down stairs, ran up to say the overseer had advised us all to leave, as the place was not safe; and that I must pack up instantly, as unless we got off before the Essex came up, it would be impossible to leave at all. All was commotion; every one flew to pack up. Phillie determined to go to her friends at Grosse Tête,[44] and insisted on carrying us off with her. But I determined to reach Miriam and Lilly if possible, rather than put the Federal army between us.

All en déshabillé I commenced to pack our trunk, but had scarcely put an article in, when they cried the Essex was rounding the point, and our last opportunity passing away. Then I flew; and by the time the boat got opposite to us, the trunk was locked, and I sat on it completely dressed waiting for the wagon. We had then to wait for the boat to get out of sight, to avoid a broadside; so it was half past ten before we set

44. Small town about fifteen miles west of Baton Rouge.

of[f], fortified by several glasses of buttermilk apiece. All went in the
carriage except Ginnie, Lilly [Nolan], and me, and we perched on the
baggage in the wagon.

Such stifling heat! The wagon jarred dreadfully, and seated at the extreme [p. 19] end, on a wooden trunk traversed by narrow slats, Ginnie
and I were jolted until we lost our breath, all down Arkansas lane,
when we changed for the front part. I shall never forget the heat of that
day. Four miles beyond, the carriage stopped at some house, and still
determined to get over the river, I stepped in the little cart that held
our trunk, drove up to the side of it, and insisted on mother's getting
in, rather than going the other way with Phillie. I had a slight discussion, and overcame mother's reluctance and Phillie's objections with
some difficulty; but finally prevailed on the former to get in the cart,
and jolted off amid a shower of reproaches, regrets, and good byes. I
knew I was right though; and the idea reconciled me to the heat, dust,
jarring, and gunboat that was coming up behind us.

Six miles more brought us to Mr Cain's,[45] where we arrived at two
o'clock, tired, dirty and almost unrecognizable. We were received with
the greatest cordiality in spite of that. Mother knew both him and his
wife, but though I had never seen either, the latter kissed me as affectionately as though we had known each other. It was impossible to cross
when the gunboat was in sight, so they made us stay with them until
the next morning. A bath, and clean clothes soon made me quite presentable, and I really enjoyed the kindness we met with, in spite of a
"tearing" headache, and a distended feeling about the eyes as though
I never meant to close them again—the consequence of my vigil, I presume. O those dear, kind people! I shall not soon forget them. Mr Cain
told mother he believed he would keep me; at all events, he would
make an exchange, and give her his only son in my place. I told him
I was willing, as mother thought much more of her sons than of her
daughters.

I forgot to say that we met Genl Allen's[46] partner a mile or two from
Dr Nolan's, who told us it was a wise move; that he had intended recom-

45. Dempsey P. Cain, a West Baton Rouge planter. His son Dempsey J. Cain served in
the 1st Louisiana Cavalry.

46. Colonel Henry Watkins Allen of the 4th Louisiana.

mending it. All he owned had been carried off, his plantation stripped. He said he had no doubt that all the coast would be ravaged, and they had promised to burn his, and many other houses, and Dr Nolan's, though it might *possibly* be spared in consideration of his being a prisoner, and his daughters being unprotected, would most probably suffer with the rest; but even if spared, it was no place for women. He offered to take charge of all, and send the furniture in the interior before the Yankees should land, which Phillie gladly acccepted.

[p. 20] What a splendid rest I had at Mrs Cain's! I was not conscious of being alive, until I awaked abruptly in the early morning, with a confused sense of having dreamed something very pleasant. The first dream in a strange house comes true; but I tried in vain to recall it. Sometimes it was all before me, but the same instant it was gone. I only remembered writing a letter to Howell, in which I wished to tell him something that I did not wish to be seen by someone else who must first read it, and that Mr Talbot's name stood out in most extraordinary relief on the page; but what connection it had with the rest, I could not remember.

Mr Cain accompanied us to the ferry some miles above, riding by the buggy, and leaving us under care of Mr Randallson,[47] after seeing us in the large flat, took his leave. After an hour spent at the hotel after landing on this side, we procured a conveyance and came on to Mr Elder's,[48] where we astonished Lilly by our unexpected appearance very much. Miriam had gone over to spend the day with her, so we were all together, and talked over our adventures with the greatest glee. After dinner Miriam and I came over here to see them all, leaving the others to follow later. I was very glad to see Helen Carter once more. If I was not, I hope I may live in Yankee land!—and I cant invoke a more dreadful punishment than that.

Well! here we are, and heaven only knows our next move. Mother stays with Lilly, Miriam and I here. But we must settle on some spot, which seems impossible in the present state of affairs, when no lodgings are to be found. I feel like a homeless beggar. Will P. told them here, that he doubted if our house were still standing, as the fight occured

47. Luther R. Ronaldson.
48. William Elder.

just back of it, and every volley directed towards it. He says he thought of it every time the cannon was fired, knowing where the shot would go. O my lost home! Wonder if Teach left my poor little bird there? I'll never get over it if she did. Poor Jimmy! What an extraordinary waste of paper, in recording all the trifles that led to our forsaking our former haven! But if I had had the power to describe it fully (for absurd as it may seem, it is very much abridged) it would really be an undertaking.

August 13th

I am in despair. Miss Jones who has just made her escape from town, brings a most dreadful account. She, with seventy five others, took refuge [p. 21] at Dr Enders', more than a mile and a half below town, at Hall's.[49] It was there we sent the two trunks containing father's papers and our clothing and silver. Hearing that guerillas had been there, the Yankees went down, shelled the house in the night, turning all those women and children out, who barely escaped with their clothing, and let the soldiers loose on it. They destroyed every thing they could lay their hands on, if it could not be carried off; broke open armoirs, trunks, sacked the house, and left it one scene of devastation and ruin. They even stole Miss Jones' braid! she got here with nothing but the clothes she wore. This is a dreadful blow to me.

Yesterday, I thought myself beggared when I heard that our house was probably burnt, remembering all the clothing, books, furniture etc that it contained; but I consoled myself with the recollection of a large trunk packed in the most scientific style, containing quantities of night gowns, skirts, chemises, dresses, cloaks, in short our very best, which was in safety. Winter had no terrors when I thought of the nice warm clothes; I only wished I had a few of the organdie dresses I had packed up before wearing. And now? It is all gone; silver, father's law papers without which we are beggars, and clothing! Nothing left! I could stand that. But as each little article of Harry's came up before me (I had put many in the trunk) I lost heart. Father's slippers that I made his last birthday, Hal's little gifts to me, the Tennyson I prized more than I

49. Magnolia Mound, the plantation home of George O. Hall just below Baton Rouge, today a museum operated by the Foundation for Historical Louisiana. Hall and his family were in France at this time; Dr. Enders may have been occupying the place because it was safer than his own home.

could say, all that—the teapot that he used as he lay dying, and his shirt I would not have washed after, and his cap—O when I came to that I dropped my head and cried.

They may clothe their negro women with my clothes, since they only steal for them; but to take things so sacred to me! O my God teach me to forgive them! Hal, father! I could lose all cheerfully, if I had only those little tokens! It is hard to bear this patiently. Our dresses that we loaded with lace by way of saving it, are now doing active duty on the sylph like form of some negro women. O men! to disgrace you[r] country, cause, and name by such unheard of outrages! to pillage a whole country to procure apparel for vile negroes! what a stain on humanity!

Poor Miss Jones! they went in her clothes bag and took out articles which were certainly of no service to them, for mere deviltry. There are so many sufferers in this case, that it makes it still worse. The plantation just below[50] was served in the same way; whole families fired into before they knew of the intention of the Yankees; was it not fine sport?

I have always been an advocate of peace—if we could name the conditions *ourselves*—but [p. 22] I say War to the death! I would give my life to be able to take up arms against the vandall[s] who are laying waste our fair land! I suppose it is because I have no longer any thing to lose, that I am desperate. Before, I always opposed the burning of B.R., as a useless piece of barbarism in turning out five thousand women and children on the charity of the world. But I noticed that those who had no interests there, warmly advocated it. Lilly Nolan cried loudly for it; thought it only just; but the first shell that whistled over her father's house, made her crazy with rage. The brutes! the beasts! how cruel! wicked! etc. It was too near home for her, then. There is the greatest difference between *my* property, and *yours*.

I notice that the farther I get from town, the more ardent are the people to have it burned. It recalls very forcibly Thackery's cut in the Virginians,[51] when speaking of the determination of the Rebels to burn the cities; he says he observed that all those who were most eager to burn N. York, were inhabitant[s] of Boston; while those who were most zealous to burn Boston, had all their property in New York. It is true all

50. The plantation of J. M. Williams.
51. Thackeray's novel *The Virginians*.

the world over. And I am afraid I am becoming indifferent about the fate of our town. Anything, so it is speedily settled! Tell me it would be of service to the Confederacy, and I would set fire to my home—if still standing—willingly! But would it?

August 17th.

Another Sunday. Strange that the time, which should seem so endless, flies so rapidly! Miriam complains that Sunday comes every day; but though that seems a little too much, I insist that it comes twice a week. Let time fly, though; for each day brings us so much nearer our destiny, which I long to know.

Thursday, we heard from a lady just from town, that our house was standing the day before, which somewhat consoled us for the loss of our silver and clothing; but yesterday comes the tidings of new afflictions. I declare we have acted out the first chapter of Job, all except that verse about the death of his sons and daughters. God shield us from that! I do not mind the rest. "While he was yet speaking, another came in and said 'thy brethren and kinsmen gathered together to wrest thine abode from the hand of the Philistines which pressed sore upon thee; when lo! the Philistines sallied forth with fire and sword, and laid thine [p. 23] habitation waste and desolate, and I only, am escaped to tell thee.' "[52]

Yes! the Yankees, fearing the Confederates might slip in unseen, resolved to have full view of their movements, so put the torch to all eastward, from Col. Matta's, to the Advocate.[53] That would lay open a fine tract of country, alone; but unfortunately, it is said that once started, it was not so easy to control the flames which spread considerably beyond its appointed limits. Some say it went as far as Florida St.; if so, we are lost, as that is half a square below us. For several days the fire has been burning, but very little can be learned, of the particulars. I am sorry for Col Matta. Such a fine brown stone front, the finest in town. Poor Minna![54] poverty will hardly agree with her. As for our home, I hope against hope. I will not believe it is burnt, until some-

52. The first and last words of this quotation are from Job 1:16.

53. The home of Colonel Andrew Matta was on the north side of North Street in the block just east of Third. See Charles East, *Baton Rouge: A Civil War Album* (Baton Rouge, 1977), 41. For a list of the residences and other buildings burned, see *Weekly Gazette and Comet*, October 22, 1862, p. 1.

54. Minna Matta, Colonel Matta's daughter.

body declares having been present on that occasion. Yet so many frame houses on that square must have readily caught fire from the sparks.

Wicked as it may seem, I would rather have all I own burned, than in the possession of the negroes. Fancy my magenta organdie on a dark beauty! Bah! I think the sight would enrage me! Miss Jones' trials are enough to drive her crazy. She had the pleasure of having four officers in her house, men who sported épaulets and red sashes, accompanied by a negro woman, at whose disposal all articles were placed. The worthy companion of these "gentlemen" walked around selecting things with the most natural airs and graces. "*This*," she would say, "we *must* have. And some of these books, you know, and all the preserves, and these chairs and tables, and all the clothes, of course; and yes! the rest of these things." So she would go on, the "gentlemen" assuring her she had only to cho[o]se what she wanted, and that they would have them removed immediately. Madame thought they really must have the wine, and those handsome cut glass goblets.

I hardly think I could have endured such a scene; to see all I owned given to negroes, without even an accusation being brought against me of disloyalty. One officer departed with a fine velvet cloak on his arm; another took such a bundle of Miss Jones' clothes, that he had to have it lifted by some one else on his horse, and rode off holding it with difficulty. This I heard from herself, yesterday, as I spent the day with Lilly and mother at Mr Elder's, where she is now staying. Can anything more disgraceful be imagined? They all console me by saying there is no one in Baton Rouge [p. 24] who could possibly wear my dresses without adding a considerable piece to the belt. But that is nonsense. Another pull at the corset strings would bring them easily to the size I have been reduced by nature and bones. Besides, O horror! Suppose instead, they should let in a piece of another color? That would annihilate me! Pshaw! I do not care for the dresses, if they had only left me those little articles of father's and Harry's. But that is hard to forgive. If I cry at the thought of Hal's shirt and cap, what would I do if I saw them worn?

Aug 18th.

If I dared keep the diary that is ever in my thoughts, what a book this would be! But it is not to be thought of. Wandering about the world as I now am, with no sacred or convenient spot where I can place any thing with security, it would [be] impossible to do so with any pleasure; for there are some inward thoughts which I would shrink from having rudely exposed. Not that I imagine that any one here would take the trouble to look at this, but because I am told that there are people in the world who might do it from mere curiosity, and I do not know how long it will be before I am thrown among such. So I keep to myself all that is worth recording, and industriously compile a whole volume of trash which even I will never have the patience to review, and which curiosity mongers would soon abandon as a fruitless undertaking. And yet, if I gave away to impulse, I *could* write a diary! Such a one perhaps, that I could actually look over again. But pshaw! throw such ideas to the wind, and save your paper; for really when this is gone, journalizing is at an end; for even if I could procure another book, I cannot carry so many volumes around the world. And if I should lose my greatest consolation under all afflictions—my pen—I really think I would fall victim to despair.

Spendthrift that I am! In fourteen days I have wasted twenty two sheets! this will never do my darling! restrain your ardor against the Yankees, and be more economical with your writing material. How I regret my great, well stocked old desk, with the pigeon holes and drawers! The negroes will hardly need it, so perhaps Col. Dudley will spare it. If Genl. Williams was alive, I would feel secure about our house; for I know he would not suffer it to be plundered as he is one of the few gentlemen who came over in the land force to B.R. The naval officers all appear like gentlemen, and certainly produced that impression on all who saw them; but Heaven defend me from the majority of the "Land forces" as I dubbed them, thinking they merited the title in more ways than one. If our house could be spared—if I could have the faintest hope of ever again beholding it, I think I could be reconciled to my present vagrant life, for a few months.

Father used to say that I had so few wishes, that it would be hard indeed if he could not satisfy them; he believed me so content, in my disposition! I *was* then, but it was because he supplied my wants before I knew them. Dear father! how many discussions we had, as to whether my cheerfulness and contentment arose from my "happy disposition," as he insisted, or from his kindness and indulgence in never letting me want for anything, as I [p. 25] argued! And I was right, O father! for the sunshine died out of my heart when you were taken away! there is no longer the cheerfulness, the amiability there, which you thought existed, though I have often struggled to obtain it; for it was yours, shining on me, that made me appear worthy of love in your eyes, and when that light was withdrawn, it left me in darkness, father. There is nothing worthy of regard or esteem in me. Selfishness, and all evil passions gain on me day by day.

O father when I recall those words so full of care for me "All I regret now, is Sarah. You and Miriam will not want; but I had hoped God would spare me to be with her the few years she has to live; this world will be too hard for her—" O then I cry why was I not taken first? I could have died when Hal went, without an earthly regret; I believed I was more than willing to go, but father's anxious, troubled face haunted me, in my selfish wish. Should he mourn over two? Would I bring tears to his eyes, and bow down his grey head, through mere selfish indifference as to my fate? Ah! how wicked that was! I lived to stand by and hold his hand in mine as he died, I saw him lowered in his grave; by what I felt, I knew what he would have suffered had he stood in my place. I thanked God for the comfort of having been with him; I was grateful that I had been spared. Spared, but for what? Is my life to be spent in selfishly sacrificing the comfort of others, to my own? am I only to seek my own comfort, and follow my own selfish impulses? am I to toil night and day to gain support for a life whose object is not worth the labor bestowed? What labor is it I am to turn to? What am [I] fit for? What can I do?

There is but one question the answer to which is plain before me. That question is Shall I be dependent? and the answer comes with an energy that makes my head throb, Never! take drudgery, take teaching which you abhor, and which will speedily lay you in your grave; take hard crusts and bitter words; take poverty, and hardships; take all that God sends, cheerfully, bear all patiently; but dependence, Never! Death first! Yes! that is the only thing I can plainly see; all else is dark. We are not the only ones beggared by this war; it may not be so bad after all; but if mother was where she could not feel it, if Miriam and I were alone together, I would not mind poverty. I think I could make it a merry jest. It is hard for mother though. I wait, I hope, I strive to look cheerfully forward; but you were right. O father! this world is too hard for me!

Aug 19th

Yesterday two Colonels, Shields & Breaux,[55] both of whom distinguished themselves in the battle of Baton Rouge, dined here. Their
personal appearance was by no means calculated to fill one with awe,
or even to give one an idea of their rank; for their dress consisted of
merely cotonade pants, flanel [sic] shirts, and extremely short jackets,
(which, however, is rapidly becoming the uniform of the Confederates
[sic] States) but still my terror of strangers grew so strong, that when
I got half way down stairs I found it impossible to proceed; and while
endeavoring to conquer my fear by holding fast to the bannisters and
telling myself I was a fool, my position was made doubly embarrassing
by Genl. Carter coming out of the parlor after me, and carrying me in
before I regained my breath. By a queer smile I noticed, I perceived
one of them knew I was frightened; but bah! the introduction over, and
the bow made, and I am afraid of no one! and in five minutes I found
myself again, and congratulated myself on the [p. 26] discovery.

My alarm brought vividly to mind the disgrace I incurred just two
years ago, on a similar occasion, and more than one, reminded me of
the circumstance, which I think I shall never forget. It was in August/
60, when Miriam and I spent four very happy weeks here, that it occurred. Two young gentlemen that we had as yet not met, sent us word
they would call in the evening. Now I never consider that visits are intended for me; I take it for granted that they are meant for Miriam;
but any how I dressed [?] myself, as it was thought necessary for me
to appear. Miriam never looked handsomer; no wonder she was in fine
spirits; I cast one look at the glass—vanish every feeling except self
contempt, which is really a strong [illegible] plaster on sensitive nerves!
I had put the last pin in Miriam, and watched her run down to the
parlor, to await her visiters; then I turned with a sigh to my own toilet,
which consisted merely of a blue organdie with a lace cape, all of which
I put on by myself, until presently Helen Carter came in, reviewed it
all, arranged what she did not like, settled the rest, and with a kiss that
I was really grateful for, pronounced it—some thing or other—which
failed to set me at ease, however, as I felt it was undeserved.

55. Colonel Gustave A. Breaux was in command of the 30th Louisiana and Lieutenant
Colonel Thomas Shields second in command. Breaux practiced law in New Orleans before and after the war. See sketch in *Biographical and Historical Memoirs of Louisiana*,
1:314.

With orders to go down instantly, she left me; but instead of obeying, I sunk on a chair, for at that moment I heard the clank of strange boots in the hall, and had not courage to meet the dread visiters. Shaking with fear, and nervous apprehensions—I really dont know how I happen to be such a fool—I turned to a book to steady my nerves, and soon forgot the ordeal which sooner or later must be passed through, in the interest I took in its pages, when presently my nerves received a shock as of a galvanic battery: a carriage was driving to the door! another one followed! and *was* that a buggy?

I was now desperate; come what may, I shall not go down, I resolved; and after hearing all the strange footsteps enter the parlor, and the bustle of their reception, I sank back in my chair, satisfied that I had escaped the fiery furnace, and had now only to make myself happy and forget my fears; so I was soon absorbed in my book. But the sanctity of my asylum was soon disturbed; voices below repeated my name, I heard some one coming; there was no escape except through the windows, which would allow the strangers to see me in my fall, so I had to stand still. I have not an idea of who it was that forced me to go down; I remember reaching the last step, when with the speed that only desperation can lend, I turned and fled to my room again where I fell in a chair unable to stand.

Again I was forced to the steps, and half way down, I stopped still, and pleaded with all the pathos of a condemned criminal to be allowed to remain up stairs. I did not care for the people! just let me go! I dont know how one could resist such entreaties; it would have melted a heart of stone; but my captors were obdurate; and I found myself downstairs again. I caught Mrs Carter's hand, and begged for mercy as I never begged before. I believe I was crazy. She reasoned, she argued, she threatened, by turns; and I still pleaded wildly. "How can you be so foolish?" she asked. "Shame on you. *You* a girl who [words lined through]" (I came "out" before I was [word lined through])[56] "*you* act so childishly? What [p. 27] would your sister Beatrice say? I'll write to her and tell her how you behave and let her know that after all her trouble with you in New Orleans, you are afraid to meet eight or ten country people! did you act this way in the city?" "O" I would sob, "Sister made it so easy for me! She used to hold my hand until I got

56. Sarah wrote "seventeen" and then lined through it and wrote "sixteen I was."

to the door. I was not afraid with her. Please let me go." "I'll write to your father!" "Father would never force me to go in! O do let me go!" I know I had her sympathy, but she thought she was doing her duty, so she insisted.

Worn out with my pleadings, no longer able to resist, I consented to surrender on my own terms, which were that she should hold my hand tightly, and introduce me to the married lady next to whom there was a vacant Chair, and by degrees introduce me to the rest, or rather leave me to speak to them as I felt inclined. No! I must be introduced formally. With my horror of introductions, imagine the effect of this sentence on me! It was too late though; I was at the door; some sixteen pair of eyes were on me; I grasped for the promised hand; it was gone! scarcely less afraid than I, Helen Carter had escaped, and I was making my entrée with Mrs Badger! I heard "Dr Purnell, Miss Morgan, "Mrs Purnell, Mr Newport, Mr Sambola, Mr—"[57] hear [sic] I lost all sense of sight and sound.

Unable to endure the torture, unfitted for anything except my room, after the previous scenes, conscious that I was making myself ridiculous, and disgracing myself by such shocking behavior; with the dim idea of cold eyes and strange faces looking at me with contempt in them for my strange conduct; that Miriam was justly angry at my shocking appearance, and Sister disgraced in me, as a chaperon; feeling I had forfeited all claims to respectability and regard, I fell back motionless on the door which was thrown wide open as it is now (I am sitting on the very field of my disgrace) and knew nothing, felt nothing, except that I was disgraced for ever. I no longer saw the stony eyes; I saw only blank space before me. Presently a warm, friendly hand took mine, and led me to a large arm chair in which my trembling limbs dropped me without the slightest effort on my part; another was drawn near; some one was bending over so as to screen me from part of the faces, and was talking without asking for answers. It was Will Pinkney to the rescue!

Heaven bless him for that kind deed! my heart swells every time

57. Dr. George W. Purnell and his wife Mary lived near Port Hudson. Robert Newport was the son of Simpson W. Newport, a nearby landowner. He and Anthony Sambola of New Orleans had graduated from Centenary College in the class of 1857, and no doubt were the two young gentlemen who had come calling.

I think of what I suffered, and how he comforted me. I had waited so long, that refreshments followed a few moments after my appearance. They needed comfort after the shock I had given them! Will piled my plate with almonds, raisin[s], cakes, and industriously peeled my peaches and spread a napkin over my dress, and tried to talk me out of my apathy. But it was hopeless. Seeing I was in no condition to be tempted by the peaches, etc, he whispered "Will you go on the gallery?" I found my voice "O yes" I said eagerly, regaining my feet. He offered his arm, and followed by the surprised look of the whole assembly, took me on the balcony where I managed to regain my self possession, and acted like a christian for the first time during the evening.

No argument could again induce me to enter the parlor, and none could make him leave me, so we stood out there and talked until the younger portion of the company came out and proposed a walk to the sawmill. Will looked at me and said "Let me walk with you." "Yes indeed!" I said heartily, thankful to have escaped the company of one of [p. 28] those who had witnessed my disgrace. How I hated them for having seen me and how I despised myself for my folly! I never spoke to one until they bowed good bye which salute I returned with alacrity. Miriam walked with the two first arrivals, I followed with Will, the rest came behind. I sang Hallelujahs in my heart, though still ashamed of my conduct; I was thankful that Will, at least, was not ashamed of me. And that is the story of the severest mortification I ever endured. Miriam afterwards told it to father, but I had all his sympathy. He said it was a foolish timidity I should strive to overcome, but did not reprove me for a weakness he knew came woven in my very bones. I have struggled hard to overcome it, but whatever the outside may be, the inside is as weak as ever.

Just three lines back, three soldiers came in to ask for molasses. I was alone down stairs, and the nervous trepidation with which I received the dirty, coarsely clad strangers who however looked as though they might be gentlemen, has raised a laugh against me by the others who looked down from a place of safety. I dont know what I did that was out of the way. I felt odd receiving them as though it was my home, and having to answer their questions about buying, by means of acting as telegraph between them and Mr Carter. I confess to that. But I know I talked reasonably about the other subjects.

Playing hostess in a strange house! Of course it was uncomfortable! And to add to my embarrassment, the handsomest one offered to pay for the milk he had just drank! Fancy my feelings, as I hastened to assure him that Genl Carter never received money for such things, and from a soldier, besides, it was not to be thought of! He turned to the other saying "In Mississippi we dont meet with such people! Miss, they dont hesitate to charge four bits a canteen for milk. They take all they can. They are not like you Louisianians." I was surprised to hear him say it of his own state, but told him we thought here we could not do enough for them.

Miriam is angry because my hands were cold when I went upstair[s]. She says it is nothing but stupidity that makes me timid. Perhaps; but should she not be more lenient, since both the flesh and the spirit are weak? Now I understand the meaning of Genl Carter's words, when speaking of the difference between Miriam and me, the other night. She was a Woman, he said; and I never would be one; if I lived to be old, still I would die a child. Strange! many have said that. Dr Woods says that at thirty my face will be as young as now; and a few months ago, Mr Lusher [?][58] who had not seen me since I was seven years old, greeted me with "I cannot mistake you; you have never changed!" Well! if I can preserve the child heart, with the child face, I do not care to be a Woman.

Aug 20th.

Last evening, after hard labor at pulling molasses candy, needing some relaxation after our severe exertions, we determined to have some fun, though the sun was just setting in clouds as watery as New Orleans milk, and promised an early twilight. All day it had been drizzling, but that was nothing; so Anna Badger,[59] Miriam and I set off through the mud, to get up the little cart to ride in, followed by cries from the elder ladies of "Girls! Soap is a dollar and a half a bar! Starch a dollar a pound! take up those skirts!" We had all started stiff and clean, and it

58. Sarah may be recalling Robert Mills Lusher, clerk of the U.S. district court in New Orleans, later a well-known educator. He was the nephew of Charleston architect Robert Mills.

59. Daughter of Wallace and Mary Badger, and niece of General Carter. Anna was 16 when Sarah wrote this.

did seem a pity to let them drag; so up they went—you can imagine how high when I tell you my answer to Anna's question as to whether her's were in danger of touching the mud, was "Not unless you [p. 29] sit down."

The only animal we could discover that was not employed, was a poor old pony, most appropriately called Tom Thumb, and him we seized instantly together with a man to harness him. We accompanied him from the stables to the quarter where the cart was, through mud and water urging him on with shouts and cries, and laughing until we could laugh no longer, at the appearance of each. The cart had been hauling wood, but that was nothing to us. In we tumbled, and with a driver as diminutive as the horse, started off for Mr Elder's, where we picked up all the children to be found, and went on. All told, we were twelve, drawn by that poor horse who seemed at each step about to undergo the ham process, and leave us his hind quarters, while he escaped with the fore ones and harness. I dare say we never enjoyed a carriage as much, though each was holding a muddy child.

Riding was very fine; but soon came the question of how shall we turn? which was not so easily solved, for neither horse nor boy understood it in the least. Every effort to describe a circle brought us the length of the cart farther up the road, and we promised fair to reach Bayou Sara [60] before morning, at that rate. At last after fruitless efforts to dodge under the harness and escape, pony came to a standstill, and could not be induced to move. The children took advantage of the pause to tumble out, but we sat still. Bogged, and it was very dark already! Wouldn't we get it when we got home! Anna groaned "Uncle Albert!" Miriam laughed "the General!" I sighed "Mrs Carter!" we knew what we deserved; and darker and darker it grew, and pony still inflexible! At last we beheld a buggy on a road near by and in answer to Morgan's shouts of "uncle! uncle! [61] come turn our cart!" a gentleman jumped out and in an instant performed the Herculean task. Pony found motion so agreeable, that it was with the greatest difficulty we prevailed on him to stop while we fished seven children out of the mud, as they pursued his flying hoofs.

60. An important shipping point on the river near St. Francisville.

61. In the South, elderly black males were commonly addressed as "Uncle."

Once more at Mr Elder's, we pitched them out without ceremony, and drove home as fast as possible, trying to fancy what punishment we would receive for being out so late. Miriam suggested, as the most horrible one, being sent to bed supperless; Anna's terror was the General's displeasure; I suggested being deprived of rides in future; when all agreed that mine was the most severe yet. So as we drove around the circle, those two set up what was meant for a hearty laugh to show "they were not afraid" which however sounded rather shaky to me. I dont think any of us felt like facing the elders; Miriam suggested anticipating our fate by retiring voluntarily to bed; Anna thought we had best run up and change our shoes any way; but at last with her dare devil laugh Miriam sauntered in the room, where they all were, followed by us, and thrusting her wet feet into the fire that was kindled to drive away the damp (follow[ed] also by us) commenced a laughable account of our fun—in which we, of course, followed too. If I had fancied we were to escape scott free, we would most assuredly have got a scolding. It is almost an inducement to hope always for the—worst! The General did not mention the hour! did not prohibit future rides!

While we were yet toasting, a negro came in with what seemed a bank note and asked his master to see how much it was, as one of the women had sold some of her watermelons to the three soldiers of the morning, who had give[n] that to her for a dollar. The General opened it. It was a pass! So vanish all faith in human nature! They looked so honest! I could never have [p. 30] believed it of them! But it looked so much like the "shinplasters"[62] we are forced to use, that no wonder they made the mistake. To discover who had played so mean a trick on the poor old woman, the General asked me if I could decipher the name. I threw myself on my knees by the hearth, and by the flickering light read "S. Himes [?]. By order of C.! H.!! Luzenberg!!![63] Provost Marshal!!!! Okolona Miss.," with a gasp of astonishment that raised a burst of laughter against me. Thought he was taken prisoner long ago!

62. Small paper notes issued by merchants and others as change. They took the place of coins during wartime, and were usually in denominations ranging from five cents to fifty cents.

63. Lieutenant (later Captain) Charles H. Luzenberg, a young New Orleans attorney, served in the 13th Louisiana. Obviously Sarah was acquainted with him. He was the son of Dr. Charles A. Luzenberg, a well-known surgeon who had died some years earlier.

At all events, I did not know he had turned banker, or that his valuable autograph was worth a dollar!

Aug 21st.

Helen Carter and I had a curious conversation yesterday, the subject of which I promised her to record here, by way of remembering, this, certainly the greatest compliment I ever received. Speaking of second marriages, she strongly expressed her disapprobation of them, in which I could not agree, as I think it perfectly natural. She went on saying that there was but one person on earth she would be willing to have as a successor, and that one was—I!! Talk about compliments! Can any thing equal this? Where is there a woman, who in perfect health and fine spirits, of a jealous disposition and adoring her husband, could seriously and ernestly recommend a friend to take her place after her death? It is a perfect farce. She told me I must always remember it was her most ernest wish, and if I did not marry him, she would haunt me for ever afterwards. I answered that it was too serious a charge to commit to memory; but I would record it, to bear it in mind! O Helen Carter! what a mistaken woman you are, in regard to my merits. But bah! Serious as she tried to be yesterday, if I remind her of it two years from now, she will be as surprised then, as I am now. At least it has the merit of originality.

Miriam and mother are going to Baton Rouge in a few hours, to see if anything can be saved from the general wreck. From the reports of the removal of the Penetentiary machinery, State Library, Washington Statue, etc.,[64] we presume that that part of the town yet standing is to be burnt like the rest. I think though, that mother has delayed too long. However, I dreamed last night that we had saved a great deal, in trunks; and my dreams sometimes come true. Waking with that impression, I was surprised a few hours after, to hear mother's sudden determination. But I also dreamed I was about to marry a Federal officer! That was in consequence of having answered the question, whether I would

64. Books and paintings in the State House as well as the Hiram Powers statue of Washington that stood in the rotunda were crated up and shipped to New Orleans by order of General Butler. From there the statue was sent to Washington, D.C., where it was on display in the Patent Office. It was eventually returned to the state, but was destroyed in an 1871 fire in New Orleans.

do so, with an emphatic "Yes! if I loved him," which will probably ruin my reputation as a patriot, in this parish. Bah! I am no bigot!—or fool either.

I hate to record mean things even about mean people; but I must say this about master Henry Walsh,[65] as I mean to make him feel his insolence if I ever have the pleasure of beholding his amiable countenance again. Will Pinkney asked him if the reports that were so industriously spread in the country about our receiving Federal officers were true. The gentleman answered "O yes! but they repented afterwards, and are now behaving very well, I believe." Mr Henry Walsh! [words lined through] entirely from those who are supposed to be most intimate with us. Hang such friends. Here are [p. 31] these Hope Estate people,[66] our near relatives, knowing we had no place to go to after we were forced to fly from our home where we were hourly exposed to alarms of all kinds, knowing we could barely save our most necessary clothing, and that we three women were totally unprotected, never offered to take charge of the smallest parcel of valuables for us, never offered us an hour's shelter under their roof, never asked whether we were alive or dead though the young men our cousins were in town daily, except once, when aunt Adèle sent a negro woman to ask if we were frightened! which considerate message I returned by a defiant "Tell her not in the least!" that I hope the woman imitated.

Hang such people! And yet, let us get back to our house, let peace be established, and we have our natural protectors once more, and I would bet a thousand to one, that they would call daily, and kiss us too, and also lunch with us as they used to do; and it would be Cousin this, and that, as affectionate as possible. Hang such people I cry!

Thank heaven, no debt of gratitude or *anything else* lies on our side. Think of Waller Fowler[67] coming from N.O. after its fall, where he saw mother and all of them; coming to B.R., where I was ignorant as to whether Jimmy had died from his severe illness, had escaped, or had been taken prisoner; when nothing but a letter arriving on that

65. Of Hope Estate.

66. Sarah is referring to her aunts Caroline Morgan and Adèle Fowler and their children, who lived at the Hicky plantation.

67. A first cousin, son of Sarah's Aunt Adèle Fowler.

Thursday, by the last mail that was brought to town, saved me from the misery of believing he had been lost on the McRae; when I was in ignorance of his fate, as well as of that of mother, and Miriam, whom this amiable and considerate youth told strangers was lying extremely ill (which was of course instantly reported to me) this model Cousin calls daily on the most utter strangers in town, without approaching me, (though he knew how I was situated, for he could not have turned a corner with out hearing the story of our suspense) parades the streets daily, and never so much as sent me word that Jimmy was alive. I did not want to see him; but there was not a negro in town who would not joyfully have taken the message to me, out of common charity; and if Mr Fowler could not have spared a dime, I would have give[n] all I had to repay the trouble.

After waiting three weeks for one token of still dwelling in his highness recollection, finding none came, I sent him a message of thanks for his courtesy by Bena. She must have made it considerably worse, for he afterwards told mother he dared not approach me after. Nor did he, until six weeks after his arrival, when he called one morning to ask my opinion as to whether Mrs Brunots house was in danger of being seized during her absence. I gave my opinion of No; at all events, I would warn her. Exit Lieut. Fowler whom I have never since beheld, and whom I care never more to see.

With all my soul, I cry hang such people! I refrained from all words at the time; now, involuntarily they have formed themselves here. The door is open; a vent is found; my rage has burst forth and deluged kin in—ink. All is over, and the country safe! I believe I could kill Waller honestly, if he would only give me the opportunity of telling him what I think, to his face. But is he man enough to listen? Bah! let him rest. He is not worth the paper and ink I have wasted; so here is an end of him.

Aug 23d.

Yesterday Anna and I spent the day with Lilly and the rain in the evening obliged us to stay all night. Dr Perkins[68] stopped there, and repeated the same old stories we have been hearing, about [p. 32] the

---

68. Dr. Jehu Perkins, whose plantation was a few miles southeast of Baton Rouge, on what became known as the Perkins Road.

powder placed under the State House and Garrison, to blow them up, if forced to evacuate the town. He confirms the story about all the convicts being set free,[69] and the town being pillage[d] by the negroes and the rest of the Yankees. He says his own slaves told him they were allowed to enter the houses and help themselves, and what they did not want, the Yankees either destroyed on the spot, or had it carried to the Garrison and burned. They also bragged of having stopped ladies on the street, cut their necklaces from their necks, and stripped the rings from their fingers, without hesitation. It may be that they were just bragging to look great in the eyes of their master; I hope so; for heaven help them if they fall in the hands of the Confederates, if it is true.

I could not record all the stories of wanton destruction that reach us. I would rather not believe that the Federal Government could be so disgraced by its own soldiers. Dr Day says they left nothing at all in his house, and carried everything off from Dr Enders. He does not believe we have a single article left in ours.[70] I hope they spared Miriam's piano. But they say the soldiers had so many that they offered them for sale at five dollars a piece! We heard that the town had been completely evacuated, and all had gone to N.O. except three gunboats that were preparing to shell, before leaving.[71]

This morning Withers' battery[72] passed Mr Elder's on their way to P. Hudson, and stopped to get water. There were several buckets served by several servants; but I took possession of one, and filled the canteens as fast as the soldiers handed them to me, to their great amusement. What a profusion of thanks over a can of water! It made me smile, and they smiled to see my work, so it was all very funny. It was astonishing to see the number of Yankee canteens in the possession of our

69. On August 18, 1862, Colonel Halbert E. Paine, about to evacuate his men from the city, wrote that he had "released the prisoners from the penitentiary and confined them on a transport." See "Manu Scripta Minora." An August 20 order quoted in the same source reveals that the prisoners were taken aboard the *Laurel Hill.*

70. On August 13, 1862, Colonel James W. McMillan wrote General Butler from Baton Rouge: "This place has been nearly completely sacked by the soldiery. Scarcely a single house has escaped, all the citizens having fled. . . . Even officers' tents are filled with furniture from deserted houses." *OR,* ser. I, 53:533–34.

71. The Union army withdrew from the city on August 21, 1862, but returned the following December.

72. The 1st Mississippi Light Artillery commanded by Colonel William T. Withers.

men. Almost all those who fought at B.R. are provided with them. In their canvass, and wire cases, with neat stoppers, they are easily distinguished from our rough, flat, tin ones.

I declare I felt ever so important in my new situation as waiting maid! There is very little we would not do for our soldiers, though. There is mother, for instance, who got on her knees to bathe the face and hands of a fever struck soldier of the Arkansas, while the girls held the plates of those who were too weak to hold them and eat at the same time. Blessed is the Confederate soldier who has even [a] tooth ache, when there are women near! What sympathy and remedies are volunteered!

I always laugh, as I did then, when I think of the supposed wounded man those girls discovered on that memorable Arkansas day. I must first acknowledge that it was my fault; for seized with compassion for a man supported by two others who headed the procession, I cried "O look! he is wounded!" "O poor fellow!" screamed the others while tears and exclamation flowed abundantly, until one of the men, smiling humorously cried out "Nothing the matter with him!" and on nearer view, I perceived it was laziness, or perhaps something else, and was forced to laugh at the streaming eyes of those tender hearted girls. I am afraid I have very little feeling. All the girls had wet cheeks and red noses and—handkerchiefs—(which I certainly had not) when the officers joined us, except myself. Cold hearted!

[p. 33] Aug 24th Sunday.

Soon after dinner yesterday two soldiers stopped here, and requested permission to remain all night. The word "soldier" was enough for us; and without even seeing them, Anna and I gladly surrendered our room, and said we would sleep in Mrs Badger's, instead. However, I had no curiosity to see the heroes, and remained up here reading until the bell summoned me to supper, when I took my seat with out looking at them, as no introduction was possible, from their having refrained from giving their names.

Presently I heard the words "That retreat from Norfolk was badly conducted."[73] I looked up, and saw before me a rather good looking man covered with the greatest profusion of gold cloth and buttons,

73. The Confederates had withdrawn from Norfolk, Virginia, on May 9, 1862.

which I instinctively felt he was proud of, and for which I intuitively despised him. The impulse seized me, so I spoke. "Were you there?" "No; but near by. I was there with the first La.[74] for 'most a year." "Do you know George Morgan?" "Know George? yes indeed! you are his sister." This was an assertion; but I bowed assent and he went on "Thought so, from the resemblance. I remember seeing you ten years ago, when you were a very little girl. I used to be at your house with the boys; we were schoolmates." I remarked that I had no recollection of him. "Of course not," he said, but did not inform me of his name. He talked very familiarly of the boys, and said he had met them all at Richmond.

Next he astounded me by saying he was a citizen of Baton R., though he had been almost four years in N. York before the war broke out. He was going to town to look after "the property," hearing his father had gone to France. An inhabitant of that city, who was so familiar with my brothers and me, and with whom I was not acquainted! Here was a riddle to solve. Let us see who among our acquaintances had gone to France! I could think of none. I made up my mind to find out his name if I had to ask it.

All through supper he talked, and when, in country style, the gentlemen left us at table, I found the curiosity of the others was even more excited than mine. I was determined to know who he was, then. In the parlor, he made some remark about never having been in ladies' society the whole time he was in Virginia. I expressed my surprise, as George often wrote of the pleasant young ladies he met everywhere. "O yes!" said monsieur "but it is impossible to do your duty as an officer, and be a lady's man; so I devoted myself to my military profession exclusively." "Insufferable puppy!" I said to myself. "Does he mean that George neglected his duties?" (my heart got beating so at the thought of his insolence that I could scarcely control myself.) I said to myself again "This is a low, ill bred man, who suddenly inheriting a military coat, thinks to impose on me, for a gentleman, by contrasting George's privilege, as a gentleman by birth, of visiting his equals, with his own 'devotion to his profession' to which he was compelled to resort, by a cold shoulder, occasionally. He is a puppy by birth and education."

One piece of insolence stung me to the quick, and I came very near

74. The 1st Louisiana Infantry (Volunteers).

putting myself on an equality with him, by uttering the words that quivered on my lips, and that certainly would have left an impression on him. I said we had never yet heard whether George had been engaged in a battle; it was long since he had written. Adjusting his gold cuffs the man said "O George's position as Adjutant [p. 34] relieves him from that kind of thing. You should not be uneasy about him. The General's fancy staff are relieved from fighting, unless they want to." I curbed the words on my tongue, and merely said "My brother would hardly shirk a fight, sir." "O yes! but it is not his place, you know," he hastened to inform me. How dare he say that about my brother, than whom a braver man never lived? I trembled with anger. "This man is *very* low" I said to my confidant Sarah. "He is a brave among women, and not quite the thing among men. Yes! he must be from the basse classe."[75]

Then he told me of how his father thought he was dead, and asked if I had heard of his rallying twenty men at Manassas, and charging a Federal regiment, which instantly broke. I honestly told him No. "Iagoo,[76] the great boaster," I decided. Abruptly he said there were very few nice young ladies in B.R. "Probably so, in *his* circle" I thought, while I dryly remarked "Indeed?" "O yes!" and still more abruptly he said "Aint you the youngest?" "Yes." "Thought so! remember you when you were a wee thing, so high" placing his hand at a most insultingly short distance from the floor. "Really I must ask your name" I said. He hesitated a moment and then said in a low tone "St Martin." "St What?" I absurdly asked, thinking I was mistaken. "William St. Martin" he repeated. I bowed slightly to express my satisfaction, said "Anna, we must retire" and with a goodnight to my newly discovered gentleman, went up stairs where I made Helen Carter laugh heartily at my story.

I had been talking with Alex. St. Martin the brewer's son! No wonder I did not remember him! What's the price of small beer? I might have asked him. He omitted to say "the property" consisted of a beer garden, and vats and empty bottles. However his father went to France to claim an immense fortune, and perhaps he thought I might mistake him for a gentleman, knowing his "Great expectations;" pas si bête![77] I always know the parvenu. He is the one I heard George speak of last

75. Lower class.
76. Character in Longfellow's *Song of Hiawatha*.
77. Tell me another!

December when he was here, as having been court martialed, and shot, according to the universal belief in the army;[78] that was the only time I ever heard his name, though I am quite familiar with the beer cart of St Martin, père, which daily perambulates the streets.

My first impressions are seldom erroneous. From the first, I knew that man's respectability was derived from his buttons. That is why he took such pride in them, and contemplated them with such satisfaction. They lent him social back bone enough to converse so familiarly with me; with out the effulgence of that splendid gold, which he hoped would dazzle my eye to his real position, he would have hardly dared to "remember me when I was a wee thing, so high." Is he the only man whose coat alone entitles him to respectability? He may be Colonel for all I know; but still he is W. St Martin to me. He talked brave enough to be General of the—home brewed.

This morning I met him with a cordial "good morning *Mr* St Martin," anxious to atone for several "snubs" I had given him, long before I knew his name (last night); you see I could afford to be patronising now. But the name probably, and the fluency with which I pronounced it, proved too much for him and after "good morning Miss Morgan," he did not venture a word. We knew each other then; his name was no longer a secret.

[p. 35] August 25th. About 12 at night.

Sleep is impossible after all I have heard, so after vainly endeavoring to follow the example of the rest, and sleep like a stoic, I have lighted my candle and take to this to induce drowsiness. Just after supper, when Anna and I were sitting with Mrs Carter in her room, I talking as usual of home, and saying I would be perfectly happy if mother would decide

78. William St. Martin had enlisted as a first sergeant in Company F, 1st Louisiana Volunteers, but transferred to Company H, which later became part of a Kentucky regiment. His father operated the Baton Rouge Brewery.

to remain in Baton Rouge and brave the occasional shellings, I heard a well known voice take up some sentence of mine from a dark part of the room, and with a cry of surprise, I was hugging Miriam until she was breathless. Such a forlorn creature! so dirty, tired, and fatigued, as to be hardly recognizable.

We thrust her in a chair, and made her speak. She had just come with Charlie, who went after them yesterday; and had left mother and the servants at a kind friend's, on the road. I never heard such a story as she told. I was heart sick; but I laughed until Mrs Badger grew furious with me and the Yankees, and abused me for not abusing them. She says when she entered the house, she burst into tears at the desolation. It was one scene of ruin. Libraries emptied, china smashed, sideboards split open with axes, three cedar chests cut open, plundered, and set up on end; all parlor ornaments carried off—even the alabaster Apollo and Diana that Hal valued so much. Her piano, dragged to the center of the parlor, had been abandoned as too heavy to carry off; her desk lay open with all letters and notes well thumbed and scattered around, while Will's last letter to her was open on the floor, with the Yankee stamp of dirty fingers.

Mother's portrait half cut from its frame stood on the floor. Margret who was present at the sacking, told how she had saved father's. It seems that those who wrought the destruction in our house, were all officers. One jumped on the sofa to cut the picture down (Miriam saw the prints of his muddy feet) when Margret cried "For God's sake, gentlemen, let it be! I'll help you to anything here. He's dead, and the young ladies would rather see the house burn than lose it!" "I'll blow your damned brains out" was the "gentlemans" answer as he put a pistol to her head, which a brother officer dashed away, and the picture was abandoned for finer sport. All the others were cut up in shreds. Up stairs was the finest fun. Mother's beautiful mahogany armoir, whose single door was an extremely fine mirror, was entered by crashing through the glass, when it was emptied of every article, and the shelves half split, and half thrust back crooked. Letters labeled by the boys "Private," were strewn over the floor; they opened every armoir and drawer, collected every rag to be found and littered the whole house with them, until the wonder was, where so many rags had been found. Father's armoir was relieved of every thing; Gibbes' handsome Damascus sword with the silver scabbard included. All his clothes, George's, Hal's, Jimmy's, were appropriated.

They entered my room, broke that fine mirror for sport, pulled down the rods from the bed, and with them, pulverized my toilet set, taking also all Lydia's china ornaments I had packed in the washstand. The débris filled my basin, and ornamented my bed. My desk was broken open. Over it was spread all my letters, and [p. 36] private papers, a diary I kept when twelve years old, and sundry tokens of dried roses, etc., which must have been *very* funny, they all being labled with the donor's name, and the occasion! Fool! how I writhe when I think of all they saw; the invitations to buggy rides, concerts, "Compliments of," etc.—! Lilly's sewing machine had disappeared; but as mother's was too heavy to move, they merely smashed the needles.

In the pillaging of the armoirs, they seized a pink flounced muslin of Miriam's, which one officer placed on the end of a bayonet, and paraded around with, followed by the others who slashed it with their swords crying "I have stuck the damned Secesh! that's the time I cut her!" and continued their sport until the rags could no longer be pierced. One seized my bonnet, with which he decked himself, and ran in the streets. Indeed, all who found such, rushed frantically around town by way of frolicking, with the things on their heads. They say no frenzy could surpass it. Another snatched one of my calico dresses, and a pair of vases that mother had when she was married, and was about to decamp, when a Mrs Jones[79] jerked them away, and carried them to her boarding house, and restored them to mother the other day. Blessed be heaven! I have a calico dress! Our clothes were used for the vilest purposes, and spread in every corner—at least those few that were not stolen.

Aunt Barker's Charles[80] tried his best to defend the property. "Aint you 'shamed to destroy all dis here, that belongs to a poor widow lady who's got two daughters to support?" he asked of an officer who was

79. Mrs. S. E. Jones operated The Central House, a boarding house, in a two-story residence on the north side of Laurel Street between Church and Third not far from the Morgan home.

80. Charles Barker appears to have been a slave or former slave of Sarah's Aunt Barker. The widowed Ann Morgan Barker had returned to the North sometime before the war. Charles may have lived on or near the Morgan property.

foremost in the destruction. "Poor? Damn them! I dont know when I have seen a house furnished like this! look at that furniture! *they* poor!" was the retort, and thereupon the work went bravely on, of making us poor indeed.

It would have fared badly with us, had we been there. The servants say they broke in the house crying "Where are those damned Secesh women? We know they are hid in here, and we'll make them dance for hiding from Federal officers!" and they could not be convinced that we were not there, until they had searched the very garret. Wonder what they would have done? Charles caught a Captain Clark,[81] in the streets, when the work was almost over, and begged him to put an end to it. The gentleman went readily, but though the devastation was quite evident, no one was to be seen, and he was about to leave, when insisting that there was someone there, Charles drew him in my room, dived under the bed, and drew from thence a Yankee Captain, by one leg, followed by a lieutenant, each with a bundle of the boys' clothes, which they instantly dropped, protesting they were only looking around the house. The gentleman Captain carried them off to their superior.

Ours was the most shockingly treated house in the whole town.[82] We have the misfortune to be equally feared by both sides, because we will blackguard neither. So the Yankees selected the only house in town that sheltered three forlorn women, to wreak their vengeance on, just as our own people would have done, thanks for the reports of our kind relatives at Hope Estate, who Mr McHatton[83] says, satisfied him that we were all Yankees. Bless their kind hearts!

[p. 37] From far and near, strangers and friends flocked in to see the ravages committed. Crowds rushed in before, crowds came in after, Miriam and mother arrived, all apologizing for the intrusion, but saying they had heard it was a sight never before seen. So they let them

81. Possibly Captain Charles E. Clark of Company D, 6th Michigan, or Captain John Clark, identified by John Dougherty as being from Boston and one of General Williams's aides. See Dougherty diary, entry of May 30, 1862.

82. Another Baton Rouge woman, Eliza McHatton, described the looted Morgan home in a memoir written after the war. She wrote that the scene left her "heart-sick and indignant." See Eliza McHatton-Ripley, *From Flag to Flag* (New York, 1889), 49–50.

83. James A. McHatton, a prominent Baton Rougean whose plantation, Arlington, was on the river a few miles south of the city. His wife Eliza later married a New Englander, Dwight Ripley.

examine to their hearts content; and Miriam says the sympathy of all was extraordinary. A strange gentleman picked up a piece of mother's mirror, which was as thick as his finger, saying "Madame, I should like to keep this as a memento. I am about to travel through Mississippi, and having seen what a splendid piece of furniture this was, and the state your house is left in, should like to show this as a specimen of Yankee vandalism."

William Waller[84] flew to our home to try to save it; but was too late. They say he burst into tears as he looked around. While on his kind errand, another band of Yankees burst into his house, and left not one article of clothing to him, except the suit he had on. The whole talk is about our dreadful treatment at the Yankees hands. Dr Day, and Dr Ender's, in spite of the assertions of the former lost nothing.

Well! I am beggared! Strange to say, I dont feel it. Perhaps it is the satisfaction of knowing my fate, that makes me so cheerful that Mrs Carter envied my stoicism, while Mrs Badger felt like beating me because I did not agree that there was no such thing as a gentleman in the Yankee army. I know Major Drum[85] for one, and that Capt. Clark must be two, and Mr Biddle is three, and Gen Williams—God bless him where ever he is! for he certainly acted like a Christian. The Yankees boasted loudly that if it had not been for him, the work would have been done long ago.

And now, I am determined to see my home, before Yankee shells complete the work that Yankee axes spared. So by sunrise, I shall post over to Mr Elder's, and insist on Charlie taking me to town with him. I hardly think it is many hours off. I feel so settled, so calm! just as though I never meant to sleep again. If I only had a desk—a luxury I have not enjoyed since I left home,—I could write for hours still, without being sleepy; but this curved attitude is hard on my stiff back, so good night, while I lie down to gain strength for a sight they say will make me faint with distress. Nous verrons! if I say I Wont, I know I'll not cry.

The Brunots' lost nothing at all from their house, thank heaven for the mercy! Only they lost all their money in their flight. On the door,

84. Sarah's cousin.
85. Her brother-in-law.

on their return, they found written "Ladies, I have done my best for you," signed by a Yankee soldier, which they suppose to be the one who has made it a habit of continually passing their house.

Forgot to say Miriam recovered my guitar from the Asylum, our large trunk and father's papers (untouched) from Dr Ender's, and with her piano, the two portraits, a few mattresses (all that is left of housekeeping affairs) and father's law books, carried them out of town. For which I say in all humility, Blessed be God who has spared us so much. How ungrateful I would be, to complain when we have been so fortunate after all. Have I cause to complain? True, the house, furniture, clothing, etc., are lost but—trust in God!

[p. 38] Thursday Aug. 28.

I am satisfied. I have seen my home again. Tuesday I was up at sunrise, and my few preparations were soon completed, and before any one was awake, I walked over to Mr Elder's through mud and dew to meet Charlie. Fortunate was it for me that I started so early; for I found him hastily eating his breakfast and ready to leave. He was very much opposed to my going; and for some time I was afraid he would force me to remain; but at last he consented—perhaps because I did not insist— and with wet feet, and without a particle of breakfast, I at length found myself in the buggy on the road home. The ride afforded me a series of extraordinary surprises. Half the time I found myself half way out of the little low necked buggy when I thought I was safely in, and the other half, I was surprised to find myself really in, when I thought I was wholly out. And so on, for mile after mile, over muddy roads, until we came to a most terrific cross road, leading to the plank road,[86] where we were obliged to pass, and which is best undescribed. Four miles from town we stopped at Mrs Brown's to see mother, and after a few moments' talk, went on on our road.

I saw the first Yankee camp that Will Pinkney and Col. Bird had set fire to the day of the battle. Such a shocking sight of charred wood, burnt clothes, tents, and all imaginable articles strewn around, I had never before seen. I should have been very much excited, entering the

86. The road from Clinton to Baton Rouge, a distance of some thirty miles. The Baton Rouge and Clinton Plank Road Company was incorporated in 1853 with Sarah's father listed as one of the commissioners. See *Acts of the Legislature, 1853*, pp. 312–13.

town by the route our soldiers took; but I was not. It all seemed tame and familiar. I could hardly fancy I stood on the very spot where the severest struggle had taken place. The next turn of the road brought us to two graves, one on each side of the road, the resting place of two who fell that day. They were merely left in the ditch where they fell, and earth from the side was pulled over them. When Miriam passed, parts of their coats were sticking out of the grave; but some kind hand had scattered fresh earth over them when I saw them.

Beyond, the sight became more common. I was told that their hands and feet were visible from many. And one poor fellow lay unburied, just as he had fallen, with his horse across him, and both skeletons. That sight I was spared, as the road near which he was lying was blocked up by trees, so we were forced to go through the woods, to enter, instead of passing by the Catholic graveyard. In the woods, we passed another camp our men destroyed, while the torn branches above, testified to the number of shells our men had braved to do the work. Next to Mr Barbee's,[87] were the remains of a third camp that was burned; and a few more steps made me suddenly hold my breath, for just before us lay a dead horse with the flesh still hanging, which was hardly endurable. Close by lay a skeleton, whether of man or horse, I did not wait to see.

Not a human being appeared until we reached the penitentiary, which was occupied by our men. After that, I saw crowds of wagons moving furniture out, but not a creature that I knew. Just back of our house [p. 39] was all that remained of a nice brick cottage—namely, four crumbling walls. The offense was that the husband was fighting for the Confederacy; so the wife was made to suffer, and is now homeless, like many thousands besides. It really seems as though God wanted to spare our homes. The frame dwelling adjoining was not touched, even. The town was hardly recognizable; and required some skill to avoid the corners blocked up by trees, so as to get in at all.

Our house could not be reached by the front, so we left the buggy in the back yard, and running through the lot without stopping to examine the store room and servants' rooms that opened wide, I went through the alley, and entered by the front door. Fortunate was it for this record that I undertook to describe the sacking only from Miriam's

87. Oscar Barbee, whose home was east of the State Penitentiary.

account. If I had waited until now, it would never have been mentioned; for as I looked around, to attempt such a thing seemed absurd. I stood in the parlor in silent amazement; and in answer to Charlie's "Well?" I could only laugh. It was so hard to realize. As I looked for each well known article, I could hardly believe that Abraham Lincoln's officers had really come so low down as to steal in such a wholesale manner. The papier maché workbox Miriam had given me, was gone. The baby sacque I was crocheting, with all knitting needles and wool, gone also. Of all the beautiful engravings of Annapolis that Will Pinkney had sent me, there remained a single one. Gentlemen, my name is written on each!

Not a book remained in the parlor, except Idylls of the King,[88] that contained my name also, and which, together with the door plate, was the only case in which the name of Morgan was spared. They must have thought we were related to John Morgan, and wreaked their vengeance on us for that reason.[89] Thanks for the honor, but there is not the slightest connection! Where they did not carry off articles bearing our name, they cut it off (as in the visiting cards) and left only the first name. Every book of any value or interest, except Hume and Gibbon, was "borrowed" permanently. I regretted Macaulay more than all the rest. Brother's splendid French histories went too; all except L'Histoir de la Bastille.[90] However as they spared father's law libraries, (all except one volume they used to support a flour barrel with, while they emptied it near the parlor door) we ought to be thankful.

The dining room was *very* funny. I looked around for the cutglass celery and preserve dishes that were to be part of my "dot" as mother always said, together with the champagne glasses that had figured on the table the day I was born; but there remained nothing. There was plenty of split up furniture though. I stood in mother's room before the shattered armoir, which I could hardly believe the same that I had smoothed my hair before, as I left home three weeks previously. Father's was split across, and the lock torn off, and in the place of

88. Tennyson's *Idylls of the King*.

89. Colonel (later General) John Hunt Morgan, whose raids into Tennessee and Kentucky had begun to make him a legend.

90. Sarah is probably referring to the 8-volume *Histoire de La Bastille* by Auguste Arnould and Alboize du Pujol.

the hundreds of articles it contained, I saw two bonnets at the sight of which I actually sat down to laugh. One was mother's velvet, which looked very much like a foot ball in its present condition. Mine was not to be found, as the officers forgot to return it. Wonder who has my imperial? I know they never saw a handsomer one, with its black velvet, purple silk, [p. 40] and ostrich feathers.

I went to my room. Gone was my small paradise! Had this shocking place ever been habitable? The tall mirror squinted at me from a thousand broken angles. It looked so knowing! I tried to fancy the Yankee officers being dragged from under my bed by the leg, thanks to Charles; but it seemed too absurd; so I let them alone. My desk! What a sight! The central part I had kept as a little curiosity shop with all my little trinkets and keepsakes, of which a large proportion were from my gentlemen friends. I looked, and of all I had left, found only a piece of the McRae, which, as it was labled in full, I was surprised they had spared. Precious letters, I found under heaps of broken china and rags; all my notes were gone, with many letters. I looked for a letter of poor ———, in cipher, with the key attached, and name signed in plain hand. I knew it would hardly be agreeable to him to have it read, and it certainly would be unpleasant to me to have it published; but I could not find it. Miriam thinks she saw something answering the description, somewhere, though.

Bah! what is the use of describing such a scene? Many suffered along with us, though none so severely. Indeed, the Yankees cursed loudly at those who did not leave anything worth stealing. They cannot complain of us, on that score. All our handsome Brussles [*sic*] carpets, together with Lydia's four, were taken too. What did they not take? In the garret, in its darkest corner, a whole gilt edged china set of Lydia's had been over looked; so I set to work and packed it up, while Charlie packed her furniture in a wagon, to send to her father. It was now three o'clock; and with my light linen dress thrown off, I was standing over a barrel putting in cups and saucers as fast as I could wrap them in the rags that covered the floor, when Mr Larguier[91] sent me a nice little dinner. I had been so many hours with out eating—19, I think, during three of which I had slept, that I had lost all appetite; but nevertheless I eat [*sic*]

---

91. Isidore Larguier, a Baton Rouge merchant.

it, to show my appreciation. If I should here-after think that the quantity of rags was exaggerated, let me here state that after I had packed the barrel and china with them, it made no perceptible diminution of the pile.

As soon as I had finished my task, Charlie was ready to leave again; so I left town without seeing, or hearing, any one, or any thing except what lay in my path. As we drove out of the gate, I begged Charlie to let me get my bird, as I heard Charles Barker had him. A man was dispatched, and in a few moments returned with my Jimmy. I have since heard that Tiche deserted him, the day of the battle, as I so much feared she would; and that Charles found him late in the evening and took charge of him. With my pet once more with me, we drove off again. I cast many a longing look at the graveyard; but knowing Charlie did not want to stop, I said nothing, though I had been there but once in three months, and that once, six weeks ago. I could see where the fence had been thrown down by our soldiers as they charged the Federals, but it was now replaced, though many a picket was gone.

Once more I stopped at Mrs Brown's, while Charlie went on to Clinton, leaving me to drive mother here in the morning. Early yesterday [p. 41] after seeing Miriam's piano and the mattresses packed up and on the road, we started off in the buggy, and after a tedious ride through a melting sun, arrived here about three o'clock, having again missed my dinner, which I kept a profound secret until supper time. I declare, by next Ash Wednesday, I will have learned how to fast without getting sick! Though very tired, I sat sewing until after sunset, dictating a page and a half to Anna, who was writing to Howell.

August 29. Clinton, La.

Noah's *duck* has found another resting place! Yesterday I was interrupted while writing, to pack up for another move, it being impossible to find a boarding house in the neighborhood. We heard of some about here, and Charlie had engaged a house for his family, where the servants were already settled, so I hurried off to my task. No easy one, either, considering the heat, and length of time allowed. This time I eat [*sic*] dinner as I packed, again. About four, finding Miriam did not come to Mr Elder's as she promised, I started over to Gen. Carter's with her clothes; and found her just getting in the buggy to ride over, as I arrived warm, tired, hardly able to stand. After taking her over, the General sent the buggy back for Mrs Carter and myself, and soon we were all assembled waiting for the cars.[92]

At last determining to wait for them near the track, we started off again, Gen. Carter driving me in his buggy. I love Gen. Carter. Again, after so many kind invitations, he told me he was sorry we would not remain with him; if we were content, he would be only too happy to have us with him; and spoke so kindly, that I felt as though I had a Yankee ball in my throat. I was disposed to be melancholy anyway; I could not say many words without choaking. I was going from the kindest of friends to a country where I had none at all; so could not feel very gay. As we reached the track, the cars came shrieking along. There was a pause, a scuffle during which the General placed me and my bird in a seat, while Lilly, Charlie, Miriam, mother, five children and two servants, with all the baggage, were thrown abord [*sic*] some way, when with a shriek and a jerk we were off again, with out a chance of saying good bye, even.

I enjoyed that ride. It had but one fault; and that was, that it came to an end. I would have wished it to spin along until the war was over, or we in a settled home. But it ended at last, to Jimmy's great relief; for he was too frightened to move even, and only ventured a timid chirp if the car stopped, as though to ask "Is it over?" Nothing occurred of any interest except once a little boy sent us slightly of[f] the track, by meddling with the breaks [*sic*].

Landed at sunset, it is hard to fancy a more forlorn crew, while waiting at the depot to get the baggage off, before coming to the house. We burst out laughing as we looked at each lengthened face. Such a procession through the straggling village, has hardly been seen before. How we laughed at our forlorn plight as we trudged through the hilly

92. The Clinton and Port Hudson Railroad crossed the Carter plantation and ran very near Linwood itself.

streets—they have no pavements here—looking like emigrants from the Ould Counthry, as we have watched them in New Orleans! At the house we found Tiche laid up. The loaded wagon, with its baggage, four mules, three grown servants and four children,[93] was precipitated from a bridge [p. 42] twenty five feet high, by the breaking of the before mentioned causeway, and landed the whole concern in deep water below. Wonderful to relate, not a life was lost! The mattress on which the negroes remained seated floated them off into shallow water. The only one hurt was Tiche, who had her leg severely sprained. The baggage was afterwards fished out, rather wet. On the mud next morning (it happened late at night) Dophy found a tiny fancy bottle that she had secreted from the Yankees; a present from Clemmy Luzenberg,[94] it was, and one of two things left in my curiosity shop by the Yankees.

After seeing every thing in, we started off for the hotel, where we arrived after dark, rather tired, I think. Not a comfortable house, either, unless you call a bare unfurnished, dirty, room without shutter or anything else, comfortable; particularly when you are to sleep on the floor with four children and three grown people, and a servant. After breakfast we came here, until we can find a place to settle in, which Mr Marsden[95] has promised to attend to for us. It is rather rough housekeeping yet, but Lilly has not yet got settled. Our dinner was rather primitive. There was a knife and fork to carve the meat, and then it was finished with spoons. I sat on the floor with my plate, and a piece of corn bread (flour not to be bought at any price) and eat [sic] with my fingers—a new experience. I found that water can be drank [sic] out of a cup! Ouf! I am tired!

Aug 30th.

Still no prospect of a lodging; so here we remain. I never before lived in a house without a balcony, and have only now found out how inconvenient it is. The whole establishment consists of two rooms on each

93. Two other servants traveled with the family by train. There appear to have been nine slaves with them in all.

94. Clementine Luzenberg of New Orleans, age 20 in the 1860 census. She was the sister of Charles H. Luzenberg.

95. Henry Marston, banker, landowner, and leading citizen of Clinton.

side of a passage as wide as the front door; and as it has a very low
ceiling, with no opening, and no shade near, it is decidedly the warmest spot I ever inhabited. We all sleep on the floor and keep our clothes
in our trunks—except Lilly who has an armoir without doors. Knives
and forks for dinner to day, though the table still consists of a single
plank. The house really has a suffocating effect on me, there is such
a close look about it.[96] The front is fully a foot below the level of the
street, while quite a flight of steps leads from the back door to the yard.
In fact, the whole town consists of abrupt little mounds. It is rather a
pretty place; but Heaven save me from the misery of living in it!

Miriam is crazy to remain; even advocates that dirty, bare, shutterless
boarding house where we passed the first night, from what attraction I
cannot imagine. I am just as anxious to get in the country. I would hate
the dull round of this little place; I prefer solitude where I can do as I
please without being observed. Here we are as well known by people
we never before heard of, as though we were fellow citizens; the whisper "These are the Miss Morgans" being by no means unusual. I hear
a stir in the narrow entry, and the names of Mrs & Miss Marsden.[97]
Fortunately they are taken to Lilly's room; there is no escape out of this
except through the window; suppose I must go in and be presented.
Wish I was at home! Will I ever, ever, see Baton Rouge again? Please
God send the day speedily!

[p. 43] Aug 31st.

I find that Mattie & Mollie Castleton have preceeded us here, and
have, as we expected from the latter, spread their stories, which are as
consistent with the truth as heretofore. I hear that we not only entertained Federal officers daily, but besides walking the streets daily with
them, gave many a cozy dinner and supper party in their honor. What
a pity poor Mollie has not a friend kind enough to tell her that apart
from her soul's salvation, she is ruining her reputation by petty lies
which are only credited by those of her own character! I am sorry to
see her disgrace herself so unnecessarily. Poor girl! what a pity she has

96. In a letter written a few weeks after this, while he was in Louisiana recuperating
from a war wound, Sarah's brother Gibbes referred to it as "a nutshell of a house." Letter
to George Morgan, October 7, 1862, Dawson Papers, Duke University.

97. Henry Marston's wife Abigail and one of their daughters.

no mother. I hardly think Mattie aids her by more than silent acquies-
cence, or a few phrase[s] that you may distort if you please. She is too
great a coward to do anything openly; she cannot bear the consequence
of detection. Mollie, though—well there is really something worthy of
admiration in the bravery with which she upholds what she knows to
be false. What energy of character is misapplied, by her! it would not
take half the trouble to state merely the truth.

I wonder if she would not be mortified if she knew how little her
stories were credited by those for whose opinions we care? She certainly
deserves credit for the trouble she has taken to circulate the report.
From Mississippi, Tennessee, Kentucky, Virginia, and Alabamah [*sic*],
the same story has come back to us, from the same source. The other
states remain yet to be heard from. Certainly it will be told where ever
there is a garrison; think how many "beaux" it will gain her! I have
said enough to hang me, anyway.

A young lady remarked to me when the report first started—not that
she credited it, but to show her horror of the thought of the deed—that
if any of the young ladies of B.R. so much as spoke to a Federalist, her
name should be marked, and the young men should not call on her
when they returned from the war. It struck me as so extremely contemptible and petty, that I exclaimed with that involuntary sneer said
to be peculiar to Brother and me, "What a severe punishment to a girl
with any self respect!" Wo unto me if Mollie heard it! Poor Sarah! you
would die an old maid sure enough! Let the poor girl rest. She has not
done me half the injury she has inflicted on herself.

I was sorry to find all at Linwood so very harsh on Will Pinkney. It
pained me very much. He was unfortunate enough to make some remark about "free fighters" and "independents" (a prejudice he shares
in common with every organised corps in the army) which drew on
him the wrath of the whole family. His mother spoke still more harshly
of him, about his marriage, until I was completely bewildered by the
change the opinions of each had undergone. Lilly was very angry with
him, because he lauded me to the skies, talked of me as being—well!
something I decidedly am not, and ended by saying he had always
loved me more than he did Miriam. This she thought flagrant injustice to the latter, and consequently ventured battle in her defense. If he
chose to fancy he liked me so much, why not let him follow his whim?

Neither his wife, or Miriam object to it, and they are the two most nearly concerned.

I have heard sundry insinuations that if the person speaking was Col. Pinkney's wife, they would decidedly [p. 44] object to his correspondence with a girl young enough to be her daughter. But as the before mentioned correspondence extends to two letters a piece since his marriage, I hardly think it can be so very indecorous—particularly as Mrs Pinkney receives my letters, and mother and Miriam read his. I hardly think Lilly was pleased at my resisting the general feeling against Will. I knew that she and Charlie were much prejudiced against him, and I made allowance for her feelings without allowing them to influence mine. So Miriam and I listened in silence to the tide of abuse heaped on him by every one, his mother included, and then said, "Poor Will has not a friend left; let us two remain true to our old impressions, and think kindly of him until he proves himself unworthy of our regard." So Miriam, who is the soul of generosity, agreed, and I, who follow impulse as usual, satisfied the compact, and here we stand alone, the two solitary friends that remain to the favorite Will of two years ago. Pool Will! I have half a mind to answer that last letter of his, to show he is not forgotten by Miriam and me, at least.

September 1st. Monday.

I wake up this morning and, to my great surprise, find that summer has already passed away, and that we have already entered the first month of fall. Where has the summer gone to? Since the taking of Fort Jackson, the days have gone by like a dream. I had hardly realized spring, when now I find it is autumn. I am content to let the time fly, though, as every day brings us nearer Peace—or something else.

How shockingly I write! Will I ever again have a desk or a table to write on? At present, my seat is a mattress, and my knee my desk; and that is about the only one I have had since the 2d of Aug. This is the dreariest day I have seen for sometime. Outside, it has been raining since daybreak, and inside, no one feels especially bright or cheerfull. I sometimes wish mother would carry out her threat and brave the occasional shellings at B.R. I would dare anything, to be at home again. I know that the Yankees have left us little besides the bare house; but I would be grateful for the mere shelter of the roof.

I often fancy how we will miss little articles that we thought necessary to our comfort before, when we return. How shall I dispense with my old work box? so well furnished with embroideries, pieces of lace, buttons, and all other things! Wonder what Yankee girl will inherit it? And my dumb bells? And the shoes I paid five dollars for, and wore a single time? I am wishing I had them now that I am almost barefooted, and cannot find a pair in the whole country. A Yankee girl cannot get much use out of them; that is one consolation. Would it not be curious, if one of these days while traveling in the North (if I ever travel again) I should find some well loved object figuring in a strange house as a "trophy of the battle of Baton Rouge"? I should have to seek for them in some very low house, perhaps; respectable people had very little to do with such disgraceful work, I fancy. Suppose I should see father's cigar stand, for instance, or Miriam's little statues? I wonder if the people would have the conscience to offer to return them?

A young lady passing by one of the pillaged houses, expressed her surprise at seeing an armoir full of women's and children's clothes being emptied, and the contents tied up in sheets. [p. 45] "What can you do with such things?" she asked a soldier who seemed more zealous, than the rest. "Aint I got a wife and four children in the north?" was the answer. So we, who have hardly clothes enough for our own use, are stripped to supply Northerners who have no need of them!

One would think that I had no theme save the wreck of our house, if they should see this. But I take it all out, in here. I believe I must be made of wood, or some other tough material, not to feel it more. I sometimes ask myself if it is because I did not care for home, that I take it so quietly now. But I know that is not it. I was wild about it before I knew what had happened; since I learned all, few are the words that have escaped by lips concerning it. Perhaps it is because I have the satisfaction of knowing what all women so crave for—the Worst. Indeed it is a consolation in such days as these, when truth concerning either side is difficult to discover. The certainty of any thing, fortune or misfortune, is comfort to me.

I really feel sorry for the others who suffered; but it does not strike me that sympathy is necessary in our case. Mrs Flynn[98] came to Lilly's

---

98. Mother of William and Theodore Pinkney.

room, when she heard of it, well prepared for sympathy, with a large
handkerchief and a profusion of tears, when she was horrified to find
both her and Miriam laughing over the latter's description of some
comical scene that met her sight in one of the rooms. Seems to me that
tears on all occasions come in as the fortieth article, to the articles of
belief of some people. Miriam was inquiring as to the probability of
boarding at a Mrs Netterville's.[99] "You wont like her" said Mrs Flynn.
"She is such an unsympathetic person. Never cries at funerals, you
know"! If the lady is "unsympathetic" I must be a brute, in Mrs. Flynn's
opinion. Perhaps I do not feel the full force of it yet; I can hardly fancy
anything more forlorn than our present condition. But wait until the
reaction comes, and we are once more at home! Wont I suffer then?
And yet, Mrs Flynn will hardly find me in tears, either!

Sept 3d.

A night of rather unpleasant sickness and chilliness has left me rather
unwell to day. And yet I will not go to bed. I'll sit up as long as I can.
I never yet was so sick, that going to bed did not make me worse. If
there was only a breathing spot in the house, where fresh air could
be obtained, I would soon conquer this dizziness; but there is no such
place within, and the sloppy condition of the streets has made it impossible for me to venture out since Saturday. Still, we are unsuccessful
in finding lodgings. We have met many kind friends, in this strange
country, thanks to our father's name; for all here seem to have known
him. Old Mr Marsden in particular, has proved his regard for father,
in his attention to his children. "Cast thy bread upon the waters;"[100] it
is coming back to us, father!

I wonder if it because I think so constantly of Sis, that her name appears so seldom here? However, hers is not the only name slighted; as I
look back, I see nothing but Sarah, Sarah, as though there was no one
living, save myself. Bah! I am trying to persuade myself that "Sarah" is
worth thinking of! Poor child! if she does not praise and vaunt herself,
who is there to do it for her? So in revenge for not being a favorite of

99. Perhaps Mrs. Elizabeth Netterville. The Netterville plantation was in East Baton
Rouge Parish, but she may have refugeed in Clinton to get beyond reach of the Union
army.

100. Ecclesiastes 11:1.

the whole world, and feeling acutely the want of sympathy, or approbation, sometimes (though I dare say she has more than she deserves) she naturally takes to petting herself and says—on paper—"O what a very nice girl you are, my dear!" just as though she believed it, or [p. 46] could thereby fool others into believing it too! Sarah is a humbug, there is no doubt of it; but then this is her diary; and has she not a right to show herself off in the most amiable light, for her own edification, since the book is her own property and work? And she makes such a very poor show elsewhere, that it is hardly fair to deny her the pleasure of a display on paper. So she talks of her dear self constantly, and very little of what she has nearest to heart, or most at stake. Let her have her way.

Political news it would be absurd to record; for our information is more than limited, being frequently represented by a blank. Of the thirteen battles that Gibbes has fought in, I know the names of four only: Bull Run, Stonebridge, Port Republic and Cedar Run. Think of all I have yet to hear! Today comes the news of another grand affair, the defeat of McClelland, Pope & Burnside [101] combined. If I dared believe it! But accounts are too meagre as yet. Both Gibbes & George were in it, if there *was* a fight, and perhaps Jimmy, too. Well! I must wait in patience. We have lost so much already, that God will surely spare those three to us. Ah! if they come again, if we can meet once more, what will the troubles of the last six months signify? If I dared hope that next summer would bring us peace! I always prophesy it just six months off; but do I believe it? Indeed I dont know what will become of us, if it is delayed much longer.

If we could only get home, it would be another thing; but boarding, how long will mother's two hundred and fifty last? And that is all the money she has. As to the claims, amounting to a small fortune, she might as well burn them; they will never be paid. But if we get home, what will we do for bedding? The Yankees did not leave us a single comfort, and only two old bars, and a pair of ragged sheets, which articles are not to be replaced at any price, in the Confederacy, so we must go without. How glad I am that we gave all our blankets to our soldiers last summer! So much saved from the Yankees!

101. George B. McClellan, John Pope, and Ambrose E. Burnside, Union generals.

Poor Sis! She fancies us comfortably settled at home; I dare say she spends all her time in picturing to herself what we may be doing, and recalling each piece of furniture the rooms contained. Wonder if she would not be shocked if the real scene were suddenly revealed to her, and she should see the desolated house, and see us fugitives in a strange town. Wonder how the cry of "Where are those three damned Secesh women?" would have struck her, had she heard the strange oaths, and seen the eager search which followed? I dare say it would have frightened her more than it did me, when I was told of it. William Waller says it is God's mercy that we had escaped already, for we certainly would have suffered. I hardly think we would have been harmed, though, and shall always regret that we did not return immediately after the battle. It took them from that day, to the evacuation, to finish the work; and I rather think that our presence would have protected the house.

Our servants they kindly made free, and told them they must follow them (the officers). Margret was boasting the other day of her answer "I dont want to be any free-er than I is now. I'll stay with my mistress," when Tiche shrewdly remarked [p. 47] "Pshaw! dont you know that if I had gone, you'd have followed me?" The conduct of all our servants is beyond praise. Five thousand negroes followed their Yankee brothers, from the town & neighborhood;[102] but ours remained. During the fight, or flight, rather, a fleeing officer stopped to throw a musket in Charles Barker's hands, and bade him fight for his liberty. Charles drew himself up, saying "I am only a slave, but I am a secesh nigger, and wont fight in such a d—— crew!" Exit Yankee, continuing his flight down to the riverside.

Sept 4th.

I hear to day that the Brunots have returned to Baton Rouge, determined to await the grand finale there. They and two other families alone remain. With these exceptions, and a few Dutch[103] and Irish who

---

102. There is no way to confirm Sarah's figure on blacks who sought freedom. In a letter dated August 31, 1862, Colonel Halbert E. Paine told his wife that he "gave freedom to over 500 slaves," and that he brought most of them back with him to New Orleans when he evacuated the Union army from Baton Rouge on August 21. Letter in collection of Fred G. Benton, Jr.

103. Germans.

cannot leave, the town is perfectly deserted by all except the Confederate soldiers. I wish I was with them! If all chance of finding lodgings here is lost, and mother remains with Lilly as she sometimes seems more than half inclined, and Miriam goes to Linwood as she frequently threatens, I believe I will take a notion too, and go to Mrs Brunot! I would rather be there, in all the uncertainty, expecting to be shelled, or burnt out every hour, than here.

Ouf! what a country! Next time I go shopping, I mean to ask some clerk, out of curiosity, what they *do* sell in Clinton. The following is a list of a few of the articles that shop keepers actually laugh at you, if you ask for. Glasses, flour, soap, starch, coffee, candles, matches, shoes, combs, guitar strings, bird seed—in short, everything that I have heretofore considered as necessary to existence. If any one had told me I could have lived off of corn bread, a few months ago, I would have been incredulous; now I believe it, and return an inward grace for the blessing, at every mouthful. I have not tasted a piece of wheat bread since I left home, and shall hardly taste it again until the war is over.

I do not like this small burg. It is very straggling, and pretty, but I would rather not inhabit it. We are as well known here as though we carried our cards on our faces, and it is peculiarly disagreeable to me to over hear myself spoken about by people I dont know, as "There goes Miss Morgan" as that young man, for instance, remarked this morning to a crowd, just as I passed. It is not polite, to say the least.

Will Carter[104] was here this morning, and told me he saw Theodore Pinkney in the streets. I suppose he is on his way home, and think he will be a little disappointed in not finding us at Linwood as he expects, and still more so to hear he passed through the very town where we were staying, without knowing it.

Beech Grove. Sept 6th. Saturday.

Another perch for Noah's duck! Where will I be in a week or two from this? I shall make a mark, twenty pages from here, and see where I shall be when I reach it. Here, most probably; but O if I could then be at home! Gen. Carter who spent the evening with us day before yester-

104. William P. Carter, nephew of General Albert G. Carter. When the 1860 census was taken, Will Carter was 19 and living in the household of his half sister Esther Worley and her husband Caleb Worley.

day, remarked that the first thing he heard as he reached town, was that all the gentlemen and ladies of Clinton were hunting for country [p. 48] lodgings for us. It was pretty much the case. The General was as kind as ever, bless his grey head! and made us promise to go back to Linwood with him, when he passes back next week.

This is the way we keep the promise—coming out here. Early yesterday morning we received a note from Eliza Haines, one of our indefatigable agents, saying her grandmother Mrs McKay [105] had consented to receive us, and would come for us in the evening. Immediately my packing task was begun. But imagine my disappointment when just as I had finished one trunk, to hear mother announce her determination to let us go alone, while she remained with Lilly! Prayers, entreaties, tears, arguments, all failed; and we were forced to submit. So with a heart fuller than I can express, I repacked the trunk with Miriam's, and my clothing, and got ready to depart.

In the evening the carriage drove up to the door with Eliza and her grandmother, and with a hasty, and rather choaky goodbye to Lilly & mother, we were hurried in, and in another moment were off. I fancied the house would be north of Clinton, so of course the horses took the road south. Then I decided on a white cottage to the left of the road, and about two miles out, found that it was to the right, not painted, and no cottage at all, but a nondescript building, besides. "Twas ever thus from childhood's hour!" [106] When did I ever fancy anything exactly as it was? But the appearance does not affect the house, which is really, very comfortable, though apparently unfinished. The same objection might be made to it, that I made to Mrs Moore's,[107] for there is not a shutter on the place. But fine shade trees take their place, and here, I do not feel the want of them so much, as our room is in the back of the house, to the west, where the rising sun cannot salute my nose as it did at Mrs Moore's. As to what effect the setting sun has, I must wait for evening to decide, though I always enjoy that. At Greenwell, we used to walk a mile away from home to see the sun set in an open field.

105. Mrs. Eliza McCay (sometimes spelled McKay), a widow. Mrs. McCay's daughter Delia was the wife of the Clinton lawyer Bythell Haynes.

106. Thomas Moore, *Lalla Rookh*.

107. Mary E. Moore operated a hotel opposite the Masonic Hall in Clinton.

I find Mrs McKay an excellent, plain old lady, with neither airs or pretentions, and very kind hearted. Here she lives alone, with the exception of an orphan girl called Jane,[108] whose position, half menial, half equal, it would be hard to define. Poor girl! the name of orphan alone, was enough to make me sorry for her. She must be "Friday's child" she is so "ready and willing."[109] Eliza, who it seems stays a great deal with her grandmother, is one of the brightest little girls I have seen for a long while. I know no child I was ever more prejudiced against by report, or one who was more interesting on acquaintance. She is about thirteen, with a very pretty and expressive face, all annimation and life. I envy her her short dresses as I see her run around the grass without holding them up—only I should not like mine to be so *extremely* short. She sings and plays on the piano with a style and assurance that I can only mutely covet. Why cannot I have the confidence I see all others possess? She took me to the gin house last evening though I could not see much, as it was almost sunset when we arrived. An early tea, and singing, and music after, completed our evening, and then we were shown to our room.

I had but one fault to find, [p. 49] and that, in my opinion is a serious one; there was no foot tub in the room. Accustomed as we are to bathing every night before lying down, in summer and winter, we have felt the lack of such accommodations very much since we left home; except at Linwood, where our partiality for water is well known, and we are always liberally supplied. I would have impressed a tooth-mug though, rather than do without; but fortunately, contented myself with a "swim" in the basin. When I am away from home, and I am not offered a tub of water, I always think it so an imputation on my cleanliness that I must look as though I disliked the article, to my entertainers.

Mrs. McKay has only room for us two so it is fortunate that mother would not come. She says she wants us to spend a few days with her, to see if we like it, or if we will be willing to be separated from mother. In the mean time, we can look around for lodgings in a larger and more comfortable place where we can be together. She tells such stories

108. The census of 1860 shows Jane Forester, age 15, living in the household of Eliza McCay.

109. In the more common version, Friday's child is "loving and giving."

about the house Lilly lives in, of its age, and unhealthiness, that I am frightened about mother. She says she will die if she stays there this month. Miriam and Eliza have gone to town to see them, and are then going to Mrs George's[110] to see if she can accommodate us. Nannie Davidson[111] is staying there, and was crazy for us to get there too. I hope they will succeed. I cannot live without mother, any more than without Miriam. I am as homesick at leaving her, as I am when I think of Baton Rouge. There now!

I wanted to have a splendid dream last night, but failed. It was pleasant though to dream of welcoming George and Gibbes back. Jimmy I could not see; and George was in deep mourning. I dreamed of fainting when I saw him (a novel sensation, since I never experienced it awake) but I speedily came to, and insisted on his "pulling Henry Walsh's red hair, for his insolence," which he promised to do instantly. How absurd! Dreams! dreams! That pathetic "Miss Sarah, do you ever dream?" comes vividly back to me sometimes.

Dream? Dont I! Not the dreams *he* meant; but royal, purple dreams, that De Quincy could not purchase with his opium; dreams that I would not forgo for all the inducements that could be offered. I go to sleep, and pay a visit to heaven or fairy land. I have white wings, and, with another, float in 1osy clouds, and look down on the moving world; or I have the power to raise myself in the air without wings, and silently float where ever I will, loving all things, and feeling that God loves me. I have heard Paul preach to the people, while I stood on a fearful rock above. I have been to strange lands and great cities; I have talked with people I have never beheld. Charlotte Brontë has spent a week with me—in my dreams—and together we have talked of her sad life. Shakespeare and I have discussed his works, seated tête-à-tête over a small table. He pointed out the character of each of his heroines, explaining what I could not understand when awake; and closed the lecture with "*You* have the tenderest heart I have ever read, or sung of" which compliment, considering it as original with him, rather than myself, waked me up with surprise.

I see father and Harry in dreams. Once I walked with Hal through a

110. Possibly Frances George, wife of John F. George.
111. Sister of Fanny Davidson Trezevant.

garden of Paradise. Fountains, [p. 50] statues, flowers, surrounded us, as we wandered hand in hand. We stopped before a statue that held a finger to its lips, when he said "Did you ever see Fitch's celebrated picture of Eternity? No? Well let me show it to you. Nothing but that picture can give you an idea of the vastness of this eternity. Come!" I followed him through beautiful alleys until he stopped before an immense chrystal [*sic*] wall. He held my hand without speaking, and we watched together. In the chrystal, or the otherside, forms were moving, ever, always. What they were, I could not say; I only know that they were real, and forever moving! Over all, above, below, beyond, hovered a Something; a Something too great, awful, and mysterious for me to comprehend, though I struggled to understand. Striving still, I suddenly waked up, and the chrystal painting disappeared. Dreams! who would give up the blessing? I would not care to sleep, if I could not dream.

Clinton. Sept 9th. Tuesday.

Back again! For how long, I know not. At sunset Saturday, Eliza and Miriam returned to Mrs McCay's with Nannie Davidson. Mother had proved obdurate, and refused to leave Clinton; so they had all gone on, and spent the day with Mrs Haynes instead of going to Mrs Georges'. After my quiet, solitary day, I was glad to see them again, particularly as they brought confirmation of the great victory in Virginia. It is said the enemy were cut off from Washington, and that we were pursuing them. O my brothers! If God will only spare them! I envy Lydia who is so near them, and knows all, and can take care of them if they are hurt. It will be several days at least, before we can hear from them, if we hear at all; for Jimmy has never yet written a line, and George has written but once since the taking of the forts, and that was before the battle of Chickahominy. We can only wait patiently. Perhaps Genl. Carter will bring us news.

Mrs Haynes sent a very pressing invitation for us to spend the next day with her, so although it was Sunday, we went. I am becoming dreadfully irreligious. I have not been to church since Mr Gierlow went to Europe last July. It is perfectly shocking; but the Yankees have kept me running until all pious dispositions have been shaken out of me; so they are to blame. Like Heathens, we called on Miss Comstock as we passed through town, and spent an hour with her. Landed at Mr Haynes', we had ample time to look around, before he and his wife got back from church. Here again I found what seems to be the prevailing style of the country, wide spread doors and windows, with neither blinds nor shade trees to keep off the glare of the sun. The dining room was a wide hall, where the rising sun shone in your face at breakfast, and at dinner, being directly overhead, seemed to shine in at both ends at once. A splendid arrangement for a Fire Worshipper; but I happened to be born in America, instead of Persia, so fail to appreciate it.

Sept 10th.

Yesterday I was interrupted to undertake a very important task. The evening before, mother and Lilly happened to be in a store where two officers were [p. 51] buying materials for making shirts, and volunteered to make them for them, which offer they gladly accepted, though neither party knew the other. They saw that they were friends of Charlie, so had no scruples about offering their services; the gentlemen saw that they were ladies, and very kind ones, besides, so made no difficulty about accepting. Lilly undertook a purple merino, and I took a dark blue one. Miriam nominally helped her; but her very sore finger did not allow her to do much. Mother slightly assisted me; but I think Lilly and I had the best of the task. All day we worked, and when evening came, continued sewing by the light of these miserable home made candles. Even then we could not finish, but had to get up early this morning as the gentlemen were to leave for Port Hudson at nine o'clock. We finished in good time, and their appearance recompensed us for our trouble. Lilly's was trimmed with folds of blue from mine, around collar, cuffs, pockets, and down the front band; while mine was pronounced a chef d'oeuvre,[112] trimmed with bias folds of tiny red and black plaid. With their fresh colors, and shining pearl buttons, they were really very pretty.

We sent word that we would be happy to make as many as they chose for themselves or their friends, and the eldest, with many fears that it was an "imposition" and we "too good," and much more of the same kind, left another one with Charlie for us. We cannot do too much, or

112. Masterpiece.

even enough for our soldiers. I believe that is the universal sentiment of the women of the south.

Well, but how did we get back here? I hardly know. It seems to me we are being swayed by some kind of destiny which impels us here or there, with neither rhyme or reason, and whether we will or no. Such homeless, aimless, purposeless, wandering individuals are rarely seen. From one hour to another, we do not know what is to become of us. We talk vaguely of going home "When the Yankees go away." When will that be? One day there is not a boat in sight; the next, two or three stand off from shore to see what is being done, ready at the first sight of warlike preparation to burn the town down. It is particularly unsafe since the news from Virginia, when the gunboats started from Bayou Goula,[113] shelling the coast at random, and destroying everything that was within reach, Report says.

Of course we cannot return to our homes when commissioned officers are playing the part of pirates, burning, plundering and destroying at will, with neither law or reason. Donaldsonville they burned before I left B.R., because some fool fired a shotgun at a gunboat some miles above; Bayou Sara they burned while we were at Genl Carter's, for some equally reasonable excuse.[114] The fate of B.R. hangs on a still more slender thread. I would give worlds if it were all over, one way or the other.

At Mrs Haynes', we remained all night, as she sent the carriage back without consulting us. Monday we came to town, and spent the day with Lilly. How it was, I cant say; but we came to the conclusion that it was best to quit our then residence, and either go back to Linwood, or to a Mrs Somebody who offered to take us as boarders. There was no objection to be made to our staying out there, except that Miriam found it rather dull, and I missed [p. 52] my bucket of water every night more than I can say. How people can dispense with such a necessary article in such a climate, I cannot understand. Yet I have seen many

113. Town on the west bank of the Mississippi River below Plaquemine.

114. On August 9, 1862, Farragut burned hotels, wharf buildings, and some residences in Donaldsonville because citizens of the town had "pursued a uniform practice of firing upon our steamers," and he promised to burn more if the firing continued. On August 23 a party of Union sailors sent ashore from the *Essex* burned residences and other buildings in Bayou Sara after they were fired upon by guerrillas. See *ORN*, ser. I, 19:141, 181.

respectable people who did not seem to have the slightest partiality for it. We went back to Mrs McCay's to tell her of our determination, and in the morning took leave of her, and came back home. I expect it must have been a great inconvenience to the old lady to have us there, living alone as she does; so perhaps it was best for both parties. Where we will be next, it is hard to say. I'll go crazy if I do not reach my own home before long.

We hear so much news, piece by piece, that one would imagine some definite result would follow, and bring us peace before long. The Virginia news, after being so great and cheering, has suddenly ceased to come. No one knows the final result. The last report was that we held Arlington Heights. Why not Washington, consequently? Cincinnati at last accounts, lay at our mercy. From Covington Kirby Smith had sent over a demand for its surrender in two hours.[115] Would it not be glorious to avenge New Orleans by such a blow? But since last night, the telegraph is silent. News has just come of some nice little affair between our militia in Opelousas, and the Yankees from New Orleans, in which we gave them a good thrashing, beside capturing arms, prisoners, and ammunition.[116] "It never rains but it pours" is George's favorite proverb. With it comes the "rumor" that the Yankees are preparing to evacuate the city. If it could be! O if God would only send them back to their own country, and leave ours in peace! I wish them no greater punishment than that they may be returned to their own homes, with the disgrace of their outrages here, ever before their eyes. That would kill an honest man I am sure.

Sunday Sept 14th 1862.

I have been so busy making Lieut. Bourge's [117] shirt, that I have not had time to write, besides having very little to write about. So my industry saved my paper, and spared these pages a vast amount of trash. I would not let any one touch Lieut. Bourge's shirt, except myself; and last evening when I held it up completed, the loud praises it received

---

115. General Edmund Kirby Smith's thrust into Kentucky in the late summer and early fall of 1862 did threaten Cincinnati, but what began as an invasion ended in withdrawal into East Tennessee.

116. The action Sarah is referring to occurred at Boutte Station.

117. Probably Lieutenant Ernest Bourges of the 30th Louisiana Infantry.

satisfied me it would answer. Miriam and Miss Riply[118] declare it the
prettiest ever made. It is dark purple merino. The bosom I tucked with
pleats a quarter of an inch deep, all the way up to the collar, and stitched
a narrow crimson silk braid up the centre to hold it in its place. Around
the collar, cuffs, pockets, and band down the front, the red cord runs,
forming a charming contrast to the dark foundation. Indeed I devoted
the sole article the Yankees let fall from my two workboxes—a bunch
of soutache—to the work. Large white pearl buttons completed the description, and my shirt is really as quiet, subdued, and pretty a one as
I ever saw. I should first hear the opinion of the owner, though. If he
does not agree with all the others, I shall say he has no taste.

I got a long, sweet letter from Sophie on Friday, that made me happy
for the whole day. They were about leaving [p. 53] for Alexandria.[119] I
was glad to hear they would be out of danger, but still I was sorry they
were going so far away. I have been laying a hundred wild schemes to
reach Baton Rouge and spend a day or two with them, which is impossible now. Sophie writes just as she talks—and that means remarkably
well—so I can at least have the pleasure of corresponding.

At Dr Carnal's[120] they will be out of the reach of all harm and danger; so I ought to rejoice. But suppose they do not come back again?
How would I exist in Baton Rouge without the Brunots? What singular
tie of friendship is it that attaches us, I wonder? Congeniality of tastes,
Sophie says; but even there we differ. They have their favorite authors;
I have mine; and each sustains her favorite. They uphold America, I,
England, as the greatest country in the world. (They have since substituted the Confederate States.) In the autumn of 1860, they were as
wild secessionists, as I was strong Union. Now, they are as bitter and
uncompromising as the most rabid, while I am as quiet and hopeful as
the most liberal of the Once conservatives. Certainly there is no congeniality of taste on political subjects. They, violent Democrats; I, a
subdued, though strong Whig, quietly adopting all father's sentiments,
though rarely expressing them. They, devout Catholics; I, a member
of the Episcopal Church. What can be the tie that preserves order and

118. Sarah Ripley, age 17 in the 1860 census and living in the home of her maternal
grandmother, Mrs. Rebecca Whitaker.

119. Alexandria, Louisiana, in the center of the state and still within the Confederacy.

120. Dr. Robert Carnal, who married Louisa Brunot, Sophie's oldest sister.

concord in such opposite natures? Certainly they are the best friends I ever had; and Hal said I would never find any [others] as true.

I wonder if our clubs, which Yankee rule put an end to, will ever be again resumed? Every fall they would open, and continue until the warm days came again, or until Miriam or I would go to the city. Twice a week we would meet about nine o'clock, and each read aloud half an hour, from some Essayist or Poet. Half an hour allowed for lunch, and discussing the question while we took our repast, brought us to twelve o'clock, when we would fold up our knitting and sewing, and take our leave, as we happened to meet at their house, or they, at home. It was at least a rational way of spending the time. No sweethearts or rivals were discussed, so it had the merit of originality, at least. How many pleasant days we spent in that way!

Still no authentic reports of the late battles in Virginia. I say late, refering to those fought two weeks ago. From the Federal accounts, glowing as they usually are, I should gather the idea that their rout was complete. I cannot imagine why we can hear nothing more from our own side. There is one thing in which Sophy and I agree, and that is in making Stonewall Jackson our hero. Talk of Beauregard! he never had my adoration; but Stonewall is the greatest man of the age, decidedly. O War how I wish you were over! How thankful I will be when all this fuss and trouble is done away with, and the boys come home!

It is but a step from the sublime to the ridiculous. Absurd [p. 54] as it may seem, I think my first act on my return home, will be to take a cup of coffee, and a piece of bread, two luxuries of which I have been deprived for a long while. Miriam vows to devour an unheard of number of biscuits, too. How many articles we considered as absolutely necessary, before, have we now been obliged to dispense with! Nine months of the year I revelled in ice, thought it impossible to drink water without it. Since last November, I have tasted it but once, and that once by accident. And O yes! I caught some hail stones one day at Linwood! Ice cream, lemonade and sponge cake was my chief diet; it was a year last July since I tasted the two first, and one since I have seen the latter. Bread I believed necessary to life; vegetables, useless. The former I never see, and I have been forced into cultivating at least a toleration of the latter. Snap beans I can actually swallow, sweet potatoes I really like, and one day at Dr Nolan's I "bolted" a mouthful of tomatoes, and afterwards kept my seat with the heroism of a martyr. These are the minor trials of war. If that were all—if coarse, distasteful food were the only inconvenience—!

When I think of what Sis must suffer so far from us, and in such ignorance of our condition, our trials seem nothing in comparison to hers. And think how uneasy Brother must be, hearing of the battle, and not knowing where we fled to! For he has not heard of us for almost two months. In return we are uneasy enough about him and Sister. If New O. is attacked, what will become of them with all those children?

From interesting, turn we to uninteresting subjects. Theodore came from his home on Friday, to see us, and afterwards took a long walk with us in the evening during which I had an opportunity of seeing a new portion of the village. I am wofully tired of it, and sincerely wish I was in my own town, though Soph begged me not to return yet.

Tuesday. Sept 16th.

Yesterday Miriam determined to go to Linwood, and consequently I had a severe task of trunk packing, one of my greatest delights, however. I hate to see anyone pack loosely or in a slovenly manner. Perhaps that is the reason I never let anyone do it, if I am able to stand. This morning was appointed as our day for leaving, but I persuaded her to wait until tomorrow, in hopes that either the General, or news from Virginia should arrive this evening. Bless this village! It is the meanest place for news that I ever was in. Not a word can be gathered, except what is false, or unfounded; and they are even tiring of that, in the last few days.

Talk of Baton Rouge turning Yankee, as the report went here! Of the three or four there who took the oath, not one can be compared to some loyal citizens of this small burg. Why I talked [p. 55] to two gentlemen yesterday, who, if it were not for the disgrace and danger incurred by bearing the name, I should style Union men, and talked, or rather listened to them, until my spirits were reduced to the lowest ebb. People were shocked at our daring to believe there lived gentlemen and Christians in the North—I mean those wild fanatics who could only take in one idea at a time, and rarely divested their brains of that one, to make room for a newer one, were shocked at our belief; but if they should converse with a few here, that I could point out, our gnat of common sense would be swallowed by this behemoth of heterodoxy.

This morning Mrs Bar, Miss Bernard, and a Miss Mud[121] came to town and surprised us by a most unexpected visit. They spent the day with us, and have just now driven off on their return home, through this drizzly, misting evening. A while ago, a large cavalry company passed, at the corner, on their way from Port Hudson to Camp Moore, the report is. They waved their hats to us, seeing us at the gate, and we waved our handkerchiefs in return, each with a silent God bless you, I am sure.

As though to prove my charge unjust, news comes pouring in. Note we a few items, to see how many will prove false. First, we have taken Baltimore without firing a gun; Maryland has risen en masse to join our troops; Longstreet & Lee are marching on Washington from the rear; the Louisiana troops are ordered home to defend their own state—thank God! if it will only bring the boys back! Then comes tidings of nine gunboats at Baton Rouge, Ponchatoula on the railroad taken by Yankees,[122] Camp Moore and three batteries, ditto. Not so cheering! If that is so, Clinton lies within reach, being thirty five miles off.

Leaving much the most valuable portion of our clothing here, the Yankees will probably appropriate what little they spared us, and leave us fairly destitute; for we take only summer clothes to Linwood. I have plenty of underclothes; but the other day when I unpacked the large trunk from Dr Enders, I found I had just two dresses for winter. A handsome blue silk I bought two years ago last spring, and one heavy blue merino that does not fit me. What an out-fit for winter! Miriam has two poplins and a black silk, and mother a wine colored merino, only. But each of us are blessed with a warm cloak, and are correspondingly grateful. I was confident I had saved my green, dark blue, and brown silk dresses; but the Yankees saved them instead, for me—or their suffering sweethearts, rather. On the other hand, taking so many

121. Sarah is referring to Mrs. Cornelia Barr and to one of the daughters of General Joseph Bernard, a wealthy Baton Rouge landowner. Miss Mud has not been identified.

122. The day before, a Federal force drove the Confederates from Ponchatoula on the railroad to Jackson, Mississippi. However, when the Federals withdrew, the Confederates returned.

necessary articles to Linwood, the risk of losing them is the same. An attack on P. Hudson is apprehended, and if it falls, Genl. Carter's house will be decidedly unsafe from Yankee vengeance. The probability is that it will burn, as they have been daily expecting ever since [p. 56] the Yankees occupied B.R. The risk seems equal, either way. Go or stay, the danger seems the same.

Shall we go, then, for variety, or die here of stagnation while waiting for the Yankees to make up their minds? I would rather be at neither place just now; in fact I could hardly name the place I should like to be in now, unless it were Europe or the Sandwich Islands; but I love Linwood and its dear inhabitants, and under other circumstances, should be only to[o] happy to be there. I was regretting the other day that our life was now so monotonous; almost longed for the daily alarms we had when under Yankee rule in Baton Rouge. Stirring times are probably ahead. Will these blank pages record any experience worth remembering, or will they be as dull as these, I wonder?

Night. O Sarah! I address myself to you, and ask you to answer candidly. Ancient maiden that I shall suppose you to be when this question is put to you, tèll me, do you still suffer that very severe pang of feeling that you are very hateful and extremely disagreeable to people? If so, if it is to keep up all those years, poor creature! you had best keep out of the world even more than you do at present. "I have not loved the world, nor the world me." [123] Byron, I can with good reason adopt your words. Was there ever a greater martyr to strangers than I? Have I not cause to hate them? Do they not gain me almost every cross word I get from Miriam? Do they not procure me a scolding from mother, every time their strange footsteps cross the threshold?

O Strangers! have I not at least as much reason to hate you, as you have for hating me? I hear a ring at the door, and strange voices; my heart beats faster than it has ever yet beat at the whistle of a Yankee shell close to my ears. My doom is sealed. Before these people I am to appear, and make a very stiff and ridiculous bow. Miriam and the others will do the talking; I may as well keep quiet, for if I make an abrupt remark, they will probably snub me, or elevate their eyebrows and coolly stare. They can only hate me, and they have already learned

123. *Childe Harold's Pilgrimage.*

to do that; they will never learn to tolerate me, so efforts to dispell their dislike would be thrown away. Besides, what care I for universal favoritism? I want to be loved only by those whom I can love in return, whose friendship is worth obtaining. Would theirs repay the trouble? What benefit will be derived from overcoming the prejudice of those who dislike me, and whom I do not care for? Let them hate me if they will. Pharisee that I am, I love only those who love me. Let those cold grey eyes look as indifferently at me as they will. They will find that mine can return the gaze with a ray of defiance in it.

To me, receiving strangers simply means that I am to be very disagreeable and uncomfortable for a certain length of time. I am to produce on them the impression of being unnaturally dull, stiff and awarkward [sic], as well [as] [p. 57] uninteresting. I am to be very uncomfortable and wretched, and then they are going away saying "What a charming girl the eldest Miss Morgan is! how entertaining and pleasant! her sister, I think, must be a fool." While they comment, mother and Miriam are railing at me for my conduct. "How can a girl of your understanding" etc, cries mother. "Sarah invariably makes herself absurd in company" interrupts Miriam. "Cant you be like other people? Cant you act like a Christian? Are you an idiot to sit silent when all are talking? You talk enough at home! It is vanity! You think they are all thinking of you! You think they are not worth talking to! Really you must learn to behave, and not act like a baby!"

And so they go on, until O strangers! dont I hate you for the punishment your visits bring? Dont I hate your name and company! Who made you a judge over me? Why are you prejudiced against me before you know me? Now recess the case, and ask yourself the same thing about strangers. What is this antagonism that exists between us?

Linwood Sept 17th. Wednesday.

Still floating about! This morning after breakfast General Carter made his appearance, and in answer to his question as to whether we were ready to leave with him, Miriam replied "Yes indeed" heartily, glad to get away from Clinton, where I have detained her ever since the day Theodore returned home, to her great disgust. As our trunk was already packed, it did not take many minutes to get ready; and in a little while, with a protracted goodbye, we were on our way to the depot which we reached some time before the cars started. Though glad to leave Clinton, I was sorry to part with mother. For ten days she has been unable to walk, with a sore on her leg below the knee; and I want to believe she will miss me while I am away. I could not leave my bird in that close, ill ventilated house. He has never sung since I recovered him; and I attribute his ill health, or low spirits, to that unhealthy place, and thought Linwood might be beneficial to him, too; so brought him with me to see what effect a breath of pure air might have.

We were the only ladies on the cars, except Mrs Brown,[124] who got off half way; but in spite of that, had a very pleasant ride, as we had very agreeable company. The train only stopped thirteen time[s] in the twenty miles. Five times to clear the brushwood from the telegraph lines, once running back a mile to pick up a passenger, and so on, to the great indignation of many of the passengers aboard who would occasionally cry out "Hello! if this is the 'cleaning up' train, we had better send for a hand car!" "What the devil's the matter now?" until the General gravely assured them that it [p. 58] was an old habit of this very accommodating train, which in summer time, stopped when ever the passengers wished to pick blackberries on the road.[125]

Many soldiers were aboard, on their way to P. Hudson to rejoin their companies. One gallant one offered me a drink of water from his canteen, which I accepted out of mere curiosity to see what water from such a source tasted of. To my great surprise, I found it tasted just like any other. The General introduced a Mr Crawford to us, who took the seat next to me, as the one next to Miriam was already occupied, and proved a very pleasant and talkative compagnon de voyage. General Carter's inquiry as to my industry since he had seen me, brought my acknowledgement of having made two shirts, one of which I sent

124. Probably Elizabeth Keller Brown, wife of Dr. A. Porter Brown.

125. Some of the soldiers called the train the "tri-weekly," saying it "would go to Clinton one week and try weakly to get back the next." Quoted in Hewitt, *Port Hudson*, 23.

yesterday. Who to? was the next question. I gave the name, adding that I did not know the gentleman, and he was under the impression that it was made by mother. "I'll see that he is undeceived!" cried the General. "Hanged if I dont tell him!" "30th Louisiana, you say?" queried Mr Crawford. "That is the very one I am going to! I will tell him myself!"

So my two zealous champions went on, the General ending with "See to it, Crawford. Mrs Morgan shall not have the credit!" as though there was any great merit in sewing for ones country men! Our new acquaintance handed me from the cars as we reached Linwood, and stood talking while the accommodating train slowly rolled out its freight. He told me he was going to send me a tiny sack of coffee, which proposition, as it did not meet with the slightest encouragement, will of course never be thought of again.

I noticed too, on the train, one of the Arkansas' crew. The same who, though scarcely able to stand on a severely wounded foot, made such a fuss about riding in a carriage while "real ladies" had to walk. Of course he did not recognise us, any more than we would have known him, if Dr Brown[126] had not pointed him out. I hear all of them are now at P. Hudson. Anna told us as we got here, that Dr Addison[127] (the one I disliked because he was so scrupulously neat and dandified while the others were dressed, or rather *un*dressed, for working) was here yesterday, and inquired for the Miss Morgans, saying they were the most charming young ladies he had ever met. On what he founded his opinion, or how he happened to inquire for us in this part of the country, I cannot imagine.

The General brings news of the boys from Jackson. He there met an officer who left Stonewall Jackson's command on the 2d inst, and says Gibbes was unhurt, God be praised! Another saw George a week ago in Richmond, still lame, as the cap of his knee had slipped in that fall, last spring. Of Jimmy we hear not a word, not even as to where he is. It seems as though we are destined never to hear again.

126. Dr. A. Porter Brown, an East Feliciana physician who served in the military hospital at Port Hudson.

127. Dr. W. J. Addison, the surgeon who came aboard the Confederate ram *Arkansas* at Vicksburg and who is referred to as "the doctor" in Sarah's entry of August 6, 1862. He does not appear in the list of the *Arkansas*'s officers in *ORN* because he came to the vessel late. However, his name does appear on a Jackson, Mississippi, roster alongside some of the other officers. See *ORN*, ser. II, 1:318.

[p. 59] Sept 20th. Saturday.

Last evening as Miriam, Wallace,[128] Theodore and I were riding out on the P. Hudson road, I met with quite an accident. Coming back, I fell behind with Wallace, and let the others ride ahead. The horse, more eager to get home than I, started to run, which game I soon put an end to, when he changed to a very rough, uneven gait, and before I could put an end to that, the saddle which had been very loose all the evening, commenced turning. In vain I threw myself to the left, and tried to replace it. It was going over backwards, and I was going— going—gone! Over I went, as quietly and unresisting (when I found I *must* go) as a child. Not a cry or exclamation escaped me, though I was satisfied that I would not reach the ground alive. I merely said in a low tone "Help me The [Theodore]! the saddle has turned" which he, being a few yards ahead, did not hear, so he and Miriam rode on unconscious of my accident.

It took me a long while to reach the ground. When I did, my right eyebrow was ploughing up the dirt, then thump! scrape! went my shoulder, while four legs and a dark body above, satisfied me I was in a dangerous place. I dont know that I ever felt more placid, more resigned, in my life. I knew I would be killed if I did not extricate my foot from the stirrup, noticed that my dress still concealed my feet, pulled on the reins I still held until the horse almost stopped, disengaged my foot, and down came my right hip on the ground, with a blow that satisfied me I was still alive up to the last accounts, at least. Convinced of that, I threw down the reins to pick myself up, and the abruptness of my movements startling him, away he galloped, carrying Miriam the first tidings of my misfortune by showing an empty saddle, just as Wallace found voice to call out to them.

After answering satisfactorily all questions concerning broken bones, The put me up behind Miriam, and so I rode for a mile, when we overtook my horse grazing by the roadside with the saddle reversed. Wallace captured, The saddled, and I mounted him again, and we continued on our way. Theodore, declaring that if I had continued to ride with him, the accident would never have happened, kept close to me, determined that it should not occur again. And so, as it was very late, we took a short cut through the fields, where the grass was only up

128. Wallace Badger, Anna's younger brother.

to the saddle, and the path invisible besides, while the assurance of several pitfalls rendered us still more secure. However, here we have arrived, I having sustained no injury beyond a dirty face and dress, a bruised hip, and the loss of my cameo pin, which I regret much more than the fall. So after all, my long story ends in—nothing!

Genl Carter has just received a letter from Lydia which contains what, to me, is the most melancholy intelligence—the news of the death of Eugene Fowler [129] who was killed on the 22d of Aug., in some battle [p. 60] or skirmish in Virginia. Poor Eugene! The only one of the whole tribe of Hope Estate boys, with the single exception of Gibbes, that I cared a cent for! And I did love Eugene. The death of any of the rest would not have distressed me one tenth part as much as his. I have looked forward to meeting him again, anticipating so much pleasure; and now he will never come! He was always so good and affectionate to Miriam and me, and was so much at home, that we shall miss him sadly. Ah Eugene! you will never hang over my chair, and snatch a kiss from your "own cousin" again! Waller, Phil, Jimmy Mather, or Morris, in my estimation could much better have been spared. [130] Does it not seem that this war will sweep off all who are nearest and dearest, as well as most worthy of life, leaving only those you least care for, unharmed?

Sept 21st

After supper last night, by way of variety Anna, Miriam & I came up to our room, and after undressing, commenced popping corn, and making candy in the fireplace. We had scarcely commenced, when three officers were announced, who found their way to the house, to get some supper, they having very little chance of reaching Clinton before morning, as the cars had run of[f] the track. Of course we could not appear; and they brought bad luck with them, for our corn would not pop, and our candy burned, while to add to our distress the odor of broiled chicken and hot biscuits was wafted upstairs, after a while,

129. One of her Hope Estate cousins, son of her Aunt Adèle Fowler. Eugene was a year older than Sarah.

130. Waller Fowler, the oldest of her Fowler cousins, was 25; Philip, the youngest, was 16. James Mather was 19, and Morris Morgan, not quite 27. She means she could have given them up easier than she could have Eugene.

in the most provoking way. In vain we sent the most pathetic appeals by each servant, for a biscuit apiece, after our hard work. Mrs Carter was obdurate until tired out with messages, she at last sent us an empty jelly cup, a shred of chip beef, two polished drumsticks, and half a biscuit divided in three. With that bountiful repast we were forced to be content, and go to bed.

At sunrise this morning, Mrs Carter left to go down to her father's in Iberville,[131] to see her step-mother who is expected to die. Scarcely had she gone, when six more officers & soldiers came in from the still stationary cars to get their breakfast. We heard that Mr Marsden too, was down there, so the general sent him a nice breakfast, and I sent my love with it; but he had already breakfasted at Mr Elder's. As soon as they left, we prepared for church, and just as we were ready, Capt. Brown[132] & Dr Addison were announced. The Doctor greeted us with an elegant bow, but they did not remain long, as we were about going out.

A long, stupid sermon from that insufferable bore, Mr Garie,[133] gave me a dreadful head ache. Does it not seem that the ministry is overstocked with fools? I grew perplexed and weary of his never ending stupidity, and assiduously read my hymnbook and would have learned it by heart, if his voice had not been so aggravating. He repeated everything at least three times. First "Christ died to save sinners, my breathren" then "Yes, brethren, Christ died [p. 61] that sinners might be saved" next "O christian friends, to save sinners Christ died" until I was wild with irritated nerves and impatience. Invariably, the most beautiful passages of the bible, those I cry over alone, appear absurd from his lips. I dont feel like a christian; I shall not go to hear him again. Better remain at home, than feel so wickedly disgusted in church. Besides, I cannot pray standing. The only thought of prayer that entered my tired head, dull with the monotonous trickling of an unending sermon, was when I dropped on my knees at the final close, in defiance of rules, to render thanks for having heard the last of it.

Many officers were in church, and as I passed out, Col. Breaux joined

131. Helen Carter's father, Edward E. Moore, in Iberville Parish.

132. Very likely Lieutenant Isaac N. Brown, the captain of the *Arkansas*, who had come down from Mississippi and rejoined his officers at Port Hudson.

133. Rev. John M. Geary, pastor of the Plains Presbyterian Church.

me, and escorted Miriam and me to the carriage, where we stood talking some time under the trees before getting in. He gave us a most pressing invitation to name a day to visit the camp that he might "have the pleasure of showing us the fortifications," and we said we would beg the General's permission to do so. Charming Col. Breaux! like all nice men, he is married, of course. He and another officer drove just behind our carriage in coming home, until we came to the fork of the road. Then leaning from their buggy, both gentlemen bowed profoundly, which we as cordially returned. Two more behind followed their example, and to our great surprise, ten, who were seated in a small wagon drawn by two diminutive mules, bowed also, and, not content with that, rose to their feet as the distance between the two roads increased, and raised their caps, though in the most respectful silence. Rather queer; and I would have said impertinent, had they been any others than Confederates fighting for us, who, of course are privileged people.

Monday, 22d. Sept.

I do not know when I have passed a more delightful morning. After an early breakfast we started out on a walk to the woods with our reading and sewing to get full benefit of the fresh air. I took the precaution of borrowing a pair of india-rubbers, as my poor old shoes are by no means a protection from chips and briars, and worn as they are, I can find none to replace them. A walk of a mile or more, half of our way lying through the field we traversed the other evening, brought us to a beautiful shady spot where Anna and Miriam instantly took possession of two splendid grape vines, and reclining at ease the first drew out one of the weakest of Mrs Southworth's weak novels, and the second produced a copy of Thorndale,[134] and then both gave themselves up to the delights of reading.

I was not so fortunate in finding a seat there, so I wandered off to a place some distance from them, discovered a grand vine which served as arm chair or lounge, suspending me some four feet from the ground, and taking instant possession, I threw myself back, at my ease, drew

---

134. The popular novelist E.D.E.N. Southworth. Miriam was reading *Thorndale; or the Conflict of Opinions* by William Henry Smith, first published in 1857.

Thompson from my pocket, and soon forget [*sic*] everything except
[p. 62] the pleasure I was enjoying. Every now and then I would take up
a little pair of pants I was embroidering for Fred Worley,[135] and think
over what I had read while sewing. A muddy little stream or ditch near
my feet, bordered with wild flowers, suggested the Lotus Eaters,[136] and
I let chance, or inclination guide me to the rest.

And what a pleasure it was, to sit alone on my perch sewing in hand,
and book on knee, reading snatches aloud, to the great edification of
Fido who wagged an approving tail, and nondescript birds that came
in with a Caw! Caw! as a chorus. Now and then the low hum of distant
talking reached me, and I heard Anna's loud laugh, or Miriam's; but
I was alone, save for an occasional visit Anna would pay, to discover if
I really was content, saying incredulously that Miriam told her I was
much happier than I would be if surrounded by a crowd. She could not
credit it, so charitably came to see me once in a while to be sure I was
comfortable. We were all sorry when it was time to go home. And halfway, a drizzle overtook us which turned into a brisk rain as we reached
here, when tired, warm, dirty and wet, we were greeted by Charlie who
had stopped on his way to Baton Rouge.

The General offered us five dollars a piece if we would walk to
P. Hudson to see dress parade, and we were all eager for the frolic until
he stipulated we should walk back, too. Eleven miles is too much for
our shoes, as well as our bones. I hardly think we will try it. I declare we
are dreadfully spoiled, and are wonderously at home here! The General is as kind to us as it is possible to be; too good, I am afraid, for
it will unfit us for the rough old life that lies ahead. We roam around,
and do just as we please, with no questions asked. We just got up a
cart for a nice ride when the rain recommenced; and rather than be
disappointed in giving trouble, Miriam and Anna searched the store-
room for pop corn, and despatched half a dozen negroes to the sugar
house for "sirop" to make candy to night. Here the cart comes again
for another trial.

135. Age 3 in the 1860 census, son of Caleb and Esther Worley.
136. Probably a reference to Tennyson's poem "The Lotos-Eaters," whose subject is
drawn from the *Odyssey*.

Sept. 23d.

We had our ride, after all, yesterday, and with it, fun enough for a week. Whenever we met people on the road, in carriage or on horseback, our old mule would plant four dogged legs in the earth, and neither cries nor blows could move her until she thought she had allowed ample time to inspect us; when, with an abrupt leap she would keel us almost over, and start off again. In front of Dr Dortche's [137] we met two buggies and a carriage filled with ladies, while half a dozen gentlemen stood around. Miss Mule came to her usual halt, and of course everybody laughed aloud, so to testify her joy, madam kicked up her heels with delight, and every one laughed still more. We joined in; for it was very amusing to us, as well as them. I dare [p. 63] say there was more enjoyment in our cart, than in their carriages.

But coming back, we had [a] disagreeable experience to mar our pleasure. We were coming through the woods when it was quite late, and Wallace ran us over a stump that came near laying passengers and team in the mud. A severe bump, a lurch to one side which threatened to send us out, and he thought no more of it, until a few yards beyond, an ominous creaking warned us that all was not safe. In an instant we sprang out, and discovered that the wheel was in the act of coming off. Here was a predicament! We were in the woods, half a mile from home, in a fine drizzle, with no alternative save a long walk for we three girls alone, to send help to the two boys and their broken vehicle. Wallace & Charlie were not over brave about it, either, as the latter declared having met a runaway just there, a while earlier. But there was no help for it, and we started off at a brisk pace, and I may answer for myself, at least, that the only thing [that] alarmed me was the certainty of being injured by the rain.

We all shared an equal anxiety about what the General would say, and anticipated his most severe displeasure for breaking his indispensable cart. "O I wish we had staid at home!" was the constant exclamation, and we redoubled our lamentations as we drew nearer the house. At the quarter, we dispatched a negro to help the boys, when lo! here they were behind us. They had taken out the mule, and both had mounted; but even then had not been able to overtake us. We must

137. Dr. Caleb Dortch, a physician, half brother of Will Carter.

have flown. As we reached the house the General's voice (it was too late to see him) greeted us with "Hello! have you won your wager? Just from the Port?" No, we said we had been riding. "In what?" "Your little wagon." "Why did you not order the ambulance?" "Didn't like to without your permission. Besides, O General! we broke down! Ran over a stump and the wheel came off!" "Easily mended" was the answer, and that was our only reproof.

If Helen Carter had been with us, she would have expired of alarm at the idea of the General's displeasure. Pshaw! I dont know why his children stand in such awe of him. A better, or kinder man than he does not live. Our father was such a companion to us, that it seems strange to see them feel so differently here. There is such a thing as having too much reverence for one's parents. Miriam and I, mere strangers, take more liberties, and laugh and talk more familiarly with him, than any one of his own children. We agree, or disagree with him, just as we please, and argue our side of the question where one of the others would have utter[ed] a respectful "Yes sir" and nothing more. Why are people so differently constituted? Every day we say "Thank God that father was always our best friend." I wont be afraid of Genl Carter any more, what ever the others may be. He has been the kindest friend we have had for many a long day, and after father and our brothers, I love him better than any man in the world, God bless him!

[p. 64] Sept 24th   Sis' Wedding Day, 1850[138]

Yesterday the General saluted us with "Young ladies, if you will ride in a 'Confederate' carriage, you may go to dress parade this evening." Now, in present phraseology, "Confederate" means anything that is rough, unfinished, unfashionable or poor. You hear of Confederate dresses, which means last year's. Confederate bridle, means a rope halter. Confederate silver, a tin cup or spoon. Confederate flour, is corn meal, etc. In this case, the Confederate carriage is a Jersey wagon with four seats, a top of hickory slats covered with leather, and the whole drawn by mules. We accepted gladly, partly for the ride and sight, partly to show we were not ashamed of a very comfortable conveyance; so with Mrs Badger as chaperon we went off in grand style.

138. The year appears to have been written in later.

I must say I felt rather abashed, and wished myself at home as we drove in town,[139] and had the gaze of a whole regiment rivetted on us. But soon the men fell in line, and I did not feel so painfully conspicuous. I was amused at a contrast nearby, too. There was but one carriage present, besides ours, though there were half a dozen ladies on horseback. This carriage was a very fine one, and in it sat three of the ugliest, dowdiest, worse [sic] dressed females I ever saw. We three girls sat in our rough carriage as comfortable as could be, dressed—well! we could not have been dressed better—and looking our very best. Sans mentir,[140] I think the Confederates were much the most respectable. And what a sad sight the 4th La. was, that was then parading! Men that had fought at Shiloh and Baton R., were barefooted. Rags was their only uniform, for very few possessed a complete suit, and those few wore all varieties of colors and cuts. Hats could be seen of every style and shape, from the first ever invented, down to the last one purchased evidently some time since. Yet he who had no shoes, looked as happy as he who had, and he who had a cap, had something to toss up, that's all.

Four or five that we knew gathered around our vehicle and talked to us. Mr. Hueston[141] told me he heard I had been thrown, severely injured, had a narrow escape, etc. Was *not* thrown! Saddle turned! A few steps off we recognized Mr. Scales.[142] He would stare very hard at us, and if we turned towards him, would look quickly the other way, as though afraid to meet our gaze. Presently he gave us an opportunity, and we bowed. He came forward eagerly, blushing deeply, and looking very much pleased, and shook hands with us, and remained some time talking. He said he had not heard of our arrival, but would call as soon as possible. Mr Talbot had joined Breckenridge. Having seen the last of that parade, he invited us to see that of his sailors, which was next; but it was too far; so we turned off to see Col. Breaud's, a mile away. His, the 30th La., is a beautiful encampment on a large open common. Parade was almost over as we reached there, and soon the Colonel came to meet us.

139. Port Hudson.

140. To tell the truth.

141. Probably Eli Huston, listed as age 24 and a medical student in the 1860 census. The family lived near Port Hudson.

142. Midshipman Dabney M. Scales, one of the *Arkansas*'s officers.

Sarah Morgan, probably on the eve of the war.

Judge Thomas Gibbes Morgan, Sarah's father.
From *A Confederate Girl's Diary*.

The State Asylum for the Deaf and Blind, where the Morgans sought refuge during the shelling of the city. Gouache by Adrien Persac dated 1859, courtesy of the Anglo-American Art Museum, Louisiana State University.

Facing page, top: A photograph of Church Street in Baton Rouge taken in the spring of 1863. The Morgan home is in the center of the picture, largely hidden by the foliage. *Bottom:* A view of the same block and the home as it looked in the 1890s after the front had been altered. Louisiana and Lower Mississippi Valley Collections, LSU Libraries.

Union army encamped at Baton Rouge, just to the east of the Morgan home. A. D. Lytle took this photograph from the upper floor of the Heroman Building.

The Union ironclad *Essex* in the river at Baton Rouge. Louisiana and Lower Mississippi Valley Collections, LSU Libraries.

Ruins of the State House after the fire of December 28, 1862. Completed in 1850, the building stood on the site of an earlier Morgan home. Louisiana and Lower Mississippi Valley Collections, LSU Libraries.

Ruins of Baton Rouge homes burned by the Union army following the battle of August 5, 1862. Anticipating a second Confederate attack, the Federals cleared several blocks around their positions. Louisiana and Lower Mississippi Valley Collections, LSU Libraries.

April 26th 1862.

There is no word in the English language which can express the state in which we are all now, and have been for the last three days. Day before yesterday news came early in the morning of three of the enemy's boats passing the forts, and then the excitement commenced, and increased so rapidly on hearing of the sinking of eight of our gunboats in the engagement, the capture of the forts, and last night of the burning of the wharves and cotton in the city, while the Yankees were taking possession, that to day the excitement has reached almost the crazy point. I believe that I am one of the most self possessed in my small circle of acquaintance, and yet, I feel such a craving for news from Miriam, and mother and Jimmy, who are in the city, such patriotic and enthusiastic sentiments, etc, that I believe I am as crazy as the rest, and it is all humbug when they tell me I am cool. Nothing can be heard positively, for every report except that our gunboats were sunk, and theirs coming up to the city, has been contradicted, until we do not really know whether it is in their possession or not. We only know we had best be prepared for anything; so day before yesterday Lilly and I secured what little jewelry we had, that may yet be of value to us if we must run. I vow I will not move one step, unless forced away! I remain here, come what will. We went this morning to see the cotton

A page of the diary. In order to save space, Sarah wrote to the edges of the book.
Courtesy of the Manuscript Department, Duke University Library.

The *Arkansas*, from *Official Records of the Union and Confederate Navies in the War of the Rebellion.* No photographs of the Confederate ironclad are known to exist, but several drawings survive.

Black refugees uprooted by the war, photographed in a contraband camp in Baton Rouge in the early months of 1863. Former slaves in areas occupied by the Union army were known as contrabands. Louisiana and Lower Mississippi Valley Collections, LSU Libraries.

General Thomas Williams, in command of the Union army at Baton Rouge in the summer of 1862, offered protection to the Morgans.

Union General Benjamin F. Butler, better known as "Beast Butler" to the citizens of occupied New Orleans. Library of Congress.

Admiral David G. Farragut's fleet attempting to pass the Confederate guns on the bluffs at Port Hudson, from a drawing in *Harper's Weekly*. Courtesy of the Louisiana State Library.

General Albert G. Carter.
"A better, or kinder man than he
does not live," Sarah wrote. Courtesy
of Evelyn M. Lambert.

Lydia Carter Morgan,
daughter of General Carter and wife
of Gibbes Morgan. Courtesy of Ed
and Jo Ann Hackenberg.

The train that Sarah rode, photographed at the Clinton and Port Hudson Railroad depot in Clinton in the 1880s. *Right:* Colonel I. G. W. Steedman, one of the officers who came to Linwood to call on her. Louisiana and Lower Mississippi Valley Collections, LSU Libraries.

Left: Linwood, prior to renovation and restoration in the 1980s. The gable was added by Sarah's nephew Howell Morgan after he acquired the plantation in the early 1900s. Courtesy of Ed and Jo Ann Hackenberg.

Some of the New Orleans citizens who registered as enemies of the United
States were allowed to leave the city early in 1863. This drawing from *Harper's
Weekly* shows them departing from Port Hickok, the point of arrival for the
Morgans on their journey to New Orleans.

Harper's Weekly drawing showing Confederate officers imprisoned in the
Customhouse in New Orleans following the surrender of Port Hudson.

Sarah Morgan Dawson in 1886, when she was forty-four. Courtesy of the Manuscript Department, Duke University Library.

Portrait of Sarah taken at Asheville, North Carolina, probably in the late 1880s. Courtesy of David Madden.

Sarah Morgan Dawson on her deathbed, Paris, 1909. Courtesy of the Manuscript Department, Duke University Library.

I did not look at the drill. I was watching the hundreds of tents—it look[ed] like a great many—and was wondering how men could live in such places, and was trying [p. 65] to fancy what George's, or Gibbes's looked like. It was pleasant to watch the barefoot soldiers race around like boys let loose from school, tossing caps and chips at two old grey geese that flew in circles around the encampment, just as though they had never had more ernest work. One grey headed man stood in the door of his tent, while a black headed young one danced before him, to his own whistle, with his arms akimbo. Altogether it was a very pretty picture; but poor men! how can they be happy in these tents?

Col. Breaud as charming as ever. He said he had made the engineer explain all the works to him, for the express purpose of showing them to us, himself; and that as soon as he returned from B.R., where he was going in the morning, he would call, and get us to appoint a day to ride down on horseback. We came home liking him *worse* than ever. Camp fires were begining to be lighted as we drove off; and the General, giving the driver his horse to ride, took his place and drove us down those steep hills with a speed, and recklessness, that occasionally took my breath away. I forgot to say that for the first time, I saw the process of locking a wheel, an operation that filled me with surprise, to sage Miriam's great pity and compassion. The General dispensed with the precaution, however.

I know I have no business writing at this hour of the night, and in bed, too, but still I am doing it. I have been too sick all day, so try it now that every one has been asleep for hours, and Mirian has gone to stay all night with Mrs Worley.[143] Miriam decided I should ride after breakfast, so ride I did, though so nauseated as hardly to be able to speak. I stood it for almost four miles, when I felt it was useless to contend, and turned my horse homeward. By the time I got here, I hardly dared think. I jumped down, ran up to my room, and before I could get my clothes off, found myself clinging to the bed post as sick as sick could be. After I tumbled on the bed, Miriam and Mrs Badger found me, recommended me to my bed for the rest of the day, ordered four gallons of scalding water for my feet and a quart of scalding tea for my throat, together with several quilts, this warm day, all of which I

143. Esther Worley, age 26 in the 1860 census. She was General Carter's niece.

patiently submitted to, though I cannot remember the last time I spent the day in bed.

After being killed with kindness, I got up this evening and started off riding in the little wagon again, which broke down for the second time, a quarter of a mile away. We had it fixed up, got in again, broke down, refixed, and afraid to turn directly back, resolved to go around by Mrs Elders, a perfect triangle, to avoid another accident. Just as we got at the farthest part of the angle away from home, off rolled the wheel, and we were forced to jump out and walk. A heavy rain had fallen, it was dark again, and in spite of the hot baths, here I was expose[d] to all that could kill me, and Anna too, had a very bad cold. But with the three boys we marched bravely along in spite of all. And with another cup of Mrs Badger's tea, and another bath, here I am writing in bed when I should be asleep. Good night, Almost Sleepy!

[p. 66] Sept 26th. Friday.

My mark finds me at Linwood,[144] though I had not the slightest idea that it would. Wonder where twenty pages beyond, will find me? At home, I hope and pray, though I am as happy here as I could possibly be in any place on earth.

Stirring news from our armies comes pouring in. Sunday, Col. Breaud told us of Wool's defeat, and the great number of prisoners, cannon, and the large supplies of stores and ammunition that we had captured.[145] Then Tuesday we heard of three great battles in Maryland, the third one still continuing; but no particulars of any of them. Yesterday came tidings of our having recrossed the Potomac, and to day we heard that McClellan's army has been cut to pieces; but whether it is the same old fight or a new one, I cannot as yet learn; for reliable information is not easily obtained in America at this period.

Did I ever record how little truth there was in any of that last Clinton news? It speaks for its self, though. Not a boat lay at B.R., Camp Moore was not even threatened, Ponchitoula Station was burned, but the one

144. When she was writing the entry of September 6, Sarah wondered where she would be twenty pages hence—and made an X in the margins there.

145. Sarah may be referring to the surrender of the arsenal at Harpers Ferry earlier in the month, a defeat some blamed on General John E. Wool. A veteran of the War of 1812, Wool was in his eighties.

battery was retaken by our men the same night. But still these false reports cannot equal the Yankees. Take, for instance the report of the Captain of the Essex. I give Genl. Carter for my authority. The Captain reports having been fired on by a battery of thirty six large guns, at Port Hudson, some weeks ago, when he opened fire, and silenced them, one after the other, from the first to the last. Not a shot from the "rebel" batteries reached them, and not a casualty on their side occurred.[146] But the loss of the Confederates must have been awful. He came within—I forget how many—yards from the shore, and there was not a live man to be seen. Keen! [he] did not mention if there were any dead ones!

Now for the other side. There were but four guns mounted there at the time. Shot & shell from those four certainly reached something, for one was seen to enter a port hole, from whence issued frightful shrieks soon after, and it is well known that the Essex is so badly injured by "something" as to be in a sinking condition, and only kept afloat by a gunboat lashed on either side. If she is uninjured, why did she not return and burn Natchez as she announced? In leaving P. Hudson, where "not a live man was to be seen" (nor a dead one to be found) she stopped at Mr Babin's,[147] just below Dr Nolan's, where she remained the rest of the day. After she left, being curious to discover the reason of her short stay, Mr Babin walked to the place where she had been, and discovered sixteen fresh graves on the bank.[148] If they buried them as they did at B.R. and Vicksburg, four in a grave, how many would they be? But granting there were but sixteen, would that prove the veracity of the Captain? Poor man! Perhaps he is related to Pope, and cannot help himself.[149]

146. In his report to the secretary of the navy, William D. Porter wrote that the Confederates "opened on us a vigorous fire with heavy siege guns" and that the *Essex* was struck fourteen times, but "without material damage." He said he had reason to believe the enemy was considerably damaged by fire from his vessel, but concluded: "A land force will be necessary to complete the destruction of this fort." *ORN*, ser. I, 19:181–82.

147. The Pierre Paul Babin plantation, but the senior Babin had died and it is not clear which Mr. Babin she means.

148. Nothing in *ORN* or elsewhere confirms this.

149. Sarah is referring to John Pope, recently removed from command in Virginia. The controversial Union general's penchant for writing tactless general orders and blaming others for his errors had earned him contempt in the South.

[p. 67] Sept 27th.

I often wonder how lies first came in the world, and whether those who originate them do not believe them as firmly as any one else would believe truth. Lying seems to be the common creed of children and servants. If one lies, believing firmly what they say, is it a sin to him? On that plea only can I excuse the Castletons, who I am loath to believe take willful pleasure, or have the barefacedness to deliberately concoct all their tales about us and our affairs. Perhaps they still retain the vivid imaginations, together with the common habit of small children—all the world knows what an innocent child Mollie is—and believe they are telling the truth; which they probably are, to the best of their ability. Here is a specimen of the glory they have achieved. Nannie went to Capt. West[150] in great distress about the report of our being so very friendly with the Yankees. "Who says it is so?" he asked. "The Castletons. You know they are very intimate, and Mrs Stith says she was present when a Federal officer called, herself. And she says they are received by those young ladies every day." "Stith! Castleton! then dont you know it is only a lie?" was the not very gentlemanly reply.

Why will I persist in recalling the names of those girls? I never think of them unless some other train of thought brings them. A falsehood, or rather idle fabrication I have just heard of, suggested their name as any thing false invariably does; and made me think of them. I was wondering if their error preceeded [sic] from ignorance, and lack of reason, as this harmless story does. Anna told me of having hear[d] Lennice[151] telling the other servants that she knew there were spirits, because I often talked to them. Every morning and evening I walked to the graveyard with a basket of flowers, and would sit by father's and Harry's graves and call their spirits to me; and they would all fly to me, and talk and sing with me for hours until I would tell them goodbye and go home, when they would go away too. I suppose the ignorant girl, having foundation enough from my frequent visits there, which were most often alone, made up the rest to account for my never seeming to like company out there. The fervent "Good Lord!" with which the tale

150. Probably Captain Edward West of the 4th Louisiana.

151. One of the Carter slaves. Her earlier presence in Baton Rouge suggests that she was attached to the household of Lydia Carter Morgan when Lydia and Gibbes lived next door to his father.

was received by the other servants, and the full credence they gave it, might have proved unpleasant if further circulated; and I believe some members of the family found it necessary to put an end to it at once.

And speaking of the graveyard recal[l]s something I heard for the first time last night. Miriam was telling me that Tiche had asked if we knew that Mr Sparks had visited Harry's grave? That he had got a basket of flowers from the Davidsons, and had made their driver carry it for him. And the man had [p. 68] told her that after filling the vases with roses, and spreading them over the grave, he had thrown himself on it with a shriek of despair, calling on Harry to forgive him; that it was only because forced by his father that he had killed him; and calling on God to prove that he would give his life gladly to recall Harry's. The man thought him a raving maniac and fled in terror. Miriam asked Fanny[152] if it was true, and she said yes; she had gathered the flowers for him herself. I saw them there, but little knew whose hand had brought them. I perceived at once that they were not mine and touched even to tears by so silent an offering from an unknown person, I said "It is some woman's work; God bless the hand that laid them there!" I cannot say how much that little tribute affected me. And Mr Sparks, I do not retract the blessing now! No! "God have mercy on him" has been my prayer ever since I knew what an awful loss you had caused us. God knows that I never even desired *this* revenge—remorse standing over his grave. It has ever been "God pity and forgive!" never yet for an instant "God pursue and avenge!"

Sept 28th.

We were roused up at four o'clock last night by the arrival of Lydia and Eugene Carter,[153] the first from Virginia and the second from Tennessee and of course there was very little sleep for any of us, so anxious were we to hear the news they brought. First I learned that Gibbes was safe up to the seventeenth, that George in spite of the advice of his surgeon had rejoined Stonewall Jackson in Maryland, and Jimmy was midshipman on the iron clad Palmetto State at Charleston. How

152. Fanny Davidson, later Fanny Trezevant.

153. Eugene Carter, General Carter's son by his first marriage, was Lydia's half brother. He had come home on leave from Tennessee, where the 1st Louisiana Cavalry was then operating.

thankful I was to hear that much, I need not say. Lydia said they all three looked remarkably well; Jimmy, handsomer than ever. After that, news of all kind[s] came indiscriminately. The boys were very anxious about us, but had no idea of our misfortunes, or whereabouts. They believed us still in Baton Rouge, and feared we had been there during the battle. Lydia only heard of our house having been plundered when she reached Alabamah so of course they are still ignorant of it. They were all very homesick, but said that we were their only trouble.

A few of the "Castletonia" had reached them through brother officers; and George swore to make himself understood by the ladies if he ever saw them again. A gentleman from Cooper's Wells [154] told Lydia that they never tired of repeating their stories to every new arrival; and no man was suffered to depart without having heard a few. If a gentleman friend of ours, or the boys inquired if they knew the Miss Morgans of B.R., "O yes!" would be the answer. "Intimately! But you know they have turned Yankee. Received Federal officers every day, and placed all their property under Yankee protection. I" (or "my [p. 69] sister" as it happened who was retailing the lie, meaning Mrs Stith) "slept in their house when it was surrounded by a Yankee guard. O they are perfectly in favor of the Yankees," and so on, as long as they could lie without pausing to collect their ideas, or could get any one to listen to them. The gentleman said he had taken the liberty to denounce it as a lie, when he heard it publicly discussed in bar rooms.

I dont mind Mattie's lying; it hurts only her; but we owe her a grudge for having our name bandied about in billiard saloons and at camp mess tables by people who have no right to pronounce it, even. Notoriety may be to her taste, though hardly to ours. Think of a common, low soldier who stopped for buttermilk somewhere where Anna was, introducing the subject. "It is all false!" Anna interrupted. The man answered "O miss! you dont suppose we believe it? We would not believe such stories of *any* young ladies, much less these; for if they are true, their conduct must have been perfectly disgraceful. But though we know these stories to be lies, it does not prevent their being discussed by the soldiers in camp."

This we owe you, Mrs Stith; you who with your sister played the

154. Popular resort near Raymond, Mississippi, south and west of Jackson.

part of hypocrite and liar through so many years when you called our father's house "home" and almost daily eat [sic] his bread! His daughters, your "intimate friends," you hold up as proper subjects of discussion among people who, how ever suited to *your* rank, have hardly associated with them. In trying to put yourselves on an equality, misguided women! have you dragged us down, or are you sunk still farther in the mire? Let them rave!

Lydia saw Mr McGimsey too, at Lynchburg, who sent me his "regards." Poor fellow! he says he still has "Dreams." He told her a few, but she says they were chiefly about meeting me at a ball, when I always treated him with the most freezing coldness. The same old nightmare! How often he has told me of that same dream, that tormented him eighteen months ago! He says he often thinks of me now. And he still "dreams" of me! "Dreams are baseless fabrics whose timbers are mere moon beams." [155] Apply your own proverb! And Gibbes complained that I never wrote now, and said something so sweet about my letters that in future I shall be afraid to write, conscious of how undeserved his praise is, and desiring to merit it too much to be willing to lose it altogether. After swearing me to secrecy, Lydia told me he had confessed having read my letters out to the officers of his regiment, who professed to be highly edified, and who would often ask if he had received another letter from his "smart, pretty little sister." Ah Gibbes! What idle tales you tell on me!

[p. 70] Bless the boys! how many good, honest people have they caused to be disappointed in their "Little sister"! When I first came out in N. Orleans, I found I was only another being, under the same name. I would make my first bow to a perfect stranger who would greet me with "Ah! I know you already! your brothers have told me all about you! Dr. Morgan [156] says you are devoted to your books. And your brothers Gibbes and George have talked of you too. They told me of your magnificent hair, and I see they were right. They said—" this, that, or the other, no matter what! Suffices it to say they flattered me so as to invariably caused [sic] their friends to be disappointed in me. Where they [sic] boys got their delusion, that of believing I had even common sense,

155. Sarah echoes Shakespeare, *The Tempest*.
156. Harry Morgan.

I cannot imagine. One of these days when they open their eyes, what a surprise it will be to them!

Gibbes told Lydia again that he was satisfied I would never marry. When asked his reason, he answered something about never finding one to suit me, and my being too well satisfied with my present lot. Right, as to the latter, O Gibbes! As to the former, dont let us boast; wait and see. But not yet, O Gibbes! not yet, for worlds! I have but one life, one heart; shall I throw away both on one who values neither half so much as one of you? I am content with my brothers; what do I care for a stranger? At all events, not yet! This life will answer for me now; and after a while I will adopt some motherless niece or nephew, and prove God has not made me in vain—that I am worthy of a better life than this. I was not made for a wife; but I was destined to be an old maid in my cradle. This is my path in life: the adopted mother of some orphaned child, and the housekeeper at the hearth of some widowed, or bachelor brother. Would that be a useless life? I rather fancy it. And—

A clatter of horse hoofs down the road! And bent over the window sill which is my desk, my fingers are not presentable with the splattering of this vile pen in consequence of my position. Two hours yet to sundown, so of course I am not dressed. They come nearer still. Now I see them! Dr Addison and Mr Milligan![157] I shall not hurry my toilette for them. It will take some time to comb my hair, too. Wish I could remain up here!

Tuesday Sept 30th.

It required very little persuasion to induce those gentlemen to stay to supper the other evening, and it was quite late before they took their leave. Dr Addison I was very much pleased with, and so were all the rest. Mr Milligan, none of us fell desperately in love with. He is too nonchalant and indifferent, besides having a most [p. 71] peculiar pronunciation which grated harshly on my ears, and that no orthography could fully express. Garb, for instance, was distorted into gairb, yard into yaird, Airkansa, and all such words that I can only imitate by a violent dislocation of my lower jaw that puts Anna in convulsions

157. Samuel Milliken, acting master of the *Arkansas*.

of laughter—only she would laugh the same if it was *not* funny. This Kentuckian pronunciation grates "hairshly" on my Southern ears.

Miriam addressed herself exclusively to the Doctor, so I was obliged to confine my attention entirely to neglected Mr Milligan, in which pious duty I was ably and charitably assisted by the General. Speaking of the bravery and daring displayed by the Southern soldiers during this war, Mr Milligan mentioned the dangerous spot he had seen us in the first day we went down to the "Airkansas" and said that, lying directly across the point, from the Essex, they expected every instant to see one of her shells explode among us, and were very uneasy about our position as we did not seem to know the danger. I asked him if he had observed anything peculiar among the dozen planters and overseers standing a short distance from us, when the Captain sent us word that our position was a very dangerous one as they expected the Essex to open fire every instant, and we had best stand below the levee, higher up where we would be safe from shells. "I noticed that before any of you understood your position, that every man had disappeared as though by magic."

Now I had noticed that myself. When I turned, under shelter of the levee, our gallant planters were galloping off in the distance. While Ginnie and I looked and laughed, we suddenly found ourselves the sole objects on the horizon; the other girls were in the road below, going carelessly towards the carriage; so we followed, having lost sight of the brave representatives of Southern Chivalry, being the last to leave the supposed field of danger. To my former remark, let me add that there is only one set who take better care for their safety than married women; and that set is composed exclusively of the "Home Guard." Timid girls, either through ignorance or fun, compose the majority of the brave "men" that the volunteer service has not absorbed.

The General brings a message from Col. Breaux saying he will "do himself the pleasure of spending the evening with the Miss Morgans this week." Too exclusive by half! Mrs Badger laughingly suggest[s] that the rest of the family should retire to bed, since their company is not desired. Not so! In case there should be another visiter, the most uninteresting is sure to fall to my lot, and I will need at least one aid-de-camp to sustain me. It is just my luck. If there is one fool in a crowd, that fool will invariably be paired off with me; if they are all fools, I am sure to get the biggest one. The man who is most distasteful to me is sure to be the one who loves me most.

(Here let me be candid and confess that hating is the effect produced by [t]his confession, [p. 72] and not the cause that leads to the result by some strange contradiction. The man who says to me "I love you" must be a fool to say such a thing, as a man of understanding could not be guilty of such folly as loving such a girl as I, when he sees so many thousand around me wiser, better, and handsomer than I. I have an unbounded contempt for fools; the man who says he loves me is a fool; ergo I have for him a pity that is more than akin to contempt, and I would not marry unless I had the highest respect for the individual. Walking with Jimmy one evening last Spring, we discussed this question, he laughing at my fastidiousness. "If you hate a fellow for telling you he loves you, I dont see how the devil you will ever marry unless you tell him so yourself!" was his perplexed exclamation. I laughed aloud. "That is it! but I might despise him if he should say 'Yes;' so Jimmy you see you are bound to have an old maid sister!" "You are a strange girl" was his final comment.)

All this parenthesis à-pro-pos of my distressing destiny in bearing burdens too trivial to be imposed on others! Let me try to recall a few more which I have borne so long that I would feel injured if deprived of now. I never in my life rode on the back seat of a carriage if it contained more than one person besides myself. I never went riding with a small party that I did not mount the meanest horse and most uncomfortable saddle—except once, when I rode Will Carter's race horse for hunting in spite of Miriam's disapprobation and displeasure; when she declared I would be thrown out and killed; and instead, I kept ahead of the rest, with Will C. and the hounds, and she got pitched, herself, over a fence nine inches high. But the pleasure of that one ride was turned into misery by knowing I was on a finer horse than she. And I wondered if she felt such dreadful compunctions on all other occasions, as I suffered then; and dismounted satisfied that the pleasure, turned into pain by the consciousness of being more comfortable than others, was not worth purchasing a second time, nor have I since experienced it.

Mother buys us dresses, and invariably the greatest number and the prettiest go to Miriam. I am glad of it; I could not be happy if my dress were prettier than hers. At home, when we would dress for the evening, I would wait to see what she would wear, and would put on a plain or handsome dress just as she would. But if I dressed first, and wore a plain, simple one, she would put on her handsomest and look like a queen while I played the barmaid. You see she does not notice pretty things as I do. I have a little soul, which picks up trifles and builds a world of them. She has a great one which over looks my molehill, and can compass a mountain. I could perform no act of selfsacrifice, unless it happened once a year and was the veriest trifle the performance of which would be more agreeable than otherwise. Tell Miriam to lay down all comfort, happiness, her life—she can comprehend you; it is worth an effort; it is at your service! She will not hesitate.

[p. 73] October 1st. Wednesday.

Just after sunset yesterday, Anna and I were walking down the road towards the sugar house, she reading occasionally from Abbott's Napoleon,[158] and then pausing for me to explain the *very* difficult passages she could not understand, when we suddenly became aware of the approach of a horse, and raising our bowed heads, beheld Colonel Breaux and another before us, to our infinite surprise and astonishment. The Colonel sprang from his horse and advanced on foot; his companion slowly followed his example, and was introduced as Capt Morrison.[159] We adjourned our historical fit for some future period, and walked home with the gentlemen. Miriam did not get back from her excursion to the cain patch until it was quite late; when, after sitting down a few moments, she ran upstairs to change her dress. She had just put it on an hour before, but nothing would do but she must dress up fine; so she put on her handsomest organdie. In vain I pointed to my simple pink muslin with a white body that I had worn all day, and begged she would not make the contrast between us more striking than ever, as I felt I could not change it without exciting remark. She was obdurate; dressed herself in gorgeous array, and, as usual, I looked like her lady's maid.

Col. Breaux was even more entertaining than usual. O what a charm-

158. John S. C. Abbott's *History of Napoleon Bonaparte.*
159. Captain Charles E. Morrison of the 30th Louisiana.

ing companion! It is really a treat to listen to a man who converses so well, and who speaks as though he believed you capable of appreciating what ever subject he is discussing. Capt. Morrison I can briefly describe in the following sentence: he fell *exclusively* to my lot. Farther explanation would be superfluous. I made incredible exertions. I started every subject imaginable, except books. I felt that would be hopeless, and kept it as a dernier resort.[160] Every thing else failed; that remained, so I asked if he could get any thing to read in camp, etc. I thought for an instant that he *would* exchange an idea; but no; he described the store where he bought them,[161] and skipped over the books.

Col. Breaux paid my hair the most extravagant compliments. He said he could not say his prayers for looking at it in church Sunday before last. Perhaps that is the reason St Paul said a woman should not worship in church with her head uncovered! But as the Yankees stole my bonnet, I am reduced to wearing my black straw walking hat with its curled brim, trimmed in black ribbon with golden sheaves of wheat. Two years ago this fall, father threw me a banknote at table, and I purchased this with it. Now it is my only headgear, except a sunbonnet. When I heard Col. Breaux speak of it, I am ashamed to confess I was foolish enough to regret the fourteen inches I was induced to cut from the length of my hair this summer. It is only to my knee now, and I am ashamed of it. Before leaving, which was not until quite late, this evening was named for our ride to the fortifications, to our infinite delight, as we have dreamed and [p. 74] talked of nothing else for a week. The natural consequence to me will be a stupid companion and very dull time, as I have anticipated so much fun.

A dispatch just received from Gibbes, from Mobile, on his way home. I am so happy! But what can bring him? I fear—

Lydia has gone to Clinton to meet him at Lilly's.

Oct 2d. Thursday

With what extraordinary care we prepared for our ride yesterday! One would have thought that some great event was about to take place.

160. Last resort.

161. Another Louisiana diarist, Robert Patrick, who was in one of the regiments then at Port Hudson, wrote on January 4, 1863, that he "went down in town to-day and bought several novels from Barton, who has opened a book store." *Reluctant Rebel: The Secret Diary of Robert Patrick, 1861–1865*, edited by F. Jay Taylor (Baton Rouge, 1959), 74.

But in spite of our long toilette, we stood ready equipped almost an hour before Col. Breaux arrived. I was standing in a novel place—up on the banisters looking over the fields to see if he was coming, and not perceiving him made some impatient exclamation, when lo! he appeared before me, having only been concealed by the wood-pile; and O my prophetic soul! Capt. Morrison was by his side! Before I could spring to the ground, I knew my destiny; it was patent.

There was quite a cavalcade of us: Mr Carter and his wife, Mrs Badger & Mrs Worley, in two buggies; the three boys who of course followed on horseback, and the two gentlemen, Miriam, Anna & I riding also. It was really a very pretty sight, when Capt. Morrison and I, who took the lead going, would reach the top of one of the steep hills, and look down on the procession in the hollow below. Fortunately it was a very cloudy evening; for starting at four, it would have been very unpleasant to ride that distance with the sun in our faces. As we reached the town we heard the loud report of two cannon which caused the elder ladies to halt and suggest the propriety of a return. But if it was a gunboat, that was the very thing I was anxious to see; so we hurried on to the batteries. It proved to be only practising, however.

At the first one we stopped at, the crew of the Arkansas were drilling. After stopping a while there, we followed the river to see the batteries below. It was delightful to ride on the edge of a high bluff with the muddy Mississippi below, until you fancied what would be the probable sensation if the horse should plunge down into the waters; then it ceased to be so pleasant. The great, strong animal I rode could have carried me over without a protest on my part; for the ridiculous bit in his mouth was by no means suited to his strength; and it would require a more powerful arm than mine to supply the deficiency.

Miriam had generously sacrificed her own comfort to give him to me; and rode fiery Joe instead of her favorite. But it was by no means a comfort to me. Then Anna was not reconciled to her pony while I was on such a fine horse, until I proposed an exchange, and gladly dismounted near an old mill two miles and a half below P. Hudson, as we returned home and succeeded in convincing her that pleasure and comfort are not always to be found on the handsomest horse, without saying a word on the subject. Well, if I had kept my horse, she would always have felt ill used, [p. 75] and that I was better mounted and enjoying myself more. I gave him to her; and now she thinks it was self sacrifice on her part to take him and merely did it to accommodate me. Perhaps we have an equal right to the feeling; but I must not assert it.

In leaving the town, we lost sight of the buggies as there was no carriage road that might follow the bluff; and though there was one just back, we never saw our buggies again. Once, following a crecent [sic], far below us lay the water battery concealed by the trees that grew by the water's edge, looking, from where we stood like quite a formidable precipice. Then still beyond, after leaving the river, we passed through a camp where the soldiers divided their attention equally between eating their supper and staring at us in the most profound silence. Then, through an old gate, down a steep hill, past a long line of rifle pits, a winding road, and another camp where more men stared and cooked their supper, we came to the last battery but one, which lay so far below, that it was too late to visit it. We returned highly delighted with what we had seen, and our pleasant ride. For I found that my escort could exchange an occasional remark; the slightest incidents of the ride elicited a few. Besides, the night before I omitted two topics which he *could* talk about—War, and the fortifications; though he had nothing original to say about either. Still, I found him extremely amiable and accommodating.

It was late when we got back, as altogether our ride had been some fifteen miles in length. As soon as we could exchange our habits for our evening dresses, we rejoined our guests at the supper table where none of us wanted for an appetite except poor Capt. Morrison who could not be tempted by the dishes we so much relished. After supper, Col. Breaux and I got into a discussion, rather, *he* talked, while I listened with eyes and ears, with all my soul. It was long since I had met such a man; I know but four such as he: father, Brother, Harry, & Mr Smith. No one had talked so to me since father died. The mind recalled his, and I listened with double pleasure. What would I not give for such knowledge! He knows every thing, and can express it all in the clearest, purest language, though he says he could not speak a word of English at fourteen![162]

---

162. A biographical sketch published long after the war states that Breaux spoke only French during his boyhood and that "it was for the purpose of giving him an opportunity to learn the English language that he was sent to a northern school." *Biographical and Historical Memoirs,* 1:315.

The discussion commenced by some remark I made about physiognomy; he took it up, and passed on to phrenology—in which he is no great believer. From there he touched on the mind, and I listened entranced, to him. Presently he asserted that I possessed reasoning faculties, which I fear me I very rudely denied. You see, every moment the painful conviction of my ignorance, grew more painful still, until it was most humiliating; and I repelled it rather as a mockery. He described for my benefit the process of reasoning, the art of thinking. I listened more attentively still, resolving to profit by his words. I would strive to obtain this great gift. But how could I, weak, unreasoning, ignorant, helpless as I am? You must be educated for it; and I—?

O folly! to presume that I could be otherwise than the fool I am! The Will is not lacking; but the Means? He touched on Philosophy, and talked like—like Col. Breaux! Then he turned [p. 76] the conversation on quite another theme. Health was the subject. He delicately alluded to my fragile appearance, and spoke of the necessity of a strong constitution to sustain a vigorous mind. If the mind prevailed over the weak body, in its turn it became affected by decay, and would eventually lose its powers. It was applicable to all cases; he did not mean that I was sickly, but that my appearance bespoke one who had not been used to the exercise that was most necessary for me. Horseback rides, walks, fresh air, were necessary to preserve health. No man had greater disgust for a freckled face than he; but a fair face could be preserved by the most ordinary precautions and even improved by such exercise.

He illustrated my case by showing the difference between the flower growing in the sunshine, and that growing in a cellar. Father's old illustration, and very words, when he so often tried to impress on me the necessity of gaining a more robust frame than nature had bestowed! And a letter he had made Hal write me, showing the danger of such neglect, rose before me. I forgot Col. Breaux; I remembered only the ardent desire of those two, who seemed to speak to me through his lips. It produced its effect. I felt the guilt I had incurred by not making greater efforts to gain a more robust frame, and putting on my sunbonnet as I arose from the breakfast table this morning, I took my seat here on the wide balcony where I have remained seated on the floor ever since, with a chair for a desk, trying to drink an extra amount of fresh air.

I was sorry when Col. Breaux arose to take his leave. As he took my hand, I said ernestly "Thank you for giving me something to think about." He looked gratified, made some pleasant remark, and after talking a while longer, said goodnight again and rode off. While undressing, Miriam and I spoke of nothing else. And when I lay down, and looked in my own heart and saw my shocking ignorance and pitiful inferiority so painfully evident even to my own eyes, I actually cried. Why was I denied the education that would enable me to be the equal of such men as Col. Breaux and the others? He says the woman's mind is the same as the man's, originally; it is only education that creates the difference. Why was I denied that education? Who is to blame? Have I exerted fully the natural desire To Know that is implanted in all hearts? Have I done myself injustice in my self taught ignorance or has injustice been done to me? Whose is the fault? I cried. Have I labored to improve the few opportunities thrown in my path, to the best of my ability?

Answer for yourself. With the exception of ten short months at school where you learned nothing except Arithmetic, you have been your own teacher, your own schollar, all your life, after you were taught by mother the elements of reading and writing. Give an account of your charge. What do you know? Nothing! except that I am a fool! and I buried my face in the sheet. I did not like even the darkness to see me in my humiliation.

One thing I comprehend; I can readily understand how Mrs Breaux happened to marry such a man. One thing I would rather *not* realize, and that is, how a woman must feel who sees her husband in his society, and perceives his inferiority of mind. That must be the gall of bitterness! I would feel more keenly for his [p. 77] deficiency, than I do for my own. A woman should feel her husband to be immeasurably her superior. Let her see him under such circumstances, and if she can appreciate the difference, she will feel infinitely "taller" than he. Then, Heaven help her!

We found on our return that Mr Scales had called to see us, and hearing of our expedition, had started off with the expectation of joining us; but he must have taken the other road, since we did not meet him, which would have been a difficult matter, in all our turns.

Oct 3d.

As we got ready to pay a visit to a neighbor last evening, just as the others got seated in their vehicle, and before Miriam and I could mount our horses, a carriage drove up with visiters. The rest instantly got out; but determined to have a ride at least, we ran to the stable door where our two horses stood, and mounted in haste. The block was in sight of the parlor, so I just put my foot in Eli's[163] hand and got tossed up like an arrow in my saddle. Frank again fell to my lot; and leaving word for one of the boys to join us on the road, away we went with the most shameful disregard of politeness, and travelled over ten miles of road before we returned. Of course it was rude; but then they did not see us until we were riding off. Besides, with a free choice between a splendid canter in the open air, and an insciped [*sic*] companion in a close parlor, who could resist the temptation of the former?

Then my "constitution"! Why at this rate, the day is not far distant when Helen Carter will no longer be able to pinch my waist into nothing with her two hands, and will be obliged to forgo her chief amusement at present, that of thrusting her arm down my back after my corsets are laced! Perhaps I will yet be obliged to wear corsets to make me smaller, rather than to make me larger, which is my present object in wearing them. Perhaps old Mrs McCay will no longer have reason to exclaim as she did some time ago, "Why child you have all run into hair!" Dont care if I did! It is as nice a thing to "run" into as I know of! Vive fresh air and exercise! I'll have a constitution yet!

Oct 4th. Saturday.

While Anna and Miriam went out riding last evening, just as I put down my pen, I went out for a solitary walk down the road that Gibbes would have to pass; but saw nothing of the carriage. When I got back,

163. One of the Carter slaves.

they told me he was wounded. My fears were well founded then. With what anxiety we then waited for his coming, then, it would be impossible to describe. Every wagon rattling through the fields made us stop and listen; every cain stalk waving in the moonlight brought us to our feet. At last, after supper, far off in the clear light we saw the carriage. I could not sit still. I walked down the steps and stood under the tree in front, followed by Anna. I did not like her to stand nearer the spot where it would stop, than I, even. All the rest remained on the balcony.

We did not know how serious the wound might be; we must be careful. Eugene Carter advised caution for more reasons than one. [p. 78] "Look out!" he cried. "Suppose it should be Col. Breaux?" "Then I am afraid the Colonel will get a kiss," I answered, nervously shuffling from one foot to the other. "But suppose it is Mr Milligan?" he persisted. "O thank you for the caution! I will look carefully before I greet him!" I returned, moving to the other side, for nearer around the circle drew the carriage. I heard his voice; "Oh Gibbes, where is it?" "Left shoulder; mere scratch," he answered. The carriage stopped. "Gibbes! Gibbes!" I cried. "My darling!" and he had his great strong arm around me; the left was hanging in a sling. Slowly the others moved down the steps towards him.

What a meeting! My heart was in my throat, I was so happy. Every one caught the well hand and kissed him again and again, and every one shrunk from that left side. I had almost forgotten my "gear Lygia" in my excitement. We followed him on the balcony and put him in a chair near the steps. I pulled off his hat and coat and knelt in front of him with my arm across his lap, to get near enough. Miriam stood on the steps with his arm around her shoulder, and Lydia near. The others stood around, and altogether, it was a happy group that performed in the tableau of "The soldier's return." Presently the negroes gathered too. "How is you, Mass' Gibbes?" in all imaginable keys and accents was heard, while the Captain shook hands with each and inquired into their own state of health. But even wounded soldiers can eat; so supper was again prepared. I am afraid it gave me *too* much pleasure to cut up his food. It was very agreeable to butter his corn bread, carve his mutton and spread his preserves, to me; but I doubt whether it could be so pleasant to a strong man accustomed to do such small services for himself.

We listened to him talk, but though it was evident from his slow, deliberate speech, so different from his ordinary habit, that he was suffering, yet I felt impatient when he was interrupted by any commonplace observation by one of us. I wanted to learn something of his exploits. Much knowledge I obtained! He was wounded at Sharpsburg[164] on the 17th Sept, at nine in the morning. That is all the information I got concerning himself. One would imagine that the seventeen months that have elapsed since we last met, had been passed in a prolonged picnic. Concerning others, he was quite communicative. Father Hubert told him he had seen George in the battle, and he had come out safe. Gibbes did not even know that he was in it, until then. Our army, having accomplished its object, recrossed the Potomac, after what was decidedly a drawn battle. Both sides suffered severely. Hardly an officer on either side escaped unhurt. Mr McGimsey is wounded, and Major Herron reported killed.[165] I expect the list will contain the names of many friends when it comes.

I have just come from seeing Gibbes' wound dressed. If that is a scratch, Heaven defend me from wounds! A minié ball struck his left shoulder strap, which caused it to glance, thereby saving the bone. Just above, in the fleshy part it tore the flesh off in a strip three inches and a half, by two. Such a great raw, green, pulpy wound, bound around by a heavy red ridge of flesh! Mrs Badger who dressed it, turned sick; Miriam turned away groaning; servants exclaimed with horror; it was the first experience of any, except [p. 79] Mrs Badger, in wounds. I wanted to try my nerves; so I held the towel around his body and kept the flies off while it was being washed. He talked all the time, ridiculing the groans of sympathy over a "scratch" and O how I loved him for his fortitude! It is so offensive that the water trickling on my dress, has obliged me to change it.

Thirty two years ago this day, mother was married. This day last year—

164. The bloody Battle of Antietam, where McClellan turned back Lee's invasion of Maryland.

165. Major Andrew S. Herron, a Baton Rouge attorney serving in the 7th Louisiana, was wounded, but recovered.

Oct. 5th.

I am afraid Col. Breaux will begin to think me rather an untamed young lady, as he has the fortune always to find me in some unusual situation. Yesterday, Anna and I after getting a supply of sugar cane walked out to the railroad and sat on the rails while we eat [*sic*] it. Coming home in the early moonlight, she stopped presently and refused to walk unless I would sing a "funny" song. I humored her, and walked on singing until we got almost to the house, just by the horse rack, when I stopped in the middle of the "Wild tremendous Irishman" hearing her exclamation of "See! A horse with a Mexican saddle!" Sure enough, there was the horse, and a few more steps, the rider, Col. Breaux advanced from the balcony to meet us. I felt ashamed of my display, and my "Nasty, ugly Irishman" but made no apology for either.

Presently Miriam & Lydia came in from their ride, and then Gibbes & Mr Carter, and as Col. Breaux and Gibbes are old friends, I forgot to feel foolish while listening to them talk. Again we had the pleasure of his company to tea, and he spent a long, and very pleasant evening with us. He, Mrs Badger, & Gibbes talked so much, that poor Miriam's tongue was forced to take a temporary rest. Imagine how fast they must have talked, if she had not a chance to say a word! Before leaving, Col. Breaux asked Miriam and me to name a day that he might come out and ride with us, and we appointed to-morrow. Was it not sweet in him? I should have thought that one evening's experience was sufficient. I hope to enjoy the ride; but of course the least agreeable part will be reserved for me. Tomorrow will prove.

Monday, Oct. 6th

I shall begin really to believe that my soul *is* prophetic. See the situation of affairs at 12 M. Of course we asked Anna to accompany us on our ride, though Col. Breaux, owing doubtless to her having been absent at the moment, had omitted to mention it. This morning, while discussing the horses we were to ride, one was discovered to have a sore back, and to be consequently hors de combat.[166] That one, by the law of the star that presided over my birth, falls to my lot. Miriam rides Joe, Frank carries Anna, the other horse carries—a sore back, and

166. Disabled.

I stay home. Miriam is angry, as she invariably is when I am what she calls "imposed on;" Anna is lazily sympathetic; I, comparatively indifferent. Alone here, I can take my book out under the trees, and be happy. Riding, I would infallibly have an extremely uninteresting companion—a Capt. Morrison, if none less congenial could be found, and would have very little pleasure beyond that derived from being in motion. A copy of Shakespeare will afford me more instruction than the ride. It is best as it is.

[p. 80] Last night I actually drew from Gibbes the outlines of Jackson's campaign. After supper (he sits next to me) I smuggled in an Atlas, and turning to Virginia, besought an explanation of his movements, which he cheerfully pointed out, as far as the small map would allow. Then he told me of some heroic deeds of his fellow soldiers; but of his own, not a word. For that very reason, I know that he has been among the bravest of the brave. He carries it stamped on that magnificent head of his. I have seen his name too often in the papers to believe that he has no deeds of his own to relate, if he only would; though I like him a thousand times more for his silence.

5. P.M. Well! they have gone at last. I dont hesitate to confess *here* that I am bitterly disappointed, what ever I may say aloud. About dinner time, when the state of affairs was comprehended by the family in general, great was the excitement occasioned. Mrs Carter, of course, warmly advocated my claims, to my great distress. She even told Anna that she had no business to go, if I had to stay at home in consequence. Mrs Badger took it up, and offered me Anna's horse, and said she should give up her place to me, if I would go. Anna began to get in "the dumps," and while almost crying with disappointment, made all imaginable difficulty about going without me.

At dinner, again it was brought up. Something was said about my not going, when Gibbes said yes I was, for I should ride his horse. "Anna has already selected him, Gibbes," I said. "Has she? Well dont mind it, and I will take It out riding my own self, when I get well!" he answered, throwing his arm around my neck. I did *not* mind it, so long as I knew I was right, and that he approved. A nice old sheep that could do nothing but gallop, and could not even do that, without a thrashing, was suggested, which I laughingly declined.

After I left, I think Mrs Carter gave another lecture, for while I was combing, Anna came up and insisted on giving me Frank; she would stay home, and I go with Col. Breaux; of course he would prefer my company, etc. I really felt sorry for her. She had so set her heart on going, that the thought made her cry, and she was by no means amiable, besides. I firmly declined the sacrifice. Then, since I would not go, she would stay to keep me company. I turned from the glass and said "Tell me what company you will be to me? Do you not know I am so selfish as to prefer my own company to all other? (O what a story! to *some*, only) Dont you know that if you stay, you will be in a dreadful humor, when I would rather *not* be with you? Dont you see it will seem to Col. Breaux that I, being of a very jealous, spiteful nature, have prevented you from going because I could not go too? I value Col. Breaux's opinion, understand. I beg you will not be the cause of my forfeiting it. Go, like a reasonable creature, and do not make yourself both disagreeable and disobliging by remaining."

I said much more; too much, I fear, for she had lost her temper, and swore to stay just where she was, no matter what I wanted, etc. I went to Mrs Carter, told her I should feel very badly if at this late moment she would retract, and tell Col. Breaux it was on my account that it was a sacrifice that would always be held up to me, and one I would not submit to. Any way, I got her to undo her work. Her mother readily agreed. I [p. 81] hope I am not uncharitable; but both Miriam and I have been forced into observing that Mrs B. is not altogether satisfied with the marked attention we receive from the Colonel. Let it pass, though. Anna and Miriam got ready. I put on an evening dress, and descended to meet Col. Breaux. I did not mention it until all were assembled, when Mrs Badger made explanations, such as, that my horse had a sore back, and Anna was distressed to leave me at home, but as one was obliged to remain, it could not be helped as I would not take her horse, to her great distress. The Colonel was in distress, too; such mutual concessions and amiability deserved a reward; he wished he had a horse to offer, etc.

Mrs Badger called me off. She said she had supposed that he would have brought another gentleman; but since he had not, I had best even now take Anna's place, as the Colonel prefered my society. She had not thought he would be alone, or would not have consented to her going. I declined, as before, saying I, for my part, prefered his society to that of his friends, and would certainly have enjoyed the arrangement, if I had happened to be of the party. I went back. Col. Breaux again expressed his regret. I felt flattered, and all the more as Gibbes repeated "Never mind! I'll take her soon." I saw them go off, I think I may say without envy. I was sorry for poor Anna. She was really beginning to feel it, as her dejected air expressed. She tearfully assured me it was only to please me that she had at last assented. I consoled her, and they went off. Poor girl! how little she will enjoy herself!

Wonder where they are now? As they disappeared Gibbes turned to me saying "Remember, in future that when there is any question about riding, that my horse is yours. Do you hear?" Dear Gibbes! he feels my disappointment as much as I. Gibbes is very proud of his little sister. Why, I wonder?

Oct 7th.

Perhaps I was more than recompensed for my ride, by the friends that my disappointment gained me. I wrote the latter portion of the upper half of this page quite in the dark. Then I joined Lydia at the piano, and sang with her and Mrs Carter, with Gibbes and Mrs Worley for an audience, for some time. It was a magnificent evening. The moon was so bright that you could see far over the fields in every direction. I watched for them, and after some time perceived them by the sugar house. They looked so happy, pacing up the road. I met them on the steps as they dismounted, and felt happy too. Anna's placid face expressed content; Miriam's looked bright with pleasure; I was satisfied. The Colonel began to express his great regret that I was forced to stay at home, and to say how much he had missed me. I answered with truth that the pleasure of having been missed, more than atoned for my disappointment.

Miriam told me after, that he had talked constantly of me; and he told me that Anna had spoken incessantly of me, while Anna said the same of Miriam. Altogether, they agreed that I had been constantly in their thoughts. Was it not sweet in them? Anna with a smile of good humor confided to me that she was *so* happy. Why, I asked. "O because I pleased you by going!" she answered. Brother would have exclaimed "The naïveté of the rising generation is perfectly refreshing!" I smiled approbation. [p. 82] Mrs Badger, passing by me, called me by some

nick name and patted my cheek; a motion so unexpected, that my
heart bounded to my throat with gratitude; I felt like hugging her. Col.
Breaux crossed over the balcony and sat by me, talking in his peculiar
way. He seemed to wish to atone for whatever pleasure I had lost in the
ride. Certain it is, he remained by me for the rest of the evening, and
made himself as interesting as usual. Yes! and he once addressed me
as "My little philosopher!" Was I not amused? But was it not sweet?
O Col. Breaux! If all the unmarried men were as charming, what a
pleasure society would be!

Will Carter has been down stairs this hour. I have not left my place
out on the upper balcony for him. I cant listen to his loose, illiterate,
rambling, stupid talk while the taste of Col. Breaux['s] conversation
lingers on my mental palate. There he goes (Glad of it, though I will
get a lecture for my rudeness in not appearing). But *he* knows that my
admiration for him, mentally or morally, is not great enough to cause
me to take the trouble of pretending to a toleration I do not feel.

"Our" Colonel (Mrs Badger caught me up last night, for saying "My
Colonel" when we girls were undressing, so I substitute "our") told me
that as soon as he returned from Camp Moore, he would come out to
take me, *especially*, out riding. It should be called "Miss Sarah's ride"
and no contretemps would be allowed to interfere. Gallant Col. Breaux!
What unmarried man would put himself to so much trouble merely to
gratify foolish girls? I am right in my predilection for married men;
they are worth all the others put together. Any how, there are very, very
few of them I do not like; whilst as to the single ones—

"Our" Colonel has just written the sweetest note to Miriam, asking
for her riding whip which he insisted on having mended, last night.
He says "Je l'ai complêtement oubliée au moment de mon départ hier
soir; oubli, au reste, que je ne saurais regretter dès qu'il me procure
l'occasion de témoigner à M'elle, ainsi qué à sa gentille soeur, encore
une fois ma respectuéuse estime." [167] Now I appeal to an impartial judge
(which I certainly am not), can any thing be sweeter? Charming Col.
Breaux! Why are not all men wise, brave, gallant, preux chevaliers,[168]
in one word Cols Breaux?

167. "I had completely forgotten it at the time of my departure last night; an oversight,
moreover, that I could not really regret since it provided me the occasion to express to
mademoiselle, as well as to her amiable sister, once again my respectful esteem."

168. Valiant knights.

Oct 9, Thursday.

Miriam laughingly asks if I know how many friends I gained by my "heroic sacrifice." I cannot but notice it in one or two instances; but I put to her the question that perplexes me: why should a deed in which I had no choice but to submit, gain me such extraordinary, though silent, regard? What else could I have done, but stay at home, when I had no choice in the distribution of the animals? "All true," she says; "*You* could not have acted differently; the glory of such things depend[s] upon whether they are done with good grace or not; you chose your own part, and came out a heroine. It is really touching to see the affection you have gained!" Miriam is a tease; but some things *are* funny.

It is astonishing what a quantity of fresh air has been consumed by me since I formed that wise resolution. The supply must be largely increased, to keep up with the demand; perhaps that is the cause of all these clouds and showers; I must be making a severe drain on the economy of heaven. From breakfast to dinner I remain on the balcony, [p. 83] and read aloud several Chapters of the Mémoire of Dumas,[169] by way of practice. A dictionary lies by me, and I suffer no word to pass without a perfect definition. Then comes my french grammar, which I study while knitting or sewing, which takes very nearly until dinner time. After that, I do as I please, either reading or talking until sunset, when we can ride, or walk; the walk being always sweetened with sugar cain. The evening, we always spend on the balcony. Is that grand air enough? O mon teint! je serai joliment brune![170]

We three girls occupy the same room, since Gibbes' arrival, and have ever so much fun, and not half enough sleep. I believe the other two complain of me as the cause; but plead not guilty. I never was known to laugh aloud, no matter how intense might have been my mirth; "it wont come," as Gibbes murmured last night while reading aloud Artemus Ward's[171] last letter, when we discovered it was suppressed laughter, rather than suppressed pain that caused him to writhe so. On the other hand, Anna and Miriam laugh as loud and lustily as daughters of the Titans—if the respectable gentlemen *had* daughters. I confess to doing

169. *Mes Mémoires* by Alexandre Dumas père.

170. O my complexion! I will be awfully brown.

171. Pseudonym of Charles Farrar Browne, whose series of humorous newspaper letters enjoyed a wide following.

more than half of the talking, but as to the laugh that follows, not a bit.

Last night I thought they would go wild, and I too laughed myself into silent convulsions, when I recited an early effusion of my poetic muse for their edification. Miriam made the bedstead prance, fairly, while Anna's laugh sounded like a bull of Bashan[172] with his head in a bolster case. I only testified my amusement by an occasional kick and chuckle; but I dare say none enjoyed the laugh at my expense more than I. When, pretending to have been swallowed by Miriam's good night kiss, in a deep, sepulchral voice I sent affecting messages to my friends in general, and "our" Colonel in particular, from my supposed seat in Hades, they got [to] laughing immoderately again. From her solitary bed Anna would quip "O you are *so* funny! but please stop! it sounds so dreadful in the dark! I'm sure to have awful dreams! O please!" Anna is like some others I know; she would laugh if it is funny or not, if you just give her the key to laugh on. An amiable quality; but one not calculated to inspire much respect for the mental calibre of the person who possesses it, besides being one that is by no means flattering to the vanity of the person who incites the outburst, as one would naturally object to having a good joke received with the same applause that is bestowed upon a poor one.

Saturday Oct 11th.

Miriam went off to Clinton before daylight yesterday, with Mr Carter & Mrs Worley. She would not let me go for fear mother should keep us. At midnight they got back last night, tired, sleepy and half frozen, for our first touch of cool weather came in a strong north wind in the evening which grew stronger and stronger through the night, and they had worn only muslin dresses. I shall never cease to regret that I did not go too. Miriam says mother is looking very sad. Sad, and I am trying to forget all our troubles, and am so happy here! O mother! how selfish it was to leave you! I ask myself whether it were best to stay there where we would only be miserable without adding anything to your comfort or pleasure, or to be here careless and happy while you are in that horrid hole so sad and [p. 84] lonesome. According to my theory, Miriam would remind me that I say it is better to have three miserable

172. Psalms 22:12.

persons, than two happy ones whose happiness occasions the misery of the third. That is my doctine only in peculiar cases; it cannot be applied to this one. I say that if, for example, Miriam and I should love the same person, while that person loved only me, rather than make her unhappy by seeing me marry him, I would prefer making both him and myself miserable, by remaining single. She says "Fudge!" which means, I suppose, nonsense.

But our happiness here does not occasion mother's unhappiness. She would rather see us enjoying ourselves here, than moping there. One proof is that she did not suggest our return. She longs to get home, but cannot leave poor Lilly alone, for Charlie is in Granada.[173] O how willingly I would return to the old wreck of our home! All its desolation could not be half so unendurable as Clinton. But Lilly cannot be left. Poor Lilly! When I look at her sad young face, my heart bleeds for her. With five helpless little children to care for, is she not to be pitied? I think that such a charge, in such dreadful days, would kill me. How patiently she bears it! God bless and help you, dear, noble hearted Lilly! May God comfort you; for He only knows your heart. O Lilly! such a good, pure, noble soul deserves a happier lot. Will it ever come? If by one word I could express the pity, the love I feel for you—! Such things are never told though. But though not expressed, do I feel it the less?

O what a dream I had last night! I have not yet recovered from my terror. I dreamed that I was to be married. Awful, was it not? But worse still, my heart misgave [?] me at the last moment. I was standing in mother's room, dressed in bridal array, with the exception of my veil, when a vision passed before me. I saw myself walking up the aisle of the church with my hand on the arm of my bridegroom. Behind me followed four bridesmaids with as many groomsmen. I saw the altar I was approaching, and the minister with his book; I saw a sea of faces turned towards mine, that was bent down, and deathly pale. A silent horror crept over me. With a gasp of terror the phantom of myself disappeared from before my distended eyes. I was still standing in mother's room holding a wreath in my hand, which I cast away crying "O mother I cannot! Save me!" Mother smiled and continued her toilette.

I turned to Miriam who was putting on a lace dress, and begged her

173. Grenada, Mississippi. Charlie LaNoue worked in the government commissary there.

to save me. "From what? You promised of your own free will." "But only to please mother!" I sobbed. "And now I find I cannot! I'll die! Save me! tell him I am crazy! It will be true, for I shall be crazy if you force me into it! Save me, Miriam!" Miriam pinned my wreath on, by way of reply. "Too late. The supper table is spread, and looks beautifully, too. They say the church is already crowded. Would you have them disappointed? Dont make your eyes red; you have just half an hour" and she pointed to the clock.

"Let them have the supper without the wedding! Cant they enjoy the feast without the sacrifice? Save me! tell him I did not know how much courage it required! I'll die! O Miriam, I'll die!" Just then I heard footsteps. "There he is, and Gibbes too! Hurry; you are wanted," I heard. Again I pleaded wildly; in my agony I threw myself on the ground, and besought her [p. 85] to tell him I could not marry him; that I had only discovered I hated him at the last moment. "And if you refuse, I solemnly swear that when the clergyman asks if I Will, I will answer No! with an energy which will startle him, and scandalize the congregation!" I burst forth, rising from my knees with a determined air.

"If you really feel so—" Miriam began; but I stopped further remark by a torrent of tears and protestations, that convinced her of my real feelings, while I pushed her towards the stairs. I heard her as she reached the parlor, heard her voice first in astonishment, then in anger, and hugged myself for joy crying "Saved! saved!" His [*sic*] voice ceased. I suddenly found myself near a corps[e]. Whose, I do not know. I kept repeating "First I dreamed of a wedding, then of a funeral. One destroys the other; neither will follow. Thank heaven I am saved! Blessed be heaven, I am not married! Free! free!" And my ecstacy of joy was disturbed by the voice of the servant who called me to get up for breakfast. A tame ending, but my horror at the thought of marrying that man has not yet deserted me. I am glad I did not, even in my dreams. And his name was John! Bah!

Evening. I think it was about eleven o'clock when I shut up this book, and induced Miriam and Anna to take a walk with me. It was a splendid day for it. Dark grey clouds were piled up like feather beds over the sky, and smothered the sunshine, while the wind blew with a will over the fields and threatened to nip our noses. Pinning our dresses up until they fell only to our knees—for calicoes are dearer now than silk—we started off each with a knife and two or three sugar cains under our arms, to follow the railroad towards P. Hudson. The cain did not encumber us long; it is surprising how much easier it is to carry it *in*ternally, than externally. When we got a mile and a quarter away, we had nothing to carry except our knives, which could not be as easily disposed of as our cane.

We found walking inside the track so delightful, that we all declared we would go on to Port Hudson, and tell the General when he comes back that we had won the wager. But just where our cain gave out, came a railroad bridge. It was quite high, or rather the ravine was quite deep, as well as wide; and here arose a difficulty. I was the only one brave enough to cross the extraordinary chasm. Half the way there was a line of planks; the rest, you must cross over and walk on the beam that held the rail. I performed the feat several times to show its practicability, and at last induced Anna to cross while holding on to me. I got Miriam started, but she grew so dizzy and frightened that I had to conduct her back, followed by Anna. Determined to cross, these two heroines scrambled down the side of the ravine through mud and briars, and climbed the other side while I retained my perch shouting after them "Ole Abe and his underground railway!" to their great disgust.

Once over, there is no knowing how far we would have gone, had we not perceived some distance beyond a figure advancing. One said it was a [illegible] one, a man, the other cried "Road walker!"[174] when each instantly turned to hurry home. I dont know what a "road walker" is; but have seen Mrs Carter turn so pale at the name, that we fancied it must be something. Running at full speed we then reached the dreaded bridge; but as we put our foot on it, came the whistle of the cars. Which to do, go back and meet the road walkers (for the case had resolved itself into three men, now) or run the risk [p. 86] of meeting the cars on the bridge? The others ran towards the men, but I called them back, insisting we could cross. There was no time to scramble down the gulley; this time the danger must be braved; so Miriam nerved herself to the task, and held trembling on to me, while Anna stepped cautiously before.

I got my sheep on terra firma; but where stand even now? It was

174. Men employed by the railroad to walk the tracks and inspect them. Evidently those in the vicinity of Linwood had an unsavory reputation.

a high embankment, with not three feet of earth on either side of the rails, bordered by a thick cane brake, and woods below, the thick branches of the trees being on a level with us. Fortunately we espied two small posts on the steep side of the embankment, which might support us until the cars passed. Presently they came on slowly, for we had been seen, and the engineer was watching that we should be in no danger. Far off, on the platform of the first car, we perceived among several officers, Col. Breaux! At the same moment he recognised us. He is too well bred to show surprise, or doubtless he would have made some exclamation. The others evidently were astonished. "Are you lost, young ladies?" was his inquiry as he came within hearing, smiling in the sweetest way imaginable at our escapade. "O no!" we answered, with a corresponding smile. "Are you afraid?" he asked, bending over the car, as he came directly opposite. I shook my head laughing; "But O Col. Breaux! the road walkers!" I exclaimed, pointing down the road with my knife.

I dont know that he heard; for at the instant logic Anna laid her hand on my shoulder; my log turned slightly, and I was threatened with a flight backwards down in the canebrake, which I checked by a profound obeisance to the last car, which just missed grazing my nose. We sprang in the road again and looking after the retreating cars, there stood our Colonel on the extreme verge of the platform, leaning over to see us, and waving his hand. What an excitement there was among our veils and handkerchiefs! I twisted my hand in my enthusiasm; but both parties only ceased when we lost sight of each other.

"Bless our Colonel! was there ever such a man? Did he not look splendidly? and did you ever hear anything as sweet as those few words?" Such was our conversation coming home; we could not say enough, or walk fast enough either, for closer and closer came our road walkers. Soldiers! and we were safe! Confederate buttons, where ever found, are the protectors of women. So well is it known, that it is almost proverbial. A day or two since, Anna and Miriam were sitting in our favorite place on the railroad in front of the big gate, eating cain, when a negro man approached. Anna, frightened, yet wishing to appear at ease and protected, commenced talking to her mother, as though she were behind the hedge, instead of in the house. The negro paused and civilly took off his hat, when Anna cried "Oh uncle! I was afraid of you!" "Miss!" he exclaimed in turn, "didn't you see what buttons I had? Dont be 'fraid of *dese* buttons!" Like many another man, all his claims to respectability were founded on his buttons, for he wore an old soldier coat, which he seemed to consider as a passport, as many a white man does.

Our soldiers walked behind us as far as the gate, and never by word or look, annoyed us, for the which they have our sincerest thanks.

[p. 87] Thursday Oct. 16th

It seems an age since I have opened this book. How the time has passed since, I have but a vague idea, beyond that it has passed very pleasantly. Every evening, has followed the same old routine, which loses no attraction by repetition; that of a visit to the cain field where we cut a large supply of cane which we afterwards carry to our favorite seat on the railway, where it speedily disappears, leaving nothing to tell its story save a melancholy heap of peelings, and some extremely dry and well masticated substance, which an old pig carefully removes for us, immediately after, so that each evening, our attempt to leave a monument of defunct canes by the road side has to be recommenced.

Once since, I have been with Mrs Badger to a Mr Powell[175] who has started quite an extensive shoe making establishment, in the vain attempt to get something to cover my naked feet. I am so much in need, that I have been obliged to borrow Lydia's shoes every time I have been out since she returned. This was my second visit there, and I have no greater satisfaction than I had at first. He got my measure, I got his promise, and that is the end of it, thus far.

His son, a young man of about twenty four, had the cap of his knee shot off at Baton Rouge.[176] Ever since, he has been lying on his couch, unable to stand; and the probability is that he will never stand again. Instead of going out to the manufactory, Mrs Badger has each time stopped at the house to see his mother (who, by the way, kissed me and called me Sissie to my great amusement) and there I have seen this poor young man. He seems so patient and resigned, that it is really

175. Mordecai Powell, an East Feliciana planter.

176. Littleton M. Powell, 17 in the 1860 census. See Michael F. Howell, *Feliciana Confederates* (St. Francisville, 1990), 152.

edifying to be with him. He is very communicative too, and seems to enjoy company, no matter if he does say "her'n" and "his'n." Wonder why he doesn't say "*shisen*" too? The girls are highly amused at the description I give of my new acquaintance, but still more so at Mrs Badger's account of the friendship of this poor young cripple, and his enjoyment of my visits. Of course it is only her own version, as she is very fond of jokes of all kinds.

Night before last Lydia got [to] playing the piano for me in the darkened parlor, and the old tunes from her dear little fingers sent me off in a sea of dreams. She too caught the vision, and launched off in a well remembered quadrille. The same scene flashed on us, and at each note, almost, we would recall [a] little circumstance charming to us, but unintelligible to Anna, who occupied the other side. Together we talked over the dramatis personae. Mrs Morgan, Jr., in dark blue silk with black flounces, a crimson chenille net on her black hair, sits at the piano in her own parlor. On the Brussels carpet, stand, among others, her Majesty, queen Miriam, in a lilac silk, with bare neck and arms save for the protection afforded by a bertha of appliqué lace trimmed with pink ribbon, with hair à la madonna, and fastened low on her neck. Is she not handsome as she stands fronting the folding doors, her hand in tall Mr Trezevants, just as she commences to dance, with the tip of her black botine just showing?

Vis-à-vis stands pretty Sophy, with her large, graceful mouth smiling and showing her pretty teeth to the best advantage. A low neck and short sleeved green and white poplin is her dress, while her [p. 88] black hair combed off from her forehead carelessly, is caught by a comb at the back and falls in curls on her shoulders. A prettier picture could not be wished for, as she looks around with sparkling eyes, eager for the dance to begin. There stands calm Dena in snuff colored silk, looking so immeasurably the superior of her partner, who, I fancy rather feels that she is the better man of the two, from his nervous way of shifting from one foot to the other, without saying a word to her. Nettie in lilac and white, stands by the mantle laughing undisguisedly *at* her partner, rather than with him, yet so good humoredly, that he cannot take offense, but rather laughs with her. Lackadaisical Gertrude whose face is so perfect in the daytime, looks pale and insipid by gas light, and timidly walks through the dance, not gracefully, withal. Stout, good natured Minna smiles and laughs, never quite completing a sentence, partly from embarrassment, partly because she hardly knows how; but still so sweet and amiable that one cannot find fault with her for so trifling a misfortune.

At this point Lydia suggests "And Sarah? do you forget her?" I laugh; how could I forget? There she stands in a light blue silk checked in tiny squares, with little flounces up to her knee. Her dress fits well, and she wears very pretty sleeves and collar of appliqué. Lydia asks if that is all, and how she looks. The same old song, I answer. She is looking at Miriam just now; you would hardly notice her, but certainly her hair is well combed. That is all you can say for her. Who is she dancing with? A youth fond of "dreams," futile ones, at that, I laughingly reply. He must be relating one just now, for there is a very perceptible curl on her upper lip, and she is looking at him as though she thought she was the tallest. Lydia dashes off into a lively jig. "Ladies to the right!" I cried. She laughed too, well knowing that that part of the dance was invariably repeated a dozen times at least. She looked slyly up: "I am thinking of how many hands I saw squeezed" she said.

I am afraid it did happen, once or twice. At all events, she invariably had the benefit of it. Not a hand was squeezed, word whispered, or glance exchanged, that demure little Lydia was not in the secret. Her knowledge sometimes startled me. The day after some such little reunion she would tell me all she had observed, to my great astonishment, as I have the fortune or misfortune to notice nothing that is not perfectly plain, and only half that is obvious to others. Par example, Major Haskins[177] visited at home for a year, before I perceived that he had but one arm; and even then, someone attracted my attention to it by calling him "the one armed Major" which charge I indignantly denied until they pointed to his empty sleeve. With such a defect in my powers of observation, of course she had a great deal to tell me that had innocently passed just under my nose, without attracting my attention.

Eighteen months ago! What a change! One who was prominent on

177. The U.S. Army officer in command at Baton Rouge when state troops seized the Arsenal early in 1861. Major Haskin was popular with the townspeople. William Watson wrote that many of them regarded the circumstances of his leaving "with sorrow and indignation, although they dared not openly express their feelings." *Life in the Confederate Army,* 79.

such occasions—Mr Sparks—they tell me is dead.[178] May God have mercy on his soul, in the name of Jesus Christ! I did not ask even this revenge.

[p. 89] Oct 17th

As I laid down my pen at sunset, I saw Col. Breaux coming, and hastened to meet him. We were expecting him, for the day before Gibbes had called on him just as he was about starting to come out, and had prevented him from paying the intended visit, so he sent word he would be out the next evening. Capt. Morrison accompanied him, to my infinite disgust.

Let me record the sweetest deed imaginable; of course the actor was Col. Breaux. He brought me a book to read, since I have questioned him a great deal on the subject, Abercrombie's Intellectual Philosophy.[179] Was it not kind to think of affording me such pleasure? He said he had sent to B.R. and Clinton, hoping to procure a copy that he might present to me; but had failed, when Professor Miller[180] had that morning lent him this one. I hastened to assure him that I appreciated the attention as much as I would have appreciated the gift, and thanked him for his kindness. The Colonel bowed and smiled, offered his services to explain or help me in case I should find any difficulty in my new study, and completely won my heart by his unexpected attention. He says a question I asked him the last time he was here, has caused him to think a great deal about the subject, and confessed it was a hard one to answer. Wonder if he thought as much of it as I have *tried* to think of some subjects he has suggested to me, by way of exercising my memory?

I had Col. Breaux all to myself, and he was talking about everything that possessed the greatest interest for me, yet I could not fully enjoy it. For opposite me sat odious Capt. Morrison, stiff, silent, stupid as

178. This may not be so. A James H. Sparks died of yellow fever in New Orleans in 1867. See mortuary report in New Orleans *Daily Picayune*, September 8, 1867, p. 3.

179. John Abercrombie's *Intellectual Philosophy.*

180. Before the war John C. Miller had been president of Centenary College, which was forced to suspend classes in 1861. The following year he became provost marshal at Port Hudson. See William Hamilton Nelson, *A Burning Torch and a Flaming Fire: The Story of Centenary College of Louisiana* (Nashville, 1931), 167–68.

ever, and my conscience reproached me for being so selfish as to be
exclusively entertained by Col. Breaux while the others had such a task
before them. Then, listening with one ear to what the Colonel would
say, the other was strained to catch some sound addressed to the Captain, while internally I would ejaculate "Why dont she talk to him!" as
I observed Miriam listening attentively to what was addressed to me,
instead of doing her duty to the other. It destroyed half my pleasure.

The Colonel gave me a piece of consolation for my timidity, which,
being the first I have ever received, I am correspondingly grateful for.
They were teasing me about it, in a way which was by no means calculated to make me feel more assured, and I was endeavoring to promise
amendment, when the Colonel said "Miss Sarah, if you only knew how
beautiful, in the eyes of refined men, is this same timidity they are
teasing you about, you would thank God that he made you gentle and
modest, rather than bold and assured." Saying such a kind thing, in
such a frank, [words lined through] way, at a time I most felt the need
of the approbation of some one, was unspeakably grateful to me. One
feels sympathy to be necessary occasionally.

Uncivil Capt. Morrison drew out his watch, and suggested a return
to camp at nine o'clock, the heathen! Col. Breaux had not an idea of
leaving for at least an hour to come, if it had not been for the wretch!
Before leaving he told me he was ready for "our" ride any day that I
would name. I did not name one just then, from a conviction that it
would never come off; so postponed it indefinitely. Mark this: It will
[p. 90] never come off.

Mrs Worley dislikes Col. Breaux; why, we cannot imagine. She said
to me last evening that she did not like to see married men so attentive
to young girls. There was poor Mrs Breaux pining away at home, groaning over the troubles and hardships of her dear Colonel, and being
wretched herself because she believed him to be the same, while he,
forsooth, was flying around the country after two young ladies, riding
out with them and paying them the greatest attention as though there
was no weeping Mrs Breaux at home! Of course I flew to arms. Colonel
Breaux was formed for society; his taste and refinement lead him to
prefer that of ladies, to that of rough men. What harm was there in his
visiting us, and being kind to us, so long as we understood his attentions to be those of an intelligent and refined married man, who, in

the absence of his wife, naturally prefered our society to that which he probably found in his camp? That we were the only ones thus honored, was probably an evidence of bad taste on his part; but our vanity was not increased by it, any more than it would be by the attentions of an elder brother.

As to me, Col. Breaux was almost old enough to be my father.[181] And was it not rather a compliment to Mrs Breaux, that he should appreciate her so much, that he should seek during her absense, in others of her sex some of the attractions which he had learned to admire in her? I was sure she must be a most estimable lady, from the fact of his selecting her among all others. Would she be selfish enough to begrudge him the few pleasant evenings he could spend out of camp? Mean enough to wish him to keep all his attentions for her only? Disgusting enough to want him to sit within four damp canvass walls, himself damper than the tent with tears shed over their separation? No! Col. Breaux's wife could never be such a disgusting, mean, selfish, horrid woman! Such a charming man was too much for one, anyway; she should not begrudge the light of his countenance to his friends who were less fortunate than she.

Last night the Colonel told me he had strong hopes of getting his wife out of New Orleans before many days. I was so glad for him! But Miriam would not join with me; she says she is *not* glad, and cant be a humbug!

Oct 18th Saturday.

Last night mother arrived from Clinton with Gibbes and Lydia who had gone there the day before to get her to go to Baton R. Accompanying them was—Waller Fowler! He looked tired and sick; I thought of poor Eugene; vanish all my dislike! I kissed him! Of course I could not cherish prejudice after that. Mother is looking badly, thanks to vile Clinton. I tried [to] be kind to Waller, if not affectionate; I was sorry for him. We all turned out of our room, and slept on the floor in Mrs Carter's room to accommodate him; a ceremony Miriam and I have been accustomed to from our earliest years, for Waller must always have the most comfortable bed.

181. The colonel was born December 28, 1828, and therefore was thirteen years older than Sarah.

[p. 91] Clinton Oct 19th Sunday.

What an unexpected change! I am surprised myself! Yesterday as the Baton Rouge party were about leaving, Miriam thought Lilly would be lonesome alone here with her sick baby, and decided that we should leave by the cars, and stay with her until mother returned. There was no time to lose; so dressing in haste, we persuaded Anna to accompany us, and in a few moments stood ready. We walked down to the overseer's [182] house to wait for the cars, and passed the time most agreeably in eating sugar cain, having brought a little negro expressly to cut it for us and carry our carpet bag. Three young ladies who expected to be gone from Saturday until Wednesday, having but one carpet bag between them! Can it be credited? But then we knew we had clothes here, and depended upon them for supplies, when we now find they are in the trunk, and mother has the key.

We walked aboard alone, on the crowded train, and found ourselves in the only car reserved for ladies which was already filled with a large party returning from P. Hudson, consisting of the fastest set of girls that I have seen for some time. Anna and I had to content ourselves with a seat on a small box between the benches, while Miriam was established on the only vacant one, with a sick soldier lying at her feet. The fast girls talked as loud as possible, and laughed in a corresponding style in spite of the sick man. They must have been on a picnic, from the way they talked. One in a short dress complained that she had not seen her sweetheart. A pert little miss of thirteen cried "You can bet your head *I* never went to any place where I did not see one of *my* sweethearts." One of about seventeen, a perfect beauty, declared she would die of thirst. "So will I! And I vow I dont want to die before I get a husband!" exclaimed her vis-à-vis.

They evidently expected to produce an impression on us. At every brilliant remark (stupid understood) they looked at us to see what we

182. David D. Jackson was the Carter overseer.

thought. All of them sat with bare heads in the strong light, an unfailing proof of la basse classe [183] on steamers and cars. Every time my
veil blew aside, they made no difficulty about scanning my features
as though they thought it might be agreeable. I must confess I was
equally impolite in regard to the beauty; but then her loveliness was
an excuse, and my veil sheltered me, besides. While this young Psyche
was fascinating me, with her perfect face and innocent expression, one
of her companions made a remark—one that I dare say is made every
day, and that I never imagined could be turned into harm. My beauty
uttered a prolonged "Oh!" of horror, and burst out laughing, followed
by all the others. My disgust was unspeakable. Mock modesty is always
evident. A modest girl could not have noticed the "catch;" the immodest, on the lookout for such an opportunity, was the only one who could
have perceived it. Well! after all, no one can be perfect; this may be the
single stain on my [p. 92] Beauty, though I confess I would rather have
any other failing than this, almost.

Putting this aside, I hardly know which I was most amused by: the
giddy, lively girls to my right, or the two ladies to my left who were
as cross and ill natured as two old cats and railed unmercifully at the
silly creatures behind them, and carried their spite so far as to refuse
to drink because the conductor (the husband of one of them) gave the
young ladies water before passing it to their two elders. Didn't the poor
man get it! She wouldn't tast[e] a drop of that nasty dirty drippings, that
she wouldn't! Might have had the decency to 'tend to his kinfolks, before them creatures! And why didn't he wait on those two young ladies
behind her? He did ask them? Well ask them again! they must want
some! Poor Henpecked meekly passed the can again, to be again civilly
declined. I confess the "drippings" were too much for me also, though
I did not give it as my excuse. Mrs Hen recommended her pecking;
poor Mr Hen at last surlily rejoined "For Heaven sake dont make a
fuss in the cars" with an emphasis on the last word that showed he was
accustomed to it at home, at least. With my veil down, I leaned against
the window, and remembering Col. Breaux's remarks two nights before concerning cross people, I played his "little philosopher" for the
remainder of the journey.

At sunset we walked in at Lilly's gate, and astonished her by standing

183. The lower class.

before her as she sat alone with her poor sick little Beatrice in her arms.

I laugh at Anna for the great improvement that has already taken place in her. She always talked to me alone, but here she has actually learned to talk freely to every one. She is seventeen to day. I tell her perhaps she has finally determined to profit by the lectures Miriam and I have given her, and appear in the new light of a reasonable creature on her birthday in our honor. I hear Miriam in the next room tell Lilly how surprisingly I have improved. She says "I have no trouble with her now. You remember how she used to make so much difficulty about going in the parlor? Now, she gets there as soon as I do, without a word of trouble, thanks to having seen how badly it looks in Anna." True, Oh Miriam! If I had not had a specimen of such behavior in others, I verily believe I would still make a difficulty about going in company. Now, no matter what I feel, I keep quiet to set a good example to Anna. I hear Miriam telling her the true cause now.

We went to church to day, and heard a great [illegible] sermon from the methodist minister. Our Colonel went to hear Mr Garie, and we know he will be disappointed in not seeing us!

Wednesday 22d Oct. Linwood.

We left Clinton this morning, and have just now arrived by the cars. Charlie came in last evening, to our great surprise, so we did not scruple to leave Lilly, though mother has not returned. Dellie's distress at my departure was only equaled by her delight on seeing me when I first came. I dont know when I have been more [p. 93] gratified than I was at her extravagant demonstrations of joy on seeing me last Saturday. The cold, old fashioned child seems to keep the warm corner of her heart for me. We saw dear old Mr Marsden every day, and this morning he came around to tell us goodbye again. Such a dear, kind old gentleman! And I love him all the more because I know that we owe all his kindness and attention to his friendship for father.

We were the only ladies on the car crowded with soldiers; but as some of them stood up the whole way in order to accommodate us, we suffered no inconvenience beyond being naturally most painfully obliged. Accustomed as I have always been to see this done in the South, I have never yet recovered from feeling the most painful gratitude, doubly painful, because unexpressed.

Mr Carter greeted us with a doleful face, saying "Have you heard the awful news?" My heart went below zero. I could not think what calamity had befallen us, until he exclaimed "Mrs Breaux is at Ponchatoula!" Bless Mrs Breaux! Honesty is the best policy. With Miriam, I confess I am—sorry! Mrs Badger condoles with me, on the loss of my ride. Oh! my prophetic soul! But she consoles me—rather *endeavors* to console—by telling of the visits that have been paid during our absence; among others, a gem of a Captain, and an Admirable Crichton of an *un*married Colonel (Col. Steedman) [184] who promised to repeat their visit when we should return. Bah! They cannot be as nice as "our" Colonel! It would be folly to fancy such a thing possible. What's the use of wives, except to be a bother and spoil fun? "O my Colonel! mine no more!" O this dreary getting married! O you odious Mrs Breaux! Quick! where is my philosophy? We'll drown our sorrows in—a teaspoon full of Abercrombie! Vive la philosophie! Vive le Colonel! A bas la jalousie, et Madame Breaux! [185]

Night. Philosophy and sugar cane having somewhat settled my nerves, I return to record a fact which Mrs Badger omitted to mention when speaking of other visits. The General told me at dinner, that our Colonel called Sunday evening, but did not stay long after finding that we were absent. That is what I call a good joke on Mrs Badger! Let her tease me about Mrs Breaux's arrival, and I'll mention the Colonel's *first* short visit! Bless the General for giving us the information! I do believe they did not mean to tell us! Mrs Badger and I are always fighting about our Colonel. Love taps, of course; for she is certainly as kind and affectionate to me as she can possibly be; bless her kind heart.

The Baton Rouge party returned late this evening. In spite of all preparation, Gibbes was horrified at the appearance of home.[186]

Friday Oct 24th

Last evening we were agreeably surprised by a visit from the Colonel, who stopped on his way after his wife, and took tea with us before con-

184. Colonel Isaiah George Washington Steedman, who commanded the 1st Alabama— and the left wing of General Franklin Gardner's army during the siege of Port Hudson.

185. Long live the philosophy! Long live the Colonel! Down with jealousy, and Mrs. Breaux!

186. Writing from Linwood while on leave, Gibbes Morgan told his brother George: "The Yankees destroyed every-thing we had . . . . If it is ever my fate to go into another action I intend to take a musket, to feel sure that I have some of their bad blood on my individual hands." Letter dated October 7, 1862, in Dawson Papers, Duke University.

tinuing his journey. He looked so supremely happy in anticipation of the meeting that I felt right happy through sympathy. And though he had a live wife at Clinton, he inquired about my progress [p. 94] in philosophy, and peeled cane for me just like an angel, and as though Mrs Breaux were in New Orleans! He spoke of his disappointment in not seeing us Sunday, and assured us that he would not forget us now that his wife had arrived in our neighborhood; on the contrary, she would be but another attraction added to those already here. Was it not sweet? I was glad that mother should have an opportunity of seeing our new hero.

Before he left, came a letter from Jimmy, the first we have received since New Orleans fell. It was dated the 10th inst., and he spoke of being on the eve of running the blockade, and going to Liverpool "to represent our unfortunate navy" as he says, though I am at loss to imagine what he can mean. He speaks of a kind friend, a Mr Geo. Trenholm [187] whose kindness has been perfectly extraordinary. He has befriended him in every way.

Charlie has just come by the railroad, bringing other letters from him, to mother and Lilly. In mother's, is his last goodbye on the 12th. Again Mr Trenholm is the theme. I could not help crying over my dear little brother's manly, affectionate letter. He says he is sure God will still care for him; He has raised him up friends where ever he has been. He says he lost all his clothing in going to Charleston. There, among many other kind people, he met this gentleman, who carried him to his house, where he has kept him ever since, treating him like his son, and forced him to accept a magnificent outfit as a present from him. He procured the appointment which sends Jimmy abroad (I wish Jimmy had been more explicit concerning it; we hardly know what it is, or how long it will keep him). The money he received to pay Jimmy's passage (received from the Government) he in turn obliged Jimmy to accept, as he sails in one of Mr Trenholm's steamers, and not satisfied with that, gives him carte blanche on his house in England, to be filled up with any amount he chooses to name.

Jimmy feels the unparalelled [*sic*] confidence and kindness deeply; and says that when he attempts to thank his friend, the answer is that

187. George Trenholm, wealthy Charleston merchant and shipping magnate, later to become secretary of the treasury in the Davis cabinet.

the only return expected, or desired, is that when once in England he shall study hard and make a man of himself. The poor little fellow laments that [while] we are suffering, he should be living in a palace; for his friend is worth at least four millions and a half. "Good bye mother, I am going to make a man of myself." God grant it, my darling brother! God watch over you, and send you back to comfort us. O Jimmy! may God bless and prosper you!

Accompanying the others, comes a letter to mother from Miss Trenholm,[188] saying he got out the night of the 12th. She speaks of him in the highest terms, and the strong attachment they had formed for him, and of his cheerful and amiable disposition which had endeared him to all. She adds that she had addressed a photograph which he desired to have sent to me, to Jackson, Miss.[189] Charlie promises to get it there, and send it on. One he sends to mother, represents him as very tall and stout, considering, and much changed. I am to answer Miss Trenholm; I hope to express my thanks as fully as I feel them. All this good news come[s] on my dear [p. 95] Harry's birthday. God bless him in his lonely grave!

Mother went back to Clinton with Charlie this evening, to my great distress; for she hates that odious place as much as I, and I know the life will kill her if it lasts six months longer. How happy I would be, if it were not for the thought of her uncomfortable position there! Lilly agrees with me, that once out of it, she never wishes to see the vile place again. Margret says that when the Lord had finished all the world and all the people, he had some scraps left, and just thought he'd "batch" up Clinton with them. Perhaps she is right.

Sunday 26th Oct.

Every one having gone to church except Lydia and me, I have at last a leisure moment; and closing the door, with my feet in the fire (for it turned extremely cold yesterday, and there is ice this morning) I shall take advantage of the unnatural quiet to write to Miss Trenholm—if I can find a writing table; for this writing on one's own knee does not

188. George Trenholm's daughter Helen. She would become the wife of Jimmy Morgan in 1865.

189. Presumably Jimmy Morgan had told her to address the letter to Sarah at Jackson, Louisiana.

improve the handwriting, as this whole book can testify. I suppose by the time I get back to my desk I will not be able to write at all.

This place is completely over run by soldiers passing and repassing. Friday night five staid here, last night two more, and another has just gone. One, last night, a bashful Tennessean, had never tasted sugar cane. We were sitting around a blazing fire, enjoying it hugely, when in answer to our repeated invitations to help himself, he confessed he had never eaten it. Once instructed, though, he got on remarkably well, and eat [*sic*] it in a civilized manner, considering it was a first attempt.

Every thing points to a speedy attack on P. Hudson. Rumors reach us from N. Orleans of extensive preparations by land and water, and of the determination to burn Clinton as soon as they reach it, in revenge for the looms that were carried from B.R. there, and which can soon be put in working order to supply our soldiers, negroes, and ourselves with necessary clothing.[190] Of two evils, if Baton Rouge is to be over run by Yankees, and Clinton burned, I would rather await them at home. I would stand another four months of Yankee rule, rather than live that long in Clinton. Yes! and would undergo a weekly shelling besides. But when it comes to taking Yankees, Clinton, and burning altogether, I confess it is too much for me. One would be quite sufficient for a life time, and I hate Clinton a thousand times more than I do the Yankees. The three combined would be a climax of misery.

Give me my old home, and there is no army of Yankees that could prevent me from being perfectly content in it, or that could again coax me to run out of it to undergo a Clinton experience, unless they carried me out as they did Miriam's dress, on the point of a bayonet. I lived in town surrounded by ten thousand of them, and did not find them a bit more disagreeable than Clinton is. They never caused me the slightest annoyance by their individual behavior, and that place has caused me many, very great annoyances; how, it is unnecessary to explain.

[p. 96] Thursday. 30th October
Company, company! is so constantly the cry, that I have never thought of mentioning those who pass in and out incessantly. Yesterday, the

190. The looms at the State Penitentiary were dismantled and taken to Clinton after the Union army withdrew from Baton Rouge late in August.

General invited several officers from P. Hudson to dine with us; but only one, Capt. Fenner,[191] could come. This we did not know until dinner time however, so great was the excitement and bustle of preparations. Determined to call on Mrs Breaux at all hazards, Miriam and Mrs Badger started off at one o'clock alone. I could not go, but had my hands full, at all events. First I combed Mrs Badger to her satisfaction, and saw them get ready; then Miriam bequeathed her collar and cuffs to me, to arrange during her absence; then I braided Mrs Carter's hair, with Anna sitting by, insisting on my teaching her to knit gloves at the same time, impatient that she could not learn fast enough, and professing herself glad that she could not braid, so nobody would bother her. A singular kind of bother, truly. What is the use of living, if you please no one but yourself, and please yourself only halfway?

At the same time, Mrs Badger left me the superintendence of a flannel shirt that was to be altered for the young soldier who staid here last night, and as soon as I finished, I had Anna's hair to comb, and succeeded in pleasing her also. By the time I got through, Capt. Fenner had arrived, and I had the room to dress in alone, as every one went down and left me alone in my glory to finish my toilette to please myself. A few moments before dinner, I made my bow to the gentleman. I suppose that it was because Gibbes was particularly anxious for me to shine, that, like all wilful children, when desired to show off, I remained strikingly indifferent and stupid, with little to say, and that little, said very coolly and distinctly. The gentleman is by no means astonishing, either physically or mentally, though decidedly good looking, and really, several times, made little speeches in which the compliment was so insinuating, and so delicately veiled, that I was startled into remarking it to Gibbes, who is always my next neighbor at table.

One remark, one of the best turned speeches that I ever heard, passed unnoticed by all except Gibbes and me. "Answer with your prettiest speech" he whispered; but I remained mute. Fact is, while observing its delicacy and insinuating address, I forgot what it was! And now, I

191. Captain Charles E. Fenner commanded a battery of light artillery attached to the brigade of General S. B. Maxey. An attorney who practiced in New Orleans before and after the war, Fenner also later served in the legislature and became an associate justice on the state supreme court. See *Confederate Military History*, 13:410–11.

cannot imagine what it referred to; so how was I to reply? However, I found him very agreeable and pleasant, when I thought about him at all.

At twilight as we assembled around the parlor fire after he left, the General asked each their opinion. Every one thought him so nice! so intelligent and agreeable! The question came to me. I looked up from the socks I was knitting for Gibbes's soldiers. (I must record my industry at the expense of a parenthesis and a break in my narrative; I knit down to the heel of one yesterday, in addition to my other feats.) "He talks as though he were lying down, General" was my [p. 97] comment. All burst out laughing and acknowledged the truth of the remark. "I'll swear! what a girl! it is original, at least!" the Gen. exclaimed. Well, the man did talk as though he were reclining mentally, singular as it may seem. The Gen. says I am too hard to please, that I think no one is agreeable unless they are Col. Breaux. I acknowledge that I *have* a taste for nice people, and that the Colonel is certainly one of them.

By daylight I was up to write to Howell, at the General's request, and never raised my head until I finished the last word. I wish I had had time to write him a nice letter; but breakfast came and interrupted, or rather hurried me, so I was forced to despatch it in haste. As we arose from table, Eugene Carter and the young soldier took their leave, to join their regiments in Kentucky. I like partings to be made as cheerful as possible; but one glance at the tear stained faces around me showed me that my only safety lay in retreat, which I hastily performed as soon as Mass' Gene had given me my good bye kiss.

Sunday November 2d.

Yesterday was a day of novel sensations to me. First came a letter from mother announcing her determination to return home, and telling us to be ready next week. Poor mother! She wrote drearily enough of the hardships we would be obliged to undergo in the dismantled house, and of the new experience that lay before us; but n'importe! I am ready to follow her to Yankeeland, or any other place she chooses to go. It is selfish for me to be so happy here while she leads such a distasteful life in Clinton. In her postscript though, she said she would wait a few days longer to see about the grand battle which is supposed to be impending; so our stay will be indefinitely prolonged. How thankful I am that we will really get back, though! I hardly believe it possible however; it is to[o] good to be believed.

The nightmare of a probable sojourn in Clinton being removed, I got in what the boys call a "perfect gale" and sang all my old songs with a greater relish than I have experienced for many a long month. My heart was open to every one. So forgiving and amiable did I feel, that I went down stairs to see Will Carter! I made him so angry last Tuesday, that he went home in a fit of sullen rage. It seems that some time ago, some one, he said told him such a joke on me that he had laughed all night at it. Mortified beyond all expression at the thought of having had my name mentioned between two men (I, who have thus far fancied myself secure from all remarks good, bad, or indifferent of men) I refused to have anything to say to him until he should either explain me the joke, or, in case it was not fit to be repeated to me— until he apologized for the insult.

He took two minutes to make up a lie. This was the joke, he said. Our *milkman* had said that that Sarah Morgan was the proudest girl he ever saw; that she walked the streets as though the earth was not good enough for her. My milkman making his remarks! I confess I was perfectly aghast with surprise, and did not conceal my contempt for the remark, or his authority either. But one cant fight one's milkman! [p. 98] I did not care for what he or any of that class could say; I was surprised to find that they thought at all! But I resented it as an insult as coming from Mr Carter, until with tears in his eyes fairly, and in all humility, he swore that if it had been anything that could reflect on me in the slightest degree, he would have cut the man's heart out; and that if I would forgive him, he would thrash the next man who mentioned my name.

I was not uneasy about a milkman's remarks, so I let it pass, after making him acknowledge that he had told me a falsehood concerning the remark which had been made. But I kept my revenge. I had but to cry "Milk!" in his hearing to make him turn crimson with rage. At last he told me that the less I said on the subject, the better it would be for me. I could not agree. "Milk" I insisted was a delightful beverage. I had always been under the impression that we owned a cow, until he had informed me it was a milkman; but was perfectly indifferent to the

annimal [*sic*] so I got the milk. With some such allusions, I could make
him mad in an instant. Either a guilty conscience concerning the lie
told, or the real joke, grated harshly on him, and I possessed the power
of making it still worse. Tuesday I pressed it too far. He was furious,
and all the family warned me that I was making a dangerous enemy.
But I dread his opinion no more than that of my milkman.

Yesterday he came back in a good humor, and found me in unimpaired spirits. I had not talked even of "curds" though I had given
him several hard cuts on other subjects, when an accident happened
which frightened all malicious fun out of me. We were about going
out after cane, and Miriam had already pulled on one of her buckskin
gloves dubbed "Old Sweety" from the quantity of cane juice they contain, when Mr Carter slipped on its mate, and held it tauntingly out to
her. She tapped it with a case knife she held, when a stream of blood
shot up through the glove. A vein was cut and was bleeding profusely.
He laughed, but panic seized the women. Some brought a basin, some
stood around; I ran after cobwebs, while Helen Carter held the vein
and Miriam stood in silent horror, too frightened to move.

It was indeed alarming, for no one seemed to know what to do, and
the blood flowed rapidly. Presently he turned a dreadful color, and
stopped laughing. I brought a chair, while the others thrust him in it.
His face grew more deathlike, his mouth trembled, his eyes rolled, his
head dropped. I comprehended that these must be symptom[s] of fainting, a phenomenon I had never beheld. I rushed after water, and Lydia
after cologne. Between us, it passed away; but for those few moments, I
thought it was all over with him, and trembled for Miriam. Presently he
laughed again and said "Helen, if I die, take all my negroes and money,
and prosecute those two girls! dont let them escape!" then seeing my
long face he commenced teasing me. "Dont ever pretend you dont care
for me again! here you have been unmerciful to me for months, [p. 99]
hurting more than this cut, never sparing me once, and the moment
I get scratched, it's O Mr Carter! and you fly around like wild to wait
on me!"

In vain I represented that I would have done the same for his old
lame dog, and that I did not like him a bit better; he would not believe
it, but persisted that I was a humbug and that I liked him in spite of
my protestations. As long as he was in danger of bleeding to death, I

let him have his way; and frightened out of teasing, spared him for the rest of the evening.

Just at what would have been twilight but for the moonshine, when he went home after the blood was staunched and the hand tightly bound, a carriage drove up to the house, and Col. Allen [192] was announced. I cant say I was ever more disappointed. I had fancied him tall, handsome and elegant; I had heard of him as a perfect fascinator, a woman killer. Lo! a wee little man is carried in, in the arms of two others—wounded in both legs at B. Rouge, he has never yet been able to stand. Monsieur struck me as being the last person one could be fascinated by. A dough face stood in the place of a handsome one; and as I looked at it, I could not help thinking "My friend, I know nothing of your history or tastes; but if you are not vicious, then I shall no longer believe in intuitive aversion."

He was accompanied by a Mr Bradford,[193] whose assiduous attentions and boundless admiration for the Colonel, struck me as being unusual in a man. His kindness showed a woman's heart; but something struck me disagreeably, and mentally I classed them as the Lion and his jackal, however uncharitable it might be. I had not observed him otherwise, until the General whispered "Do you know that that is the brother of your old sweetheart?" Though the appellation was by no means merited, I recognized the one he meant. Brother to our Mr Bradford of eighteen months ago! My astonishment was unbounded, and I alluded to it immediately.

He said it was so; that his brother had often spoken to him of us, and the pleasant evenings he had spent at [our] home. I mentioned one evening not so pleasant, when he had spoiled my fun completely at the party given by the officers at the garrison, and had quarreled with me all the way on our long walk home, and how we had parted, he in wrath, I in disgust, standing on the steps at home that beautiful moonlight night which it seemed a sin to desecrate by such a display of temper, and how we had never met since, adding that he was one of those who could make themselves the most agreeable, or disagreeable

192. Colonel Henry Watkins Allen of the 4th Louisiana had been badly wounded in the Battle of Baton Rouge. He would become governor of Confederate Louisiana and at the end of the war would go into exile in Mexico City.

193. J. McPherson Bradford, called Mac, brother of J. B. (Buck) Bradford.

of men, just as he pleased. His brother laughed and said that the last remark described his brother so perfectly that he could not have mistaken who I meant. Poor Buck had an unfortunately irritable temper, but was *so* good! and besides, liked us so much—I hastened to assure him that I appreciated his talents, and bore no malice towards him for his lecture; and that I was only sorry I could not see him again to tell him I forgave him. O how he bothered me at that party!

Though I clung to Gibbes' arm, he made me [move] over to Mr Bradford, and against my will, I had to go with him. Once there, like my wraith, he never lost sight of me. A red rose bud was given me emblematically, accompanied by a corresponding speech. Silly enough [p. 100] it was; all remarks of the kind are, and consequently one dislikes to have them over heard. I was leaning against the window at the time swinging the flower carelessly in my fingers. Before I committed myself by an answer, I turned, and beheld Mr Bradford on the other side! Fancy my sensations! A while later, some one brought me a white bud, with the emblem—too young to love. A voice startled me saying "Emblematically again, Miss Sarah?" It was my shadow again! Imagine if I had cause to hate him! What wonder that our walk was anything but pleasant, I feeling that I had been under a strict surveillance, he feeling that I was anything but pleased with him? Shall I ever forget that walk?

November 3d.

I suppose I would have written forever if I had not been called to take a ride. I had never before thought of riding on Sunday, but Mr Bradford and Will Carter suggested it, and as the General sent for the horse, Miriam and I got ready. It was just sundown as we started, and we promised ourselves a splendid ride by moonlight. I had but one objection, and that was going so slowly. Both gentlemen decidedly objected to getting home too soon, and made us walk slowly through the light and shadow of the road.

Poor Will exerted himself to entertain me, and deplored my cruelty. "You are so smart! you see *clean* through a fellow, and then tell him what a fool he is to boot! Heaven knows I have stood more from you, than from any girl in the world. You cut me to pieces, turn me in ridicule just as coolly as though I were nobody, and then I swear I'm angry, and then to-morrow come back as humble as a dog, and go through it all again! 'Tisn't fair! You know I only stand it because I love you and your sister more than anyone in the world, and that I would make any other girl suffer for it. You are too hard on a fellow! Indeed you are!" and so on until he convinced me of my ferocious disposition, and made me promise to be more lenient. All the way coming back he would exclaim "*Aint* it nice? First time in four years we have met without your cutting me! And yet I have spent the day with you! Please let us keep it up!" just as though it was not his miserable disposition that caused him to find fault with me!

I like Mr Bradford more than I thought I would; he is so excessively amiable. There is a quiet fun about him, too, that I like very much. Pity he and his brother did not each give the other a piece of their amiability and temper. A mild half and half would make fine men out of each.

November 4th 1862.

O what a glorious time we had yesterday! First, there were those two gentlemen to be entertained all day, which was rather a stretch, I confess, so I stole away for a while. Then I got the sweetest letter from Miss Trenholm, enclosing Jimmy's photograph, and she praised him so, that I was in a damp state of happiness and flew around showing my picture to everybody, Mr Bradford included, who pronounced him a noble boy, and admired him to my satisfaction. Then came a letter from Lilly, saying mother had decided to remain in Clinton, and [p. 101] wanted us to join her there. O my prophetic soul! My heart went below zero! Then Col. Allen sent to P. Hudson for the band to serenade us, and raised my spirits in anticipation of the treat.

While performing my toilette in the evening, Waller Fowler arrived, on his way to Vicksburg, bringing a letter to Miriam from Major Drum! Heaven only knows how it got here! Such a dear, kind letter, dated sixth of August only! Affairs were very different then, and he said that Sis' distress about us was such, that he must try to send her nearer to us. And such an unexpected piece of news! Oh my heart fails me! I cannot fancy Sis as a mother. Either her child never lived, or she is dead. I was wild about it. Think, three whole months have passed since, and that she is either a happy mother now, or lying in her distant grave! And we so ignorant of it! O Sis! Sis! You cant know what a load that is on my heart. Slowly I dressed myself, and still more slowly I combed Anna. I could think of nothing else until I heard Miriam and Mr Bradford call us to take a walk, when we hurried down to them.

A race down to the railroad, a merry talk standing on the track mingled with shouts of laughter in which I tried to drown fears for Sis, made the early sunset clouds pass away sooner than usual, to us, and moonlight warned us to return. Mrs Worley passed us in her buggy, coming to stay all night; and half way a servant met us, saying two soldiers had come to call on us. Once there, I was surprised to find that one was Frank Enders,[194] the one I least expected to see. The other was a Mr Harold.[195] I need not describe him, beyond this slight indication of his style. Before half an hour was over, he remarked to Anna that I was a *very* handsome girl, and addressed me as—Miss Sallie! That is quite sufficient. Then Will Carter came in, and joined our circle. His first aside was "If you only knew how much I liked you last night, you would never be cruel to me again. Why I thought you the greatest girl in the world! Please let's part friends tonight again!" I would not promise, for I knew I would tease him yet. And at supper, when I insisted on his taking a glass of milk, his face turned so red that Mrs Carter pinched my arm blue, and refused to help me to preserves because I was making Will *mad*! But Waller helped me, and I drank my own milk to Mr Carter's health with my sweetest smile.

"Confound that milkman! I wish he had cut his throat before I stumbled over him," he exclaimed after tea. But I had more amusing game than to make him angry then; I wanted to laugh to get rid of the phantom that pursued me, Sis. I would only think of her as alive and happy; but the moment the laugh ceased, my thoughts went back, while Anna in alarm begged me to laugh again.

The evening passed off very pleasantly; I think there were some eigh-

194. Frank Enders had enlisted as a private in Captain Fenner's battery, Louisiana Light Artillery, a few weeks before. He was detached to the medical department at Port Hudson and in December of 1862 was sent to Clinton as a nurse in the Soldier's Home Hospital. Enders was very likely a son of the Paducah, Kentucky, merchant and banker Henry Enders. He studied medicine after the war and in 1873 went to practice in Maui, in Hawaii, where he died in 1884. I am grateful to Janine Volkmar of the Hawaii State Library Staff for locating his obituary in the *Hawaiian Gazette*, December 17, 1884, p. 2.

195. In his notes to the 1960 edition of *A Confederate Girl's Diary*, James I. Robertson, Jr., identifies Mr. Harold as Lieutenant B. Morgan Harold, an artillery liaison officer on General Martin L. Smith's staff. Obviously he is referring to B. Morgan Harrod. I have ruled out Harrod, but have not come up with an identification of my own.

teen of us in the parlor. About ten, the General went to the sugar house (he commenced grinding yesterday) and whispered to me to bring the young people down presently. Mr Bradford and I succeeded in moving them, and we three girls retired to exchange our pretty dresses [p. 102] for plain ones, and get shawls and Nuages, for our warm week had suddenly passed away, and it was quite cold out.[196]

There was quite a string of us as we straggled out in the beautiful moonlight, with only Mrs Badger as an escort. Mr Enders and I had a gay walk of it; and when we all met at the furnace, we stopped and warmed ourselves, and had a laugh before going in. Inside, it was lighted up with Confederate gas, in other words, pine torches, which shed a delightful light, neither too much, or too little, over the different rooms. We tried each by turns. The row of bubbling kettles with the dusky negroes bending over in the steam, and lightly turning their paddles in the foamy syrup, the whole under the influence of torch light, was very interesting; but then Mr Enders and I found a place more pleasant still. It was in the first purgery, standing at the mouth of the shoot through which the liquid sugar runs into the car, and taking the place of the car as soon as it was run off to the coolers, each armed with a paddle, scraped the colon[197] up, and had our own fun while eating. Then running along the little railroad to where the others stood in the second room over the vats, and racing back again all together to eat sugar cain and cut up generally around our first pine torch, we had really a gay time.

Presently Puss wants a corner[198] was suggested, and all flew up to the second staging, under the cain carrier and by the engine. Such racing for corners! such scuffles among the gentlemen! such confusion among the girls when springing forward for a place, we would find it already occupied! All dignity was discarded. We laughed and ran as loud and fast as any children, and the General enjoyed our fun as much

196. Writing diagonally across the page, Sarah added: "Some of the gentlemen remarked that very few young ladies would have the courage to change pretty evening dresses for calico, after appearing to such advantage. Many would prefer wearing such dresses, however inappropriate, to the sugar-house. With his droll gravity Gibbes answered: 'Our girls dont want to be stuck up.'"

197. In *Recollections of a Rebel Reefer* (p. 12) James Morgan identifies *colon* as taffy.

198. Popular nineteenth-century game in which the players exchange places and one, designated Puss, tries to secure a corner by rushing to any place that is vacant.

as we, and encouraged us in our pranks. Waller surpassed himself; Mr Bradford carried all by storm, Mr Enders looked like a school boy on a frolic, Mr Carter looked sullen and tried lazily not to mar the sport completely, while Mr Harold looked timidly foolish and half afraid of our wild sport. Mrs Badger laughed, the General roared, Anna flew around like a baloon, Miriam fairly danced around with fun and frolic, while I laughed so that it was an exertion to change corners. Then forfeits followed, with the usual absurd penalties in which Mr Bradford sentenced himself unconsciously to ride a barrel, Miriam to make him a love speech going home, Mr Enders to kiss my hand, and I to make him (Mr Enders) a declaration, which I instantly did, in french, whereby I suffered no inconvenience as Miriam alone comprehended.

Then came more sugar cane and talk in the purgery, and we were horrified when Mrs Badger announced that it was twelve o'clock, and gave orders to retire. O the pleasant walk home! Then of course followed a last goodnight on the balcony, while the two young men mounted their horses and Frank Enders vowed to slip off [p. 103] every time he had a chance, and come out and see us. Then there was a grand proposition for a ride to Port Hudson on horseback, and in order to secure a pledge that we would pass by Gen. Beale's headquarters,[199] Mr Enders wrapped my nuage around his throat, declaring that I would be obliged to stop there for it, though, if prevented, he would certainly be obliged to bring it back himself. This morning though, the married ladies made so much difficulty about who should go, and how, that we were forced to abandon it, much as we would have enjoyed it. I am afraid to say how late it was when we got to bed. I know it was almost ten when we left the breakfast table this morning, so I suppose it must have been quite late before we retired. To Col. Allen's, as well as to our own great disappointment, the band could not come on account of sickness.

November 5th. Wednesday.

Col. Allen and Mr Bradford have just left, to our great regret, for both have made themselves so agreeable, that we young people will miss them very much. Last evening accompanied by Mr Bradford and

199. At this time Brigadier General William N. R. Beall, an Arkansan, was in command at Port Hudson.

Waller, we went again to the sugar house after supper, and spent as pleasant, though not quite so noisy an evening as we had the night before. The chief fun consisted in sitting on the edge of the coolers, where we could constantly replenish our paddles without the trouble of moving, and held firmly by the adhesive powers of sugar, we laughed unrestrainedly at any thing amusing that presented itself, confident of not falling in the warm mixture so long as syrup could stick. Mr Bradford afforded us the greatest amusement. Not that he is by any means brilliant, but his amiability added to his quiet fun and evident desire to please, could not fail to make him a pleasant companion; and besides, when one is determined to be amused, it must be a dull person indeed who fails to interest you. I think he was decidedly struck with Miriam. The Colonel told us while taking leave, that if we returned to Clinton while he was there, he would promise us a splendid serenade.

November 6th.

We three girls fancied a walk last evening, and immediately after dinner prepared to walk to Mrs Breaux's, only a mile, and get her to come to the sugar house. But as we put on our bonnets, Captain Bradford,[200] brother of the one who left in the morning, was announced, and our expedition had to be abandoned. This is the third of the five brothers that I have met, and if it were not for the peculiarity in their voices, I should say that there was not the most distant relationship existing between them. This one is very handsome, quiet, and what Dickens calls "in a high shouldered state of deportment." He looks like a moss covered stone wall, a slumbering volcano, a—what you please, so it suggests anything unexpected and dangerous to stumble over. A man of indomitable will and intense feeling I am sure. I should not like to rouse his temper, or give him cause to hate me.

[p. 104] A trip to the sugar house followed as a matter of course, and we showed him around, and told him of the fun we had had those two nights, and taught him how to use a paddle like a Christian. We remained there until suppertime, when we adjourned to the house,

200. Captain James L. Bradford, in command of Battery F, 1st Regiment Mississippi Light Artillery. A native of Georgetown, he grew up in Mississippi, where the 1860 census lists him as a law student age 26 and living in Raymond, in Hinds County. After the war he practiced in New Orleans. See obituary in *Times-Picayune*, January 6, 1919, p. 5.

where we spent the remainder of the evening very pleasantly. At least I suppose he found it so, for it was ten o'clock before he left.

Fickle Miriam instantly turned. In the morning, there was no one like Mr Bradford; I came near being thrashed by both her and Anna for saying I did not think him by any means intelligent. At night it was O *Captain* Bradford! How charming! how intelligent! How much more agreeable than his brother! I ventured a word in defense of the morning star; but the rays of the evening star had blinded her to all others. I came near being sent to Coventry for asserting that the forgotten one was as handsome as the new favorite! Anna of course took part with the one she thought could talk loudest, while I took pleasure in defending the abused one; not that I so much admired him, but merely because he *was* abused. However, I think I shall like this one better on acquaintance; I am satisfied there is something in him.

Just now I was startled by a pistol shot. We three girls have just returned from Mrs Breaux's, who by the way was not at home, and leaving them to go in Helen Carter's room where Will Carter was waiting to see us, I came here to write. Threatening to shoot her, Mr Carter playfully aimed Miriam's pistol at her, and before he could take fair aim, one barrel went off, the shot grazing her arm and passing through the armoir just behind. Of course there was great consternation. Those two seem doomed to kill each other. She had played him the same trick before. He swore that he would have killed himself with the other shot if she had been hurt; but what good would that do her?

We did a foolish thing this morning which I am ashamed to record; but here it is. The railroad which we followed to Mrs Breaux, passed just before her door. As we stood on the gallery the cars passed crowded with soldiers. An impulse seized us, and we just gave the least little flap to our veils, to make the poor creatures feel cheerful, since they were fighting for us. Instantly every cap was tossed up, and repeated cheers and hurrahs from the whole regiment startled us into consciousness of our folly. The more enthusiastic they became, the more frightened we were; and each made the other promise not to tell what had happened, we were so ashamed. I'll never wave again, if it is even to those who capture New Orleans.

Sunday Nov. 9th.

How the time flies! one would suppose the calendar was composed of Sundays. Our exile passes gaily here. In Clinton I should grow mad. But who could be unhappy at Linwood? Does not the dear General treat us like his own children? Are they not all as devoted and kind as brothers and sisters? Added to their dear loving hearts, who could be unhappy where there is space and fresh air? And fun and frolic too? Does not the General pass me all the ducks and fowls to carve, just as my [p. 105] own dear father did, and does he not praise my skill, as father did too? And does he not like me to read the papers to him occasionally? That must be because I take such interest in the news, invariably sitting down to read the papers just as he and Gibbes do. And who does he call to help him on with his over coat, when he goes out in the fields? Who but me? Bless the General! He is too good.

I hardly know how these last days have passed. I have an indistinct recollection of rides in cain wagons to the most distant field, coming back perched on the top of the cane singing "Dye my petticoats" to the great amusement of the General who followed on horseback. Anna and Miriam comfortably reposing in corners were too busy to join in, as their whole time and attention was entirely devoted to the consumption of cane. It was only by singing rough impromptues on Mr Harold and Capt. Bradford that I roused them from their task long enough to join in the chorus of "Forty thousand Chinese." I would not have changed my perch, four mules, and black driver, for queen Victoria's coach and six. And to think old Abe wants to deprive us of all that fun! No more cotton, sugar cane, or rice! No more old black aunties or uncles! No more rides in mule teams, no more songs in the cain field, no more steaming kettles, no more black faces and shining teeth around the furnace fires!

If Lincoln could spend the grinding season on a plantation, he would recall his proclamation.[201] As it is, he has only proved himself a fool, without injuring us. Why last evening I took old Wilson's place at the baggasse shoot,[202] and kept the rollers free from cane until I had thrown

201. The Emancipation Proclamation was not issued until January 1, 1863, but on September 22, 1862, Lincoln made public a preliminary draft, and this is the proclamation Sarah is referring to. The document freed slaves in territory under Confederate control.

202. Bagasse is the fiber of cane remaining after the juice has been extracted, a by-product of the sugar-making process. Sarah means *chute.*

down enough to fill several carts, and had my hands as black as his. What cruelty to slaves! And black Frank thinks me cruel too, when he meets me with a patronising grin, and shows me the nicest vats of candy, and peels cane for me! Oh! very cruel! And so does Jules, when he wipes the handle of his paddle on his apron, to give "Mamselle" a chance to skim the kettles and learn how to work! Yes! and so do all the rest who meet us with a courtesy [sic] and "Howd'y young missus!"

Last night we girls sat on the wood just in front of the furnace—rather Miriam and Anna did while I sat in their laps—and with some twenty of all ages crowded around, we sang away to their great amusement. Poor oppressed devils! why did you not chunk us with the burning logs instead of looking happy, and laughing like fools? Really, some good old Abolitionist is needed here, to tell them how miserable they are.[203] Cant mass Abe spare a few to enlighten his brethren?

I must not forget that this is Brother's birthday. One year ago yesterday that father was taken with that dreadful attack of asthma that killed him. In what agony we spent this day last year, when they told us he must die in half an hour! O dear father! as the days wear on, it grows harder and harder to realize your death. If it were not for the hope that every Christian has, of meeting those we love here after, I could never have borne it so. But why should I murmur when God takes, and calls me to follow? Father! Harry! I'll meet you again, pleas[e] God, where I shall never be called on to cry over another parting! This one is so short; why should I grow impatient?

[p. 106] November 10th Monday.

In spite of its being Sunday, no sooner was dinner concluded yesterday than we adjourned as usual to the sugar house to see how much damage we could do. Each took from a negro his long paddle, and for more than half an hour skimmed the kettles industriously to the amazement of half a dozen strange soldiers who came to see the extraordinary process of sugar making. At one time the two boys taking

203. Others observed the black view of slavery differently. One Union soldier who was in Baton Rouge in the early months of 1863 wrote in his diary: "Questioned a boy about fourteen, about being a slave, found him very well informed. . . . I asked him if he wished he was white, he said yes, because he would be free. He understands freedom, and slavery, as all that I see do." Diary of William H. Nash, Company D, 50th Regiment Massachusetts Volunteers, April 17, 1863, Louisiana State Library.

possession of the other two paddles, not a negro was at the kettles, but stood inspecting our work. The hardest part we found to be charging the batteries, which none of us could do without their assistance.

We had no sooner relinquished our paddles than some one announce[d] two gentlemen at the house. While we were discussing the possibility of changing our dresses before being seen, enter Mr Enders & Gibbes Morgan of Fenner's Battery.[204] No retreat being possible, we looked charmed and self possessed in spite of plain calicoes and sticky hands, and led the way to the purgery, our usual drawing room at present. When we had fairly got in a humor for fun, Col. Breaux was announced. Ah ça! I did not bargain for him too! I felt more bashful of his seeing me than the two young men; so while Miriam ran up to the boiling room where all the family were assembled, I remained with the others in the purgery. However in a little while Miriam reappeared accompanied by the Colonel, and I went down the railway to meet him just as though I were not ashamed of my plight.

Really, I dont know why I was ashamed, for certainly I was neatly dressed, and had a well combed head; I rather think it was because I did not like Col. Breaux to see me enjoying so much the society of two not very profound young gentlemen and dancing around a vat of candy after Mr Enders who had carried off my pop corn, as though it was the highest pleasure I was capable of enjoying.

I think we each felt that he was the tallest, for presently Mr Enders chalenged [*sic*] me to a walk to the cane carrier where we were closely followed by Anna and Gibbes, and where we remained having our own fun until long after sunset when we rejoined the others around the pine torches before coming up to supper. Mr Enders very conveniently forgot to bring my nuage. He says he started expressly to do so, but reflecting that I might then have no inducement to pay that visit to P. Hudson, he left it for another time. He and Gibbes sat on each side of me, and as I had to entertain both as Anna had nothing to say, I could not say more than a word or two to Col. Breaux, who fell to Miriam's lot. We afterwards agreed that the two varieties did not accord very well in the same room. As I rattled away, I was always thinking "What a fool the

204. Henry Gibbes Morgan, Sarah's cousin, son of her Aunt Caro. He was 19 when she wrote this.

Colonel must think me to hear me talk such nonsense!" while Miriam felt that it would not do to talk rationally on such an occasion, and felt incapable of doing her duty to either side. All this time the Colonel talked as kindly as possible, but I just felt—young people may do for an hour; but it is the rational after all that are the most agreeable and who can make a big day short.

We arranged a visit to Gibbes, and Mr Enders made me promise to call at Gen. Beale's head quarters for a pass. "They will want you to go to the [p. 107] Provost Marshall's for it, but you just come to Gen. Beale's, and send a courier for me, and I will bring it myself!" And half in fun, half in ernest, I promised.

Nov. 12th Wednesday.

Once more a cripple, and consigned to my bed, for how long, heaven only knows. This is writ[t]en while in a horizontal position, reposing on my right arm which is almost numb from having supported me for some sixteen hours without turning over. Let me see if I can remember how it happened. Last evening we started out to see Gibbes, just Miriam and Anna in one buggy, and Mrs Badger and I in the other. Gibbes proper, that is, the Captain, and the General both approved, but neither could accompany us. It is useless to say how much I objected to going without a gentleman. Indeed, when we reached the road which formed the fourth side of the square formed by Col. Breaux's, Capt. Bradford's and Capt. Fenner's camps, I thought I should die of terror on finding myself in such a crowd of soldiers on parade. My thick veil alone consoled me, but I made a vow that I would not go through it again, not if I never saw Gibbes, Junior, again on earth.

His camp lay far off from the road, so that we had to drive out to it between the other two, and asked a soldier to tell him that we were there. Presently he came up looking so pleased, that I was almost glad we had come; and then Capt. Fenner appeared, looking charmed, and Lieut.

Harris[205] who looked more alarmed and timid than I. Capt. Fenner exerted himself to entertain us, and seeing how frightened I was, assured me that it was an every day occurrence for young ladies to visit them in parties without gentlemen, and that it was done all through the Confederacy, which however did not comfort me for the hundreds of eyes that were looking at us as our small party stood out in front of the encampment around a cannon. I think he can throw more expression in his eyes than any one I ever saw.

Miriam suggested sending Gibbes to the Provost to get our pass, in order to avoid the crowd that might be there. Eager to leave the present one for a more retired spot, I exclaimed "O no! let us go ourselves! We cant get in a worse crowd!" I meant *a greater;* but Capt. Fenner looked so comically at me, that I could scarcely laugh out an apology, while he laughed so that I am sure he did not listen to me. What a comical mouth! I liked him *very* much, this time. He promised to come out to day, or tomorrow, and have a game of Puss wants a corner in the sugar house. But now I cant join in, though it was to me the promise was made!

But to the catastrophe at once. As we left, we insisted on taking Gibbes to get our pass, and made him get in Miriam's buggy, where there was space for him to kneel and drive. I was to carry out my promise to Mr Enders. We had to pass just by the camp of the 1st Alabamah, Col. Steedman's, where the whole regiment was on parade. We had not gone thirty yards beyond them, when a gun was discharged. The horse instantly ran off. I dont believe there could be two cooler individuals than Mrs Badger and I were. I had every confidence in her being able to hold him so long as the bridle lasted. I had heard that there was more danger in jumping at such moments, than in remaining quiet, so I sat still. There was nothing to hold to, as it was a no top, or what I call a [p. 108] "low neck" buggy; so my hands rested quietly in my lap. Presently I saw the left rein snap close to the horse's mouth. I knew all was over then, but did not utter a word. Death seemed inevitable, and I thought it was as well to take it coolly. The horse turned abruptly, I felt that something impelled me out, followed the impulse, saw Mrs Bad-

205. Lieutenant Thomas B. Harris of the 4th Louisiana. He was detailed on the Clinton and Port Hudson Railroad.

ger's white cape fluttering above me, received a blow on the extremity of my spine that I thought would kill me before I reached the ground, landing however on my left hip, and quietly reclining on my left elbow, with my face to an upset buggy whose reversed wheels spun around in empty air.

I heard a rush as of horses; I saw men galloping up; I would have given worlds to spring to my feet, or even to see if they were exposed; but found I could not move. I had no more power over my limbs than if they were iron; only the intense pain told me that I was still alive. I was perfectly conscious, but unable to move. My only wonder was why Miriam, who was in front, did not come to me. My arm was giving away. Dimly as through a haze, or dream, I saw a soldier bending over me, trying to raise me. The horse he had sprung from rushed up to his master, and reared up over me. I saw the iron hoofs shining above my body; death was certain this time, but I could not move. He raised his arm and struck him, and obedient to the blow the animal turned aside, and let his feet fall without crushing me. Mrs Carter, when she heard it described, offered a fabulous sum for a correct drawing of that most interesting tableau, the gallant Alabamian supporting a helpless form on one arm, while he reined in a fiery charger with the other. I was not aware of the romance; I was conscious only of the unpleasant situation.

Dozens crowded around, and if I had been a girl for display, here was an opportunity, for thirty pair of soldier arms were stretched out to hold me. "No! Gibbes! Gibbes!" I whispered, and had the satisfaction of being transfered from a stranger's, to my cousin's arms. Gibbes trembled more than I, but with both arms clasped around me, held me up. But for that I would have returned to my original horizontal position. "Send for the doctor!" cried one.

"A surgeon, quick!" cried another. "Tell them no!" I motioned. I was conscious of a clatter of hoofs, and cloud of dust. One performed a feat never heard of before. He brought a glass of water at full gallop which I instantly drained by way of acknowledgement. I think I felt the unpleasant situation more than the pain. Not being accustomed to being the centre of attraction, I was by no means pleased with the novel experience. Miriam held my hand, and questioned me with a voice tremulous with fear and laughter. Anna convulsively sobbed or giggled some question. I felt the ridiculous position as much as they. Laughing was agony, but I had to do it to give them an excuse, which they readily seized to give vent to their feelings, and encouraged by seeing it, several gold band officers joined in, constantly endeavoring to apologize or check themselves with a "Really, Miss, it may seem unfeeling, but it is impossible—" the rest was lost in a gasp, and a wrestle between politeness and the desire to laugh.

I dont know what I was thinking of, but I certainly paid very little attention to what was [p. 109] going on. I only wanted to get home, away from all those eyes; and my ernest wish made me forget them. The first remark I heard was my young Alabamian crying, "It is the most beautiful somerset I ever saw! Indeed it could not be more gracefully done! Your feet did not show!" Naif, but it was just what I wanted to know, and dared not ask. Some one ran up, and asked who was hurt, and I heard another reply "I am afraid the young lady is seriously injured, only she won't acknowledge it. It is worth while looking at her. She is the coolest, most dignified girl you ever saw," and another was added to the already too numerous audience.

Poor Mrs Badger, having suffered only from torn clothing, received very little sympathy while I got more than my share. I really believe that the blow I received was from her two hundred and forty pound body, though the Alabamian declares he saw the overturning buggy strike me as I fell. To her, and others I am indebted for the repetition of many a remark that escaped me. One bold soldier boy exclaimed "Madame, we are all warriors, but we cant equal that! It is braver than any man!" I had to laugh occasionally to keep my spirits up, but Miriam ordered me to quit, saying that I would go off in hysterics.

I had previously repeatedly declared to the Doctor that I was not hurt, and seeing him idle, and hearing Miriam's remark the Alabamian— I am told—cried "O Doctor! doctor! cant you do something? Is she going to have hysterics?" "Really" said the Doctor. "The young lady objects to being examined; but as far as I can judge, she has no limbs broken." Every body ordered me to confess at once my injury; but how was I to inform a whole crowd that I had probably broken the tip of my backbone, and could not possibly sit down? So I adhered to my first affirmation, and made no objection when they piled the cushions up and made Gibbes put me down; for I knew he must be tired.

I am told I remained there an hour; I know they talked to me, and that

I answered; but have not an idea of the subject. A gentleman brought a buggy, and offered to drive me home; but a Capt. Lenair[206] insisted on running after the ambulance. Arrived there, Mr Enders says he rushed in crying "For God's sake Gen. Beale, lend me the ambulance! There is a dreadful accident, and I am afraid the young lady will die!" Coming back he exclaimed "By Jove! boys if you want to see a sight, run down and see her hair! The prettiest auburn (?) you ever looked at, and sweeps the ground! I wouldn't mind such a fall if I had such hair to show. Come look at it, do!" Mr Enders says he was sure that it was I, as soon as hair was mentioned, and started out as soon as he had finished a duty he was obliged to perform.

My garter, a purple silk ribbon, lay in the centre of the ring. By the respectful silence observed, I saw they recognized its use, so, unwilling to leave such a relic behind, I asked aloud for my "ribbon" where-upon Anna says the officers pinched each other and smiled. Up came the ambulance, and I was in imminent danger of being carried to it, when with a desperate effort I regained my feet with Gibbes' help, and reached it without other assistance. Beyond, I could do no more.

Capt. Lenair got inside, and several others lifted me up to him, and I sunk motionless on the floor. [p. 110] All bid me goodbye, and my little Alabamian assured me that he was proud of having been the first to assist me. President Miller whispered to Mrs Badger for permission to accompany us, which she readily granted, and raising me on the seat, he insisted on putting his arm around me to hold me up. It was useless to decline. "Now Miss Morgan, I assure you I am an old married man! I know you are suffering! let me have my way!" And the kind old gentle-man held me so comfortably, and broke the force of so many jolts, that I was forced to submit and acknowledge that had it not been for him I could not have endured the rough road.

At the gate that leads to Gen. Beale's headquarters, I saw half a dozen figures standing. One was Frank Enders who hailed the driver. "Hush!" said one I recognized as Capt. Lenair. "The young lady is in there, and the Provost too!" "I dont care if it is Jeff Davis, I'll find out if she is hurt!" he answered. Miriam and Anna recognized him, as they

206. Later Sarah refers to this officer as Captain Lanier. See entry of August 16, 1863. At that time she believed he was one of the Port Hudson officers imprisoned in New Orleans.

followed behind us, and called to him. Without more ado, he jumped in
their buggy, finding them alone, and drove them home. He asked me
something as he passed, but I could not answer. The road was dreadful.
Once the driver mistook it, and drove us within two steps of an embankment six feet high, but discovered the mistake before the horses
went over.

What I most dreaded was explanations, when we should arrive.
Miriam stepped out an instant before, and I heard her telling the accident. Then everybody big and little, white and black gathered around
the ambulance. The Provost thought himself privileged to carry me,
Gibbes insisted on trying it with his one arm, when the General picked
me up and landed me on the gallery. He wanted me to lie down in
old Mrs Carter's room, but confident that once there I could not get
up, and feeling that perhaps the gentlemen would take advantage of
its being on the ground floor to suggest calling on me, I struggled up
stairs with Helen's assistance.

A dozen hands undressed me, and laid me on my face in bed, which
position I have occupied up to the present, 3, P.M. I heard them talking
below, and was told that Miriam's friend Mr Halsey[207] was there also.
Every body sent me messages, and twice the General and Gibbes came
up to see me. Mrs Badger insisted that she would rather be in my condition than have her clothes torn; but Gibbes declared that he wished I
had had my clothes torn off me, rather than have me so injured. Frank
Enders declared he would not leave the house without seeing me, and
readily accepted the General's invitation to stay all night, in hopes of
seeing me in the morning. But later, the Provost carried him off, and
among a dozen messages, he sent this: "Tell her I never would have left
without seeing her if it had not been for President Miller." Well! every
body troubled themselves so much about me, and was so kind, that I
was distressed that they did not share their sympathy with Mrs Badger,
who professed herself willing to exchange her torn clothes for my broken back, to my astonishment, for I would gladly have dispensed with
the suffering.

207. John H. Halsey, a young Pointe Coupee Parish lawyer, enlisted as a second lieutenant in the 1st Louisiana Cavalry on October 8, 1861, but resigned the following April
to accept a commission as captain and raise a company. Instead, he ended up as a private
(later sergeant) in Captain James L. Bradford's battery, 1st Mississippi Light Artillery,
enlisted by Bradford himself. Halsey was a native of Virginia, age 27 in the 1860 census.

Unable to turn, all night I lay awake lying on my face, the least pleasant of all positions; but though the slightest motion tortured me, I had to laugh as we talked it over. Of course this has [p. 111] been written in snatches, and in my same position, which will account for many blots. This morning I was interrupted by mother's unexpected arrival, she having come with Dellie and Morgan[208] to spend the day. Of course she is horrified at the accident of that "unfortunate Sarah!"

Saturday Nov. 15th

I think I grow no better rapidly. Fortunately on Wednesday night they succeeded in turning me over; for my poor elbows, having lost all their skin, were completely used up. Now, if I go slowly and carefully, I can turn by myself at the cost of some little suffering. Au reste, I am well enough off, for there is my dinner that I can eat, if I only had the appetite, and there are books to read, besides, when I get tired of doing nothing. There is poor Anna who was taken with a slight fever the day after I was laid up, who has been there ever since unable to eat or read, and who groans loud enough for forty. I think her's is the least enviable position. Ah me! how much more cheerfully I would have borne the breaking of an arm! Not *more* cheerfully. I may do myself the justice to say that I make no complaints, and am always ready for a laugh. But I would gladly exchange the back for an arm. Spare me my feet! Merciful Father let me walk once more! Anything, save a helpless cripple!

Yesterday Col. Steadman [*sic*] of the 1st Alabamah called with his father.[209] He sent me many messages of condolence, and the rather unpleasant advice to be cupped and scarified.[210] His profession was that of a physician before he became Colonel. His surgeon, whose name is Madding,[211] told him he was satisfied that I was seriously injured though I had not complained. This Colonel is the same who called when we were in Clinton. They readily accepted an invitation to dinner, and remained until late in the afternoon, when Capt. Bradford came in.

208. Two of Lilly's children.

209. Reuben Steedman, a South Carolinian. See sketch of his son in *Confederate Military History*, 12:416.

210. It was common medical practice of the time to bleed patients, and this is the treatment Sarah describes. Vacuum cups provided suction.

211. Dr. Robert F. Madding.

More messages of condolence and sympathy upstairs, which produced no visible effect on my spine, though very comforting to the spirit. Then up came a negro from Fenner's battery. Mr Morgan could not obtain leave, but sent his love, and wanted to know how his cousin was.

At twilight while Anna groaned, I lay quietly thinking of this sad day last year, which had haunted me all day, when Phisse [?][212] ran up. "O the young man with the shiny hat has come, and asked for miss Sarah. And when I said she could not be turned in her bed, he said, 'Whew!' and walked in with his mouth screwed up. And the other one asked where was Miss Anna and said 'You dont say so!' when I told him she was sick too!" So Miriam, not inquired for, was the only one able to receive! Followed more messages of regret and disappointment, to our solitary room, until Miriam vowed that it was the last time she would entertain other girls' beaux, and told them they must not come until we got well again. Of course it was Mr Harold and Mr Enders, one not fancying that Anna could ever get sick, and the other never dreaming that such a neat upset could have serious consequences.

Mr Enders sent me a pencil to write to him, and lying on my side, I managed [p. 112] I managed [*sic*] to scribble off a whole page of nonsense for his benefit. Mr Harold I understand was very anxious to read it, but Mr Enders fortunately refused. I say fortunately, for among other stupidities, I said that Anna was talking in her sleep either about "John" (Mr H.) or "bananas," I could not understand which, but knew it was about something *green* and *soft*. He would never have forgiven me! The bananas were apropos of a nice little bunch that a Major Bennett[213] had sent the young ladies with his compliments, and regrets that he could not call in person and inquire of my health. I believe it was he, instead of the Capt. Lenair who went after the ambulance. I have an indistinct idea of having seen the latter every time I looked, which, however, was not often. Major Bennett sent word by Mr Enders that he was sorry that he could not have accompanied me in the ambulance; but that he could not get Gen. Beale's consent. Capt. Lenair says the same. At that rate, there would have been a crowd of us!

212. One of the Carter slaves.

213. Major William K. Bennett, a Tennessean, was quartermaster on the staff of General Beall at Port Hudson. See *Confederate Veteran* 32:129.

I lay here solitary and alone, for Anna had fallen asleep, listening to the laughter downstairs, without other occupation. Once the two young men came to the foot of the stairs and called out something to me, and after talking a while, I heard them go with Miriam and Mrs Badger to the sugar house. O how I envied them the power of walking! Last Monday I spent the day in there, skimming kettles and throwing off strikes[214] with the girls, working as hard as any; and to day—! [Lines drawn through] because they have no better sense; not because I make an effort to catch them. They are as welcome to go—more so—than to come. I always ask myself Le jeu, vaut il la chandelle?[215] and in the answer—Pouf! ma chandelle s'éteint vraiment.[216]

Poor Mrs Breaux's misfortune distresses me beyond measure. She is perfectly mad. The doctors say hopelessly so; but the Colonel thinks she will be well in a few day[s]. They agree that it was in consequence of her anxiety and want of sleep during the illness of her little girl last week, while over the river. The Colonel has told me that she was the most nervous woman he ever saw. Added to that, they kept up her strength with the strongest coffee, fed her on peppered dishes that only Creoles could eat, and ended by throwing her nerves in such a state that sleep became impossible. Monday she came home, perfectly crazy from the whole combined. Miriam has been several times to see her, and represents her condition as most distressing. Poor Col. Breaux! It would be better for him that she should die rather than live in such a state. They say his devotion to her is perfectly beautiful. Poor man! poor woman! I hardly know which I pity most.

Nov. 16th

I was interrupted yesterday morning by Mrs Badger who wished to apply a few dry cups to my back, to which I quietly submitted, and was unable to move afterwards with[out] pain, as a reward for my patience. But towards sunset came two dear letters that made me forget what I had suffered; one from George, and one from Jimmy dated Bermudas. For the first [p. 113] time I know what my dear little brother suffered

214. Batches of boiling syrup skimmed from kettles during the sugar-making process.
215. The game, is it worth the candle?
216. Pouf! my candle really is going out!

during those long months when we could not hear if he were dead or alive. He kept the secret until he no longer needed either friends or money; and now he tells it with a simplicity that made me cry fit to break my heart when I was left alone in the twilight with no one to see. Dear little Jimmy! what a noble heart! Please God send our darling back again! He tells me he keeps a "log" for my especial benefit. Indeed I will prize it, my little brother! George comforts me with hopes of Peace, and a speedy return. If it could only be!

Will Carter was unceremoniously ushered in here at sunset. At least six times he has asked to come up, and as often have I declined, when this time they did not ask my permission, and in he walked. I have been more agreeably surprised. It was quite dark, when having been alone for some time, Miriam came back to me, and announced that Dr Dortch was down stairs. She and the General had laid a plot to have me butchered, and in my helpless state I had to submit. Only I notice that the Doctor first strengthened himself with a hearty supper and allowed me to do the same before commencing, and that about that time the General disappeared. I got the doctor laughing before he commenced, for I was in a glee myself. He ran a gamut down my spine as though it were a flute until a convulsive twitch told the spot without my troubling myself to speak. "Ah!" I heard, and then a pause. I raised my head and beheld an ugly machine about to be applied, and made the doctor laugh until he could hardly adjust it.

Miriam shut her eyes and she and Anna groaned in concert; I laughed; click! it went and two dozen shining, cutting teeth were buried in my flesh. Six different mouthfuls it took, and as often every one most absurdly groaned, except myself, as there was no more necessity for a groan over that, than over a flea bite, and if there was, I had sponsors enough to answer for me. Then came great cups over the cuts that I thought loosened the roots of my teeth with their tremendous suction power, and which I dare say pulled my hair in at least a foot. Followed more groans from Miriam, and plenty of blood.

I had more fun than any, except perhaps the doctor who, laughing himself, ordered me to hush the same bad practice, and turning to Mrs Carter said he would give anything for a blank book to take down my remarks. How easily he must be amused! Only, the heathen! didn't he put one vile old tumbler four times on the same sore spot? Perhaps that was to try me. But I don't mind it, as he praised my fortitude extravagantly, and called me a young soldier, as though I deserved it. I like to be thought brave. I asked if I were seriously hurt. "Not permanently, I hope" was the doubtful answer, though he promised that I might stand up in a week. Well! I ought to be satisfied.

Anna alone is a study that could amuse me some days longer. To see her frisk around one minute, and the next call that shrimp of a Malvina[217] to lay her down, is as good as a farce. One dish after another she orders, and when brought, perhaps the one that was not made; these are nasty. After talking awhile, she breaks out in the most awful groans, and when I ask in alarm what is the matter, answers "O nothing!" with a voice and indifference that bear witness to her words; "she just wants to, that's all." Yesterday her mother scolded her for it, and besought her to follow my example. "See how Sarah suffers! and who has heard her groan?" "O! Pshaw ma! She's used to it!" was the [p. 114] feeling reply. Salt water she constantly requires; she believes she would like to throw up. If she succeeds, I am constantly called on to testify how often it has been, and as my nights are more than half spent awake, I am requested to state how often she was awake too.

Poor Anna! She is right; there *is* something in being used to suffering. She would think me inhuman if I laughed at her as she did at my overturn; but sometimes I feel like it. Everybody laughs at everybody's accident, except their own. Mrs Badger was furious with her and Miriam for laughing at P. Hudson, the more so when a soldier remarked "Those two young ladies take it coolly! Wonder if they would have cared if the other had been killed?" I say he must have been a cross man who could not have a keen sense of the ridiculous; whoever refused to laugh inwardly, at least, would have been more or less than human. However no one attempted it until Miriam commenced, and then it was only a quiet smile outwardly, whatever they felt inwardly.

Every day I hear more and more about the romantic scene. I confess I did not notice much of it. I made Dr Dortch roar with laughter, telling how timidly the young doctor ventured to put out his hand, and how foolishly he withdrew it at my desire, and stood there looking red

217. A slave, Anna Badger's maid, though she may have been the property of Anna's uncle, General Carter.

and frightened, willing to serve, but afraid to venture. They tell me that when Capt. Lenair asked permission (of Miriam) to hold me, as he advanced to carry it in execution, I stopped him with a wave of my hand which rooted him to the spot. I must have looked like a lion at bay! If I was sparing of words, and abrupt of gesture, it must be attributed to my horror of scenes. I had no idea of reclining in the arms of any man. My helplessness may have served as an excuse to them, but not to me; for I was never yet in that situation where, however weak or sick, I could not make just *one* effort more.

People may talk as they please of the tableaux of "the young Alabamian;" the pale girl supported in her cousin's arms while her "auburn" hair "swept the ground;" the frame formed for the picture by the uniforms and épaulettes of handsome officers while the privates formed a cordon around the whole, looking on with anxious faces; but bah! I'll change with any one who was not there! Anything, rather than be camp talk! Whoever likes affecting scenes, is more than welcome to take my place. I feel disgraced every time I think of it.

This morning the boom of Yankee guns reached my ears; a sound I had hoped never to hear again. It is only those poor devils (I can afford to pity them in their fallen state) banging away at some treasonable sugar houses that are disobedient enough to grind cain on the other side of the river. I hear that one is Mrs Cain's.[218] The sound made my heart throb. What if the fight should come off before I can walk? It takes three people to raise me whenever it is necessary for me to move; I am worse than helpless. What will become of me? Port Hudson, I prophesy, will fall. I found my prediction on the way its defenders talk. I asked a soldier the other day if he thought we could hold it. "Well if we dont, we know so many bypaths that we can easily slip out" was the answer. I was shocked. That is no way for our soldiers to talk, "Slip out!" I expected the answer that always makes my heart swell with enthusiasm, "We'll conquer or we'll die!" Fancy my disappointment! Defended in that spirit, Port Hudson is lost. What follows?

[p. 115] Tuesday Nov. 18th

Last night came a nice letter from Howell. He assures me that in the midst of the battle I am still remembered, for which compliment I shall

218. Mary Ann Cain, wife of Dempsey P. Cain, the West Baton Rouge planter. The Cains would eventually become refugees in Texas.

make him a courtesy [*sic*] the next time we meet, if I ever stand on my feet again. O that reminds me! A note just came from mother, telling me that the most awful Yankees were coming to burn Linwood and take P. Hudson, and so this evening I must walk down to the cars with a chair to rest in until they came, and must certainly be in Clinton to night. Delightful arrangement! I wrote to ask if she knew that my legs were of no more service to me than they are to her?

Dr Dortch has again been murdering me. All the old gashes recut, some twice, and the bed bathed in blood. He comforted me with praises of my fortitude, and pronounced it perfect butchery. My back is so em-broidered that Miriam and Mrs Badger declare they can trace "Dellie," "Dixie" and "Frank" in the gashes. The doctor says *perhaps* I can stand by Sunday. If the Yankees come before—

Here comes a great paper of candy from Will C. I like it better than his company, for he has been to see me every day, and candy has not. I like variety.

Yesterday as though to punish me for my unkind remarks, Anna grew decidedly worse, and I am really uneasy about her. Her mother has her hands full with both of us, though poor Miriam is indefatigable in her attendence on me. Anna and I must get well in time to nurse them if they give away.

Friday night. Nov. 21st.

Lying on my face, as it were, with my poor elbows for a support, I try to pass away these lonely hours. For with the exception of old Mrs Carter who is down stairs, and the General who is elsewhere, Anna and I are the only white people on the place. The cause of this heartless desertion is a grand display of Tableaux Vivants[219] at Jackson, for the benefit of the Soldiers' Hospital,[220] and of course it would be sinful to stay away, particularly as Anna is a great deal better, and I need no great care. I have had company enough to day, to make amends for all that I have missed since I have been disabled. First, came two ladies to spend the day. I was not much interested, I confess. I much prefered

219. Living Pictures. In such *tableaux* the costumed participants struck poses, usually to the accompaniment of songs or narration.

220. On orders of General Beall, the dormitory buildings at Centenary College had been converted to a hospital to handle the overflow from the military hospitals at Clinton and Port Hudson.

continuing my Napoleon, if only to tease Anna; for in two days I have read more in it than she has in two months, and she is not a little annoyed at seeing me pass her. But after a while the cars whistled, and to my intense astonishment, in walked Lilly.

I am afraid I let mother know my condition too plainly in my note, and the small hope I had of ever being strong again; for Lilly says she cried bitterly over it, and made her instantly write for Dr Enders [221] to come up to me, and examine my spine. But I am as unhappy about her as she can be about me, for Lilly tells me she has a very painful and sore hand, the swelling of which has gone up to her elbow. It makes me wretched to think of what she suffers. But she forced Lilly to leave her, in order that she might be satisfied about me, and in the dear little woman walked, God bless her loving heart! and made me happy for the rest of the day. And she brought a letter from [p. 116] Sis, of only the 15th of Sept. Sis has a daughter! I could thank God heartily. Poor Sis must be so proud and happy! She calls it Harry. Is this selfishness? I dont like anyone to bear his name. It goes to my heart. But I must overcome this to please her. I am so thankful that she is well and happy! [222]

I did not see half enough of Lilly; but believe I laughed enough for her to carry back a good account to mother. She says every one we know in Clinton, and many that I do not know, make constant inquiries about my state, and seem very solicitous. I think I have received the condolences of the whole of these two parishes, certainly. If sympathy cures, I ought certainly to recover. Even dear little Dellie sent her contribution—her love and a bundle of pralines. But before I heard enough, or said enough, the cars came back, and Lilly went back to mother, carrying her, I hope, more encouragement than I feel. If I could only know if she is better, now. I am very, very uneasy about mother.

Dinner was just over when Lilly left, and at the same moment Frank

221. Dr. Peter M. Enders.

222. On the day Sarah wrote this, she turned back to the entry of August 10 and wrote the following note in the margin at the top of the page: "November 21st 1862. Night. I am persuaded (though I have not the slightest foundation for such a belief as Sis did not say how old her baby was, or mention the date of its birth) that little Harry was born that Sunday, 10th Aug, when we were flying from the Yankees. I made a note to see if I am not right in my supposition."

Enders was announced. Miriam received him, being the only presentable one. I should think she would grow tired. Last night she entertained Capt. Bradford until long after twelve. Mr Enders begged to be
allowed to see me, and instantly all the ladies decided that he should.
I naturally felt decidedly averse to it at first, but Miriam argued that
there was no one to entertain him while she dressed for the Tableaux,
and I reflected that as I see Will Carter every day, it would make very
little difference. So at last they picked me up in their arms and carried
me in Mrs Carter's room, as Anna was not presentable, with her salt
water and fever, and laid me on the bed in my white gown, with a quilt
thrown over me. At the last moment, I was ashamed of receiving visiters
in that style, and begged them to carry me back; but they only laughed
at my entreaties until it was too late, and Miriam ushered him in. His
look of intense pity made me laugh, and I held out my hand.

As we talked, one by one the ladies disappeared in the adjoining
rooms to dress, and left me to entertain him alone. He asked me if I
knew what he had come for? To go to the Tableaux, I suppose, I answered. "Indeed I didnt!" he said. "I thought you surely were well by
this time, and expected to find you downstairs. I joined the tableaux
party when they said you could not see me. But I hate to go now. Will
you let me spend the evening here?" I laughed at the surprising request. What a vastly agreeable visit he would have had in the place of
the grand sight at Jackson!

Presently Gibbes, the General and Will C. came in, and I had quite
a levee. The General shook his head at me for getting ahead of him,
for he has constantly threatened me with the announcement that he
means to bring all the gentlemen up here, who call; but I pleaded that
I was tired of my own company; and believed he did not mean to carry
his threat in execution, so he forgave me for stealing a march on him.
I am satisfied of Mr Enders' sympathy. He talked very bravely to me,
but every now and then he would turn to [p. 117] Gibbes and say "*Isn't
it hard to see her lie there in perfect health, and yet so helpless?*" as
though he really felt it. And then he would say to me "Capt Lenair tells
me that you laughed to give them a pretext for laughing, declared you
were not hurt and would not let them touch you!" He seemed to think it
extraordinary, but added he was sorry he had not been there; he would
not have asked my permission to support me; it was *too* unreasonable

to make believe I was able to sustain myself. Glad he was not there, but dare say I would have ruled him as I did the rest!

It was almost sunset when every one appeared, dressed, each looking lovelier than the other. Mrs Carter, Mrs Worley, Mrs Badger, Lydia, Miriam, and Ida Smith (I saw her for the first time to day) each stood by the bed to show me their dress, kissed me, and went off. Will Carter was pathetic in his regrets over my misfortune, and generously offered to remain with me; but I put his offer by with the other, and told them goodbye cheerfully. And now it is late enough for me to say good bye to this pen too, for tonight.

Monday Nov. 24th

Yesterday Col & Mrs Breaux came over to see us. The Colonel has called several times to inquire for me, though I have not seen him; but this is the first time I have seen his wife. She is thought to have recovered from her late unfortunate attack, but occasionally I saw slight indications that her mind was not entirely settled. I hardly know whether it is right for me to mention what others discuss so freely; but undoubtedly she is a very jealous woman. Some unthinking people judged proper to tease her about the Colonel's visits here, as soon as she arrived, and jestingly alluded to his attentions to Miriam. I hardly think she liked it. It was an unreasonable jest, at all events; for it is well known here that if the Colonel liked one better than another, it was me. I do not say this through vanity, but through justice to Miriam. She talks more than I, is a greater favorite abroad, so of course all her admirers thought that like themselves, Col. Breaux must admire her most. I dare say he did. But still it is an acknowledged fact that the Colonel, whose chief pleasure is the society of ladies, paid much more attention to me than he did to her, perhaps because I was a better listener, and was not quite so talkative; every one who is conscious of conversational powers likes an attentive listener.

But is it not absurd to imagine it possible for a married man to really *like* a girl? He may laugh and talk with them, play the gallant and devoted (which Col. Breaux did *not* do) but still a married man is a married man, and the idea of flirting with such is preposterous. Perhaps Mrs Breaux thinks differently.

When she came, Mr. Halsey and Capt. Bradford were spending the day with Miriam, and tired of being alone, I asked to see her up here. I found her a nice little lady, with a perfect Creole face, speaking English with a French accent, and just a soupçon of English occasionally heard in her French. Almost her first remark was "Are you Sarah? The Colonel raved about your beautiful hair until I so wished that mine was light!" I thought it funny; but as he had praised it several times to me, turned it by speaking of her own black hair.

[p. 118] A long while she talked rationally if you will, but with a restlessness and vivacity that alarmed me. She was sitting on my bed at sunset, just where I could look in her large hazel eyes. "You might [?] not walk for months" she said. "Let me take your place in the riding party." I told her certainly; that the Colonel owed me a ride which I would cheerfully make over to her. Looking at me earnestly with her great eyes, she said as simply as though such a thing were within the realms of possibility "Dont fall in love with my husband." I fancy I opened mine a little wider with astonishment. But I laughingly assured her that I had never yet been in love, not being at all susceptible; but that Miriam was the flirt of the family. "I am more afraid of you" she returned more earnestly than ever.

Afraid of me! In my surprise I raised myself on my elbow and looked steadfastly at her. "Yes!" she said. "I am afraid because you are so natural! You are true!" "Isn't Miriam?" I asked in growing wonder, for I did not believe any one would dare say my dear Miriam was anything save one of God's noblest and truest women. She clenched her hands and drew her breath in with a hissing sound while exclaiming vehemently "No! No! but you are! Shall I tell you what my husband says?" Bending over me she whispered "He says he admires you more than he does your sister. He likes you best." Abruptly she kissed my cheek and ran out of the room. And there terminated this surprising interview between two strangers.

Poor little woman! A jealous heart and unsettled brain! what misery! They tell me the Colonel looks perfectly wretched, which does not surprise me. With such a melancholy object before him, how could he be otherwise? What cause she has for jealousy, especially about Miriam, I cannot imagine. It is too unreasonable. Poor Miriam has many other sins to answer for. Here is Will Carter just crazy enough about her to blow his brains out, and acknowledging that nothing but his horror of compromising her, keeps him from putting an end to his misery. Talking of Will Pinkney's unhappiness while at F. Jackson last year, Waller said when last here "Sometimes I thought him crazy. I would take my oath that either you or Miriam caused it. Sometimes I was led to believe it was one, sometimes the other. One of you two will have to answer for it." Answer, Miriam. You know best.

Tuesday 25th. Night.

I cannot sleep without recording my extraordinary feat. For a whole second, I stood alone to day! Rather a shakey "stand" to be sure; but still it was something. And they put me in a rocking chair too! All this is thanks to the inhuman cupping and bleeding I underwent yesterday. How thankful I will be if I can ever walk again!

I have not seen Miriam since dinner, as she has been entertaining Mr Halsey all this time; and as we three were alone on the place, all the others having gone out to spend the day, Anna and I would have had a lonesome time if Mrs Breaux had not come over to see us. What a frank, impulsive little woman! She seems to like me, to my great surprise; I did not expect it. "Ah!" she exclaimed, "Think! I was so jealous, I thought, of Miriam! It was a mistake! I did not remember the right name! Enfin, everybody talked of her, she was so gay, so handsome & [p. 119] such a fine performer, such a universal favorite, how was I to think after all, that it was cette petite violette blanche?[223] Miriam the most fashionable, Sarah the most interesting? You see, ma violette, you are too modest! You dont know your worth!" Pray, who told her I had any worth knowing?

Such a lively, rattling little woman! She says her visits are intended for me alone (a strange way of being jealous) and promised to spend the day with me to-morrow. She asked if I would not like to be carried downstairs in a day or two; I said yes, but it was too much trouble. "Where is Gibbes?" I said he can use but one arm, and besides, was going away with the General on Thursday to be gone several days. "Oh!" cried the impulsive little woman "Gustave will carry you! It is no trouble! He would like to do it!" Merci, I said, but [I] prefer depending on myself. "Think!" she would say "of my being so jealous

223. This little white violet.

of Miriam, mistaking her for you!" Her frank speech amuses me; she talks so childishly and oddly.

Gibbes comes in, bringing me many kind messages from Gen. Beale and others. The General sends word he has tried in vain to discover the man who fired that unlucky gun, to punish him for it. I hope he will never find him. What good would it do? No punishment they could inflict on him would heal my poor spine. The Doctor confesses that he fears it is beyond his skill, and that it is more serious than I allow others to suppose. What then? Am I to be a cripple for life? O my God! I who love earth and air so much, who am never so happy as when wandering alone with Thee and Nature, is this to be my end? I, so independent, am I to depend on others for each little office I was once so proud of being able to perform for myself? How shall I who abhored helplessness submit to being waited upon? Shall Miriam, so fond of pleasure, be chained down by my sick bed, with my miserable pale face to haunt her where ever she goes and mar all enjoyment? Shall mother mourn over me, hardly a woman, yet ready to die, and see me fade away day by day before her? The burden and sorrow falls on them.

Dear Lord! for their sake let death come first! I could stand it better than this torturing helplessness that gives such pain to others. My heart swells when Gibbes looks at me so sadly. And shall George come back to find me weak and helpless, a cripple on his hands for the rest of my days? And Jimmy—Oh dear little Jimmy! no more romps around the old parlor! no more walks or rides with you by me! no more gay songs at twilight when you used to lay your head in my lap and bid me sing! Dear Jimmy, this will be sadder to you than it is to me. Lord, Thou knowest if I have loved life; how I have blessed Thee that I have lived, each day; how I cling to it still. With all my soul, I love this beautiful earth—each blade of grass that grows, every flower of the field that God made. I would not lightly give it up; yet if this must be my fate, dear Lord, in mercy to those who must suffer with me, let me die!

Who would believe I here laid down my pen to sing until every one laughed at my cheerfulness? All except Miriam. She knows me. And when ever I sing she always asks "Where hurts you, Sarah?" Dying swan!

[p. 120] Thursday December 4th.[224]

As Miriam, Anna, and Mrs Carter are spending the day with Mrs Worley, I had resigned myself heroically to that most dreadful trial—spending a lonely day without a book within reach—and was suffering the ennui most sublimely, when about eleven o'clock a message came up—Mr Enders begged permission to see Miss Sarah. Mrs Badger has promised me for a week past that the next time any one came she would have me carried down in the parlor; but then part of the time they have been in Clinton, and the rest, nobody came that I cared very much about seeing except Col. Breaux and Mr Halsey, Sunday, and I did not feel able to endure the fatigue just then. But to day I was lonesome, and determined to see Mr Enders, so got up and slipped on my salmon colored schallie [*sic*] morning dress, faced with blue silk, which I have never had an opportunity of wearing before. But he sent Mrs Badger up with such a vehement request that I should not risk such a journey, that she persuaded me to keep [to] my room; and brought him up here instead.

I hate to play the invalid! So very interesting to be reposing in an arm chair looking "pale" and "spiritual" and playing with cords and tassles! Very nice, but I would rather be the observer, than the observed; or better still, I would rather be up and away, galloping over the hills with the pure air of heaven around me. That reminds me of a kind offer—

224. In the 1913 edition Warrington Dawson noted: "A page is here torn from the Diary. It evidently related the beginning of an incident of which my sister and I have often heard our mother tell: how, after the Jackson tableaux, our aunt Miriam laughingly staked herself in a game of cards with Will Carter—and lost. The sequel follows, the scene at the house of his uncle, General Carter, beginning in the middle of a sentence." The page removed from the diary (presumably by Sarah herself) in fact followed manuscript page 120, which was cut by the 1913 editor. Dawson began his cut on manuscript page 115, deleting most of the entry of November 21, both the November 24 and November 25 entries, and the first page of the December 4 entry. It is clear that what he assumed to be the continuation of the December 4 entry is instead what remains of the original entry of December 6.

Mr Enders places his nice little pony at my command, and say[s] he will send it out as soon as I can venture to ride, requesting me to consider it mine during the remainder of my stay. But, dear me! When I am able to ride, I must be able to go to Clinton, that small Paradise! I was so glad to hear how *very* much I was missed at the concert! I like to be missed—only it is not everybody who cares what becomes of me.

By the way, that same journey to Clinton came near costing me Miriam's life, in the grand smashup and running off a railroad bridge. But for the calmness of the ladies, and the heroic deed of Major Bennett who alone supported the toppling car until the others could brace it, they would all have been killed. As it was, as soon as they had been safely removed, the end of the bridge gave way and carried the car down. At least that is the story as plainly as I can make it out, from the confused accounts.[225] I am so thankful that Miriam was spared to care much about the particulars.

Mr. Enders did not take his leave until one o'clock, so I suppose that the united efforts of Mrs B. and myself succeeded in entertaining him, though Miriam was not here to talk. He told me that he had written me several letters, to wile [*sic*] away the lonely hours I must spend, but had been afraid to send them. O rare timidity! We shall hardly see so much of him now, as he is ordered to Jackson; however he promised to spend the evening with me to-morrow.

Last night I was waked from the most exquisite dream, by still more exquisite music. It was Capt. Bradford, Mr Halsey, and others with the band of the 4th Regt. I could find but one fault with the serenade; [end of p. 120; two manuscript pages that originally followed this page are missing]

[December 6th] [226]

[p. 121] it would be only the absurd tableau I agreed to, with plenty of fun, and nothing more. So I tried to be merry and content, and

225. Robert Patrick was on the train when the accident occurred and mentions it in his diary: "The passenger car ran off the track while crossing a bridge, tearing up the track behind it. . . . We were forced to leave the passenger car on the track and proceed to town without it. There were several ladies in the car at the time the accident occurred and it is a great wonder that they all escaped without being hurt." *Reluctant Rebel*, 60–61.

226. Although the first part of this entry is missing, what remains reveals that it was written on the day following the incident Sarah describes, and the presence of Frank

so I should have been, for there was plenty to talk about, and every one was so solicitous for my comfort, and there was Mr Enders who would wheel my chair for me where ever I wished it, and was as kind and attentive as a brother. Surely my first trip should have been a gay one! Miriam sat down by the piano, Mr Enders drew me by her, and we three sang until dark together. A Mr Morse, his wife and mother who are spending a week here were our audience. The first two retired at candle light, while the latter, present at the play the night before, remained to the last.

But while we sang, every noise at the parlor door caused us to turn with the apprehension of we hardly knew what. A dozen times Mr Enders consulted his watch, and telegraphed his fears to me, though I persisted in thinking it only the fun that had been intended. Half past six came, and with it, Mrs Worley. Now, she knew better. For Dr Dortch had come to see me, and was guiding me in my game of Euchre in which I was not even as wise as my partner Mr Enders, when her note came. Instantly we put down our cards, while Miriam begged him to write instantly and tell her the true story. He wrote, and we all read it. Not only that, but Miriam added a postscript which I think was this, word for word: "Mrs Worley, it is only a bet at cards, intended as the merest joke. There is not a word of truth in it, and I will consider it the greatest favor if you will contradict the report where ever you may hear it!"

Explicit enough, one would think, but still she came, and sent word in the parlor that one of the ladies present when Will made the announcement, had sent her contribution to the evening's fun. It turned out to be a complete bridal suit worn by the lady a year ago! That was too serious a jest. Miriam went in the other room to speak to Mrs Worley, who cold as an icicle refused to receive or make explanations beyond "I wont kiss you; this is too cruel." There was nothing to do; she returned laughing, but certainly feeling herself the injured one, and so she was.

In fifteen minutes, another stir. I held my breath with expectation. Lydia introduced—Mr Garie! Ten miles he had ridden through

---

Enders places the incident after his visit to Linwood on December 4, when he left at one o'clock in the afternoon.

mud and water that freezing evening, at Will Carter's request to perform the ceremony between him and Miriam! Lydia laughed until
she could hardly introduce him. He, hat in hand, bowed around the
convulsed circle with a countenance shining with the most sublimely
vacant expression. O that man's idiotic face, and solemn, portentous
look, brought a writhe even to my trembling lips! Mr Enders would
have given one an excellent idea of the effect produced by a real old
piney woods chill; he shook as with suppressed laughter. But when
the—tremendous—preacher (tremendous because composed of gigan-
tic Nothing) turned his lugubrious face [p. 122] toward Mrs Morse, and
addressed her as Mrs Morgan under the impression that she had come
down to see her daughter married, Miriam's risibles could no longer
stand it; and she flew from the room in time to avoid a disgraceful
explosion.

I was growing frightened. Mr Enders was leaning over my chair and
involuntarily it burst from me with a groan "For God's sake help me
save her!" "Hush! lay back in your chair! I will!" he whispered. "But
for the love of Heaven save my sister!" "I'll do what you will, if you
will only keep still and not hurt yourself. I'll do my best." It was all
whispered that the minister and Mrs Morse might not here [*sic*]. "If it
were your sister, what would you do?" "My God! I'd meet him on the
front gallery and kick him out! then I'd know one of us must die to-
morrow!" "But under the circumstances it is impossible for Gibbes to
act!" I urged, while we agreed that it was the most unwarrantable piece
of impudence ever perpetrated. While we talked, Gibbes had seized
Miriam, and without interfering or advising further, advised her to
keep [to] her room, and not meet Will.

But I skipped the most important part. She came back when she had
recovered her composure, and sat by me. Mr Enders, when I asked what
were best to do, whispered that to spare Will's feelings, and avoid a
most painful scene, as well as to show that she had no serious intentions
whatever, she should see that the minister was put in full possession of
the facts before it went any farther. He felt keenly his unpleasant situation, and it was only our ernest request that induced him to remain,
or give his advice. Who should explain? Certainly not the General. He
thought the joke carried too far, and retired to his room before Mr
Garie came. How take part against his own nephew? Not Gibbes either,

for he had gone up stairs too worried and annoyed to talk to anyone; besides, it was his wife's cousin. Who then?

Miriam is one woman in a thousand. Rising, she crossed the room slowly and as dignified as though she only meant to warm herself. I think I see her before me now, as she stood before the fire, facing Mr Garie, looking so handsome and stylish in her black grenadine with the pale green trimming, telling her story. Plainly, ernestly, distinctly, without hurry or embarrassment, in the neatess [sic], prettiest, most admirable speech I ever heard, she told everything just as it was. Bravo for Miriam! There lives not the woman in this state who could do so painful a thing in such a beautiful way. I felt like hugging her. Oh it was magnificent!

He heard her in surprise, but when once satisfied of its truth, he said "Well, Miss Morgan, when you stand on the floor, when I ask if you Will, it is your privilege to answer 'No.'" Miriam is not one to do so cruel a thing; she is too noble to deceive him so far and wound him so cruelly before all, when he believed himself so near happiness. She said that was mockery; she would not suffer him to believe for an instant that she meant to marry him; if he believed it, he was deceiving himself wilfully, for he already knew that she had told him it could never be. He agreed to take it only as a jest, promised that he would not feel hurt, [p. 123] and with the most admirable tact, Miriam, the trump (I have been playing Euchre, excuse me), settled the minister, and the wedding, by her splendid behavior, with no trouble.

A rapid step was heard in the hall; the bridegroom had come! I know he must have killed his horse. He certainly did not leave his house before one o'clock; it is twenty miles by the road to Clinton; he went there, procured his license, and was here at seven, in full costume. He bounded up stairs to meet the bride elect. Fool! I can fancy him going to Clinton, doubting, fearing, believing against all evidence, yet trembling; securing the license at last, persuading himself that she would not dare refuse when the deeds were recorded in court, and he held them in his hand;—and very few women would have been brave enough, too; he did not know My Miriam! I can fancy the poor horse lashed through the heavy mire, tired, foaming, panting while his strong arm urged it on, with whip and spur; I can hear the exulting beating of his heart, that wild refrain that was raging as his death knell—"Mine! mine at last!" I could hear it, I say. It rung in my ears all night.

He held her in his power; she must be his; hastily, yet carefully he performs his toilet; I dare say he stopped to think which cravat she liked best. "Mine! mine!" the song is ringing in every stroke of his throbbing breast. Mount! mount! two miles fly past. He sweeps through the moonlight like Death riding on a pale horse;[227] yonder shine lights in the parlor; and that above, is it hers? He throws himself from his horse; his hour has come, hers too; with the license and minister, his own adoration—and she must love him too!—he will win. Show him the way to her! she is his for ever now!

His? my God! had I not reason to cry "In God's name, save her, Frank!" He reaches Mrs Carter's room, and triumphantly throws the license on her table. He is ready now; where is his bride? Some one meets him. "Will!" The story is told; she is not to be won by force; she has appealed to the minister; he has carried the jest too far. The strong man reels; he falls on the bed in his bridal array in agony too great for tears. I dare not ask what followed; they tell me it was awful. What madness and folly to dream of forcing her to marry him! Why if she had loved him, the high handed proceeding would have roused the lion of her spirit! He is no mate for her. He has but one thought, and at last words come. Miriam! Miriam! Call her for the love of God! one word! one look! Oh she will take pity on him in his misery! Let her come for an instant! she cannot be so cruel! she will marry him if only to save him from death, or worse! And fortunate it was that he was not armed; one of the two would have died; perhaps both. The heart broken prayer goes on. The exulting "mine! mine!" has changed to the groan of despair "Miriam! for the love of God! come to me!"

And where is the bride? Gibbes has her caged in the next room, this one where I am now lying. He has advised her not to appear; to go to bed and say no more. Sent to bed like a baby on her wedding night! She says that she laughed aloud when the door closed on her. She laughing in here, [p. 124] he groaning in there, it is to be hoped they each drowned the voice of the other. At last she went out like a spoiled and petted baby just being whipped for a first error. "Please Gibbes let me go down! I wont do anything more!" She ran down with the permission; he lay writhing in agony up here. In whispers we young people talked it over. I was suffering agony myself but in a different way. His

227. The image comes from Revelation 6:8.

of the heart, mine of the back. As Mr Enders say[s] "Which would you rather be, Miss Miriam; you or Miss Sarah?" I refused to listen to their entreaties until the minister said good night. He disclaimed all feeling of pique; he felt chiefly for the young lady—and the disappointed groom. (Ouf!)

I sent to ask Will to come to me alone for one moment; no; he could not see me; write to him. Slowly as though an aged, infirm, tottering man, we heard him descending the steps. How different from the step that carried him up! We, conscience striken [*sic*] sat within, with doors closed. He was off. He has again mounted his horse, and the broken hearted man, hardly less cruel than the expectant bridegroom, dashes the rowells [?] in his side and disappears like a whirlwind. I turned to Anna who had imbibed the idea from her mother that Miriam would feel herself obliged to do it, and would certainly marry him, and who had been very anxious to know where the bridal chamber should be prepared, and thoughtlessly said "Poor Anna! all your preparations are useless!" Unfortunately Mr Enders caught the joke; at least he spoke this morning about Anna's "disappointment" to Miriam.

I would have stayed up forever, in spite of my suffering, if Mr Enders had not at last drawn my chair to the stairs, and insisted on my being taken to rest, with a long sermon on the danger of overexertion, etc. My back was nothing! I was too unhappy about poor Will. Yet how inconsistent! When they laid me on my bed, and I thought of his careful toilet, I burst out laughing. What a cruel farce!

Miriam came at last, and again we discussed it. It was first a burst of laughter, then a gasp of "Poor Will!" Miriam was wretched, and yet how she laughed! She jumped in bed. Thank Heaven for my old bedfellow! I cried, whereupon I came near being kicked out. Mrs Badger would have given all her teeth for that match; she would give them even now. "Miriam," she said. "If you had been let alone, you would have married Will tonight." Hump! I *sneezed* and pinched my bedfellow's plump arms. "Yes! Cant tell me that any girl in this world would act as coolly and independently as you did, unless they had some body to back them. Some one put you up to it, or you would now be Mrs Carter, as you should be." Slap for me, slap for Frank! I corresponded with Miriam by means of pinches, and got kicks for answers. Aloud, I said of course no other girl could have acted so discreetly, but this was

Miriam! But O my duck! would it be treason to ask just in here, whether you would not have collapsed with all that outside [?] pressure if Frank and I had been absent? [p. 125] Not that we said much, but was there no feeling of necessity lent her by the certainty of the approbation of at least two present?

We laid awake for hours. Often Miriam would start up with a shriek of laughter, when I would subdue her with a "Think of poor Will!" Very little sleep awaited any of us; but there was no dearth of thoughts while waking. I roused her this morning with a "Good morning Zuleika." Why Zuleika, she asked. "What? have you forgotten the bride of Abydos, that bride that was never married?" [228] Miriam thought it such an excellent joke, that she carried it down to Mr Enders who of course thought it fine, and declared that between him and myself she should carry the name to her grave. I have already taught her to answer to it quite naturally. She tells too many of my jokes to Frank; one in particular that I regret, as mother forbid my using the word, which I forget at the moment.

While I was teasing my Bride of Abydos, I asked for my pill box, which was not to be found, or my comb either; so I said "Since such marriages are fashionable, I would not be surprised if my pill box had run away with the comb—or some other rake." I always thought "rake" meant wild, drinking boys, like Will, until mother told me one day that I must never say it again. And Miriam's description of Frank's intense amusement leads me to believe that mother was right, and that I should not have said it. But if put on oath, I could give no other definition of it, so there is no harm meant.

I can fancy mother's and Lilly's agony when they hear of the wedding. All Clinton knew it last night, and if they did too, I know there was as little sleep for them as for us. I know mother shrieked "my child! my child!" while Lilly cried. How could he believe she meant to marry him, without even sending word to mother when he was going to the very town? Bah! What a jolly go if those two got hysterics about the supposed Moral Suicide! Glad I was not at the tea party!

Well, fearing the effect of such a shock in mother's nervous state,

228. Zuleika, engaged to marry a wealthy bey she has never seen, dies of grief when her father kills the man she loves, her cousin Selim. See "The Bride of Abydos" by Lord Byron.

Gibbes advised Miriam to go on the cars this evening, and convince her that it had not occurred, court records, and licenses and minister to the contrary notwithstanding; so my duck, my angel, she whom I call my Peri[229] with the singed wings (children who play in the fire must expect to be burned), set off on her pious errand, *without* the protecting arm of her bridegroom. Here I am deserted, in spite of my work! When Mrs Badger asked me this morning *why* I did not like so suitable a match, I said by way of evading the *true* cause "Hum! Think I want Will to take my 'treasure?' Good gracious! Who would I have to wait on me or rub my back?" "I do believe it is disgusting selfishness!" ejaculated she. But a disappointed woman! Que voulez vous?[230] I bear no malice; disappointment must have some vent, and bless her dear heart! she has been so good to me that I'll let her thrash me!

[p. 126] Sunday 7th December

I wrote enough yesterday to last a week, in spite of my strict orders to lie still all day. I do lie still, only not quite in the required position. From eight in the morning, to almost sunset, I lay face downwards, writing all that had occurred, struggling with a splattering pen and clotted ink, and only stopping occasionally to talk to, or about the Bride of Abydos. It was no light task. At last orders came at sunset that I was to be transported again to the parlor to receive Capt. Ross.[231] Down with my old pen, and out with my finery. Oh how I longed for Miriam! I cared not in the least to see anyone; but Mrs Carter undertook to dress me. My morning gown comes in play now. As an invalid I am entitled to wear it in the evening. Opening over the embroidered skirt, with a delicate lace collar fastened with my diamond cross, and my hair hastely [*sic*] coiled in one roll, she pronounced me ready, had me carried down, placed in a large chair, and wheeled in the parlor, where I was presented to the gentleman in this novel style. But I did not enjoy my visit. I was anxious, uneasy, miserable. I thought only of Miriam

229. Tiny fairylike creature. Sarah was familiar with Thomas Moore's *Lalla Rookh*, in which they appear in one of the tales.

230. What do you expect?

231. Captain T. A. Ross, ordnance officer on the staff of General Beall. Ross was a Mississippian. See *Confederate Veteran* 32:175.

and the scene of the night before, and only occasionally of the guest. Fortunately there were others to talk; but how much I missed Miriam!

It was late before he left, to my great disappointment, and when the General rubbed his hands and said "Now for fun! let's hear your criticisms!" I had actually nothing to say! Had discovered no points to praise, no peculiarities to laugh at! Then the General knew I must be suffering, which I candidly acknowledged, and begged to be taken to bed; and glad was I to lie down again. Such dreams haunted me! All kinds of misfortunes. One of my few superstitions is dreaming of teeth; trouble or death seem inevitably to follow. And I dreamed a front tooth fell out, which in endeavoring to replace, I inserted upside down. Then another grew in its place and dropped too, and in trying to restore it, I twisted all the others out sideways.

I have had a shock! While writing alone here (almost all have gone to church) I heard a step ascending the stair. What, I asked, if it should be Will? Then I blamed myself for supposing such a thing possible. Slowly it came nearer and nearer, I raised my head, and was greeted with a ghastly smile. I held out my hand. "Will!" "Sarah!" (Misery discards ceremony.) He stood before me the most woe begone, heart broken man I ever saw. With a forced laugh he said "Where is my bride? Pshaw! I know she has gone to Clinton! I have come to talk to *you*. Wasn't it a merry wedding?" The hollow laugh rung again. I tried to jest, but failed. "Sit down and let me talk to you" I said.

He was in a wayward humor; cut to the heart, ready to submit to a touch of silk, or to resist a grasp of iron. This was the man I had to deal with, and get from him something he clung to as to—not his life, but—Miriam; and I know so little how to act in such cases, know so little about dealing gently with wild natures! He alarmed me at first. His forced laugh ceased; he said that he meant to keep that license always. It was a joke on him yesterday, but with that in his possession, the tables would be turned on her. He would show it to her occasionally. It should keep her from marrying any one else. I said that it [p. 127] would be demanded though, he must deliver it. The very devil shot in his eye as he exclaimed fiercely, "If any one dares demand it, I'll die before giving it up! If God Almighty came, I'd say no! I'll die with it first!"

O merciful Father! I thought; what misery is to come of this jest! he must relinquish it. Gibbes will force him into it, or die in the attempt; George would come from Virginia and cut his heart out for the mere threat; even Jimmy would cross the seas and run the blockade to avenge Miriam! And I was alone in here to deal with such a spirit! I commenced gently. Would he do Miriam such a wrong? It was no wrong he said. Let him follow his own will. You profess to love her? I asked. "*Profess?* Great God! how can you? I adore her! I tell you that in spite of all this, I love her not more—that is impossible; but as much as ever! look at my face and ask that!" burst from him with the wildest impulse.

"Very well. This girl you *love* then, you mean to make miserable. You stand for ever between her and her happiness, because you *love* her! Is this love?" He was sullenly silent. I went on: "Not only her happiness, but her honor is concerned. You who love her so, do her this foul injury." "Would it affect her reputation?" he asked. "Ask yourself! Is it quite right that you should hold in your hands the evidence that she is Mrs Carter, when you know she is not, and never will be? Is it quite honorable?" "In God's name would it injure Miriam? I'd rather die than grieve her." My iron was melted, but too hot to handle; I put it on one side, satisfied that I and I only had saved Miriam from injury, and three brothers from bloodshed, by using his insane love as a lever. It does not look as hard here as it was in reality but it was [one] of the hardest struggles I ever had. It will never go beyond this page; but indeed it was desperate.

I had touched the right key, and satisfied of success, turned the subject to let him believe he was following his own suggestions. When I told him he must free Miriam from all blame, that I had encouraged the jest against her repeated remonstrance, and was alone to blame, he generously took it on himself. "I was so crazy about her" he said "that I would have done it any how. I would have run any risk for the faintest chance of obtaining her," and much more to the same purpose that, though very generous in him, did not satisfy my conscience. But he surprised me by saying that he was satisfied that if I had been in my room, and he had walked into the parlor with the license, she would have married him. What infatuation! He says, though, that I only, prevented it; that my influence by my mere presence, is stronger than his words. I dont say that is so; but if I helped save her, thank Heaven!

It is impossible to say one half that passed, but he showed me his determination to act just as he has heretofore, and take it all as a joke, that no blame might be attached to her. "Besides, I'd rather die than not see her; I laugh, but you dont know what I suffer!" Poor fellow! I saw it in his swimming eyes. At last he got up to go before they returned from church. "Beg her to meet me as she always has. I told Mrs Worley that she must treat her just the same, because I love her so. And—say I go to Clinton to-morrow to have that record effaced, and deliver up the license. I would not grieve her; indeed, I love her too well." His voice trembled as well as his lips. He took my hand saying "You are hard on me. I could make her happy I know, because I worship her so. I have been crazy about her for three years; you cant call it a mere fancy. Why are you against me? But God bless you! good bye!" and he was gone.

Why? O Will, because I love my sister too much to see her miserable merely to make you happy!

[p. 128] Monday 8th December.

I saw company enough yesterday. I was carried down again, and had the pleasure of seeing Col. & Mrs Breaux, Capt. Bradford, Mr Halsey, and Mr Enders again. They all came before four o'clock, and if they all missed Miriam as I did, I dare say they did not enjoy themselves. But they knew she was not here; why did they come? Wasn't I glad to see the Colonel! I did not observe it myself, but afterwards Mr Enders told me his wife never took her eyes off of me, and declared that she was jealous of his attention.

Folly! I am afraid a very foolish attempt of mine will cost me a few weeks' more suffering. When all the gentlemen had left the room except the Colonel and Mr Enders, the latter by way of jesting on what he supposed to be an impossibility, laughingly asked me to take the vacant chair by him, as he wished to speak to me, and I was so surrounded that he could not approach. I do not like the thought of being helpless; so to prove my ability to do what ever I pleased to undertake, in utter disregard of the Colonel's remonstrances, and the small screams of the ladies, I arose and slowly and falteringly walked not towards Mr Enders, but the fireplace. I never saw a whiter, more terrified face. Both hands were put out towards me, while he sat in silent horror.

For the first few steps I felt the Colonel's grasp on my dress, then I passed beyond reach while he still leaned forward as though to catch me. I gained the mantle, held on as I turned, got half way back when—was the room tottering, or was it I? Certainly one of the two was going over. Further effort was impossible; over—over, I was going when Mr Enders sprang up and caught me with a cry of "O Miss Sarah!" the next instant Col. Breaux had me too, with the single ejaculation "Rash girl!" I would rather have had him scold me! But when I was again safe in my chair, and he begged me not to do so again, when I professed myself willing to receive a scolding from him, he said O no! he never was cross to those he liked very, *very* much, his entreaties must suffice me! Mr Enders says Mrs Breaux did not lose a word. How very unreasonable! Cant a body say nice things occasionally without another body's caring? And the Colonel was ever so kind to me yesterday! [Words lined through]!

Soon after sunset only Mr Enders was left. He declared he had intended only to stop for a single instant; he really must go; yet there he sat playing with one end of my long tassles while I held the other, as though he never meant to go. We talked the Wedding all over again, with many a burst of laughter. Will told him too, that if it were not for me, Miriam would marry him; but I was too strong for him; he would give all he owns if I had been in my room that night, where she could not see me. And Mr Enders alarmed me by saying that he feared Will would win yet, if she wavered for an instant; once firmly resolved, she was safe; hesitate an instant, and she is lost. He does not know her as well as I. People think Miriam so self reliant, resolute, and independent—she thinks she is too; that nothing can turn her. I can, if I dont let her know it, though. She is as easily led as a child, and in spite of protestation, as dependent on others—more so—than I am. Hers is a tender heart; not willing to pain anyone, or anything. She believes she is firm and unalterable, now; take away external support, the countenances of those of [end of p. 128; two pages of the diary that followed this page (one book page, front and back) are missing]

[p. 129] Friday 12th December

I have gone through a lively ordeal! Dr Martin [232] examined me thoroughly on Wednesday, and I think understands my state. The result is

232. Dr. Amzi Martin, the surgeon credited with saving the "life and limbs" of Colonel Henry Watkins Allen after he was wounded in the Battle of Baton Rouge. See Sarah A. Dorsey, *Recollections of Henry Watkins Allen* (New York and New Orleans, 1866), 146.

not very enlivening. He says no important organic change has taken place as *yet;* but that I must be carefully watched. Besides my spine, there is danger of paralysis in the left leg, which I have not thought worth complaining of yet. He spoke very plainly, saying he did not believe I was in any immediate danger; but that only the most violent counter irritants could save me. Accordingly blisters were instantly applied; and if that dont succeed, I am settled for life.

How do I take it? I hardly know. These things are hard to realize until we are brought face to face with them. I'll not know how I bear it until the day my doom is read in a powerless limb. Then I can tell all about it. But at present, hope is stronger than the almost certainty. I want to believe I will yet recover; I wont look at the other dreadful side. Courage! Fifty years from now, one leg more or less, and no spine at all will make very little difference to an old skeleton that has mouldered in the grave for forty nine years and six months. Neither will interfere in the slightest degree with its grace or agility! And yet—! My God! what a beautiful life I had fancied before me! Courage! let the sad facts come once distinctly and irrevocably upon me, I'll have one desperate struggle that no one will ever hear of, and then meet it like a christian, I know. Wait!

This is gloomy. Lets talk of something more amusing. My cripple friend that I mentioned ever so far back,[233] continues to send me the most affecting messages. "He is really wretched about me; never was more distressed; thinks of nothing else;" and so on through the whole list. To cap the climax he sends me word that he can now walk on crutches, and the first time he can venture in a buggy, means to call on me. Que le ciel m'en préserve![234] What could we talk about? "Hisn" and "hern's" several misfortunes. Thats too bad! Every one teases me unmercifully about my new conquest. I cant help but be amused; and yet beware, young girls, of expressing sympathy even for soldiers! There is no knowing what effect it may produce. O Sarah! Sarah! this is *too* bad. But still I have to laugh at the affecting messages! This is rare.

In spite of my blisters, I had a delightful time last night. Several officers we have not yet met, sent word they would spend the evening with us, though they unaccountably deprived themselves of the pleasure,

233. See entry of October 16, 1862.
234. Heaven protect me from that!

tant pis pour aux![235] However I got up to dress, for the first time since Sunday, as we expected others; and my toilette was not a little hastened by a message from Col. Breaux saying he would be there early, and insist on carrying me down himself, to be certain that I should receive no farther injury. Of course I hurried then, and made the servants carry me down before he could arrive. I had no idea of putting him to such trouble. He came with Mrs Breaux and Mrs Boyle,[236] and soon after, Capt. Bradford and Mr Halsey entered.

Mrs Breaux has taken a fancy to rave about me in the most unreasonable style. I am her darling Sarah! her angel! the most innocent, artless child! Her little perfection! such a dear little creature! Hopes I'll grow up as innocent and holy; I cant be yet sixteen! Oh how [p. 130] I laugh! [Words lined through]! that's a little too much! But as long as it amuses her—! She smothered me with kisses. "O the Colonel was so distressed about my [sic] attempt to walk! He said it made him wretched to think of it. He says he loves you like a daughter!" I told her I was sure I liked him as a brother, also. The giddy, light headed little creature would call the girls off in a corner, and looking at me with her head on one side, would call on them to pronounce if I was not perfectly beautiful. Fortunately for her taste, the poor little lady is hardly to be considered responsible for what she says. Yet it only shows itself in the giddiness. I was not aware of her comments however until this morning when the girls told me of them.

I did not say a single word beyond "good evening" to Mr Halsey on Sunday, so I took a fancy to surprise him last evening. Think I succeeded! He opened his eyes in amazement a dozen times. I was so *very* different from other young ladies! He sat down by me when he first came, and with the exception of an occasional stroll to the piano when I talked to Capt. Bradford, remained by me until he left, which,—tell it not in Gath![237] was at the early hour of 1, A.M. Miriam melancholily confesses herself cut out. What a triumph—if one only appreciated it. He evidently thought at first that my taste was decidedly of the yellow

235. Too bad for them.

236. Very likely the wife of Captain Roger T. Boyle of Company C, 30th Louisiana Infantry (Colonel Breaux's regiment).

237. 2 Samuel 1:20.

back novel style. My ignorance made him doubt. He went up a step higher, and higher still, when at the name Macaulay, I launched out in a warm panegyric on my favorite of all writers, ancient or modern, which caused him to pause and stare at me. Macaulay! Addison! Pope! Hume! Where had I acquired such tastes? A young lady to enjoy "dry" reading! He had never heard of such a thing! It was my time to stare, and take *him* down, which I did in one sentence: "What *very* intelligent young ladies you must have associated with!" After that, we understood each other.

Col. Breaux looked so very unhappy that he distressed me. I was about the only one he spoke to, and as he gave up his seat to Mr Halsey, he said scarcely a word to any one the rest of the evening, after. Poor Col. Breaux! I can understand that a man whose wife labors under such a great misfortune should be very, very wretched. He and the two ladies left at about ten, leaving the other gentlemen to finish off the evening. He told me he was coming some morning to have a long, quiet talk with me, which I know I shall enjoy.

Capt. Bradford has some of the most amusing peculiarities. He has the most affectionate way of saying "Eumph?" when he has not heard a question, that can be imagined. It strikes me as being excessively absurd. I asked Mr Halsey if it did not sound like "What, my love?" at which he laughed immoderately. I'll make an enemy of the Captain, if I do not take more care. I did him several cruel injuries last night, one of which was unpardonable; I know *he* thinks so. He proposed a conundrum, which was to strike us all as very amusing, if we could only guess it. He had hardly finished it, when the answer flashed across me, and without farther ceremony I announced it. It was a blow to the Captain, who evidently expected to make a decided hit with it. Seeing his disappointment, I hastily resolved never to come between a man and his pun again. It's worse than interfering between husband and wife.

Mr Halsey begged leave to send me some books to while away the tedious hours in a sick room, etc. Wonder what style he would select? I'd consider the yellow backs as a *very* poor compliment!

Sunday December 14th

Yesterday evening, sometime before sunset, Mr Enders was announced, to our great surprise, as we knew he had been in Clinton all the week, having been transfered there instead of to Jackson, as he threatened. He was the most miserable, unhappy creature one could possibly imagine; even too melancholy for me to laugh at him, which expresses the last degree of wretchedness. To all our questions, he had but one answer, that he had had the most dreadful attack of "blues" ever since he was here Sunday; that he had waited every evening at the cars, expecting us, and at last, seeing that we had no intention of coming, he could no longer stand the temptation, so got permission to come down for a day to P. Hudson so he could come out and see us.

His melancholy was almost ludicrous. I asked him what he had done to recover. "Do? What *could* I do? I could not study; I sat there by the hour not knowing what I was reading, so gave it up. I could not talk; I did not care to talk to the men, and declined visiting the ladies. I was so wretched that I wanted to do something desperate; so I just attended to my patients [238] and eat [*sic*] candy all day." Can a more melancholy picture be drawn? I laughingly asked what sensation such an alarming state of affairs produced, when he informed me he felt very much as though he was desperately in love and had been rejected! Poor Frank! I declare it distressed me to see him so sad.

Before we could fairly get him cheerful, Will Carter and Ned Badger, who returned only this week from Kentucky, entered. Will was in a bad humor, and wanted to vent it on us; so after waiting some time, he proposed that the two young men should go with him, pocketing at the same moment the cards which had won Miriam, and saying they would have a nice game together, and just the rarest old whiskey! He looked around to see the effect produced. We girls did not move, but Mr Enders said he must really return immediately to P.H., and start for Clinton from there in the night. Will thought it would be such a triumph over us to carry him off, that he insisted. They'd have a fine time! cure the blues! etc. Ned was more than willing; and at last Mr Enders said well! he felt just so desperate that he did not care what he did; he believed he would go.

I saw he was in a reckless humor, and that Will knew it too, and I promised to make at least an effort to save him. To go with Will, meant to get tight; at least Will meant that to be the consequence. I thought if

238. Soldiers in the military hospital in Clinton.

it was Jimmy—! and resolved I would. Miriam spoke to him apart; but he said he had promised now; he must go. Will ran down triumphant, to mount his horse, calling him to follow. All ran out to see him off, when Frank came back to tell me good bye. I seized the opportunity, and didn't I plead! I told him I would not ask him to stay here, though he knew we would be happy to have him stay; but begged him to go back to the camp, and leave Will alone; Will only [p. 131] wanted to make him tight. He said he believed he did not care; if it were not for the thought of his mother, he would not mind getting tight by way of variety; now he was so miserable! I suggested other resources; talked of his mother whom he idolizes, pleaded like a grandmother, and just as I wound up came Will's voice from below "Why the devil dont you come, Enders? Hurry!" He moved a step, looked at me, I dropped my head without a word.

Here I must confess to the most consummate piece of acting; I am sorry; but as long as it saved him from doing what I knew he would have cause to regret, I am not ashamed of having tried it. Will called impatiently again, as he stood hesitating before me; I did not say "stay," I just gave the faintest sigh imaginable. His mother would not blame me; for it decided him. He went down and told Will he would not go! Of course Will went off in a rage with us.

I was glad I had saved him! After that, it did not take long to talk him into cheerfulness. I was carried to the parlor, where we sang and talked, and had a nice time. He made the oddest speech. He was holding one of my tassles as usual, and talking of his home, when he said that Miriam and I reminded him so much of it that he always felt as though we were his sisters: "As for you, I have the most irresistible desire to catch you up and play with you; its all I can do to keep my hands off; a dozen times this evening I have been on the point of laying my hand on your head; I'd give anything if I could do it! But when I think that you might be angry—!" Of course I expressed the hope that the impulse would be *altogether* beyond control. But he said it so oddly! Just as though it were *so* natural. I felt as though I would be contaminating innocence by telling him it was not *quite* the thing! He was easily induced to remain all night; and a lively evening we all spent! Think of that! lively with neither cards nor whisky! Will could hardly credit it.

I had won a great point, had heard several of just the queerest, funniest things one likes to hear, and when at last I was carried up to my room, I had a hearty laugh all to myself. A while after, I heard Frank tell Miriam to kiss Miss Sarah good night for him, and as she came in the room at the first look we burst out laughing. I whispered to her after a while, to ask what she thought was the matter with Frank. "In love, I verily believe!" "What a coincidence! So do I!" I answered. "But with whom?" Miriam was puzzled; she said "That's it! One moment I think it is me, the next I *know* it is you!" I laughed again at this second coincidence. Pshaw! we said. The poor boy was lonesome, homesick; felt desolate and forsaken, longed for a sight of his mother's, or some other loved face, and comforted himself with trying to fall in love with the first one who recalled his home to him. We must try to cheer him up. Oh yes! and I was sorry for him; but I just buried my face in the pillows and laughed again. Poor, poor Frank! Yet it was *so* odd!

I fell asleep laughing; I awaked at daylight laughing again, so seized a book to settle my nerves before the girls waked up too. Before breakfast came a note from Frank. He too had been reading for some two hours; he asked if I was able to come down; "Make haste, and let me see you; for nothing but the light of your own bright eyes can dispell this gloom that has again settled around me."

Mrs Badger was dressing my blisters at the time it came, and I dare say was startled at my uncontrolable burst of laughter under such circumstances. But it was *so* much more amusing than the blisters! Under such distressing circumstances, of course "the light of my eyes" could not be refused; so about an hour after breakfast, I arose, and signified that I was prepared to receive visiters; so Miriam brought him up. I did not ask his opinion of the light of my eyes, but he looked full into them for fully a half hour without moving, telegraphing with one hand the deaf and dumb alphabet signs which read "I love you." Of course though, thats all nonsense.

He needs a mother or sister to talk to him more than any one I know of, except perhaps Jimmy, who I know is as crazy for us to kiss him and pet him, and make a fuss over him, as any mortal can be. I look at Frank so home sick, and think of how my poor little brother suffers just the same, and wish I could tell him how sorry I am for him. He says he cant stand it. If he dont get some one to say a kind word occasionally, treat him like a brother, and care for him, and let him think he really has a home or a friend, he says he just means to desert, or cut his throat. He is just going to Clinton and ask mother if [words lined through]; he is sure he [words lined through]. He shall ask her if he cant come see us as often as he pleases and if he cant just touch our hand occasionally, and please to let us call him Frank; it is a hard case to stand on ceremony with him, when he feels as though he ought to be our brother. If he does tell her that, I can fancy mother's surprise! She does not understand this platonic affection. *I do* though. And—I am sorry for poor Frank.

How he begged us to come to Clinton! If we were not there this week, he was coming after us himself. I should not be dull an hour! he'd come and talk to me, and we'd have such splendid duets on the guitar and piano! Yes! and he'd bring me books, and read to me too, as long as I wished, if we would *only* come! He was so lonely! Ah Frank! fine promises! Once there, you and Miriam would find such gay times visiting and walking, that both would forget the poor cripple sitting solitarily at home. I asked myself just a foolish question, not for vanity or self love, but just to see how such things end, and here is the answer: "Which of the two does he like best, if either have the preference?" "Would it be vain to say that perhaps it is I?" "Which will he end by liking best?" "Miriam undoubtedly!" That is my conviction, though to be sure it matters very little, as every one, except a very, very few prefer her to me, and serve[s] me right.

In spite of intentions, Frank did not leave until an hour before sunset. We had the satisfaction of making him cheerful again, seeing him spend the liveliest, happiest day he has probably had for a long while, and at last say a reluctant good bye, and go off in much better spirits than he had arrived in, at the same hour the evening before. Poor Frank! Indeed he needs a mother or sister!

[p. 132] Friday December 26th. 1862.

Eleven days have passed since I opened this, days passed for the most part in very great pain, yet which had their fun and pleasure, nevertheless. Of course my inability to move was the signal for a perfect rush of visiters. The very day that terrific blister was applied, ([a] blister which drew an exclamation of horror even from Mrs Badger, skilled as she is in such matters) came two strangers, Frenchmen, one of whom, Mr Guiole, is to be my future cousin,[239] and the other, M. Robleaux, was an old friend of Harry's in Paris. They say he looks like him, too.

O how I wanted to see him when I heard that! But instead, I was forced to keep [to] my lonely room, sitting in my large chair with my hands grasping the arms, trying to drown the sound of laughter and music from below by losing myself in Macaulay's Essays, and subduing every quiver of pain with a whispered "Nonsense! there is no such thing as pain! Cant you stand more?" until I was quite in a talking humor when Gibbes and the General paid their nightly visit, by way of proving to myself that suffering is all imagination that Will can subdue. But when they had said goodnight and Malvina had slipped off as she invariably does when Mrs Badger passes the door, and I was left alone, alone with Macaulay and a candle for company, when it grew worse and worse, until I could no longer see to read even my beloved essayist, and stretched my hands out to grasp thin air, and battle against the strange, unearthly feeling that was stealing over me, and asked myself if it was really possible I was about to faint, I who prided myself on my self control, I think I came nearer acknowledging to myself in that awful hour that pain was a reality, and no fiction, than I ever came before.

But when the footsteps sounded on the steps, and a chorus of voices asked how I fared, I was a skeptic again. If I suffered, why did I not groan? That is the way every one shows it. This must be a humbug. So I listened to the stories of the fun downstairs, and forgot the past struggle until another chorus, of horror, this time, was chanted over the deeply burned patch of raw flesh Mrs Badger was attending to, and these poor girls with sighs and exclamations labored to convince me that I was a perfect martyr. Then I asked myself "*Is* this suffering? I could stand more!" I tell Anna that I was convinced, until this last blister, that like herself, I could *lie* in any position; but now I find she has an advantage over me. That is unjust, of course, for she is a dear good girl, and only fibs occasionally; I only said it to make her laugh, and succeeded.

So it happens I have not been carried down very often, though Sun-

239. Mary Morgan, daughter of Sarah's Aunt Caro, would marry Leonce P. Guyol in 1864.

day I was taken down to see Col. Breaux and Mr Halsey. And then Monday Dr Woods and Mr Van Ingen[240] stopped, just from their regiment in Kentucky, and on their way home, and I begged so hard to see the Doctor, and promised so faithfully to retire if I suffered too much, that Mrs Badger yeilded [*sic*], like an angel, and I carried my point.

The Doctor! We looked in vain at each other, I for my dandy friend in irreproachable broadcloth, immaculate shirt bosoms and perfect boots, he for the brusque, impulsive girl who in ordinary circumstances would have run dancing in the parlor, would have given him a half glad, half indifferent greeting, and then either have found occasion to laugh at him, or would have turned elsewhere for amusement. We looked, I say, in vain. Before me stood my pattern of neatness in a rough uniform of brown homespun. A dark flannel shirt replaced the snowy cambric one, and there was neither cravat nor collar to mark the boundary line between his dark face and the still darker material. And the dear little boots! O ye gods and little fishes! they were clumsy, and mud splattered!

If my mouth twitched with laughter as I silently commented, the doctor's did not! I who always danced on my way, came in lying back on my pillows, and wheeled in by a servant. The doctor's sympathy was really touching. I never felt my helplessness so keenly as when he condoled with me. And poor consolation he gave when he heard the story. "You will recover, to a certain extent; but will feel it more or less all your life." God's will be done; I can bear that too. And the doctor melted to more than ordinary kindness; so kind, that I forgot to tease him, and so gentle and considerate that twice he arose and arranged my footstool for me. The Doctor whom I never suffered to pick up my handkerchief in the old days! Wonder kept me silent.

And there was Mr Van Ingen, more quiet and subdued than when I last saw him, looking very sad in fact, and telling me he needed my advice very much, yet not giving me fair play to lecture him. I am the ruin of all these puns; the gentlemen will hate me; I must learn to ignore their conundrums until they answer them themselves, and to wait patiently for the pun instead of catching it and laughing be-

240. Dr. A. V. Woods, who had attended Sarah's father and who was now surgeon of the 1st Louisiana Cavalry, and J. S. Van Ingen, a private. Van Ingen appears in Booth as "Van Jugen," obviously a mistranscription.

fore it is half spoken. Why cant I do as the others do? There was Mr Van Ingen with his constant stream of them, that I anticipated several times. He said to me "If I were asked what town in Louisiana I would rather be in this evening, what would my answer be?" I should have looked perfectly innocent, and politely inquisitive; but I did neither. I saw the answer instantly, and laughed. "Ah you have guessed! I can see it in your eyes!" he said. Of course I had; but I told him I was afraid to say it, for fear he might think I was flattering myself. Then we both laughed. The place he prefered was Bayou, Sarah.[241]

It was like old times looking at the doctor again. He looked so very natural that I could hardly think ten whole months had elapsed since we had met. And his sympathy was so unaffected! Miriam says it is quite touching; *she* knows! They required very little pressing to remain all night. I think they were rather pleased. But I was carried up soon after supper, and did not see them again.

[p. 133] Yesterday, being a beautiful day, I was carried down in honor of Christmas, to meet Capt. Fenner and Mr Duggan[242] who were to dine with us. The cars had brought Miriam a beautiful little set of collar and cuffs from Dellie, and the oddest, sweetest little set for me, from Morgan, for our Christmas gift. It is all Lilly. If we were a thousand miles away she would never rest until she had sent us some little token of the day. God bless her sweet eyes! I dont believe she ever thinks of herself. It made me happy all day to think of the kind heart that suggested such a sweet thing to those little children. What did I ever do for her? A blank will answer the question.

The General insisted on my being wheeled to the table. A table! I had not seen one all these long weeks. It looked right odd to see all those faces around it. But the novelty took away my appetite even for a Christmas dinner. Capt. Fenner thinks my accident was a punishment for having objected so much to visiting his camp; I think it was a judgement for having gone in spite of my protestations, and believe it, too.

We had an exquisite Christmas gift the night before, a magnificent

241. A pun on Bayou Sara.

242. Lieutenant Thomas J. Duggan, one of the officers in Captain Fenner's battery. See biographical sketch in *Confederate Military History*, 13:398. Duggan married Bena Morgan.

serenade, a compliment from Col. Breaux. It very singularly happened that Miriam, Anna, and Ned Badger [?] were sitting up in the parlor, watching alone for Christmas, when the band burst forth at the steps, and startled them into a stampede upstairs. But Gibbes, who came with the serenaders, caught them, and brought them back in the parlor, where there were only *eight* gentlemen, and in this novel, unheard of style, only these two girls, with Gibbes to play propriety, entertained all these people at midnight while the band played without. What would Mrs Grundy say?[243] Who ever heard of such a reception for serenaders? The Colonel sent me so many kind messages! Among others, that if the music had added in the slightest degree to my pleasure, he would consider himself more than repaid for the ride. Was it not sweet to think of me in particular?

I commenced writing to day expressly to speak of our pleasant Christmas; yet it seems as though I would write about any thing except that, since I have not come to it yet. Perhaps it is because I feel I could not do it justice. At least, I can say who was there.

At sunset came Capt. Bradford and Mr Conn,[244] the first stalking in with all the assurance which a handsome face and fine person can lend, the second following with all the timidity of a first appearance and conscious unattractiveness, which rather prepossessed me. The Captain was overpoweringly gracious to me, and bestowed the light of his radient countenance upon me with the same serene benevolence that the moon might shine down on a small glow worm. Not that it cared in the least, but just because the worm happened to be there, and was just as convenient to shed its rays on that as on nothing. Shame! How can I when he tried to be so interesting! Did we not discuss Byron?—at least the *binding* thereof—and theaters [?] and all that? And didn't he make several *very* pointed allusions to Mr Halsey which should have been *very* funny, only they failed? I am a humbug! Why did I talk and look pleased if he did not interest me?

Again, after a long pause, the door swung open, and enter Mr Halsey

243. Expression whose source is a late-eighteenth-century English play by J. M. Morton. Mrs. Grundy was the personification of the prig.

244. First Lieutenant John D. Conn, 4th Louisiana Volunteers. The *Daily Picayune* (July 15, 1863, p. 2) lists Conn as one of the Port Hudson officers brought to New Orleans as prisoners following the surrender of the garrison.

who bows and takes the seat on the other side of me, and Mr Bradford, of Col. Allen memory, once more returned to his regiment and
his dear Miriam, who laughs, shakes hands all around, and looks as
happy as a school boy just come home for the holidays, who has neverending visions of plum cakes, puddings, and other sweet things. How
absolutely pleased he looks! I laugh aloud as he grasps my hand, pours
out a torrent of questions and condolence, he was so distressed at my
accident! never was more concerned! but I look so splendidly! I'll surely
recover! Allow him! Is that pillow *quite* comfortable? May he arrange
it? Exertion is the very worse [sic] thing for me. Is my foot stool conveniently placed? I answer yes and no rapidly, in order to keep up with
him, as he throws himself in his brother's just vacated chair, and talks,
talks, not more profoundly, but more amusingly, at all events, than
the other, on two *very* interesting subjects, himself, and myself, which
however soon lose their attraction for me. I had heard enough of both.

There was the General who had already made a dozen journeys
across the room to say he knew I was suffering and had I not better
retire, while I fibbed and begged off, and asked how he knew, and got
a reprieve, and the information that though I controled my face very
well, that there was occasionally an intensely quiet look that betrayed
me. I promise you I did not pause a moment after that. And there was
Mr Conn studying my face, (I could see by means of the mirror that
reflected him only at that angle) and questioning Anna about me in a
voice that was not so low as to escape my attention entirely. And all the
rest, strangers and family, were strangely kind and gentle to me, until I
feared I might get vain with all their kindness, and so wanted to forget
myself a while, and Mr Bradford too.

I turn to Mr Halsey, and soon the other spies a vacant chair by
Miriam, which he instantly seizes. It is a perfect game of Pussy wants a
corner with the gentlemen, only it is Pussy wants a chair, instead. Only
Mr Halsey keeps his place without moving. O Miriam! Miriam! I've
stolen your John from you decidedly!

While all goes on merrily, another rap comes, and enter Santa Claus,
dressed in the old uniform of the Mexican war, with a tremendous
cocked hat, and preposterous beard of false hair, which effectually conceal the face, and but for the mass of tangled short curls no one could
guess that the individual was Bud. It was a device of the General's,

which took us all by surprise. Santa Claus passes slowly around the circle, and pausing before each lady, draws from his basket a cake which he presents with a bow, while to each gentleman he presents a wine glass replenished [p. 134] from a most suspicious looking black bottle which also reposes there.

Leaving us all wonder and laughter, Santa Claus retires with a basket much lighter than it had been at his entrance. Follows more talk, music, and laughter, and all seem in the best of humors, and ready for any fun. Amiable Mr Bradford is in a perfect gale of good humor. One would not be surprised to hear him say something really good, after a while; so many attempts should not all be fruitless. His brother the Captain is seated just opposite the mirror; no wonder he is temporarily silent. But hush! he begins to speak! Patience! he will complete the sentence after a while; give him time. The request is that Miriam shall sing "No ne'er can thy home be mine." Why did he not ask for "There is the happy land," or "Hush a bye baby"? I thought I should have expired during his first visit, when he asked her to play. She selected Prudent's Lucie,[245] played magnificently, and as the last chord died away, while I still listened to the vibration, he slowly and deliberately asked "Can you play the Copenhagen Waltz?" Heathen!

And there is Anna talking away to Mr Conn as she has hardly ever talked before, exerting herself to entertain him, and evidently pleased with her success. Miriam talks to all while I am chiefly occupied with Mr Halsey. "John" is tant soit peu égoïst;[246] but that amuses me. When I tire of it, I forget him, which piques his vanity, then we make mutual concessions, and I doubt if there is a gayer corner in the well filled room, than that occupied by my invalid's chair. And Mr Halsey must needs get pitched out of a buggy two days before, and get his arm sprained so he can appear with a sling, and look interesting too, and share the sympathy bestowed on me. I assure him he is more than welcome to the sympathy, and injury, too.

Then follows refreshments, and more and more talk and laughter until the clock strikes twelve, when all these ghosts bid a hearty good night and retire, all reluctantly, but with a dim sense of propriety. Mr

245. The French pianist and composer Emile Prudent.

246. Just a little egotistical.

Conn comes to assure me of his sympathy once more, and beg a promise for a horseback ride as soon as I recover. I make a very safe engagement; I fear me the horse that will next carry me is not yet born. Mr Bradford heartily assures us he means to come again very soon, and very often, while Mr Halsey slowly rises and says he supposes he must go too. And I am glad to get up stairs again. Nine hours I have been sitting up dressed, an unheard of feat for me; and thankfully I fall on my pillows again. And as a punishment for the excess of yesterday, to day I under go my sixth and last blister. Ever since breakfast I have been lying on my face, and here at early candle light I lay down my pen to discover if such a thing as a change of position is practicable.

December 30th Tuesday.

O dear me! I fear me I am a very bad girl! A wicked, cruel, unchari-table one! Peccavi! Yet why should I cry out against my wickedness, when I have not made an effort to retract it? The letter has not yet left the house; why do I not burn it? What! and let Miriam be unavenged? But could she not avenge herself? Undoubtably. With more grace, dig-nity, ability, judgement and discretion than I; but then imperfect as my revenge is, I cant forgo it. If the woman had tried it on me, I would never have thought of her after her note had been tossed in the fire. But it is Miriam she dares insult, *Miriam!* "Revenge! Timoleon cries!" I never felt it before. *Is* it revenge? I would not pull a red hair from her ugly head; I would not add another scratch to her freckled face; I would not move a step to look at, or flee from her; I would not talk about her for worlds, or give her additional cause to hate me. I vow I would not make a face at her! Isn't that what they call hate, revenge, etc.? I dont feel any of that; I just feel that I must write to her. And I did. I felt it to be a right I could not forgo; it was for Miriam; who had a better right?

The cause of the outburst is an individual whom I have never had the felicity of beholding, though Miriam met her long ago, somewhere or other. This personage, Miss Jane Stone,[247] or Miss Jenny Stone as she subscribes herself, or Miss Donkey Brickbats, as I would christen her if the ceremony had not been performed between thirty and thirty

247. Jane Stone, age 20 in the 1860 census, daughter of Dr. John Wilmer Stone and step-daughter of Franklin Hardesty of Clinton. Sarah obviously thought her to be much older.

five years ago, under the charitable appearance of comforting mother when she was so wild about Miriam, fearing rather believing she had married Mr Carter, put her charitable visit to two excellent uses. Besides comforting, she endeavored. to gain material for future gossip. With the will, one cannot lack the opportunity of lying. Soon the most extraordinary falsehoods were circulated by "a witness," such as that Miriam, mounted on the front steps, made a speech to fifty persons the evening she got to Clinton, which she concluded with an appeal to the applauding crowd of "Gentlemen, would it not take a heroine to refuse fifty thousand dollars and a handsome husband, to live in such a coop as this?" Which remark needs no refutation beyond the simple quotation as coming from her; it bears "lie" to[o] plainly to require contradiction.

The "witness" was the beauteous Miss Stone. That, and all remarks of the same class Miriam paid no attention to, until a week ago she heard that the young woman's stepfather, on her authority, had told Gen. Carter that Miriam, in Miss Stone's presence, had told mother that "the General and the whole family were down on her for not having married Mr Carter." Distressed at so base a falsehood, which, beside reflecting on Gen. Carter's self respect and honor, affected her reputation for veracity, Miriam in a most modest and temperate note begged Miss Stone to contradict a report which was sanctioned by her name, though utterly baseless, which brought so serious a charge against Gen. Carter, telling her that she was sure she could never have so misunderstood her, and—O everything that was proper and lady like on the occasion.

Yesterday came the most impudent, uncalled for answer, that can be possibly conceived. Neither affirming, nor denying honestly the charge, but evading scrupulously any approach to straightforwardness and candor, naturally feeling shy about such utter strangers. O but the impudence of that note! Its insolence can only be surpassed by my reply. Miriam trembled with rage. I grew beligerent, looking at her face. Miss Stone might pile up such notes on me, and I would not care; but Miriam—! I seized a pen and dashed off an answer. Miriam applauded, but objected to it as coming from me. I insisted, she resisted, I pleaded, feeling my revenge grow dearer as it seemed [to be] passing away, and at last prevailed.

I feel better now it is over. But is it christianly? Pshaw! I dare say it [p. 135] will not hurt her as much to read it as it does me to send it now it has been written. Besides, she is sure to have some devilish prank in reserve which will make me think I have been even too lenient. Dare say she'll send it back—after she has read it! Confound her ugly red head! How dare she write so insolently to Miriam? Think I have settled her this far, though, and Miriam thinks so too, which more than consoles me. Of course the woman will repay me. I am a novice in such matters, and who ever triumphed over a red head?

Turn we to more interesting subjects. Most of our visiters of Christmas have since repeated their visit, though my blessed blister had confined me to my room ever since. I tell Miriam that during these few days I fear me she has regained her "John." At best, we are only half and half in possession. And what do I want with a demi-John?

While recording my wonderous deeds and witticisms, let me tell of one I propounded to her and Anna two nights ago, after the candle was out, of course, as I could not have perpetrated such folly if either the light of reason or a tallow candle had been shining about me. I asked with the hesitation peculiar to modesty and native genius, What should be the first question of a young man who is looking out for a wife? "Will you marry me?" they might have suggested, only they were too busy guessing to think of it. At last I was called on for the answer, which consisted of either one, or three words, as you please; it was "Am-i-able?" Enough! Light the candle! Return, Reason! Where's Anna's night cap? Good night!

January 1st. Thursday. 1863.

1863! Why I have hardly become accustomed to writing '62, yet! Where has this year gone? With all its troubles and anxieties, it is the shortest I ever spent. '61 & '62 together would hardly seem three hundred and sixty five days to me. Well, let time fly. Every hour brings us nearer our freedom, and we are two years nearer peace now, than we were when South Carolina seceded. That is *one* consolation! Do see how, while prosing here, I am forgetting the economy I have been forced to practice with my paper![248] Only one page left, and I cant return to Clinton for several days to come. Where will I find space to relate a hundred things I am dying to tell? Must such wonderous revelations be allowed to perish unrecorded?

We had a merry time, watching the old year out. Besides four strangers who were to stay all night, Capt. Bradford and his brother came out to help us welcome the New Year in. I prefered remaining up here; but Miriam had me carried down against my inclinations, and indeed I did not afterwards regret it. O didn't Mr Halsey send me the most beautiful white Camelia for my New Year's gift! What is it I love better than flowers? Not human beings, certainly! I would not let it go down stairs; I kept it up here where I could look at it all the time without moving. I believe I love God better when I see flowers; this one looks as though He had not yet taken his finger off of it.

Mr Bradford tried to be *so* witty at Mr Halsey's expense, that it is a pity I did not reward him by believing his nonsense. He gave what was supposed to be the most accurate imitation of how Mr Halsey disturbed them at night by talking about me in his sleep, and by pacing up and down the tent repeating my name aloud; in fact, related absurdities that only Mr Bradford could utter, and which would be unendurable from any one less amiable and good humored than he. Of course I took it just as it was meant, in fun; but what was my surprise when we got up in our room, when Anna told me that the Captain had told her it was all true; that he feared Mr Halsey was seriously "struck," and moreover believed that he had told me so—and Heaven knows what else; I have written enough trash without increasing the budget.

Such jokes may do for Mac Bradford, but is his brother mad, that he should jest so? There is not a word of truth in it; they just want me to hate a man who has never done me anything that could justify me in disliking him, and have taken the surest way. And the worst part is that all of them here have the story, and deal with it unmercifully. These girls kept me awake ever so long, calling "Sarah!" in their mock sleep by way of teasing me, as though I cared!

After my wasting all that paper on miss Brickbats the letter that

248. Sarah's handwriting is much smaller than usual on the last pages of this book—so tiny in fact that it can be read only with difficulty. But she managed to crowd a great deal into these pages.

troubled my conscience so did not go. Gibbes thought that only Miriam should fight her own battles, so she wrote herself. Sorry I cant do the woman something mean, now!

I learn, to my unspeakable grief, that the State House is burned down. Those blessed Yankees have been in the town some three weeks, and this is the result, confound them![249] Adieu, Home and Happiness! Yankees inhabit my first, and have almost succeeded in destroying my second. Let the whole town burn, now; without our State House, it is nothing. Without its chief ornament, what does our poor little town look like? Do wretched Yankees, standing in the little room at home, look through the single window without seeing the white towers against the blue sky? How can Baton Rouge exist without our pride? I can hardly fancy it. Though desecrated, mutilated, pillaged, almost destroyed within by the Yankees in their previous visit, still we had the outside left untouched, at least, until this crowning act of barbarism. Our beautiful gardens! Our evening walks! Oh Yankees! If you were only in glory! You'd have fire enough there, to induce you to dispense with the burning of our beautiful State House!

I can never realize it until I see it myself. Would it not be awful to come before it unexpectedly, and, opening your eyes, look at the white walls and glittering windows, meet instead that awful [p. 136] void, that blue nothing that hangs between our beautiful gardens and heaven? Baton Rouge is ruined forever now; let it burn; I would hardly cry. O my home! Our "city of bowers"! I wish you had been laid low before you were desecrated by the touch of Yankee heathens! Nothing but fire can purify you now. Burn, then, and may the Yankees burn with you!

Sunday January 4th. Sis' birthday.

Did I have a Happy New Year? Cant tell, though I have repeatedly asked myself the question. Rather think I did not, but am not quite certain. Capt. Bradford and his brother dined with us; that certainly

---

249. The Union army reoccupied Baton Rouge on December 17, 1862. On the night of December 28 the State House burned to the walls. The fire was not, however, a deliberate act of war, or arson, as Sarah first supposed. At the time it started, Union soldiers were quartered in the building and Confederate prisoners were being held there. The historic structure was restored twenty years later and was used once more until the new State Capitol was built in the early 1930s.

did not add to my felicity, if it did to Miriam's and Anna's. Then they were mean enough to accept an invitation to a small party, and cooly made their arrangements to leave me alone for the rest of the evening, having invited the two gentlemen to escort them. That I did not care for, though I thought they could have quite as pleasant a time here. But just before they left, Mr Halsey entered, and then I fervently hoped that they would either remain to entertain him, or take him with them. But in answer to their invitations, he only said he had come out expressly to spend the evening with me, and believed he prefered remaining. I did not like him for it!

So they departed, and here I was left alone to entertain Mr Halsey, for Mrs Carter had to divide her time equally between little Lilly[250] who was sick, and myself, who really needed the help of her dour countenance, at least. And hour after hour passed, and still Mr Halsey talked—I believe he could talk forever—and still I chimed in, until twelve o'clock struck, when I felt very much like a disobedient little Cinderella, and he at last said good night and rode off. The others did not get back until long after three, too late for the gentlemen to return to camp, so they remained all night.

I waked up in the morning with a vague sense of something disagreeable. What it was, I could not define, even to myself. In answer to Miriam's inquiry, I told her I had had a very pleasant time, but contradicted myself by exclaiming in the same breath "O Miriam! I *dont, dont*, like your Mr Halsey!" Why not, I wonder? Had it occurred to me while he was there? I dont know; I felt it when I said it, and the more I thought of it, the stronger the aversion grew, until I almost hated him. Miriam laughed, and said she knew he must have said something I disliked; I vowed he did not! She laughed and teased unmercifully, and only made me dislike him more, until every now and then I would exclaim involuntarily "O Miriam! I hate your Mr Halsey with all my heart!" I dont believe I do, but I dont, dont like him, [even] if he is ever so kind and obliging to me. I am indebted to him for a very pleasant evening, which, but for him would have been a very lonely one; but still, I dont, cant, wont, *shant* like him! It is just the natural perversity of the animal!

250. Daughter of Eugene and Helen Carter, age 3 in the 1860 census.

One just from B.R. tells us that my presentiment about our house is verified; Yankees do inhabit it, a Yankee Colonel and his wife. They say they look strangely at home on our front gallery, pacing up and down as though at home. O my garden! do they respect you? I lay here in my sick bed, longing for a spray of Heliotrope, or leaf of Geranium that grows there, when in all probability neither now exist. Does my honeysuckle still climb over the galleries? Well, perhaps it would be for the best if my garden is destroyed. It may be vanity, but I often think that when I die it will be painful to mother to see it. All the work of my hands, and mine only, always and always, early and late, she will see me working in my garden, singing over my violets and roses and training my vines. I can fancy that she would feel just as I would if I returned there when she was dead. I should always see her pacing up and down in the twilight on the gallery, always hear the echo of the short, dry cough. A feeling of awe creeps over me when I think of it. I will be afraid of the twilight gallery when mother dies, if I then live.

And a stranger and a Yankee occupies our father's place at the table where he presided for thirty one years. The table that has been surrounded by his children and friends so long, the table sacred to our pleasant dinners, and long, quiet or gay, and delightful after supper talks. And the old lamp that shone in the parlor the night I was born, that lighted up so many eager, laughing faces around the dear old table night after night; that with its great beaming eye watched us one by one as we grew up and left our homes; That witnessed every parting and every meeting; by which we sang, read, talked, danced, and made merry; the lamp that Hal asked for as soon as he beheld the glittering chandeliers of the new innovation—gas; the lamp that all agreed should go to me among other treasures, and be cased in glass to commemorate the old days, our old lamp has passed in[to] the hands of strangers who neither know nor care for its history. And mother's bed (which, with the table and father's little ebony stand, alone remained uninjured) belongs now to a Yankee woman!

Father prized his ebony table. He said he meant to have a gold plate placed in its centre, with an inscription; and I meant to have it done myself, when he died so soon after. A Yankee who has neither ancestors or family to be proud of, now sips his tea over it, just where some beau or beauty of the day of Charles the II may have rested a laced sleeve or dimpled arm on it.[251] "What a fall was there, my country!"[252] From Morgan hands down to—Yankees! Poor debased table! It will drive me mad to think of those people [illegible] in our house, peering in the garret and reading all our letters and papers. Wonder what Sis would think? Give the devil his due. Bless Yankees for one thing; they say they tried hard to save our State House.

I have just heard that Mattie has lost her husband.[253] God help her. I am more than grieved for her.

Who comes down the road in the twilight? Mr Halsey they tell me, so I must dress to go down. Wonder if he brought the poetry he promised?

[p. 137] Friday January 9th 1863.

This last fly leaf of my journal shall be devoted to the last pleasant event of these most pleasant days. And this last event was—a party! Chose extraordinaire for these times, chose almost inoui;[254] for Linwood, besides being the first I have attended since Harry died. It happened that the girls attended another dance on Monday, and came back so fascinated and delighted, that the General proposed having one here for our own benefit. Such crazy people as all became! Such excitement, such heart flutterings and heart burnings for fear some favored and especial "He" should be omitted! I think they were half wild.

Isidore Comstock, Miss Dickson and Sarah Ripley were sent for from Clinton, and arrived in the morning by the cars to join us in our fun. This Sarah is one of the dearest, sweetest, most fairy like little creatures imaginable; one of these kind, affectionate little ladies one cant help loving, who spent the day sitting on my bed patting my hand, kissing my cheek, and calling me "poor dear little thing" as though she were twice as large as I. But all of them did that; there was a strange pity in

251. In a footnote to the 1913 edition Warrington Dawson wrote: "This 'little ebony table'—which happened to be mahogany so darkened with age as to be recognized only by an expert many years after the war—and a mahogany rocking-chair are the two pieces of furniture which survived the sacking of Judge Morgan's house and remain to his descendants to-day. Such other furniture as could be utilized was appropriated by negroes."

252. Echoes Shakespeare, *Julius Caesar.*

253. Lieutenant James H. Stith, with the 1st Louisiana Heavy Artillery but on detached duty, died near Vicksburg the previous month.

254. Something extraordinary for these times, something almost unheard of.

each face as one by one leaned over me, a silent sympathy in the pressure of each hand laid on mine that expressed more than words, and caused me to hold my breath more than once for fear that a trembling lip or choaking sob should betray me.

Ah me! how keenly I felt it! All were to dance and be merry, all save me; my foot was once as light as any there; for the first time in my life I was to look on the dance, without participating. It was no little sacrifice, and keeping it to myself did not diminish the pain. All day to watch them dancing in and out, to hear their foot falls on the stairs, in the hall, to see them gay and merry, running around after dresses and flowers, and to lay here echoing their laughter and talking as fast, with that dreadful pain fastened in my back like shark's teeth, and never to dare, or be willing to acknowledge it, was one of those little penances I delight in inflicting on myself. If I cried "Please God!" wildly in spirit, I only laughed aloud "O girls!" and delighted in watching their swift movements. Then to see them dress so prettily! to lay here and see one by one arrayed in all their glory, and know I could not assist! Ah how I longed for my feet again!

They were all so beautiful. Yet to console me, each told me I looked lovely in my night gown, and playfully begged me to be carried down in it, if I wished to look my *very* best. I kept my own counsel. When all had gone below, I called Malvina and alone performed my toilet. The morning dress that all the gentlemen rave about I selected as the most becoming and appropriate, as I could hardly be expected to appear in full dress. An embroidered skirt, wide open undersleeves with a fall of rich lace, a delicate lace col[l]ar and handkerchief to correspond, and I was ready. I hesitated a moment before I added a jet bracelet and pinned a tiny blue bow to my braided hair just at my temple. I did not wait to look again. It was useless to compete with the other girls; I would not try.

I heard the guests come, and then the music and dance begin; and then the General sent for me to come down. He had considerately waited until they had deserted the parlor to dance in the large dining room, so I was spared the mortification of a public entrée. Yet I had no sooner been wheeled to my place near the dining room door where I could see at least part of the dancing, than I found Mr Halsey at my elbow, with ever so much to say. Among other things he told me of a most amusing little circumstance that had occurred in the morning. It seems that he had procured a very beautiful little bird for me, and after spending an hour in the composition of a most extraordinary note written with the greatest care imaginable, he addressed it with my name and residence in full, and fastened it under its wing with pink ribbon. But unfortunately as the messenger approached to receive it, the bird made an effort to regain its liberty, and darted away.

Mr Halsey says he watched it in blank disappointment with a dozen others as it flew off towards Gen. Beale's headquarters, doubtless to obtain a pass; but whether it was granted or refused, is not known, as it never returned to tell. He wonders into whose hands the note so legibly addressed in full will fall, I wonder if it is not very painful to the poor dear little creature to carry so much paper and ribbon under its wing, poor thing!

I had a good opportunity to criticise the dresses of the young ladies as they passed before me. Besides those mentioned already, there was only Ida Smith who has been spending a week with us, and Miss Purnell and Miss Flower.[255] But every woman in the room, married and single, wore snow drops in her hair, and snow drops in her dress. I believe I was the solitary exception. Each looked their very best; I never saw Anna appear to such advantage before; but Miriam was the handsomest, and Sarah Ripley the prettiest there.

The dance over, all the gentlemen I had met previously came to speak to me, and those I had never before seen, to be introduced, until there was quite a crowd around me, with inquiries and condolence in profusion. All my friends insisted on my dancing with them, to tease me. Only one made the mistake in reality, a stranger, Col. Crockett.[256] I had thought my costume would be a sufficient explanation; but discovering my error, I simply said that I was compelled by an unfortunate accident to play invalid just at present. He bowed and retired; but at the end of five minutes, which he must have spent in making inquiries, he returned with the most overwhelming apologies for having so heedlessly wounded my feelings by reminding me of my misfortune. I laughingly

255. Mary Purnell, daughter of Dr. George Purnell, and Lucy Flower, daughter of Richard Flower.

256. Colonel Robert H. Crockett, son of the legendary Davy Crockett, commanded a regiment in Beall's brigade. See Edmonds, *The Guns of Port Hudson*, 2:212.

assured him that it was a very pardonable mistake, and I did not mind it, etc, but the man seemed really touched, and could not do or say enough. He said he had just discovered that he was the only one in the whole army who did not know it, and could not comprehend why Gibbes whom he saw every day, had never told him of—if I would excuse the expression—such a very interesting case.

Perhaps Gibbes, like myself, shrinks from making my accident so very public. But why do they call it "interesting?" That is what Izzie Comstock called it, and indifferent Miss Dickson, and a dozen others I could not help overhearing. What is there interesting in premature decay? What would I not give for a pair of strong feet again?

I was never more agreeably disappointed in a gentleman than in Col. Crockett. I had heard of him as a wild, reckless, dissipated man, who thought nothing of kissing a girl when he was introduced to her, and made up my mind to hate him cordially, and not to look at the odious wretch. That was the ideal Col. Crockett. The real one stood before me, short, stout, very handsome, with a ferocious moustache, rather a sailorish costume, with a flesh colored sash wound around his waist, altogether quite [?] a piratical looking little craft. His compassion and sympathy at first disarmed [p. 138] me, and by the time I remembered I was to despise him, I could find nothing to hate for he was amusing me so.

His respectful behavior surprised me. Was it possible that this man so very defferential to me was in the habit of kissing girls whenever he wished, and saying impudent things to them? At last I could no longer resist the temptation of asking if there were two Col. Crocketts. He laughed heartily. "I see my reputation has preceeded me. Yes, there are two Col. Crocketts, for two different tastes. I perceived that folly and familiarity were not to your taste, and am now expending on you what little wisdom and dignity I possess."

I appreciated the compliment when, later in the evening, I saw him play the buffoon with the other girls and swing them around in the dance. After his first mistake, every other set he called mine, and drawing up his chair would talk incessantly to me. He is unfortunately deaf; but singular to say could hear my words though spoken in the lowest tone; so we got on very well together.

I hardly ever heard more genuine sympathy expressed; he could not condole enough with me. Would I let him come out to see me *very* soon, and *very* often? Might he come just when he felt like it, at any hour, and read to me, talk to me? Might he bring me books to amuse me? He considered it the sacred duty of all my friends to devote their whole time to lessening my sufferings and ennui. I did not tell him that suffering I did not care for, and ennui I had never yet experienced; I only spoke of all the kindness that was lavished on me by those who surround me. But he could talk of nothing else. I was surprised to find any one take such interest in anything so stale and trite as me, but it was really gratifying to receive such great sympathy.

If I was pleased with him, I was rather disappointed in Col. Steadman [*sic*]. I was prepared to fall in love with him instantaneously; I had heard such extraordinary accounts of him. But I only saw a very plain and unpretending man, which was not exactly what I expected. He also made himself very agreeable, and assured me that there was no doubt of ultimate recovery, citing several desperate cases, each of which had miraculously recovered. His experience must differ from mine. I have scarcely touched a book or paper since I have been sick, in which there is not some mention of some one thrown from a horse or buggy, who pined away and died a year or two after, in a most interesting way. One of the gentlemen mentioned a novel he had just been reading—Vivian, I believe—in which the heroine languished for a year or two from a similar accident, and then got married—just as Miss Sarah will do!

Capt. Steadman I found one of these dear, nice, clean, innocent little creatures, in other words a ninny. But my extreme aversion, which I had reserved for Col. Crockett, I bestowed on a Major Buckner.[257] I must confess that perhaps Frank Enders prejudiced me against him. I have heard him express his opinion. But I was willing to think the best of him until I observed a singular peculiarity about him, which was that it seemed as though he could never get close enough to a young lady when turning her in the dance, or speaking to her. Imagine my horror when he leaned over my chair to speak to me, and came so alarmingly near, that a lock of his odious red hair reposed warm on my molasses candy locks! Agitation and aversion made my answers unusually brief;

257. Major D. P. Buckner, a Louisianian and one of the officers on General Beall's staff. Captain Seth D. Steedman was Colonel Steedman's brother.

but he did not appear to observe it. Retreat was impossible; so there I sat with that odious, odious lock resting on mine, mentally endorsing every thing Frank had said, and so indignant and embarrassed that I could hardly speak. The worse part of it is that the wretch has short hair! Good gracious! I really felt beligerent.

Capt. Fenner I liked better than ever; that is saying a great deal. But the one who amused me most of all was Mr Duggan. I believe I had more fun with him, than with any of the rest. I had more fun talking to him alone than when half a dozen surrounded me. He has the oddest way of saying "Miss Sarah!" when he thinks I am giving reins to my imagination, that I ever heard. It amuses me so, that I have been practicing it all day on Anna. Indeed I had a delightful time, though a miserable old cripple. The girls accuse me of having monopolized more than my share of their beaux; but I consider the accusation unjust; I saw none who suffered for want of them.

About twelve o'clock the General told me he wished to move me. I submitted, fearing I was perhaps to be sent to bed. But I was soon undeceived; it was only supper time, and as usual the dear General thought first of me. Mr Duggan accompanied me, to table, that is to say walked by my chair, and established himself next to me as my cavalier, and then the others followed. The table was spread on the back gallery which was enclosed with curtains, and presented a beautiful appearance. Every thing was unexceptionable. I cant imagine where so fine a supper could be procured in such days of scarcity, and at so short a notice. Then the cordon formed by some thirty five happy looking faces around, was by no means the least interesting feature. Every one seemed determined to enjoy themselves and make the best of every thing. I really enjoyed myself exceedingly; and while trying to talk as fast and amusingly as Mr Duggan, Col. Crockett would write me toasts from his end of the table, and make me feel "good." Such a gay, gay time! I like Mr Duggan.

I hate Mr Halsey. Indeed I do; so I dont mind telling something foolish on him. It was after supper, when they were again dancing, and I happened to be talking to him alone, that we were discussing the extraordinary powers of observation some people possess. I mentioned Lydia whom I imagined was too far off to hear me as she was watching the dance, and said I was sure that nothing ever escaped her attention; that she perceived every look and gesture that passed in the room. "Nonsense!" said he. "Do you suppose she would know it if I squeezed your hand? Let me try! please do! I know she wont know it!" It is unnecessary to add that I did not put her powers of observation to the test; but whether she really overheard, or Miriam told the story on me, both repeated it to day in full conclave to my great annoyance. Wonder if he would think she was an observing little creature if he heard her tell the story?

It was five o'clock, a most heathenish, *indecent* hour, before they ceased dancing and took their leave. I remained [?] to the last, in spite of Col. Crockett's protestations that I was surely in great pain (wonder how he guessed?), and can candidly say I have seldom enjoyed myself more. Then the fun of discussing the guests and comparing notes up in our room, was almost equal to the pleasure of the evening.

"And now my tongue the secret tells—" Why do you suppose I have been writing all this? I commenced it just with the view of testing my patience. To begin then, Yesterday Sarah Ripley told me that Frank Enders had written me a long note by her, which he had afterwards torn up, but that he sent me word he was coming to see me to day. This morning the cars brought him. Instead of getting them to carry me down stairs, I quickly commenced writing as though I had nothing else to do. One by one the girls came in and asked if I knew Mr Enders was down stairs. "Yes," and I continued my self appointed task without looking up. I would not go down until he asked especially for me, if he staid a week. I shut my ears to the sound of voices down stairs, and wrote rapidly when the girls would let me alone.

About half an hour before the cars returned, Mrs Badger came up with the message that Mr Enders begged permission to come up to see me, if I was not able to come down. That sufficed, particularly as all the others then joined in, and said it was singular that I refused to go down when Mr Enders had informed them that he had come down expressly to see me, and no one else, and had requested each in turn to ask me to come down if I was well enough. Singular that they had forgotten to mention it until then! But I coolly got up and dressed without further remark, and was carried down stairs. Frank looked glad to [p. 139] see me, indeed he did! He imagined that I had not made my appearance because I was too indisposed, but I quietly told him that I was waiting for him to ask for me. He looked slightly astonished. He had come expressly to see me; had they not told me? he had asked each in turn to inquire if I could come down. I shrugged my shoulders. They had forgotten to tell me.

We had not talked ten minutes before dinner was announced, and again I was drawn to the table. Frank eat [*sic*] by me, and we tried to talk enough to make up for lost time, but hardly succeeded. Miriam had already told all the news, and a dozen shocking stories on me. Frank surprised me by informing me he meant to pull that ugly lock of red hair out of Major Buckner's head, for his impudence, threatened to knock down Mr Halsey and thrash Mr Duggan, just as the latter had threatened to do him the night before. While he was asking when I was coming back to Clinton, and begging me to hurry, the cars whistled, and abruptly terminated the dinner. All the party were to return, and Miriam was [words illegible] them in spite of the rain that had poured incessantly all day.

Then came a hurried leave taking, all except Mr Enders. I had punished him by not coming down, I punished myself by not telling him good bye. It was all the most absurd piece of folly imaginable. I dont know how I could be [page torn] foolish. But twice he came to say good bye, and extended his hand, and twice I refused to offer mine in return and saw him depart not of course, hurt, but [page torn] calling dignity and pride to his assistance. I could bite myself for playing the fool so. What harm did it do him? What good did it do me? Why did I not put out my hand honestly and frankly, instead of putting on absurd airs?

Sarah, I have lost all respect for you! A man comes twenty miles to see you; you do not make your appearance until just before he leaves; you talk and look just as you feel—glad to see him—and then when he bids you a [word lined through] goodbye, you turn a cold shoulder not quite in the style of "The hand of Douglas is his own," [258] but something very like it. What does this contradiction mean? I am angry, and ashamed of you! Why distress myself about a piece of folly he has forgotten by this time? He neither remembers nor cares for it, yet you are allowing the mere thought to annoy and distress you as though it were of importance. Is it the first time you have played the fool? Hush, then!

258. Sir Walter Scott, *Marmion*.

Hearken to Mrs Badger's remonstrances and shut up your book. Extinguish the hardly lighted candles, and let us have a pleasant dream by the flickering fire light. Adieu Mr Enders! I'll recall more agreeable thoughts! [The bottom half of p. 139 is missing; apparently it was removed before Sarah used the top for her entry.]

[p. 140] Jan. 11th. Sunday.

I kept my promise. I closed my eyes to the dancing firelight and dull grey sky. I closed my conscience to the recollection of my folly and Mr Enders and with the music of pattering rain drops, launched into a sea of rosy dreams. At last I was startled by the name "Sarah!" coming from the other side of the room, and hastily roused myself. The grey sky had disappeared; it must have been late; by the flickering firelight I saw Mrs Badger lying on the other bed. Again the voice called me. "Sarah, do you know Mr Halsey is in love with you?" I gave a scream of horror as I cried "O Mrs Badger!" All my pleasant dreams to be disturbed by such an assertion! Why had she spoken? And to say that above all things! I was angry, mortified. "Yes" she went on. "He is desperately in love with you, and you know it, too. I am not to be deceived; and even if I had not eyes to see for myself, the extreme aversion you have recently conceived for him would have satisfied me of it. Lydia and Miriam say it is an unfailing sign, that you invariably hate those who acknowledge, or show they love you. Dont deny it; cant I see?"

But I did deny it vehemently and earnestly, though to no purpose. "Pshaw! little girl, I was not born yesterday! I am not to be fooled!" was the only response elicited. "I have never yet [ink spot] been mistaken in such affairs; it would take a smarter man than Mr Halsey to mislead me; I could take an oath that it was so."

I represented that the individual was thirty years old; a confirmed old bachelor; one who had never met me until recently, and who, if he ever meant to fall in love, had probably succumbed to Miriam. She would not listen to me; she knew what she was saying. "And do you know that you are unconsciously encouraging him?" Another cry of "Mrs Badger!" as I struggled half way up on my elbow, in my distress. "Yes; I watched you last [?] night, together, and saw you bestow so many smiles on his nonsense, that I was provoked with you, and was just about giving you a hint about coquetry, when you turned from him to answer Capt. Fenner." I wrung my hands in distress. Is it possible that I could be so dishonest? Indeed I was unconscious of trying such capers! And I was sorry, so sorry! I had deemed myself incapable of doing such a thing. My idol Self had fallen, fallen! What could I do? Of course Mrs Badger is mistaken. But I hate him! Oh I hate him!—

Whose voice is that in the hall below? I will *not* go down! "Shut shut the door good John!" Say I'm sick! I'm dead! I *shall not* see him.

Pour tant I was well enough to go down to see Capt. Fellows and Capt. McClure[259] last night. But I will not see Mr Halsey this morning. Go down Anna and say I am just expiring! And so I am—with disgust! [The bottom half of p. 140 is missing; apparently it was removed before Sarah used the top for her entry.]

259. Captain John R. Fellows, assistant adjutant general on the staff of General Beall, and Captain James L. McCleur, quartermaster on the staff of General Franklin Gardner.

Book Four

Book Four

[p. 1] From my sick bed, this 15th day of January 1863. Linwood. Thursday.[1]

Am I not glad to get another blank book! On Sunday my old one gave out to my unspeakable distress, and I would have been desolée if I had not had three or four letters to answer, as writing is my chief occupation during my tedious illness. O that unfortunate trip to Port Hudson! Have I not cause to remember and regret it? Two months last Sunday since I have been lying here a cripple, and I am not yet able to take a step. However on Monday mother sent me Dr Woods as my fourth physician, and I have made up my mind that either he or Nature will effect a cure before long. Wonder how it feels to walk? It makes me uneasy to see others try it; I always fear that the exertion must be very painful—an absurd idea which I endeavor to keep to myself, and which certainly does not keep me from putting all those around me to the trouble of waiting constantly on me. How patiently they submit! Where all are so devoted it is unfair to mention one without all; but I must speak of Mrs Badger who has been a perfect mother to me— as tender and gentle as my own—and my dear Miriam, who is a full fledged angel to her poor smashed up sister.

What extraordinary sympathy this "interesting" state of affairs brings me! That is what they all call it, though the word comes like a mockery to me. What is there "interesting" in having a whole life blighted? I receive the sympathy with gratitude, but reject the sentimentalism which sees only the romance of creating a great excitement by being dashed out of a buggy in a crowd of men, and the delights of receiving the pity and condolence of the whole country.

1. The word puzzles that Sarah mentions in her March 20, 1863, entry appear on two unnumbered pages at the front of this book.

397

Just hear Col. Crockett talk of it, if you want to realize how sad it is! Miriam says that at the party last Tuesday he brought the tears to her eyes while expatiating on the "interesting" theme. What an odd man he must be! I have seen him but once, at our pleasant party here on the 8th, yet how he talks of me! He tells Miriam that he never before experienced such intense sympathy for any one. So young! The loveliest creation! (Good Gracious! that alone would suggest his having come from Arkansas or the Hoosier State! Or else he was looking at her.) Such an extraordinary mind! (On what occasion did he prove it? Is he clean daft to talk so?) The most charming, amiable, fascinating, interesting girl— Pshaw! why record Col. Crockett's nonsense? He swears he loves me better than anything on earth after his wife and children— loves me like a sister! What an unexpected burst of affection! Yet is it not sweet in him?

I dont know which to attribute it [p. 2] to, compassion for my unfortunate accident, or genuine admiration for my toilette, which he and all present raved about as the most becoming, heavenly, appropriate, and exquisite in the world. Rather humiliating to be forced to acknowledge that all extravagant admiration and praise bestowed upon me is due entirely to sympathy for me, and a pretty dress, is it not? Yet such is the case. If I did not owe it to a strained back, I would not receive it at all; so I patiently endure the one for the sake of the other. It *is* nice to receive forty thousand messages of condolence and sympathy! Only when I remember the price I pay for them, I cry "O men! keep your sweet speeches, and pray Heaven with me, that I may soon be placed beyond the need of this overwhelming sympathy!"

Monday. Jan. 19th. 1863.

That blessed Mr Halsey (what a different strain from the one I sang in my last diary!) like an angel of mercy sent me Kate Coventry [2] yesterday, just when I was pining for a bonne bouche [3] of some kind, I did not care what, whether a stick of candy or an equally palatable book. It is delightful to have one's wishes realized as soon as they are made. I think it rather caused me to relent towards Mr Halsey; I did not feel

2. Novel by George John Whyte-Melville.
3. Tidbit.

half so beligerent as I did just the Sunday before. At all events *I felt well
enough to go down in the evening when he called again,* though I had
been too indisposed to do so on a previous occasion. (O Sarah!) Yes! I
actually put away sweet, naïve Kate Coventry, and arraying myself like
Solomon in all his glory, I signified that I was ready to be carried down
stairs.

Once in the entry, placed in my chair, I was wheeled in the parlor
where I beheld not my friend alone, but several other individuals whose
presence rather startled me. I found myself undergoing the terrors of
an introduction to a Col. Locke,[4] and to my unspeakable surprise the
individual I had formerly stigmatized as "odious Major Buckner" was
claiming the privilege of shaking hands with me, and Col. Steadman
was on the other side, and—*was* that Mr Halsey? O never! The Mr
Halsey I knew was shockingly careless of his dress, never had his hair
smooth, let his beard grow as it would, and wore a most ferocious
slouched hat. This one had taken more than one look at the glass, a
thing I should have imagined the other incapable of doing. He had
bestowed the greatest care and attention on his dress, had brought his
beard within reasonable limits, had combed his hair with the greatest
precision, and held lightly in one hand an elegant little cap that I am
sure must be provokingly becoming. Why he was handsome!

Ah ça! Some mistake surely, I cried to myself. *My* Mr Halsey was not,
certainly! "If it be I, as I hope it may be, I've a little dog at home who
will surely know me" I kept repeating. I resolved to test the little dog's
[p. 3] sagacity, so I pretended to know this apparition, and thanked
him for the pleasure he had afforded me by sending me Kate Coventry.
He looked conscious and pleased! the "little dog" then had found out
his identity! I was more puzzled than ever. How account for this wonderous change? What does it mean? What metamorphosis has "John"
undergone? What change has come over the spirit of his dream? I am
really alarmed! What has happened?

It did not take ten minutes to find out that Col. Locke was more afraid
of me than I could possibly be of him. He is a perfect Major Dobbins;[5]

4. Lieutenant Colonel Michael B. Locke, an Alabamian, second in command of the 1st
Alabama, Colonel Steedman's regiment.
5. Captain Dobbin, in *Vanity Fair*.

such a perfect picture of that dear, good, noble hearted, innocent individual, that I thought I was reading Vanity Fair every time he spoke. And Major Buckner was not half so odious as I had resolved to think him. Indeed I would have been most ungrateful if I had persisted in my opinion; for did he not do all in his power to entertain me? True, [his] quotations did not show profound research or study, though used with the greatest profusion, but it was not his fault if I knew they were coming a few moments before they were due, and it was only accident if he was forced to apply to me occasionally to help him out. At all events, I deferred forming a decisive opinion of his merits or demerits until further acquaintance. Yet Frank Enders hates him, and he ought to know!

Ah! Col. Steadman! Yes! I like *him*! He made as many inquiries concerning my accident as though he had been my physician,[6] and tells me I may possibly be well in six month[s]. And he alarmed me too. I had told him early in the evening that I was being treated Homeopathically, and several hours after, while giving me some salutary advice, he startled me by saying "All depends on the course you pursue; in two months your fate for life will be decided, and I fear me miss Sarah you will find yourself a cripple." Comforting, under the circumstances! I was naturally alarmed; but he explained his meaning at my earnest request by saying he had no faith in homeopathy himself. My alarm subsided as I perceived the prejudice of his class. How expect an Allopathic physician to agree that a homeopathist was even a christian?[7]

Major Dobbins did not venture a word to me, at least until he was unfortunately seated next to me at supper, when he remarked he was very, very sorry for me, which original remark led to nothing more interesting, and there the "conversation" ended.

But metamorphosed "John" talked! He was expatiating at a most extraordinary rate, and had been doing so for an hour after supper, when

6. A physician, Dr. Steedman had practiced in Wilcox County, Alabama, before the war. He was in his twenties and unmarried. "Our Col. is a great Ladies man," one of Steedman's men wrote his wife from Port Hudson. See A. H. Beauchamp letter dated November 3, 1862, in vertical files, Port Hudson Commemorative Area.

7. The established school of medicine was allopathy, a name given it by homeopathists. Homeopathy was a nineteenth-century system of medicine that treated disease by use of drugs which produced the same symptoms in the patient as the disease itself—quinine for malaria, for example.

Gibbes drew his chair near me,[8] whereupon timid Mr Halsey drew his slightly back, and very soon after asked for his horse. Ah! Gibbes you wretch! What an amusing tête-à-tête you spoiled, you innocent! And the General [p. 4] of course only waited for his exit before beginning to tease me unmercifully. I must put an end to this; they shall not bring such unjust charges against him. Yet how am I to make them see reason?

Night. I am more pleased to night than I could well express. I have been talking to an old and dear friend, no other than Will Pinkney! His arrival was as unexpected as it was agreeable. The cry of "Here comes Will Pinkney" sent me back to August/60, when the words were always the fore runner of fun and frolic. It recalled another scene in my life; I saw before me that Sunday morning in January, two years ago, when Will stood like an apparition before me in the parlor at home. It recalled the traitor feeling I then experienced, of having been the sole cause of his misery—of having broken off the engagement between him and Miriam, while pretending to be his best friend. So I was, in one sense. I suffered none to abuse him, I liked him myself, but not enough to be willing to see Miriam marry him.

I remember how I shrunk from telling him what I knew must come from me; for Miriam was sick at the time and unwilling to see him. How we both avoided it that morning, though each had no other thought! Mother was sick in bed, as well as Miriam, and I was father's little housekeeper; so every time the subject seemed unavoidable, I would rattle my keys, and discover that father's tea had been forgotten, or else his toast was not prepared. That kept me alive until father appeared. And then the misery of sitting opposite that dismal face and know[ing] that no matter how long I delayed, sooner or later the letters must be returned and the story told! And while father unsuspectingly read his papers, Will and I exchanged dull nothings, and looked—O unutterable things! Until a great black cloud that looked as though it had come from the lower regions made the dismal morning blacker still, and burst into a perfect deluge of rain, which, with the wind and darkness, appalled me so, that my lips blanched as I cried "Father! father!" while he cried "Nonsense, little daughter!" and Will gloomily wished it

8. Above the line Sarah wrote: "(Gibbes likes to hear what visiters say to his little sister)."

would rain and hail forever; suited *his* feelings perfectly! O that gloomy morning! And breakfast was over at last, and father went out, and Will and I confronted each other alone!

Why is it that Miriam's adorers always remain my best friends? What reason has Will for being so? Yet he tells me to day that I am the favorite now; that he thinks of me as his truest friend. Yet Miriam still lives. What strange contradictions this? I confess to being rather surprised when after being for some time down stairs, [lines drawn through]

[p. 5] [Top of page missing] followed a long, quiet talk, while he told me what he called his secrets; of how he had been treated by the war department (which has indeed behaved shockingly towards the Colonel) and of how happy he was with his wife though she was so many years his senior (twelve at least)[9] and what a beauty his little boy was. Then he commenced a long panegyric on myself, which half amazed, half amused me. Has the whole world conspired to turn my head? What induced Will to laud me so? Am I expected to believe that I am the greatest girl in the world? the best, sweetest, smartest, dearest, and heaven knows what else? No; fortunately posterity will exonerate me from all blame if I modestly doubt he is quite sane on the subject.

And he has taught his wife to love me too, he says; and he must have my daguerreotype, please. And I really shall write to him! he cant dispense with my correspondence. The letters I wrote him before his marriage, he saved in his flight, and he and his wife agree to destroy all letters save these; even her's he burns; but mine shall be kept, and some day published under the title of "Letters to a young man" as a pattern for all girls to follow. O Will! Will! you humbug! En attendant his wife keeps them just in front of her armoir, where she can read them occasionally; "she loves them as much as I do." Will, you absurdity! If you were still the Will Pinkney of two years ago, I might put all this down as impudence and fun; but a staid married man! Why flatter me, and pretend that you believe I am such a paragon? Well! let others abuse him as they choose; to me he is the same frank, honest, friendly Will, and as such I shall always like him.

9. Another wartime diarist, Julia LeGrand, mentions "Mrs. Colonel Pinckney" in an 1863 entry and identifies her as "a daughter of an officer in the old United States' army, . . . brought up in garrison circles." *The Journal of Julia LeGrand: New Orleans, 1862–1863,* edited by Kate Mason Rowland and Mrs. Morris L. Croxall (Richmond, 1911), 232.

Sunset had passed into twilight before he arose to say good bye. "You will be well soon I know. If your doctor cared as much for you as I do, he would tie you in bed, and force you to be careful." Just as though I am not! "No Will," I answered "I will never be well again. My life is told." It was almost sport to hear him declaim; he winds up with "You *shall* get well! Remember how you used to like to waltz with me? We'll have many a glorious dance yet!" "Not unless you engage me for the first quadrille in Heaven, Will; I'll never dance on earth again." I meant the laugh which accompanied the remark to pass it off as a joke, but Will took it seriously, just as I felt it.

It is too dark to see his face distinctly, but he takes my hand in both [p. 6] [top of page missing] of the long past sunset streams through Mrs Carter's western windows and touching them with the faintest hue of rose color throws their shadows on the entry wall, is waving me good-bye, and in another moment only the blank wall and open doorway is left; they are running down stairs side by side, that strange pair whose "Might have been" presents such a singular contrast to their actual Is.

By what caprice of Chance is it that these people find themselves face to face in this house this evening? Here is Will Carter who for three years has been wild about Miriam, and who so short a time ago was fool enough to imagine that with the minister in the parlor and a license in his pocket he could force her to change the "No" into "Yes" and oblige her to marry him; here is Will Pinkney who two years ago last summer was wilder still, and believing himself the Destined one, was in the seventh heaven until—well! until the blow was struck, and after the first forerunner of the storm to come had prepared him for what was to follow, he and I looked at each other with moist, damp eyes, one rainy morning in January, and he came down the ladder of happiness and took a plunge into the sea of Misery below. And here too is Dr Woods, who came down again to day, meeting these two others for, I believe, the first time. Perhaps I have no right to touch on the subject as far as he is concerned.

Mr Carter, having forfeited all title to her respect and regard, and having received her orders concerning it, dares not for his life address the slightest remark to her, but hangs around fretting, swearing and cursing, mad with jealousy and rage, assuming the independent style and looking the bully to perfection, until the very sound of his heavy boots stamping through the hall fills me with disgust.

Will Pinkney, married to a lady, who, however estimable, is very little younger than his mother, carries his own heart secrets and struggles of which he only is aware; and yet I think that very, very often that picture of the "Might have been" comes before him with startling vividness, which it requires more than one effort to efface. Unconsciously he reveals it. "I thought I could revisit Linwood without recalling the past; but the first glimpse of the sugar house made my heart bound to my throat. I came through the big gate down the road, pass [sic] the cooper shop—do you remember the bank of shavings where we used to sit? You & Howell, Miriam and I—I cant tell you what I felt. The brick kiln, the [p. 7] little hollow in the road, the circle before the house—Sarah, I lived my life over again while coming here this evening!" And I dare say he had, yet he tells me he is happy. Kismet! It is Destiny that rules us and orders all things.

These two face Dr Woods. If ever he loved woman—and that dark, cold, calm looking man certainly has some fire under that quiet face— that woman is Miriam. If ever she loved a man, that man is Dr Woods. What is it that should come between them? Why does she not marry him and be happy? Because it would make misery, and not happiness, and she knows it. Because there is the implied disapprobation of brothers she loves, and is willing to please; because she respects mother's opinions, and remembers the dear father that sleeps in his grave, and the brother that lies by his side, with skeleton hands crossed on his noble breast. Harry! Harry! Help me my God! Shall I murmur now, I who have borne it so quietly? Now as ever, Thy will be done!

Yes! she will remember those two who lie so peacefully in the grave yard, and while she still remembers—and Miriam loved them—she will never marry him, for the sake of the love she bears them. No, never! She will laugh and dance, flirt and be merry, until in some reckless moment she will throw herself away on some man she does not care a cent for, and then she will plunge herself in a perfect sea of dissatisfaction and break her husband's heart with a smile, or her own without a groan, and that is Miriam's fate, if this strange demon which sometimes possesses her, is not exorcised. Miriam, my idol, God's noblest woman! What a life! Kismet! It is Destiny! What can we do? "It is hard to kick against the pricks!" [10]

10. Acts 9:5.

Thursday 22d Jan.

What a rush of visiters last night! One would imagine they had all come by appointment, expressly to have an impromptu dance, which they certainly enjoyed, by the way. There was little Capt McClure, the Susceptible and Simple, who so innocently says "I seen" & "I done it" without the faintest suspicion of the peculiarity, and looks so sweet, and guileless, and amiable, and soft, that I cant help wondering if he would be sticky if I touch him. Indeed, I think his hands stick, at least; for when he told me good bye, it was with the greatest difficulty that I extracted mine from his grasp (he having forgotten to return it during a long farewell address) and even when I succeeded in recovering it, by being almost rude, it was not released without a *very* sensible pressure from the putty, or what ever it is that is so tenacious. I am afraid it is rather a habit of his, which has lost all force or meaning by being too frequently repeated.

Then there was a horrid little wretch, vulgar and underbred, (to *my* idea) to whom I was introduced as Mr Gwynn.[11] My astonishment was unbounded; Anna having captivated him at a small party, boasted loudly of her conquest to me, and extolled her victim, until I was prepared to greet an exquisite. However, this morning I picked him to pieces for her [p. 8] amusement, and succeeded in making him rather ridiculous; so now of course she vows she always *did* think him common, always despised him, and never *never* told me she liked him, and never talked of him either, not she! and as I attempt to remonstrate, she shuts her ears and gives a shrill scream. "She wont listen, it aint true!" and looks so thoroughly simple, confused, and ashamed, that I cease out of mere pity. Even now if I would say "What a charmer is Mr Gwynn! So elegant and refined!" she would exclaim "*Aint* he? But dont take him away! remember he belongs to me!" Bah! Some women—

But here is Lieut. Duprés,[12] whom I have not yet introduced, though we have met before. Tall, good looking, a fine form, and not a sparkling face, I am inclined to believe that his chief merit lies in his legs. Cer-

11. Possibly First Lieutenant William Gwynn, 10th Arkansas Volunteers, one of the Port Hudson officers sent north to prison following the surrender of the garrison. He also appears as Gwin and Gwinn in Confederate military records.

12. Lieutenant Alcée Louis Dupré, a Louisianian and an aide to General Franklin Gardner. He was the brother of Lucius Jacques Dupré, who served in the Confederate Congress.

tainly, when he dances, he puts his best foot forward, and knows it, too. Miriam who adores dancing is flirting openly with this divinity of the "Deux temps" [13] and polka, and skims around with his arm about her— (position sanctified by the lively air Lydia is dashing off on the piano) with a grace and lightness only equalled by his own. And Lieut Duggan with his good, honest, clever face which so unmistakably proclaims him "Tom," we know already, so no further description is needed. Capt. Fenner too, is well known, with his short, though graceful figure, his good humored, intelligent face, irresistible imperial, and that roguish expression about that large mouth which displays such handsome teeth, which seems to say "Dont trust me too far." I like these two last the best. The others "bore" me.

Little Capt. McClure tells me a long story about how Col. Steadman had come to him and asked if he believed it possible that Miss Morgan had put her life and happiness in the hands of a homeopathic physician; how he considered her fate sealed; and what a shame it was to trifle with such a sad affair—at my age too, ruined for life! It was dreadful! Too sad! Hereupon, as continuing the story, he remarks that being asked his opinion by the Colonel, he agreed perfectly and thought with him it was an appalling sacrifice, and O, all sorts of things! Anything, just to make me miserable and unhappy!

Well! what is written will come to pass. First comes a Doctor with a butchering apparatus who cups and bleeds me unmercifully, says I'll walk ten days after, and exit. Enter another. Croton oil and strychnine pills. That'll set me up in two weeks, and exit. Enter a third. Sounds my bones and pinches them from my head to my heels. Tells of the probability of a splinter of bone knocked off my left hip, the possibility of paralysis in the leg, the certainty of a seriously injured spine, and the necessity for the most violent counter irritants. Follows blisters which sicken even disinterested people to look at, and a trifle of suffering which I come very near acknowledging to myself. Enter the fourth. Inhuman butchery! wonder they did not kill you! Take three drops a day out of this tiny bottle, and presto! in two weeks you are walking! [p. 9] A fifth, in the character of a friend, says "My dear young lady, if you do, your case is hopeless."

13. "Two-Step."

What wonder that I am puzzled? A wiser head would be [illegible] confused. I want to believe all, but how is it possible? "What will be, will be." Of this I am satisfied: if Dr Woods thought me beyond his skills, he has too much regard for me to trifle with my life, and if he had not, would not risk the happiness of one dear to Miriam. He shall have his trial with the rest; believing as I do that each has advised to the best of his knowledge, what follows shall not be attributed to ignorance or neglect, but to the will of God.

So I am glad to turn from the little Captain, to Mr Duggan who has not left my elbow all evening, knowing perhaps that his conversation was more agreeable to me than that of most of the others, and who remains firmly at his post in spite of some of the gentlemen who endeavor to enter into army discussions. So I talk to him, while I listen to the music of Capt. Fenner's spurs as they clink, clink in the dance, like miniature triangles. All the gentlemen wear them, but there is a faint silvery, merry chime in his that has a peculiar effect. I never liked spurs before. And when Mr Duggan talks, I listen to Miriam's lively rattle, or Anna's silly prattle on the other side of the room, and wonder how they can talk so freely when everyone hears them. For my part, under certain circumstances it kills me. Perhaps it is because many auditors embarrass me, that all the family have such a fancy for my end of the room. Let me be talking as gaily as I please, as soon as two or three of the family gather around my chair I feel foolish, and have nothing to say. I dont know why.

There is Anna who can flow on in one uninterrupted stream of small talk at the top of her voice, about gloves, and shoes, and complexion, and beaux, and tell the most absurd stories à-pro-pos of nothing at all, without being embarrassed. I cant talk on any of those topics; dont know exactly what I do talk about, when I get interested, or forget that other people are listening; but I am always throttling myself mentally and crying "Fool! fool!" while she dribbles on with a self complacency that is truly astounding. I dont want to arrogate to myself any credit for being wiser than she; perhaps I'd be a monstrous big fool if I was her inferior; but if I had heard myself make some remarks that she made last night, I would have been making faces at myself all day. Yet I see her smiling! Well, well! it is not fair to judge her by my ideas. They tell me that I am an odd, peculiar girl, though I feel stereotyped.

Bon! here comes a note from Mr Halsey! Ah ça! Lend him Zaidee? [14] Certainly! Here is a postscript three times the length of the note; voyons.[15] Will Miss Sarah make the annotations he requested, in Kate Coventry? He is anxious to have the lady's opinion on the questions of taste and propriety which so frequently occur in the book. Or if I would prefer—a short criticism on the merits of the work, as an appendix would no doubt be very [p. 10] instructive. He hopes the suggestion will suffice. Ma foi![16] Is he sane? Will she? Not if she knows herself!

What possessed him with the idea that I had any taste that way? Criticise one man to be criticised in turn by another? A laugh at my expense would annihilate me. No, no! I told him on Sunday that it was a sport I never indulged in. Think I'll get Anna to do it for me! What a jolly go! Wonder if she would hesitate? Miséricorde![17] Does the man mean to make fun of me? No, no, I'll not attempt such a display; yet there are several passages I am dying to mark. One in particular, speaking of the peculiarities of men, of how they are always more at ease when they have their hands employed, drawing confidence, and even conversation from a paper knife and book to tumble, a pair of scissors and a thread to snip, or even from imbibing the head of a cane [?], I am anxious to call his attention to. If I dared add to the list "or a cord and tassle to play with"! This nervous Mr Halsey is wearing out my pretty blue tassles that Frank admires so much; he says he can talk better when he dangles it. Think the hint might save it in future!

Friday night. Jan. 23d.

What a strange sensation is this, being alone! All have gone away; another dance is the attraction, and I now enjoy the pleasures, the delights of solitude, that I pretend so much to relish. Do I like being alone so much? Yes—sometimes! Nonsense! I like it *very* well. So delightful to shut one's eyes and recite aloud without fear of being overheard, or dream golden dreams without the dread of being disturbed; or better still, write page after page with none to cry "Put down that pen before you kill yourself" or read some favorite author as long as one chooses,

14. *Zaidee: A Romance* by the English novelist Margaret Oliphant.

15. Let us see.

16. Really!

17. Mercy on us!

without having the extinguisher placed over the candle as a night cap. Yes! I enjoy it hugely. It would have been positive pain to see them stay. They anticipate so much pleasure, and married and single looked so sweet and lovely, that it was almost like going myself, to look at them, so happy and smiling. Then, though I could not join them, it was so pleasant to make them wear this or that little article of mine that they fancied, to wonder if they were ever as becoming to me, and if I would ever, ever need them again. No, that part was not pleasant, but watching the girls was. My dear Miriam will be the handsomest there to night; she always is. I think I should die without Miriam; I like to think that I must go first.

If it was not for disturbing a dozen babies (more or less) I would try my guitar. Mother sent it like an angel, by Lilly and Charlie when they came down to see me on Tuesday, for she thinks this poor Sarah must be dreadfully low spirited, and wofully in need of consolation. [p. 11] Ah no! mother! It would be black ingratitude if I grew melancholy and unhappy! Because God has seen fit to afflict me, that would not justify me in complaining. Thank Heaven, *this* far I have not murmured, and with the blessing of God, I will keep a smile and cheerful word for those around me as long as He gives me strength. Would groans and tears diminish the pain I suffer?

I am particularly happy to day, for we have just heard from Brother for the first time since last July. And he is well, and happy, and wants us to come to him in New Orleans, so he can take care of us, and no longer be so anxious for our safety. If we only could—!

To be sure the letter is from a gentleman who is just out of the city, who says he writes at Brother's ernest request; still it is something to hear, even indirectly. One hundred and fifty dollars he encloses, with the request that mother will draw for any amount she wishes. Dear Brother, money is the least thing we need; first of all, we are dying for want of a home. If we could see ours once more!

During the time we have heard incidentally of Brother; of his having taken the oath of allegiance—which I am confident he did not do until Butler's October decree [18]—of his being a prominent Union man, of his

18. Sarah is probably referring to Butler's General Orders No. 76, issued September 24, 1862, which required those who had not sworn their allegiance to the Union to report to the nearest provost marshal with a descriptive list of all their property. They would then be given a certificate of registration showing them "claiming to be an enemy of the

being a candidate for the Federal Congress, and of his withdrawal; and finally of his having gone to New York and Washington, from which places he only returned a few weeks since. That is all we ever heard. A very few people have been insolent enough to say to me "Your brother is as good a Yankee as any." My blood boils as [I] answer "Let him be President Lincoln if he will, and I would love him the same." And so I would. Politics cannot come between me and my father's son. What he thinks right, Is right, for him, though not for me. If he is for the Union, it is because he believes it to be in the right, and I honor him for acting from conviction, rather than from dread of public opinion.

If he were to take up the sword against us to-morrow, Miriam and I at least, would say "If he thinks it his duty, he is right; we will not forget he is our father's child." And we will not. From that sad day when the sun was setting for the first time on our father's grave, when the great, strong man sobbed in agony at the thought of what we had lost, and taking us both on his lap put his arms around us and said "Dear little sisters dont cry; I will be father and brother too, now," he has been both. And we love him as such, dont we Miriam? He respects our opinions, we shall respect his!

I confess my self a rebel, body and soul. *Confess?* I glory in it! Am proud of being one; would not forego the title for any other earthly one! Though none could regret the dismemberment of our old Union more than I did at the time, though I acknowledge that there never was a more unnecessary war than this in the beginning, yet once in ernest, from the [p. 12] secession of Louisiana I date my change of sentiment. I have never since then looked back; forward, forward! is the cry; and as the Federal States sink each day in more appalling folly and disgrace, I grow prouder still of my own country and rejoice that we can no longer be confounded with a nation which shows so little fortitude in calamity, so little magnanimity in its hour of triumph.

Yes! I am glad we are two distinct tribes! I am proud of my country; only wish I could fight in the ranks with our brave soldiers, to prove my enthusiasm; would think death, mutilation, glorious in such a cause; cry "war to all eternity before we submit!" But if I cant fight, being

United States." Failure to register made them subject to fine or imprisonment at hard labor, or both, and to confiscation of their property. See *OR*, ser. I, 15:575–76.

unfortunately a woman, which I now regret for the first time in my life, at least I can help in other ways. What fingers could do in knitting and sewing for them, I have done with the most intense delight; what words of encouragement and praise could accomplish, I have tried on more than one bold soldier boy, and not altogether in vain; I have lost my home and all its dear contents for our Southern Rights, have stood on its deserted hearth stone and looked at the ruin of all I loved without a murmur, almost glad of the sacrifice, if it would contribute its mite towards the salvation of the Confederacy.

And so it did, indirectly; for the battle of Baton Rouge, which made the Yankees, drunk with rage, commit outrages in our homes that civilized Indians would blush to perpetrate, forced them to abandon the town as untenable, whereby we were enabled to fortify Port Hudson here, which now defies their strength. True they have reoccupied our town; that Yankees live in our house; but if our Generals said burn the whole concern, would I not put the torch to our home readily, though I love its bare skeleton still? Indeed I would, though I know what it is to be without one. Dont Lilly & mother live in a wretched cabin in vile Clinton while strangers rest under our father's roof? Yankees, I owe you one for that!

Well! I boast myself Rebel, sing Dixie, shout Southern Rights, pray for God's blessing on our cause, without ceasing, and would not live in this country if by any possible calamity we should be conquered; I am only a woman, and that is the way I feel. Brother may differ. What then? Shall I respect, love him less? No! God bless him! Union or Secession, he is always my dear, dear Brother, and tortures should not make me change my opinion.

Friday. Jan. 30th.

A whole week has past [*sic*] since I opened this book, a week certainly not spent in idleness, if not a very interesting one. For I have kept [to] my room almost all the time, leaving Miriam and Anna to entertain their guests alone. Even when Mr Halsey called on Sunday, I declined going down. Why, I wonder? I felt better than usual, was in a splendid humor for talking, yet—my excuses took my place, and I lay quietly in bed, dreaming by the fire light, and singing hymns to myself. Once in a while the thought would occur to me "Why dont I go down?" but it was always answered [p. 13] with a wry face, and the hymn went on. Yet I knew he had come expecting to see me.

On the table near me stood a bunch of snow drops that Miriam had culled for her *beloved* Capt Bradford. An idea struck me so suddenly that my voice died instantly. The spirit of mischief had taken possession of me. Laughing to my self, I caught them up, drew three long bright hairs from my head—they looked right *gold-dy* in the fire light—and tied them around the flowers—I thought I should never get to the end while wrapping them. Thus secured, a servant carried them into the parlor with "Miss Sarah's compliments to Mr Halsey." Poor Miriam's cry of surprise at finding her flowers thus appropriated reached my ears and caused me to laugh again. It *was* rather cool! But then it was better fun than going down. And then didn't it flatter his vanity! O men! you vain creatures! A woman would receive a whole bunch of hair and forty thousand bouquets without having her head turned; while you—

Well! I heard enough from Miriam to amuse me, at all events. And a day or two after, Capt. Bradford had a long story to tell her—what he called a good joke on Mr Halsey. Of how he had found him kissing three long bright hairs in rapture, and on asking where he got them, received as an answer—"From the God-blessed*est* little angel that ever wore long hair!" This *blessedest* little angel did not intend it as a souvenir, and is consequently annoyed about stories of three hairs, intended as a string, and nothing more, being wrapped in tissue paper and treasured up—so goes the tale—instead of being thrown in the fire as I certainly expected.

I kept [to] my room until Wednesday, when I left my self inflicted retirement, to go down to see Capt. Fenner & Mr Duggan; for by tacit consent the latter is always left to my care, and Miriam tells me he is rather neglected in my absence; so of course I made a sacrifice of my feelings in order to show him that his visits were appreciated by *me* at least. He had been out riding with Anna in the evening, and I fear both were dreadfully bored; he wanted to ride with Miriam, Anna prefered Capt. Fenner (both of whom were enjoying themselves ahead, not thinking of them) and so they did not have a very pleasant time. They tell me he had not had a word to say until I came down; certainly he looked relieved when he drew his chair next to mine and commenced to talk as though his tongue was rather glad to be exercised again.

And we certainly were having some fun, when after supper Anna introduced a pack of cards, and eagerly seconded by Miriam, suggested Euchre. If there is anything that I would pronounce a perfect nuisance, it is Cards. Not that I object to a sound game occasionally, when people are too stupid to think of anything more interesting, or to see just one or two couples dreadfully bored throw away an hour or two over tiresome paste board when they have nothing else to do; but I do think that when a party of rational young people [p. 14] cannot find amusement enough in music and conversation to make the evening pass pleasantly, they had better confess themselves fools—or better still—bring out the Cards, and that will save them the trouble of making the acknowledgement. I pronounce them a most intolerable nuisance, fit only for elderly people who like quiet, and silly young ones who have not sense enough to enjoy anything else.

Miriam would vote it a loss if she was excluded from the game, and Anna could not very well endure it herself; so I who despise cards, and pride myself on being able to stand what they could not, volunteered a most extraordinary sacrifice, and looked on while they played their intolerable nonsense, until tired of the everlasting "Trumps!" "Right Bower!" I seized a very learned article on the American War, and just as I finished the third column, Mr Duggan left the card table with a dolorously bored expression and once more commenced talking like a Christian. I saw but one effect produced by Cards, and that was that they put an end to all pleasure for the rest of the evening. If they had been intended to produce such a result, they succeeded admirably.

Ah me! In my rôle of invalid how many curious little by-plays I am present at! I can look on now; and have a better opportunity of judging than when I participated. Last night Anna and Miriam sat on my bed at twilight playing cards while I tried my guitar, when Capt. McClure, Major Spratley,[19] and Lieut. Duprés were announced. Quick,

19. Captain (later Major) James W. Spratley, an Alabamian, became chief quartermaster at Port Hudson early in 1863. See General Orders No. 12 issued by General Gardner on January 24, 1863, in General and Special Orders, Port Hudson, 1862–63, chap. 2, vol. 198, Record Group 109, National Archives.

down went the cards as they sprang to their feet to throw off their neat calicoes. Where was Miriam's comb, and grenadine, and collar and belt? Good gracious where was her buckle? On the bureau, mantle, washstand, or under them? Please move a moment, Anna! In such a hurry, do!

There was Anna: "Wait! I'm in a hurry too! Where is that pomatum? You Malvina! if you dont help me, I'll— There! take *that*, miss. Now fly around!" Malvina, with a faint dingy pink suddenly brought out on her pale sea green face, did fly around, while I, hushing my guitar in the tumult, watch each running over the other in silent amazement, wondering if order can come out of such confusion, and if the people down stairs were worth all that trouble.

Tired out with an extraordinary task I had finished that day, I lay quietly in bed until after supper. By the way I must not forget to record my industry. The General wanted two pair of socks knit for Howell, and paying me the, I confess, undeserved compliment of calling me the most reliable, asked me to knit one pair while the other two girls knit the other. Wednesday morning we commenced; at sunset I finished my first sock, leaving Anna just beginning to divide for the heel of her's, while Miriam's was about half way down the leg. That night Anna knit her heel in the parlor, in [p. 15] an unparalleled fit of industry, and Thursday as she threw off the stitches preparatory to beginning her foot, I threw on the first stitches for my second sock at a quarter to four. I held up my pair, finished not ten minutes after she finished her's. Not so bad for an invalid, as knitting in a horizontal position is a novel experience. Two socks to her one is not so very slow, either. As to Miriam, I had to finish her's today, she having grown desperately tired of knitting the mate to Anna's. Maybe the General did not praise my industry!

When I finally made my appearance in the parlor, it was with the conviction that I would have a dreadfully stupid time, and Capt. McClure too. However though at first I had both, soon only the last was left me. Some one suggested calling the Spirits, which game I had imagined "played out" long ago, and we derived a great deal of amusement from it. Six of us around a small table invoked them with the usual ceremony. There was certainly no tricks played; every finger was above the board, and all feet sufficiently far from the single leg to insure fair play. Every rap seemed to come exactly from the centre of the table, and was painfully distinct, though not loud. When asked if there was a writing medium present, it indicated Capt. McClure. I observed that he seemed averse to trying it, but yielded at length and took the pencil in his hand.

Our first question of course was how long before peace? Nine months was written. Which foreign nation would recognize us first? France then England—in eight months. Who was Miriam to marry? Capt. of a Battery. Who? we all shouted. "Capt. C. E. Fenner" was written again. When? In ten months. I believe Capt. McClure to be honest about it. He seemed to have no control over his hand, and his arm trembled until it became exceedingly painful. Of course I do not actually believe in Spiritualism; but there is certainly something in it one cannot understand; and Mrs Badger's experience is enough to convert one, alone.

Each was startled in turn by extraordinary revelations concerning themselves; Gibbes was to be transferred to the Trans Mississippi Department,[20] George would come home, and all the gentlemen had the name and address of future sweethearts written in full. The question was asked who will Sarah Morgan fall in love with? Every eye was on the pencil as a capital H was traced. As the "a" followed, I confess to a decided disgust at Spirits, and was about to beg it might be discontinued when the rest followed rapidly until in three separate line[s] appeared "Has not seen him yet" (here came an exclamation of surprise from Lydia and Miriam who knew how true it was, and even Gibbes looked astonished). "Captain, in Virginia.[21] Capt. Charles Lewis." A perfect buzz of comments followed; every one asked every one else if they knew any one by that name, and every one said no.

[p. 16] Gibbes was decidedly more interested than I. That odd "Has not seen him yet," expressing so exactly the fact that I pride myself upon, carried conviction in the truth of Spirits, *almost*. Who will she marry? asked Gibbes. (He has a pet belief, in which I encourage him, that I will never marry.) Again came the name as distinctly as before, of

20. Later note by Sarah, above the line: "(So he was—in a coffin, January 1864)." The Trans-Mississippi Department embraced those parts of the Confederacy west of the Mississippi River.

21. Later note by Sarah: "So he was (F. W. Dawson), Purcell's Battery, for a few hours."

Capt. Charles Lewis. When will she marry him? In June 1864 was the answer. I was to meet him in New Orleans. November followed after a period.

Of course the Spirits produced some slight commotion which made the time pass pleasantly until Miriam commenced to waltz with her Monsieur Deux temps. Then Captain McClure told me why he had been unwilling to try it; of how his father believed so strongly in it that he had very nearly been made crazy by it, and how he had sworn to abandon the practise of consulting them, seeing the effect produced. He did not believe in Spirits himself; but could not account for the influence he was under, when he saw his hand involuntarily write things he was totally unconscious of, himself. However he proposed that we two should have a private conversation with them, which I opened by asking when I should again see my home. I know he did not know anything about it; but on the paper appeared—"Five months have gone— five months more." It is *just* five months since I did see home. I think it was the 26th of Aug. that Charlie took me there.

He asked if he should ever marry. "Never. You will be jilted by the lady you love in Missouri, Miss Christina P." I pointed it out to him, as he happened to be looking at me when it was written. It surprised him into saying "Why I'm engaged to her!" I asked whose spirit was communicating with us. He was watching the dance when his hand wrote John McClure. I laughed and asked if there was such a person, pointing to the name. He looked actually sick as he said "Yes; my brother; he is dead." I had not the heart to talk of spirits again; so we took to writing poetry together, every alternate line falling to my lot. It made an odd jingle, the sentimental first line being turned to broad farce by my absurd second one; but still it was amusing.

Before that, the Spirits had told me an odd thing. Capt. McClure does not know Mr Halsey. They told me that the latter loved me, and just below, wrote "Heart of a friend," what ever that may mean. No; I do not believe in Spirits. Only wish I could; am more than willing to be converted. But there is certainly something that is not to be accounted for in it. Though of course I dont believe a word of what they said, particularly as far as my Capt. Lewis is concerned. You err, Spirits. The man I could marry does not exist. If he does, you are right in one respect: *I have not seen him yet*, which Heaven grant!

I looked in vain for any trace of the commotion which had [p. 17] disturbed the girls up stairs. Anna, smiling and simpering, looked the very personification of amiability as she prattled to Major Spratley (Ye gods and little fishes! what a name!) and her hands reposed so innocently in her lap that I was inclined to believe that she was not the same girl who had so unnecessarily slapped her little maid before going down. And stylish, lively Miriam—was she the same who had so completely upset the room to find that elegant toilette, and had so buried me under cast off skirts, cards, and dresses that Malvina, with her cheek still tingling with the slap of her ungrateful mistress, had to come to the rescue, and excavate me from the chaotic mass under which my *inhuman* sister had left me, before I could be visible? Mal and I should have sympathized;—only we didn't. She dressed me without the slightest difficulty occurring, while I had only an occasional Thank you to say, which was the extent of our conversation. She would break her neck for me, while strange to say, she would rather disobey Anna than to eat her dinner.

But while I silently commented on the girls' present appearance, the thought suddenly struck me "What if they were also speculating on me? Is there no other face for my sick room, or am I always the same?" Unable to answer, and fearing that they might know more funny things about me than I knew about them, I prudently refrained, remembering that people who live in glass house[s] should not throw stones. Besides, a little ebulition of temper occasionally is pardonable; and if Miriam was too excited to see I was overwhelmed, would not the arrival of her divine Alcée Duprès be a sufficient excuse for a first offense? Suppose I heard my Capt Lewis was down stairs, wouldn't I slap Mal, and Miriam too, in my excitement? Good Gwacious [*sic*]! What a row to make! Yes! after boxing my maid and pinching my sister (bless her honest eyes!) I dare say I'd skip down, and putting that same right hand in his, cry "Dearest Charley!" with the sweetest smile on lips that had just angrily cried "You ugly beast!"

Tuesday Feb. 3d.

Dont think I was in ecstacies Saturday night when Capt. Bradford and Mr Halsey were announced. Have been made much more happy in my life; but still as a matter of duty I made my appearance, and tried to look pleased. I had to do it in order to take the vanity out of

Monsieur about those three poor hairs, which vanity I found to be—disagreeable, to say the least. Didn't I cool him down when he alluded to it in a style I did not like? Think I can do pretty much as I please with "John" though of course it would never do to let him, or anyone else know it. "Discipline must be preserved." He is not a stupid man by any means; yet he says some dreadfully foolish things to me sometimes; *so* foolish that I dont like to tell on him because I know he has better sense and feels ashamed of it afterwards. And [p. 18] he is not so dreadfully bashful either; yet if I speak to him when he does not expect it, or if I make one of my brusque speeches which he thinks so very bold, the blood rushes to his face like a girl. Altogether he is very, very funny, and I cannot quite understand him—perhaps there is nothing to understand about him.

Miriam had her Captain in to entertain, so Mr Halsey was left to me. Anna soon found it a bore, and retired to bed, gradually followed by the others, until only Gibbes and mass 'Gene were left to play propriety. They seemed [to be] expiring from ennui, at which I was not astonished; for both the gentlemen seemed to prefer an undertone to carry on the conversation, which rendered it impossible for their remarks to reach the other side of the room, so they could not have been very well entertained. Before long to my unspeakable horror they fell asleep in their chairs, while we four had all the fun to ourselves during the slumbers of our two married gentlemen. Half past twelve had passed before Capt. Bradford suggested the propriety of returning to camp; I had begun to think that he meant to wait till breakfast. Gibbes roused himself in order to "speed the parting guests," and before they had mounted their horses fairly, picked me up in his arms and carried me up to my room without a moment's delay, thinking very properly that I had had enough to kill me for one evening.

Just after dinner on Sunday Mrs Badger ran up here calling out before she had entered the doorway "Sarah! Little girl, your dog's dead!" "What dog?" I asked in astonishment. "Why when a fellow rides five miles [on] such a rainy, horrid day to see a girl, *I*'d say he was gone, certain!" I cant say how it jarred on my nerves. It isn't, isn't true! and apart from that, there was the almost certainty of his having heard her. No wonder I did not want to go down! Hadn't I seen enough of him the night before? So I made up my mind that I would be invisible; but just at sunset, fancied having some fun, so I went down. Didn't I talk, laugh at, and tease him? And he took it so good naturedly, that it was only another inducement to ridicule him still more. Why does he blush so when I first talk to him? It is *so* foolish!

Yesterday Miriam took me to task about flirting; *think*! *Miriam* to reprove me for such a vice, her own peculiar weakness! I vow I am innocent of it; dont even know how it is done; and when I asked how people went about it, she said "Why, just as you did Mr Halsey Sunday night! The only difference is that you are a sly flirt, and I am an open one!" Indeed that is unfair! If I was a flirt, or had any taste that way, *wouldn't* I lead John Halsey a dance? Ignorant as I am, it would not be so very difficult even now! Only I have not the taste or courage for it. I cannot conceal my aversion when a gentleman shows his preference for me. When he comes to plain words it is because he wont take a silent hint; I would gladly save both the pain. But if I could make believe like Miriam, [p. 19] I know I'd have some fun! What a misfortune it is to be so *very* honest!

The General did me the meanest thing last night! He came gravely to my bedside, and after talking awhile about my visitor (they always call him mine) said "I have a request to make. Dont you engage your self, that is to say if you meant to say yes, without consulting your mother." Fancy the sensation of a modest young woman! "For heaven's sake General! dont jest that way!" I cried in the most unfeigned distress. "Jest? I am in sober ernest! I want you to remember what I say." Unfeeling General! I declare it is not modest to jest on such subjects! And this wicked Miriam sat there aiding and abetting him, enjoying my distress—for even if I do dislike Mr Halsey myself, I hate to hear people attribute such bad taste to him. And it isn't, isn't true! They may preach for a hundred years, and this tease of a Miriam may say what she will, but they cant make me believe this nonsense. He cares no more for me, than—I do for him; and everyone knows what that means! No! no! I must put an end to this! Yet how?

Feb 5th, Thursday night.

A letter from Sis has come to me all the way from California. How happy it made me, though written so long ago! Only the 30th of June! Sis has changed, changed. There is a sad, worn out tone in every line; it sounds old; as though she had lived years and years ago and was writing as though she were dead and buried long since. Sis, whose letters used to keep me in sunshine for weeks at a time! Well! no wonder she is sad. All these dreary years from home, with so faint a hope of ever again seeing it, and all these sorrows and troubles that have befallen us, combined, are not calculated to make her happy. But I wish she had kept her cheerful heart. Well, perhaps it is easier for us to be cheerful and happy knowing the full extent of our calamities, than it is for her, knowing so little, and having just cause to fear so much.

Courage! Better days are coming! and then I'll have many a funny tale to tell her of the days when the Yankees kept us on the qui vive,[22] or made us run for our lives. It will "tell" merrily; be almost as lively as those running days were. One of my chief regrets over my helplessness is that I will not be able to run in the next stampede. I used to enjoy it. O the days gone by, the dreary days when, cut off from our own people, and surrounded by Yankees, we used to catch up any crumb of news favorable to our side that was smuggled in town, and the Brunots and I would write each other little dispatches of consolation, and send them by little negroes! Those were dismal days. Yet how my spirits would rise when the long roll would beat, and we would prepare for flight!

O you mean Miriam! I had promised myself a long quiet evening with my Tennyson and this, and here you [p. 20] interrupt my plan! For Mr Halsey is down stairs; has been there more than an hour—almost two, for it is now after supper. I had resolved not to go down, dont like to be teased, and dont want to see him either. Yet while I lay on my pillows by the fireside just now, Miriam came running up. She said I must go, and gave so many good reasons, and drew such a picture of what he would think if I did not, that I gave a reluctant consent, and have sent for Mal to help me dress. Dont want to go! Meant to have such a quiet evening! But suppose he should attribute my non appearance to ill humor? That is worse than what Miriam suggested! Never! I'll martyrize myself rather than let him think me ill tempered!

Anna is in a dreadful one; so bad off that she has been telling stories (downright falsehoods) on Miriam. I had to play loudly on the guitar to keep from hearing her; I didn't want to know of such a contemptible

22. On the alert.

trait, but could not help suspecting it, from the tone of her voice, and have since had my suspicions confirmed. Yet Miriam tells me she met her with her amiable, honest, good natured face, and loving words, before Mr Halsey just now. I dont understand this. A hypocrite besides? O Sarah! you fool! How can she? Ask yourself how can *you*! Dont you know that in ten minutes you will meet Mr Halsey with a smile, and the same hand that just wrote "dont want to see him" will be extended to him in token of welcome? Is that honest? "Thou who sayest a man should not steal, doest *thou* steal?" Go down stairs, say "Mr Halsey, I dont like you *very* much, and wish you would not like me, because then I'd like you better; and please dont come so often, 'cause I am not at all glad to see you" and then I'll call you an honest woman, and make you judge over Anna.

Late—ever so late. Hypocrisy apart, had a delightful evening, and Mr Halsey was so agreeable, that when he left, and Gibbes was carrying me up stairs again, I beat the devil's tatoo on my dear brother's shoulder as I lay in his arms, and half way acknowledged to myself with an odd grimace that I *did* like Mr Halsey a little better!

Monday Feb. 9th 1863 Night

A letter from my dear little Jimmy! How glad I am, words could not express. This is the first since he arrived in England, and now we know what has become of him at last. While awaiting the completion of the iron clad gunboat to which he has been appointed,[23] like a trump, he has put himself to school, and studies hard, which is evident from the great improvement he already exhibits in his letter. How he raves about the Yankees! What bloody vengence [sic] he swears on them for the destruction of our home! I had to laugh at his intense hatred. Poor devils! what good would vengence do? Better leave them to God and their own conscience. Remorse would be torture enough, if they happen to be honest men. And he is [p. 21] is [sic] keeping a journal for me, the duck! *Won't* I prize it!

One extraordinary occurrence he mentions, which I shall transcribe

23. The cruiser *Georgia*, which was secretly being built for the Confederate navy. Jimmy boarded it at sea after it had sailed from Greenock.

as it relates to Spirits, being, I am afraid, almost willing to be converted
to the belief myself. Certainly if such a thing happened to me, I should
hardly dare doubt again. Jimmy is so honest and matter-of-fact in his
disposition as to place the supposition of the story being fictitious, or
the result of mere imagination, beyond belief. I would sooner doubt
the evidence of my own eyes, than his slightest word. He says, a few
evenings before, he was thinking of how absurd the belief (in spirits)
was, when suddenly it must have been the devil that prompted him, he
asked aloud "If there is a spirit in the room, let it rap."

Rap, rap, came from the corner. Again he repeated the request, when
the rapping recommenced violently. He says he wished to see if he
looked pale, or frightened, and walked to the glass, when what was his
horror at seeing not his own face but another's reflected there! He adds
he did not *run*, but just changed his base for his bed in a very short
time, a mere strategic movement. He laughs, but I should have felt
rather shaky about it. I called on the Spirits to rap for me this evening
when I was alone, but they would not come. I wonder why they are so
exclusive?

My delight at hearing from Jimmy is overcast by the bad news Lilly
sends of mother's health. I have been unhappy about her for a long
while; her health has been wretched for three months; so bad, that
during all my long illness she has never been with me after the third
day. I was never separated from mother so long before; and I am home
sick, and heart sick about her. Only twenty miles apart, and she with
a shocking bone felon in her hand and that dreadful cough, unable to
come to me, whilst I am lying helpless here, as unable to get to her.
I feel right desperate about it. This evening Lilly writes of her having
chills and fevers, and looking very, *very* badly. So Miriam started off
instantly to see her. My poor mother! She will die if she stays in Clinton, I know she will! And I cannot, cannot live without her. O God will
spare her to me; I pray he will! My dear dear mother what would life
be without you? I cant stand this. I must get to her by some means.

To hear that young scamp of a Jimmy talk of Lord this, and Lord
that, is a good joke. "My friends, Lord Dunmore and Lord Runfort [?]"
comes as naturally as possible. He talks of being out fox hunting with
them, when he was spending ten days at the Earl of Sheffield's—that
must have been a sly vacation, my young rascal! And his "Lady Maria

Fielding"! O Jimmy! Jimmy! Pray Heaven that all your kind friends and good fortune may not turn that dear head!

[p. 22] Sunday Feb. 15th. 1863.

Tired! Worn out! Feel as though I had been unburied and galvanized into a half way state of existence. This is thanks to the surprise party Friday night which has all but annihilated me with fatigue. I never anticipated an unusual amount of pleasure, that I was not most grievously disappointed. Consequently day before yesterday when we received at dinner time the intimation that we might expect a surprise that night, from the very visions of extraordinary pleasure that we all conjured up, I might have been satisfied of having a stupid time.

Fortunately Miriam returned from Clinton that morning; it would have been an intollerable bore without her; but even she could not save it from being rather stupid. At least it was dull to us, though the other young ladies present seemed to enjoy themselves. The fact of the matter is that "our set" was not present. Each family in the neighborhood has its peculiar one, but ours is conceded to be just a *little* superior to the others. Indeed we would not tolerate some of their favorites. So as the affair was got up among them, "our set" was necessarily left out, or rather out of the few invited, only half the number, the whole of two, came. Those two were fortunately favorites of mine—Capt. Fenner and Mr Duggan. If it had not been for them Miriam would have expired, whilst I would not have appeared at all.

As to the others who represented the genus Man, I had best not express my opinion about them. Late in the evening I ventured to whisper it to the General, and emboldened by his assent to every proposition, expressed it fully. I began with "General—I dislike Capt. McClure more and more every time I see him." "So do I!" exclained he as though he was rather glad to have a confident [*sic*]. I looked at the little absurdity dancing with all his soul—(no! that is not much! say with all his feet and arms and that will express his intense absorption in the arduous undertaking as being tremendous) and wondered how he could endure his own society. No wonder he is subject to such awful fits of "the blues"! Why I would think him pardonable for cutting his throat in one of his attacks. The strange lady he was dancing with, I ventured to pronounce ill tempered, which the General endorsed with a nod of his head which satisfied me I was right. A red faced, irritable, dissipated looking man was her vis-à-vis, with a modest, gentle, shy girl, the sweetest and most unaffected imaginable. A strange quartette, truly.

But there was one who disgusted me even more than did Mr Gwyn. He looked as though he was made of day before yesterday's soup, which had been thrown in the slop barrel when just half congealed. O the wretch of a man! He looked like a great rough bear, besides, when he danced with a pretty, doll faced girl. The couple strongly reminded me of the old story of Beauty & the Beast. Only I was sure that no powers of enchantment could bring a [p. 23] respectable man out of, or induce him to stay in such a form if he had a right to a more decent one.

"General, I think that the two gentlemen among our guests are decidedly Capt. Fenner and Mr Duggan. I would not give much for the others." A hearty assent was vouchsafed, and here our conversation was interrupted by the dance breaking up, and Mr Duggan approaching again to talk to me. I dont know what I would have done without him. Most probably I would have fallen asleep. For with the other individuals I would have nothing to do, and Capt. Fenner I cannot talk to. It is perfectly incomprehensible to me, but nevertheless most true. Perhaps it is because I am anxious not to appear a fool before him, that I invariably prove myself to be an extraordinary one. I become so easily confused, that the simplest word in the language escapes my recollection. I was so completely baffled by that most extraordinary of words— medium,—that I remained at a dead stand, in the most painful silence until he kindly suggested it, which made me silently lash myself and shriek inwardly "Fool! fool!" After that, I could not talk to him; I felt disgraced. Is "medium" a word seldom used by me? Why should I make a greater display of ignorance to Capt. Fenner than to any one else? I can talk enough to Mr Duggan, bless his honest face!

There was that horrid little Mrs McPhaul,[24] three feet high by two feet wide, simpering and giggling with all her silly little soul, and telling me she was sure I was having a dull time; "We never enjoy ourselves when our *particular* friends are absent. John will regret it very much too; but he has been over the river for several days." I was aware of that

24. The sister of John Halsey. In the 1860 census she is listed as the widow M. E. McPhaul, residing with her brother in Pointe Coupee Parish. Court records identify her as Mary Elizabeth McPhaul.

distressing fact already. Gibbes had taught his little boy[25] the lesson, and bringing him to my bed side before I commenced to dress, made him break the dread intelligence gently with his baby lips stammering "Sady—John Hawdy gine ober yibber." As I did not faint or scream, I hardly needed his sister's sympathy. I looked in amaze at her winks and nods with which she endeavored to give additional force to her meaning, and let the question "Are you fool or crazy?" appear very distinctly on my face. But still she simpered, giggled, nodded, winked, and said she was *very* sorry John could not be there; I would enjoy myself *so* much more. Evidently somebody is being fooled! It isn't *I* either!

Just then Mr Duggan laid his hand on my chair, and remarked he was going to wheel me to table, supper having just been announced. "Leave me here please, and as a *favor* take Mrs McPhaul!" I entreated. After a short demur he complied with my request, and I was left in peace with Mrs Carter for five whole minutes, at the end of which time he reappeared, bearing my supper in his own hands, like an angel. Mrs McPhaul could not have seen much of him during her repast!

I stood it until half past five o'clock in the morning. I was suffering, tired, and [p. 24] so weary! Ah me! I felt as though I should die of fatigue. Yet still they danced with as much spirit as ever, until it seemed that they would never leave off. I was so weak and tired that I could hardly summon energy to talk. Presently Mr Duggan, who had disappeared, reappeared with a fan and commenced fanning me gently. He is so kind! Such a tender, womanly heart that he has! He never says he is sorry for me; yet his manner shows more sympathy than the words of half the rest. So when he saw me sick and weary, and began to fan me with an air that said "Poor child! poor child!" at every wave of the fan, somehow, it made me feel sorry for myself, a sensation that does not often occur to me, and self pity threatened to bedew my eyes; but I shut them a moment or so, and when he said "This is too much for you; you must go up stairs" I opened them with a laugh, and the announcement that I meant to see the fun out. He said No; I said Yes; but he conquered, and I left them still dancing.

It was broad day before the girls came up, and found me lying still awake. Anxiety for mother, fears about my ultimate recovery which

25. Thomas Gibbes Morgan III, born November 2, 1860. He would die at the age of 12.

had been until now resolutely suppressed, kept me awake. I was too selfish too [*sic*] keep my fears from Miriam, so made her as miserable as I, about my blessed spine. Tears would come; it is hard to give up life at my age without a struggle. So my pillow grew wet—Heaven forgive me for the weakness; but I have *tried* to be patient and brave heretofore—and there I lay awake, awake, watching the slumbers of the others, and with unwinking eyes waiting for the breakfast bell to rouse the slumbering household, with a feeling of intense resignation after I once repressed the rising despair, [word lined through] almost indifferent as to whether I ever slept again.

But late in the evening when Will Pinkney came to see me (he has just returned home with his wife) I was myself again, and with him and Miriam sitting by my bed, spent a delightful evening. I was glad to see a gleam of his old self appear. We had such a pleasant, old time talk! Ah! bah! Twilight overtook me a while ago, and here comes the summons to go down to receive Mr Halsey! Dont know why I should martyrise myself! If I *must* though, here goes! What a bore!

Tuesday Feb. 17th.

I got the sweetest note and present last night! A splendid copy of Poe, beautifully illustrated, sent by—Col. Steadman! I confess to being slightly amazed. But the note was the crowning point to my delight. Dont know which I would rather have. One is so acceptable, being one of my favorites, the other so flattering, that really it is hard to tell, both chime so well together, whether either would be acceptable without the other.

Listen how it goes. [p. 25] Of course there is some kind of beginning, then follows: "Having the highest appreciation of your intellectual capacities and of the finer and deeper feelings of your heart, I would beg you to accept this copy of Edgar Poe's Poetical works as a slight testimonial of my highest regard and warmest friendship—hoping that during your painful illness you may find some consolation or recreation in some of Poe's ethereal productions. Ernestly hoping for your early recovery—" Well all that! It comes to an end of course. But isn't it as sweet as it is undeserved? And how unworthy you are of the praise, you only, Sarah, can fully know. This high minded, whole souled, honest Col. Steadman to be so deceived? Ah! he was laughing at my "intellectual capacity." Wonder if he knows I could not recall the word "medium" the other night? No matter! that wont prevent me from appreciating Poe, or Col. Steadman, either!

Lydia jumps rapidly to conclusions. I was looking over my favorite pieces while I handed Gibbes the note, when with her roguish brown eyes sparkling with mischief she asked if I would *marry* him if he addressed me! Really, my little sister, there are some questions too startling to answer! As to this one, I should like to pinch your plump arms by way of punishment. Dont marry me off to every man who is civil to me, or you will have your hands full.

"He" has not come yet. "*Aint*" he *going* to? I am sometimes tempted to ask. What is he doing all this time? If he had come before, I should not have been here—would not have gone to Port Hudson to gratify a whim of Miriam's and Anna's, consequently would not have been thrown just by Col. Steadman's camp, and ergo, my future husband is responsible for my misfortune, as it is only the result of his delay. O Wretch! what martyrdom you have caused me. One hundred days in this bed! Ingrate! Forlorn I languish, while at this moment he (Capt. Lewis) is doubtless swearing eternal devotion to some hale and hearty damsel who never had the misfortune to be pitched out of a runaway buggy![26] The ingratitude of these men! One of these days he will even have the cruelty to reproach me with my misfortune! And it is all his fault; why dont he come? Rather why did he not? For it is too late now. Nevermore! Nevermore! Ah! Capt. Lewis, Nevermore! "The dirges of my hopes, the melancholy burden bore, of Nevermore! of Nevermore!"[27]

Frank Enders has been with us all day. He staid with us last night, but I did not see him until this morning when he came up to say goodbye and vaccinate me at the same time. But the goodbye was not said until after dinner. He always says he cant tear himself away from Miriam and me under twenty four hours. So he spent the day sitting by [words lined through] talking to us. Really, this novel style of receiving visiters [words lined through].

26. Later note by Sarah: "(So he was! 1896)." Obviously she is referring to the man she married, Francis Warrington Dawson.

27. Echoes Edgar Allan Poe's *The Raven*.

[p. 26] Reposing is not quite to my taste, but dressing is rather a fatiguing task, and being carried down stairs is rather an alarming journey—altogether, it does not always pay; so as it is only Frank, I dont mind it so much, having tried it on half a dozen others, such as the Doctors, Will, and one or two others. There is Ned Badger who exclaimed "By Jove! I didn't know how pretty she was before!" in evident surprise at his discovery, when he paid me his first visit after his return from his regiment. All of them tell me that invalidism is wonderously becoming to me, particularly when reposing on my pillows; so why deny myself the pleasure of seeing an old friend from mere absurd scruples about etiquette, especially when one can combine perfect rest with the becoming?

Wednesday Feb. 18th.

Gibbes has gone back to his regiment. I cant say how dreary I felt when he came to tell me good bye. I did not mean to cry; but how could I help it when he put his arms around me and sobbed so bitterly. Gibbes loves his little sister. Dear brother, I have never deserved it! But he cried like a child—as though we were never to meet again; and I cried too, just because I knew what he was thinking. The tears of forty thousand women would not affect me as much as the single sob of a man. The former have nothing but tears to occupy them; but one expects such firm self control from the latter, that it is heartrending to see them give away to the impulse; it is like breaking up the fountains of the vasty deep. May heaven spare me the frequent repetition of the sight! I dont readily get over it.

Miriam has been laughing at Gibbes for two day[s] about what she calls his "conceit" about Col. Steadman's note. She complains that he is infinitely more flattered and pleased than I. Why should he not [be]? If I were conceited, it would argue that I was unaccustomed to such a thing; but if *he* was, it would prove that he was proud of his little sister, that is all. A dozen times he has walked in asking if I had torn it up yet. "*I'd* paste it in the book! Think! if he wrote it while talking to me, what it would have been if he had taken time to think about it, Suke!"[28] he says, pulling his tawny beard, and laughing quietly, half at me, half at

28. Gibbes's nickname for Sarah was Suke (Sook), sometimes spelled Sukey.

himself, and then tells me what a manly, quiet, rigid disciplinarian the Colonel is, as though that concerned me!

Sunday Feb. 22d. 1863

Mother has come to me! O how glad I was to see her this morning! And the Georgia project which I dared not speak of for fear it should be mere talk, and nothing more, is a reality—yes! we are actually going! I can hardly believe that such [p. 27] good fortune as getting out of that wretched Clinton really awaits us. Perhaps I shall not like Augusta either; a stranger in a strange city is not usually enchanted with everything one beholds; but still—change of scene—a new country—new people—it is worth while! Shall we *really* go? Will some page in this book actually record "Augusta, Georgia?" No! I dare not believe it! Yet the mere thought has given me strength within the last two weeks to attempt to walk. Learning to walk at my age! Is it not amusing? But the smallest baby knows more about it than I did at first. Of course I knew one foot was to be put before the other; but the question was how it was to be done, when they would not go? I have conquered that difficulty however, and can now walk almost two yards, if some one holds me fast. But O my unspeakable horror of walking alone! The fear of falling will probably retard my progress; but with the idea that every step takes me so much nearer to Georgia, I shall probably overcome that too.

Sunset. Will[29] has this instant left. Ever since dinner he has been vehemently opposing the Georgia move, insisting that it will cost me my life, by rendering me a confirmed cripple. He says *he* could take care of me, but no one else can, so I must not be moved. I am afraid his arguments have about shaken mother's resolution. Pshaw! it will do me good! I must go. It will not do to remain here. Twenty seven thousand Yankees are preparing to march on Port Hudson, and this place will certainly be either occupied by them, or burned. To go to Clinton is to throw myself in their hands, so why not one grand move to Augusta? Railroad travelling will not be half so hard on me as Yankees. And staying in Clinton will actually kill me.

Words cannot express the unutterable horror and intense hate I feel

---

29. Will Pinkney. Pinkney survived the war, but died young. See death notice in New Orleans *Daily Picayune*, November 13, 1875, p. 4.

for that place. Yet it is just my fate. O my prophetic soul, bright as the prospect now is, you will never reach Georgia! As soon as you arrive in that blessed Clinton, obstacle on obstacle will arise, and the project [will] be quietly laid on the shelf. Clinton is death to me; yet I feel that there my journey will end. And the disappointment will kill me, if that vile spot is to be my future residence. Well! if I feel so keenly the anticipated disappointment, what will the real one be? I am afraid I shall lose my temper in my despair. Anything, except a life in Clinton! And there my journey will end! I feel like gnashing my teeth at the thought. In the mean time, let us go down and receive *that* Mr Halsey and Capt. Fogg.[30]

[p. 28] Monday Feb. 23d.

Here goes! News has been received that the Yankees are already packed, ready to march against us at any hour. If I was up and well, how my heart would swell with exultation. As it is, it throbs so with excitement that I can scarcely lie still. Hope amounts almost to presumption at P. Hudson. They are confident that our fifteen thousand can repulse twice the number. Great God!—I say it with all reverence—if we could defeat them! *If* we could scatter, capture, annihilate them! My heart beats but one prayer—Victory! Victory! I shall grow wild repeating it. In the mean time though, Linwood is in danger. This dear place, my second home; its loved inhabitants; think of their being in such peril! O I shall cry heartily if harm comes to them! But I must leave before. No use of leaving my bones for the Yankees to pick. Better sing Dixie in Georgia. To-morrow, consequently, I go to that earthly paradise, Clinton, thence to be reshipped (so goes the *present* programme) to Augusta in three days. And no time for adieux!

Wonder who will be surprised, who vexed, and who will cry over the unforseen separation? Not a single "good bye"! Nothing—except an old brass button that Mr Halsey gave me as a souvenir in case he should be killed in the coming assault! It is too bad! Ah! Destiny! Destiny! Where do you take us? During these two trying years, I have learned to feel myself a mere puppet in the hands of a Something that takes me

30. A Captain Fogg appears on Port Hudson rosters for February and March 1863 in connection with duties performed for General Beall, General John Gregg, and General S. B. Maxey. See chap. 1, vol. 106, Record Group 109, National Archives.

here, to day, to-morrow there, always unexpectedly, and generally very unwillingly, but at last lands me somewhere or other, right side up with care, after a thousand [word lined through] troubles and distresses. The hand of Destiny is on me now; where will it lead me?

Tuesday [February] 24th.

Meeting Miriam by mere accident on the road last evening, and hearing of our surprising journey to Georgia, Mr Halsey came to spend a last evening with us, and say good bye. What a deluge of regrets, hopes, fears, etc! Perfectly overwhelming. Why had I not told him of it the night before? All our friends would be so disappointed at not having an opportunity of saying good bye. If the Yankees would only postpone their attack so he might accompany us! But no matter; he would come on in two months, and meet us there. And would we not write to him?

Thank you! Miriam may, but I shall hardly do so! We had such a pleasant evening together, talking over our trip. Then we had a dozen songs on the guitar, gay, sad, and sentimental, [p. 29] then he gave me a sprig of jessamine as a keepsake, and I ripped open my celebrated running bag to get a real *for true* silver five cents—a perfect curiosity in these days—which I gave him in exchange, and which he promised to wear on his watch chain. He and Miriam amused themselves examining the contents of my sack and laughing at my treasures, the wretches! Then came—Good-bye. I think he was sorry to see us go. Well! he ought to miss us! Ah! these farewells! To day I bid adieu to Linwood. "It may be for years, and it may be forever!"[31] *This* good bye will cost me a sigh.

Wednesday Feb. 25th.

Here we are still, in spite of our expectations. Difficulty on difficulty arose, and an hour before the cars came, it was settled that mother should go to Clinton and make the necessary arrangements, and leave us to follow in a day or two. Two days more! Miriam no more objected than I did, so mother went alone. Poor Miriam went to bed soon after, *very* ill. So ill that she lay groaning in bed at dusk, when a stir was heard in the hall below, and Col. Steadman, Major Spratley, and Mr

31. Julia Crawford, *Kathleen Mavourneen.*

Dupré were announced. Presto! Up she sprang, and flew about in the most frantic style, emptying the trunk on the floor to get her prettiest dress, and acting as though she had never heard of pains and groans. When we leave, how much I shall miss the fun of seeing her and Anna running over each other in their excitement of dressing for their favorites! Anna's first exclamation was "Aint you glad you didn't go!" and certainly we were not sorry, from mere compassion; for what would she have done with all three?

If I laughed at their extra touches to their dresses, it did not prevent me from bestowing unusual attention on my own. And by way of bravado, when I was carried down, I insisted on Mrs Badger lending me her arm, to let me walk in the parlor and prove to Col. Steadman that in spite of his prophecies I was able to take a few steps at least. Such a surprised set of faces as I made my bow! The Colonel sprang to his feet to congratulate me and shake hands, and the others came forward to follow his example, and I felt my face flush with my extraordinary achievement as I sunk in the nearest chair. Miriam was absorbed in her dear Alceé, or Armété as Mass 'Gene calls him, Anna appropriated by Major Spratley, and the Colonel left exclusively to me, so I hope we were all satisfied; certain it is that I did not envy either of them. What they can see to admire in Monsieur Deux temps, I cannot imagine. Stout (though graceful, I confess) with a good looking, rather dull face, and [p. 30] altogether rather a heavy expression, I cannot appreciate fully the charms of this Adonis and watch them go crazy, perfectly unmoved. As to Major Spratley—Anna is welcome to him.

I believe I am the greatest fool in the world. Will I never be a woman? I had no sooner got settled in my chair, than a feeling of the most painful embarrassment came over me, which came near suffocating me. In vain I attempted to talk to Col. Steadman; every answer was at random, and the consciousness increased my misery. Fortunately supper put an end to my sufferings, and with a desperate effort I conquered the mauvaise honte which was fairly crushing me, and managed to talk collectedly to the Colonel, who was again by me at table.

The conversation turned upon our trip to Georgia, upon which he evinced some slight surprise. "Tell me what you think of it" I asked, thinking, with some reason, that it would be a relief to him to express his opinion, which I saw in his face. No danger of those steadfast, firm, honest, deep, grey eyes evading a question! They look to me as true as Harry's. He fixed them on mine, until I felt them looking almost through me, and answered with a peculiar emphasis that startled me "Perfectly outrageous!" I had expected a candid answer, but not one so abrupt, but I laughed, and he went on: "You cannot intend committing such a rash act. I had hoped to see you restored to the world and your admiring friends"—(here my lip twitched involuntarily; maybe they are not as numerous as he supposes!) "But your fate is sealed if you undertake such a journey; it will cost you your life. I beg of you to think of it again."

He talked until I was almost disheartened about the move. Arguments without number he brought to prove the danger, and at last I grew so undecided and uneasy that I hardly knew whether I prefered dying by inches in Clinton or taking the risks of a journey to Georgia. Imagine how preoccupied I was, when I say that I did not mind it when the wretch caught my beautiful dress on his spur and tore the most heartrending gash—a rent that absolutely appalled me this morning when its magnitude fully struck me. Pshaw! Spurs after all are not such graceful things! In these, at least I have not discovered the music that Capt. Fenner jingles out of his. These are only engines of destruction. "Well! 'tis well that I should bluster"—having been so amiable about it at the time! My revenge is accomplished now.

I rather conquered my timidity after that, and managed to come out of my shell long enough to bask in the sunshine of conversation. It was not so difficult to take my share [end of p. 30; the two pages of the diary that follow are unnumbered and the top half of each is missing] of my disagreeable [words missing] me to feel once more "The hand of Douglass is his own"—instead of Col. Steadman's, and added considerably to my comfort, though I felt as though I was putting wicked ideas in his head about it. His last words "You *wont* go, will you? Think once more!" sent me up stairs wondering, thinking, undecided and unsatisfied, hardly knowing what to do, or what to say. Every time I tried to sleep, those calm, deep, honest grey eyes started up before my closed ones, and that ernest "You *wont* go, will you? Think once more!" rang in my ears like a solemn warning.

Hopes of seeing Georgia grew rather faint that night. Is it lawful to risk my life? But is it not better to lose it while believing that I have still a chance of saving it by going, than to await certain death calmly and unresisting in Clinton? I'd rather die struggling for this life, this beautiful, loved, blessed life that God has given me! When the hour comes, I shall, with His help, give it up without a murmur; but now— away from home, from Sis, from the boys—! "Spare me a while! Lift up my drooping brow! I am content to die—But Oh! not now!" Yes I am, whenever He calls. God have mercy on me—God forgive me— God take me to thy holy rest! [unnumbered page; top half missing] knowledge?

I look back on the past, and shake my head. Will experience bring it? No; there is a moral blindness weighing down my mental eyes so that I cannot read the lessons so plainly written by past experience, and grow no wiser, no better from its teachings. I will Never be any wiser, Never any better. And yet "I have immortal longings within me"![32] It is better not to be, than to remain stagnant. I can never remember feeling differently from what I do now. At eight, I felt the same strange, un-accountable shyness, and shrinking, even sometimes from those that are nearest and dearest to me, that I do now. I was the same shallow, unimpassioned creature, with all my feelings and thoughts on the sur-face, all reflected in my face, for which I was consequently supposed to be *very* deep and far sighted by scheming people who said "If so much is on the surface, how much more must be below!"

Perhaps this believing that I was so simple, and so easily read, made me think it less necessary to express my opinions, as they must, I thought, be easily seen. For to this hour I can never rid myself of the feeling that I am made like glass, I am not speaking exaggeratingly, or figuratively. I feel as though made of clear, transparent material in reality, so that every throb, every wish of my heart could be open. Espe-cially when anyone looks at me fixedly, [p. 31] with their eyes on mine, I feel like chrystal; as though they saw all the workings of my brain, and read the half formed thought as soon as I. This makes me think it useless to repeat what they must already see, and so by reserving my opinions under this delusive belief, earn the reputation of being secretive, and deep, O *so* deep! under that innocent face of mine.

32. Shakespeare, *Antony and Cleopatra.*

This is the way some people judge. What a world of meaning they find where there is hardly a passing thought! What a hypocrite I must be to deny the hypocrisy of the world! How am I to know whether the world is made up of hypocrites or not? My life has been spent almost entirely at home, and there, certainly I could not learn the lesson. Let the world be good or bad; what matters it to me? My life has had very little to do with it, and promises gloomily to have still less.

Give me my home, my old home once more—place me where my dear father can show me the right from wrong, and laying his beautiful hand on my head say those words so frequent then, but which I would almost give my life to hear now—"God bless my little daughter"—give me back Harry, O give me my noble brother again! let me hear his words of praise and encouragement, let me feel his dear hand in mine, and his ernest eyes looking into my very soul once more—give me Harry to love me and be proud of me—and with the blessings I have now, what more could I wish? What would the opinion of the world matter to me? O my home, my home! I could learn to be a woman there, and a true one, too. Who will teach me now?[33]

March 10th. Tuesday.

My darling little brother's eighteenth birth day. Wonder if he is thinking of us, and remembers it? I always feel nearer Sis on such anniversaries; she and I pay more attention to them than the others. So to day I feel as though she were looking over my shoulder. Mustn't abuse her, for fear she is listening, then. Col. Steadman had knocked Georgia completely out of my head, and for three days I have had a nervous fever thinking of a probable sojourn in Liberty,[34] when to day a letter from Gibbes knocks the original idea in again, and I breathe once more. Heaven only knows our final destination. Because the mere thought of Liberty makes me sick, of course I'll land there before many days are over. Think I'll be sorry to leave Linwood, which has been my more than home in these days of trouble. And all our "admiring

33. The following day Sarah returned to this entry and wrote in the space remaining on the line: "John Halsey. Aged 30. 26th Feb. 1863."

34. Liberty, Mississippi, in the county adjoining East Feliciana Parish.

friends"! What a heartrending separation! Frank says he cant spare us; [we] mustn't go. All unite in lamenting our departure, for Miriam and I are wonderous favorites about. Wednesday we leave.

Thus far had I gone—I had so many nice things to say, which are now, alas, knocked for ever from my [p. 32] head—when news came that the Yankees were advancing on us, and were already within fifteen miles.[35] The panic which followed reminded me forcibly of our running days in B.R. Each one rapidly threw in trunks all clothing worth saving, with silver and valuables to send to the upper plantation. I sprang up, determined to leave instantly for Clinton so mother would not be alarmed for our safety, but before I got half way dressed Helen Carter came in, and insisted on my remaining, declaring that my sickness and inability to move would prove a protection to the house, and save it from being burned over their heads. Put on that plea, though I have no faith in melting the bowels of compassion of a Yankee, myself, I consented to remain as Miriam urgently represented the dangers awaiting Clinton. So she tossed all we owned in our trunk to send to mother as hostage of our return, and it is now awaiting the cars.

My earthly possessions are all reposing by me on the bed at this instant, consisting of my guitar, a change of clothes, running bag, cabas, and this book. For in spite of their entreaties, I would not send it to Clinton, expecting those already there to meet with a fiery death—though I would like to preserve those of the most exciting year of my life. They tell me that this will be read aloud to me to torment me, but I am determined to burn it if there is any danger of that. Why I would die with out some means of expressing my feelings in the stirring hour so rapidly approaching. I shall keep it by me.

Such bustle and confusion! Every one hurried, anxious, excited, whispering, packing trunks, sending them off, wondering negroes looking on in amazement until ordered to mount the carts waiting at the door, which is [sic] to carry them too away. How disappointed the Yankees will be at finding only white girls instead of their dear sisters and brothers whom they love so tenderly! Sorry for their disappoint-

35. The day before, Union cavalry attacked Confederate pickets at the bridge across Monte Sano Bayou four miles north of Baton Rouge. General Banks's advance on Port Hudson did not, however, begin until March 13, and Banks ordered a retreat two days later.

ment! They say they are advancing in overwhelming numbers. That is nothing, as long as God helps us, and from our very souls we pray His blessing on us in this our hour of need. For myself, I cannot yet fully believe they are coming. It would be a relief to have it over. I have taken the responsibility of Lydia's jewelry on my shoulders, and hope to be able to save them in the rush which will take place. Down at the cars Miriam met Frank Enders, going to Clinton in charge of a car full of Yankees, deserters who came into our lines. [p. 33] He thinks just as I do, that our trunks are safer here than there. Now that they are all off, we all agree that it was the most foolish thing we could have done.

These Yankees interfere with all our arrangements. I am almost ashamed to confess what an absurdly selfish thought occurred to me a while ago. I was lamenting to myself all the troubles that surround us, the dangers and difficulties that perplex us, thinking of the probable fate that might befall some of our brave friends and defenders in P. Hudson, when I thought too of the fun we would miss. Horrid, was it not? But worse than that, I was longing for something to read, when I remembered Frank told me he had sent to Alexandria for Bulwer's "Strange Story"[36] for me, and then I unconsciously said "How I wish it would get here before the Yankees!" I am *very* anxious to read it, but confess I am ashamed at having thought of it at such a crisis. So I toss up the farthing Frank gave me for a keepsake the other day, and say I'll try in future to think less of my own comfort and pleasure.

Poor Mr Halsey! what a sad fate the pets he procures for me meet! He stopped here just now on his way some where, and sent me a curious bundle with a strange story, by Miriam. It seems he got a little flying squirrel for me to play with (must know my partiality for pets) and last night while attempting to tame him, the little creature bit his finger, whereupon he naturally let him fall on the ground, (Temper!) which put a period to his existence. He had the nerve to skin him after the foul murder, and sent all that remains of him out to me to prove his original intention. The softest, longest, prettiest fur, and such a duck of a tail! Poor little animal couldn't have been larger than my fist. Wonder if its spirit will meet with that of the little bird which flew heavenward with all that pink ribbon and my letter from Mr Halsey?

36. Novel by Bulwer Lytton published in 1862.

I declare I am indebted to my friends for all the kind and flattering messages they send. Some people fear it may turn my head. Pas si bête![37] Dont I know if it had not been for that unlucky toss out of the buggy which has rendered me "an interesting invalid" I would never have acquired the reputation of being a ———? Wont say what; ashamed to expose their folly. Anna says she'd *break* her back to be loved, admired, petted, and talked of as I am. Silly thing! I'd give all to be myself once more. Flattery cant supply the place of a back bone to *me;* besides, it palls wofully on the moral palate. Shockingly conceited to mention this, but Miriam has just been asking me if I was conscious of what a favorite I was among the gentlemen, and telling me so many things, that I—feel like a fool.

[p. 34] Saturday March 14th. 5 o'clock P.M.

They are coming! The Yankees are coming at last! For four or five hours the sound of their cannon has assailed our ears. There! that one shook my bed! O they are coming! God grant us the victory! They are now within four miles of us, on the big road to B.R.[38] On the road from town to Clinton, we have been fighting since daylight at Redbridge, and have been repulsed. Fifteen gunboats have passed Vicksburg, they say. It will be an awful fight. Gant[39] badly beaten at Redbridge. No matter! with God's help we'll conquer yet! Again! the report comes nearer. O they *are* coming! Coming to defeat, I pray God.

Only we seven women remain in the house. The General left this morning, to our unspeakable relief. They would hang him, we fear, if they should find him here. 'Mass' Gene has gone to his company. We are left alone here to meet them. If they *will* burn the house, they will

37. I am not such a fool!

38. Banks's army was advancing up the Bayou Sara Road. His tactic was to create a diversion while Admiral Farragut got his ships past the guns that commanded the river from the bluffs at Port Hudson.

39. Lieutenant Colonel George Gantt, 9th Tennessee Cavalry Battalion.

have to burn me in it. For I cannot walk, and I know they shall not carry me. I'm resigned. If I *should* burn, I have friends and brothers enough to avenge me. Create *such* a sensation! Better than being thrown from a buggy—only I'd not survive to hear of it!

Letter from Lilly to day has distressed me beyond measure. Starvation which threatened them seems actually at their door. With more money than they could use in ordinary times, they can find nothing to purchase. Not a scrap of meat in the house for a week, no pork, no potatoes, fresh meat obtained *once* as a favor, and poultry and flour, articles unheard of. Besides that, Tiche crippled, and Margret very ill, while Liddy has run off to the Yankees. Heaven only knows what will become of them. The other day we were getting ready to go to them (Thursday) when the General disapproved of my running such a risk, saying he'd call it a d—— piece of nonsense, if I asked what he thought, so we remained. They will certainly starve soon enough without our help; and yet—I feel we should all be together still.

That last superfluous word is the refrain of Gibbes's song that is ringing in my ears, and that I am chanting in a kind of ecstacy of excitement—"Then let the cannon boom as it will, We'll be gay and happy still—" And we will be happy in spite of Yankee guns! Only— my dear This, That and the Other, at P. Hudson, how I pray for your safety! God spare our brave [p. 35] soldiers, and lead them to victory! I write, touch my guitar, talk, pick lint, and pray so rapidly that it is hard to say which is my occupation. I sent Frank some lint the other day, and a bundle of it for Mr Halsey is by me. Hope neither will need it![40] But to my work again!

Half past One o'clock A.M. It has come at last! What an awful sound! I thought I had heard a bombardment before; but Baton Rouge['s] experience was child's play compared to this.[41] At half past eleven came the first gun—at least the first *I* heard, and I hardly think it could have commenced many moments before. Instantly I had my hand on

40. The lint was used to dress wounds.

41. What Sarah heard was the fire from the Confederate river batteries and the ships of the Union fleet as Farragut attempted to pass Port Hudson. Two of the vessels made it past; the others were forced to fall back. Colonel Steedman, watching from the bluffs, would remember it as "the grandest, most sublime and terrible scene of my life." Steedman to his son George F. Steedman, June 1, 1891, letter in *Civil War Times Illustrated* Collection, U.S. Army Military History Institute, Carlisle Barracks, Pa.

Miriam, and at my first exclamation, Mrs Badger and Anna answered. All three sprang to their feet to dress, while all four of us prayed aloud. Such an incessant roar! And at every report the house shaking so, and we thinking of our dear soldiers, the dead, and dying, and crying aloud for God's blessing on them, and defeat and overthrow to their enemies. That dreadful roar! I cant think fast enough. They are too quick to be counted. We have all been in Mrs Carter's room, from the last window of which we can see the incessant flash of the guns, and the great shooting stars of flame, which must be the hot shot of the enemy. There is a burning house in the distance, the second one we have seen to night. For Yankees cant prosper unless they are pillaging honest people. Already they have stripped all on their road of cattle, mules and negroes—Like unto like—hope they like their companions.

Gathered in a knot within and without the window, we six women up here watched in the faint star light the flashes from the guns, and silently wondered which of our friends were lying stiff and dead, and then shuddering at the thought, betook our selves to silent prayer. I think we know what it is to "wrestle with God in prayer"; we had but one thought. Yet for women, we took it almost too coolly. No tears, no cries, no fear, though for the first five minutes every body's teeth chattered violently. Mrs Carter had her husband in Fenner's battery, the hottest place if they are attacked by the land force, and yet to my unspeakable relief she betrayed no more emotion than we who had only friends there. We know absolutely nothing; when does one ever know anything in the country? But we presume that this is an engagement between our batteries and the gunboats attempting to run the blockade.

Firing has slackened considerably. All are to lie down already dressed; but being in my night gown from necessity, I shall go to sleep, though we may expect at any instant to hear the tramp of Yankee cavalry in the yard.

[p. 36] Sunday March 15th.

To my unspeakable surprise, I waked up this morning and found myself alive. Once satisfied of that, and assuring myself of intense silence in the place of the great guns which rocked me to sleep about half past two this morning, I began to doubt that I had heard any disturbance in the night, and to believe I had written a dream within a dream, and that no bombardment had occurred; but all corroborate my statement, so it must be true, and this portentous silence is only the calm before the storm. I am half afraid the land force wont attack. We can beat them if they do; but suppose they lay seige [*sic*] to P. Hudson and starve us out? That is the only way they can conquer. We hear nothing still that is reliable.

Just before daylight there was a terrific explosion which electrified every one save myself. I was sleeping so soundly that I did not hear anything of it, though Mrs Badger says that when she sprang up and called me, I talked very rationally about it, and asked what it could possibly be. Thought that I had ceased talking in my sleep. Miriam was quite eloquent in her dreams before the attack, crying aloud "See! see! what do I behold?" as though she were witnessing a rehersal [*sic*] of the scene to follow.

Later. Dr Kennedy who, just passed through, and was within the fortifications last night, brings news which is perhaps reliable, as it was obtained from Gardener.[42] It was as we presumed, the batteries and gunboats. One we sunk, another, the Mississippi, we disabled so that the Yankees had to abandon and set fire to her,[43] thirty nine prisoners falling in our hands. It was her magazine that exploded this morning. Two other boats succeeded in passing, though badly crippled.[44] Our batteries fired gallantly. Hurrah! for Col. Steadman! I know his was by no means the least efficient!

Clinton they say will inevitably be sacked. Alas for mother and Lilly! What can we do? The whole country is at the mercy of the Yankees as long as Gardener [*sic*] keeps within the fortifications. Six miles below here they entered Mr Newport's,[45] pulled the pillow-cases from the beds, stuffed them with his clothes, and helped themselves generally.

42. Major General Franklin (Frank) Gardner, the officer in command at Port Hudson. A native of New York and a West Pointer, Gardner had commanded a brigade at Shiloh and later participated in the Confederate invasion of Kentucky. He arrived at Port Hudson late in December.

43. The *Mississippi* was the only ship lost. The famous old sidewheeler that had carried Admiral Matthew Perry to Japan ran aground and had to be abandoned. Later she drifted downstream burning and disappeared in an explosion that could be heard for more than fifty miles.

44. Neither the *Hartford* nor the *Albatross* was badly damaged, though the *Hartford* lost one man killed and two wounded, and the *Albatross* one killed.

45. Simpson W. Newport.

What can we expect here? To tell the truth I should be disappointed if they did not even look in at us, on their marauding expedition.

March 17th.

On dit the Yankees have gone back to B.R., hearing we had [p. 37] sixty thousand men coming down after them. I believe I am positively disappointed! I *did* want to see them soundly thrashed! The light we thought was another burning house was that of the Mississippi. They say the shrieks of the men when our hot shells fell among them, and after they were left by their companions to burn, were perfectly appalling.

Another letter from Lilly has distressed me beyond measure. She says the one chicken and two dozen eggs Miriam and I succeeded in buying from the negroes by prayers and entreaties, saved them from actual hunger; and for two days they had been living on one egg apiece and some corn bread and syrup. Great Heaven! has it come to this? Nothing to be bought in that abominable place for love or money. Where the next meal comes from, nobody knows. Father, wife and children to suffer this! No wonder I cried in my dreams Sunday "I curse the day I ever saw Clinton!" So I would, if it would only get mother and Lilly out of it. I implore such a blessing as would bring down fire and brimstone on that meanest spot of the whole earth! I feel that the day we entered it we lost caste.

Mother in her state of health to endure privation of the most necessary articles to sustain life! Miriam sat down and had a cry. I tried to think how we could get out of it, but see no way as long as Lilly is unprovided with a home elsewhere; and it seems as though Charlie is not finding one very rapidly. Brother, Sis, and Jimmy feasting in strange countries while they are actually starving here! This war if it is ever over, will make gluttons of us all.

One cant help regretting one's accustomed food. Last Sunday, being rainy and dismal generally, gave us all an intense longing, after some wonderful delicacies of old. Lydia, lying by me, sighed for a single oyster; Miriam thought some fruit would complete her happiness; Anna talked most pathetically of the delights of roast chicken, while I thought that a piece of bread, and a cup of coffee would be the greatest treat in the world. Words cannot express how I miss those two articles. Yet if it was put to the vote, "Corn bread in the confederacy, or wheat in the Union," I think I'd cry "Sawdust and Independence for ever!" Yet I cant help regretting the days of spunge [*sic*] cake and ice cream, to say nothing of more ordinary things. Pshaw! I am allowing my invalid's capricious appetite to make me think too much about such things. I am disgusted at having mentioned it.

[p. 38] Wednesday March 18th

Miriam [words lined through]. Gibbes will be twenty eight on the 21st inst, Charlotte ten on the same day, Susie[46] thirteen on the 24th, and there the anniversaries for this month end. Enough of them, certainly.

Mr Halsey came out last evening about four o'clock to see us once more before the fun begins; for the rumor this morning is that the Yankees are advancing again. He brought me a letter he had written me, saying he meant to post it, but thought it would be a better excuse to bring it himself; and I did not object to the arrangement; for verily the probability of his being knocked on the head in the coming attack has almost removed my prejudice against him. If he is really killed, I will doubtless persuade myself that I always did like him. So I would, if they let me alone; but sometimes I hate him.

This practice of teasing young ladies about the attention of gentlemen is inexpressibly shocking to me. Besides the bad taste displayed, on young and inexperienced girls it has a most injurious effect, making them believe in an affection which does not exist save in the imagination of the third party, and in many instances, I venture to say, has caused many a warm hearted, confiding girl, to bestow her love where it was uncalled for and unappreciated. This has come several times under my own observation; and often I have wondered if there was no remedy for this social torment. Delicacy of feeling, or one touch more of refinement might remove the annoyance; but these two virtues are not generally diffused, and the evil spreads.

Mind, this is not an appeal in behalf of my own unrequited affections, a plaintive cry from my own harrowed soul; I have no affections to bestow, consequently they have never been trifled with. To my shame be it said, "I still rove in maiden meditation fancy free."[47] So certainly I have no cause to complain of a grievance that has never assailed me.

46. Sarah's nieces Charlotte Morgan and Susie Emily Drum.
47. Shakespeare, *A Midsummer-Night's Dream.*

But I feel keenly the injury inflicted on others younger, more impulsive, and more susceptible than myself, and tremble to think that nothing but a matter of fact nature, and the peculiarity of feeling an instinctive aversion for those who profess, or are supposed to do more than admire me, have saved me from perhaps bestowing my gushing affections where they are equally unthought of, and unvalued. Thus far I have escaped; but if I had been susceptible to the insiduous [sic] insinuations, more than once I have been placed in the dangerous situation from which only common sense and a naturally reserved disposition has heretofore saved me. But all girls are not so [p. 39] stony hearted; and wo [sic] to the one who gives away under such circumstances to her first rêve de jeune fille![48]

It will be seen from this that my heart is still safe and untouched. If it was not, I could not talk of it this way. After all, what has this absurd dissertation to do with the visit I commenced speaking of? Nothing at all, as far as I can see, except that our little world has unanimously agreed in making John Halsey over to me, body and soul, and I dont like even the reputation of being his captor, and in consequence of being unmercifully teased about him, I have grown in the belief that the said practise of teasing is almost indelicate under such circumstances, and have accordingly entered a vehement protest against it, in the Court of Love.

Au reste,[49] what is it to me whether he cares for me or not, so long as I never think of him, except when spoken of? No woman has a right to place any construction on a gentleman's attentions, or believe he loves her until he actually falls on his knees and cries "Jane! I adore you!" Time enough then to think what this look, or that sigh meant! They call me a coquette; they say I am more dangerous than Miriam (impossible!) because she flirts openly, while I look so innocent that it seems criminal to suspect me.

What malicious slander! Of course mother's daughter must have a slight taste for such amusements; but as to my ever practicing them, never, never! I have not the tact, even if I had the inclination. And I wish the men would let Mr Halsey alone about me, and the women let me alone about him. I dont like their taking so much for granted.

48. Dream of a young girl.
49. Besides.

Friday March 20th.

Confound John Halsey! I have just received the most amusing letter from him, but, confound him for his meanness in picking me to pieces! The other day, against my wishes, Miriam gave him the two enigmas[50] that I wrote on the first page of this book, to solve. The first, a slap at Capt. Bradford, he though[t] excellent; could not praise it enough. The second, a panegyric on Col. Steadman, he criticises unmercifully, and ridiculed it until I grew weak from laughter. But what amused me most was his slap at the unfortunate subject of my wretched attempt. (He might have spared me, considering they were first attempts.) He says that considering the scarcity of pen, ink, and paper in the Confederacy, he would advise him to omit the "George Washington" in his name until after the war, when he may add to it "Stonewall Jackson." Good Gracious! His first name is bad enough; but when those *four* are added to Isaiah—!

Jealousy! jealousy! Miriam says, and nothing else! He thinks the Colonel is ahead! *I* say [p. 40] nothing. What can I say? A man must be in love before he grows jealous; and I insist that no such cause exists here. But it is very odd that he thought my unprovoked and absurd ridicule of his most *intimate* friend, Capt. Bradford, so extremely good, while a single word of praise of an utter stranger to him should call forth such a *stunning* criticism! But really the whole was very good, and I think I shall keep it to remember both, the critic and martyr. Suppose me to mean Colonel Steadman by that last epithet, for he is the most injured party, after all, while I have miraculously survived the cruelty of my false friend.

Wednesday March 25th.

I dont know how it happened that I find myself insensibly entering into a correspondence with Mr Halsey. I certainly did not mean to do so. But the above mentioned note required an answer—and a flaming one it deserved—and Tuesday came a long letter which required as speedy a one, so that is the way it began. I had a quiet laugh to myself when he came out Sunday in spite of the driving rain to see us. What would mother say to my corresponding in this off hand style with a gentleman? I wrote to her about it though, and she said nothing at all,

50. Word puzzles which were popular at this time.

which probably implies that what her dear daughter thinks proper must necessarily be so. I must prepare myself for a terrific assault of evil. My last was calculated to draw down a perfect thunderbolt of wrath on my head, and Mr Halsey is hardly the one to let such a fine opportunity for retaliation pass unnoticed. Perhaps I was too severe. N'importe! He is fully capable of annihilating me in this game that two can play at. Maybe I will be the first to cry "Hold! Enough!"[51] At this stage of the game, I think he has the worst of it. Time will show the victor.

I shall cease making puns for these girls; they either will not or cannot appreciate them. It is useless to waste bon mots in my bed room that other people would make a reputation with in the parlor. Puns *are* low, though, and it is proof of a higher order of wit to be innocent of them. Anna! I forgive you for your reception of my second, yesterday. She was reading Mr Halsey's letter, when she exclaimed "Why Sarah! he turns his y's in the wrong way!" alluding to a very peculiar style he has, which is not to be imitated. "Is he the only man wise the wrong way, Anna?" I asked. I met the fate I merited for so wretched an attempt. She received it in perfect silence, and half an hour after, exclaimed "O me! It is Wise! Miriam did you hear that?" That is enough to kill one with stronger wit than mine. Damning with faint praise! From some sources, *any* kills.

[p. 41] Friday March 27th.

Am I still alive? Is it possible I have survived this dreadful blow? O Sarah are you made of stone that you bear this so quietly? What! No word! no sigh! not a groan to betray the agony within? What *are* you made of? Shed just one tear to prove there is still some feeling left in you, callous girl! Not one to spare? Go, heartless wretch! I blush for your indifference. "Twas ever thus from childhood's hour, I've seen my fondest hopes decay;[52] I never had a beau, or eat [sic] sour Grapes, but that there was the devil to pay! I never nursed a pleasing thought, To cheer me in an hour of gloom, But the hand of fate with evil fraught, Consigned it to an early tomb! I never had flirtation sweet, To wile the weary hours away, But when my swain was at my feet, He was not harshly torn away!"

Even so! Cruel Destiny (or Gen. Gardener) with ruthless hand has

51. Shakespeare, *Macbeth*.
52. Thomas Moore, *Lalla Rookh*.

torn assunder [*sic*], etc, etc. "And now there's nothing left but weeping," but I never weep; what! spoil mes jolies yeux bleu? No indeed! I'll change the strain and sing "O hearts that break and give no sign," that must be my condition; for verily I can perceive no outward token of the commotion that should reign within my bleeding heart. He is gone! he is gone! I must take to singing the "Long long weary day" in despair; maybe consolation is to be found in its melancholy strain.

How were the awful tidings disclosed? Hush! throbbing heart be still! and let me calmly here record my woes.

'Twas on a balmy eve in early spring When winds of heaven kissed the smiling plain; When geese— Hold! what have they to do with the song I sing?— Why, fool! a goose is the hero of your plaintive strain! There! the secret is out now! No need of further concealment! If g-o-o-s-e dont spell his name it is because old Cadmus did not know what he was about when he invented the Alphabet. At all events I improve on the old gentleman's invention and decree that in future G-O-O-S-E shall stand for John Halsey. Yes! it is he who has departed!

Early last evening the tremendous clatter of a sword that made such unnecessary noise that one might imagine that the owner thereof had betaken himself to the favorite pastime of his childhood, and was prancing in on his murderous weapon, having mistaken it for his war steed, announced the arrival of Capt. Bradford, who with two friends came to say adieu. Those vile Yankees have been threatening Ponchitoula [*sic*], and his battery, with a regiment of infantry, was on its way there to drive them back. I never make my appearance when [p. 42] the Captain calls; he bores me, and I take no pains to conceal it; and so I always withdraw the light of my countenance unless he is accompanied by some one more agreeable to me—which happened not to be the case on this occasion. But he sent me word of the distressing departure, with many assurances that he would take good care of "my" John.

Scarcely had he departed when lo! John arrives, and speaks for himself. Yes! he is going! Only a moment to say good bye. Sorry he had not time to answer that note (maybe I felt relieved!) but would I let him write to me from Ponchitoula? He would be very happy, etc.

That last enigma of mine had baffled him completely. For four hours he had puzzled over it in vain, until he got so impatient that he fairly lost his temper at last. He will have his revenge yet!

Sunset approaches. Well! he must say good bye now! Chorus of young ladies: "O will you not spend the evening with us? You can easily over-take the Battery later!" Chorus of married ladies: "You must not think of going! Here is a comfortable room at your service, and after an early breakfast you can be on the road as soon as the others." No necessity for prayers; he readily consents. And yet as the evening wore on, when we laughed loudest, I could not help but think of poor little Mrs McPhaul sitting alone and crying over her brother's departure, fancying his pre-cious bones lying on the damp ground with only the soldier's roof—the blue vault of heaven—above, while two miles away he sat in a comfort-able parlor amusing himself, apparently without a thought of sister or war to mar his pleasure. Yet they are perfectly devoted to each other.

And I just thought—wonder if my brothers do the same? I would not be jealous of other girls that they bid adieu to, now; but I would be just a *little* bit jealous if one parted from me in tears, and went off and had a gay time with others afterwards. And the thought of that little widow came often and often when we were playing our absurd games; I felt as though we were all doing her an injury. We grew shockingly undignified, playing Crambo, What's my thought like, and—but no! we played too many ridiculous games; I for one am ashamed of myself. As it was the last time though, it mattered very little.

Then we had the guitar, and at Mr Halsey's request I wrote for him the words of "I'll watch for thee" which he always asks to hear, and then came good bye in ernest; he was to leave before we were up. Good bye John Halsey! Is this the last time you cross my path? Will you—the remainder of my soliloquy was lost in a gap, and I fell asleep without finishing it.

About sunrise, while the most delightful dreams floated [p. 43] through my brain, a little voice roused me exclaiming "Sady! Sady! John Hawsey say so! Say give Sady!" I opened my eyes to see little Gibbes standing by me, trying to lay some flowers on my cheek, his little face sparkling with delight at his own importance. A half opened rose bud with the faintest blush of pink on its creamy leaves—a pink, and a piece of Arbor Vitae all sprinkled with dew, this was my bouquet. The servant explained that Mr Halsey had just left, and sent me that with his last good bye. And he has gone! "And now there's nothing left but weeping! His face I ne'er shall see, and naught is left to me, save"—putting away my book and all recollections of nonsense. So here goes!

Tuesday March 31st.

"To be, or not to be; that is the question,"[53] Whether 'tis nobler in the Confederacy to suffer the pangs of unappeasable hunger and never ending trouble, or to take passage to a Yankee port, and there remaining, end them. Which is best? I am so near daft that I cannot pretend to say; I only know that I shudder at the thought of going to New Orleans, and that my heart fails me when I think of the probable consequence to mother if I allow a mere outward sign of patriotism to over balance what should be my first consideration—her health. For Clinton is growing no better rapidly. To be hungry is there an every day occurrence. For ten days, mother writes, they have lived off just hominy enough to keep their bodies and souls from parting, without being able to procure another article—not even a potato.

Mother is not in a condition to stand such privation; day by day she grows weaker on her new régime; I am satisfied that two months more of danger, difficulties, perplexities, and starvation will lay her in her grave. The latter alone is enough to put a speedy end to her days. Lilly has been obliged to put her children to bed to make them forget they were supperless, and when she followed their example, could not sleep herself, for very hunger. The inhabitants of that abode of bliss would not put themselves out to sell them a mouthful to keep them from starving, such is their idea of Christianity. So with money enough to purchase a comfortable home among respectable people, they find it as serviceable as so many rags, and live on from day to day with empty stomachs and full pockets. Can any thing more aggravating be imagined?

We have tried in vain to find another home in the Confederacy. After three days spent in searching Augusta, Gibbes wrote that it was impossible to find a vacant room for us, as the city was already crowded with refugees. A kind Providence must have destined that disappointment in order to save my life, if there is any reason for Col. Steadman's fears. We next wrote [p. 44] to Mobile, Brandon,[54] and even that horrid little Liberty, besides making inquiries of every one we met, while Charlie too was endeavoring to find a place, and every where received the same answer—not a vacant room, and provisions hardly to be obtained at all.

53. Shakespeare, *Hamlet.*
54. Brandon, Mississippi, near Jackson.

The question has now resolved itself to whether we shall see mother die for want of food in Clinton, or, by sacrificing an outward show of patriotism, (the inward sentiment cannot be changed) go with her to New Orleans, as Brother begs in the few letters he contrives to smuggle through. It looks simple enough. Ought not mother's life to be our first consideration? Undoubtedly! But suppose we could preserve her life and our free sentiments at the same time? If we could only find a resting place in the Confederacy! This, though is impossible. But to go to New Orleans; to live surrounded by Yankees; to cease singing Dixie; to be obliged to keep your sentiments to yourself—for I would not wound Brother by any Ultra Secession speech, and such could do me no good and only injure him. If he is as friendly with the Federals as they say he is—to listen to the scurrilous abuse heaped on those fighting for our homes and liberties, among them my three brothers—could I endure it? I fear not. Even if I did not go crazy, I would grow so restless, homesick and miserable, that I would pray for even Clinton again.

O I dont, dont want to go! If mother would only go alone, and leave us with Lilly! But she is as anxious to obtain Dr Stone's advice for me, as we are to secure her a comfortable home; and I wont go any where without Miriam, so we must all go together. Yet there is no disguising the fact that such a move will place us in a very doubtful position to both friends and enemies. However all our friends here warmly advocate the move, and Will Pinkney and Frank both promised to knock down anyone who shrugged their shoulders and said anything about it.

But what would the boys say? The fear of displeasing them is my chief distress. George writes in the greatest distress about my prolonged illness, and his alarm about my condition. "Of one thing I am sure" he writes, "and that is that she deserves to recover; for a better little sister never lived." God bless him! my eyes grew right moist over those few words. Loving words bring tears to them sooner than angry ones. Would he object to such a step when he knows that the very medicines necessary for my recovery are not to be procured in the whole country? Would he rather have mother dead, and me a cripple in the Confederacy, than both well out of it? I feel that if we go we are wrong; but I am satisfied that it is worse to stay. It is a distressing dilemma to be placed in, as we are certain to be blamed which ever course we pursue. But I don't want to go to New Orleans!

[p. 45] Before I had time to lay down my pen this evening, Gen. Gardener & Major Wilson[55] were announced; and I had to perform a hasty toilette before being presentable. The first remark of the General, was that my face recalled many pleasant recollections; that he had known my family very well, but that time was probably beyond my recollection; and he went on talking about father and Sis, until I felt quite comfortable, with this utter stranger. But the Major I could not talk to. He was as diffident as I, and I searched my brain in vain to find some topic which would lead to a conversation. Every time I thought I might almost suggest one, and would raise my eyes to take a preliminary view of affairs to see if I might venture, I found his fixed on me; and with a feeling of suffocation and despair, mine would burn until I felt and looked like a fool. It was too provoking! but I could not overcome the embarrassment, so I was dumb to him.

But the most aggravating part of it was that he is decidedly the handsomest gentleman who has yet called—I should judge from the occasional glimpses I caught—and I could not contemplate his features at leisure because I felt sure of meeting his eyes! How often I called myself Fool, it would be impossible to say. The very fact of being at ease, and able to talk to Gen. Gardener, added to my distress. For I was constantly thinking "Suppose he thinks that I am afflicted with 'Buttons on the Brain' and pay homage only to the number of stars a coat collar may hold! If he should think I neglect him because he has not as high a title!" Such thoughts succeeded in making me miserable, without affording a subject for conversation; so at last in a fit of desperation I asked him if Mr Dupré spent his time in dancing at headquarters; and in the laugh that followed I drew my horns in, and rested satisfied with having done my duty towards him, and having made a fool of myself, which was just what was expected of me.

I rather liked Gen. Gardener. I would prefer his speaking of "our" recent success at P. Hudson to "my"; for we each, man, woman, and child feel that we share the glory of sinking the gunboats and sending Banks back to B.R. without venturing on an attack;[56] and it seemed odd

55. Major T. Friend Wilson served on Gardner's staff.

56. Part of his army remained in Baton Rouge, but by the time Sarah wrote this General Banks had returned to his headquarters in New Orleans and had carried the war to the

to hear anyone assume the responsibility of the whole affair and say "my success" so unconsciously. But this may be the privilege of Generals. I am no judge as this is the first Confederate General I have had the pleasure of seeing. Wish it had been old Stonewall! I grow enthusiastic every time I think of the dear old fellow!

I am indebted to Gen. Gardener for a great piece of kindness though. I was telling him of how many enemies he had made among the ladies by his strict regulations that now rendered it almost impossible for the gentlemen to obtain permission to call on them, when he told me if I would signify to my friends to mention when they applied that their visit was to be here, and not elsewhere, that he would answer for their having a pass whenever they called for one. Merci du compliment; mais c'est trop tard, monsieur![57]

[p. 46] Tuesday April 7th.

I believe that it is *for true* that we are to leave for New Orleans via Clinton and Ponchitoula this evening. Clinton at least, I am sure of. Lilly came down for me yesterday, and according to the present programme, though I will not answer for it in an hour from now, we leave Linwood this evening, and Clinton on Thursday. I am almost indifferent about our destination; my chief anxiety is to have some definite plans decided on, which seems perfectly impossible from the number of times they are changed a day. The uncertainty is really affecting my spine, and causing me to grow alarmingly thin. So thin, that pulling on my stockings without the slightest obstacle from my ankle to my knee, I remarked to Miriam the other day with more pathos than delicacy that if I was a cow I would certainly go dry, for I had lost my *calf*. So any change, [just] so I am sure of it, would perhaps restore some flesh to my bones which threaten to stand out with the most shameless disregard of modesty and covering.

Teche country, west of the river. It would be May before he made his next move against Port Hudson.

57. Thank you for the compliment; but it's too late, sir!

Wednesday, Clinton. April 8th 1863.

Our last adieux are said, and Linwood is left behind, "it may be for years, and it may be forever." My last hours were spent lying on the sofa on the gallery, with Lydia at my feet, Helen Carter sitting on the floor at my side, while all the rest were gathered around me as I played for the *last time* "the Centre of attraction." I grew almost lachrymose as I bid a last adieu to the bed where I have spent so many months, as they carried me down stairs. Wonder if it will not miss me?

It must have been at least five before the cars returned. Mrs Carter grew quite pathetic as they approached, while poor little Lydia with streaming eyes and choaking sobs, clung first to Miriam and then to me, as though we parted to meet only in eternity. All except her and her mother started in a run for the big gate while I was carried to the buggy through the group of servants gathered to say good-bye, when the General drove me off rapidly.

What a delightful sensation is motion, after five months' inaction! The last time I was in a vehicle was the night Gen. Beale's ambulance brought me to Linwood a helpless bundle, last November. It seemed to me yesterday that I could again feel the kind gentleman's arm supporting me, and his wondering, sympathetic tone as he [p. 47] repeated every half mile, "Really Miss Morgan you are *very* patient and uncomplaining!" Good, kind President Miller! As though all the trouble was not his, just then! But stopping at the gate roused me from my short revery, and I opened my eyes to find myself stationary, and in full view of a train of cars loaded with soldiers, literally covered with them; for they covered the roof, as well as filled the interior, while half a dozen open cars held them seated one above the other in miniature pyramids, and even the engine was graced by their presence.

Abashed at finding myself confronted with so many people, my sensation became decidedly alarming as a dozen rude voice[s] cried "Go on! we wont stop!" and a chorus of the opposition cried "Yes we will" "No!" "Yes!" they cried in turn, and as the General stood me on the ground (I would have walked if it had been my last attempt in life) I paused irresolute, not knowing whether to advance or retreat before the storm. I must say they are the only rude soldiers I have yet seen in Confederate uniforms. But as I walked slowly, clinging to the General's arm half from fear, and half from weakness, they ceased the unnecessary dispute, and remained so quiet that I was more frightened still, and actually forgot to say good bye to Mrs Carter and Mrs Worley as they stood by the road.

How both the General and I escaped being hurt as he raised me on the platform, every one present is at a loss to account for. I experienced only what may be called slight pain, in comparison to what I *have* felt; but really fear that the exertion has disabled him for to day. It must have been very severe. Some officer led me to my seat, Lilly, Miriam, and Anna got in, the General kissed us heartily with damp eyes and kind wishes, the cars gave a whisle [*sic*], and I put my head out of the window to see Mrs Carter industriously applying white cambric to her face, which occupation she relinquished to call out last good byes; another whistle and a jerk, and we were off, leaving her and Mrs Worley surrounded by children and servants, using their handkerchiefs to wipe tears and wave farewell, while the General waved his hat for good bye. Then green hedges rapidly changing took their place, and Linwood was out of sight, before we had ceased saying and thinking God bless the kind hearts we had left behind. Can I ever forget the kindness we have met among them? To see green trees and wild flowers once more after such an illness, is a pleasure that only those long deprived of such [p. 48] beauties by a similar misfortune can fully appreciate.

It was a relief to discover that what I had thought shocking rudeness in the soldiers had not been reserved for me alone. For every time we stopped the same cry of "No waiting for slow people" was raised, varied by constant expostulations with the engine for drinking ponds dry, and mild suggestions as to taking the road the other side of the fence, which would no doubt prove smoother than the track. These Arkansas troops have acquired a reputation for roughness and ignorance which they seem to cultivate as assiduously as most people would their virtues. But rudeness does not affect their fighting qualities.

A Capt. Packwood[58] was very kind to us on the way, and did every-thing he could for our comfort. When we arrived at the dépôt the car-riage we expected to take me to the house was not there; but Miss Dickson was kind enough to offer her's, which Lilly accepted; and having called a negro to carry me out of it, just as I was prepared to go, Capt. Packwood insisted on helping me, and deliberately picking me up, carried me off as though I were a feather. "Good Gracious!" I thought. "What would Mrs Packwood say!" But before I had time to think much more about it, I was safely deposited in the carriage, and had barely time to thank him for his trouble before Lilly and Mr Marston were seated by me, and we drove off.

No sooner had the carriage stopped at the door than a rush of little feet, and a cry of "Aunt Sarah!" in a variety of keys told me that the little children had not forgotten me in my long sickness, and eight or ten little arms threatened to interfere seriously with my organs of res-piration. When I had once more been carried in the room and laid on the bed, dear old Mr Marston, after contemplating me for several min-utes with the most satisfied look imaginable, stooped down suddenly and kissed me as heartily as my own dear father would have done. The unexpected demonstration, the light falling on his white hair, and the figure so much reminding me of father, brought tears to my eyes for the first time that day, as I thought what he would have felt if he could see me lying so helpless there. I wonder if the dead can see us? I would rather he and Harry should not know.

Madisonville[59] Sunday, April 12th. 1863

We arrived here about five last evening, and strange to say the jour-ney, fatiguing as it was, has not altogether disabled me. But I must go

58. Captain George H. Packwood raised a company called the Packwood Rifles which became a part of the 4th Louisiana Infantry. See Howell, *Feliciana Confederates,* 143–44.

59. On the north shore of Lake Pontchartrain.

back to Clinton to account for this new change. [p. 49] It would never do to take more than a hundred miles at a single jump without speaking of the incidents by the way. Numerous and pleasant as they were, some way, they have unaccountably paled; and things that seemed so extremely amusing, and afforded me so much pleasure during these four days, now seem to be absurd trifles half forgotten.

I now remember lying in state on Lilly's bed Wednesday talking to Mrs Badger (who had been several days in town), Anna, Sarah Ripley and the others, when Frank suddenly bolted in, just from Port Hudson, to say another good bye, though I told him good bye at Linwood Sunday. Presently the General entered, just from Linwood, to see us off, then Mr Marston & his daughter, and Mr Neafus,[60] all as kind as possible, until a perfect levee was assembled, which I, lying all dressed with a shawl thrown over me, enjoyed all the more as I could take my ease and have my fun at the same time. Frank, sitting by my pillow, talked dolorously of how much he would miss us, and threatened to be taken prisoner before long in order to see us again. Mr Neafus, who for l'amour des beaux yeux de Miriam[61] had taken no end of trouble, together with Mr Marston, to secure us a carriage, surrendered himself to her care, while the elders conversed apart, the two girls having left us to go to a candy pulling, or some such nonsense. Though we were to leave at seven in the morning, it was quite late before our visitors left, promising to return in the morning to see us off; and after all else had withdrawn Mrs Badger and Mr Neafus remained an hour longer, as though inclined to wait for daybreak before saying good evening.

When we were finally left alone, I fancy there was very little sleep in the house. As to me, I lay by Lilly wide awake, thinking how lonely she would be without us, and perfectly désolée at the idea of leaving the Confederacy (the dear grey coats included) so when it was almost sunrise there is [*sic*] no necessity of rousing me to dress, as I was only to[o] glad to leave my sleepless bed. Before I got dressed, Anna, her mother, and Sarah Ripley came in again, then Miss Comstock, and just as I had put the last touch to my dress the gentlemen of the night before entered, and we had almost an hour and a half's respite before the carriage, less punctual than we, drove to the door.

60. George Neafus, a Clinton merchant.
61. The love of Miriam's beautiful eyes.

We waited so long, that Mrs Badger and Anna were forced to leave us, to get to the cars in time to go back, anxious as they were to carry the news of our actual departure to Linwood. Poor Anna went through her last adieux with such a woe begone face, and such sad eyes, and damp cheeks, that I really [p. 50] feared that I should catch cold from the shower bath at that hour of the morning. Mrs Badger had great red rims like crimson spectacle[s] around her eyes as she kissed me good bye. Seems to me she should have been glad to be rid of the constant care and trouble I had given her ever since I was injured. Bless her dear kind heart! How good she has been to me!

When the carriage finally came, only Frank and the General remained; and after a long goodbye to each of the children, beginning with Beatrice and ending with Dellie, the latter picked me up in his arms and carried me once more to the carriage. Then the servants had to say goodbye, then Lilly, very quiet, very red, and, disolved [*sic*] in tears, clung to me almost with out a word, hardly able to speak, whilst I, distressed and grieved as I was, had not a tear in my eyes—nothing but a great lump in my throat that I tried to choak down in order to talk to Frank who stood at the window by me, after she left. People must think me very unfeeling. I could see Lilly crying on Miriam's neck in the narrow little entry, hear her sobs, yet for all the outward tokens of distress visible about me, I could well have passed for stone.

With an ear for every sob within, and a twitch at my heart for poor Lilly, I sat laughing with Frank heartily; for the subject under discussion was whether I was to kiss him goodbye or not. A proper subject for dispute between young ladies and gentlemen! I laughingly promised to see about it, and Frank, evidently thinking it all right, asked mother if I could not kiss him. To my unspeakable surprise, with a cool air which struck me aghast, mother said—certainly! I thought I had carried the joke too far then, and regretted that I had encouraged the discussion as I had not the slightest idea of committing such a breach of propriety. But the harm was already done. Frank advanced to claim his kiss, when I said "O wait awhile! Let me kiss the General first, then *may be* I will kiss you." The General kissed me, and then Frank advanced the second time. Again I put him off telling him to kiss Miriam first. She acted like a sensible girl, throwing aside her veil, and going through with it with the same grace and nonchalence she would have showed if it had been George.

He turned to me. "Now, Miss Sarah!" Now, not for an instant had I thought to do anything so much against my principles; and like a flash came the remark he made Sunday: that he would rather kiss me than any girl he knew, for the very reason that he knew no man on earth would dare take such a liberty with me, and the recollection only strengthened my resolution. His face was within six inches of mine when I [p. 51] drew back with a frightened look I fancy, and a cry of "O Frank! dont please!" that sent him back a step of [*sic*] two. I must have been alarmed, for I did not look at him until the General said "Why shame on you! you have made him turn pale with disappointment!" Disappointment could have had very little to do with it; but as I looked at him, I saw he had become perfectly white with mortification. I would not have hurt his feelings for worlds; and a painful feeling of contrition came over me as he exclaimed "*Why* did you say you would? This is too unkind!"

"Kiss him, you silly thing and be done with it!" cried the General. "Sarah you are absurd," Miriam remarked. "You are behaving badly" said my accommodating mamma. "Kiss Frank this instant! You might as well object to kissing your brother!" Dear tender hearted mother! What? and let Frank think that he at least could do what no one else dared? Never! So without heeding the running stream of scolding that I had brought on my own head, I put my face to the window, and my hand out, saying "I cant kiss you, Frank, and am more than sorry I jested about it. Let us part friends." So we shook hands heartily after three minutes of reproaches and mutual declarations of forgiveness and friendship, which was interrupted by a sudden jerk as the driver cut the dispute short by starting off. And my last view of Frank showed him waving his handkerchief after the retreating carriage, where upon I kissed my hand to him, which should have settled the difficulty. I am sorry it should have occurred; he looked so hurt.

Didn't I tease Miriam along the road about her breach of propriety! Every now and then I would ask if she really had kissed Frank, and how it felt, until she voted me a torment, and said I deserved a slap for my absurd conduct. I differ from her; I was right. No woman has a right to kiss a man she does not intend to marry. Even if she is engaged to him it is improper; for if one had to marry every one they engage themselves to, heaven help some households! And those things are so uncertain besides! Wonder how a girl feels when it is broken off, when she meets dearest Edward who has enjoyed so many delightful kisses? If it is wrong when you are engaged, it is worse when you are not. This is the belief that has saved me from "many a foolish thing."

I am either to marry, or remain single. If I am to marry, some blessed man was destined for me. He may be at my elbow, or at the antipodes, it matters not; for go where I will, do what I will, sooner or later, at the time appointed by heaven we will meet, and nothing will prevent it. Ergo, I am to consider myself virtually engaged, though the lucky individual for whom this prize in the matrimonial lottery is reserved [p. 52] is yet a stranger to me. Now, is not an engaged woman guilty of a breach of faith if she indulges in sundry little flirtations during the absence of her beloved? If so, how very reprehensible all these little brotherly kisses she may choose to allow, to pass away the dreary hours of her weary watch for him! When the bridegroom comes at last, what would he say to the traces of molasses and treacle left on those ruby lips by Tom, Dick and Harry who have tasted them before him? He can never wipe it off; he will taste it ever more, and for ever more, in spite of soap and water; for there are some things, airless and immaterial though they be, that can never be washed away.

"No!" I say in answer to Miriam's lecture. "I have nothing to give the man I marry except a pure heart." That is my sole dower; is it fair to de-fraud him of it by dulling [?] my scruples of delicacy until they become so blunted that the sharp edged sword that guards the entrance is no longer a safe guard? If I kiss Frank because he is good, and a perfect brother to me, why should I not kiss Mr Halsey who is quite as good, and as kind as it is possible to be? The line must be drawn somewhere, so I draw it this side of nothing at all, and try to keep myself unspot-ted from the world, kisses, and other quicksands—there is no knowing where the next step will take you to.

When the marriage ceremony is over with, and not before, I want to be able to say to my dear "Capt. Louis"[62] "Dearest Charles, here is a mouth, not pretty to be sure, but which nevertheless possesses one beauty;—yours will be the first lips that ever touched it." And if he is not charmed with the gift, I shall say he is a brute of a man, and un-

62. The "Captain Charles Lewis" that Sarah was told she would fall in love with.

worthy of the trouble I have taken in preserving unpoluted what was to be his future treasure!" If to this it is objected that he may tarry so long that I will forget how to kiss by the time he comes, I say I will keep in practice by kissing the girls, and dear old grandfathers. Besides, it is so easily learned, that a very few lessons from the Captain would suffice!

What an absurd dissertation, and how far I have wandered from my journey! Good bye Frank! Sorry I hurt your feelings, but [I] am satisfied you think none the less of me. I have retained your respect, as well as my own. This *is* a comfort! How the distance lengthens between us! I raise up from my pillows and find myself at Camp Moore at four o'clock. Forty miles are passed over, good bye Frank!

From Camp Moore we had to go three miles back, to find Capt. Gilman's[63] house where we were expected. The gentleman is a friend of Gibbes' though I had never seen any of them before. [p. 53] Such a delightful place, with every thing looking so new, and cool, and such a hospitable hostess that I thought every thing charming in spite of my fatigue. I had hardly a moment to look around; for immediately we were shown to our rooms, and in a very few minutes Miriam had me undressed and in bed, the most delightful spot in the world to me just then. While congratulating myself on having escaped death on the roadside, I opened my eyes to behold a tray brought to my bedside with a variety of refreshments. Coffee! Bread! Loaf sugar! Preserves! I opened my mouth to make an exclamation at the singular optical illusion, but wisely forebore speaking, and shut it with some of the unheard of delicacies instead. That was the only exertion I had to make. Presently the two ladies came in to see me, and kept me company for a long while, and leaving me willing enough to sink in the invited [*sic*] arms of Morpheus, for I was tired enough of my journey.

Early the next morning the same routine was gone through of Thursday morning. Again the carriage drove to the door, and we were whirled off to Camp Moore where the engine stood snorting with impatience to hurry us off to Ponchitoula. Here again I was fortunate enough to have nice old married gentlemen to put me in the cars—but that was the

63. Samuel H. Gilman. The house is still standing. Captain Gilman's account of his wartime activities is in the Louisiana Historical Association Collection at Howard-Tilton Memorial Library, Tulane University. See "Narrative Incidental to the late unpleasantness in the family of Uncle Sam."

last time. At the other end of the railway—oh! After seeing us settled, Col. Hatch[64] and Capt. Gilman told us good bye, and soon we were steaming down the track, I, reclining on my pillows in an interesting state of invalidism, sadly abashed now and then at the curious, wondering gaze of the soldiers who were aboard. Having very little idea of the geography of that part of the country, and knowing we were to take a carriage from some point this side of Ponchitoula, fancying how surprised Mr Halsey would be to hear we had passed him on the way, I took a card from my travelling case, and wrote a few words for "good-bye" as we could not see him again. I sealed it up, and put it in my pocket to send to the first post office we passed.

About twelve o'clock we stopped at Hammond,[65] which was our place to disembark. Mother sent out to hire a negro to carry me off the platform; and while waiting in great perplexity, a young officer who had just seated himself before me, got up and asked if he could assist her, seizing an arm full of cloaks as he spoke. I got up and walked to the door to appear independent and make believe I was not the one, when mother begged him not to trouble himself; she [p. 54] wanted a man to assist her daughter who was sick. Calling a friend, the gentleman kindly loaded him with the cloaks, etc, while he hurried out after me. I was looking ruefully at the impracticable step which separated me from the platform. The question of how I was to carry out my independent notions began to perplex me. "Allow me to assist you" said a voice at my elbow. I turned and beheld the handsome officer. "Thank you; I think I can get down alone." "Pray allow me to lift you over this place." "Much obliged but your arm will suffice."

"Sarah let the gentleman carry you! you know you cannot walk!" said my very improper mother. Really what will she suggest next? Thursday I was to kiss Frank, Friday to be carried by an officer who was a

64. Francis H. (Frank) Hatch was collector of customs for the port of New Orleans at the beginning of the war. Following the Union occupation of the city, he moved into the Gilman home, which a Union intelligence officer described as "a kind of headquarters for smugglers from New Orleans." *OR*, ser. I, vol. 48, pt. 1, p. 639. In his "Narrative" S. H. Gilman identifies Hatch as the "C.S. Depository of this department." See biographical sketch in *Jewell's Crescent City Illustrated*, edited by Edwin A. Jewell (New Orleans, 1873), 85.

65. At this time Hammond was little more than a station stop on the New Orleans, Jackson & Great Northern Railroad, later the Illinois Central.

perfect stranger. I disobeyed once, I would try it twice. I respectfully declined the renewed offer. "Dont pay any attention to her. Pick her up just as you would a child," said my incorrigible mother. The gentleman turned very red, while Miriam asserts I turned extremely white. The next thing I knew, by passing his arm around my waist, or taking me by my arms—I was so frightened that I have but a confused idea of it— I was lifted over the intervening gulf and landed on the platform!

Hammond boasts of four houses. One, a shoe manufactury, stood about twenty or thirty yards off, and there the gentleman proposed to conduct me. Again he insisted on carrying me, and resolutely refusing, I pronounced myself fully equal to the walk, and accepting his proffered arm, walked off with dignity and self-possession. He must have fancied that the injury was in my hand; for holding my arm so that my entire weight must have been thrown on him, not satisfied with that support, with his other hand he held mine *so* respectfully, and so carefully that I could not but smile as it struck me, which, by the way, *was not until I reached the house*!

Discovering that he belonged to Colonel Simonton's[66] command, I asked him to take Mr Halsey the note I had written an hour before. He pronounced himself delighted to be of the slightest service, and seeing that we were strangers, travelling unprotected, asked if we had secured a conveyance to take us beyond. We told him no. He modestly suggested that some gentleman might attend to it for us. He would be happy to do anything in his power. I thought again [p. 55] of Mr Halsey, and said if he would mention we were at Hammond, he would be kind enough to see to it for us. "May I ask your name?" he asked, evidently surprised to find himself asking a question he was dying to know. I gave him my card, whereupon mother asked *his* name, which he told us was Howard.[67]

We had been talking for some ten minutes, when feeling rather uncomfortable at being obliged to look up at such a tall man from my low seat, to relieve my neck, as well as to shade my face from any further scrutiny, I put down my head while I was still speaking. Instantly, so

66. Colonel John M. Simonton of the 1st Mississippi Infantry commanded a consolidated regiment that included cavalry and light artillery as well as infantry. General Gardner had ordered him to Ponchatoula after a Union raid on the town three weeks before.

67. Possibly Second Lieutenant Robert J. Howard, Company A, 1st Mississippi Infantry.

quietly, naturally, and unobtrusively did he stoop down by me, on one knee so that his face was in full view of mine, that the action did not seem to me either singular or impertinent—in fact I did not think of it until mother spoke of it after he left. After a few moments it must have struck him; for he got up and made his parting bow, departing, as I afterwards heard, to question Tiche as to how I had been hurt, and declaring that it was a dreadful calamity to happen to so "lovely" a young lady.

Monday April 13th.

Having nothing else to do, I may as well go on with the history of our wanderings. When the cars were moving of[f] with the handsome Mr Howard, mother turned to a gentleman who seemed to own the place, and asked to be shown the hotel. He went out, and presently returning with a chair and two negroes, quietly said he would take us to his own house; the hotel was not comfortable. And without listening to remonstrances, led the way to a beautiful little cottage, where he introduced his wife Mrs Cate,[68] who received us most charmingly, and had me in bed before five minutes had elapsed. I dont know how any one can believe the whole world so wicked; for my part I have met none but the kindest people imaginable; I dont know any wicked ones.

Before half an hour had passed, a visiter was announced; so I gathered up my weary bones, and with scarcely a peep at the glass, walked to the parlor. I commenced laughing before I got there, and the visiter smiled most absurdly too; for it was—Mr Halsey! It seemed so queer to meet in this part of the world, that we laughed again after shaking hands. It *was* odd. I was thinking how much amused the General would be to hear of it; for he had made a bet that we would meet when I asserted that we would not.

After the first few remarks, he told me of how he had heard of [p. 56] our arrival. A gentleman had walked into camp, asking if a Mr Halsey was there. He signified that he was the gentleman, whereupon the other drew out my note saying a young lady on the cars had requested him to deliver it. Instantly recognizing the chirography, he asked where I

68. Mrs. Cate was the wife of Charles E. Cate, pioneer settler who operated a shoe factory in Hammond as well as a sawmill.

was. "Hammond. This is her name" replied the other, extending to him my card. Thinking, as he modestly confessed, that I had intended it only for him, Mr Halsey coolly put it in his pocket, and called for his horse. Mr Howard lingered still, apparently having something to say, which he found difficult to put in words. At last as the other prepared to ride off, with a tremendous effort he managed to say "The young lady's card is mine. If it is all the same to you, I should like to have it returned." Apologizing for the mistake, Mr Halsey returned it, feeling rather foolish, I should imagine, and rode on to the village, leaving, as he avers, Mr Howard looking enviously after the lucky dog who was going to see *such* a young lady.

He told me something that slightly disgusted me with Capt Bradford, or rather added to my previous disgust. It was that when he reached the bivouac the next morning after leaving Linwood, the Captain had him put under arrest for having staid there all night. It was too mean, considering that it is more than probable that he himself remained at Mrs Fluker's.[69] We discovered too that we had missed two letters Mr Halsey had written us, which *of course* is a great disappointment. One, written to both, the other, a short note of ten pages for me, which I am sure was worth reading.

It was not until after sunset that we exhausted all topics of conversation, and Mr Halsey took his leave, promising to see us in the morning. And to be sure, as soon as I was dressed on Saturday, he again made his appearance, followed soon after by the carriage. Taking a cordial leave of Mrs Cate, with ma[n]y thanks for her hospitality, we entered our conveyance, and with Mr Halsey riding by the side of the carriage, went on our way. He was to accompany us only as far as Ponchitoula— some six miles; but the turning point in his journey seemed to be an undetermined spot; for mile after mile rolled away—rather the wheels rolled over them—and still he rode by us, talking through the window, and the sprays of wild flowers he would pick for me from time to time were growing to quite a bouquet, when he proposed an exchange with the farmer who was driving us, and, giving him his horse, took the reins himself.

69. Isabella Fluker, widow of David J. Fluker. Asphodel, the family home, was a few miles from Jackson and not far from Linwood. Captain Bradford's interest there was Mrs. Fluker's daughter Mary, whom he later married.

I think Miriam and I will always remember that ride. The laughter, the conversation, the songs with the running accompanyment of the wheels, and a thousand incidents pleasant to remember [p. 57] though foolish to speak of, will always form a delightful tableau in our recollections. I have but one disagreeable impression to remember in connection with the trip, and that occurred at a farmhouse two miles from here where we stopped to get strawberries. I preferred remaining in the carriage, to the trouble of getting out, so all went in, Mr Halsey dividing his time equally between Miriam in the house and me in the carriage, supplying me with violets and pensées one moment, and the next showing me the most tempting strawberries at the most provoking distance, assuring me they were exquisite.

The individual to whom the carriage belonged, who had given up the reins to Mr Halsey, and who no doubt was respectable enough for his class in his part of the country, would allow no one to bring me my strawberries, reserving the honor for himself. Presently he appeared with a large saucer of them covered with cream. I was naturally thankful, but would have preferred his returning to the house after he had fulfilled his mission. Instead, he had the audacity to express his admiration of my personal appearance, without a pause gave me a short sketch of his history, informed me he was a widower, and *very* anxious to marry again, and finally—Lares and Penates of the house of Morgan ap Kerrig, veil your affronted brows! You will scarcely credit that the creature had the insolence to say that—he would marry me to-morrow, if he could, and think himself blessed; for the jewel of the soul must be equal to the casket that contained it! Yes! this brute of a man had the unparalelled audacity to speak to me in such a way!

Just then, mother, remembering her invalid, came to the gallery and asked how I was enjoying my lunch. "I'm courting her!" cried the wretch. "Glad she did not go in! Swear she's the prettiest girl I *ever* saw!" At that moment Mr Halsey came sauntering out with a handful of violets for me, and turning my shoulder to the creature, I entered into a lively discussion with him, and at last had the satisfaction of seeing the wretch enter the house. Annoyed and insulted as I felt, I told him of the amazing liberty the creature had taken in addressing such language to me, as though it was a good joke, instead of expressing my real disgust; he tried to look amused, but failed, and I am satisfied that he did not like it any more than I, though neither expressed our private opinions.

As an aggravation of his previous offense, yesterday the "creature" had the assurance to send me a beautiful bouquet, while a few roses loosely tied together accompanied the more pretentious offering, intended for Miriam.

What a vulgar style mine must be to attract the admiration of such people! I felt like taking a "swim" in a [p. 58] briar bush, until I reflected that there was no longer any necessity for such precaution as it is probably the last time we shall be thrown in contact with such people. A drive through the straggling, half deserted town brought us here to Mrs Greyson's,[70] a large, old fashioned looking house so close to the Tchefuncta (I think that is the name of the river) that I could throw a stone in it from my bed, almost.[71]

A ride of twenty six miles, bolt upright in the carriage over such bad roads, had almost used me up; and I retired to bed in a state of collapse, leaving Miriam to entertain Mr Halsey alone. After supper though, I managed to put on my prettiest dress, and be carried down to the parlor where I rejoined the rest. Several strange ladies were present, one of whom has since afforded me a hearty laugh. She was a horrid looking woman, and ten minutes after I entered, crossing the room with a most laughable look of vulgarity attempting to ape righteous scorn, jerked some articles of personal property from the table, and retired with the sweep of a small hurricane. I thought her an eccentric female; but what was my amazement yesterday to hear that she sought Mrs Greyson, told her it was impossible for her to stay among so many elegantly dressed ladies, and that she prefered keeping [to] her room. Next day, she told her that she was entirely too attentive to us, and rather than be neglected in that way, for other people, would leave the house, which she did instantly. Rather an amusing character!

There was a singular assembly of odd characters in the parlor Saturday night, six of whom looked as though they were but so many reflections of the same individual in different glasses, and the seventh

70. The widow of General John B. Grayson, a soldier of the Mexican War who had died at his post in Florida in 1861. Grayson's body was brought back to New Orleans for burial. See *Daily Picayune*, October 29, 1861, p. 1.

71. The Tchefuncta runs into Lake Pontchartrain at Madisonville.

differed from the rest only in playing exquisitely on the banjo—"Too well to be a gentleman," I fear. These were soldiers, come to "call" on us.[72] Half an hour after we arrived, a dozen of them took possession of the bench on the bank of the river, one with his banjo who played and sang delightfully. Old Mrs Greyson who is rather eccentric called out "Ah Mr Carter! Have you heard already of the arrival of the young ladies? You never serenade *me!*"

The young man naturally looked foolish; so she went out and asked him to come around after dark and play for the young ladies. So after a while he came, "bringing six devils yet worse than himself" as the old scriptural phrase has it,[73] all of whom sat on the same side of the room, and looked at us steadily when they thought we were not [p. 59] looking. All had the same voice, the same bow, the same manner—that is to day none at all of the latter. One introduced an agreeable variety, saying as he bowed to each present separately "Happy to make your acquaintance ma'am." Mr Halsey just managed to keep his face straight, while I longed for a Dickens to put them all together and make one amusing picture out of the seven. I troubled myself very little about them, prefering Mr Halsey's company, not knowing when we would meet again. It would not have been quite fair to leave him to himself after he had rode [*sic*] such a distance for us; so I generously left the seven to Miriam, content with one, and rather think I had the best of the bargain.

The one with the banjo suggested that we should sing for them before he played for us, so Miriam played on the piano, and sang with me on the guitar half a dozen songs, and then the other commenced. I dont know when I have been more amused. There was an odd, piney woods dash about him that was exceedingly diverting, and he went through comic, sentimental, and original songs with an air that showed his whole heart was in it. Judging from the number of youth too timid to venture in, who peeped at us from the windows, I should say that young ladies are curiosities just now in Madisonville.

72. At least four of these soldiers may have been in Company K, 1st Mississippi Cavalry, commanded by Captain William V. Lester. See note 107, page 496. Company K and Company H of the same regiment were under the command of Lieutenant Colonel H. H. Miller, then at Ponchatoula.

73. Sarah misquotes Matthew 12:45 and Luke 11:26.

The novelty of the scene made the evening pass rapidly to me, and forgetting my fatigue entirely, I found myself talking as though there was no such thing as a weak back, when the clock struck twelve. What was my horror when I asked for a servant to take me up stairs, to be told that all had gone to bed! Words cant say what I felt when Mr Halsey insisted on helping me. I almost cried with vexation. But calling the only young man left in the room, with his assistance he took up my chair, and carried me up, crimson with mortification, and feeling a ferocity and rebelliousness about my misfortune that I had never experienced, and put me down in the centre of the room, too vexed at being obliged to accept their services to thank them with graciousness, or even politeness. But the young man covered my deficiencies by vehement assurances that he was charmed to be of the slightest service to me, redoubling his professions with increasing zeal as he bowed himself out backwards, most of which I lost; for as Mrs Greyson, holding the candle, nodded and smiled for me, Mr Halsey put out his hand to say good bye, and I turned from the absurdity to take a last look at "John," as he was to leave early in the morning, and I was not to see him again.

This *must* be the last time we meet, though he said if we could [p. 60] possibly go over[74] under a flag of truce, he would obtain permission to accompany us. But it is very doubtful if the flag of truce will be granted; and Mr Halsey had no business to come even this far—though I am glad he did—so we meet no more—sorry to lose so kind a friend—but good bye! "It may be for years and it may be forever." I watched him pass out at the door with a last good bye, and as the solitary candle was withdrawn at the same moment, I may say the light died out of my firmament in the plainest sense of the word; for I was left in utter darkness through Mrs Greyson's over zealousness, now smiling at odd thoughts, now making the most ferocious grimaces at myself when I thought of having been obliged to accept such a service from him, until mother came in with a light, putting an end to my chief amusement when vexed with myself, when I hastily got to bed and under the friendly covers made faces to my hearts content until sleep put an end to my vexation. Will I never, *never* be independent again? No one knows how this helplessness galls me.

74. To New Orleans.

Tuesday April 14th.

Ah! another delightful glimpse of society has been offered to our charmed view. Such a treat has not often fallen to our lot. Good Mrs Greyson, in her anxiety to make all around her happy, determined we should have a dance. I should say "Miriam"; for Mrs Bull and Mrs Ivy [75] never indulge in such amusements, and I cant; so it must have been for Miriam alone. Such a crew! The two ladies above mentioned and I almost laughed ourselves in hysterics. Poor Miriam with a tall slender Texian who looked as though he had chopped wood all his life, moved through the dance like the lady in Comus; only, now and then a burst of laughter at the odd mistakes threatened to overcome her dignity. We who were fortunately exempt from the ordeal, laughed unrestrainedly at the mêlée. One danced entirely with his arms; his feet had very little to do with the time. One hopped through with a most dolorous expression of intense absorption in the arduous task. Another never changed a benign smile that had appeared on entering, but preserved it unimpaired through every accident.

One female apparently of the tender age of thirty, wore a yellow muslin, with her hair combed rigidly à la Chinoise, and tightly fastened at the back of her head in a knot whose circumference must have been fully equal to that of a dollar. In addition to other charms, she bore her neck and chin in a very peculiar manner, as though she were looking over the fence, Mr Christmas remarked. Mr Christmas had rode [sic] all [p. 61] the way from Ponchitoula expressly to see us, and if it had not been for him, Mr Worthington, and Dr Capdevielle [76] who came in after a while, I think I should have expired, and even Miriam would have given up in despair. The Doctor was an old friend of Harry's, though we never met him before; and that alone would have commanded our favor, even if he had nothing to recommend him himself.

The contrast of a refined man among so many Piney Woodsmen was ludicrous in the extreme. Mr Christmas laughed himself into an almost

75. Probably Mrs. Andrew G. Bull and Mrs. Edward Ivy, both New Orleanians trying to make their way back into the city. Presumably they had fled after the occupation of New Orleans the previous year.

76. Mr. Worthington is later referred to as Lieutenant Worthington. Company H, 1st Mississippi Cavalry, commanded by Captain Gadi Herren, was operating in the area at this time with Lieutenant W. M. Worthington as one of its officers. Dr. Auguste Capdevielle, a native of France, practiced medicine in New Orleans in the years after the war.

apoplectic state, all the more severe as it was necessary to endeavor to suppress it. Dr Capdevielle, addressing himself exclusively to Miriam and me, was congratulating himself on his good fortune, when his rejoicing was changed into lamentation. I was telling him that this was my first glimpse of the demi monde. "*Demi* monde, Mademoiselle? Je dirais que ce n'est pas un quart!" [77] he exclaimed, and launched into a stream of ridicule in which I am sorry to say I was encouraging him, when Mrs Greyson came up. "You must dance, Dr Capdevielle."

"Certainly Madam," he said turning to Miriam expecting to dance with her. "La vielle dame m'a pres par le collet" [78] he afterwards piteously remarked, and turning him the other way said in a tone that always tells you you are expected to dance with such a one, "Miss Perkins, Dr Capdevielle." "Grand Dieu!" [79] he murmured, casting a heartrending glance at me as he bowed to the Venus in yellow muslin who sat simpering with anticipation. My sympathy was never more aroused. He bore himself with the dignity of a martyr; walked through the dance bravely, and when it was over, handed her to her chair, where he left her with the most exquisite bow, and a sigh of relief that proclaimed a man who had performed his duty, though conscious that none would applaud him for the sacrifice.

Thursday April 16

While I was writing Tuesday morning, about twelve o'clock I heard a footstep on the lower gallery, which was so familiar to me that instantly I said "Mother, Mr Halsey is down stairs," where upon she said nonsense, as a matter of course; and I, satisfied I was not mistaken, waited yet a few moments, when word was brought that he was below. It was very kind in him to come so far, but it was such an awful bore to dress and go down! Besides, Mr Christmas had just sent me a basket of splendid strawberries, and it had taken so long to help all the ladies to a dish, that I had not had time to finish my own; and the idea of [p. 62] leaving strawberries to see *any* one is preposterous. But this headstrong Miriam thinks I belong to her; so she had me taken down stairs im-

77. "*Half* world, Mademoiselle? I would say that this is not even a fourth!"
78. "The old lady has me close by the collar."
79. "My goodness!"

mediately, and laid on a sofa in state, because feeling decidedly worse was one of my excuses for not going down until after dinner.

On the whole I did not care much after I was once settled; for while Miriam practiced, Mr Halsey read aloud to me from "Sword and Gown" which he gave me at Hammond, while we each marked our favorite passages. I do not like the book; there is very little of a "story" about it, and that little, hardly developed, besides not being *very* moral; but it is splendidly written, and abounds in the most striking true-isms. The story reminds me very much of the author's (is it the same?) Lucille; so much so, that it is singular that he should make both hero-ines so much alike; both love married men, and both go as sisters of Charity to the Crimea.

Mr Halsey brought us each a little tortoise shell ring he had made for us by his camp fire, as a keepsake, and of course we promised to wear them for him, *particularly* as they make our hands look as white as pos-sible. Towards sunset, in spite of prayers and entreaties from Miriam who insisted that I was too feeble to attempt it, I insisted on walking out to the bench by the river to enjoy the cool breeze; and was rather glad I had come, when soon after Dr Capdevielle made his appearance with two beautiful bouquets which he presented with his french bow to us, and introducing his friend Mr Miltonberger,[80] entered into one of those lively discussions about nothing which Frenchmen know how to make so interesting. The fresh air, or conversation, revived me miraculously. I felt so much improved, that when Dr Capdeviellle offered his arm, declaring a short walk would be of service to me, I accepted it, and walked half a square and back! "Voila un miracle![81] I have brought the dead to life!" he exclaimed, bringing me back to Miriam triumphantly. It certainly was a prodigious feat for me; and if harm comes of it, he shall bear the blame.

No sooner had they left than to our infinite surprise, the immor-tal seven of Saturday night walked in. Wonder what fun they find in

80. One of the sons of the wealthy New Orleans commission merchant Alphonse Milten-berger. Ernest, 26 in the 1860 census, and James, 22, would seem the likeliest pos-sibilities. Late in the war Ernest Miltenberger carried a letter from Governor Henry Watkins Allen to Napoleon III in Paris. See "Polignac's Mission: An Interesting Chapter in Confederate History," *SHSP* 32 (1904): 364–71.

81. What a miracle!

coming? I see none. For we rarely trouble ourselves about their presence; there are but two I have addressed as yet; one because I am forced to say yes or no to his remarks, the other because I like his banjo which he brought again, and feel obliged to talk occasionally since he is so accommodating, and affords me the greatest amusement with his comic songs.

I was about retiring unceremoniously [p. 63] about twelve o'clock, completely worn out, when they finally bethought themselves of saying good night, and saved me the necessity of being rude. Wonder if that is all the fun they have? I should say it was rather dry. It is mean to laugh at them though; their obliging disposition should save them from our ridicule.

Last evening Mr Halsey succeeded in procuring a large skiff, whereupon four or five of them offered to row, and took us way down the Tchefuncta through the most charming scenery to a spot where Echo answered us in the most remarkable way; her distinct utterance was really alarming. Not being aware of the secret, I thought the first answer to the halloo was from pickets. Mr Halsey has a magnificent voice; and the echoes came back so full and rich, that soon we appointed him speaker by mutual consent and were more than repaid by the delightful sounds that came from the woods. The last ray of the sun on the smooth waters; the soldiers resting on their oars while we tuned the guitar and sang in the still evening until twilight, slowly closing over, warned us to return, forms another of those pictures indescribable, though never to be forgotten.

It was quite dark when we returned to the house, when I fell back on my sofa, glad to be in repose again. Mr Halsey, wandering up and down the parlor with rather a mischievous expression in his eye, after inviting Mrs Greyson to play a game of chess with Miriam (for which cruelty the latter rewarded him with a piteous look of entreaty), drew his chair by me, and spent the remainder of the evening in uninterrupted conversation. Miriam's calm look of resignation amused me, though I was sorry for her; and I could not conceal my delight at the righteous retribution when about ten o'clock the old lady, not satisfied with one victim, insisted on a game of Euchre with Mr Halsey. Excuses, apologies, promises to play the next time he came, nothing sufficed. Have him she would, and have him she did. He walked like a lamb to the sacrifice, while I made no attempt to conceal my relish of his unpleasant position. Just then mother summoned me up stairs; and following me to the steps, he bade me a last good night while, as usual, I went laughing to bed.

Ah! but a few hours ago I told him good bye for good and all. He said he would come back on Sunday; but I rather think we will not meet again. Three days leave of absence having been taken instead of the one and a [p. 64] half granted, will hardly entitle him to another furlough so soon. So when, after talking for an hour or two to me from below, while I sat on the gallery above, he mounted his horse and rode off with my red rose in his button hole, saying "Au revoir," I said good bye for true this time.

Miriam likes him so much, mother has conceived such a high regard for him, that I wonder why I dont like him too? I cannot conceal from myself the shocking fact that it is not the *good* man I like. It is the elegant, the worldly, with a slight touch of the devil that I find myself unconsciously looking for. Perhaps Heaven will send a judgement on me for the sin, yet. But good men— Pshaw! it is true; paragons are not to my taste.

Bonfouca.[82] Saturday, April 18th.

When I paused on Thursday to rest a few moments before bringing the above interesting subject to a close, while I gathered strength to pursue my reflections on my own wickedness and worldliness, how little idea I had of its never being brought to a close, and that the rest I was taking would soon be required for another journey! It was agreed among us, with our fellow travellers, Mrs Bull & Mrs Ivy, whom we met at Mrs Greyson's endeavoring to reach the city like ourselves, that

82. Plantation home on the northeastern shore of Lake Pontchartrain which took its name from the nearby Bayou Bonfouca. Sarah originally wrote "Bonfoucard" and then came back later and corrected it here and elsewhere (with one exception).

we would wait there until we could receive our passports from Gen. Pemberton.[83]

When this journey was first seriously contemplated, Miriam wrote to Col. Szymanski[84] representing mother's state of health, and my unfortunate condition, the necessity of medical advice for both, and the impossibility of remaining in famishing Clinton, and asked him to apply to the General for a pass to go to Brother. The Colonel sent word through Eugene La Noue[85] that we should obtain it in a few days, and advised us to go by way of Ponchatoula. Tired of delay, and hearing that we could pass as readily on Gen. Gardener's order, we obtained one, and started off without waiting for the other. The first news on arriving at Madisonville was that no one should pass except on Gen. Pemberton's order. Pleasant intelligence for those who had come that far without! The other two ladies were in the same dilemma. They were told that they should have a pass if they would wait. Waiting, at the expense of four dollars a day for each, Mrs Ivy with two very sick babies, Mrs Bull with all her property in New Orleans at stake, Tiche with her broken foot, mother with a powerless [p. 65] hand, and I with [page torn] (to use a [illegible] expression) and injured spine, was anything but agreeable under the circumstances; though nothing could be more pleasant, apart from this sense of restriction, than our stay at Madisonville.

Gen. Pemberton took his leisure about the affair, which is not surprising as our generals have more weighty matters than women's passports to attend to. Still, pleased as we were with our residence there, it was necessary to get on as soon as possible. So as I rested from my labors about one o'clock on Thursday, Mrs Bull came in to suggest a new plan to mother. It was to leave immediately for a plantation called Bonfoucard [sic], thirty miles off, where schooners came twice a week, and where we would be allowed to embark without a pass. Carriages that had just brought a party of ladies from Mandeville were waiting on the other side of the river, which could take us off immediately, for there was not a moment to lose.

83. General John C. Pemberton, the officer in command of Confederate forces in Mississippi and East Louisiana. Pemberton's headquarters were in Jackson, Mississippi.

84. Colonel Ignatius Szymanski, an officer on Pemberton's staff.

85. Charlie LaNoue's brother.

Instantly we resolved to hazard the undertaking, encouraged by Mrs Greyson's advice, who thought it the best plan, though she professed herself distressed to lose the company of the young ladies. "They are such comforts; and some how all the flowers seem to follow them," she said sniffing daintily one after the other of our array of bouquets. As soon as we could dress, and get our trunks packed (much I had to do with the latter arrangement!) I scribbled off a last word to Mr Halsey while I waited for my hat. It was only just; for here was Mrs Greyson who has taken such an extraordinary fancy for him, setting her heart on giving us a dance Saturday night when he would arrive, and promising him a most delightful visit. And I knew that he would naturally be rather disappointed when he found only a deserted house instead of the gaiety promised. So it was nothing but proper that we should leave a word of adieu behind.

About three we got in the large scow to cross the Tchefuncta, in a party numbering five ladies, four children and four servants. One of the devoted pickets ("devoted" because they form a never failing source of amusement to me and are consequently "devoted" by me to ridicule), after setting me carefully in the most comfortable place, asked permission to accompany me as far as the carriage; he was sure he could assist me more carefully than the drivers. And without further parley, he followed. Before we turned [p. 66] the point, Mr Worthington [page torn] the dim distance, rowing up the stream in the direction of Madisonville. What if he had perceived us, and was hastening after us, deeming it his duty to arrest us for trying to get away without Gen. Pemberton's order? As the idea was suggested, there was rather a nervous set of ladies on board.

The half mile that we had to go before reaching our landing place was passed over in nervous apprehension. At last the spot was reached. Mr Worthington had not appeared, and we reached terra firma without being "nabbed," as we confidently expected. The obliging picket put me in the carriage, bade me a most friendly adieu, and returned to the village, leaving us with every prospect of getting off without serious difficulty, in spite of our serious apprehensions. With two little children and Tiche with me, our carriage started off some time before the others. Two or three miles from our starting point, I perceived three gentlemen riding towards us, one of whom I instantly recognized as

Dr Capdevielle. Instantly I stopped the carriage to speak to him. His look of astonishment when satisfied of my identity rather amused me; but my amusement was changed to a slight feeling of disappointment when he commenced talking.

Was it possible I was leaving Madison? O how distressed he was! He was promising himself so much pleasure! And to leave so unexpectedly! He had just come with his friends from—somewhere. They had planned a surprise party at Mrs Greyson's for us that evening, and had been after the supper they had procured—somewhere, as I before observed, and were just now returning. And now we were deserting them! He had invited Monsieur Berger, Monsieur Pollock,[86] Monsieur— Mais enfin des Messieurs![87] he exclaimed with a comical emphasis and smile that brought vivid recollections of the other party before my eyes, by force of contrast I suppose. And wasn't I sorry we had left! We fairly condoled with each other. Twenty minutes elapsed before I had so far recovered from the disappointment as to bethink myself of the propriety of continuing my journey. And then with the assurance of being mutually désollé [sic], we parted with a hearty good bye, and he rode on to rejoin his companions, while I went the way he had come.

Two miles beyond, I met three others of the six gentlemen he had mentioned, riding in a little dog cart which contained [p. 67] champagne baskets in which the supper was evidently packed, each gentleman elegantly dressed, holding between them a little basket of bouquets that my prophetic soul told me was intended for Miriam and me. I was not personally acquainted with the gentlemen, or I should have told them of the disappointment that awaited them. It *must* have been a disappointment! Dont tell me they did not feel it! I know I could have made faces at myself with vexation; and their sensation I hope was quite as disagreeable. It was aggravating to see them so gay and lively. "Wretches!" I mentally exclaimed as one gracefully toyed with a bouquet, "Do you know that your supper and your elegant selves are passing your expected guests on the road?" I felt a kind of exultation when I thought that an hour later Dr Capdevielle would tell them that

86. Sarah probably means Miltenberger, the same gentleman referred to in the previous entry. Monsieur Pollock was no doubt one of the Pollock brothers, possibly James or George, Jr., both associated with A. Miltenberger & Co.

87. But at last the gentlemen!

the carriages they passed contained the young ladies they were going to see.

Was it not too provoking to miss all that fun when the next morning would have answered as well for our journey? In the midst of profound reflections about fate, vanity of human wishes and calculations, friendships formed on the road side in the journey through life (or from Clinton), I raised my eyes to behold Lake Ponchartrain, and to find myself in Mandeville, just seven miles from the Tchefuncta. Looking at the dreary expanse of water which suggested loneliness and desolation, first recalled my own situation to me. Here I was in this straggling place, with Tiche a cripple like myself, and two little children, under my care, without an idea of where we were to go. Any one as timid and dependent as I to be placed in such a position as pioneer to such a tremendous company, would feel rather forlorn. But some step had to be taken, so I consulted the driver as to where we could obtain board, and followed his suggestion. One house after the other we stopped at, and with my veil down and my heart beating as though I were soliciting charity, or some other unpleasant favor, I tried to engage rooms for the company without success. At last we were directed to a Frenchman, who, after the usual assurance of "nothing to eat" (which we afterwards found to be only too true) consented to receive us.

"Taking possession" seemed to me such a dreadful responsibility that for some time I remained in the carriage, afraid to get out before the others arrived. But there was [p. 68] still no signs of them; so I gathered my children and Tiche, and prepared to dismount with the Frenchman's assistance. I have read descriptions of such houses and people, but have not often seen them. The man and his wife were perfect specimens of the low Canadian,[88] speaking only french. No sooner had they discovered that I was "blessée"[89] as they supposed, than each seized an arm and with overwhelming exclamations of sympathy, half way dragged me in the room, where they thrust me in a chair. Their family seemed to consist only of cats and dogs who seemed to agree most harmoniously, and each of whom conceived the liveliest affection for us.

88. Sarah probably means Acadian, or Cajun.
89. Injured.

As we were leaving Mrs Greyson's, a stranger just from the city brought to our room a paper of ham, tongue and biscuits for "the sick young lady" (heaven only knows how she heard of her), saying she had just travelled the road herself, and knew I would find nothing to eat; so she would insist on putting this in our basket. It was done in a manner that put all refusal out of the question, so it had to be accepted. I was feeding little Jenny Ivy and Minna Bull[90] on this lunch for want of something else to do, when the affection of the cats and dogs became overpowering. Six of them jumped at us, licked Jenny's face, eat [*sic*] Minna's ham, and what with sundry kicks and slaps, I had exercise enough to last a week, and was rapidly losing all my strength when the woman came to my rescue and called her pets off just as the rest of the party drove up to find me almost exhausted.

I dont mean to grumble; but in spite of the kindness and attention lavished upon me, how much pleasure I am deprived of by this sickness! Throwing aside cloaks and bonnets, all went to walk on the lake shore, leaving me thankful enough to be in bed, but still with a slight feeling of regret that I could not join them.

Such a bedroom! There was a narrow single bed in which mother, Jenny, and I slept, a decrepit table on which stood a desèased mirror, a broken lounge without a bottom, and a pine armoir filled with— corn! In the centre stood the chief ornament, a huge pile of dirt, near which Miriam's matress was placed, while the sail of a boat flanked it in on the other side, arranged as a bed for Tiche. The accommodations in the other [bedroom] were far inferior to ours. Then the mosquitoes swarmed [p. 69] like Pandemonium on a spree, and there was but one bar in the house which the man declared should be only for me. I would rather have been devoured by the insects, than enjoy comforts denied to the others; so I made up my mind it should be the last time.

Our supper was rare. "Nothing like it was ever seen in Paris" as McClellan would say. It consisted of one egg a piece, with a small spoonfull of rice. A feast, you see! Price, one dollar each, besides the dollar paid for the privilege of sleeping among dirt, dogs and fleas.

90. Children of Mrs. Ivy and Mrs. Bull. Virginia (Jenny) Ivy was 3. See New Orleans births, 1859, Vital Records. Minna Bull's age is 4 in the 1860 census.

Sunday April 19th.

Friday morning we arose at daylight and prepared to resume our journey for Bonfoucard, twenty three miles away. The man walked in very unceremoniously to get corn from the armoir as we got up, throwing open the windows and performing sundry little offices usually reserved for femmes de chambres,[91] but with that exception every thing went on very well. Breakfast being a luxury not to be procured, we got in the carriages before sunrise, and left this romantic abode of dogs and contentment. Again our road lay through Piney Woods, so much like that from Hammond to Ponchatoula, that involuntarily I found myself looking through the window to see if Mr Halsey was there. It lacked only his presence to make the scene all in all the same. But alas! this time the driver picked me wild flowers, and brought us haws. Mr Halsey, in blissful ignorance of our departure, was many, and many a mile away. The drive was not half as amusing. The horse would not suffer any one except Miriam to drive, and at last refused to move until the driver got down and ran along by the carriage. Every time the poor boy attempted to occupy his seat, the obstinate animal would come to a dead stop and refuse to go until he dismounted again. I am sure that he walked nineteen miles out of the twenty three, out of complaisance to the ungrateful brute.

All equally fatigued and warm, we reached this place about twelve o'clock. Mrs Bull had arrived before us; and as the carriage stopped, her girl Delia[92] came to the gate the personification of despair crying "You cant get out, ladies. They say we cant stop here; we must go right back." The panic which ensued is indescribable. Go back when we were almost at our journey's end, after all the money we had spent, [p. 70] the fatigue we had undergone, to be turned back all the way to Clinton, perhaps! "With my sick babies!" cried Mrs Ivy. "With my sick child!" cried mother. "Never! you may turn us out of your house, but we will die in the woods first! To go back is to kill my daughter and these babies!" This was to the overseer who came to the carriage. "Madam, I have orders to allow no one to pass who has not written permission.

91. Chambermaids.

92. Probably a servant.

Lieut. Worthington sent the order two days ago; and I am liable to imprisonment if I harbor those who have no passport," the man explained. "But we have Gen. Gardener's order," I expostulated. "Then you shall certainly pass; but these ladies cannot. I cant turn you away though; you shall all come in and stay until something can be determined on."

This much granted was an unlooked for blessing. He showed us the way to a large unfurnished house, one room of which contained a bed with one naked matress, which was to be our apartment. Mrs Bull sat down in a calm, dignified state of despair; little Mrs Ivy disolved in tears; we all felt equally disconsolate; the prospect of getting off was not so pleasant when we thought we should be obliged to leave them behind. Our common misfortunes had endeared us to each other, strangers as we were a week ago. So we all lamented together, a perfect Jérémiade of despair.

The overseer is very tender hearted; he condoled, comforted, and finally determined that if there was any way of getting them off, they should go. A glimpse of sunshine returned to our lowering sky, and cheerfulness reigned once more, to be violently dethroned some hours later. Three of the Madisonville pickets were announced approaching the house. Of course they were coming after us! O that vile Mr Worthington! We always *did* hate him! There was always such a sneaky look about him! Hypocrite! we always felt we should hate him! O the wretch! "I wont go back!" cried mother. "I shall not" said quiet Mrs Bull. "He shall pay my expenses if he insists on taking me back!" exclaimed Mrs Ivy. "Spent all my money! Mrs Bull, you have none to lend me, remember, and Mrs Morgan you *shan't*! O that Worthington! let's make him pay for all!" We smothered our laughter to sit trembling within as the pickets stepped on the gallery. I believe we commenced praying.

Just think! Thus far, our journey has cost mother two hundred and twenty dollars. It would cost the same [p. 71] to get back to blessed Clinton, and fancy our spending that sum to settle there again! Besides, we gave away all our clothes to our suffering friends; and what would we do there now?

After half an hour of painful suspense, we discovered that it would have been as well to spare poor Mr Worthington; for the pickets were not after us, but had come to escort Mrs. Ryan,[93] a woman who was taking the body of her son who was killed at Murfreesboro, to the city for interment. Poor woman! she rode all this distance sitting on her child's coffin. Her husband was one of those who with Breedlove stole that large sum of money from father which came so near ruining him. She speaks of her husband as of a departed saint. I dare say she believes him innocent of the theft in spite of his public confession. The grave has wiped out even the disgrace of the penetentiary where he expiated his offence. Low, vulgar, unrefined, she has lived in affluence. Father was made an old man before his time by the wicked deed, and spent many years in my early life, bowed down by poverty. When I told Tiche who the woman was, she clasped her hands, saying "The Lord is good! Years and years master suffered while she grew rich, and now *her* time comes! The Lord dont forget!" I cant feel that way. It is well for the narrow minded to look for God's judgement on us for our sins; but mine is a more liberal faith. God afflicted her for some wise purpose; but if I thought it was to avenge father, I should be afraid of her. As it is, I can be sorry, oh *so* sorry for her!

As usual I find myself taken care of at the expense of the others. There are but two [mosquito] bars on the place; one, the overseer said, should be for me, the other for the children. Sheets were scarce, covers scarcer still. Tired of being spoiled in this way, I insisted on being allowed to sleep on a matress on the floor, after a vigorous skirmish with mother and Miriam, in which I came off victorious. For a bar, I impressed Miriam's grenadine dress, which she fastened to the door knob and let fall over me à la Victoria tester arrangement. To my share fell a double blanket, which, as Tiche had no cover, I unfolded, and as she used the foot of my bed for a pillow, gave her the other end of it, thus, (tell it not in Yankee land, for it will never be credited) actually sleeping under the same bed clothes with our black, shiny negro nurse!

We are grateful [p. 72] though even for these discomforts; it might have been so much worse! Indeed I fear that our fellow travellers do not fare as well. Those who have sheets have no bars, those who have

---

93. Mrs. Ryan has not been identified, but her son was very likely Private James Ryan, 20th Louisiana, who died in October 1863 while nursing in the military hospital at Murfreesboro, Tennessee.

blankets have no sheets, and one woman who has recently joined us has nothing except a matress which is to do the duty of all three. But then, we got bread! Real, pure, wheat bread! And coffee! None of your potato, burnt sugar, and parched corn abomination, but the unadulterated berry! I cant enjoy it fully though; every mouthful is cloyed with the recollection that Lilly and her children have none.

As usual, as Mrs Greyson says, the flowers follow us; yesterday I received three bouquets, and Miriam got one too. In this out of the way place such offerings are unexpected; and these were doubly gratifying coming from people one is not accustomed to receiving them from. For instance, the first was from the overseer, the second from a servant, and the third from a poor boy for whom we have subscribed to pay his passage to the city.

Wednesday April 22d New Orleans

Yesterday we arrived; I thought we should never get here. Monday we had almost given up in despair, believing the schooner would never return. But in the evening when all were gathered in our room discussing our hopes and fears, a sail was perceived at the mouth of the bayou, where upon every one rushed out to see the boat land. I believe I have not mentioned that this Bonfouca is on a bayou of the same name, that runs within a few yards of this house. It is an Indian name signifying Winding river, which struck us as very appropriate when we watched the schooner sailing now to the left, now to the right, apparently through the green fields; for the high grass hid the course of the stream so that the faintest line was not perceptible, except just in front of the house. All was now bustle and confusion, packing, dressing, and writing last words to our friends at home, until half past eleven when we embarked.

This is my first experience of schooners, and I dont care if I never again behold another. The cabin where Mr Kenedy[94] immediately

94. Possibly the overseer at Bonfouca.

carried me, was just the size of my bed at home (in the days I had a home) and just high enough to stand in. On [p. 73] each side of the short ladder, there was a mattress two feet wide. One of them Mrs Ryan had possession of already, the other was reserved for me. I gave the lower part of mine to Minna and Jennie who spent the rest of the night fighting each other and kicking me. Just before twelve we "weighed anchor" and I went on deck to take a last look at Dixie with the rest of the party. Every heart was full. Each left brothers, sisters, husband, children, or dear friends behind. We sang Farewell dear land with a slight quaver in our voices, looked at the beautiful starlight shining on the last boundary of our glorious land, and fervently and silently praying, passed out of sight.

God bless you, all you dear ones we have left in our beloved country! God bless and prosper you, and grant you the victory in the name of Jesus Christ.

I returned to my matress, and this is the way we spent the night; Mrs Ryan, rocking and moaning as she sat up in bed, whined out her various bodily ills with a minute description of each, only ceasing the recital to talk of her son's body which lay on deck. (Yesterday morning she was sitting crying on his coffin while a strange woman sat on its head eating her bread and cheese.) Mrs Bull, one of the most intelligent and refined ladies I have yet met, who is perfectly devoted to me, sat by me, laughing and talking, trying her best to make every one comfortable and happy in her unobtrusive way. Mother talked to Mrs Ryan and cried at the thought of leaving her children fighting & suffering.

The space between the two beds was occupied by three Irish women, and Mrs Ivy's two babies. The babies had commenced screaming as the[y] were brought into the pen, at which I was not surprised. Having pitched their voices on the proper key, they never ceased shrieking, kicking, crying, throwing up, and going through the whole list of baby performances. The nurses scolded with shrill voices above the bedlam that had hushed even Mrs Ryan's complaints, Jennie and Minna quarrelled, kicked and cried, and as an aggravation to the previous discomforts, a broadshouldered, perspiring Irishwoman sat just by my head, bracing herself against my pillows in the most unpleasant style. I endured it without flinching until about half past three, when the condensed odor of a dozen [p. 74] different people and children became unendurable, and I staggered up on deck where Miriam and Mrs Ivy had been wise enough to remain, without venturing below. They laid me on a bench in the stern, rolled me up in shawls, to keep off the heavy dew, and there I remained until day light with them, as wide awake as ever.

At daylight there was a universal smoothing of heads, and straightening of dresses, besides arrangements made for the inspection of baggage. Being unwilling for any christian to see such a book as this, I passed a piece of tape through the centre leaves, and made Miriam tie it under her hoops. At sunrise we were in sight of the houses at the lake end. It seemed as though we would never reach land.

I forgot to speak of our alarm as we got in the lake. No sooner had we fairly left the bayou, than the sky suddenly became threatening. The captain shook his head and spoke of a very ugly night for the lake, which sent everybody's heart to their throats, and alarmed us immeasurably. We got [to] talking of the sailor's superstition of crossing the water with a corpse, until we persuaded ourselves that it was more than probable we would founder in the coming storm. But the severest storm we met was the one in the cabin; and all night the only wind was a head-breeze, and the spicy gale from below.

When we at last entered the canal,[95] I beheld the animal now so long unseen, the Yankee. In their dark blue uniforms they stood around, but I thought of the dear grey coats, and even the pickets of Madisonville seemed nobler and greater men than these. Immediately a guard was placed on board, we whispering before he came "Our dear Confederates, God bless them." We had agreed among ourselves, that come what would, we would preserve our dignity and self respect, and do anything rather than create a scene among such people. It is well that we agreed. So we whispered quietly among ourselves, exhorting each other to pay no attention to the remarks the Yankees made about us as we passed, and acting the martyr to perfection, until we came to Hickock's Landing.

Here there was a group of twenty Yankees. Two officers came up and asked us for papers; we said we had none. In five minutes one came back, and asked if we had taken the oath. No; we had never taken *any*.

95. The schooner would have entered the New Basin Canal after crossing the eastern end of Lake Pontchartrain.

He then took down our names. Mother was alone in the coop. He asked if there was not another. [p. 75] The schooner had fifteen passengers, and we had given only fourteen names. Mother then came up and gave her name, going back soon after. From that moment I knew she was preparing for a scene. While one went after our passes, others came to examine our baggage. I could not but smile as an unfortunate young man got on his knees before our trunk and respectfully handled our dirty petticoats and stockings. "You have gone through it before," he said. "Of course the Confederates searched it." "Indeed they did not touch it!" I exclaimed. "They never think of doing such work." "Miss, it is more mortifying to me than it can be to you," he answered. And I saw he was actually blushing.

He did his work as delicately as possible, and when he returned the keys, asked if we had letters. I opened my box and put them in his hand. One came near getting me in serious trouble. It was sent by some one I never saw, with the assurance that it contained nothing objectionable. I gave it sealed to the man, who opened it, when it proved to be rather disagreeable I judged from his language. He told me his captain must see it before he could let me have it, and carried it off. Presently he came back and told me it could not be returned. I told him to burn it then, as I neither knew the writer, the contents, nor those it was written to. "I may save you some difficulty if I destroy it" he remarked, whereupon he tore it up and flung it in the canal. I have since found I had cause to be grateful; for just after came an officer to see the young lady who brought that letter. I showed the pieces in the water, saying the young man had torn it up, which seemed to annoy him; it was to be sent to headquarters, he said.

Then came a bundle of paper on board carried by another, who standing in front of us cried in a startling way "Sarah Morgan!" "Here." (*very* quietly) "Stand up!" "I cannot." (firmly) "Why not?" "Unable." (decisively) After this brief dialogue, he went on with the others until all were standing except myself, when he delivered to each a strip of paper and informed the people that Miss, or Mrs So and So had taken and subscribed the oath as Citizen of the U.S. I thought that was all, and rejoiced at our escape. But after another pause he uncovered his head and told us to hold up our right hands. Half crying I covered my face with mine and prayed breathlessly for the boys and the Confederacy, so that I heard not a word he was saying until the question [p. 76] "So help you God?" struck my ear. I shuddered and prayed harder. There came an awful pause in which not a lip was moved. Each felt as though in a nightmare until throwing down his blank book, the officer pronounced it "All right!" Strange to say, I experienced no change. I prayed as hard as ever for the boys and our country, and felt no nasty or disagreeable feeling which would have announced the process of turning Yankee.

Then it was that mother commenced. He turned to the mouth of the diminutive cave, and asked if she was ready to take the oath. "I suppose I *have* to, since I belong to you" she replied. "No madam, you are not obliged; we force no one. Can you state your objections?" "Yes. I have three sons fighting against you, and you have robbed me, beggared me!" she exclaimed, launching into a speech in which Heaven knows *what* she did not say; there was little she left out, from her despoiled house to her sore hand, both of which she attributed to the at first amiable man, who was rapidly losing all patience. Miriam endeavored in vain to stop her, Mrs Bull expostulated, Mrs Ivy entreated. But mother had been preparing herself for just such a scene, and faint with hunger, dizzy with sleeplessness, she had wrought on her own feelings until her nerves were beyond control. She was determined to carry it out, and crying and sobbing went through with it.

I neither spoke nor moved, knowing that at such moments mother is not to be controled by any one on earth except father or Brother, and that neither could come to her. The officer walked off angrily and sent for a guard to have mother taken before Gen. Bowens.[96] Once through her speech, mother yielded to the entreaties of the ladies and professed herself ready to take the oath, since she was obliged to. "Madam, I did not invite you to come" said the polite officer, who refused to administer the oath, and putting several soldiers on board, ordered them to keep all on board until one could report to Gen. Bowens. Mother retired to the cabin crying still, and thinking every one against her, while we still kept our seats above.

O that monotonous, never ending canal! We thought it would go on

96. A former president of the Erie Railroad, General James Bowen was provost marshal general of the Department of the Gulf under General Banks.

for ever. At last we came to the basin in the centre of the city. Here was a position for ladies! Sitting like Irish emigrants on their earthly possessions, and coming in a schooner to New Orleans, which a year [p. 77] ago would have filled us with horror.

Again the landing was reached, and again we were boarded by officers. I dont know how they knew of the difficulty mother had made, but they certainly did, and ordered that none should leave until the General's will was made known. Mrs Bull and Mrs Ivy, after a long delay and many representations, at last prepared to leave. I was sitting in the spot I had occupied ever since before daylight, with nothing to support me above my hips. All of us had fasted since an early and light supper the night before, none had slept. I was growing so weak from these three causes, and the burning sun (for it was now twelve), that I could hardly speak when they came to tell me good bye.

Alarmed at my appearance, Mrs Bull entreated the officer to allow me to leave the boat. No, he said; it was impossible; we should remain on board until Gen. Bowens could come. We may get an answer in half an hour, or we may not get it for some time; but there we must stay until it came. "But this young lady has been ill for months; she is perfectly exhausted, and will faint if she is not removed immediately" pleaded Mrs Bull. She did not know my powers of self control. Faint! I would have expired silently first! The officer said those were his orders; I could not leave. "Do you think you are performing your duty as a gentleman and a Christian? This young lady has obtained her pass already, without the slightest difficulty" she persisted. Still he said he was acting according to orders. Not to be baffled, she begged that she might be allowed to take me to Brother, telling him who he was, while our trunk, Miriam, Tiche, and mother would remain as hostages. Then he gave a reluctant consent on condition I left my number, so he could go after me when I was wanted.

I dont know what good came of the consent, for there I was to remain until something, I dont know what, happened. I only know I was growing deathly sick and faint, and could hardly hold myself up, when some time after Mrs Bull and Mrs Ivy left (under the impression that I was to go immediately) a gentleman in citizen's clothes came to me and said he had obtained permission for me to wait Gen. Bowens orders in his office a few steps from the schooner. Thankful for that much, I accepted his arm, and slowly dragged myself along to the first shelter I had seen that day. By some wonderful [p. 78] condescension Miriam and mother (the sole offender) were allowed to follow; and with the guard at the door, we waited there for a half hour more until our sentence could be received.

Miriam had written a line to Brother as soon as possible, telling him of the situation mother had placed us in by her rash conduct, and while we were waiting in this office, I half dead with fatigue, a carriage dashed up to the door, and out of it stepped Brother. I felt that all our troubles were over then. He looked so glad to see us, that it seemed a pity to tell the disagreeable story that yet remained to be told. But once heard, he made all go right in a few moments. He got in the carriage with mother to take her to Gen. Bowens, while we got in another to come to the house. I saw no more of the guard or officer.

When we arrived Sister was too astonished to speak. She did not believe we would come when it was ordered that all should take the oath on entering. If we had only realized it I dont think we would, either. In half an hour mother got back. Supported by Brother's presence she had managed to hold up her right hand and say "Yes" to the oath, which was more than any of us had done. If she had done it at first, she would have spared us a most painful scene, and saved me from fatigue that threatened to annihilate me for some time. I thought Miriam would have a brain fever. Brother found an officer at the door who had been ordered (before he took mother to the General) to arrest her and confine her in the Customhouse.[97] I suppose Miriam and I would have shared the imprisonment with her. But Brother has a way of making all these things right; and the man was sent back without accomplishing his mission.

Sunday April 26th

I am getting well! Bless the Lord O my soul! Life, health, and happiness dawn on my trembling view again! Is not this delight worth the five months and a half of suspense and pain? Yes! I am getting well!

On Thursday, [a] day to be marked with a white stone in my memory, for the first time since the eleventh of November I discarded my

97. A four-story granite structure which covered an entire block on Canal Street near the river. Work on the building began in the 1840s and was still continuing when the war came.

nightgown, put on a dress, and—walked to breakfast! And better still, scorning the bed that has been my best friend and inseparable companion through all [p. 79] these long months, I adopted this shell-like easy chair instead, and have never, since that day, laid down for an instant in the day time! Tell it not at Linwood or Clinton, lest you be denounced as an exaggerator! No one there would believe I have made but one step from sickness to health, from my nightgown to a dress, not put on for a few hours to receive particular friends, but for all day. Yes! I am getting well! Dr Stone[98] came to me a few hours after I arrived; two days after, he called again; this morning I walked out to meet him when he was announced, and he asked me how my sister was! When I assured him I was myself, "God bless my soul! You dont say so!" he exclaimed, evidently astonished at the resurrection. He attributes it to Belladonna and gentle exercise; I say thank God and dont care to know why or wherefore. Why, yesterday I walked up stairs to see Hicky and Harry[99] who have Scarlet fever!

Ah Mr Halsey! I shall never again be forced to accept your help! I am so thankful for that! And Mr Howard, I do believe I could get off the cars without that strong right arm so carefully, respectfully, delicately, yet withal so unpleasantly encircling my waist! I dont like to think of that. Yet it was very kind in him, for I certainly would have remained there without his assistance. And though it was over before I could draw a breath, yet it is one of those things that make people make faces at themselves when they think of it in the dark. One of those unpleasant obligations that make you hate the one who assists you. I believe I am an ungrateful wretch.

Thursday April 30th.

Was not the recollection of this day bitter enough to me already? I did not think it could be more so. Yet behold me crying as I have not cried for many and many a day. Not for Harry; I dare not cry for him. I feel a deathlike quiet when I think of him; a fear that even a deep

98. Dr. Warren Stone, the well-known New Orleans surgeon. See biographical sketch in *Standard History of New Orleans, Louisiana,* edited by Henry Rightor (Chicago, 1900), 218–20.

99. Hicky and Harry Hays Morgan were Sarah's nephews, sons of Philip Hicky Morgan. Harry, 4 at this time, would grow up to become a diplomat and father of the famous Morgan twins, Gloria, who married Reginald C. Vanderbilt, and Thelma, Lady Furness.

drawn breath would wake him in his grave. And as dearly as I love you, O Hal I dont want you in this dreary world again! Not here, O Hal! Not here! Stay where you can look down on these pitiful mortals and smile at [p. 80] their littleness. But I would not have you among them, Hal! Stay there, where maybe one day God will call me. I will go to you, but dont wish to be back here, Harry. Long long ago I learned to say "Thy will be done," and almost to be thankful you were in your grave. Two years ago to day Hal, you folded your hands and died so quietly and meekly.[100] Two years of trials and hardships have been spared you. Say thank God, Harry! O safe, safe, in the haven above pray for us, pity us, miserable creatures that we are!

To day came to us the proclamation which should link the name of Yankee to those of the inhabitants of the lower regions. Talk of the Revocation of the Edict of Nantes! Talk of Louis XIV! Of— Pshaw! my head is in such a whirl that history gets all mixed up, and all paralels [sic] seem weak and moderate in comparison to this infamous outrage. To day, thousands of families, from the most respectable down to the least, all who have had the firmness to register themselves enemies to the United States, are ordered to leave the city before the fifteenth of May.[101] Think of the thousands, perfectly destitute, who can hardly afford to buy their daily bread even here, sent to the Confederacy, where it is neither to be earned, nor bought, without money, friends, or a home. Hundreds have comfortable homes here, which will be confiscated to enrich those who drive them out. "It is an ill wind that blows no one good." [102]

Such dismal faces as one meets every where! Each looks heart broken. Homeless, friendless, beggars, is written in every eye. Brother's face is too unhappy to make it pleasant to look at him. True, he is safe;

100. Sarah always thought of April 30 as the anniversary of her brother's death, a date confirmed by both the New Orleans *Daily Delta*, May 1, 1861, and the *Daily Picayune* of the same date (Afternoon Edition). The May 1 date on Harry's gravestone must be an error.

101. General Orders No. 35, issued April 27, 1863. See *Daily Picayune*, May 1, 1863, p. 2. A total of 3,101 New Orleanians had come forward and registered as enemies of the United States the previous September. About one-third of those left the city when they were given the opportunity. Now, 1,015 of the remaining number left. Elisabeth Joan Doyle, "Civilian Life in Occupied New Orleans, 1862–65" (Ph.D. dissertation, Louisiana State University, 1955), 223–26.

102. John Heywood, *Proverbs*.

but hundreds of his friends are going forth destitute, leaving happy homes behind, not knowing where the crust of bread for famishing children is to come from to-morrow. He went to Gen. Bowen and asked if it were possible that women and children were included in the order. Yes, he said; they should all go, and go in the Confederacy. They should not be allowed to go elsewhere.

Penned up like sheep to starve! That's the idea! With the addition of forty thousand mouths to feed, they think they can invoke famine to their aid, seeing that their negro brothers dont help them much in the task of subjugating us. And these are the men who cry Liberty, Equality, [p. 81] Fraternity! These are the men who hope to conquer us! Ever unite with them? Never, never! Defenders of Charleston, Savannah, Mobile! *These* are the foes who are striving to overcome you! Deliver your cities in their hands? Die first!

O that from the Atlantic to the Rio Grande their vile footsteps should have been allowed to press our soil! Give up to them? Rather than submit, I would that, all gathered together, we should light our own funeral pyre, and old men, brave soldiers, fair women and tender children should all perish hand in hand in the bright flames we would send up to Heaven as a memorial of our toil, sorrow, and suffering.

If I was a man! O if I was only a man! For two years that has been my only cry, and to day I fairly rave about it. Blood, fire, desolation, I feel ready to invoke all, on these Yankees. Miriam and I are both desperate. If we could only get back, even to Clinton! It seems base treason to remain apparently under the protection of this hateful flag, while all of our own creed and country are sent out to starve. We would endure any thing, if we could only get mother's consent. If she would only stay with Brother, and let us go back to Clinton! For she cannot endure the privations we would have to undergo, while we could stand anything, just to get out of sight of these Yankees again. But she wont listen to it. So we will have to remain patiently here, and consequently labor under the suspicion of belonging to a side we abhor with all our souls. George and Gibbes will be frantic about it. If we could only, only get away!

Evidently, Banks had been whipped in the Attakapas.[103] In spite of his fanfaronade of trumpets, I believe he has been outrageously beaten

103. The Teche country in South Louisiana, principally Iberia, St. Mary, and St. Martin parishes. Banks had in fact driven General Richard Taylor back into the interior of the state, had taken Opelousas, and by May 7 would occupy Alexandria.

(as usual) and turns round to punish women and children for his defeat. The "Union" is certainly on its last legs when its generals resort to such means as getting negroes to fight its battles seeing how white men fail,[104] and take to running women and children out of the land. You have roused the Devil in us, Banks! We women will tear you to pieces yet!

Dont care who knows I smuggled in a dozen letters! Wish I had had more!

[p. 82] Tuesday May 12th.

It was just six months yesterday since I took that unlucky flight through the air which has disabled me for so long. Six months! Time to get well, one would think! Yet, when I look back, it seems only a few weeks—less than that, even. Could it be more than a dream? Three weeks ago I thought [I was] never to walk again further than across the room; this evening I expect to walk almost a mile. Miriam says she feels as though she had been shamefully imposed on; as though she had wasted the greatest amount of sympathy where it was uncalled for, and had distressed herself very unnecessarily about the final result. I am too glad, to begrudge the months of doubt, suffering and apprehension that have at last ended in this. It is almost worth the affliction I have undergone. And affliction made as easy as that, is not so difficult to be endured.

When I think of the kind, devoted hearts that surrounded me at Linwood, my heart swells with gratitude for their kindness. Nowhere will we find better friends. One by one every day I recall them, and wonder if I can ever forget their devotion and ceaseless watching over me. My own mother could not have nursed me more faithfully than Mrs Badger; I doubt if she could have done as much. Early and late, whatever a kind heart could suggest, she was ready to do for me. Even to getting up in the night, when she thought I must be tired of one position, and

104. Early in 1863 Union General Daniel Ullmann was sent to New Orleans to raise a brigade of Negro troops. Three black regiments had been formed during Butler's time in New Orleans. More were formed that spring under Banks. But there were doubts about whether blacks made good fighters until the 1st and 3rd Louisiana Native Guards proved themselves in the Union assault of May 27, 1863, at Port Hudson. "They fought splendidly!" Banks wrote his wife. See Hewitt, *Port Hudson*, 147–50, 175–79.

turning me, in those first few weeks when I could not help myself, she was always cheerfully by me, before I had silently formed the wish to move. They should have been wofully tired of such tedious sickness; but no word or sign showed it. If we mentioned it, a torrent of reproaches overwhelmed us. And day after day, there sat Lydia and Helen, ready to talk or wait on me, while Mrs Carter dragged herself upstairs when ever she was able, and every evening the General paid his visit, to tease me and bring me flowers or candy. O the dear, kind hearts at Linwood! What a debt of gratitude we owe them!

But I am getting well. No need of more care, petting or waiting on, now. Miriam, my sister, friend, comforter, waiting maid, slave, I dismiss you from your post with the sincerest recommendation [p. 83] to those who have been afflicted as I, and need a nurse who combines every requisite of heart and brain. And to think that the only feeling the wretch shows, is disappointment at my recovering so rapidly! I may have been very "interesting" (to those who did not suffer) but I have had enough of that, and am much more willing to bestow sympathy than receive any more.

I met a perfect stranger the other day, who surprised me by asking about my accident. Knowing that she knew none of my friends, and had probably never heard of me before, I could not resist the temptation of asking how she knew of it. She surprised me by saying it had been published in the True Delta here, how Miss Morgan, riding through P. Hudson, with a Confederate officer, had been thrown from her horse and very seriously injured. I had no idea of its having obtained such notoriety; but these papers, what wont they do for a paragraph? [105]

With the exception of a few inaccuracies, it is only too true, however. Only I wish it had not gained such a disagreeable publicity. It is not pleasant to have every one know it. And when people express their surprise to my friends, at not finding a hump on my back, or congratulate them on my having preserved my mind unimpaired through it all, it becomes anything but agreeable.

105. New Orleans newspapers published under difficult circumstances during the war, especially at the hands of General Butler, who was ever ready to suppress any paper which criticized his policies. See Gerald M. Capers, *Occupied City: New Orleans Under the Federals, 1862–1865* (Lexington, Ky., 1965), 176–81.

Sunday May 24th 1863

I wonder why I could never keep a respectable diary? I have a very amusing one in my brain, though no one would credit it after seeing such a specimen; but some how I keep it all there, afraid to commit it to paper, partly for fear it should fall in the hands of those it is not intended for, and partly because it would be too much trouble to write all I should like to remember, as I should like to have it written. This compromise between laziness and inclination I consider safe from all eyes, even though it should pass through Yankee hands as all my other papers did; for as long as I, the writer, could not be induced to wade through it, even the liveliest Yankee curiosity which considers the most sacred letters as public property, would hardly consider itself repaid for the fatigue of such a task.

I have tried to look back here and there, to find one redeeming touch, one description as interesting or amusing as the original, but have been forced to relinquish the search from sheer disgust. Every thing is so trite, so stale, [p. 84] so tedious and matter of fact, so dry and uninteresting, that I am strongly tempted to throw it in the fire every time I look at it. There is but one thing that withholds me; and that is the fact of its being the work of my sick hours, of those tedious months when writing and reading were my chief resources. Written for the most part while suffering severely, and while fighting desperately against blank despair that threatened to overcome all hopes of recovery, I may as well keep it to remember the dark hours when pen and ink proved my best friends, and soothed many an ache for me. One should not forget tried friends; then Vive pen and ink!

Then I'll keep this as a souvenir of my dark days—those days when Hope threatened to unfold her wings and leave me a cripple on this fair earth, and I struggled boldly to make the world believe she had not gone yet, and did not mean to. But as to keeping it for its own sake, or from any idea of wanting to read it some day, never! One page would be an infliction not to be borne. I wonder if it is because "Blessings brighten as they take their flight" or from contrast with this deserted place, that little scenes, and tableauxs briefly mentioned here, or silently passed over, now seems [sic] so bright and pleasant to me? Certain it is that I chiefly live in recollections of the past six months. There are few scenes here to distract me. A solitary Yankee or group of negroes passing the window is all the attraction I find without; and within, the occasional visit of young lady friends, and Brother, and Sister's conversation form my chief amusements. God bless them both! I say every time I look at them. How kind, and more than kind and considerate they are!

Mais revenons à nos moutons,[106] or diary, rather. What a bore this is! How signally it has failed if it aimed at being interesting! There is that week at Madisonville; who, reading this, would imagine that that was one of the pleasantest weeks I have ever spent? Miriam & I will always look back to it with pleasure; yet what is there here to show for it? Why Mrs Greyson herself would require two or three pages to do her justice. Fancy the daughter of Sir Francis Searle, the widow of Gen. Greyson, the belle of N. Orleans in her young days, settled down [p. 85] into a hotel keeper on a small scale, with stately ladies and gentlemen looking down in solemn surprise at her boarders from their rich portrait frames on the parlor walls!

Fallen greatness always gives me an uncomfortable thrill. Yet here was the heiress of these shadows on the wall, gay, talkative, bustling, active, with a word of caution, or a word of advice to all, polite, attentive, agreeable to her guests, quarrelling and exacting with her servants, grasping and avaricious with all, singing a piece from Norma in a voice about the size of a thread No. 150 that showed traces of former excellence, or cheapening a bushel of corn meal with equal volubility. What a character! Full of little secrets and mysteries; "Now my dear, I dont ask you to tell a *story*, you know; but if the others ask you if you knew it, just look surprised and say 'O dear me! When did it happen?' Cause I promised not to tell; only you are such favorites that I could not help it, and it would not do to acknowledge it. And if any one asks you if I put these candles in here, just say you brought them with you, that's a love, because they will be jealous, as I only allow them lamps." Eccentric Mrs Greyson! Dont tell a story; that is wrong; but above all, dont tell the truth, because that might lead to harm! Many an hour's amusement did she afford me with her evasions and subterfuges.

And the visiters she so kindly provided for our amusement! We laugh at them yet! The young man by the uncomfortable name of Coffin; the polite Mr Salisbury with his "happy to make your acquaintance,

106. But let us return to the subject . . .

ma'am;" the diffident Mr Mays whom Mr Carter parodied,[107] accompanied by his banjo for our edification, who twisted his toes in his boots, and twirled his fingers around and round with a "Hang it, Carter, that's too bad! before these ladies too!" The unmentionable crowd of others besides, how we laugh to recall them now! That was our first boarding-house experience; if all are as amusing, vive the institution!

What a pity it is, that the most pleasant incidents, and those that afford most amusement at the time, are those that cannot be put in words, but only hang like a picture before you. I mentioned one of these brain pictures to Miriam to day, and at the first words, before an idea was presented, we both burst out laughing. It was [p. 86] the most absurd affair imaginable, as it occurred; but as I before remarked, it is one of those incidents that cannot be clothed in words; you might read it here, and think it very flat; but Miriam, Mr Halsey, and I have thought of it more than once, since then, I am sure. I notice that I passed over it very hastily at the time, so I shall give a brief sketch of it here. Only we three, who saw the whole affair, can possibly understand the fun of it though, or know when to laugh.

Well then, it has been already recorded, that Mr Halsey's second visit began on a Tuesday, and that I pleaded indisposition, which was perfectly true, as an excuse for not going down so early in the day. It has also been mentioned that Miriam obstinately dressed me, had me carried down, and laid on the sofa in the parlor, where we spent a very pleasant day, etc. Here begins the odd part. Ever since an early dinner, Miriam had been practicing at the piano, while Mr Halsey read to me, now stopping to mark whatever pleased him, now to listen to my suggestions, or to talk. Hours passed in this way, until just before sunset, when the book had been laid by for some time, I found myself growing desperately sick. Miriam ran to me in alarm at my pallor, Mr Halsey was very kindly anxious and uneasy, while I could give no account of myself beyond saying I felt very unwell, and would probably be better in a few moments if they would leave me. That only redoubled their

107. The presence of these four names on the rolls of one of the cavalry companies operating in the area suggests that the men Sarah is referring to may have been Henry Salisbury, Hugh Mayes (also spelled Mays), William Carter, Jr., and R. L. Coffin or L. E. Coffin, privates in Company K, 1st Mississippi Cavalry. See Compiled Service Records of Confederate Soldiers from the State of Mississippi for the regiment.

solicitude; Mr Halsey commenced fanning me, while Miriam made me drink an incredible quantity of water, in spite of my protesting against both.

Embarrassed at being overwhelmed with kindness where I felt it was undeserved, it was then that I announced my determination of walking to the bench by the river to enjoy the cool breeze, when Miriam so urgently represented the folly of such fatigue in my weak state. Mr Halsey was always ready to oblige me, so he offered his arm, and suggesting that the fresh air might revive me, he won Miriam over to "our" side, and carefully conducted me to the bench under the trees. Here one of the pickets joined us, vainly endeavoring to enter into a conversation with each or all of us, and receiving very little satisfaction from any. The extent of Mr Halsey's conversation with me was this: he remarked "What a beautiful stream!" and I returned Beautiful, [p. 87] with due emphasis, whereupon we both looked attentively at the old broken warf [sic] just beyond, in dead silence. I was still too "ill" to talk.

About this time came Dr Capdevielle. "Mademoiselle!" I summoned energy to smile at the flowers he presented. He took the seat Mr Halsey had risen from, while Mr Miltonberger sat by Miriam. I made room for Mr Halsey on the other side; Thank you, he preferred standing behind me. In my weak state, I could not be expected to remember every one at once, so by turns I gave the Dr six words, and Mr Halsey one. But I was unaccountably growing better. The flowers had a wonderous revivifying effect, where Mr Halsey's strawberries failed to tempt me. I spoke rapidly! I smiled at the doctor's french compliments! I laughed, positively at his remarks! I retaliated with spirit! Those flowers must have been medicated! Talking brought the color to my face, and I turned laughing to Mr Halsey as I remembered he had been forgotten for five [108] minutes, and found him as silent and serious as I had been a short time before. Maybe he felt ill too! He had probably inherited my little indisposition. He briefly and simply agreed to my appeal; of course I was right.

Just then in the distance we beheld Mrs Greyson, running frantically after her old cow, attempting to drive it in the gate. "Shoo!" she cried "Scat, there!" jumping now to the right, now to the left as the ani-

---

108. Sarah later inserted: "(long measure)."

mal stupidly turned one way or the other, evidently not comprehending what course it was expected to take. At every jump she (the old lady, not the cow) plainly displayed her white stockings to our astonished gaze, and valiently brandished a stick at the bovine animal. "The daughter of Sir Francis!" I wonderingly said to myself, too astonished to laugh. Dr. Capdevielle chuckled unmistakably. Mr Halsey slowly and deliberately walked to her assistance, drove the cow through the gate, held it while the old lady followed, shut it gently, and coolly walked down the street and around the corner as though he lived in the village, and was only going home. I respected him for it! At that moment I would have taken his part bravely on the slightest provokation. It was manly! it was independent! Dr Capdevielle with his french airs would not have dared do it! He would have dreaded our ridicule too much to attempt it.

It was then that Dr Capdevielle suggested the walk that was to [p. 88] be of so much benefit. As we were about to return, Mr Halsey came from around the corner. "Have I not improved?" I asked, amused at his surprise. "The doctor is working wonders; I am glad to see you looking so much better," he returned coldly. The Doctor made some remark in french, I returned, and again Mr Halsey was forgotten, nor did I see him again until the visiters had departed. Then he came back, congratulated me on my recovered health, and was as good as it was possible for man to be for the rest of the evening, with the exception of a slight allusion to the affair every now and then. And that is the story that makes us laugh so now.

There are three versions of it, however. The story "John" knows, as he felt it, the story Sarah tells as she knows it, and the story Miriam remembers as she witnessed the byplay, or at least one part of it, for she saw nothing after we were under the trees except Mr Miltonberger. The first story, I am afraid, does not acquit me of all malice; the second proves it a mere series of incidents brought about by accident or impulse; the third—let Miriam speak for herself.

I ventured to day to ask what light she saw it in; this was the answer: "I think the illness was partly natural from your long suffering and sickness, but very much aggravated by a feeling of ennui that you allowed to over come you. Perhaps you were to[o] weak to struggle against it, perhaps you did not care if you did show that you were not interested in Mr Halsey's conversation. At all events, I think it was *real*. Then perhaps the fresh air of the river made you feel better, and Dr Capdeveille's conversation could not fail to enliven you, and so, and so—you forgot that you were sick, and consequently recovered rapidly. On the other side, Mr Halsey felt keenly, I think, that a rattle brain frenchman had accomplished what all his kindness and attention could not, and was rather mortified at the result, and saw only that you had reserved a cold shoulder for him. I saw he was mortified. One [*sic*] the whole, if asked to classify your disease, I should pronounce it unmistakably Bore!"

She ended with a laugh at the scene, in which I heartily joined. It *was* odd! Died of Mr Halsey, resurrected by Dr Capdevielle. Yet was it that? Is it possible that that sick, deathlike feeling was only the disease known by the vulgar name of "bore"? Perhaps that did have something to do with it; [p. 89] but O how sorry I should be to think he felt it to be so! Snubbed on all occasions by me, I might have spared him the mortification of that last scene, at least. When I think over my conduct since I first met Mr Halsey, a feeling of genuine disgust comes over me. With all humility I acknowledge to myself that I behaved shockingly towards him, on all occasions, and wonder how he ever had so much consideration for me, when I showed so little for him. What a disgust I must have given him for myself! John Halsey, one acknowledgement is due to you—I am unworthy of even the regard of so good a man. Bah! Vive la méchanceté![109] For I *dont* like saints and paragons, and enjoy your devil-may-care mischief immensely, on the other hand.

Chaqu ún à son gout;[110] you are not to mine; and there's an end to the question! Yes! an end in more senses than one; for where ever this book falls open, I see the name of Halsey staring me in the eyes, and am getting tired of the unfailing subject. So I shall drop it here, and never allude to it again until—I have occasion to mention it once more.

That occasion presents itself immediately; for I have not yet said how sorry I was to break the ring he put on my finger with a wish, just after supper that evening I have been writing about. I was sorry, because I wore it as a badge of the Confederacy, without thinking of the donor or the wish; and when I broke it while playing with the children a few days[111] ago, I felt as though the last souvenir of our dear land was gone. I put away the débris, resolved to keep them until we were free; and the

109. Long live the naughtiness!

110. Each to his own taste.

111. Sarah wrote "weeks," then came back and changed it to "days."

day peace is declared and we become as worthy of liberty in the eyes
of the Yankees as negroes are, I shall throw it in the river just as I now
throw to the winds all recollections of John Halsey. Adieu! One word!—
Wonder if he is "dreaming of those blue eyes" now? Nonsense! "Forward! March!" is the order. After skirmishes and marches, doubtless
"John" is too glad to throw himself down under the trees and forget all
things mundane in sleep—even "those blue eyes." This beautiful moon
that I was admiring a while ago, if she could speak of the scene she is
shining on somewhere between Ponchitoula and Camp Moore at this
moment, would probably represent him as oblivious of all protestations
and old promises, and report the wretch as—snoring!

[p. 90] Saturday May 30th.
    Yesterday they left. Who? Why I forget that I have not yet mentioned
the subject that has agitated the household for two weeks. I allude to
Sister's departure for California. What a surprise it was when first spoken of! Long before we came, the question had been discussed whether
she should visit Europe or the North this summer, and after we arrived, it was again a perplexing question whether she should leave us
her children, or take them with her. Two weeks ago she decided finally;
it was to take advantage of her first, and probably last oppertunity of
seeing her mother who left here eight years ago, and go to California
with Nellie and Charlotte, leaving the other children with us. Yesterday
morning they sailed in the "Morning Star" for New York.
    Each of us have quietly taken possession of our different depart-
ments already. Miriam is Chancellor of the Exchequer, and Housekeeper General; Brother, President of Financial Affairs; Mother, nomi-
nal guardian of the children, and Inspector General of servants and
house cleaning; I hold no place of importance; I am only Tutrix to
Lavinia and Hicky (made over to me formally by their mother), Arbi-
ter of innumerable disputes, General Sympathizer with infantile distresses, Keeper of the Wardrobe, Chief of the Mending Department,
and Restorer of Buttons. I have done an incredible amount of the latter
to day.
    Miriam presides with grace and dignity; but she will grow grey if
she keeps up her intense devotion to her task in this way. I have no
talent that way; I could not receive the complaints of each servant with

civility, and promise instant redress to each, complacently. The cook says if the wet nurse has milk in her tea at lunch, she will have it too; the washwoman and nursery maid insist on having all the privileges of the cook; dining room servant objects to washing dishes, so appoints Tiche to her place; mother objects to the abuse of furniture while cleaning up, and nursery maid objects to being interfered with by her, and so it goes. Miriam keeps her temper, preserves peace, quells disputes, holds the keys, and is recognized as Supreme Head by children and servants, bidding fair rule with a [end of p. 90; the two pages of the diary that followed (one page of the book, front and back) are missing]

[p. 91] June 9th. Tuesday.

My dear Brother, who is always seeking to make somebody happy, arranged a dinner party at the lake for us Saturday. There was quite a number of us, as besides ourselves and the five children, we had Mrs Price[112] and her children, Mrs Bull, and three nurses. And such an elegant dinner Brother had ordered! Every thing was perfect, from the fresh air, down to the Champagne. There never was a man better fitted to preside at table than he. No one can feel constraint when he wills you to be at ease; so our visit was one of unalloyed enjoyment. It was so good of him to invite Mrs Bull. It pleased us more than anything else. She is so unprotected and friendless here, that we feel the greatest sympathy for her; and it was gratefying [*sic*] to see how delighted she was with every thing.

Mrs Price was much harder to please; I think Brother was several times mortified by her brusque remarks, though he is too well bred to show it. After he had ordered what we thought an unexceptionable dinner, consulting as far as he could the taste of his guests, what was our surprise to hear her ask the waiter if the soup was all he had, and why he had no gumbo! Mrs Bull looked aghast, while Brother apologized saying he had not specified what soup or gumbo was to be served, but the hotel keeper, knowing he always called for this, had thought it would be equally to the taste of the others. The other courses passed off without comment, until the mutton chops and green pease; she pushed

112. Almedia Price, wife of George R. Price and sister of Helen Carter. The Price children were May and Maud.

her plate away; she never eat [*sic*] such a thing. As to the dessert, it all went wrong with her. The strawberries were well enough, but where were the cakes? And what was the sense of that pyramid of ice-cream and sherbet? She never touched sherbet!

All this was in sudden dashes, between laughter and conversation. She would stop any one who was speaking to make such inappropriate remarks. Yet she seemed to enjoy it as much as we, and was certainly in higher spirits than any of us. But what amazed me, was her asking Brother why he had brought no gentlemen to meet us. It would have been rather a difficult task in the present state of affairs. There are no Southern young men left in town, and those who remain would hardly be received with civility [p. 92] by Miriam and myself. Of the Yankees, Brother has so much consideration for us, that he has never invited one to his house since we have been here, though he has many friends among them who visited here before our arrival. Such delicacy of feeling we fully appreciate, knowing how very few men of such a hospitable nature would be capable of such a sacrifice.

Thinking we need company, Brother frequently invites what he calls "a safe old secessionist" (an old bachelor of fifty three who was wounded at Shiloh) to dine with us; thinking it a fair compromise between the stay at home youth, and Yankees, neither of which this extremely young man could be confounded with. Therefore, it would be rather difficult for him to invite those who would have been agreeable to all of his guests, a thing that is essential to the well being of all dinner parties; so he wisely refrained from inviting any, which was the most agreeable conclusion to the others of the party.

But these remarks seem to proceed from want of tact, or good breeding, on Mrs Price's part; her heart I am sure is a good and kind one; only polish is wanting. I could not but contrast her with her sister. One so dashing, fast, brusque, and fashionable, the other so timid, modest, and unpretending. Both are frank enough; but Helen Carter is a true friend to those she loves, whether they be of the highest or lowest. Frequently I, her pet and dearly beloved on other occasions, have encountered her most serious remonstrance for venturing to remark that some good, honest, common, ignorant country woman was hardly refined enough for my taste. Her belief is that who ever is a member of the church, is entitled to the rank and consideration of a lady, no matter what her station may be.

But Mrs Price on the contrary has an idea that none can be entitled to respect who do not patronize Olympe.[113] I had a laughable illustration of her taste in fashionable matters. We were drinking coffee with our bonnets on, while waiting for the cars, and Mrs Bull, praising the taste mine evinced, called it "sweet seventeen." The selection was Sister's, and a present from her. Olympe required an accurate description of my age, style, and person, which Sister gave, saying after minute details of complexion, eyes, etc, that I was *just seventeen*. Here it came, the sweetest, freshest, most [p. 93] girlish thing imaginable. I was naturally pleased with Sister's taste. Observing Mrs Price's critical eye examining the structure as Mrs Bull spoke, I appealed to her to know if Sister had not good taste. "Pretty enough" was the cool reply; "but the cape is at *Least* half an inch too short for the fashion. Why I venture to say that that bonnet is at least a month old!" I smilingly acknowledged that it had reached that venerable age, and also that it had been worn very nearly eight times. My confession was received with the advice to have it instantly altered by Olympe.

"O beloved Confederacy!" I thought; "Blessed abode of maidens who scorn not to worship in church with bonnets that had passed their prime three years ago, and in sunbonnets of unbecoming hue, would that I were once more within your limits, where Fashion is held in such contempt, that perchance I might be cut for wearing this very bonnet, the tail of which only, Mrs Price can condemn!"

No! Helen Carter is worth twenty such as her sister. She would love me the same if my sole article of clothing consisted of a Confederate grey blanket; while Mrs Price will hardly be reconciled to me until that extra half inch is appended to that tail.

---

113. The fashionable millinery shop of Mrs. Boisse Olympe at 154 Canal Street also offered fancy dry goods. But Eliza Ripley wrote that "her specialty was imported *chapeaux*." *Social Life*, 60.

Sunday June 14th.

The excitement about Port Hudson & Vicksburg is intense. When I heard on Friday that the last attack was being made on the former place,[114] I took to my prayers with a delirium of fervor. If I was a man, if I had the blessed privilege of fighting, I would be on the breast works, or perchance on the water batteries under Col. Steadman's command. But as I was unfortunately born a woman, I stay home and pray with heart and soul. That is all I can do; but I do it with a will.

In my excitement, I was wishing that I was a Catholic that I might make a vow for the preservation of Port Hudson, when a brilliant idea struck me. It was this: though vows are peculiar to Catholics, bed-bugs are common to all sects. From that arose this heroic scheme: I said "Hear me Miriam, thou who knowest that I have slept undisturbed but three nights out of seventeen, four hours out of each [p. 94] of the other fourteen having been spent in destroying my insatiable foe. Thou seest that nightly vigils are turning me pale and weak, thou knowest what unspeakable affection I have for the youth yclept by the ancients Morpheus. Yet listen to my vow: If Port Hudson holds out, if our dear people are victorious, I offer up myself on the altar of my country to Bed-bugs, and never again will I murmur at their depredations and voracity." Talk of pilgrimages, and the ordinary vow of wearing only the Virgin's colors (the most becoming in the world) there never was one of greater heroism or more sublime self sacrifice than this.

And as if to prove my sincerity, they have been worse than ever these last two nights. But as yet I have not murmured; for the Yankees who swore to enter P. Hudson before last Monday night, have not yet ful-

114. On May 22 Banks's army—in all, more than 30,000 men—surrounded the garrison at Port Hudson, and five days later the general launched a major assault that was repulsed by the Confederates. The June 11 action Sarah mentions was a preliminary to the assault that occurred on the day she wrote this. Like the one of May 27, it failed. However, the siege continued.

filled their promise, and we hold it still. Vive vows and bed bug, and forever may our flag wave over the intrenchments! We will conquer yet, with God's blessing!

A week or ten days ago came a letter from Lydia, who is placed within the lines by this recent raid. She writes that the Sugar house and quarters have been seized for Yankee hospitals,[115] that they have been robbed of their clothing, and that they [the Yankees] are in pursuit of the General, who, I pray heaven may escape them. She wrote for clothing, provisions and a servant, and after we had procured them all, and were ready to send them, we discovered that they would not be allowed to pass; so I hardly know what the poor child will do unless she accepts Brother's invitation to come down to him immediately, if she thinks it right.[116]

O Dear Linwood! Couldn't the Yankees spare you either? Think of their occupying the Sugar house where we received our friends in grinding season. Walking in the footsteps of our Confederates! Wonder if our ghosts will disturb the sick men, playing Puss wants a corner at night, with shrieks of laughter, as we used to do before I was hurt?

O the days gone by, the days gone by! When I am an old woman I will not think more of them than I do now. They will never seem brighter or dearer than at present. Linwood was always a tender spot in my [p. 95] heart. As I look back, I wonder which loved it most; Howell, Theodore, Will, Miriam or I. And we had cause to love it; for surely that August 1860 was the happiest, as well as to some of us the most painful of our lives. Will gnashes his teeth over it sometimes, perhaps; Miriam I am sure makes a wry face at some recollections, reasonable enough then, but unpleasant to recall now. And The [Theodore]—! I wonder if there is a punishment in reserve for callous hearts, hereafter? If so, tremble O my soul! For I behaved like a heathen! Tant pis pour lui![117] What

---

115. In an unpublished memoir, Sarah's nephew Howell Morgan wrote that during the siege of Port Hudson the sugar house at Linwood was used by the Federals as a hospital and that "pyramids of arms and legs . . . could be seen from our front gallery." Morgan, born during the siege, is obviously passing along what was later told to him by older members of the family. Quoted in Cecil Morgan, "A Profile of My Father."

116. Instead Lydia and her children, together with her mother, joined her father in Georgia and waited out the war in the town of Cuthbert.

117. Too bad for him!

right had he to like me, still less to tell me so? I am sure I tried my best
to prevent him. He cannot blame me there. But a little less frankness,
a little less severity, Sarah, was that impracticable too? O The! if there
was a silent mode of making reparation that would not encourage false
hopes, I would be almost be [sic] willing to atone for the misery I caused
unwittingly, by a kind look, at least.

One scene I shall always remember with a queer feeling of embarrassment. It was a cloudy evening, when Miriam and Will had gone
walking down the road and I was left alone on the balcony, as Howell
had gone off to get me peaches, and The had not approached the house
since, for the fourth time—best leave such tales untold. The General
came in and accosted me with "Are you not ashamed to [words ex-
cised]; but the General was not to be deceived; "Couldn't make him
believe that, when he had proof to the contrary. For three days The had
been hanging around his circular saw with a recklessness that nothing could justify save—" I waited for no more, but with an indignant
denial of being concerned in his folly, ran down the road to get out of
hearing, and to meet Miriam and Will who were coming by the cooper
shop. As I passed by the brick kiln, Will beckoned to some one on the
other side to come to him, while he secretly motioned to me to stand
still. I guessed who was on the other side, and confess that my first
thought was to take instant flight; but remembering that that would
only confirm Will's suspicions, and being determined that none should
ever hear the truth from me on that subject, I paused near the angle to
gather my courage.

In the mean time Will continued to beckon vehemently to the somebody who was [p. 96] cautiously approaching near and nearer, though
still invisible. I watched Miriam leaning on Will's arm evidently anticipating a scene, noticed Will's scarcely repressed smile, and determined
to deprive them of the anticipated fun. The step drew nearer still—
turned the angle abruptly, and The and I stood face to face. I shall
never forget his ghastly, frightened face as he sprang back in amaze,
evidently unprepared for Will's ambush. A moment's hesitation on my
part would have afforded them the pleasure of beholding the expected
comedy. But with my hand out, I ran to him before he recovered from
his surprise, said Heaven knows what, for I remember having talked
incessantly while leading the way back to the house, though I cannot

remember what I found to say. I know the first pause occurred on the steps when I said "Come in" when he spoke for the first time "I—I cant! God bless you!" and hurried off without another word.

He did not go far however, for several hours after, Howell told me he was standing at the gate, listening to our songs on the balcony. Poor The! He had but one song, that dolorous "My hopes have departed for ever," which he used to sing most pathetically, while Howell, walking around the circle [words excised] would sing in turn "I love somebody, yes I do," so that I smile involuntarily now to hear either sung. Ah boys and girls! and golden summer days! Will they never come again? Yes! they come frequently but they are like the sunsets; bright they may be; but we look on no two alike; each has a separate glory.

It is more than a year ago since I saw Howell. It was about the last of May, after we had run from bombarded B. Rouge to Greenwell, when he came out and spent the day with me. I remember his walking half way to Mrs Brunot's[118] with me when he was going away, and stopping under the tall pine trees to say a last good bye. But we agreed not to say it, so he could have it to do a few days after, so— "He turned his charger as he spake,"[119] waved a last "au revoir" and I went to where Mrs Brunot wept over her dead son, and Howell went his way, and we never met again; for two days after, I was in town.

[p. 97] June 17th.

I must write something somewhere, I dont care if dinner *is* ready, and Brother's "safe old Secesh" down stairs! I think I'll go crazy. Lydia has another boy! Letter just come, and I am demented about my new godchild! There now! feel better! One more word—it shall be called "Howell." Dear, blessed little baby! how I shall love it![120]

Sunday June 21st.

How about that oath of allegiance? is what I frequently ask myself, and always an uneasy qualm of conscience troubles me. Guilty, or not

118. Mrs. Brunot's cottage at Greenwell Springs, not the family home in Baton Rouge.

119. Scott, *Rokeby*.

120. Years later, an aging Howell Morgan read these words and wrote: "AND SHE DID!" See memoir written in 1937, in Sarah Morgan Dawson and Family Papers, LSU Collections.

guilty of Perjury? According to the law of God in the abstract, and of nations, Yes; according to my conscience, Jeff Davis, and the peculiar position I was placed in, No. Which is it? Had I had any idea that such a pledge would be exacted, would I have been willing to come? Never! The thought would have horrified me. The reality was never placed before me until we reached Bonfouca. There I was terrified at the prospect; but seeing how impossible it would be to go back, I placed all my hopes in some miracle that was to intervene to prevent such a crime, and confidently believed my ill health, or something else would save me, while all the rest of the party declared they would think it nothing, and take forty oaths a day, if necessary.

A forced oath, all men agree, is not binding. The Yankees lay particular stress on this being voluntary, and insist that no one is solicited to take it except of their own free will. Yet look at the scene that followed, when mother showed herself unwilling! Think of being ordered to the Custom house as a prisoner for saying she supposed she would *have* to! *That's* liberty! that is free will! It is entirely optional; you have only to take it quietly or go to jail. That is freedom enough, certainly!

There was not even that choice left to me. I told the officer who took down my name, that I was unwilling to take the oath, and asked if there was no escaping it. "None whatever" was his reply "you have it to do, and there is no getting out of it." His rude tone frightened me into half crying; but for all that, as he said, "I had it to do." If Perjury it is, which will God punish: me, who was unwilling to commit the [p. 98] crime, or the man who forced me to it? After all, what was it except taking down names, giving back certificates that the oath was subscribed before we had heard of it, and reading over a something that I for one did not hear, and do not now know what it was, which Something was received in utter silence, broken at last by the man who dashed down his blank book for names, with the assurance that it was "All right"! It was evident that with him at least, it was a ceremony so often performed as to have lost all force or meaning. How could he expect us to be impressed with it?

I shall no longer trouble myself as to whether the sin was his or mine, satisfied that the crime would be in keeping such an oath, with my heart on the other side, where as the merit would lay in breaking it. I hope I am not irreligious; I have reason to believe that I am rather scrupulous than otherwise; but if the Confederates should by any blessed chance dash in to-morrow, would I not be glad to see them? Would I not be delighted to aid and abet them, to give them comfort, or do any thing that loyal "Subjects of the United States" are forbidden to do? Bless the brave creatures! there is nothing in my power that I would leave undone for them! No! the crime would lie in *not* helping them. I shall break their sham oath without hesitation, on the first opportunity. I break it hourly in praying for them in my heart; I broke it before it was completed by praying so hard for them that I lost every sound of the man's voice.

Friday June 26th.

O Praise the Lord O my soul! Here is good news enough to make me happy for a month! Brother is so good about that! Every time he hears good news on our side, he tells us just as though it was on his side, instead of on ours; while all bad news for us he carefully avoids mentioning, unless we question him. So to day he brought in a budget for us. Lee has crossed the Potomac on his way to Washington with one hundred and sixty thousand men.[121] Gibbes and George are with him. Magruder is marching on Fort Jackson to attack it in the rear. One, or two of our English iron-clads are reported at the mouth of the river, and Farragut has gone down to [p. 99] capture them.[122] O Jimmy! Jimmy! suppose he should be on one of them? So near us! We dont know the name of his ship, and it makes us so anxious for him, during these months that we have heard nothing of his whereabouts.

It is so delightful to see these frightened Yankees! One has only to walk down town to be satisfied of the alarm that reigns. Yesterday came the tidings of the capture of Brashere City[123] by our troops, and that a brigade was fifteen miles above here, coming down to the city. Men

121. Lee was on his way to Gettysburg and a Confederate disaster.

122. Rumors with little basis in fact. Confederate General John B. Magruder remained in Texas, and there were no ironclads at the mouth of the river. Some Texas units had, however, joined the army of General Taylor. Farragut believed an attack on New Orleans was imminent: ". . . they have taken Berwick Bay and are marching upon New Orleans in force. I shall remain here to receive them." *ORN*, ser. I, 20:312.

123. Brashear City, on the Louisiana coast west of New Orleans, was taken by a Confederate force under Major Sherod Hunter on the morning of June 23. General Taylor's thrust into South Louisiana was aimed at forcing Banks to withdraw from Port Hudson.

congregated at corners whispering cautiously. These were evidently Confederates who had taken the oath. Solitary Yankees straggled along with the most lugubrious faces, troubling no one.

We walked down to Blineau's [124] with Mrs Price (in spite of the missing half inch she is just as kind and affectionate as ever) and over our ice cream she introduced her husband, who is a true blue Union man, though she, like ourselves, is a rank Rebel. Mr Price, on the eve of making an immense fortune, was perfectly disconsolate at the news. Every one was to be ruined; Starvation would follow if the Confederates entered; there was never a more dismal, unhappy creature. Enchanted at the news, I naturally asked if it were reliable. "Perfectly! Why to prove how true, standing at the door of this saloon five minutes ago, I saw two young ladies pass with Confederate flags which they flirted in the face of some Federal officers, unrebuked!" Verily thought I, something is about to happen! Two days ago the girls who were "unrebuked" this evening, would have found themselves in jail instead. The Confederates are conjuring the devil even out of the Yankees!

Talking of Confederates reminds me that I saw Col. Breaux' picture last evening. I was as delighted as though it were himself. We were in at Jacobs to get our cartes de visite,[125] and wandering around as I had done half a dozen times before among the pictures, to my infinite delight I recognized the Colonel! So like! I was enchanted. Jacobs, who is inclined to be very patronizing in consequence of having been in father's employ in the Customhouse before I was born, seemed much amused at my admiration. "You like the picture? You like the Col."? he kept repeating. "Yes indeed!" I would exclaim, stopping my panegyric to Mrs Price to answer him. "Very well! it is yours if you will do me the honor to accept it!" [p. 100] I laughingly declined, but he repeatedly pressed it on me.

Fact is, I was longing to accept it, when he insisted. It was a splendid, full length photograph, in a handsome frame about eighteen inches by fourteen, and was perfectly colored. I suppose it is worth about seventy dollars. But I just thought "Accept Col. Breaux's picture from Jacobs!

124. Blineau Brothers, French Confectioners, specialized in ice cream, sherbets, and chocolates. Jules Blineau was in charge of the store on Canal Street.

125. Paper photograph popular in the 1860s. The photographer was E. Jacobs.

A costly gift from one who has no right to offer me such a present, representing one whose portrait I have no right to possess! What would Brother—what would Mrs Breaux say?" That strengthened me in persisting in my refusal. I would not displease the first, and candidly I was afraid of the second. So I decidedly declined, though just dying for it; when obliging Jacobs kindly desired me to call in a few days, when he would have a nice, little copy of it, which I would certainly oblige him by accepting, and could hardly object to.

Perhaps I would be accommodating myself, as well as Jacobs! For really I never met a gentleman that I admired and respected more than Col. Breaux. His intelligence, his refinement, his deference to ladies, won my truest admiration; and being some eighteen or twenty years my senior made me feel as though he were an elder brother, rather than a stranger who was kind enough to show the greatest, and most flattering partiality for poor, shy little me.

Ah Mrs Breaux! Unkind Mrs Breaux! What tempted you to go to the Confederacy? Before you came, every thing was so charming! The Colonel was perfection! How we got on in philosophy! How fascinating he was! And how constantly he spoke of his "dear little wife," and with what delight he looked forward to her arrival! He rode twenty five miles one night to meet her a few hours sooner, rushed to Clinton eagerly to meet the "dear little wife." Madam has already heard of his visits to Linwood; she is not in an amiable mood. She herself told me the story the first time we met. These were her words: "The first thing I said, was 'See here; I have heard of your flirtations; I came because I wanted to see you; but if you dont treat me just as Samuel Lock's daughter[126] should be treated, I go right back to my father!' He looked at me so seriously and asked what I meant; but I tell you I was ernest, and told him so, too!"

[p. 101] I who had seen him setting out on his long, dark ride, could feel what a sad welcome it must have been to him after his dreams of that same meeting. In my other diary I have mentioned his having taken tea with us, and have spoken of his delight at the idea of meeting her again. Long after he left, we continued to exclaim "How happy Mrs Breaux must be! Wonder how far he is now?" And lo! the reception!

126. Emilie Breaux's father was Samuel Locke, a New Orleans merchant.

In a few weeks, from a variety of causes, chiefly it was said from ill temper, sickness, and hereditary predisposition, Mrs Breaux became perfectly crazy. The Colonel remained just what he was, a model of patience and devotion to his poor wife, humoring every fancy, and never leaving her side. By slow degrees she recovered, though I dont think she was quite sane the first time I met her. She grew reconciled to Linwood and its inhabitants, and was constantly there. I became her pet, her Violette blanche,[127] her everything—until she shared the fate of all the married ladies of the neighborhood, and received no invitation to the party the General gave us on the 8th of Jan. Then I was nothing. She abused and vilified every one on the place from the first to the last. She said Miriam neglected me, left me "writhing in agony" while she danced all night miles away; and I could not forgive her for the slander; for Miriam was everything to me, and only distressed me by being too good to me.

Col Breaux, to keep the peace, ceased visiting us after that. I used to hear of both, though. Every one was his staunch friend, no one could endure her. In fact they never spoke of her; it was her temper that at-taine[d] such notoriety. The life she led him! Socrates and Xantippe over again. His glass of hemlock has not come yet, that is the only dif-ference, as far as domestic affairs are concerned. A more thoroughly wretched man hardly exists; and yet I was told that but for the haggard face and deepening lines, one would be none the wiser of his unhappi-ness. He is a brave man, and—a philosopher! But woman's tongue, and woman's temper can wear out the most patient disposition. Socrates slipped out many a time! Mrs Breaux would make me a virago in a month. I hope she only gives the Col. an opportunity of exercising his philosophy; he has need of it all, certainly.

I [p. 102] often look back to that meeting. How the real differs from the Ideal! What a recompense for his devotion! I think of his pictured delight before, of her shocking story after, and cry with all my soul "O Col. Breaux I am sorry for you!" If he had been a worthless, unedu-cated, vicious man, he would have had a perfect wife; as it is, he has a Tartar.

May be this is uncharitable to write this, in spite of its truth. I did not

127. White violet.

mean to; but in spite of its being so late, I found my pen unwilling to stop, and so just let it have its way. Shall we leave off, my scratcher? Let us forget our uncharitable talk in sleep. I dont know which is worse; for me to have such thoughts, or for you to transcribe them. It is the old question of that Oath compelling Yankee and myself. Yankee reminds me that our troops are within ten miles of us to night. And I to be hurried off all this glorious news by Col. Breaux's grievances! Shame! Where is your patriotism? Go dream of Grey Coats!

July 8th. Wednesday.

This dreary city! I never knew how much I loved the country until this, my first summer in New Orleans. How I long for the green woods and open fields! This melancholy sight which I never expected to see— that of grass growing in the streets of this once populous city—makes me pine for the greener, fresher grass of my once home—Baton Rouge. If it could be once more what it has been—if we could again be there— if Sophie and I could once more stand hand in hand on our beautiful terraces, watching the glorious sunsets over the mighty Mississippi! And it will never, never be again!

One year ago, standing there, we wondered if our future lives would be apart, and if the day would ever come when we could talk about when we used to be friends long ago, and used to wander around the State House gardens so happily together. I can remember the yellow sunset that lighted up the grounds, the very dress Sophy wore, and the very half laughing, half sad expression of her sweet face as she asked "Will we, *must* we grow old? Can you fancy either, with other lives, other interests to draw us away from each other? Will we care no more than other people? [p. 103] O Sarah! *must* we too grow old?" To which Sarah the calm replied "Why not? What difference will age make? Would you not be still Sophy, even if your hair was white? Why should we not be friends still, though a mob cap should shade your black hair, as well as my tawny tresses?"

But Sophy with her pretty ways disliked the thought of growing old; and to comfort her, I said "and I too wish to die young." What a shudder she gave! "Die! die young! O no, let me live! I dont care for grey hair and dim eyes! let me live to the farthest limit of life! let me live! let me live! let me live to the day of Judgement! I should go mad if I

knew I had to die!" I dont know why it seemed to me so awful to hear
her talk so. I had heard her often, yet always a shudder, though not of
sympathy, passed over me. I love to think of death. "I would not live
alway[s]." I am glad that I was born to die! Death may be bitter; but
I would rather endure its pain than forego the bliss of meeting father
and Harry in the Hereafter. Harry! Harry! could I bear this, if it were
not for the sure hope of meeting you when I close my eyes for ever?

Yes! let me die, and let me die young! I dont want to out live old
friends, and sweet recollections of my youth. I dont want to be forced
into heaven through weariness of earth. I want to go while I am yet
happy and beloved, with my heart full of gratitude to God, and charity
to man; I want to go Because I love God, and feel He loves me; and I
want to go before that feeling and that faith die away. Why should we
keep our Youth and Beauty of form and heart for man, and prepare
for heaven only when both fade away? Is the dross only, a fit offering
to God?

To me there is no more pitiful sight than old age. To see others fill
the place you once occupied; to bury one by one loved forms, and dead
hopes; to live on and on with snowy hair and deepning [*sic*] wrinkles,
and to sink in a lonely grave unloved, and unloving—! Ah no! let me
die, and die young.

July 10th.

Shall I cry, faint, scream or go off in hysterics? Tell me which,
quickly; for to doubt this news is fine and imprisonment, and if I really
believe it I would certainly give way to my feelings and commit some
vagaries of the kind. My resolution is formed! I will do neither; [p. 104]
I wont gratify the Yankees so much. I have been banging at the piano
until my fingers are weary, and singing "The Secret through Life to be
Happy" until my voice is cracked; I'll stand on my head if necessary
to prove my indifference; but I'll never believe this is true until it is
confirmed by stronger authority than that of these Yankees.

Day before yesterday came tidings that Vicksburg had fallen on the

4th inst. The Era poured out extras, and sundry little pop-guns fizzled out salutes. All who doubted the truth of the report and were brave enough to say so, were fined or imprisoned; it has become a penal offense to doubt what the Era says; so quite a number of arrests were made. This morning it was followed up by the announcement of the capture of Port Hudson.[128] The guns are pealing for true, and the Yankees at Headquarters may be seen skipping like lambs for very joy. And I still disbelieve! Sceptic! The first thing I know that Era man will be coming here to convert me! But I dont, cant, wont believe it! *If* it is true—but I find consolation in this faith: It is either true, or not true; if it is true, it is all for the best, and if it is *not* true, it is better still. Which ever it is, is for some wise purpose; so it does not matter so we wait, pray, and believe.

5 O'clock P.M. I dont believe it? What am I crying about then? It seems so hard! How the mighty are fallen! Port Hudson gone! Brother believes it. That is enough for me. God bless him! I cry hourly. He is so good and considerate. He told me "Name your friends, and what can be done for them shall be attended to. The prisoners will be sent here. Maybe I cannot do much; but food and clothing you shall have in abundance for them when they arrive." God bless him for his kindness!

O dear, noble men! I am afraid to meet them; I should do something foolish; best take my cry out in private now. May the Lord look down in pity on us! Port Hudson does not matter so much; but those brave, noble creatures! The *Era* says they had devoured their last mule before they surrendered.[129]

Saturday July 10th [11th].

I cried myself to sleep last night. It was not about P. Hudson though. I was sleeping in the bed Harry died on, and with my face close pressed to the spot where his cheek grew cold, I thought of the dear dead brother

128. The surrender of the Confederate garrison was agreed to on July 8. The formal surrender ceremony took place on the morning of July 9.

129. In a letter written from Port Hudson only a few days before the surrender, Colonel Steedman told his uncle, Dr. D. J. Fox, "We have no meat but mule and horse flesh. Many are eating it, but many more prefer to live entirely upon peas, bread and molasses." Mobile *Advertiser and Register*, August 9, 1863. In the previously cited 1891 letter to his son, Steedman wrote: "The gallantry, heroism, endurance and sufferings of our little garrison of about five thousand men all told, against overwhelming odds of army and navy, can never be realized except by participants."

I would have [p. 105] given my life to save, until the tears would steal down my face. Not rebellious tears; no; I dont want you back, Hal—at least I try to believe I dont; but while waiting for that meeting above, Hal, I wonder if you will love me still in the Hereafter? Will I still be your favorite "little sister"? O Harry, does God let you see me? are you watching me now? Why cant the dead give us word or token that we are still beloved? I would brave all things for one sign that I am still remembered.

I was sitting on Brother's lap the other night, talking about father and Harry, and he cried so bitterly! How he loved Hal! how he worshiped father! It made my heart ache to see him cry so; I dont cry except when I am sure nobody will know it; I feel a quiet awe about it, as though it would disturb them. "I shall go unto them, but they shall not come unto me." Better as it is! Thank God for teaching me humbly to say "Thy will be done." Yet sometimes I am almost afraid that my resignation is akin to insensibility. I hear people sometimes say that they cannot forgive—*think* forgive!—God for chastening them. Did I not love them? Thou Lord, who seest my heart, knowest all things. Do I love them less, for saying "Thy will be done"?

With thoughts of them still in my heart, I fell asleep, and was only roused by Brother's voice at sunrise, calling me to dress quickly and be ready to breakfast with him at the lake. Mother is spending a week or ten days there for the benefit of little Miriam's [130] health, and I was already longing to see her though she only went yesterday. So, (chose inouï [131] for a young lady) as the carriage drove to the door, and before Brother was ready, I stood already dressed at the door, waiting for him. Such a splendid ride in the fresh air, and such an appetite it gave us! And when Brother would cease talking, and lie back in the carriage, I tried to trace a resemblance between the Bayou St. John [132] and the Tchefuncta (indeed it was so vivid that when I got back I told Miriam that it was just like it—couldn't tell the difference when your eyes were shut!). So in the little miniature stream, I fancied a miniature skiff,

130. Miriam Morgan, daughter of Philip Hicky Morgan, was born September 15, 1861, and thus was not quite 2 when Sarah wrote this.

131. Something unheard of.

132. A small stream that empties into Lake Pontchartrain.

and all of us floating down the stream with— "O no we never mention him!" And [p. 106] that led me to think of Port Hudson, and Brother's kind promise, and of who I would like to help, until the ride seemed a mere nothing. I am afraid P. Hudson has fallen. But if it has, Gardiner [*sic*] has been deceived in regard to Vicksburg, for I will not believe that the latter has surrendered. It is a trick, depend upon it, only we cant hear.

10 O'clock P.M. I preach patience; but how about practise? I am exasperated! there is the simple fact. And is it not enough? What a scene I have just witnessed! A motley crew, of thousands of low people of all colors parading the streets with flags, torches, music and all other accompaniments, shouting, screaming, exulting over the fall of P. Hudson and Vicksburg. The Era will call it an enthusiastic demonstration of the loyal citizens of the city; we who saw it from upper balconies know of what rank those "citizens" were. We saw crowds of soldiers mixed up with the lowest rabble of the town, working men in dirty clothes, newsboys, ragged children, negroes, and even *women* walking in the procession, while swarms of negroes and low white women elbowed each other in a dense mass on the pavement. To see such creatures exulting over our misfortune was enough to make one scream with rage.

One of their dozen transparencies was inscribed with "A dead Confederacy." Fools! The flames are smouldering! they will burst out presently and consume you! More than half, much more, were negroes. As they passed here they raised a yell of "Down with the Rebels!" that made us gnash our teeth in silence. The devil possessed me. "O Miriam help me pray the dear Lord that their flag may burn!" I whispered as the torches danced around it. And we did pray ernestly—so ernestly that Miriam's eyes were tightly screwed up; but it must have been a wicked prayer, for it was not answered.

Dr Schuppert [133] has out a magnificent display of black cotton grammatically inscribed with "Port Hudson & Vicksburg *is* ours" garnished with a luminous row of tapers, and drunk on two bits worth of lager beer, has been shrieking out all Union songs he can think of with his

133. Dr. Moritz Schuppert, a German-born surgeon, operated an orthopedic clinic at 179 Carondolet Street.

horrid children until my tympanum is perfectly cracked. Miriam wants to offer him an extra bottle of lager for the two places of which he claims the monopoly. He would sell his creed for less. Miriam is dying to ask [p. 107] him what he has done with the Confederate uniform he sported before the Yankees came. His son says they are all *Union* men over there, and will "lemonate" (illuminate) to night. A starving seamstress opposite has stuck six tallow candles in her window. Better put them in her stomach! I know it is the emptiest of the two!

And I *wont* believe Vicksburg has surrendered! P. Hudson I am sure has fallen. Alas for all hopes of serving the brave creatures! the rumor is that they have been released on parole. Happily for them; but if it *must* go, what a blessed privilege it would have been to aid or comfort them!

Wednesday July 15th.

It is but too true; both have fallen. All P. Hudson privates have been paroled, and the officers sent here for exchange. Aye! aye! aye! I know some privates I would rather see than the officers! As yet, only ten that we know have arrived. All are confined in the Customhouse. Last evening crowds surrounded the place. We did something dreadful, Ada Peirce,[134] Miriam and I. We went down to the Confectionary, and unable to resist the temptation, made a détour by the Customhouse in hope of seeing one of our poor dear half starved mule and rat fed defenders. The crowd had passed away then; but what was our horror when we emerged from the river side of the building and turned into Canal, to find the whole front of the pavement lined with Yankees! Our folly struck us so forcibly that we were almost paralysed with fear. However that did not prevent us from endeavoring to hurry past, though I felt as though walking in a nightmare.

Ada was brave enough to look up at a window where several of our prisoners were standing, and kept urging us to do like wise. "Look! he knows you, Sarah! he has called another to see you! They both recognise you! O look please and tell me who they are! they are watching you still!" she would exclaim. But if my own dear brother stood there, I could not have raised my eyes; we only hurried on faster, with a hun-

---

134. Ada Peirce and her sister Marie, daughters of lawyer Levi Peirce, were Sarah's closest friends during the wartime years in New Orleans. In *Recollections of a Rebel Reefer* (p. 254) James Morgan referred to them as "the two most beautiful girls that New Orleans could boast of."

dred Yankees eyes fixed on our flying steps. Miriam was no braver either, so we have no idea of who our friends were. The most likely story is that they were strangers to all who, struck by Ada's lovely upturned face, could not withdraw their eyes. And her natural [p. 108] modesty and humility which leads her to think every one entitled to admiration except her own sweet self, made her imagine that they were friends of mine who recognised me.

But I would not do that again—! When we passed the last Yankee, with crimson cheeks we looked at each other and asked what would tempt us to try it over; and the answer was nothing—except the *certainty* of seeing a friend. Yet crowds of young ladies have tried it yesterday, have stopped in front and waved back at the captives. Ours is not an unprecedented exploit; but still for us it was *fast*.

My friend Col. Steadman was one of the Commissioners for arranging the terms of the capitulation, I see. He has not yet arrived. When he comes, what can be done for him will be attempted. Bless them one and all! what would we not be willing to do for them? Wonder when the rest will arrive?

Dreadful news has come of the defeat of Lee at Gettysburg. Think I believe it all? He may have been defeated; but not one of these accounts of total overthrow and rout do I credit. Yankees jubilant, Southerners dismal. Brother, with principles on one side, and brothers on the other, is correspondingly distracted. Mother has cried, sobbed, fought all the battles over, knocked the war into a cocked hat, painted the dismal picture of a conquered race, and has conjured up the horrors generally while drinking a decoction of tears and chocolate for breakfast. There is no misfortune that can happen for twenty years to come, at which she cannot exclaim "I told you so!" for her presentiments are legions, and all of the most dismal hue. I could not stand it; it is a shame for women to despair while our men are fighting so bravely. I'll die shouting "Lice and the Confederates for ever"! I'll never give up the ship!

Talk of the "bottom being knocked out of the Confederacy"—Bah! if there is a screw loose somewhere, Lee will find it, and knock it in again. The skies *are* dark, but there is a bright side somewhere. Victory and defeat come in waves, now on one side, now on the other. Up to Vicksburg our prospects were glorious; now they are the reverse; but the next flood will land us on the shores of Freedom.

I was so provoked at mother's tears, that like the pious little girl in story books, I gave her a [p. 109] good lecture, which I hope will be a kind of moral shaking to her, and prevent her from crying before she is hurt again. How I blazed away! When my own faith and belief was almost exhausted, I seized the papers that induced her to despair, hunted up stray paragraphs of encouragement, followed up conflicting statements, proved the fallacy of all, gathered comfort, forced it on her, proved the decisive struggle had not come, that Bragg[135] would join Lee, and that "God would have mercy upon us and cause his face to shine upon us." I am satisfied He will; He will not desert us, He will "arise and scatter our enemies." And our brothers—! I was indignant with mother for believing that harm could come to them; but my secret belief has always been that Gibbes would die in this struggle. God grant to spare them to us.

Saturday July 18th.

It may be wrong; I feel very contrite; but still I cannot help think-ing it is an error on the right side. It began by Miriam sending Mr Conn a box of cigars when she was on Canal the other day, with a note saying we would be delighted to assist him in any way. Poor creature! He wrote an answer which breathed desolation and humility under his present situation in every line. The cigars, and unexpected kindness had touched a tender cord evidently. He said he had no friends, and would be grateful for our assistance.

But before his answer arrived, yesterday morning I took it in my head that Col. Steadman was also at the Custom house, though his arrival had not been announced, the Yankees declining to publish any more names to avoid the excitement that follows.[136] So Miriam and I pre-pared a lunch of Chicken, soup, wine, preserves, sardines, and cakes, to send to him. And, fool like, I sent a note with it. It only contained the same offer of assistance; and I would not object to the town crier's reading it; but it upset Brother's ideas of decorum completely. He said nothing to Miriam, because that was first offense; but yesterday he met

135. Confederate General Braxton Bragg.

136. The *Era*, which Julia LeGrand called "the low, vulgar tongue of the Federal Gov-ernment in this city" (p. 286), had listed earlier arrivals of officers from Port Hudson. These lists were in turn picked up by other New Orleans papers. See *Daily Picayune*, July 15 and 22, 1863, for example.

Edmond [137] who was carrying the basket, and he could not stand the sight of another note. I wish he had read it! But he said he would not assume such a right. So he came home very much annoyed, and spoke to Miriam about it. Fortunately for my peace of mind I was swimming in the bath tub in blissful unconsciousness, else I should have drowned myself.

[p. 110] He said "I want you both to understand that you shall have everything you want for the prisoners. Subscribe any sum of money, purchase any quantity of clothing, send all the food you please, but for God's sake dont write to them! In such a place every man knows the other has received a letter, and none know what it contains. I cannot have my sisters' names in every body's mouth. Never do it again!" All as kind and as considerate for us as ever, and a necessary caution; I love him the better for it; but I was dismayed at having rendered the reproof necessary.

For three hours I made the most hideous faces at myself and groaned aloud over Brother's displeasure. He is so good that I would rather bite my tongue off than give him a moment's pain. Just now I went to him unable to keep silence any longer, and told him how distressed I was to have displeased him about that note. "Dont think any more about it, only dont do it again, dear," was his answer. I was so grateful to him for his gentleness that I was almost hurried into a story. I began "It is the first time—" when I caught myself and said boldly "No, it is not. Col. Steadman has written to me before, and I have replied. But I promise to you it shall not occur again if I can avoid it." He was satisfied with the acknowledgement, and I was more than gratified with his kindness. Yet the error *must* have been on the right side!

Col. Steadman wrote back his thanks by Edmond, with heartfelt gratitude for finding such friends in his adversity, and touching acknowledgements of the acceptable nature of the lunch. His brother and Col. Lock [138] were wounded, though recovering, and he was anxious to know if I had yet recovered. And that was all, except that he hoped we would come to see him, and his thanks to Brother for his kind message. Brother had sent him word by one of the prisoners that though he was

137. One of Philip Hicky Morgan's servants.
138. Lieutenant Colonel Michael B. Locke.

not acquainted with him, yet as his sisters' friend he would be happy
to assist him if he needed money or clothing. There was no harm in
either note, and though I would not do it again, I am almost glad I let
him know he still had friends [ink spot], before Brother asked me not
to write.

And as yet we cant see them. A man was bayonetted yesterday for
waving to them, even.[139] It only makes us the more eager to see them.
We did see some. Walking on Rampart St. with [p. 111] the Peirces
yesterday, in front of a splendid private house, we saw sentinels stationed. Upon inquiry we learned that Gen. Gardiner and a dozen others
were confined there.[140] Ada and Miriam went wild. If it had not been for
dignified Marie, and that model of propriety, Sarah, there is no knowing but what they would have carried the house by storm. We got them
by without seeing a grey coat, when they vowed to pass back, declaring
that the street was not respectable on the block above. We had to follow.
Lo! there they all stood on the balcony above. We thought we recognised Gen. Gardiner, Major Wilson, Major Spratley and Mr Duprés.
Miriam was sure she did; but even when I put on a bold face and tried
to look, something kept me from seeing; so I had all the appearance
of staring, without deriving the slightest benefit from it. Wonder what
makes me such a fool?

Mr. Conn writes that Capt. Bradford is wounded, but does not say
whether he is here.[141]

139. In its July 17, 1863, issue the *Daily Picayune* reported that a citizen named William
Smith was admitted to Charity Hospital after being wounded by a sentinel at the Customhouse. "We understand that he aroused the ire of the sentinel by waving a handkerchief
and making other sympathetic signs to the Confederate prisoners now confined in the
Customhouse building."

140. Colonel Steedman was held there also. Of his imprisonment in New Orleans he
later wrote: "Gen'l Banks treated us as gallant enemies, prisoners of war, should be
treated. No insults, no indignities, and sufficient food, though we were crowded in narrow quarters, illy suited as a prison, a few weeks in the Custom House, the remaining in
banker Connor's old residence on Rampart Street." Letter to his son, June 1, 1891, U.S.
Army Military History Institute.

141. Captain James L. Bradford was severely wounded on May 28, 1863. After the surrender on July 9 he asked to be allowed to go to the nearby home of Mrs. Fluker to
recuperate, and the request was granted.

Thursday July 23d

It is bad policy to keep us from seeing the prisoners; it just sets us wild about them. Put a creature you dont care for in the least, in a situation that commands sympathy, and nine out of ten girls will fall desperately in love with them. Here are brave, self sacrificing, noble men who have fought heroically for us, and have been forced to surrender by unpropitious fate, confined in a city peopled by their friends and kindred, and as totally isolated from them as though they inhabited the Dry Tortugas.

Ladies are naturally hero worshippers. We are dying to show these unfortunates that we are as proud of their bravery as though it had led to victory instead of defeat. Banks wills that they remain in privacy. Consequently our vivid imaginations are constantly occupied in depicting their sufferings, privations, heroism, and manifold virtues, until they have almost become as demigods to us. Even horrid little Capt. McClure has a share of my sympathy in his misfortune! [142] Fancy what must be my feelings where those I consider as gentlemen are concerned! It is all I can do to avoid a most tender compassion for a very few select ones. Miriam and I are looked on with envy by other young ladies because some twenty or thirty of our acquaintance have already arrived. To know a Port Hudson defender is considered as the greatest distinction one need desire.

If they would only let us see the prisoners once to sympathise with, and offer to assist them, we would never [p. 112] care to call on them again until they are liberated. But this is aggravating. Of what benefit is it to send them lunch after lunch, when they seldom receive it? Col. Steadman and six others, I am sure, did not receive theirs on Sunday. We sent with the baskets a number of cravats and some handkerchiefs I had embroidered for the Col., which I am sure the sentinel appropriated. We behaved shockingly on Tuesday again. Walking on Canal, Miriam was resolute to purchase a bouquet for Mr Duprè. Ada fol-

142. McCluer's name does not appear on the published lists of officers brought to New Orleans. The lists appear to be incomplete, however. He was ordered to department headquarters in Jackson, Mississippi, in March, and may never have returned to Port Hudson. See General Gardner's Special Orders No. 78, issued March 17, 1863, chap. 2, vol. 198, Record Group 109, National Archives.

lowed suit for Gen. Gardener, and feeling it would be uncivil as Col. Steadman and Monsieur Deux Temps [143] occupy the same room, I got one for him. Only Marie was proper enough to refrain, and wisely too; for she knew none of them.

Mr Camack, discharged from our army on account of his health, [144] offered to escort us to the sentinel at the door. As we turned into the street, we beheld the upper galleries crowded with our friends. That frightened me into perfect unconsciousness of their identity; and with my head bowed down, I hardly dared breathe for fear they would see me. Miriam turned back to whisper that Col. Steadman was leaning over the balcony looking at us, and that quite took my breath away. I was ready to cry with shame. A low, whisky smelling snuff taking quarrelling Yankee, on Mr Camack's application, roughly said that nothing could pass in after four o'clock, and catching a whisper of "toss it through the window," fiercely proclaimed that that was unlawful, etc, and so frightened me that I implored them to pass on quickly and get away from them. Mr Camack in turn laughingly intreated me not to faint as it would be unpleasant to be obliged to call the Yankees to his assistance.

But the officers from above, leaning over to catch the purport of our parley, in dead silence, & the rough Yankees below, proved too much for my nerves, and I resolutely commenced an onward march, supported by sensible Marie, and followed by the other wild creatures. Arrived at the corner, we plunged down a side street after vain efforts to induce them to follow us, and bewailing and bemoaning our escapade, never ceased our lamentations until we found ourselves at the confectionary when we suspended it until we could imbibe an inordinate amount of soda and ice water. In the mean time, these bad girls, stopping to talk to a young lady who lives opposite the prison, and who has a cousin there with whom she corresponds by means of the deaf and dumb alphabet, [p. 113] told her the object of our expedition, which she instantly telegraphed to him, while he, signifying that he would bribe the sentinel, disappeared within, presently to return crest fallen and disappointed; and show it was hopeless.

143. Lieutenant Dupré.

144. Possibly Thomas D. Cammack, who served in Company B, Crescent Regiment, and who was discharged in June 1863.

Here [*sic*] me, Dame Propriety! If ever I so trespass on your rules again, may I suffer the remord de conscience[145] that tortured me that night! I cant wish any thing worse!

Brother should forbid those gentlemen writing too. Already a dozen notes have been received from them, and what can we do? We cant tell them "not to." Miriam received a *letter* from Major Spratley this morning, raving about the kindness of the ladies of New Orleans, full of hope of future successes, and vows to help deliver the noble ladies from the hands of their oppressors, etc. It is a wonder that such a patriotic effusion could be smuggled out. He kindly assures us that not only those of our acquaintance there, but all their brother officers, would be more than happy to see us in their prison. Position of affairs rather reversed, since we last met!

Another, from Capt. Duprè, is written in a light, playful rollicking spirit which I hardly gave him credit for. I tell Miriam he must have tasted of the Old Cognac which figured in the lunch she sent him, before he composed it. I never was more amazed than to read this sentence which sounds so little like him, that I cant believe he was sane when he wrote it: "How is Annie, O how is dear Annie?" Poor Anna! Miriam's rival in "dear Alceé's" affection! What a shock it would be to her to read those light words! Immediately after followed "my respects to Miss Sarah." Thanks, sir, for the distinction. It would annihilate me to be treated with disrespect even by those for whom I have no regard.

Monday July 27th[146]

How shall I survive it? I'm sick, trembling, apprehensive, unhappy, and every thing in a breath. That man is going to dine here! Trouble will follow, I feel. O my prophetic soul! I do believe in dreams! listen! Saturday evening Brother took me to the lake to see mother, and a sudden storm obliged me to remain all night. As usual, I named the bed posts, and prepared to remember my dream. Is it not foolish to repeat it? Nevertheless, here it is. First one passed me with three letters. The top most I knew was from Col. Steadman. "Give!" I cried. "That at *least* belongs to me, though Miriam may claim the others!" The servant smiled, and put them in Miriam's hand instead of mine. My dream

145. Remorse.
146. Sarah first wrote "Tuesday July 28" and then corrected it.

changed. I was talking to a [p. 114] Yankee officer, who told me that all our things in Clinton were lost, and that he had the diary I had before this. All kinds of troubles and annoyances followed, which I forget, until I found myself carrying somebody's baby over miles and miles of road, and at each mile, the baby grew larger and heavier, until I could scarcely carry it. I bent down to kiss its pretty cheek, and lo! instead, it turned to a great blood boil which burst on my lips. In horror I awoke, murmuring "Bless that baby; my unfailing prophecy of trouble!"

Last night, at nine o'clock, I got back. Miriam held out three letters that a man had brought in the morning. Hers were from two of the prisoners, one thanking her for things sent by me; the third only was for me, from Col. Steadman. The sweetest, kindest note, *too* kind, may be, yet I was pleased. This is a record of plain facts. I may as well state that I hardly know which kept me awake, that, or thoughts of that Yankee. Between the two however, I could not sleep until the "Wee sma' hours" were slowly passing away. O how I have prayed that Yankee may not come!

Night. He didn't! my prayers are always answered. His apologies took his place, and were more than welcome. He is not Brother's friend; he would not ask one of his; but this one has been kind to Lydia, and Brother repays such tenfold, no matter who they are. But what a relief! We sent for Ada and Marie to help us dispatch the elegant dinner that had been ordered, since there was no danger of their meeting a Yankee. My spirits were dancing then. Every thing passed off so pleasantly, until at table Brother expressed his opinion about note writing to the prisoners. A guilty conscience needs no accuser. He said just what he ought to say, and every word of it was true. He must know best. But my remorse for those I had received, (not for those written, for I have written but one) [147] made me perfectly wretched. I would not displease Brother for worlds. Yet how must I appear to him? I could have cried before all of them. They turned to other subjects, while I sat in speechless despair, mortified and contrite for sins that I am not responsible for.

Why must I suffer as much for the follies of others as for my own? Miriam laughed gaily, yet she has written a dozen. I wrote One (Mem:

147. Above the line, Sarah added: "(*answer*, I should have said)."

Written in answer to yesterday's [?], though not received by him for a week after.) and was wretched. Edmond came in after a temporary absence from the dining room; he was only waiting on table, yet my heart leaped to my throat; I felt that he had—a letter for me. I was right. He put it in Brother's hand, who reading the address put it in mine. I dont know how I felt; I only know I fixed my eyes steadily on his while I put it under my napkin. O for a good quiet cry! What made him write? I pinched the senseless paper [p. 115] under the table. How inopportune! O Brother! Brother! I would not lose your esteem for all the Confederate prisoners!

After almost four hours at table, we arose. I slipped up stairs to read the note. O why did he write it? If last night I was pleased, tonight I was grieved. Shall I say what my conscience whispered? Why not, as long as it is confined to this page? Twenty years hence, I prim maiden Sarah of the sharp face and unbending back, if the confession seem unmaidenly, throw the book in the fire, and the story will never be told. But all the house is asleep save you. No eyes except those of spirits read the words over your shoulder, eyes that see every thing, and read in the Rampart prison as well as here. Well then, my heart whispered "I wish he had not!"

The tone of his letters is changing: His monotonous life in the dull prison, his isolation, and lack of occupation are combining to lead his fancy astray. His gratitude for finding a friend in a strange land, he is learning to confound with a deeper feeling. Homesickness softens one's heart wonderfully. He is lonely, and his imagination has full play. Because it is impossible, he longs to see me, and constantly entreating me to come, "hope differed [sic] maketh the heart sick"[148] and so he thinks that "one look at that sweet face, and the music of that soft voice," etc might render consolation, etc, again. If he saw me once more, there would be an end of it. But shut up there, with nothing to think of— O I wish he wouldn't!

The letter is not like him! There is a tender vein in it that hardly belongs to so unsentimental a person. O Banks! Banks! you are doing a noble and true heart a great injustice, by keeping it alone in that dreary prison! But one course lies before me. I shall go to Brother, tell him how

148. Proverbs 13:12.

grieved I am about it, ask permission to write one last note, and in that last, while assuring him of my sincere desire to be of assistance to him, gently represent the impossibility of answering his letters in future. The remedy will either kill or cure. Best apply it in the earliest stage; it may save unpleasant consequences here after. "O, I wish he had not—!"

The girls interrupted my lamentation. "What is the matter?" asked sympathetic Ada looking at my troubled face. "Nothing; just kiss me and hug me tight; for I feel that some where I have sinned, though I dont know where or how." So for half an hour she did hold me tight and kiss me, and load me with pet names and sweet words which almost deprived me of my self control. I could have cried with distress, but for a Something that told me it would be misunderstood. What can Brother think of that note? I cannot show it to him.

Twelve O'clock! This wont do! Mother says night vigils ruin the complexion. [p. 116] Thanks, Vanity, for the recollection of that calamity. My complexion, if not fatigue, will induce me to retire. Miriam, of the guileless conscience, is sleeping as innocently as a baby. What a blessing it must be to possess such a conscience! Fool that I am! Here I sit making faces at my self, crying now and then (though mother says it spoils the eyes) and wringing my hands, whisper as though some one was near "O dont, dont! please dont! I cant stand it!" Spirits, if you are here, go elsewhere and repeat what I say. But he does not believe in you, any more than I do. I wish I could. Tell him he is deceiving himself, tell him it is unreasonable, warn him that he is betraying himself. Somebody help him! I cannot.

This is too much! If Brother knew what I suffer, surely he would be sorry for me. I must forget it, someway. I go to sleep. How unpleasant it will be to wake in the morning! That must be sinful; I never felt it before. God has always been my refuge and my strength, a present help in time of trouble. But what comfort can religion afford for sins you have never committed? This is a new phase of the question. This has been decidedly the most unpleasant day of my whole life.

I must go. And yet, O Sarah! burn this page before you sleep! You to hint such a thing, you who hold it immodest for a woman to suspect that a man cares for her, before he makes a formal declaration to that effect—*you* to write this? It may be wrong. I dont know. That letter, that letter has unnerved me! I cant reason; I cant explain. Woman's instinct has warned me that—I cant go on! "What the heart of the young girl whispered one summer night," I have vaguely shadowed forth here; it may be wrong; it may be unwomanly; it is not meant for such. I write because I must tell it somewhere, to ease my conscience; and even to Miriam I could not hint such a delicate matter. Let it remain here. Later, if all goes well, as I hope and trust, burn it, and let it perish in the ashes. No one will be the wiser of this, my midnight vigil and distress. A month hence it will be forgotten. Yet wherein have I sinned? Why must I bear the burden of another? Who suffers when I do foolish things? Certainly nobody would sit up half the night and cry about it. Fool! fool! that I am! I wish I could rid myself of this excess of sensibility for others.

I have read it twenty times, and each time I moan "Why, why did you write it?" I wish he had not! It is Banks' fault! Not mine. Shall I burn the letter?

[p. 117] Wednesday July 29th.

Shall I make faces at myself for ever? When will this torture cease? Brother sent for me just now. I went with a beating heart. A note was in his hand. What next? I thought. His first words brought me comfort. He said he had just procured a quantity of clothes for Mr Conn, and wanted to know exactly who he was before he sent them. I told him all I knew, which seemed to satisfy him. He would do anything for Gibbes' or Miriam's friend. I thought that was all; but he said abruptly "By the way, Col. Steadman will dine with you to morrow." One hears of people being knocked down by surprise; but this is the first time it occurred to me. I fell back as though struck, and was only saved from measuring my length on the floor by snatching at a friendly étagère that stood near. Involuntarily Brother laughed aloud. With an effort I recovered my self possession and footting [*sic*]. "O please dont! O Brother dont let him come! I want to go to mother to-morrow, indeed I do! I dont want to see him!"

My [Brother's] only answer was "Too late. I sent a friend of Banks', who however is a mere civilian, holding no official appointment, to ask the General to place Col. Steadman temporarily under his control as prisoner, and have invited him and his captive to dine here to morrow. He is with Banks now; in an hour or two I will receive an answer."

O Brother! Brother! I was so afraid he thought—I dare not say what! He did it to please me, thinking it would be a gratification—yet how mistaken! What made him suspect it would give me pleasure? May be I was unconsciously deceiving him. So half way crying, I put my arms around him, and told him the simple truth.

I dont want him to come! I dont want to see him! Maybe Banks will refuse. That is one consolation! I ran up stairs and groaned aloud for an hour. At last Miriam came in. What is it? you look as though something dreadful had happened. "Col. Steadman dines here to-morrow" I answered. She was wild with delight. I am not. I came out here to make faces at myself, and pinch my arms black and blue.

Thursday. [July 30th]
    Again my prayers are answered. He will not come. Banks refuses, I believe. I was glad, until just now they told me he was very ill. Now I am sorry. Praised as the bravest among the P. Hudson heroes, unseen, though often heard, sick, and in prison, so near, yet so far, if mine was a romantic or perverse [p. 118] disposition, I would be hurried into a foolish thing. Pity shall not triumph over common sense. I am neither romantic or perverse. So that neither the panegyrics of others, sympathy for his sufferings, or the fact of being forbidden to answer his letters, shall influence my reason. Pity shall not delude me into an error of the understanding.

Some day of the month, I neither know, nor care to find out which.
    An other has come—piqued, hurt, wounded evidently at my silence, when written. He has suffered some anxiety and distress? Not half as much as I have! Nous sommes quittes, à présent.[149] Yet I wish he had not been so wounded. How explain? An answer was expected; but Brother shall be obeyed; no word shall come from my pen. I called the bearer, and told him to tell his master he had seen me, and that I said I could not answer the letter *then* (I might have added—or at any other time) but that I had some books to send him in a day or two. And with that equivocation I sent him away. I feel like a—liar; there is no more gentle

149. We have quit, at present.

word for it. I feel that I have abused Brother's confidence by sending even a message, I feel that I expose myself to the most unpleasant imputations from the other, by persisting in this (to him) unaccountable silence. If the kind Lord would only send them away to be exchanged! I who was so anxious to have them sent here, now pray they may be soon be [*sic*] released.

I have his notes, he has *not* my answers; with this misunderstanding we cannot even remain friends, now. Yet I should like to retain his esteem. N'importe! What ever Is, is right; though this state of affairs is decidedly unpleasant, however proper. All my dreams run on notes, and endless annoyance proceeding from them, all day I start at the sound of the bell, fearing it announces another. This one, I read in my dreams last night; it was quite familiar to me when I broke the seal just now. Pity that I should not have respite even in dreams!

And he is grieved, grieved! Proper, it may be; but this is bad policy, Brother. This way, three of us are hurt; the other, none would be injured. But you shall be obeyed.

Miriam, working after a mid day slumber of five hours, found me just now with the letter in my hand. "What! another!" she exclaimed. For all answer I showed it to her. "You answered it, of course," was her comment. I shook my head and repeated my message by the servant. Miriam has a light way of talking which I hope she does not feel. "O you good, proper girl!" she exclaimed. "Nobody any the wiser, yet you resisted the temptation! You are more virtuous than I; *I* should [p. 119] have answered." No you would *not*, Miriam; you do yourself injustice. And as to deserving credit for resisting the temptation to write, I merit none, for I did not allow it to ammount [*sic*] even to a *desire*. If it had become temptation, I would probably have yielded to it, and would now be repenting in sack cloth and ashes.

Aug 7th.
Another still. Ha! ha! how friendly and short his notes grow! Nipped in the bud! Best so. Yet I have lost a good friend. When one has not many friends, it is not pleasant to lose one of those few. Best as it is, though. Wonder to what cause he attributes my silence? What matter whether he understands or not? I have ceased to care about it now.

After several very unpleasant days, I no longer troubled myself about what he might, or might not think. What is the difference, so long as I am conscious of doing right.

We will never, never, meet again; yet I should like him to retain at least a pleasant recollection of me.[150] That cannot be now, though. Ernestly and sincerely I hope that we may never again see each other. In that case I would have to give some explanation; this way the disagreeable duty will be spared me. Besides, he is precisely one of that large number of my acquaintance that I like best when at a distance. Put him a[t] liberty to-morrow, and he loses all claims on my sympathy. I may feel for him the respect that we involuntarily pay a brave man, but nothing more; and even that would be diminished by being brought in contact with him. So I hope that that night at Linwood when he so firmly held my trembling, shrinking hand in his grasp and entreated me to listen to his advice and "think once more" before risking my life on such a journey, will be the last time we were destined to meet. It was kind to warn me; what difference could it make to him whether it killed me or not? He, comparatively a stranger! Yes! it *was* kind. If he saw me now, he would know it was unnecessary at present.

I believe I would like to see him just *once* to show him my newly acquired independence of all assistance. And Mr Halsey is another I should like to meet *once*, and *only* once more. Just let me dance him down, or take a five mile walk with him, and I am revenged for that night he had to carry me up stairs at Mrs Greyson's. How I hate him for it! Is it an idiosyncrasy of mine, or is it a feeling common to all the world, this dislike and aversion for every man who ever rendered me a service, or pretended to admire me? I know some I almost hate.

And here is the end of my poor book. I wish two pages out of every three had never been written. I have serious misgivings about the latter part. What tempted me to make such a record? A dozen times I have debated with myself as to the propriety of throwing the whole in the fire. Suppose it should be seen by those who do not understand me as well as I do myself? It would be rather unpleasant to be misunder-

150. Sarah would see Colonel Steedman twice in the years after the war, the second time when he called on her in Charleston following the death of her husband. An 1896 note appended to Book 5 mentions that meeting and leaves the impression that Steedman, though by now married, was still in love with her. See diary page numbered 79.

stood. And yet—what is the difference? It was only written to satisfy myself, and no other could possibly have the slightest interest in it. Am I not satisfied of my opinion and sentiments on the last subject so many pages are devoted to? Yes—but would any one else believe me? What matters it? Who knows or cares about it? You are not apt to bestow un-asked for confidences. Dont burn it yet, then. Wait a year or two when every thing will assume another aspect, and if the [word lined through] allusion seems unwomanly, as you now fear, toss the whole in the fire without hesitation. Perhaps this may enable me to find a moral for the story of my life, not yet told. Keep it in spite of all, and let time prove its uses.

Book Five

[p. 1] New Orleans August 1863.
Friday 14th.

Doomed to be bored! To night Miriam drags me to a soirée musicale at Mrs McLane['s],[1] and in the midst of my toilette, I sit down with bare shoulders to scratch a dozen lines in my new treasure which has been by me for three days, untouched. I dont know what tempts me to do it, except perversity, for I have nothing to say. I was in hopes that I would never have occasion to refer to the disagreeable subject that occupied the last pages of my old journal, but the hope proves fallacious, and where ever I turn, the same subject is renewed. So there is no longer any reason in waiting until all mention can be avoided. Yesterday a little, sly, snaky creature asked me if I knew the "Hero of Port Hudson."[2] "Yes," I said briefly. "Unmistakable! I see it in your face!" she remarked. "See what?" "That you betray yourself. Do you know that every one believes that you are engaged to him?" In surprise I said no; such a thing had never been mentioned before me until then. "Well! they say so, and add too, that you are to be married as soon as the war is over." " 'They' are paying me an undeserved compliment," I returned.

Where could such a report have originated? Not, certainly, from him, and not, most assuredly, from me. Where does dame rumor spring from? He is a stranger here, and I have never mentioned his name except to the Peirces who would no more report such a thing than I would myself. I wont mind it, if it does not reach his ears; but what assurance have I that it will not? That *would* be unpleasant! Why cant "They say" let every body settle their own affairs?

1. Probably Mrs. James L. McLean. New Orleans city directories for 1861 and 1866 give the address of the McLean home as 57 Dauphine Street, in the French Quarter.

2. Colonel Steedman.

537

Here comes Miriam after me! What a bore! what a bore! and she looks as though it was a pleasure to go out! How I hate it! Glancing up the page, the date strikes my eye. What tempted me to begin it Friday? My dear Ada would shiver and declare the blank pages were reserved for some very painful, awful, uncomfortable record, or that "something" would happen before the end of it. Nothing very exciting *can* happen, except the restoration of peace; and to bring that about, I would make a vow to write only on Fridays.

[p. 2] [August] 15th.

For which of my sins was I sentenced to do penance last night? The offense is certainly expiated. What an intolerable martyrdom it was! The music and singing only, kept me awake, and there was not much of that. As to the rest, there were three or four girls as beautiful as angels, and as silly as cats, whose sole conversation consisted in whispers, giggles, and simpering, and eight or ten "stay at home" Creoles,[3] as stupid and insufferable as puppyism could make them. As I seem to possess irresistible attractions for every fool, the biggest one in the room fastened himself to me, and there remained. I abhor the man whose first remark after being introduced is "How warm, or how cold, it is." It proves either that he is a fool, or that he thinks I am one. This one expatiated on the weather. "Insufferable" I said, which might be applied to both himself and the heat.

I became very much interested in the other side of the room then, and half way turned my shoulder, to induce him to escape. But no such blessing was bestowed; he clung to me with a tenacity that speaks well for his perseverance under adverse circumstances in every day life. Every five minutes I could hear a gargle or gasp, as though he were about to make another remark; then I would let my face freeze, and immediately he would relapse into unutterable nothingness, looking very uncomfortable. In oblivion of his presence, I commenced reading a french song near me whose mispronounced words had been perfectly incomprehensible when sung. "You speak french!" cried my torment,

3. Descendants of the Europeans (principally French or Spanish) who settled in Louisiana during the colonial period. The word is sometimes understood to mean people of mixed blood, but that is not the usage here. The Creoles of New Orleans maintained their own language and customs in spite of the incursions of the "Americans."

following my eye, with an accent of surprise that was fairly ludicrous. "Certainly; all Louisianians do" I said shortly. "O! then you are some kin to the Morgans next door!"[4] "Not the slightest connection." "No? not kin to the Morgans? Why *they* speak french!" he exclaimed triumphantly as though the coincidence would confute my assertion. I very nearly laughed. Why did he not claim to be related too? It is very probable that some relationship could be established between us, from the fact that both use handkerchiefs in winter.

Since he would not desert me, I was determined to leave him; and taking advantage of a general movement towards a table of refreshments, I hastily looked around for a more agreeable companion. Not one of those creatures, [p. 3] those insufferable specimens of creolism; not one of those beautiful, simpering girls, with their shocking manners; no—standing apart was a sad, sweet faced girl in deepest black that attracted me involuntarily. "She has lost a father or mother; that yearning look in her hollow eyes shows it was some one very dear to her; she is gentle, timid, and nervous, and yes—she has a look about her which says she earns her living by her musical talents." That thought was enough for me. I staid by her until I went home. And I cant say how gratified I felt when, seeing me pass in the entry, she ran out and gave me her hand as I was going home. I was so glad of an excuse for retiring. In going up stairs I had fallen, and hurt myself enough to warrant my withdrawing at ten o'clock. Miriam, who is perfectly incomprehensible to me, prefered staying some hours later. I see neither pleasure or improvement in such meetings, and pronounce them an intolerable nuisance. If somebody would only promise to secure me from them in future, how grateful I would be!

Sunday. [August] 16th.

Coming out of church this morning with Miriam, a young lady ran up with an important air, as though about to create a sensation. "I have a message for you both," she said fixing her eyes on mine as though she sought something in them. "I visit the prisoners frequently, you know, and day before yesterday Capt. Steadman requested me to beg

4. City directories place Mrs. Sarah Morgan (no relation to the diarist) at 59 Dauphine Street, next door to the McLeans.

you to call, that he will not take a refusal, but entreated you to come, if it were only once." The fates must be against me; I had almost forgotten his existence, and having received the same message frequently from another, I thoughtlessly said, "You mean *Col.* [blank space], do you not?" Fortunately Miriam asked the same question at the instant that I was beginning to believe I had done something very foolish. The lady looked at me with her calm, scrutinising, disagreeable smile—a smile that had all the unpleasant insinuations eyes and lips can convey, a smile that looked like "I have your secret—you cant deceive *me*," and said with her piercing gaze "No; *not* the Colonel. He was very ill that day (did you know it?) and could not see us. This was *really* the Captain."[5]

"He is very kind," I stammered, and suggested to Miriam that we had better pass on. The lady was still eyeing me inquisitively. Decidedly, this is unpleasant to have the reputation of being engaged to a man that [p. 4] every girl is crazy to win! If one only cared for him, it would not be so unpleasant; but under the circumstances— Ah ça! why dont they make him over to the young lady whose father openly avows he would be charmed to have him for a son-in-law? This report has cost me more than one impertinent stare. The young ladies think it a very enviable position. Let some of them usurp it, then!

So the young lady, not having finished her examination, proposed to accompany us part of the way. As a recompense, we were regaled with charming little anecdotes about herself, and her visits. How she had sent a delightful little custard to the Colonel (here was a side glance at my demure face) and had carried an autographic album in her last visit and had insisted on their inscribing their names, and writing a verse or so. "How interesting!" was my mental comment. "Can a man respect a woman who thrusts him her album, begging for a compliment the first time they meet? What fools they must think us, if they take such as these for specimens of the genus!" Did we know Capt. Lanier?[6] Know

5. The colonel's brother, Captain Seth D. Steedman.

6. Sarah assumed that this was the officer she recalled from the day of her accident. In earlier references she spelled the name *Lenair*. There are two Laniers listed among the Port Hudson officers brought to New Orleans—First Lieutenant Charles L. Lanier, identified as a staff officer, and Second Lieutenant B. W. Lanier, who was in Miles' Legion. See *Daily Picayune*, July 15 and 22, 1863. Sarah is probably referring to the staff

him, no! but how vividly his face comes before me when I look back to that grand smash up at Port Hudson, when his face was the last I saw before being thrown, and the first I recognised when I roused myself from my stupor and found myself in the arms of the young Alabamian.

At the sound of his name, I fairly saw the last ray of sunset flashing on his handsome face, as I saw it then. No, I did not know him. He had spoken to me, begging to be allowed to hold me, and I had answered, entreating him not to touch me, and that was all I knew of him; but she did not wait for the reply. She hurried on to say that she had sent him a bouquet, with a piece of poetry and that he had been heard to exclaim "How beautiful!" on reading it. "And do you know" she continued with an air that was meant to be charmingly naïve, but which was not very successful, as naïveté at twenty nine is rather flat, "I am *so* much afraid he thinks it original! I forgot to put quotation marks and it would be *so* funny in him to make the mistake! For you know I have not much of the—of that sort of thing about me—I am not a poet—poetess, author, you know."

Said Miriam in her blandest tone, without a touch of sarcasm in her voice, "O if he has ever seen you, the mistake is natural." If I had spoken my voice would have carried a sting in it. So I waited until I could calmly say "You know him well, of course." "No! I never saw him before" she answered with a new outburst of naïveté. [p. 5] I walked on in silence, disgusted with her, and congratulating myself on never having replied to the entreaties of notes or messages by calling on the prisoners. Dear Brother, how grateful I am to you for having pointed out to me the impropriety! Miriam and I at least cannot be confounded with her set. At *her* age to make a fool of herself! Bad enough at fifteen, but then it has the merit of ignorance.

As soon as we could take leave of her, which was before she had half related her anecdotes, I said "Miriam, I am convinced from the way she speaks, that Col. St[eedman] has never paid her the compliment of appearing when she called, though she is evidently anxious to leave us under the impression that they are quite intimate, without actually

officer. However, the name *Charles L.* is a misreading of the officer's signature. He was in fact First Lieutenant John S. Lanier. See Compiled Service Records of Confederate General and Staff Officers (Microcopy 331).

saying so." "I'd stake my bracelet on it!" Miriam exclaimed. "And not only that, but she is so jealous of our knowing him, and you especially, that she cannot help showing it. Why her eyes fairly devoured you!"

Are all these women fools, or crazy? One I never beheld said to Ada the other day that it was very extraordinary that so many of those prisoners had but one topic of conversation—the Miss Morgans. That every time a lady was announced Col S[teedman] would ask if it was not Miss Sarah, and his first question after being introduced was invariably if they knew her, and if she was quite well; and Capt Duprè and Major Spratley were always asking about Miss Miriam. "In fact, we ladies all call the third story Miss Sarah's department, and the second, Miss Miriam's, since they seem to reign over the occupants of each. However it is well known that Miss Sarah is engaged to the 'Hero,' so it is all right." I wish people would let my affairs alone! Am I jealous of anybody? Who do I interfere with?

Monday Aug. 24th.

My idea of happiness is a rainy evening with a *comfortable* book to read, a solitary spot to hide one's self in with a fascinating piece of embroidery or nice piece of sewing, with a volume of Tennyson or Longfellow open before you, and Miriam playing on the piano in the distance. I have all these requisites this evening, except the comfortable book; but instead of availing myself of any of them I have selected this darkest, warmest corner, and have commenced writing without a word to say. One would imagine that under such circumstances the task would soon be ended; but it is precisely when I have [p. 6] nothing to say that it takes me the longest to say it. And I haven't a word to say this evening, though the envie[7] to write has possessed me. Clang! goes the bell! What can it be this pleasant rainy evening? May be a note from—No! he sent too many messages yesterday, to have anything left to say now. I'll go see, any way. Perhaps it will give me at least an idea.

Disappointed, yet not! A letter from Capt. Bradford to Miriam, and not as I feared. My poor Adonis, that I used to ridicule so unmercifully, what misfortunes have befallen him! He writes that during the seige [*sic*] at Port Hudson he had the top of his ear shot off (wonder if he lost any of that beautiful golden fleece yclept his hair?) and had the cap of

7. Longing.

his knee removed by a shell, besides a third wound he does not specify. Fortunately he is with kind friends. And he gives news of Lydia, most acceptable since such a time has elapsed since we heard from her. And little Florence is dead![8] I hope this is a mistake. Dear little baby! I hope Helen is not called on to bear such a severe blow as this would be.

Capt. Bradford is too bad. If I was Anna, which Pharisee like I cry "thank Heaven I am not," I should hate him. Fancy him alluding to her as "the graceful and dimpling Miss Anna Mary"! O Wretch! what insolence! Poor dear, good, logic[al], Anna! Has she been getting any fatter, or have those tortured corsets at last burst the restraint of cords and irons, and left her lungs to play freely? If they ever do get inflated, it will take a month's pulling to get the breath out of them again. For her sake, I hope the accident will not happen until she can either obtain patent pulleys, or get Malvina to screw her up again. How many days have I watched that amazing operation from my sick bed, shrinking secretly under the covers as though my blessed spine were concerned, when Anna, biting her lips white while holding her breath, would gasp faintly (for fear of taking in any air) "Harder! you Malvina, harder!" while poor Mal, as breathless, and certainly more exhausted, would tug the strong strings together still, by wrapping them around her hands, surprise them into a knot, and fall back, with an apoplectic look about her eyes, to contemplate the herculean task. Is it possible that she could have spread any more? The thing is hardly credible.

I wonder if all young ladies are subject to the cool impertinences of young men? *Would* Capt. Bradford allude to me in that way? [p. 7] I must be very vain, for though I have been his avowed enemy, and have never spared him a cut when I had the opportunity of giving him one, I do not believe he would treat me with the lazy insolence he always showed her. I cant fancy him playing with my curls—if I had any— tipping my chair backwards, or cooly saying "O shut up!" when I talked nonsense. No! I cant fancy it. But I wonder if there is any body who *can* imagine me in such a position, or if there is any one who could make such remarks about me? O I wonder if people do jest about me so? The mere fancy makes my nerves tingle! I'm glad I dont hear of it!

How blessings brighten as they take their flight! He must be under

8. Florence Carter, daughter of Eugene and Helen Carter, died July 27, 1863, at the age of 14 months.

the delusion that we were civil to each other, or friendly, even, from the messages he sends. He says "tell Miss Sarah that the last I saw of 'John' he was crossing the Mississippi in a skiff, his parole in his pocket, his sweet little sister by his side"[9] (O you wretch! at it again!) "and Somebody else in his heart." How considerate to volunteer the last statement! Then follows half a page of commendation for his bravery, daring, and skill during the seige (the only kind words he ever spoke of him, I dare say) all looking as though I was to take it as an especial compliment to myself, and was expected to look foolish, blush, and say "thanky" for it. As though I care!

Miriam and I had a warm discussion about him this morning. Wish I could like every gentleman, as she does! But I cant. Involuntarily I shrink and cry no! no! at the approach of each, while Miriam meets them with a frank face, and cordial welcome, as though she were glad to see them. She attempted to reason me into common sense to day, though she failed most ingloriously. "You aim too high!" she exclaimed impatiently "you will miss your mark, I warn you." I felt in an aggravating humor so returned "Yes; I know it. I aim at the brain, and find my arrow goes through empty nothing. I am sure I shall never find anything in the heads you have named to stop its progress."

Here she burst forth in a vehement panegyric of her two present heroes. Was not Col. [blank space] a high minded, noble, brave man, praised by all men, admired by all ladies? Was he not so good as to be wholly [sic] unconscious of his own worth, a piece of humility that was extraordinary in these days? Agreed, I said, tumbling my hair down over me preparatory to combing it. What was lacking then? Could [p. 8] I name an objection? Under cover of my tangled hair I answered Yes; a slight one. He was all that, and I admired him enough comme ça,[10] but he was not a *philosopher* to say the least, and maybe in some awful moment ever to be regretted, I might feel myself to be the taller of the two; naturally I have a contempt for those who are not superior to me.

What a storm I raised! The flood of words bore me down. I bent my head to the blast, which I really deserved for being so conceited,

9. The captain is referring to Sergeant John Halsey and his sister, Mrs. McPhaul. After the surrender of the Port Hudson garrison, men below officer rank were paroled.

10. As is.

and waited for the lull. At last it came. What had I to say to "John"? Say? why that I differed from her essentially. That I did not think him a genius, by any means, or any more than ordinarily intelligent; that neither his style, education, tastes, or manners suited me; that I had heard him say things foolish enough to make me hate him, and that altogether he did not please me. "If I liked him as much as you do," I continued, taking pleasure in being perverse, "I should look out, a dear, sweet little country girl who has no ideal besides that of a truly good man, and make him marry her. She will be supremely happy if a noble, manly heart is all she wants, and if she forsakes the world, and the devil—that is, fashion. And all he would require would be some gentle ditty chirped at a jingling piano or half tuned guitar in the twilight (I shall teach her 'I'll watch for thee'—he used to like *that*) a cheerful, placid smile across the tea table, busy fingers to make him a tomato salad for breakfast, and flying feet to meet him when he comes in, when he will give her an affectionate kiss, and contemplate her with a pleased, fond, earnest gaze. Of course she will blush, and think he is admiring her sweet eyes. But I know better. He is wondering what he will have for dinner, and if it is not most ready. Bah! Cultivate him for the little girl!"

The Colonel I should provide with a pure hearted, gentle, affectionate devoted wife; one who would think it no great sacrifice to bury herself in the country—if such a creature could be found—provided her beloved wished it. One who could worship him if necessary, and be so very meek and submissive[11] that everything would be "Isaiah" (Ye gods and little fishes! *could* she call him that?). "My love, may I do this," and "Certainly not, my dear, if you say no," as sweetly as an angel. She must adore him for his bravery and goodness—for he has both— and worship him as though he possessed the wisdom of Solomon, [p. 9] which he does not.

I would not have her very bright, or she could not be all this. She should have a limited education, very little common sense (since she

---

11. Above the line she wrote: "(1896—she was not!)" Presumably this reference to Dr. Steedman's wife reflects Sarah's conversations with him when he visited Charleston sometime after the death of her husband in 1889. Steedman married Dora Harrison of St. Louis. See his obituary in the St. Louis *Republic*, May 16, 1917, Necrology Scrapbooks, Missouri Historical Society.

is to look to him for advice and assistance, any ordinary amount of either might spoil the project).[12] No—she should not have a very bright mind—she shall be rather simple than otherwise—she may even be silly—here I was interrupted by a rude grasp on my shoulder which startled me into forgetting where I was. I threw back my veil of hair, and stupidly turned around to see what had happened. "Not here! look! look at the mirror there! You have spoken; there is the reflection of the girl you speak of!" Toute hébeteé,[13] I looked vacantly in the glass and found Miriam still grasping my shoulder, while she pointed to my staring, wondering face up in the mirror. The last I saw of myself, I was looking decidedly foolish. What an unflattering picture! O you cruel Miriam! and to seize me at that last clause, too! If you had caught me before, it would not have hurt so! Aye! I think I feel her gripe [sic] yet! On my shoulder & feelings, the pressure was severe.

Miriam's eyes grew larger with excitement. "Go!" she said. "The Lord will send a judgement on you for your ambition, yet. Beware of the crooked stick, you who turn up your nose now!" "Pride goes before a fall, and a conceited speech before a violent wrench" I muttered. Yes! I deserved the reproof, but have I not always said I was not good myself, and disliked men who were *only* good? Show me those of the world, worldly, elegant, well educated, fascinating—in short my very opposite, and then *maybe* I will bend my head to the yoke. But I hug to my heart the belief that I can stand alone, alone, and fight the battle of life out single handed. Why call in spectators to witness my defeat? I shall be Diana the huntress, the cold, calm, and independent—only I shall introduce an amendment—she had her Endymion—& from the pedestal on which my self love shall raise me, I shall look down with feigned disdain on all human frailties.

But, stop this nonsense! What trash I have written! I had better be in bed at this late hour. Any one could guess sleepiness, dim light, and fatigue from the blots and scratches of these four pages. Au revoir, then.

12. Sarah's thoughts on women and what men expect of them are echoed ten years later in the pieces she wrote for the Charleston *News and Courier*. See, for example, "The Natural History of Women" in the September 20, 1873, issue.

13. Totally bewildered.

Thursday [August] 27th.

I was surprised with the sweetest present yesterday! My eyes grow damp every time I look at it. Sitting [p. 10] in the parlor with the Peirces, we were interrupted by a violent pull at the bell. I have but one terror in these days—a note; so of course my thoughts reverted immediately to that. But no! A man entered with a huge parcel, which he said Judge Morgan had ordered to be brought to me. I knew by its shape what it was. But I was so surprised, so overcome, so amazed, that I could not undo the fastenings, but sat stupidly looking at it, until the girls took off the cover, and exposed to my bewildered gaze a most beautiful, shiny, pearl inlaid guitar! I did not know which I felt most inclined to do; to laugh or to cry. I believe I did a little of both as I hugged my precious treasure, and laid my cheek on its shining back.

O my dear good Brother! How can I ever thank him for his love and kindness! His last deed of thoughtfullness took from me all power of speech. Often, in secret, I have longed for the precious one Hal gave me, regretting I had been forced to leave it in the Confederacy, but even to Miriam I never mentioned how much I missed it. I did not even know that Brother knew I could play on the guitar, and here was this beautiful one lying on my lap, without a word of explanation or warning. It sent tears and gratitude to my eyes at once.

When ever a great, and unexpected token or word of love is given me, my first sensation is that of profound humiliation. All unpleasant words and deeds I have said, or committed, for months, and years past, rise before me with painful vividness, and a feeling of real pain surges over me, leaving me humbled and abashed at my own unworthiness. And so when I clasped my arms around my beautiful present, I thought of how he had been displeased about those notes that had been written to me, until the pain I suffered then came back to me, and I felt as though I had been the criminal and was responsible for the sin, instead of being the victim of a misunderstanding on every side. And I felt so sinful, wicked, and unhappy, that really my guitar gave me fully as much pain as it did pleasure. What pious resolutions I formed while hanging over it! How good, and gentle I would try to be, how patient and persevering under trials! How hard I would study, and how zealously I would practice that Brother's gift might not be thrown away! Remains to be seen how many of these pious resolutions will be carried out.

My dear, dear Brother! how good he is. He cant hear me thank him, for this morning he sailed for New York to meet Sister. Believe I'll take to "I'll watch for thee" myself!

[p. 11] Sunday Sept. 6th.

Marie and I say to each other almost daily with an emphasis that makes it almost ludicrous "We will never, never marry." Every one laughs at us, and prophesies that before another year has elapsed we will recant our vow at the altar. Never! We speak knowing what we say, and firmly resolved (at present) to carry out our resolution. So daily we lay our plans, and wonder when we will take possession of our cottage. It is veritably a chateau en Espagne;[14] we have decided on a home in the Pyrenees. I insist on a perfect view of sunset, she insists on a full view of sunrise; so we have compromised by selecting the top of a mountain whence both can be seen. Our house shall be as comfortable as possible; we shall have a fine library in which our days shall be quietly spent, and certain hours shall be devoted to making clothes for poor people, and embroidering for our army of neices [*sic*] and nephews. What blissful, happy, quiet days we will spend! We will grow old insensibly, without regret, live without care, and die in peace when we are called. And the secret of such bliss as this quiet life would be, is to be found in the motto to be inscribed above the door "No gentlemen or children admitted."

I thought of suggesting "Fools" as much more concise than the two before mentioned tribes, uniting them so perfectly under a name appropriate to both; but fearing that we might have a shrewd, conscientious porter who might discharge his duty so strictly as to exclude me from my proper home, I wisely refrained from offering my amendment. A place where a child's cry is not heard! Is there such a paradise as that would be, in store for me? Miriam and I have been really unfortunate in having so much to do with children. Our eldest neices were born before we were out of babydom, almost, and every year since has added one to the number, so that there has never been one day out of all these years, that the delicious harmony of an infant's voice has not cleaved our tympanum with its dulcet sounds.

14. Castle in Spain.

Let poets take [*sic*] of baby prattle! *We* know what it is! If it were not for the sure hope of some blessed haven where I may yet find rest, I would loose [*sic*] all courage. Could not children be trained to laugh out their wants?: I love them so dearly when they dont cry! Here this angelic little Hicky throws himself in my lap and with his arms around my waist calls me "my Sady" and begs a kiss, regardless of the severe strain in which I am writing. I ask him if he knows he is a [p. 12] wretch. "No; I'm your pet" he says, climbing up to my face, since I did not stoop to his. What a beautiful nature is his! I shall have to petition Marie to relax her severe rules in his favor, at least. He cant be called a child; he is an angel. What a pity this clever little Harry is not as good as he! Poor Harry is as bad as he can well be, and thinks nothing of cursing and kicking me when he is in one of his tempers.

Where ever I go, Hicky follows. Sometimes I pass him unconsciously, and am only made aware of his presence by having my hand seized and kissed. Of course then I have to stop and hug him! it is so sweet! Every morning I look out for a quiet spot (which I never find) where I can read Buckle and Thiers.[15] Before the first page is turned, my book is raised by two chubby hands, and a handsome face is substituted for it. "Dont you see I am busy? run away and let me read" I remonstrate, pleased in spite of myself at his devotion. "I'll be good, Sady! *just* let me lie down!" so he curls himself up on my lap, and I use him for a desk while he pats my hand and there he remains until I finish. So it is while I sew; it interferes sadly with speed—and neatness; but what is that, when you have any one to love you so dearly? Miriam thinks such an affectionate disposition inconvenient in warm weather; but I would rather melt, than dispense with it.

Dear, sweet little Hicky! If all children were like him what a Heaven a nursery would be! He sits next to me at table, and generally contrives to lean over and kiss me between the courses. Miriam with her strict ideas of propriety stopped him the other day with "Hicky you must not kiss your aunt at table." Instantly he turned violently red and burst into tears; it was only by kissing him regardless of regulations that I consoled him for the rebuke. Dear, loving little cherub! I'd kiss him on

15. Probably Henry Thomas Buckle's *History of Civilization in England* and Adolphe Thiers's *History of the French Revolution.*

Canal St. if he took a fancy for it. There never was such an angel of goodness and amiability before. He is absolutely faultless. Why cant all children be born with all their teeth, and five years old? I never knew one to stop crying before they had reached their fourth birthday.

Last night I was expatiating on our old maid project to mother, discovering in the most exalted strain the pleasures of single blessedness. Mother laughed at me! I was so indignant at her unbelief, that I became eloquent in my defense. *I* marry? A quoi bon? [16] I suppose falling in love would be very pleasant, though I have never tried it; and I acknowledge that it [p. 13] is very delightful to have a body fall in love with you—it is so flattering to one's vanity, for an hour or so—or until you feel it is a little too serious, and begin to shiver at the thought of being obliged to say No. Then getting married must be prodigiously amusing. Think of the delight of trying on your wedding dress, and looking over your trousseau! Who ever saw an ugly bride? there is *once* in a life time you are sure of being beautiful. And the wedding breakfast, or supper, and the congratulations, and journey—that's delightful! But then—!

Orange blossoms fade in a night, mother; after a dream comes waking. Suppose the trick played upon Jacob should be tried upon me; and after marrying my ideal, I should wake to the reality and find in the morning not the tender eyed Rachel of my imagination, but the blear eyed Leah? Do you remember that last night at Home when Hal laughed at my fastidiousness, and bade me beware of whom I married, saying I'd die of horror if my husband wore dirty socks? He was right! No I'll not run the risk! let me live single and happy! Doubtless, if I married, a gracious Providence would bestow fifteen or twenty shrieking infants upon me, as a reward for my righteousness, Heaven help me!

I left mother still an unbeliever, laughing at my plans, and assuring me that my nonsense would not upset the world. I went to sleep and dreamed she wanted to force me to marry some one I did not like. I had exhausted my tears and entreaties, and was sitting on the floor in speechless despair, when I was wakened. It might have been a continuation of my dream, for mother was standing by me, telling me somebody was down stairs. "The one you wanted me to marry?" I might have asked; but instead, I waited for her to speak, and with

16. What's the good of it?

chattering teeth she told me to get up quick; there was a robber down stairs, who had fallen over a chair. Wasn't it amusing to be called on to protect all these women so much older than myself?

I wrapped a dress around my shoulders, and went in the next room. There lay Miriam shivering in bed with terror, while these great, cowardly Irishwomen [17] cried "Lord! Lord!" in dismay, and declared they were too "scart" to move. Mother prudently chose the corner farthest from the door, and scolded them for their absurdity in putting on such "airs." She herself was trembling—but that was nothing. I sent the one most alarmed to wake up William Beanham [18] in the wing of the house. A boy of sixteen is almost as good as a man. En attendant, I, the valiant giant slayer, marched valorously down the dark stairs armed with a candle, to encounter the thief alone. As [p. 14] I put out my hand to open the dining room door, it gave an ominous click, as though the bolt were being turned on the other side. I am sorry I did not faint; but not knowing how, and William joining me at the moment, we just threw it open, and disliking to give him the precedence in such a case, I walked in first and found—what? A cat, rat, robber, ghost, escaped Confederate, or worse still, my terror, a note? No! I found absolutely—nothing!

I cant say how bitterly I was disappointed. All my daring went for nothing. We examined bolts and bars, and had to return without an adventure. It was only after I got upstairs, that it struck everybody that if it had been a robber I stood in danger of receiving a cold bullet for my trouble. I wish it had been one! I am longing for an adventure! William congratulates me on my pluck; he thinks it wonderful. I tell mother "You see I can take care of myself, so there is no necessity for my getting married."

Monday night. [September 7th]

I consider myself outrageously imposed upon! I am so indignant that I have spent a whole evening making faces at myself. "Please Miss Sarah, look natural!" William petitions. "I never saw you look cross

17. Two Irish-born domestics were living in the household of Philip Hicky Morgan when the 1860 census was taken.

18. Apparently a servant.

before!" Good reason! I never had more cause! However I stop in the midst of a hideous grimace, and join in a game of hide the switch with the children to forget my annoyance. Of course a woman is at the bottom of it. Last night while Ada and Marie were here, a young lady whose name I decline to reveal for the sake of the sex, stopped at the door with an English officer, and asked to see me in the entry. I had met her once before. Remember this, for that is the chief cause of my anger. Of course they were invited in; but she declined, saying she had but a moment, and had a message to deliver to me alone, so led me apart.

"Of course you know who it is from?" she began. I told a deliberate falsehood, and said no, though I guessed instantly. She told [me] the name then. She had visited the prison the day before, and there had met the individual whose name, joined to mine, has given me more trouble and annoyance during the last few months, than it would be possible to mention. "And our entire conversation was about you" she said as though about to flatter my vanity immensely. I prepared myself for something disagreeable then; I knew it would come. She rattled on as fast as possible—so fast that I could hardly distinguish the message from some idle compliments she repeated as having been addressed by him to me. "How extravagantly he admires you! I never heard such words! But I haven't time to tell you now. When you return my visit, I [will] tell you all he said." I wonder if she thinks me fool enough [p. 15] to care to hear anymore, and if she really expects me to call for such an object?

Hypocrite that I am, I smiled benignly through the whole of it, in spite of my internal disgust. How deceitful I must be! But was it possible, or proper to say "dear, sweet little creature, you are a mischief maker and busy body, and I suspect you of a little double dealing?" So I held my peace. She went on: "He told me *all*—" "All what?" I abruptly asked. "You know! It sounds better from his lips than from mine! I'll tell you the rest another time." "You are exaggerating, and distorting the original facts" was my mental comment, but still I held my peace. At last came the message. He must really have given her the history of those unanswered notes. What a simpleton for his trouble! Yet I was glad to hear how it had distressed him! I was glad he had been pained! That will console me for that night I cried for fear he would be hurt;

and though I cried then, for distress at inflicting needless pain, now I am glad he suffered! How very wicked I am becoming!

He told her then, that he had written repeatedly to me, without receiving an answer, and at last had written again, in which he had used some expressions, which he feared had offended my reserved disposition. Something had made me angry, for without returning letter or message to say I was not displeased, I had maintained a resolute silence, which had given him more pain and uneasiness than he could say. That during all this time he had had no opportunity of explaining it to me, and that now he begged her to tell me that he would not offend me for worlds—that he admired me more than anyone he had ever met, that he could not help saying what he did, but was distressed at offending me, etc. The longest explanation! And she was directed to beg me to explain my silence, and let him know if I was really offended, and also to leave no entreaty or argument untried, to induce me to visit the prison; he *must* see me.

As to visiting the prison, I told her that was impossible. (O how glad I am that I never did!) But as to the letters, [I] told her to assure him that I had not thought of them in that light, and had passed over the expressions he referred to as idle words it would be ridiculous to take offense at; and that my only reason for persevering in this silence, had been that Brother disapproved of my writing to gentlemen, and I had promised that I would not write to him. That I had feared he would misconstrue my silence, and had wished to explain it to him, but I had no means of doing so except by breaking [p. 16] my promise; and so had prefered leaving all explanation to time, and some future opportunity.

"But you did not mean to pain him, did you?" the dear little creature coaxingly lisped, standing on tiptoe to kiss me as she spoke. I assured her that I had not. "He has been dangerously ill" she continued apologizingly "and sickness has made him more morbid, and more unhappy about it than he would otherwise have been. It has distressed him a great deal." I felt awkwardly. How was it that this girl, meeting him for the first and only time in her life, had contrived to learn so much that she had no right to know, and appeared here as mediator between two who were strangers to her, so far usurping a place she was not entitled to as to apologize to *me* for his sensitiveness and entreat me to tell him he had not forfeited my esteem, as though *she* was his most intimate friend, and I a passing acquaintance? Failing to comprehend it, I deferred it to a leisure moment to think over, and in the mean time exerted myself to be affable.

I cant say half she spoke of; but as she was going she said "Then will you give me permission to say as many sweet things for you as I can think of? I'm going there tomorrow." I told her I would be afraid to give her carte blanche on such a subject; but that she would really oblige me by explaining about the letters. She promised, and after another kiss, and a few whispered words, left me. How my nerves jarred! I was disgusted beyond measure with him. He had no right to tell her half that he did! Maybe she exaggerated, though! Uncharitable as the supposition was, it was a consolation. I was unwilling to believe that anyone who professed to esteem me would make me the subject of conversation with a stranger—and such a conversation! So my comfort was only in hoping that she had related a combination of truth and fiction, and that he had not been guilty of such folly.

Presently, it grew clearer to me. I must be growing in wickedness, to fathom that of others, I who so short a time ago disbelieved in the very existence of such a thing. I remembered having heard that the young lady and her family were extremely anxious to form his acquaintance, and that her cousin had coolly informed Ada that she had selected him among all others, and meant to have him for her "beau" as soon as she could be introduced to him; I remembered that the young lady herself, had been very inquisitive to discover whether the reputation common report had given me had any foundation—and soon my disgust for him turned to contempt for her.

As soon as we were alone, I told mother of our conversation in the entry, and said "and now I am certain that this girl has made use of my name to become acquainted with [p. 17] him, and by representing herself as my intimate friend, has induced him to speak more freely about me than he had any right." Offering her services to make his apology and carry back my forgiveness has confirmed him in the delusion, and gives her an additional reason for repeating her visit. Let her once get a pied à terre,[19] and mademoiselle has no longer a pretext for claiming

19. Place of her own.

to be my friend, but will make her next appearance as the conqueror of the "Hero of Port Hudson." That is all she wants, and she'll have her wish too. Mean as the suspicion is, I believe it to be true. Yet she is so sweet and lovable! I want to like her.

All day that idea has pursued me, and tonight came a letter from him! He had met the young lady and, delighted to find her an intimate friend of mine, had had a very pleasant conversation with her. Then for the first time I forgave myself for having suspected her. She *had* deceived him! She had told him what was not so. I almost forgave him. He had not been able to speak to her this morning he said, as she was surrounded by visitors. Then he expected a private conversation! she had promised to bring messages from me! O Woman! woman! I can be bad, but I could not stoop to such artifices to captivate any man! Well! perhaps she is too innocent to see the shame, and maybe she did not mean it. Let us give her the benefit of a doubt on the subject. But it looks so contemptible!

Why did she use my name as a cloak? Her own attractiveness would have been more than sufficient to recommend her. What chance would poor, plain, shy, uninteresting Sarah stand by the side of this sweet little creature with her winning lisp and artless ways? She is older than I, yet so much more childish. Why, I dont know how a man could help falling in love with her! And she might possibly have won him without mentioning my name, or doing a base thing. Miriam insisted on writing to him to tell him that she was almost totally unknown to me; but I would not suffer it. It might look like pique or jealousy; and I'd die before I would do anything to make him think less of her. What is he to me? Let her win him. I have noticed that deceit has always extraordinary success for a time; but when it is discovered—Ouf! Let her have her own way!

The most unpleasant part is, that she will repeat the whole of that conversation to every one who will listen, and will make public her position as mediator between us, and have us both town talk. Then afterwards, when she has won him herself, she will have every one believe I am jilted and heart broken. That is her plot; and yet, satisfied how it will end, I will not be base enough to undeceive him about [p. 18] "my intimate friend" he has chosen to make a confidante of. I am content to let both alone, and allow things to take their own course. The young lady can rely—not on my ignorance of her motives, for secrecy,—but on my sense of delicacy, and self respect. She need not fear detection. The man won by artifice is just worthy of the woman who practices it. If my name has procured her an honor her own would have failed to secure, I am glad to have been of service to her, and my family pride is gratified; Voilà tout.[20]

Thursday 10th Sept.

O my prophetic soul—! part of your forebodings are already verified! And in what an unpleasant way! Day before yesterday an English officer, not the one who came here, but one totally unknown to me, said at Mrs Peirces[21] he was going to visit the Confederate prisoners. He was asked if he knew any. Slightly, he said; but he was going this time by request; he had any quantity of messages to deliver to Col [blank space] from Miss Sarah Morgan. "How can that be possible, since you are not acquainted with her," Ada demanded. He had the impudence to say that the young lady I have already mentioned had requested him to deliver them for her, since she found it impossible. Fortunately for me, I have two friends left. Feeling the indelicacy of the thing, and knowing that there must be some mistake that might lead to unpleasant consequences, Ada and Marie, my good angels, insisted on hearing the messages. At first he refused, saying that they were intrusted to him confidentially; but being assured that they were really intimate with me, whereas the other was a perfect stranger, and that I would certainly not object to their hearing what I could tell a gentleman, he yielded, fortunately for my peace of mind, and told all.

I cant repeat it. I was too horrified to hear all, when they told me. What struck me as being most shocking, was my distorted explanation about the letters. It now set forth, that I was not allowed to write myself, but would be happy to have him write to me; then there was an earnest assurance that my *feelings* towards him had not changed in the least— Here I sprang from my chair and rushed to the window for a breath of air, wringing my hands in speechless distress. How a word more or less,

20. That's all.

21. Clementine Hyle Peirce, wife of Levi Peirce. The Peirces are buried in Lafayette Cemetery No. 1. See the Historic New Orleans Collection's 1981 survey of historic New Orleans cemeteries.

an idea omitted or added, a syllable misplaced, can transform a whole sentence and make what was before harmless, really shocking!

Yet even in my first dismay I acquitted her of all intentional harm. My confusion at the strange reversal of our positions, my awkwardness, and singular manner of expressing myself might easily have led her into a trivial mistake; and the conversation repeated to a man of very limited understanding, might [p. 19] insensibly undergo alterations at his hands, until what was perfectly innocent when I said it, seemed revoltingly indelicate when I heard it repeated as of another person. O the man or woman who again betrays me into sending a message under such circumstances, may certainly write me down a fool! And if it had not been for Ada and Marie—! Blessed angels! they entreated him not to deliver any of his messages, insisting that there must be a mistake, that if he knew me he would understand that it was impossible for me to have sent such a message by a stranger. And though at first he declared he felt obliged to discharge the task imposed on him, (idiot!) they finally succeeded in pursuading him to relinquish the errand, promising to be responsible for the consequences.

"Ah me!" I gasped last night, making frantic grimaces in the dark, and pinching myself in disgust, "Why cant they let me alone? Why insist on lowering me in his estimation? I neither see him or write to him, while they do both. Isn't that enough for them? I care for nothing but his respect; that, every gentleman owes me. They are welcome to the rest, yet even this they try to take from me! And to destroy my own self respect by such a message—! O Women! women! I wish he could marry all of you, so you would let me alone! Take him please; but en grace dont disgrace me in the excitement of the race!" And I writhed under the lash of self reproach and contrition for others until I fairly kicked myself back to common sense, and resolutely putting away disagreeable thoughts, went to sleep.

Sunday. 20th Sept.

At a bridal dinner yesterday, much against my inclinations. The bride a bright, tiny, lovable little creature *so* glad she's married! the groom a tall, slender, sandy colored, spectacled individual, with a most amusing lisp and conceited air, and a certain je ne sais quoi,[22] which proclaimed

22. Indescribable something.

him a schoolmaster, from "down East" maybe. If it had not been for
our host and hostess, I certainly would have left Miriam to go alone; but
propriety exacted it, so I had to make my appearance. Words cannot
express how sadly against my inclinations I went. I am not fit for the
world; we have no sympathy in common; it is torture to be thrown in
contact with strangers. It turns me to a stiff iron rod, and if I unbend, I
only make a fool of myself.

Miriam, as much at home at Mrs. Lacey's[23] as she is here, did the
honors of the house in her stead, and received the bride of four days and
the invited guests with as much ease as though every thing belonged
to her. Whilst I—raved silently over my own [p. 20] folly and awkwardness, set down ever[y] one who looked at me as a mortal enemy,
and finally wrought myself into such intense contempt for poor Sarah,
mentally, morally and physically, that I was more fitted for my bed
room than the parlor. What a fool! what a fool I am! Casting my eyes
around the room, I said mentally "The greatest fool present, or the
most disagreeable one, is certain to take me to table." I singled him
out; a small, dumpy, uncomfortable looking wretch, who would have
been quite handsome had it not been for the most alarmingly crossed
eyes, which however possessed this advantage of being able to ogle two
young ladies at once. How far a compliment would go with him! A
whole room full might bow, for his oblique vision might address it to
each individual.

Dinner was announced. O my prophetic soul! Here came the destined one from the other extremity of the room, drawn as by some invisible loadstone, proferred his arm which I accepted with undisguised
repugnance, and led me to table. Some little difficulty about seating
the guests in their proper order occurred, which proved my salvation.
Mrs Lacey who has always been so kind and affectionate to me, insisted
on having me at her left hand, the bride being on the right. "You shall
sit by Miss Miriam" she said to my torment. "But I'd rather sit here"
he ventured to say. "Dont trouble yourself about me" I said nervously
clutching Mrs Lacey's hand as he said something about being unwilling to leave me, and at last with a feeling of relief I saw him retire to

23. Possibly the wife of Alfred Lacey, New Orleans commission merchant and cotton
factor.

the other extremity of the table, near Miriam, who was already trying to flirt with a Confederate Captain.

O how I longed to be at home! It seemed that the dinner would never end. At last came indications of its termination. Des[s]ert was set on table, and a toast proposed to the bride and groom. Flash! the gas died out as the last word was uttered, leaving us all in dead darkness. What an omen! "Collins," said a voice to a silent youth next to me who had never opened his mouth except to put something in it, "Miss Miriam Morgan accuses me of being afraid of the dark. I wish you would change places with me. I cant stay where I am so badly treated." Five minutes after, the returning light showed in the cross eyes of my aversion endeavoring to read welcome in my face, as he settled himself in his new place. I had none to give. The silent youth was already plying knife and fork, sublimely indifferent as to where he was placed, [just] so he had enough to eat.

My disguster's breach of politeness was more than my nerves could stand. I took refuge in [p. 21] my own thoughts, and so far forgot him, that several times the blood rushed to my face as I caught the last sound of a remark addressed to me, and became conscious that an answer was expected, and I had none to make, since I had no idea of what I was expected to say. That was being as disgusting as he; so I became very communicative, ridiculed him with a smile that made him take it all for a compliment, and soon found there is no way to rid yourself of a disagreeable man's conversation more effectually than by not allowing him an opportunity of making a remark. I talked him dizzy!

When we were once more in the parlor, I was almost resigned to my situation, and talked almost as much as Miriam—no! that is impossible!—*nearly* as much as the others. We had to dance—that was unpleasant—I have not danced before since Harry died, except once or twice lately, waltzing with Marie when we are alone. Here again I martyrized myself, and succumbed. By Wolsey's leave—if I sacrificed as much for heaven as I do for society, what a martyr's crown of glory would await me above! Isn't it too bad to suffer all this for nothing, and be thought a fool in return? I had some amusement with Miriam's Captain though. It was such a pleasure to find some one who could understand an innocent little sarcasm, after wasting such quantities of wit on that goblin of mine, that I indulged [?] in it freely; and after repeated rebuffs that would have piqued almost any one else, and have made me a deadly enemy, he would come back again, as though delighted to endure it.

It is surprising what pills men will swallow, provided they are gilded with a smile! About twelve, he came to say good night, and asked if we parted friends or enemies. "Neither, please," I answered with an affectation of ennui. "It would be such an exertion to make you an enemy, and such a bore to have you for a friend!" Monsieur is as lazy as a gentleman can decently be; he took the tap with good grace, endeavored to prolong the conversation, and came back three times to wish me good night again. One would imagine I had endeavored to please him!

Friday [September] 25th.

Write me down a witch, a prophetess, or what you will! I am certainly Something! All has come to pass on that very disagreeable subject very much as I feared. Perhaps no one in my "delicate position" would speak freely on the subject; for that very reason I shall not hesitate to discuss it. Know then, that this morning, He—the unpleasant subject of my waking thoughts, [p. 22] the nightmare of my dreams—the "Guy Vere" of his own fancy, went North, along with many other Confederate prisoners, to be exchanged. And he left—he who has written so incessantly and so imploringly for me to visit his prison—he left without seeing me. Bon! Wonder what happened? About a week ago he notified me that he had just obtained a parole, and would spend the next evening with me. I cant say that I gave an additional smooth to my hair, or took one more look at the glass than usual. I did not want to see him; had even prayed that I might not; and I felt that my prayer would be answered, and I, spared a very painful visit. So it was. Evening came, but not so he; another, still he was non est inventus;[24] another, until now a

24. Had not shown up. Sarah's Latin translates literally "was not discovered."

week has gone, and now, so has he, and I hope he is just now gloriously seasick!

What happened in the interval of so few hours to make him change his mind? My private impression is, that between that time, and the hour appointed, he met that dear little lisper. If he did—Heaven help you, poor Sarah. I would rather not know what passed. If she told him all she told the little English officer, I am not surprised that he did not make his appearance. Maybe she told him more—though I hope not. No matter who, or what it was, *Something* happened. There are four girls in this city I barely know well enough to bow to, who hate me with all their souls, and would not hesitate to injure me if it was in their power. She is one of them, and the best of the quartette too; so fancy what the others think. I dont know what cause of dislike I have given them, except that they chose to fancy their hero in love with me—to be sure that is a hanging matter during the present scarcity of beaux.

But why be so acharneé[25] against me? They used to call ever so often on him and his brother officers, whereas I have never beheld his face since he parted from me at Linwood. What they founded their delusion on, it is impossible for me to say. Ada expressed her surprise to one of the quartette that such a report should have arisen in a place where he was comparatively a stranger, and where I never mentioned his name. The young lady snappishly answered that if Ada had heard him talk of me as *she* had, she would have very little doubts on the subject. I am not at all obliged to him; having exhausted the subject of my imaginary perfections, he would really oblige me by choosing another topic of conversation. He has only succeeded in making me food for gossip, and the innocent enemy of half a dozen [p. 23] women. And now I find myself under the disagreeable necessity of playing the heart-broken, deserted, Mariana in the Moated Grange.[26] Haven't the least idea of how I am to do it, for there is no break in my heart; never yet saw any one who could make it beat faster—except when under the painful necessity of saying "No, thank you sir" to some fool who would probably have hanged himself if I had said "Yes, please." What I mean is that this fossil of mine has never yet been melted by the advances of any biped. And how am I to play a rôle I have never studied?

25. Dead set.
26. Character in Shakespeare's *Measure for Measure*.

Evening. I have learned more. He has not yet left; part of the mystery is unraveled, only I have neither patience or desire to seek for more. These women—! Hush! to slander is too much like them; be yourself. I hardly know how to stand with patience this humiliating position in which well meaning friends and designing enemies have placed me. First, all are alike employed in spreading the report that I am engaged to this man, and make it as public a theme of discussion as though it related to the Prince of Wales. I am annoyed with insinuations and inunendoes [sic] whereever I go, and sometimes with broad jests that really make me shiver. It is an insult to woman's self respect to subject her to such impertinence!

Next he is liberated for some hours every day. Instantly every one asks every one else, and the most impudent ask me, if my "Lover" has been to see me yet. I explain quietly, and as naturally to these Paul Prys,[27] that the gentleman they speak of has not been here. I owe it to him, as well as to myself, to discountenance anything that may tend to produce the impression that there is anything between us. They rush off and tell their friends, who suggest that perhaps the engagement is broken. Then I am expected to be disconsolate and heart broken. My sweet little lisper informed a select circle of friends the other night when questioned, that the individual had not called on me, and what was more, would not do so. "Pray, how do you happen to be so intimately acquainted with the affairs of two who are strangers to you?" asked a lady present. She declined saying how she had obtained her information, only ascerting [sic] that it was so. "In fact, you cannot expect *any Confederate gentleman* to call at the house of Judge Morgan, a professed Unionist," she continued. So that is the story she told to keep him from seeing me! She has told him that we had turned Yankees!

All her arts would not grieve me as much as one word against Brother. My wrongs I can forget; [p. 24] but one word of contempt for Brother I *never* forgive! White with passion I said to my informant "Will you inform the young lady that her visit will never be returned, that she is requested not to repeat hers, and that I decline knowing anyone who dares cast the slightest reflection on the name of one who has been both father and brother to me?" This evening I was at a house where she was announced. Miriam and I bade our hostess good evening and

27. Euphemism for inquisitive people.

left without speaking to her. Any body but Brother! No one shall utter his name before me with anything save respect and regard.

This young woman's father is a Captain in the Yankee navy, and her brother is Captain in the Yankee army, while three other brothers are in the Confederate. Like herself I have three brothers fighting for the South, and *un*like her, the only brother who avows himself a Unionist, has too much regard for his family to take up arms against his own flesh and blood. In this brother's house I live, it is his bread I eat; and never will I suffer anyone to speak of him with an accent of contempt for his principles. They are his; and for Him, they are right. If he was on the devil's side, I say the same; only I'd take the liberty of choosing my own party, as I do now.

Pretty, lisping, innocent little creature, poor as the choice may be, I would rather be even myself, than you. I dont know that I have ever done any one in the world an injury; if I have, it has been unconsciously. What prompts this girl to circulate all this gossip and slander? Suppose she does win him by it; le jeu vaut il la chandelle?[28] And if she not—à quoi bon tout cela?[29]

For one who has striven all her life to shun public observation, this position is unbearable. It would not have been so unendurable if it had not reached his ears; but every where I learn that the refined and delicate game of "teasing" is played on him, and my name passed from one to another in a style that would not be justified if we were to be married tomorrow. And I who have hugged myself in my self-love, vaunting that never yet had my heart been touched—I who have so zealously nursed the delusion that *my* name at least should escape the fiery ordeal of public gossip—find myself obliged to start from my dream of security, and called upon to play Ariadne to his Theseus,[30] though I have prayed daily for his departure for more than these two months. If I had given them cause to believe it, or if it was true, I would not mind the reputation of being heartbroken. But with heart untouched—Slandered—! "Ichabod! Ichabod! my glory has departed for ever!"[31]

28. The game, is it worth the candle?

29. What's the use of all this?

30. Hero of Attica in Greek myth. Ariadne's love for him was unfulfilled: he abandoned her. Later she married Dionysus.

31. Sarah echoes 1 Samuel 4:21.

[p. 25] Tuesday Sept. 29 Night

"What if I am doing that girl an injustice?" I have repeated to myself until I am ready at a moment's warning, or at the first sound of her childish lisp to fall on her neck, tell her of my base suspicions, the singular circumstances that confirmed them, and ask her pardon for wrong silently done, and unkind suspicions revealed to Miriam and mother alone. If the sin causes as much suffering to her, as the dread of having injured her in thought gives me, I am sorry for her. Maybe I am sinning against her. It would be impossible to say whether I have suffered most contrition for her or for myself. I want to think well of every one; I cannot bear malice towards even wicked people—and this seems such an artless little piece of simplicity, that it is a greater crime to suspect her of treachery than the act itself would be in her.

By what extraordinary process is it that I burden myself with the sins of others, and writhe and groan under them as though they belonged to me? Let me endeavor to harden myself against this exquisite sensibility that makes me quiver at the meanness of even perfect strangers, as though a sharp needle had been introduced into my nerves. If the Catholic belief of works of supererogation have [*sic*] any foundation, my little lisper will find enough contrition laid up in the Great Storehouse for her to dispense with the painful duty herself. Let me think kindly of her, and charitably. "Charity thinketh no evil—" [32] O how dare I write those words, when I have accused her of evil? O I want to be good! So good and pure that the dear God looking down will smile on me and take me up to his holy heaven—back to father and Harry.

Who will help me break this wall of flesh? Who will guide me to the haven where I would be? I am growing hard and ungrateful. I am aweary of my monotonous, aimless life. Something better—something beyond! My soul craves it. Was I made for this useless life? More! more! light from above, nobler thoughts, nobler aspirations, a wider, or new field in life! Something nobler, Something beyond! Earth cant satisfy me. How dare I murmur? What have I done that I call for higher wages than the rest of poor humanity, I who have never done a noble, generous, or self-denying act in my whole life? How dare I raise Pharisee hands to heaven, and call for a reward for my selfrighteousness? I am

32. 1 Corinthians 13:5.

aweary of my own folly, vanity, and blindness. I want to begin anew, and find the first error that made me the weak, insipid, despicable trash that I am now. Dear Lord help me be good! From Thy high heaven bend in mercy and take from me the [p. 26] baseness of my own nature! Make me pure, make me gentle; grant me fervent Charity; save me from myself—for without Thee I am nothing. Let my soul be beautiful in Thine eyes, and O Lord what would I care for earth?

God help me bear my life patiently, to offer it as a sacrifice to thee! The Water of Life I so madly crave this wild, tempest beaten night, cannot touch my earthly lips. But when I am purified from earthly taint, and God pronounces me clean in His mercy, let me find it above. This belief cherish, O my soul! and no earthly disappointment can cast you down: "What Will be, Will be" & "What ever Is, is right." I may seem to forget all the rest, and act at variance with my own aspirations; but mark if I still cling to this faith in the darkness and trouble through which my life threatens to take me.[33]

Tuesday October 6th.

I hope this will be the last occasion on which I shall refer to the topic to which this unfortunate book seems to have been devoted. But it gives me a grim pleasure to add a link to the broken chain of this curious story now and then. Maybe some day the missing links will be supplied me, and then I can read the little humdrum romance of What might have been, Or what I'm glad never was, as easily as Marie tells her rosary.

Well! the prisoners have gone at last, to my unspeakable satisfaction. Day before yesterday they left. Now I can go out as I please, without fear of meeting him face to face. How odd that I should feel like a culprit! But that is in accordance with my usual judgement and consistency.

Friday, I had a severe fright. Coming up Camp Street with Ada, after a ramble on Canal, we met two Confederates. Every where that morning we had met grey coats, but none that I recognized. Here, without glancing at them, I felt instantly who they were, and knew I was recognized. Still without looking, I saw through my eyelids as it were, two

33. Thirty-three years later Sarah wrote across this page of the diary: "Thank God! I have! through such Joy—through such sorrow as that poor little girl never dreamed of! July 25th, 1896."

hands timidly touch two grey caps, as though the question "May I?" had not yet been answered. In vain I endeavored to meet their eyes, or give the faintest token of greeting. I was too frightened and embarrassed to speak, and only by a desperate effort succeeded in bending my head in a doubtful bow that would have disgraced a dairy maid, after we had passed. Then, disgusted with myself, I endeavored to be comforted with the idea that they had perhaps mistaken me for some one else; that having known me at a time when I was unable to walk, they could have no idea of my height, figure, or walk. So I reasoned, turning down a side street. Lo! at a respectable distance they were following!

We had occasion to go into a daguerrean saloon.[34] While [p. 27] standing in the light, two grey uniforms watching us from the dark recess at the door attracted my attention. Pointing them out to Ada, I hurried her past them down stairs to the street. Faster and faster we walked, until at the corner I turned to look. There they were again, sauntering leisurely along. We turned into another street, mingled in the crowd, and finally lost sight of them. That fright lasted me an hour or two. Whose purse have I stolen, that I am afraid to look these men in the face? But what has this to do with what I meant to tell? How loosely and disconnectedly my ideas run out with the ink from my pen! I meant to say how sorry I am for my dear little lisper that she failed in her efforts to conquer the "Hero;" and here I have drifted off in a page of trash that does not concern her in the least. Well! she did not succeed, and what ever she told him, was told in vain as far as *she* was concerned. He was not to be caught!

What an extraordinary man! Dozens fighting for the preference, and he, in real or pretended ignorance, looking back, like Lot's wife, unconscious of the strife. One of the quartette has conceived quite a tender attachment for him. She thinks him so noble! so brave! so great! too good for her to aspire to—and yet—! imagine a line or two of sighs following. Hers is a delicate case; if she is sentimentally attracted by him, she involuntarily confesses to a deeper feeling for an equally modest Captain. I am told that between the two, she spends her time chiefly disolved in tears—idle tears! alas! for both are unconscious of the state of affairs!

34. Photographer's studio.

"She is rich, pretty, young; why dont he marry her?" I asked my informant. This was the reply: "Do you think that a man who has once loved *you* could fancy such a girl afterwards?" "Where did you ever hear such a story?" I demanded. "Why, being teased by the young lady's mamma about you, he in sheer desperation took her in his confidence, and told her how you had treated him." How I had treated him! Goose! Simpleton! who, and what would he tell next?

I must do him the justice to say he is the most guileless, as well as the most honest of mortals. He told the mother of a rich and pretty daughter what he thought of me; that my superior did not exist on earth, and my equal he had never met! Ha! ha! this pathetic story makes me laugh in spite of myself. Is it excess of innocence, or just a rôle he adopted? Stop! His idle word is as good as an oath. He would not pretend to what he did not believe. He told her of his earnest and sincere admiration—Words! words! hurry on! She asked how it was then—? Here he confessed, with a mixture of pride and penitence, that he had written me letters which absolutely required answers, and to which I had never deigned to reply by even [p. 28] a word. That mortified beyond measure at my silent contempt, he had tried every means of ascertaining the cause of my coldness, but I had never vouchsafed an answer, but had left him to feel the full force of my harsh treatment without one word of explanation. That when he was paroled he had hoped that I would see him to tell him wherein he had forfeited my esteem; but I had not invited him to call, and mortified and repulsed as he had been, it was impossible for him to call without my permission.

"In fact" said the mamma to my informant "The young lady should understand that when a gentleman of *his* dignity and high sense of honor makes such advances, and finds them so coldly repulsed, he has only his wounded pride to comfort him. He is not a man to be so trifled with by *any* one." I agree with the lady; what game of cross purposes have we been playing? I would not mind being friends with him in the least, and here he has gone off, convinced that I have grievously wronged and humiliated him! Did my little lisper change the message when the little midshipman told her it had been intercepted because too friendly? I know she met this martyred Lion frequently after that, and had many opportunities of telling him the simple truth; but she evidently *did not*.

Now all young ladies take warning by me, a victim of unanswered letters! If I had followed my own impulse, I would have answered if only to say I could not answer them. What a contradiction that would have been! And then, what would have followed? Let woman's vanity and self love veil itself in my weak nature, while with a woman's truer pride, and with honest faith, I say: "God bless Brother for not allowing me to answer those letters." One line from me would have made matters end very differently—that is to say they would have seemed more pleasant for a while, and would probably have terminated painfully for both. But I am glad it has ended this way, and shall ever be grateful to Brother for showing me the impropriety of writing to him.

He has gone away with sorely wounded feelings to say nothing more; for that I am sincerely sorry; but I trust to his newly acquired freedom, and his life of danger and excitement, to make him forget the wrongs he believes himself to have suffered at my hands. If it was all to be gone through again (which thank Heaven I will never be called upon to endure again) I would follow Brother's advice as implicitly then, as I did before. He is right, and without seeing, I believe.

They tell me of his altered looks, and of his forced, reckless gaiety which [is] so strangely out of keeping with his natural character, but makes his assumed part more conspicuous; No matter! He will [p. 29] recover! Nothing like a sea voyage for disorders of all kinds. And we will never meet again; that is another consolation.

"Notice: The public are hereby informed through Mrs ———, chief manager of the theatre of High Tragedy, that Miss Sarah M. having been proved unworthy and incompetent to play the rôle of Ariadne, that said part will hereafter be filled by Miss Blank of Blank St., who plays it with a fidelity so true to nature, that she could hardly be surpassed by the original."

O men! perverse creatures who want just what you cant get, and despise what lays at your feet, what fools poor women make of themselves for your sake! Why not like that little girl? She would suit him admirably. Yet he ignores the little thing writhing before him, and looks away, away, to a land he will never set his foot on; where all seems bright and golden because it is beyond his grasp, and where all would look dead and lifeless if he once reached it and called it his own. And he would "Sigh and look, and sigh and look, and sigh and look, and sigh again" (one would call that quotation silly if Dryden was not the author)[35] until he was turned to stone by the Medusa-head of Regret, if a watchful and benevolent Providence did not raise up the mirage of a more beautiful and more inaccessible land, which instantly obliterates all traces of the former, and wakes the throbbings of the petrifying heart once more to life. And weary miles he will toil over, towards that unattainable Happy Land, through brambles and briars, through slough and mice, over rocks and flints, until the mirage fades away, leaving him alone in the wilderness.

Then, as darkness and desolation settle around, for the first time he will perceive the patient, uncomplaining woman who has trodden in his footsteps with bleeding feet through all the weary way, fainting and thirsting for one word or look, and that woman's recompense for the agony she has undergone will be the stern command "Bind up my wounds!" Fool! fool! she asks no more than to pour "balm on a chafing spirit," to stand by the closed door and drive away the demons that seek to enter. The Holy of Holies is not for her; she is content to worship at the threshold, in storm and darkness without, forgotten, and alone, with no hope that the veil of the temple will ever be drawn aside. Fool! abandon your past! Tell him "Die untended and uncared for!" Drive your dagger to his heart, and flee from him! Step by step he will follow you over the bleak desert of Regrets, wailing and entreating your pity, and fall a suppliant across your threshold, even as you knelt [p. 30] at his before. O man! fool! fool! In your folly and perversity you are surpassed only by Woman!

Saturday October 17th.[36]

Tired and almost too warm to breathe, I throw off my bonnet after baking the whole day in the sun, and securing the only chair in this vacant room, endeavor to wile away the tedious hours by scribbling

35. *Alexander's Feast.*

36. Later note by Sarah: "We met 1888. He tried to tell." This cryptic note, probably written in 1896, may recall a meeting that occurred eight years to the day earlier—or it may instead be a postscript to the last sentence of the entry before, concerning man's folly. In either case, one might speculate that she is referring to the first of two postwar meetings with Dr. Steedman, which she alludes to in another note to the diary, and that he tried to tell her he was still in love with her.

here. Can anything be more dreary than moving? Sister and Brother came back just a week ago, and ever since then, everything has been in confusion, moving from here to a new house[37] on Camp St. This house is emptied, the other not half arranged; and both are inexpressibly dreary in their transition state. Nothing but a few beds left here, and all there seems to consist of empty armoirs and a chaos of chairs. Brother has taken for mother a house about a square below his, and there we are to keep house in state. But we cannot move until Sister is settled. I have not even seen the place yet.

Confusion did not prevent us from enjoying ourselves last night though. We had been invited by Mr Watt to meet Gen. Gardiner[38] at his house at tea, and after a hasty toilette performed with the help of a glass four inches square—the only one left in the house—we made our entrance in his parlor with the Peirces. I hope I am conquering my foolish timidity. At first it was very painful to cross the threshold; but I said "I shall!" to myself, tried to forget it was me, and in another instant found myself bowing to Gen. Gardiner, and listening to his comments on my striking resemblance to Sis before she was married, with perfect self possession.

Last night is about the only evening passed in company, that I can look back to without making a wry face and saying "Ouf!" Maybe I am growing reasonable; I hope so; "Hope differed [*sic*] maketh the heart sick;"[39] I had begun to grow tired of waiting. The few Confederates left in town, were there with the General, and also—the lately arrived English officers. I who had formed such a high opinion of England and Englishmen from their literature, as well as from some ties of blood, being a descendant of Englishmen, must confess myself thoroughly disgusted. If these are a specimen of the nation, England, with all thy faults, I may still love thee in the abstract, but I dont like my countrymen!

The most conceited, stupid, unpolished, insufferable idiots I ever had

37. Later note by Sarah: "No. 211."

38. John W. Watt, wealthy New Orleans commission merchant and cotton factor, was probably host of the tea for General Franklin Gardner.

39. Proverbs 13:12.

the misfortune to meet with. But I will not accept these as specimens of the English. They must be la basse classe même.[40] They were not *very* forward. I believe I have the honor of being the only young lady in the [p. 31] room they *solicited* an introduction to. I yawned over one for half an hour—the most uninteresting creature I ever saw. The only smile I could summon was provoked by Ada, who from the other side of the room made grimaces indicative of his stupidity, and laughed aloud at my martyrdom. Presently one sauntered up in front of me, and I heard an introduction. Mr Balfour was being presented. One would expect something, after that aristocratic name. I raised my eyes, and met those of one even less prepossessing than the one I was already burdened with, and determined not to make myself agreeable—and I didn't! Think of an Englishman being ignorant enough to confound Bulwer, Thackery [*sic*], Dickens, & Collins all in inextricable confusion, hardly knowing one from the other; and when, in hope of turning him to a subject he might be more familiar with, I spoke of my great admiration for Macaulay, he said "Oh! Ah? Which of his novels do you like best?"

Gen. Gardiner was the lion of the evening, and as such, Miriam and Ada, Marie and I, shared his company among us during the whole evening. It was so sweet in him to give us the preference over all the young ladies present. Miriam he flattered, Marie he enchanted, Ada he kissed, and while speaking to me, he quietly took my hand, and held it in his for so long, that at last feeling that several old maids were being properly shocked, and seeing he did not mean to relinquish it, I gently withdrew it.

I met him as I was coming home just now, and during the ten minutes he stopped me to tell me he had just called, and was sorry not to find us at home, and to ask the number of our new house, and I dont know what else, he held my ha[n]d just as he did last night, to the great edification of a group of Yankees standing by. And smiling to myself as I walked on, I said "Sarah my dear, you who are so apt to laugh at odd things, remember, instead of laughing the next time you see a gentleman holding a lady's hand, it may only be a dear, good, delightful Gen.

40. Of the lower class itself.

Gardiner, talking to one he considers young enough to be his daughter, almost, and dont make fun, for this is sweet enough in the General to make me feel right comfortable."

Our "Alabama" "Here we rest."[41]
From my small El Fureidis,[42] Sunday this 25th October

Last Monday we took possession of our new home, and by this time we are almost settled. What a delightful house! Three stories high for us three people, with a neverending wing that seems to extend to Magazine [?] street back, and then abruptly [p. 32] faces around transformed to a large brick stable and carriage house. The entrance to the house is rather awkward though. Fancy yourself calling for the first time, and I take you around the building. You ring at a huge, massive door on Camp St., and on its being thrown back, you find yourself in a large, open hall, paved with great blocks of stone. It is a sober light until your eye passes the arch at the extremity, and lights on the long yard, also paved in stone, that lies between the arch and the carriage house. To your right you perceive two marble steps, which you mount, and throwing open the door that bars your progress, you enter the front parlor. Black marble mantle, splendid rose wood furniture in crimson brocatelle, etagères composed of mirrors and delicate carving, fine Brussles carpet, handsome chandeliers, a magnificent mirror from floor to ceiling between the two front windows, reflecting back the one at the opposite extremity of the back parlor, until you seem to look through a neverending vista of parlors.

41. A note written in later by Sarah gives the address of the house they occupied: "No. 178? Camp St." The question mark is hers. Not long after this she wrote Jimmy Morgan: "Brother has rented a three story brick house on Camp St. for us, and we live in style. It is just a square above Odd Fellows Hall, and is elegantly furnished." Letter dated December 4, 1863, in Morgan Papers, Duke University.

42. Sarah took the name from *El Fureidis*, a romance by the American writer Maria Susanna Cummins set in Palestine.

That leads you through the open sliding doors to the second room. Same thing over again, only quite dark, and half way turned [in]to a library by the addition of two enormous book cases. Passing through a glass door you come to a square hall, with a glass door on the left leading to the stone hall, a glass door before leading to the dining room, and a long, spiral flight of steps leading above. Run up, and the first door to the left leads in to Miriam's room, the best furnished in the house, with any quantity of mirrors, and an odd little dressing closet within. Passing through, you enter mother's room. More mirrors, more furniture. Open a small door near one of her french windows, and you step into my El Fureidis.

Be careful! You see it is rather crowded, and you might upset the little table that holds my desk (a grand purple velvet, papier maché and brass inlaid affair) that stands between the open door and the long window. Above it is my hanging book case of mahogany, already supplied with books. Draw up the curtain; look over the balcony that ornaments the front of the house, at the cars and people constantly passing. How gay it is after dirty, lifeless Carondelet St.! Here is my armoir by the window—not six feet from my desk. Mahogany, with one solid mirror for a door. Next come my toilet table between the gas lights, then a tiny washstand barely large enough to hold a beautiful [p. 33] china set with a delicate design traced in gilt. All that forms the north side.

I have left out the bed just opposite all this, a fine spring one with a Victoria tester that I should so like to occupy, only mother is so nervous she cant sleep alone; so I sleep with her, and contemplate my vacant bed while I dress and undress. At its foot, between it and the desk, stands my greatest treasure, my happy land, my "tired nature's sweet restorer"[43]—not *sleep* but—easy chair. Ungainly, do you call it? Nay! just try it! Suppose yourself over strained, and with an ache in your back too great to talk about. Take up Longfellow's Golden Legend and lay back in it. Further and further! No exertion necessary! just wish it at the same angle you would describe in bed on pillow and bolster, and there you are! Now dream away! You forget yourself and time until the book is finished, and then are inclined to doubt that your back ever

43. Edward Young, *Night Thoughts.*

did ache. You move about with a softer foot fall, oblivious of pain, and dreaming of dear, holy little Elsie, and wishing she *had* died.

How beautiful it must be to die for those you love! What sublime happiness it would be! I could die for my brothers, but not for a stranger. O Hal! How gladly I would have laid down my life for you! Yesterday was his birthday. Hush! hush! Not one sob shall disturb him in his far off grave.

There! I cant go over the rest of the house with you. Pass out at my second door, between the bed and washstand, through the long, wide hall, and turn to the right, and here we are where we started from. The door to the left leads to the never endind [*sic*] wing, the stair before, up to the third story, and these at your feet are the same we ascended. I take you back to the parlors, and you bow yourself out. Good bye.

I walk around as though it was dishonorable to treat these people's things as my own, with the same feeling some of those Yankees must have had, when they broke open our doors, and standing within what was once our beautiful home, stole and destroyed everything we held dear. In our dear parlor, did any of them stop to think of the group that assembled there daily? Did the feeling of awe that ever after followed me when I entered there steal over them and whisper "On the spot where you now stand an idolized brother kissed them with a laughing 'goodbye' and went gaily away, never, never to return. In the same spot, a grey [p. 34] haired father blessed his children and peacefully closed his eyes to follow his departed son. Have pity on the widow and orphans, and spare this room at least."

But here there is lacking a certain air that one feels to pervade all homes. I cannot arrange the family group to my satisfaction. Ridiculous as it may appear considering that I know nothing whatever of the family beyond their name, I feel as though the mistress of the establishment had a loud voice, and scolded sometimes, while the master was quiet, unobtrusive, and would rather work in his office than lounge here. Every time I pass a mirror, I half expect to see a tall showy girl, lively, bold, and unrefined, who certainly must be the eldest daughter. Of course it is all sheer idleness to talk that way. Maybe fancy sways me too much. Only to my share has fallen the duty of taking an inventory of every thing in the house, for our own satisfaction; and inclination naturally led me to begin by the books. All the best Poets done up *very* new, and *very* stiff, never having been opened. Quantities of the best Biographies, Essays, etc, in the same condition. Cart loads of novels, good ones uncut, worthless ones so worn and thumbed as hardly to hold together. Stern's and Fielding's works that I have so frequently been warned against showed external signs of close application.[44] I did not take the trouble to look within, but carried them up to the study on the wing and thrust them in an old drawer where they will never be disturbed again until reclaimed by their owner.

But what disgusted me most of all, was "A Dictionary of Poetical Quotations." Human intelligence must be of the lowest order when such an auxiliary is called in. It is positively degrading. Without doubt that young lady kept it by this writing desk, and while writing sentimental letters, turned over its leaves to find something applicable to "Love," "Friendship," "Broken heart," sublimely indifferent to Webster's dictionary and the original works she might have read with more benefit, and as little trouble, as long as the scraps filled up the page. I cant help feeling that the good books were purchased because they were talked of as being popular, and the trash was bought because it suited best.

Wealthy the[y] evidently are. How then can they rent their home to strangers? All the family are in St. Louis except the [p. 35] father. He lives in the city. I wonder if he ever passes by, and looking up at our strange faces, feels half angry with us for being here, and with himself for having let his home?

Monday November 9th

Another odd link of the old, stale story has come to me, all the way from New York. A friend of mine who went on the same boat with the prisoners, wrote to her mother to tell her that she had formed the acquaintance of the most charming, fascinating gentleman among them, no other than my *once* friend. Of course she would have been less than a woman if she had not gossipped when she discovered who he was. So she sends me word that he told her he had been made to believe as long as he was on parole in New Orleans, that we were all Unionists now,

44. The English novelists Laurence Sterne and Henry Fielding. The volumes that she found in the library probably included Sterne's *Tristram Shandy* and Fielding's *Tom Jones*.

and that Brother would not allow a Confederate to enter the house. (O my little lisper! was I unjust to you?) He told her that I had been very kind to him when he was in prison, and he would have forgotten the rest and gladly have called to thank me in person for the kindness he so gratefully remembered, if I alone had been concerned; but he felt he could not force himself unasked in my brother's house. And now, she said, when she told him how false it was, he grew perfectly dismal about it. He said that from the hour he stepped on the ship he had been regretting that he had not insisted on seeing me in spite of my coldness and the warnings of others; but now it would be a regret that would terminate only with his life.

So much for listening to my four female disguised enemies! Dear me! how much trouble and annoyance one honest word would save! If I had written one line to tell him the truth, if he had boldly walked in and asked face to face "Why have you treated me so?" there would have been an end of it; and the disagreeable recollection that is left to me, and the painful one that clings to him would never have been. But pshaw! I suppose unpleasant things help make up the sum total of life; a few more or less dont matter. If people always told the simple truth, and never erred, what would become of novel writers? The only difference is that in novels the hero passes through a thousand perplexities and miseries for three volumes, and generally has them all removed in the last ten pages, leaving him in happiness and white kids,[45] with the honey moon shining on his new life; and [p. 36] and [*sic*] in real life trouble and sorrow come so stealthily and at such intervals that are all filled with rainbows of pleasure, that we hardly know what a gulf they have made in our lives until lonely and old we sit by the ashes of our deserted hearths and think sadly over the "Might have been" and the days that are no more.

Kismet! it is destiny! What ever is, is right. And it is a dear, jolly old life, if one only knew how to take it. Oh! how I love it! I am happier now than I have ever been since father died. I would be very ungrateful if I was not. I should have been content all the time; but was I? I am very selfish. I am happiest alone. This great house with its quiet nooks is Paradise to me. I shut the door when I come in here, and experience

45. White kid gloves.

the most delicious sensation of loneliness. It is bliss to be alone! to shut out all earthly sounds and faces, and sing, and read, and think, with only God to listen!

I never go out when I can avoid it. All day I am busy reading, writing, sewing, and upsetting things with a vague idea of making myself useful, and in the evenings, when Miriam and mother are out, I take my guitar way down the wing of the house and play and sing until all is dark. Nobody in the house, nobody in the yard, makes it so pleasant! Then Such curious noises are to be heard here. Wonder if I could convert myself to a ghost-seer? At every unexplained rap that I hear around me, I wonder if some dear delicious ghost means to manifest itself. But it never comes; I see but one apparition, and that is a Head that appears in the tiny window of our next door neighbor's wing, every evening at the first chord I strike, and cautiously peeps at me when it fancies I cant see. The body belonging to the Head is evidently mounted on a ladder, as the window is immediately below the ceiling. I have been unable to determine the age or sex. Understand that Yankees board there; must enquire if there is an Idiot among them.

When dark night comes, and a peel [*sic*] at the bell reminds me that mother or Miriam are coming home, and I untune my guitar and grope my way down stairs singing "Ching aring aring tum," the Head disappears too. Wonder if there is anything in it, and if so, if that little is addled?

When evening [p. 37] comes, I have had enough of loneliness. I like to sit around the gas in the parlor with the others and read until bed time.

Sunday November 15th.

Maybe too much isolation is not wholesome for human beings. Perhaps our thoughts when uninterrupted are apt to concentrate too much on ourselves, and make us selfish and egotistical. I dont know. One extreme is as bad as the other. When I am thrown in contact with people and endeavor to act like the rest of the world, it seems rather pleasant, and I can talk as fast as any one. But afterwards! Ah! how foolish you will feel to morrow for the mistakes of to day! Do people ever reach an age where they cease to care for such things? Will I ever grow self possessed enough to hurt any one's feelings quietly, or commit a gaucherie without making a face at myself? When the door closes on company, immediately the whole conversation passes in review before me. How could I reveal this thing I should have kept to myself? How dare I speak of that, that did not concern me? Whose little weakness did I make the subject of a jest? What right had I to obtrude my opinions and conversation?

O it all comes back, bitterly, bitterly! And with burning cheeks I repeat "Fool! fool! you were made for silence and seclusion! Alone, you can get in no great trouble and can injure no one; with others your tongue is apt to run away with you, and frighten away your better sense. The more you are alone, the less you will sin." But we deserve no credit for being good where there is no temptation to err. It is battling with sin, and overcoming it that earns us a crown of glory. One who sets apart, neither courting nor shunning it, looking on Sin and Goodness with an equally indifferent eye, deserves to be hung between Paradise and Tartarus forever, with no hopes of ever reaching either.

I dare not battle with the world. I know I would come out of the strife crushed and mangled. Better sit here in my window at evening looking down on the stream of people passing by, and think them all beautiful and holy because God made them. Maybe if I knew them, I would find a blemish or defect, which would become a subject for discussion between [p. 38] my next best friend and myself. No! better sit here in my cave and be able to say "Dear good people, I love you because the Lord made you, and because I have never had a chance of sinning against you."

The other day two of my four young lady haters called for the first time, evidently determined to be sociable, and intimate—if possible. They are good girls, I am sure. Intelligent, (though rather inclined to sarcasm) and evidently wishing to make themselves agreeable. The eldest is the one whose papa would so gladly have given her to a certain friend of mine, who was not of the same mind. We sat in the same room for half an hour. I had to receive them alone, as mother and Miriam were out. As usual, I kept my eye on the one I was addressing. Hers seemed unwilling to meet it, wandering over chairs and carpet instead. Yet now and then from under its dark lashes it stole a furtive glance at me which said as plainly as eye can say "What in the world did he see to admire? Nothing in her after all!" Mine flashed back (beg pardon for using a term apparently conceited, and inappropriate to all except black eyes; but Mr Halsey used to say I had a habit of "flashing" my meaning sometimes, when it was too much trouble to speak, and I used it here because there was no other expression that would answer to describe the silent telegraphing).

I apologize for this digression, and will finish my uncompleted sentence by saying I looked back. "*Very* bad taste, but we will not discuss it if you please." We understood each other perfectly. We went round and round the subject of prisoners in general, just *not* touching him in particular. Johnsons Island[46] where he is now confined; prison life and hardships, brave young men caged like wild beasts, lying heartsick and desolate in the far North; every thing we touched on, except the subject of which I said "we wont discuss it if you please." How easily a woman can *feel* what another means!

There we sat talking cheerfully and politely, to all appearance satisfied with each other, yet the unearthly feeling of Emptiness crept over me. I felt as though all we said was air, and came from airy lip. N.B. Hers *was* *h*airy, but that is not what I mean. Each of us seemed hollow, to me. Legends of German Elle maids floated through my [p. 39] mind, making all still more unreal, until I felt tempted to put my hand to the back of my head, or peep over their shoulders to see if we were not all hollow, and just painted masks, jabbering empty nothings. As soon as they left, after entreaties to be "sociable" and professions of esteem, I turned myself round and round before the nearest mirror, to convince myself that I was whole, instead of being split in two like a young spring chicken, and deprived of heart and brains. I suppose it was all right; only that I have not yet accustomed myself to a "Social" mask which seems more in vogue, worn over the heart, than veils worn over the face.

Well! that is visiting! Most women delight in it; I dont. O how I hate to be like other women! To walk in the same dull, empty, simpering round that thousands have trod before! No new piece of ground to cultivate, no new part to play—how irksome it is! All the same a thousand years ago, all to be the same a thousand years hence! But there is room to expand in, in Heaven! maybe I can find a less worn type hereafter.

In every day life I walk the beaten track apparently content to be

46. Union prison near Sandusky, Ohio, on Lake Erie.

numbered with the rest. But I am not! I wish there was a new school for woman—I dont exactly know what I want, except that it is something new.

Bah! if it is New, all the rest will adopt it. Good! then I can have the field of mediocrity to myself, without a rival or follower! It would be so delightful to find yourself just where you ought to be, without an effort! Since I cant compete with them in goodness, or rival them in wit or beauty, like a little soul, I take my revenge out of little things. All women are cowards, or conceive it their duty to be such. Ergo, *I wont.* So at twilight I sit in the deserted house, near the door of the room where they tell me an old lady died, and wonder if I cant conjure up her shadow. Crick! goes the ghostly arm chair where the old lady sat. Crack! goes Nothing at all from No Where in particular. What is that? Three times a great Shadow has darted from that corner and disappeared just as it almost touched me! Am I growing young lady like? Dont disgrace yourself! A young lady would faint, or else steal shivering over to her next door neighbors. I'll sit here until I sing three songs, and play three pieces, at least.

[p. 40] There it is again! What is It? Maybe a ghost, maybe Imagination, maybe the sudden turn of your own eye balls. Dont disturb the old lady! go on with your piece! And there I sit. Young ladies never feel their way through darkness so thick that one can almost hear it separate to let you pass, after forgotten articles up stairs when the parlor is bright and cozy. Ergo, I scorn a candle, and sail up and down stairs with only my nose for a compass, never forgetting when I come to the steps, to hug the wall, because every body else clings to the bannisters. Here at least I have a new field to cultivate! The centre is worn with the pressure of thousands of footsteps, the side nearest the wall bright with varnish. I am trying to mark out a little path of my own in that untouched spot. How foolish! When I have trampled over it and soiled it, I will wish it was smooth and bright again.

Sunday November 22d.

A report has just reached us that my poor dear Gibbes has been taken prisoner along with the rest of Hayes' Brigade.[47] I can hardly believe it.

47. Sarah's brother was captured November 7, 1863, at Rappahannock Station, Virginia, and sent to the Johnson's Island prison.

If it is so, they have taken the bravest set of men any army ever held. My dear lion-hearted brother a prisoner! God send him strength to bear his captivity! O this is too hard! Gibbes! Gibbes! if I was only a man to take your place and fight for you! I wont believe it yet; it seems hardly possible. Poor Lydia! Let us wait, and pray that it is not so.

Nov. 26th.

Yes! It is so, if his own handwriting is any proof. Mr Appleton[48] has just sent Brother a letter he had received from Gibbes asking him to let Brother know he was a prisoner, and we have heard through someone else that he had been sent to Sandusky. Brother has applied to have him paroled and sent here, or even imprisoned here, if he cannot be paroled. My dear Gibbes! How hard it seems! I hardly know how the war will continue without him; I always think Lee plans the battles, and Gibbes is the chief in fighting them. Only a piece of sisterly vanity; but he is so brave and daring! But so are all Southerners. It is nothing unusual—and plenty more left;—but O Gibbes!—

[p. 41] Monday November 30th.

Our distress about Gibbes has been somewhat relieved by good news from Jimmy. The jolliest sailor letter from him came this morning, dated only the 4th instant from Cherbourg, detailing his cruize [*sic*] on the Georgia[49] from leaving England, to Bahia, Trinidad, Cape of Good Hope, to France again. Such a bright, dashing letter! We laughed extravagantly over it when he told how they readily evaded the Vanderbilt,[50] knowing she would knock them into "pie," how he and the French Captain quarrelled when he ordered him to show his papers, and how he did not know french abuse enough to enter into competition with him, so went back a first and second time to Maury[51] when the man would not let him come aboard, whereupon Maury brought the ship to with two or three shot, and Jimmy made a third attempt,

48. Probably Thomas Appleton, a commission merchant.

49. The *Georgia* was one of the Confederate cruisers that operated in the Atlantic against merchant ships flying the U.S. flag. See Scharf, *History of the Confederate Navy*, 803–4.

50. The USS *Vanderbilt*, a steam-driven cruiser, hunted the oceans for Confederate blockade runners.

51. William L. Maury, the officer in command of the *Georgia*.

and forced the frenchman to show his papers. He tells it in such a matter of fact way! No extravagance, no idea of having been in a dangerous situation, he a boy of eighteen, on a French ship in spite of the Captain's rage. What a jolly life it must be! Now dashing in storms and danger, now floating in sunshine and fun! Wish I was a midshipman!

Then how he changes, in describing the prize with an assorted cargo that they took, which contained all things from a needle to pianos, from the reckless spirit in which he speaks of the plundering, to where he tell[s] of how the Captain having died several days before, was brought on the Georgia while Maury read the service over the body and consigned it to the deep by the flames of the dead man's own vessel. What noble, tender, manly hearts it shows, those rough seaman [sic] stopping in their work of destruction to perform the last rites over their dead enemy! One can fancy their bare heads and sunburned faces standing in solemn silence around the poor dead man when he dropped in his immense grave. God bless the "pirates"!

Saturday December 5th.

To-day closes the second week of my "scolastic course" with Charlotte.[52] What a remarkable child she is! It is really a pleasure to teach her. Sister took them all from Mad. Dérayau[53] where they learned nothing, and gave them to mother who really needs an [p. 42] occupation, on condition that Miriam and I had nothing to do with the arrangement. I listened silently, and appropriated Charlotte as soon as she was gone. From ten to half past two I teach her French and English. "What a delightful school where one can kiss their teacher in the middle of Télémaque"![54] she exclaims in her quaint womanly way.

"What so ever thou findest to do, that do as though it were unto the Lord."[55] I am glad to have found even a trifle; and have put my whole soul in this; I hope He will prosper me.

Oh! if I could do something for Brother and Sister to show them how

52. Sarah's niece, the oldest daughter of Philip Hicky Morgan.

53. Madame Desrayaux operated a school for young ladies at 39 Burgundy Street. See 1861 and 1866 city directories. The 1860 census lists her as Catherine Desrayaux.

54. Epic romance by François de Salignac de la Mothe Fénelon.

55. Sarah echoes Colossians 3:23 and 1 Corinthians 10:31.

I love them, and how gratefully I feel all they do for us—! But I will never, never be able to say even "Thank you." If I owned an empire, I'd make Brother Emperor and Sister Empress, and be content to sit forever at their gates, looking up at them so great and mighty without a wish to share their glory.

Sunday December 20th. 1863.

O my dear diary; what a dull, monotonous life this is where one cannot find a day to mark with a white stone, and say "this day is worth remembering distinctly out of the three hundred and sixty five of the year"! I never was in a place as unutterably dreary before, except Clinton. Ugh! Clinton! what made me mention that horrid place? Away with the nightmare! I find this total seclusion bliss in comparison! Fact is, I would not mind it so much on my own account, if Miriam could enjoy herself a little more. But seeing her so dissatisfied with this quiet life, and so eager for any amusement or strange face that breaks the monotony of our days, makes me restless for her. I cant blame her. We are young only once; and it is hard to feel yourself cut off from the rest of the world, when you cant live without it. If she could have a thousand visitors, a ball once a week, and company every night, I'd be satisfied to sit up stairs alone forever.

"How extraordinary to see a girl of sixteen shun society as you do!" many of my friends say. N.B. A most extraordinary mistake is made about my age. All [p. 43] married ladies say I am sixteen, and all young ladies insist that I am seventeen at least. Some go as high as eighteen. I never told a story about my age in my life, nor do I mean to. If any one will boldly ask how old I am, they will receive as straight forward an answer. But as long as people manoeuvre about it and hint they would like to know by saying "you are surely not sixteen?" I dont mean to satisfy their curiosity. I keep the secret as a reward for the first one honest enough to say "How old are you?"

And yet even I who am not fond of society, would gladly greet a familiar face within our doors. Miriam was talking the other day about those she would rather see from the Confederacy, setting apart Lilly and the boys. I believed she wanted to see every one we ever knew there. I could name but one—Col. Breaux. How I should enjoy listening to him once more!—always with Mrs Breaux' permission. All the

rest talk nonsense; he is the only one worth listening to. Why cant I
meet unmarried gentlemen whose conversation would repay one for
the fatigue of being polite to them? Are *all* the young ones fools? I dont
know any sensible ones except my brothers.

Friday December 25th. Night.

As though to punish me for thinking the city dull, this has been
almost a Merry Christmas. All the week the streets have been crowded,
and on the two days I ventured out, I saw almost every face I knew
here. What a world of reflection these Christmas expeditions would
afford to one who is fond of moralizing! But I'm not. So every time I
caught myself smiling at the bright, eager faces in the stores comparing
their purses and the coveted articles that were to give some one such a
charming surprise, and began to think of who they were intended for,
and what a beautiful custom it was, I would check myself with "Come!
no nonsense!" and come to myself just as I was forgetting what I wanted
while speculating on my neighbors. Is there anything more charming
to look at than a crowd of people all pleased with themselves and each
other? No wonder I came home feeling so [p. 44] comfortable.

Last night Sister went to a ball and the children went to another; and
as we went up to help them dress, we had bustle and fun enough even
for Christmas Eve. The children looked like angels, and Sister was as
beautiful as usual, hardly to be improved even by the magnificent diamond ear-rings Brother had just presented her. Wishing to leave my
poor little Christmas gifts (not valuable, to be sure; nothing but a mou-
choir case [56] for Sister and some trifle for Brother just to show I thought
of them) I had to wait until they had departed. Then when we came
home, I had to wait so long before mother and Miriam fell asleep so I
could hang up their stockings that midnight found me still working.

Mother made me laugh so this morning. Missing one stocking, instead of taking another pair as any one else would have done, she
immediately commenced bewailing her unhappy lot; there never was
a creature as unfortunate as she; it was her fate to have every thing go
wrong; she was the most unhappy wretch in the world, etc. Just then,
like little Bo peep she found the missing one pinned to the sofa; that

56. Handkerchief case.

was just her luck again! hastily she thrust her foot in it, and ran her toe against an extra pair of scissors which was the sole appropriate gift her practical daughter could think of. Strange to say, that only really unpleasant part of the adventure restored her spirits. I laughed heartily at the "unfortunate creature" and so did she.

After breakfast Edmond came in bearing a tray full of Christmas gifts from Brother & Sister. Besides the usual bonbons, there was a dress for mother, and two beautiful bonnets for Miriam and me. One, Miriam's, was trimmed in peach colored velvet, the other in light blue; and to the strings of each was pinned fifty dollars. Wasn't it a beautiful Christmas gift? Miriam and I fell to hugging each other, as there was nothing else to hug except the bed post, which did not even put on a pleased look when it saw us so happy. How good they are to us! Will we never—never—?

We dined with Brother alone, Sister being too sick after her party to leave her bed. And now we are back at home again, through the rain and cold, and I have [p. 45] put myself in my nightgown, writing and thinking of very different things. Every few moments I drop my head and repeat: Lilly in Macon, Miss.,[57] Sis in San Francisco, Gibbes a prisoner on Johnson's Island, George somewhere between Richmond and the Rappahannock, Jimmy at Cherbourg, father and Hal in the graveyard. O that graveyard! If I could plant my flowers there once more and train the vines—!

I dreamed last night that I was sitting by Hal's grave, only that he was buried in the earth, instead of that close vault; and that as I plucked the weeds that covered it, gradually I unburied him. O how distinctly I saw him! I dreamed he opened his eyes and said "O I have waited for you so long! I am so lonely here! Turn me in my grave; I am so weary!" And I held him in my arms, kneeling by him, and tried to comfort him. But he held out his left arm and asked me to warm it, it was so cold! Poor wounded arm! I counted the three bullet holes that shattered it, and cried over the red wounds as I would have done had it been my lot to see them before he died. And I tried so hard to warm him into life; but he did not want to come back; he only wanted me by his grave. And

57. Lilly LaNoue left Clinton with her children on June 8, 1863, and joined her husband in Macon. See letter to her brother James M. Morgan, October 11, 1863, in Morgan Papers, Duke University.

I laid him down tenderly, in my dream, and sat watching him as he slept. Hal, I wonder what I would not dare, to see your features awake as I see them in my dreams?

Thursday Night December 31st 1863.

The last of eighteen sixty three is passing away as I write. Glad, or sorry, O my soul? How stand your records? Is it not singular how sentimentally attached we become to the old year as it expires, no matter what sufferings and heart-aches it caused us in its course? Day after day we pray "Let this pang pass away, or this grief be forgotten" and sob and moan in our souls for the dawning of the day that brings respite and oblivion—and yet—when time hastening [?] to fulfill our prayers rolls rapidly away bringing the last moments of a year that has been trial and suffering, instantly it becomes "The dear old Year," "The delightful past" and we forget its stings because, forsooth, its moments are numbered, and it will not long affect us for good or [p. 46] for ill. Pshaw! it is only mawkish sentimentality, or a vague idea that all the rest of the world withdraw into their secret souls at this time and examine their past lives. Every body may make the effort; but how many are profitted by it?

Much good I derive from the retrospect! I see a great deal of severe suffering, much pleasure, and an immense tract of neutral ground before me as a landscape; but as to one step forward of soul or mind—not one! And yet I am glad to have lived it, thankful for pain as well as pleasure; it all works for good, though I dont see how, yet. Patience! I shall see yet!

Every New Year Eve since I entered my teens, I have sought a quiet spot where I could whisper to myself Tennyson's "Death of the Old Year," and even this bitter cold night I steal into my freezing, fireless little room en robe de nuit, to keep up my old habit while the others sleep. Come forth, precious Tennyson! Let me turn over your golden leaves again! Dear Tennyson! I could almost laugh as I recall the changes that each New Year brings me as I repeat your words. "He gave me a friend and a true, true love, And the New Year will take 'em away." What a significant comment on human nature it would make, if we conscientiously kept a record of the faces that rise before us each successive year as we repeat those words! No two successive ones would be the same. Is there any one frank enough to confess the shadows as they arise? Honestly, I could not, if I would.

Let me try to draw up a list. Nonsense! let them lie in their forgotten graves; there is not one worth waking. I remember them but faintly. Dim visions of half revealed Ideals, who had not prototypes of mortal form, used to look at me through celestial eyes; but I never ventured to give them human names; it seemed sacrilege. Besides, I used to think in my prim, old fashioned way, it would be treason to my To Be dearly beloved to call even a Shadow by any name but his; and his I did not know—nay, *do not* know to this hour. Yet I will not deny that earthly faces have looked smiling at me over Ideal [p. 47] heads, sometimes.

I remember once in our dear old home, before sorrow crossed the threshold, standing by the window in my room one New Year's Eve looking at a full moon shine through the frosty air [and] repeating "He gave me a friend and a true, true love, And the New-year will take them away" with a half defined shadow before me. But it was not very serious. I remember adding a line unknown to Tennyson "And he is welcome to go; he tires me; he is not my Shadow hero." And tonight, O Tennyson! I sit shivering in the cold trying to recall one friend, or one "true, true love" the New-year is not welcome to fly off with. It is all empty. Leave me the Brunots and Helen Carter, my old and tried friends (Marie & Ada you are my *new* ones) and the devil may whisk away with my "true true loves," from the first who cried, to the last who sighed. They are all welcome to gae their ain gait. Je n'en veux pas.[58] So I cannot grow sentimental over you to night, and say as I have sincerely felt many a time—

> "Old year, you shall not die;
> We did so laugh and cry with you,
> I've half a mind to die with you,
> Old year, if you must die."

No! go and welcome! Bring Peace and brighter days, O dawning New year. Die, faster, and faster, Old one; I count your remaining moments with almost savage glee. Poor old year, when each hour brings us nearer the termination of a bloody strife, who can regret your passing away? And yet—"He was a friend to me," truly. But I would rather

58. I don't want any of it.

> "Close-up his eyes; tie up his chin;
> Step from the corpse, and let him in
> That standeth there alone,
>   And waiteth at the door.
> There's a new foot on the floor, my friend,
> And a new face at the door, my friend,
> A new face at the door."

O new friend! bring happy days with you! Hark! There is twelve o'clock sounding! I have buried my Old Year! Thou who readest hearto, awake my soul to the New One in righteousness.

[p. 48]
> "Ring out, wild bells, to the wild sky,
> The flying clouds, the frosty light;
> The year is dying in the night;
> Ring out, wild bells, and let him die.
>
> Ring out the old, ring in the new,
> Ring, happy bells, across the snow:
> The year is going, let him go;
> Ring out the false, ring in the true."[59]

Jan. 2d 1864. Saturday.

Miriam and I had a most extraordinary visitor last evening. At twilight as we sat by the fireside some one rang the bell, and as the servant had gone out, I opened the door. In the uncertain light, I was sure Mr Halsey stood before me, and the idea frightened me so that I could not speak. But the first sound of the visitor's voice reassured me; it decidedly lacked the full, rich sound Mr Halsey gave each word. "You dont know me?" the gentleman exclaimed. I assured him I did not, and asked his name, which he declined giving, insisting that I *must* know who he was, or at all events would presently remember. "Very well, walk in the parlor" I said, and preceeding [*sic*] him, announced him in no very flattering manner to Miriam, saying "Miriam, this gentleman says he knows us; I have not the least idea of who he is, have you?" "The gentleman has made a mistake" she returned coldly, looking at him. There was never a more dismayed creature than our unknown. He entreated us to think once more; we certainly knew him. He mentioned things about the family that no utter stranger could know, and asked if

59. Tennyson, *In Memoriam*.

we were convinced he knew us. "You certainly *must* know us" said the inperturbable [*sic*] Miriam leaning on the guitar as though addressing a lackey. "If I thought this mere impertinence, I would order you out of the room."

"If you refuse to recognize me, I must bid you good evening" returned the fool of a man turning to leave us. Now I knew Miriam would die of curiosity if he left without telling his name, and [p. 49] I knew I would be grievously puzzled myself, so I interposed with the cool invitation "Stay at *least* until we know who you are." One would have fancied it was a command. He instantly took a chair, and entered into a discussion that proved he knew all about us. He repeatedly expressed his delight at finding me looking so well. He had heard that I had been so severely injured last winter that my recovery was hopeless—that my days were numbered—all sorts of uncomfortable things! I laughed as I assured him it was all over. He spoke of my extraordinary resemblance to Harry, in every word and look, he said. He knew my darling! Instantly my heart softened towards this unknown. He talked of his life and death to [*sic*] tenderly that even Miriam unbent from her dignity.

He said he saw Mr Sparks last Spring—a miserable wreck of a man, who could speak only of Harry—Harry—and sobbed and wept like a child at the sound of his name, protesting he loved him dearly, had fought unwillingly, forced by his father, and was the most wretched creature imaginable. Poor man! God help him! I am glad I was destined to be the only one of the family to meet him afterwards. I am thankful for the strength that was lent me from above to enable me to say "God forgive you, Mr Sparks!" as for one awful moment we stood face to face in the deserted street, when his hands seemed yet red with Harry's blood.

Our visitor spoke of Harry's love and pride for me, remarking that I was his favorite sister, addressing me as "Miss Sukey." I did not think there breathed a man impudent enough to call me by a pet name sacred only to my brothers. I thought for a few moments, and then said "I venture a last guess. You have called me by a name I never hear now, except from Judge Morgan, consequently I must have known you when my brothers were not in Baton Rouge. You must be Mr Knickerbocker."[60]

60. R. W. Knickerbocker, an attorney residing in Baton Rouge when the 1860 census was taken.

If I had paid him a compliment he could not have been more enchanted! It was he! He reminded me of the first time we met, when I was yet a little girl, at a small party at Aunt's, and how I treated him. What a silly child [p. 50] I was! How I cried and entreated Harry not to let "that creature" dance with me, until Hal had to bend over me to comfort me, & keep every one from seeing my tears, assuring me he was a good natured fellow, and I must dance for his sake! I reminded him of the dance I walked slowly through; he reminded me of my answer when he asked permission to accompany me home. "Thank you, I came with my brother, and prefer returning with him," and when he suggested Hal might wish to accompany Miss Castleton, I drew myself up to the full height of four feet eight inches and informed him that *my* brothers never neglected their sisters. What a prig I was!

But I could never endure the man. He never braved more than a dozen visits afterwards, and never received anything except ridicule and sarcasms from me, and bore civility from the rest. How he had the assurance to find us out here, is incomprehensible. However, he has one recommendation at least, which is his unsurpassed admiration [for] and adoration of the whole Morgan family in general, and your humble servant in particular. He was good to Hal; that was enough for me. So after fifteen minutes of coolness, when we were ignorant of his name, I resolved to make amends for Miriam's tactiturnity, and mother's condescending politeness by making him feel comfortable, this man I had snubbed and illtreated always.

I did not know my talent, before. In fifteen minutes, I had this man I always treated with contempt, perfectly dizzy. Mother and Miriam laughed unrestrainedly at my rôle, and his infatuation. Within an hour, by laughing at him, sympathizing with him, and soothing his vanity, I had carried him through all the phases it takes the moon a month to accomplish. Poor fellow! he forgot his dead Sophia in looking at a mad cap Sarah, and went as far as he dared, without say[ing] "Sarah I adore you!" I forgot who he was; I only remembered how long it was since I had had any fun. "I have no men to govern in this wood; that makes my only woe." When he had bowed himself out, protesting that I had improved amazingly, and too dazzled to see the fun I had made of him, "O [p. 51] mother! mother!" I cried "dont be surprised if any shoeblack addresses me! it is just my luck to have all low people fancy me, and all fools to think me smart! How dare that man admire me so openly? How dare he flatter me at Miriam's expense?"

"Why did you encourage him?" returned my reasonable mother. "Is it surprising that he presumed on his acquaintance when he found such extraordinary affability where he was accustomed to find icy reserve?" Yes! I know that this mother Eve propensity of mine to display myself though only the devil be present to admire, sometimes obscures my better sense. What demon tempted me to be civil to a man I never tolerated before? Shall I tell the whole truth? I never entirely divested myself of the idea that it was Mr Halsey; there certainly was a striking resemblance. And all this fun and coquetry was played over this man's shoulder, at Mr Halsey, hundreds of miles away, who at that time was probably lamenting much more feelingly over half rations of corn bread and molasses, than over his separation from—Miriam. Hem!

And this fool appropriated it! Bah! what else can I expect? After that affair of Mr Wilcox, I cant object to the last pedlar in creation paying his homage. Decidedly, I must have a mauvais ton[61] about me.

Sunday January 17th.

I am so sick of me, me, everlasting Me! Cant I find a new subject?

What an egotist! Poor Sarah! fighting against self contempt and that of others, raging at her own deficiencies, and at those who seek to hide them as well as at those who lay them bare, loving every body, yet unwilling to have anybody love her, what wonder if she comforts herself with the pernicious poison of the refrain of "Me, me, me," in private, for the humiliations, envyings and yearnings she suffers elsewhere? But there is too much consciousness, too much egotism about me; though heaven only knows what I could find to be conceited about. I seem to pet myself, pamper myself, and stick Me up on a high altar above everybody else, where I dress myself in rain-bow hues, burn incense and sing hymns of praise to my idol—with no one to disturb my devotions at my shrine, or to swell the chorus either.

It is very sad to hate yourself for what you are always [p. 52] apparently doing. I hate myself! Why do I thrust myself so pertinaceously on my own attention, as well as on that of others? O I am sick of me! me!

61. Lack of good taste.

of "Me's" righteousness, and manifold excellencies. Will not somebody take pity and murder this Me in order to let a comfortable "We" usurp its place? Will not some kind angel make me over again, and worthy of breathing the breath of life? Wont some body teach me to forget Me?

Saturday January 23d 1864. Night.

Oh! "Me" is so tired! Me is in one of those desperate fits in which women generally take to tears as a "calmant" for over wrought nerves. "Me" is not a woman I suppose, since it takes to writing instead—pouring out its fatigue in ink rather than water. Which aches most? Back, limbs or head? No matter! I am sitting at last. Miriam has had her dress fixed to please her, and Lalla Newcomb's little blue bows are all straight and becoming, and they have departed leaving mother and me to a dismal tête-à-tête. Lets be comfortable and rest—ah me! We sit in a chaos of cast off clothes. What is more melancholy than a room where girls have been dressing for a party? Nothing except anticipations of the same, and the next day's reflections. But it is too great an exertion to reach the parlor, even this confusion is preferable.

All this excitement is in consequence of a grand Orphans' Fair which has been in full blast ever since Thursday, and which is to conclude to-night. Miriam and Lalla are shining pillars of the concern, under Mrs Lacey's superintendence, and the most indefatigable attendants. All the city turns out, it seems, and fun is to be gathered by the bushel according to their account. I have not been, thereby shocking Mrs Lacey who was kind enough to want me to assist at her table. But as I eschew sewing societies and all places where women are managers (which means "get yourself and your neighbor in trouble") I resisted the fair also.

I must not take too much credit to myself for such heroic self denial; probably if I followed my own inclinations, I would have attended it at least one night—though hardly all the time as these girls do—; but Brother does not approve of Fairs; [p. 53] I dont suppose he will know whether I went or stayed; yet still I would not like to act against his approbation when I could avoid it. And again it was no great effort to keep out of sight of strange faces—and somebody must stay with mother— so after all inclination kept me at home. Miriam loves excitement and crowds so much, that it is a pleasure to have her go out. Such a dull,

dull life she has here, after being accustomed to constant amusement! For her sake I wish there was something to divert one's attention from four blank walls.

Well! Having denied the light of my countenance to the fair, the least I could do was to work for it. So having asked myself what I most hated doing, and having unhesitatingly replied "Dressing dolls" to the question, I immediately applied for any quantity. You see, this Sarah requires an occasional penance to keep her from laziness, and striving too eagerly to please herself only; she must suffer just a tiny bit of inconvenience once in a life time, so she chose *this* time, and dressed dolls. Ouf! how I punished her! She got fifteen to dress! Yes! and almost overcoming her repugnance for such a task, she dressed them well, too; they brought good prices, they tell me; and when a manager says that, what must the purchaser say? Last evening I ran my needle through and through the last one in an ecstasy of thankfulness and spite, and stood her on her head as a mark of contempt. O how I hate dressing dolls! How I hate them! How I hate them—hate them— Hush! As a penance you shall dress one next week for anybody who will let you. You must not give way to such fits of temper.

Well! here is the end of the week—let it go; it has not been a comfortable one. Charlotte and I dont get on very smoothly in our lessons; we have had a disturbance five days out of the seven. Poor child! I wish I could perform my duty better; but I fear that teaching is not my vocation. Her irritable temper requires a firmer hand than mine to check it, and her natural quickness and intelligence requires a stronger will to force her to perform her tasks thoroughly instead of carelessly hurrying over them. What can I do? I have repeatedly argued with her, with apparent [p. 54] success; for the child is really devoted to me; but the next day it is the same thing over again. Let her make one mistake in recitation, and angry with herself she visits the sin on me, and either remains obstinately silent, or perversely answers as incorrectly as possible throughout the whole lesson. When the book is closed "I know every word, and said it wrong on purpose" she says. "Yes my dear; I know it" I answer; and so we go.

Last week Sister scolded her, when mother told her of the tempers she indulges in. Poor child! What a rage she flew into with me! "I'll never do anything right again! I'll do you everything bad I can think of!" she cried, her eyes flashing with passion. It was sad to see so young a child with such hard feelings; I dare not leave her to fight such a battle alone, so in spite of the hard words she gave me, I staid—and endeavored to quiet her. Heaven helped her where I could not. I reasoned, entreated, spoke of Heaven only knows what, appeased her hysterics, and at last the child who commenced raving at me cried her heart out with her arms around my neck, and vowed to be good if I would forgive her. She really means to keep her promise; but occasionally the old irritability prevails. I wish I could help her, but fear that my very calmness aggravates her.

When it comes to Arithmetic, we may rely on a difficulty. I do the same sums to keep her company, and I fear me, more than half of her sums, as I have to answer all the multiplication table. Generally I stop at the third or forth [*sic*] question of "How much is three times nine?" and insist on her helping herself more. The storm betrays its coming by the intense silence that prevails. Down go slate and pencil. I work steadily on, without noticing her for an hour measured by the clock. Still not a motion from her that indicates repentence. I quietly apply myself to something else, not to get impatient. Ah! she has recovered her slate! Will she finish? Again and again it is thrust under my eyes; but knowing by the sound that she has been writing, and from her unaltered mood that it is something aggravating, I will not look for fear of losing my temper. Baffled, [p. 55] another pause ensues. The clock strikes the half hour. Suddenly she dashes off something on her slate which she give[s] me saying "Please read." I take it quietly and read as I am told "Charlotte is a very bad girl and aunt Sarah is too good to her."

Reconciliation takes place, arithmetic resumed, lesson amicably concluded. Next day same scene, lasting only one hour, and the day after, followed by a little note saying "my dear aunt I beg your pardon for being so bad yesterday, and will try to be good to day." But alas! between the hours of ten and three, there are a hundred things to try one's temper. Another repetition of our comedy. "Remember your promise!" I whisper. "O aunt Sarah! you will never believe me! but I dont mean to be bad! I am trying not to!" And so she is, I sincerely believe; but a child can hardly conquer an irritability that would be more than a match for a woman's will. And her very affection for me, and confessions of error, prove that she knows her faults and is trying to mend. I love that child dearly, and earnestly wish to help her; but what can I do? I must be perfect myself before I can hope to give her the benefit of my own doctrines. What is preaching without practice? Well well! This is a crooked week. Maybe on Monday we will get straight.

Wednesday February 3d.

Last night we were thrown in the most violent state of commotion by the unexpected entrance of—Capt. Bradford. He has been brought here a prisoner, from Asphodel[62] where he has been ever since the surrender of Port Hudson, and taking advantage of his tri-weekly parole, his first visit was naturally here, as he has no other friends. Poor creature, how he must have suffered! The first glance at his altered face where suffering and passion have both left their traces unmistakably since we last met, and the mere sight of his poor lame leg, filled my heart with compassion. I no longer felt even the desire to turn him in ridicule; and for the first time in my life, could honestly take his proffered hand, without a mental reservation to dislike him as much as ever, and to laugh at him the first time he gave me [p. 56] an opportunity.

Miriam of course was overjoyed to see him. I dont pretend to *like* him, understand; I only sympathize. That Adonis face is too hard to please my taste, and those angry eyes betray a temper the beautiful mouth is endeavoring to suppress. There is a tone about him that bespeaks a devil within that has reached the white heat of passion, in spite of icy words and deliberate speech with which he tries to hide him. I always feel I am standing over a powder magazine that may at any moment explode and annihilate me; yet I used to take a perverse delight in throwing squibs in its depths, to see how near I could come to the grand catastrophe without quite losing my head. It interested me to

62. Compiled service records of men who served in the 1st Regiment Mississippi Light Artillery show that Captain James L. Bradford was arrested at the Fluker home on January 25, 1864, on suspicion of violating his parole. He was imprisoned in New Orleans, but was soon freed and allowed to go to Baton Rouge on parole. By April, however, Bradford had made his way to Mobile, where he reentered Confederate service. The following year, a few months after the end of the war, he married Mary Fluker.

see the flash light up the icy face for an instant. But now he is a cripple, though not as helpless a one as I was when I used to tease him; and I mean to be good to him—if I can resist the temptation to be wicked.

How he hates Mr Halsey! I could not forego the pleasure of provoking him into a discussion about him, knowing how they hated each other. He would not say anything against him; understand, that as a gentleman and a companion, Mr Halsey was his warmest, and best friend; there was no one he admired more; but he must say that as a soldier, he was the worst he had ever seen—not that he was not as brave and gallant a man as ever lived, but he neglected his duties most shamefully while visiting Linwood so constantly, eluding the sentinels daily as he asked for neither pass nor permission, and consulting only his inclinations instead of his superior officer or his business. And that last night at Linwood, when he absented himself without leave, why could he not have signified to him, his Captain, that he wished to say good-bye, instead of quietly doing as he pleased? When the Colonel sent for a report of the number of men, quantity of forage and amunition, etc, and it was discovered that John Halsey was absent with out leave, with the books locked up and keys in his pocket—even after this lapse of time, the fire flashed through the ice as the Captain spoke.

Sergeant Halsey I am [p. 57] sorry for you when you reported yourself next day! All the fun that could have been crowded in an evening at Linwood could not have repaid you for the morning's scene. And after all, what was it beyond very empty pleasure, with a great deal of laughter? He could have dispensed with it just as well. Looking back, I congratulate myself on being the only one who did not ask him to stay. Only when my silence was observed, did I make the effort to say "Certainly; I would be very glad to have him spend the evening with us." Could less be said? Yes! he hates him; but if I agreed in any one proposition, he endeavored to take his part against me; and if I ventured to defend him, the latent fire broke out again. Just like Mr Halsey. He too endeavored to justify Capt. Bradford and praise him to me, yet showed the keenest relish and approbation of every slap I could give his conceit, and stopped laughing when he enjoyed the ridicule most, to declare he was a clever fellow, his best friend, etc. Neither of these men are hypocrites. What is it?

5th [February]

Not dead! not dead! O my God! Gibbes is *not* dead! Where [*sic*]

O dear God! another? Only a few days ago came a letter so cheer-ful and hopeful—we have waited and prayed so patiently—at my feet lies one from Col. Steadman saying he is dead. Dead! suddenly and without a moment's warning summoned to God! No! it cannot be! I am mad! O God have mercy on us! my poor mother! And Lydia! Lydia! God comfort you! My brain seems fire. Am I mad? Not yet! God would not take him yet! He will come again! Hush! God is good! Not dead! not dead! O Gibbes come back to us!

11th [February]

O God O God have mercy on us! George is dead! Both in a week! George our sole hope—our sole dependence.

[p. 58] March

Dead! dead! Both dead! O my brothers! what have we lived for ex-cept you? We who would so gladly have laid down our lives for yours, are left desolate to mourn over all we loved and hoped for, weak and helpless; while you, so strong, noble, and brave, have gone before us without a murmur. God knows best. But it is hard—O so hard! to give them up without a murmur!

We cannot remember the day when our brothers were not all in all to us. What the boys would think; what the boys would say; what we would do when the boys came home, that has been our sole thought through life. A life time's hope wrecked in a moment—God help us! In our eyes, there is no one in the world quite so noble, quite so brave, quite so true as our brothers. And yet they are taken—and others use-less to themselves and a curse to their families live on in safety, without fear of death. This is blasphemy. God knows best; I will not complain.

But when I think of drunken, foolish, coarse Will Carter with horses and dogs his sole ambition, and drinking and gambling his idea of happiness, my heart swells within me. He lives, a torment to himself and a curse to others—he will live to a green old age as idle, as ignorant, as dissipated as he is now.

And Gibbes, Harry, and George, God's blessings he bestowed on us awhile—are dead. My brothers! my dear brothers! I would rather mourn over you in your graves, remembering what you were, than have you change places with that man. Death is nothing in comparison to dishonor.

If we had had any warning or preparation, this would not have been so unspeakably awful. But to shut ones eyes to all dangers and risks, and drown every rising fear with "God will send them back; I will not doubt his mercy," and then suddenly to learn that your faith has been presumption—and God wills that you shall undergo bitter affliction—it is a fearful [p. 59] awakening! What glory have we ever rendered to God that we should expect him to be so merciful to us? Are not all things His, and is He not infinitely more tender and compassionate than we deserve?

We have deceived ourselves willfully about both. After the first dismay on hearing of Gibbes' capture, we readily listened to the assertions of our friends that Johnson's Island was the healthiest place in the world, that he would be better off, comfortably clothed and under shelter, than exposed to shot and shell, half fed, and lying on the bare ground during Ewell's [63] winter campaign. We were thankful for his safety, knowing Brother would leave nothing undone that could add to his comfort. And besides that, there was the sure hope of his having him paroled. On that hope we lived all winter—now confident that in a little while he would be with us, then again doubting for awhile, only to have the hope grow surer afterwards. And so we waited and prayed, never doubting he would come at last. He himself believed it, though striving not to be too hopeful lest he should disappoint us, as well as himself. Yet he wrote cheerfully and bravely to the last. Towards the middle of January, Brother was sure of succeeding, as all the prisoners

63. General Richard S. Ewell, in whose corps Gibbes Morgan served. Ewell was still in the field despite the loss of a leg.

had been placed under Butler's control.[64] Ah me! How could we be so blind? We were sure he would be with us in a few weeks! I wrote to him that I had prepared his room.

On the 30th of January came his last letter, addressed to me, though meant for Sis. It was dated the 12th—the day George died. All his letters pleaded that I would write more frequently—he loved to hear from me; so I had been writing to him every ten days. On the third of February I sent my last. Friday the fifth, as I was running through Miriam's room, I saw Brother pass the door, and heard him ask Miriam for mother. The voice, the bowed head, the look of utter despair on his face, struck through me like a knife. "Gibbes! Gibbes!" was my sole thought; but Miriam and I stood motionless looking at each other without a word. "Gibbes is dead" said mother as he [p. 60] stood before her. He did not speak; and then we went in.

We did not ask how, or when. That he was dead was enough for us. But after a while he told us uncle James[65] had written that he had died at two o'clock on Thursday the twenty first. Still we did not know how he had died. Several letters that had been brought remained unopened on the floor. One, Brother opened, hoping to learn something more. It was from Col. Steedman to Miriam and me, written a few hours after his death, and contained the sad story of our dear brother's last hours.[66] He had been in Col. Steedman's ward of the hospital for more than a week, with headache and sore throat; but it was thought nothing; he seemed to improve, and expected to be discharged in a few days. On the twenty first he complained that his throat pained him again. After prescribing for him, and talking cheerfully with him for some time, Col. Steedman left him surrounded by his friends, to attend to his other patients. He had hardly reached his room when someone ran to him saying Capt. Morgan was dying. He hurried to his bedside, and found

64. Philip Hicky Morgan's friendship with General Butler has already been documented. On one occasion during the war, when Morgan was in New York, he traveled to Lowell, Massachusetts, to call on Mrs. Butler. See her letter to her husband dated September 14, 1864, in *Butler Correspondence*, 5:133.

65. Sarah's Uncle James B. Morgan, who lived in Pittsburgh.

66. In one of his last letters written from the Johnson's Island prison, Gibbes Morgan referred to Colonel Steedman as "a ministering angel in gray clothes and brass buttons." See letter to his mother dated December 9, 1863, in Morgan Papers, Duke University.

him dead. Capt. Steedman,[67] sick in the next bed, and those around him said he had been talking pleasantly with them, when he sat up to reach his cup of water on the table. As soon as he drank it he seemed to suffocate; and after tossing his arms wildly in the air, and making several fearful efforts to breathe, he died.

O Gibbes! Gibbes! When you took me in your arms and cried so bitterly over that sad parting, it was indeed your last farewell! My brothers! my brothers! Dear Lord how can we live without our boys?

Sewed to the paper that contained the last words we should hear of our dear brother, was a lock of hair grown long during his imprisonment. I think it was a noble, tender heart that remembered that one little deed of kindness, and a gentle, pitying hand that cut it from his head as he lay cold and stark in death. Good heart that loved our brave brother, kind hand that soothed his pain, you will not be forgotten by us!

[p. 61] And keenly as we felt his loss, and deeply as we mourned over him who had fought with the bravest of the brave through more than thirty battles, to die a prisoner in a strange land—there was one for whom we felt a keener grief—the dear little wife who loved him so perfectly, whose life must henceforth be a blank before her, God help my poor little sister! "Hush, mother, hush," I said when I heard her cries. "We have Brother, and George and Jimmy left, and Lydia has lost all!" Heaven pity us! George had gone before—only He in mercy kept the knowledge of it from us for awhile longer.

On Thursday the eleventh, as we sat talking to mother, striving to make her forget the weary days we had cried through with that fearful sound of dead! dead! ringing ever in our ears, some one asked for Miriam. She went down, and presently I heard her thanking some body for a letter. "You could not have brought me anything more acceptable! It is from my sister, though she can hardly have heard from us yet!" I ran back, and sitting at mother's feet, told her Miriam was coming with a letter from Lydia. Mother cried at the mention of her name. O my little sister! you know how dear you are to us!

"Mother! Mother!" a horrible voice cried, and before I could think who it was, Miriam rushed in holding an open letter in her hand, and

67. Colonel Steedman's brother.

perfectly wild. "George is dead!" she shrieked and fell heavily to the ground. O my God! I could have prayed thee to take mother too, when I looked at her! I thought—I almost hoped she was dead, and that pang spared! But I was wild myself. I could have screamed!—laughed! "It is false! do you hear me mother? God would not take both! George is not dead!" I cried trying in vain to rouse her from her horrible state or bring one ray of reason to her eye. I spoke to a body alive only to pain; not a sound of my voice seemed to reach her; only fearful moans showed she was yet alive. Miriam lay raving on the ground. Poor Miriam! her [p. 62] heart's idol torn away. God help my darling! I did not understand that George *could* die until I looked at her. In vain I strove to raise her from the ground, or check her wild shrieks for death. "George! only George!" she would cry; until at last with the horror of seeing both die before me, I mastered strength enough to go for the servant and bid her run quickly for Brother.

How long I stood there alone, I never knew. I remember Ada coming in hurriedly and asking what it was. I told her George was dead. It was a relief to see her cry. I could not; but I felt the pain afresh, as though it were her brother she was crying over, not mine. And the sight of her tears brought mine too. We could only cry over mother and Miriam; we could not rouse them; we did not know what to do. Some one called me in the entry. I went, not understanding what I was doing. A lady came to me, told me her name, and said something about George; but I could not follow what she said. It was as though she were talking in a dream. I believe she repeated her words several times, for at last she shook me and said "Listen! Rouse yourself! the letter is about George!" Yes, I said; he is dead. She said I must read the letter; but I could not see, so she read it aloud.

It was from Dr Mitchell,[68] his friend who was with him when he died, telling of his sickness and death. He died on Tuesday the twelfth of January, after an illness of six days, conscious to the last and awaiting the end as only a Christian, and one who has led so beautiful a life, could, with the grace of God, look for it. He sent messages to his brothers and sisters, and bade them tell his mother his last thoughts

68. Dr. William S. Mitchell, surgeon of the 1st Louisiana. Dr. Mitchell practiced in New Orleans in the years after the war and taught classes at the Medical College of New Orleans.

were of her, and that he died trusting in the mercy of his Saviour. George! our pride! our beautiful, angel brother! *Could* he die? Surely God has sent all these afflictions within these three years to teach us that our hopes [p. 63] must be placed Above, and that it is blasphemy to have earthly idols!

The letter said that the physicians had mistaken his malady which was inflamation of the bowels, and he had died from being treated for something else. It seemed horrible cruelty to read me that part; I knew that if mother or Miriam ever heard of it, it would kill them. So I begged Mrs Mitchel [sic] never to let them hear of it. She seemed to think nothing of the pain it would inflict; how could she help telling if they asked? she said. I told her I must insist on her not mentioning it; it would only add suffering to what was already insupportable; if they asked for the letter, offer to read it aloud, but say positively that she would not allow any one to touch it except herself, and then she might pass it over in silence.

I roused Miriam then, and sent her to hear it read. She insisted on reading it herself; and half dead with grief held out her hands, begging piteously to be suffered to read it alone. I watched then until I was sure Mrs Mitchel would keep her promise. Horrible as I knew it to be from strange lips, I knew by what I experienced that I had saved her from a shock that might cost her her life; and then I went back to mother. No need to conceal what I felt there! She neither spoke nor saw. If I had shrieked that he died of ill treatment, she would not have understood. But I sat there silently with that horrible secret, wondering if God would help me bear it, or if despair would deprive me of self-control and force me presently to cry it aloud, though it should kill them both.

At last Brother came. I had to meet him downstairs and tell him. God spare me the sight of a strong man's grief! Then Sister came in, knowing as little as he. Poor Sister! I could have blessed her for every tear she shed. It was a comfort to see some one who had life or feeling left. I felt as though the whole world was dead. Nothing was real, nothing existed except horrible [p. 64] speechless pain. Life was a fearful dream through which but one thought ran—"dead—dead."

Miriam had been taken to her room more dead than alive—mother lay speechless in hers. The shock of this second blow had obliterated, with them, all recollection of the first. It was a mercy I envied them; for I remembered both until loss of consciousness would have seemed a blessing. I shall never forget mother's shriek of horror when towards evening she recalled it. O those dreadful days of misery and wretchedness! It seems almost sacrilege to refer to them now. They are buried in our hearts with our boys—thought of with prayers and tears.

How will the world seem to us now? What will life be without the boys? When this terrible strife is over, and so many thousand return to their homes, what will peace bring us of all we hoped? Jimmy! dear Lord, spare us that one! but I have always felt Jimmy must die young— and we have been so cast down that hope seems almost presumption in us. So we send our hearts over the waves after our last one, while our souls hardly dare pray "God spare him!"[69]

April 4th[70]

I had such a strange dream—vision—yesterday. Coming home after Communion very much exhausted, I threw myself on the bed and soon fell asleep. As I afterwards discovered, I must have slept without a thought for two hours. My first consciousness was of coming to life after death, and with such a loathing as would be impossible to describe. Yet something said "It must be." "O God!" I cried in my dream. "Let not the knowledge of sin come to my waking body!" Life seemed intolerable after what I had seen. Then came the knowledge that in waking my soul should not remember where it had been; and that reconciled me to life which had seemed insupportable before. The next instant I found myself awake whispering aloud "Let not the knowledge of sin come to my waking soul," with a vague consciousness of having been in another world, and a feeling of awe as though God had talked to my soul. Why not? Did not our Lord say He would come unto those who love him, and make his abode there? And though I am so sinful, had I

---

69. At the bottom of the page Sarah wrote brief obituary notes for her brothers who had died in the war, giving the date and place of death, the regiment and rank, and the age of each. George, she wrote, was "25 years and six months"; Gibbes, "28 years and ten months." George Morgan died at Orange Court House, Virginia.

70. This entry has been placed in chronological order. In the manuscript diary it is at the front of Book 5, on the unnumbered page facing page 1. Manuscript page 65 of course follows page 64 in the book in which Sarah wrote.

not ventured to approach His table, and did he not say he would in no wise cast out those who came to him? Let me believe it was the peace of God. It has left me with a "peace that passeth understanding."[71]

[p. 65] November 2d. 1864

This morning we heard Jimmy is engaged to Helen Trenholm, daughter of the Secretary of the Confederate States.[72] He wrote asking Brother's consent, saying they had been engaged since August, though he had had no opportunity of writing until that day—the middle of September. I cried myself blind. It seems that our last one is gone. But this is the first selfish burst of feeling. Later I will come to my senses and love my sister that is to be.[73] But my darling! my darling! O Jimmy! How can I give you up? You have been so close to me since Harry died! Alone now; best so.

No. 19. Dauphine St.
Saturday night. December 31st 1864.

One year ago, in my little room in the Camp Street house, I sat shivering over Tennyson and my desk, selfishly rejoicing over the departure of a year that had brought pain and discomfort only to me, and eagerly welcoming the dawning of the New One whose first days were to bring death to George and Gibbes, and whose latter part was to separate me from Miriam, and bring me news of Jimmy's approaching marriage.

O sad, dreary, fearful Old Year! I see you go with pain! Bitter as you have been, how do we know what the coming one has in store for us? What new changes will it bring? Which of us will it take? I am afraid of eighteen sixty five, and have felt a vague dread of it for several years past. Perhaps it is owing to that silly prophecy about the wondrous comet whose long tail is to whisk the earth out of its orbit and send it whizzing through space! Laugh if you will! Lest '65 brings some great change to me. So much for superstition!

Nothing remains as it was a few months ago. Miriam went to Lilly,

71. Philippians 4:7.

72. George Trenholm became Confederate secretary of the treasury in 1864.

73. Sarah attended the wedding of James Morgan and Helen Trenholm at the Trenholm home in Charleston in November of the following year. Her account of that visit to South Carolina reveals a genuine affection for Helen. See the unpublished Book 6.

in the Confederacy, on the 19th of October (Ah! Miriam!) and mother and I have been boarding with Mrs Postlethwaite [74] ever since. I miss her sadly. Not as much though, as I would were I less engaged. For since the first week in August, I have been teaching the children for Sister; and since we have been here, I go to them every morning, instead of their coming to me. Starting out at half past eight daily, and returning a little before [p. 66] three, does not leave me much time for melancholy reflections. And there is no necessity for indulging in them at present; they only give pain. "But what is that that I should turn to, Lighting upon days like these"?

Can I suffer this last night of the year to depart without the customary observations? The less I recall its sorrow and pain, the better it will be. With due emphasis I have repeated "He gave me a friend, and a true, *true* love, And the New Year will take them away!" He did indeed! Leaning against the frosty window pane just now, watching bright Orion coming up from the east, I whispered "It will not wait for the New One to take it away! It has perhaps expired before the Old One, with the help of my fingers!" Brave, noble heart, I never loved you, and never shall; but God have mercy on you in your loneliness, and forgive me all wherein I have erred!

April 19th. 1865. No. 211. Camp St.

"All things are taken from us, and become portions and parcels of the dreadful past." [75]

My life change, changes. I let it change as God will, feeling he doeth all things well. Sister has gone to Germany with Charlotte, Nellie, and Lavinia to place them at school, probably at Brussels. Mother and I have taken her place with the five remaining children. I am nominally housekeeper; that is to say I keep the keys in my pocket, and my eyes on the children, and sit at the head of the table. But I dont order dinner, for which I am thankful; for I would not be able to name a single article, if my reputation depended on the test. Of course I have a general idea

---

74. City directories list her as Mrs. J. C. Postlethwaite. The 1860 census identifies her as Jane Postlewaithe. The Dauphine Street address was just off Canal Street.

75. Tennyson, "The Lotos-Eaters." This was written on the day Sarah learned of the assassination of Lincoln and ten days after Lee's surrender to Grant at Appomattox Court House.

that soup, roast, baked and boiled meats are eaten, but whether all the same day, or which to be chosen, I could not decide, nor as to the kind of animal or fish. So the cook does that, though I am trying to observe every day what he provides, in order to perfect myself in the mystery.

In five days, I have twice been heart-broken about making Brother's coffee too strong. He will not complain, and I would still be ignorant of the error if I had [p. 67] not accidently observed the untouched cup after he left the table, and discovering the mistake by tasting punished myself by drinking every drop of the bitter draught. Mem. To-morrow if I fail, drink it until I learn the exact proportion.

Thursday the 13th, came the dreadful tidings of the surrender of Lee and his army on the 9th. Every body cried, but I would not, satisfied that God will still save us, even though all should apparently be lost. Followed at intervals of two or three hours by the announcement of the capture of Richmond, Selma, Mobile, and Johnson's army,[76] even the staunchest Southerners were hopeless. Every one proclaimed Peace, and the only matter under consideration was whether Jeff. Davis, all politicians, every man above the rank of Captain in the army, and above that of Lieutenant in the navy, should be hanged immediately, or *some* graciously pardoned. Henry Ward Beecher[77] humanely pleaded mercy for us, supported by a small minority. Davis and all leading men *must* be executed; the blood of the others would serve to irrigate the country. Under this lively prospect, Peace! blessed Peace! was the cry. I whispered "Never! let a great earthquake swallow us up first! Let us leave our land and emigrate to any desert spot of the earth, rather than return to the Union, even as it Was!"

Six days this has lasted. Blessed with the silently obstinate disposition, I would not dispute, but felt my heart swell repeating "God is our refuge and our strength, a very present help in time of trouble," and could not for an instant believe this could end in our overthrow.

This morning when I went down to breakfast at seven, Brother read the announcement of the assassination of Lincoln and Secretary Seward.[78] "Vengence is mine; I will repay, saith the Lord." This is mur-

76. The army of Confederate General Joseph E. Johnston.

77. New England clergyman prominent in the antislavery movement.

78. Lincoln was shot the evening of April 14 and died the following morning. News of the event did not reach New Orleans until the early hours of April 19, and most New

der! God have mercy on those who did it! A while ago, Lincoln's chief occupation was thinking what death, thousands who ruled like lords when he was cutting logs, should die. A moment more, and the man who was progressing to murder [p. 68] countless human beings, is interrupted in his work by the shot of an assassin. Do I justify this murder? No! I shudder with horror, wonder, pity and fear, and then feeling that it is the salvation of all I love that has been purchased by this man's crime,[79] I long to thank God for those spared, and shudder to think that that is rejoicing against our enemy, being grateful for a fellow-creature's death. I am not! Seward was ill—dying—helpless. This was dastard murder. His throat was cut in bed. Horrible!

Charlotte Corday killed Marat in his bath, and is held up in history as one of Liberty's martyrs, and one of the heroines of her country. To me, it is all Murder. Let historians extol blood shedding; it is woman's place to abhor it. And because I know that they would have apotheosized any man who had crucified Jeff Davis, I abhor this, and call it foul murder, unworthy of our cause—and God grant it was only the temporary insanity of a desperate man that committed this crime! Let not his blood be visited on our nation, Lord!

Across the way, a large building undoubtedly inhabited by officers is being draped in black. Immense streamers of black and white hang from the balcony. Down town, I understand all shops are closed, and all wrapped in mourning. And I hardly dare pray God to bless us, with the crape hanging over the way. It would have been banners, if our president had been killed, though! Now the struggle will be desperate, awful, short. Spare Jimmy, dear Lord! Have mercy on us as a people!

And yet what was the song of Deborah, when she hammered a nail in the head of the sleeping Sisera? Was she not extolled for the treacherous deed? What was Miriam's song over the drowning Egyptian? "Our enemies are fallen, fallen!" Was not Judith immortalized for delivering her people from the hands of a tyrant? "Pour le salut de ma patree—!"[80]

Where does patriotism end, and murder begin? And [p. 69] consid-

---

Orleanians read of it for the first time in their April 19 newspapers. Secretary of State William H. Seward was wounded in an assassination attempt, but survived the attack.

79. She is of course referring to John Wilkes Booth.

80. "For the salvation of my country—!"

ering that every one is closely watched, and that five men have been killed this day for expressing their indifference on the death of Mr Lincoln,[81] it would be best to postpone this discussion.

Saturday 22d. April.

To see a whole city draped in mourning is certainly an imposing spectacle, and becomes almost grand when it is considered as an expression of universal affliction. So it is, in one sense. For the more violently "secesh" the inmates, the more thankful they are for Lincoln's death, the more profusely the houses are decked with the emblems of woe. They all look to me like "not sorry for him, but dreadfully grieved to be forced to this demonstration." So all things have indeed assumed a funereal aspect. Men who have hated Lincoln with all their souls, under terror of confiscation and imprisonment which they *understand* is the alternative, tie black crape from every practicable knob and point, to save their homes. Last evening the Bells were all in tears, preparing their mourning. What sensibility! what patriotism! a stranger would have exclaimed. But Bella's first remark was "Is it not horrible? This vile, *vile* old crape! Think of hanging it out when"—tears of rage finished the sentence. One would have thought pity for the murdered man had very little to do with it.

Coming back in the cars, I had a rencontre that makes me gnash my teeth yet. It was after dark, and I was the only lady in a car crowded with gentlemen. I placed little Miriam on my lap to make room for some of them when a great, dark man all in black entered, and took the seat and my left hand at the same instant, saying "Good evening Miss Sarah." Frightened beyond measure to recognize Capt. Todd[82] of the Yankee army in my interlocutor, I however preserved a quiet exterior, and without the slightest demonstration answered as though replying to an internal question, "Mr Todd." "It is a long while since

81. Probably a rumor with no basis in fact. But in its April 21 issue the *Daily Picayune* does report that the police had ordered a 7 P.M. closing hour for all coffee houses "and other places of public resort," and that "all gatherings of men in the streets of more than two persons were to be dispersed."

82. Captain John W. Todd, chief of ordnance for the Department of the Gulf. In a footnote to the 1913 edition, Warrington Dawson identified Todd as "a cousin of Mrs. Lincoln." See also Winters, *The Civil War in Louisiana*, 10.

we met" he ventured. "Four years" I returned mechanically. "You have been well?" "My health has been bad." "I have been ill myself," and [p. 70] determined to break the ice he diverged with "Baton Rouge has changed sadly." "I hope I shall never see it again. We have suffered too much to recall home with any pleasure." "I understand you have suffered severely" he said, glancing at my black dress. "We have yet one left in the army, though," I could not help saying. He too had a brother there, he said.

My blood was surging within me. "Traitor to home!" I called myself. "False to Gibbes and George! Sitting by a man who has fought against them, treating him civilly, if nothing more! Tell him boldly 'do not speak to me while I remember my brothers!'" And then, icily calm without, feeling what a shocking position I would be placed in in that crowd of men if I gave one look expressive of contempt, I sat still, quietly answering the questions he chose to address to me, while internally raging at my self-command. Miriam acted with far more independence a year ago when he accosted her, and declined his acquaintance with the most perfect decorum. "O Vashti! noble Vashti!" [83] I am not Miriam though; and contrasting her conduct with my own those eight squares, made me almost wild.

He pulled the check string as we reached the house, adding unnecessarily "This is it" and absurdly correcting himself with "Where do you live?" "211. Thank you. Good evening" the last with emphasis as he prepared to follow. He returned the salutation, and I hurriedly regained the house. Monsieur stood over the way. A look through the blinds showed him returning to his domicile, several doors below. I returned to my own painful reflections. The Mr Todd who was my "sweetheart" when I was twelve and he twenty-four, who was my brothers' friend, and daily at our home, was put away from among our acquaintance at the beginning of the war. This one, I should not know. Cords of candy, and mountains of bouquets bestowed in childish days, will not make my country's enemy my friend now that I am a woman.

Strange to say, in behaving like a lady I have forfeited my self-respect. But he met me at a great disadvantage. Walking, whether in daylight or darkness, I could have [p. 71] said "excuse me" or something equally

83. Tennyson, "The Princess."

short and conclusive. But at night, alone in a car full of strangers, when you find your hand seized the natural impulse is not to create a sensation. Besides, it would require a bolder nature than mine to resent anything less than an insult from one of Abraham Lincoln's soldiers in the present perilous state of feeling here. And when the individual happens to be the cousin of the murdered man's wife—why! "Traitor, Coward," I tell myself, "considering that you invariably play the fool, perhaps after all you acted prudently!" But Miriam would have behaved better, dear blessed Miriam! And mother was so angry with me when I told her how very, very quiet I had been! What a fierce, bitter politician that meek little mother is! What astounding depths of hatred she reveals speaking of these matters!

Tuesday May 2d. 1865.

While praying for the return of those who have fought so nobly for us, how I have dreaded their first days at home! Since the boys died I have constantly thought of what pain it would bring to see their comrades return without them—to see families reunited, and know that ours never could be again, save in heaven. Last Saturday the 29th of April, seven hundred and fifty paroled Louisianians from Lee's army were brought here—the sole survivors of ten regiments who left four years ago so full of hope and determination. On the 29th of April 1861, George left New Orleans with his regiment. On the fourth anniversary of that day, they came back; but George and Gibbes have long been lying in their graves—George far away in desolated Virginia. His friend Dr Mitchell called yesterday; but we were out riding. I am almost thankful to have missed him. It will be dreadful, dreadful, the first instant we look on one who saw his dead face. And yet I so sadly long to hear from living lips of his last days on earth!

They came while I was writing—Dr Mitchell, Capt. Buckner, and Capt. Lions,[84] who were with him those days, and who saw him [p. 72] buried. Mother was far too agitated to go down. I received them alone; how, I do not know, for I was too intensely resolute to be firm to remember distinctly how I got there. I dared not ask much; and they told

---

84. Probably Captain James Buckner and Captain Isaac L. Lyons, both of the 10th Louisiana Infantry Regiment. The 10th and George Morgan's regiment, the 1st Louisiana, were part of the same army in Virginia.

me as well as they could without saying more than I was able to bear. He died happy; "trusting in the mercy of the Saviour!" Thank God! They gave me his gold buttons—the only token of him we have yet received. I have put them carefully away; they must belong to Miriam, or dear Sue.[85]

They were here an hour and a half; and I have made up my mind to like Capt. Lions, and I like Capt. Buckner *very* much without an effort; and Dr Mitchell I must *try* to like. But O George! though he was your friend, and kind to you, I thought of your dying eyes looking up to that cold face, and it pained me.

June 15th

Our Confederacy has gone with one crash—the report of the pistol fired at Lincoln. What tears we have shed over it, it is not necessary to mention. I only pray never to be otherwise than what I am at this instant—a Rebel in heart and soul, and that all my life I may remember the cruel wrongs we have suffered. It is incomprehensible, this change. Seeing familiar faces on the street is an oddity to which I cannot reconcile myself. Miriam came in from the Confederacy with Charlie, Lilly, and all the children on the nineteenth of May—O ma princesse! and since then, every one seems to follow. There is Dr Woods who seemed silently attracted to the spot, for he walked in a few days after as though we had parted hours, instead of years ago. Then in came Capt. McGimsey, O *so* naturally, that I was insensibly carried back to the days when he—rather liked me; and I came very near being ever so civil to him, to atone for past mischief. Miriam's adorer Col. Dupré came next,[86] and afforded me food for three days laughter. Clean daft about

85. Sue Covington was engaged to George Morgan. In one of the 1866 entries appended to Book 5, Sarah notes the marriage of Sue—presumably Sue Covington—to Captain Buckner.

86. In the same entry referred to in the previous note, Sarah mentions her sister's engagement to Alcée Louis Dupré. "What I have sufferred [sic] since Miriam pledged herself to this, is indescribable," she wrote.

our flirt! Our cousins Gibbes Morgan, Waller, and Phil, and dozens that we do not know so well, follow in [p. 73] rapid succession, until the unusual sensation of receiving visitors makes me dizzy. And then who should step in a week ago, but John Halsey!!!

Dear John!! How I have laughed this week! Twice a day he comes. Why I would grow alarmed if twenty-four hours passed without bringing his good, honest face.[87]

87. After the war Halsey resumed his law practice. In the early 1870s he was living in New Orleans, where city directories list him as an attorney. Later he relocated in Baton Rouge for a time before returning to Pointe Coupee Parish.

INDEX

Addison, Dr. W. J., 266, 269, 282

Albatross, 441n

Alexandria, La., 259, 437, 491n

Allen, Colonel Henry Watkins, xxii, 156n, 210, 322, 324, 364n, 376, 471n

Amite River, 184, 327–28

Antietam, Battle of, 293

Appleton, Thomas, 581

Arkansas (Confederate ram), xxi, xxii, 49n, 169, 190–91, 193–99, 229, 266, 269n, 274n, 282n, 283, 287; destruction of, 191n, 194–95

Arlington plantation, 235n

Asphodel plantation, 464n, 595

Augur, General C. C., 169n

Augusta, Ga., 429, 449

Babin, Pierre Paul, 277

Badger, Anna, xxv, 222–24, 227, 229, 241, 266, 268, 270–71, 276, 278, 280, 282–306 passim, 311, 313, 318, 324–47 passim, 352, 358, 372, 375, 376–77, 380, 381, 383, 387, 394, 405, 407–8, 411–14, 418, 420–21, 427, 432, 438, 440, 442, 446, 454, 456–57, 525, 543

Badger, C. W. (Wallace), 126, 267, 272

Badger, Francis Edmond (Ned), 92, 368, 375, 428

Badger, Mary Carter, 126n, 220, 222n, 229, 233, 236, 273, 275–76, 283, 287, 293, 294, 295–98, 305–6, 314, 318, 326–27, 333–38, 341, 343, 345, 348, 352–53, 358, 360, 370, 371–73, 391–94, 397, 418, 432, 440–41, 456–57, 492

Badger, Wallace, 92n, 126n, 222n

Banks, General Nathaniel P., xxi, 111, 436n, 438n, 451n, 486n, 491–92, 504n, 509n, 522n, 523, 527, 529–30

Barbee, Oscar, 238

Barbot, Lieutenant Alphonse, 198

Barker, Ann Morgan (aunt), xviii, 149n, 234

Barker, Charles (slave), 234–35, 240, 241, 250

Barker, Captain Thomas, xviii, 149n

Barker, Thomas (Tom), 149

Barr, Cornelia, 262

Barry, Ethel Dawson (daughter), xxxviii, xl

Barry, Herbert, xl, xli

Baton Rouge, La., xv–xxxiv passim; 43n, 46, 165, 189, 199–202, 382, 384, 513, 609; state's seizure of arsenal at, xv, 112, 307n; sickness among Union soldiers at, xxiii, 181–82; burning of cotton at, 48–49; arrival of Union fleet at, 63–64, 67; shelling of, 87–89, 94–95, 98; General Butler visits, 139–43; citizens of, arrested, 141, 143–44; population of, 181n; Confederate attack on, 183, 190–94; burning of homes in, 214; evacuation of, 228n; pillaging in, 202, 212–13, 215, 228, 233–35, 238–40, 247, 411

Baton Rouge, Battle of: 190–94, 322n, 364n, 411; casualties in, 201, 218; battlefield, 237–38

Baton Rouge *Advocate*, 214

Baumstark, Ambrose, 181, 183
Bayou Goula, La., 257
Bayou Lafourche, 52
Bayou St. John, 516
Bayou Sara, La., 223, 257, 374n
Beall, General William N. R., 327, 333, 337, 340, 345n, 351, 360n, 387, 389n, 394n, 430n, 453
Bean, Lieutenant Colonel Sidney, 97n
Beanham, William, 551
Beauchamp, A. H., 400n
Beauregard, General P. G. T., 53, 104, 107, 260
Bee, General Hamilton P., 111n
Beech Grove, 251–53
Beecher, Henry Ward, 606
Bell, Mr., 179
Belle Alliance plantation, xviii
Benjamin, Judah P., 44n, 145n
Benjamin, Solomon, 145
Bennett, Major William K., 340, 353
Berger, Monsieur, 476
Bernard, Miss, 262
Bernard, General Joseph, 262n
Biddle, Lieutenant James C., 105, 108–9, 115, 122, 124, 165, 177, 236
Bird, Mr., 208
Bird, Abraham, 9n
Bird, Thompson J., 201, 237
Blacks: in Morgan household, 17, 98, 137–38, 173n, 243, 439; Sarah's attitude toward, 72, 213, 215, 330–31, 436, 481; praise for, 91, 250; rounded up by Union army, 203, 208; seeking freedom, 250, 331n
Blineau, Jules, 510
Blineau Brothers, 510
Bonfouca, 473, 474, 479, 482, 508
Bonnecaze, Leon, 110
Booth, John Wilkes, 607n
Boswell, James, 163
Bourges, Lieutenant Ernest, 258
Boutte Station, La., 258n

Bowen, General James, 486–88, 491
Boyle, Captain Roger T., 366n
Boyle, Mrs. Roger T., 366
Bradford, J. B. (Buck), 40–41, 322–23
Bradford, J. McPherson (Mac), 322–23, 324, 325, 326, 327–29, 376–78, 381, 382–83
Bradford, Captain James L., 40n, 328–29, 330, 333, 338n, 339, 347, 348, 353, 363, 366–67, 375, 377, 381, 382–83, 412, 417–18, 445, 447, 464, 522, 542–44, 595–96
Bragg, General Braxton, 420
Brandon, Miss., 449
Brashear City, La., 509
Breaux, Emilie (Mrs. Gustave A.), 290, 309–10, 314–15, 318, 328–29, 341, 348–51, 363–64, 366, 511–12, 583
Breaux, Colonel Gustave A., 218, 269–70, 274–75, 283, 285–86, 287, 288–90, 292, 294, 296–97, 298, 300, 304, 308–10, 312, 314–15, 319, 332, 333, 341, 348–49, 350, 352, 363–64, 366–67, 373, 375, 510–13, 583–84
Breckinridge, General John C., 162n, 183, 190, 200, 274, 276
Breedlove, Mr., 481
Brooklyn, 59n, 66, 67
Brown, Mrs., 237, 241
Brown, Dr. A. Porter, 265n, 266
Brown, Elizabeth Keller, 265
Brown, Lieutenant Isaac N., 198n, 269
Brown, J. N., 30n
Brunot, Annette (Nettie), 9n, 47, 68, 96, 100, 102, 140, 161, 168, 175, 306, 420, 587
Brunot, Eugenia (Dena), 9n, 47, 78, 92, 98, 102n, 161, 168, 170, 175, 306, 420, 587
Brunot, Felix, 9, 92, 96
Brunot, James M., 9n
Brunot, Louisa. See Carnal, Louisa Brunot

Brunot, Sophia (Sophie), 9n, 26, 47, 68, 96, 98, 112, 135, 152, 161, 162, 168, 174–75, 178, 259, 260, 261, 306, 420, 513, 587

Brunot, Mrs. Sophia (Sophie), 9, 11, 23, 33, 36, 68, 78, 90, 92, 98, 100, 102, 107, 137, 152, 161, 168, 169, 173–74, 177, 184, 227, 236–37, 250–51, 507

Bryan, Mrs., 170

Bryan, Benjamin F., 64n, 145n

Buckner, Major D. P., 389, 392, 399–400

Buckner, Captain James, 610–11

Bull, Mrs. Andrew G., 469, 473–74, 478n, 479–80, 483, 486–87, 501

Bull, Minna, 478, 483

Burnside, General Ambrose E., 249

Butler, General Benjamin F., 64, 76, 85, 107, 121, 145–46, 151, 153, 158, 202, 225n, 228n, 409, 492n, 493n, 599; visits Baton Rouge, 139–43

Butler, Mrs. Benjamin F., 599n

Butler, Captain Thomas, 41, 42

Cain, Dempsey J., 210n, 344n

Cain, Dempsey P., 210

Cain, Mary Ann, 211, 344

Caldwell, Mr., 179

Cammack, Charles W., 50n

Cammack, Fanny, 50

Cammack, Morgan, 50n

Cammack, Thomas D., 524

Camp Moore, 99, 106, 160, 262, 276, 298, 460, 500

Capdevielle, Dr. Auguste, 469–71, 475, 497–99

Carnal, Louisa Brunot, 259n

Carnal, Dr. Robert, 259

Carter, Albert Eugene, 125n, 225, 279, 287, 292, 294, 300, 313, 319, 383n, 418, 432, 438, 543n

Carter, General Albert G., 8n, 21, 71n, 111, 125n, 179, 201, 218, 222, 223–24, 242, 251–52, 255, 257, 263, 264–66,

268, 270, 272–73, 275, 277, 279n, 283, 303, 317–19, 323, 326–27, 330, 333, 338, 342, 343n, 345, 347, 350–51, 352n, 355, 361, 372, 374, 376, 379, 385, 386, 401, 414, 419, 423–24, 438, 439, 453–54, 456, 457–58, 463, 493, 505–6; Sarah's affection for, 242, 252, 271, 273, 330

Carter, Eugene. *See* Carter, Albert Eugene

Carter, Florence, 543

Carter, Frances Priscilla Howell, 71n, 223, 232, 269, 338, 345, 453, 493

Carter, Helen Moore, 71, 125, 126, 211, 218–20, 225, 231, 236, 242, 269, 273, 287, 291, 295–96, 297, 303, 310, 318, 321, 325, 329, 335, 338, 342, 347, 348, 352, 357, 360, 383, 403, 425, 436, 440, 453–54, 493, 502–3, 543, 587

Carter, Howell, 21, 22, 30–32, 57, 92, 111, 125, 126, 149, 164, 185, 211, 241, 319, 344, 404, 414, 505–7

Carter, Lilly, 383

Carter, Lydia. *See* Morgan, Lydia Carter

Carter, Private William, Jr., 467, 496

Carter, William P. (Will), xxvi, 149, 251, 272n, 284, 298, 320–22, 323–24, 325, 327, 329, 342, 345, 347–50, 352n, 354–60, 361–63, 368–69, 379, 403, 598

Castle, Henry, Jr., 87, 114n, 191

Castle, Nathan, 114, 191n

Castleton, Dr. Henry, 88n, 89, 102–3

Castleton, Mattie. *See* Stith, Mattie Castleton

Castleton, Mollie, 27, 30, 70–72, 244–45, 278

Castleton, Dr. Thomas, 19n, 27n, 88n, 89, 102–3

Cate, Charles E., 463n

Cate, Mrs. Charles E., 463, 464

Catiche. *See* Tiche (slave)

Cayuga, 196n

Centenary College, 220n, 308n, 345n

Charleston, S.C., xv, xxxi, xxxiin, xxxv,
    xxxix, xl, xli, 222n, 279, 315,
    532n, 545n
Charleston *News*, xxxv, xxxvi, 82n, 175n
Charleston *News and Courier*, xxxv, xxxvi,
    xxxix, 82n, 546n
Chesnut, Mary Boykin, xxvi, xxvii
Christmas, Mr., 469, 470
Clark, Captain Charles E., 235n
Clark, Captain John, 235n
Clinton, La., xxi, xxviii, 43n, 53, 114,
    237n, 241, 255, 262, 265, 268, 286,
    300, 301, 308, 310–20 passim, 324,
    325n, 328, 345n, 346, 352, 353, 356,
    359, 361, 363, 367, 368, 371, 379, 381,
    385, 392, 411, 422, 423, 429–50
    passim, 452, 453, 456, 474, 477, 479,
    480, 489, 491, 511, 526, 583, 585n;
    description of, 242–44, 251; wartime
    shortages in, 251, 260, 439, 449–50
Clinton and Port Hudson Railroad, 43n,
    53n, 242, 265, 268, 303–4, 311, 329,
    334n, 353, 453–54
Coffin, Private L. E., 496n
Coffin, Private R. L., 496n
Columbia, S.C., xxxi, xxxii
Columbus, Ky., 37
Comstock, George C., 43n
Comstock, Isadora, 43, 255, 385, 388, 456
Comstock, Midshipman John H., 43n
Conn, Lieutenant J. D., 375, 376–78,
    520, 522, 529
Cooper's Wells, Miss., 280
Corinth, Miss., 9n, 40, 53, 104
Covington, Ky., 258
Covington, Sue, 611
Cravens, N. A., 143n, 145
Crawford, Mr., 265–66
Crockett, Davy, 387n
Crockett, Colonel Robert H., 387–91, 398
Cuthbert, Ga., 505n

Daigre, Gilbert, 9n

Daigre, Lucy, 180
Daigre, Mary C., 9n, 102, 180n
David, Seth, 45, 93
Davidson, Mrs., xxxii
Davidson, Fanny. *See* Trezevant, Fanny
    Davidson
Davidson, Nannie, 254, 255, 278
Davidson, Thomas Green, 44n, 92n, 97
Davidson, Mrs. Thomas Green, 44
Davis, Captain, 57
Davis, Jefferson, xxii, 508, 606–7
Davis, Varina Howell (Mrs. Jefferson
    Davis), 71n
Dawson, Ethel. *See* Barry, Ethel Dawson
Dawson, Francis Warrington (Frank)
    (husband), xxxivn, xxxv-xxxvi,
    xxxviii-xl, 175n, 415n, 427n
Dawson, Philip Hicky (son), xxxviii
Dawson, Warrington (son), xxxi, xxxiii,
    xxxiiin, xxxviii, xli, 352n
Day, Lavinia, 7, 130, 157, 176
Day, Dr. Richard H., 7n, 157, 167,
    228, 236
DeKay, Lieutenant George C., 153n
Desrayaux, Catherine, 582
Dickson, Miss, 385, 388, 455
Donaldsonville, La., 52n, 257
Dophy (slave), 33, 137, 144, 173n, 180,
    191, 243
Dortch, Dr. Caleb, 272, 342–43, 345,
    351, 354
Dougherty, John A., 141n, 143n, 235n
Drum, Lavinia Morgan (Sis) (sister), xviii,
    19, 20, 22, 24n, 25, 85, 104, 134, 149,
    182, 248, 250, 261, 273, 324, 325, 346,
    382, 419–20, 434, 435, 442, 451, 570
Drum, Major Richard C. (brother-in-
    law), xviii, xx, 19n, 73, 105,
    236, 324
Drum, Susie Emily (niece), 443
Duchein, Dr. Jean Bertrand, 102
Dudley, Colonel N. A. M., 202, 216
Dueling, xv-xvii, xxviii, 5, 7n, 53

Duggan, Lieutenant Thomas J., 374, 390, 392, 406–7, 412–13, 423–25
Dunnington, Lieutenant John W., 149
Dupré, Lieutenant Alcée Louis, xxxii, 405–6, 413, 416, 417, 431–32, 451, 522, 524, 525, 542, 611
Dupré, Lucius Jacques, 405n
Duralde, Joseph V., 203n
Duralde, Victorine, 203

Edmond (servant), 521, 527, 585
Elder, Ellen. *See* Flynn, Ellen Elder
Elder, Mary, 53n, 179n, 276
Elder, William, 53, 126n, 179n, 211, 215, 223–24, 228, 236, 237, 242, 269
Eli (slave), 291
Emancipation Proclamation, xxv, 330
Enders, Frank H., 70, 325–27, 332–33, 334, 337–38, 340, 346–47, 352–53, 354, 355, 357, 358, 359, 363–64, 367–71, 389–90, 391–93, 400, 408, 427–28, 436, 437, 439, 450, 457–60, 461
Enders, Henry, 325n
Enders, Dr. Peter M., 11–12, 17, 70n, 169, 212, 228, 236, 237, 262, 346
Essex, 190n, 193, 194–95, 196n, 203, 209, 257n, 277, 283
Evening Star, xxxi
Ewell, General Richard S., 598

Farragut, David G., xx, 48n, 66n, 67n, 94–95, 122n, 257n, 438n, 439n, 509
Faust, Drew Gilpin, xxvii
Fellows, Captain John R., 394
Fenner, Captain Charles E., 318, 325n, 333–34, 340, 374, 390, 393, 406, 407, 412, 415, 423, 424, 433, 440
Flower, Lucy, 387
Flower, Richard, 387n
Fluker, David J., 464n
Fluker, Isabella, 464, 522n
Fluker, Mary, 464n, 595n
Flynn, Ellen Elder, 52n, 179, 245, 247–48

Fogg, Captain, 430
Forester, Jane, 253
Fort Jackson, 47–48, 110n, 127, 143n, 144, 145, 146, 152, 157, 350, 509
Fort St. Philip, 47–48
Fort Warren, 66
Fowler, Adèle (aunt), 17, 18, 179, 226, 268n
Fowler, Eugene, 268, 310
Fowler, Henry Waller (uncle), 9n
Fowler, Philip, 268, 612
Fowler, Sarah Hunt. *See* Morgan, Sarah Hunt Fowler
Fowler, Waller, 226, 227, 268, 310, 324, 325, 328, 350, 612
Fox, Dr. D. J., 515n
Fox-Genovese, Elizabeth, xxv–xxvi
Frank (slave), 331
Frémaux, Caroline, 206n
Frémaux, Céline, 206n
Furness, Lady (Thelma Morgan), 489n

Gantt, Lieutenant Colonel George, 438
Gardner, General Franklin, 314n, 394n, 405n, 413n, 441, 446, 451–2, 462n, 474, 480, 517, 522, 524, 540n, 570–72
Garig, George, 111n
Garig, Mary Kleinpeter, 111n
Garig, William (Willie), 111, 114
Geary, Rev. John M., 269, 313, 354–56
General McClellan. See McClellan
George, Frances, 254, 255
George, John F., 254n
Georgia (Confederate cruiser), 421, 581
Gettysburg, Battle of, 519
Gierlow, Rev. John, 21, 156, 255
Gilman, Captain Samuel H., 460–61
Grayson, Caroline (Mrs. John B.), 466–70, 472, 473, 475, 476, 478, 482, 495, 497–98, 532
Grayson, General John B., 466n, 495
Greenwell Springs, La., xxviii, 45, 46, 76, 84–85, 86–87, 90, 93, 95, 97, 100, 104–

Greenwell Springs, La. (*cont'd*)
6, 107, 111, 113, 116, 124, 160, 173n,
252, 507n
Gregg, General John, 430n
Grenada, Miss., 301
Grosse Tete, La., 209
Guibourd, Mr., 26
Guyol, Leonce P., 372
Gwynn, Lieutenant William, 405, 424

Hall, George O., 212
Halsey, John H., 338, 340, 348, 350, 352–
53, 363, 366–67, 373, 375–78, 380, 381,
383, 385, 386–87, 390–92, 393–94,
398–401, 408, 412, 416, 417–21, 424–
26, 430–31, 435n, 437, 439, 443–48,
459, 461–68, 470–73, 475, 479, 489,
496–500, 532, 544–45, 579, 588, 591,
596, 612
Hammond, La., 461–64, 471, 479
Hampton, Wade, xxxii
Hampton plantation (South Carolina),
xxxii, xxxiv, xxxv
Hardesty, Franklin, 378n
Harold, Mr., 325, 327, 330, 340
Harold, Lieutenant B. Morgan. *See*
Lieutenant B. Morgan Harrod
Harris, Lieutenant Thomas B., 333–34
Harrison, Dora, 545n
Harrod, Lieutenant B. Morgan, 325n
Hartford, 66n, 67n, 87n, 94n, 441n
Haskin, Major Joseph A., 112, 307
Hatch, Francis H. (Frank), 461
Haynes, Bythell, 252n, 256
Haynes, Delia, 252n, 255, 257
Haynes, Eliza, 252–54, 255
Hemphill, J. C., xxxix
Henderson, George, 44–45
Heroman, George M., 112n, 169
Herren, Captain Gadi, 469n
Herron, Major Andrew S., 293
Hicky, Colonel Philip, xviin, xviiin, 9n
Hill, Mr., 206

Hill, Colonel James D., xxxii, xxxivn
Himes, S., 224
Hollins, Commodore George N., 37, 39,
66n, 92
Hooper, Eugene, 157
Hooper, Captain Isaac, 157
Hope Estate plantation, 177n, 226,
235, 268
Hospitals, military: in Baton Rouge, 112n,
123; in Clinton, 325n, 345n, 368; at
Jackson, La., 345; at Linwood, 505
Howard, Lieutenant Robert J.,
461–64, 489
Hubert, Father, 293
Huger, Lieutenant Thomas B., 50, 65–66,
108, 149
Hughes, Mr., 57, 59
Hunter, Major Sherod, 509n
Huston, Eli, 274
Hutchinson, S. W., 49–50
Hyams, Henry J., 143n

Iroquois, 63
Itasca, 59n
Ivy, Mrs. Edward, 469, 473–74, 478n,
479–80, 483, 486–87
Ivy, Jenny, 478, 483

Jackson, David D., 311n
Jackson, La., 24, 316n, 345, 347, 352n,
368, 464n
Jackson, Miss., 49n, 99n, 138n, 262n,
266, 316, 474n
Jackson, General Thomas J. (Stonewall),
107, 111n, 151, 161, 260, 266, 279,
295, 452
Jacobs, E., 510–11
Johnson, Samuel, 163–64
Johnson's Island (Union prison), 579,
580n, 585, 598
Johnston, General Joseph E., 77, 606
Jones, Miss, 212–13, 215
Jones, Mrs. S. E., 234

Jones, Shoe, 143n
Jules (slave), 331

Katahdin, 196n
Kelley, Mary, xxiv
Kenedy, Mr., 482
Kennebec, 94n
Kennedy, Dr., 441
Kimball, James B., 94n
Kineo, 196n
King, Grace, xl
Knickerbocker, R. W., 589–90

Lacey, Alfred, 558n
Lacey, Mrs. Alfred, 558, 592
Lake Pontchartrain, xxii, xxvii, 455, 466n, 473n, 477, 484n, 516n
Lanier, Captain, 337n, 540–41
Lanier, Lieutenant B. W., 540n
Lanier, Lieutenant Charles L., 540n
Lanier, Lieutenant John S., 540n
LaNoue, Mrs. Adelaide, 192
LaNoue, Adèle Lavinia (Dellie) (niece), 93, 129, 136, 147, 313, 339, 346, 374, 457
LaNoue, Beatrice (niece), 87n, 172, 457
LaNoue, Eliza Ann (Lilly) (sister), xx, xxi, 6, 7, 12, 15–18, 20, 22, 25, 26, 33, 38, 47, 49–50, 51, 55, 79, 87, 91, 93, 96, 98, 103, 107, 116, 129–30, 133–34, 136n, 147, 151, 154, 167, 168, 170, 172, 176, 209, 211, 215, 227, 242–44, 246, 247–48, 251, 252, 256–57, 286, 301, 311, 313, 315–16, 324, 346, 359, 374n, 409, 411, 422, 439, 441–42, 449–50, 452, 454–57, 583, 585, 604, 611
LaNoue, Eugene, 157, 474
LaNoue, Gibbes Morgan (nephew), 136, 150, 168, 223, 339, 374
LaNoue, John Charles (Charlie) (brother-in-law), xx, xxiii, 6n, 12, 14, 16–18, 20, 22, 35, 44, 47, 48–49, 55, 57, 59, 70, 87, 93–94, 103, 130, 147, 154, 157n,

158, 170, 172, 176, 183–84, 185, 192n, 201, 202, 233, 236, 237, 239–42, 246, 256, 271, 272, 301, 313, 315–16, 409, 416, 442, 449, 474n, 585n, 611
LaNoue, Louis (nephew), 38, 150, 172
LaNoue, Noemie, 192–93
LaNoue, Sarah (niece), 139, 150
Larguier, Isidore, 240
Laurel Hill, 193, 228n
Lee, General Robert E., 262, 293n, 509, 519, 520, 581, 606, 610–11
LeGrand, Julia, 402n, 520n
Lenair, Captain, 337, 340, 344, 347, 540n. *See also* Lanier
Lennice (slave), 278
Lester, Captain William V., 467n
Lévéque, Mr., 177
Liberty, Miss., 435, 449
Liddy (slave), xxvn, 173n, 439
Lincoln, Abraham, xxv, 141, 151, 239, 330, 410, 608, 610, 611; assassination of, 606–8
Lincoln, Mary Todd, 608n
Linwood plantation, xxi, xxii, xxv, xxvi, xxviii, 8, 23, 33, 53n, 56, 70n, 71, 124, 125–27, 202, 209, 211, 218, 242n, 245, 251, 252, 253, 257, 260, 261, 262, 263, 264–66, 276, 313, 344, 397, 404, 430, 431, 435, 453–54, 457, 464, 489, 493, 505, 511–12, 596; sugar-making at, 326, 328, 330–32; Christmas at, 374–78; party at, 385–91
Lobdell, Abraham, 206–9
Lobdell, Angelina Bird, 208
Lobdell, James L., 208n
Locke, Lieutenant Colonel Michael B., 399–400, 521
Locke, Samuel, 511n
Logan, Frank, xxxix
Longstreet, General James, 262
Loucks, Francis Henry, 173n
Loucks, Mary Newcomb, 173, 184
Loucks, Richard H., 173n

Loucks, Richard Newcomb, 173n
Louisa (slave), 132, 173n
Louisiana, 37n
Lovell, General Mansfield, 52, 66n
Lucy (slave), 87, 91, 92–93, 96,
    137–38, 173n
Lusher, Robert Mills, 222
Luzenberg, Dr. Charles A., 224n
Luzenberg, Lieutenant Charles H.,
    224, 243n
Luzenberg, Clementine, 243
Lynchburg, Va., 281
Lyons, Captain Isaac L., 610–11

McCay, Mrs. Eliza, 252–53, 255, 258, 291
McClellan, 141n, 169
McClellan, General George B., 107, 111,
    151, 157, 160, 186, 249, 276, 293n
McCluer, Captain James L., 394n, 405,
    406, 407, 413–16, 423, 523
McClure, John, 416
McDow, Dr. Thomas B., xxxixn
McDowell, Edward, 27n
McDowell, Philadelphia Nolan (Phillie),
    27, 178, 183, 185, 189n, 190–94,
    197–98, 200, 204–5, 206–7, 209–11
McGimsey, Dr. J. W. P., 36n, 281
McGimsey, William C., 36, 43, 47,
    293, 611
McHatton, Eliza. *See* Ripley, Eliza
    McHatton
McHatton, James A., 165n, 235
McKay, Mrs. Eliza. *See* McCay,
    Mrs. Eliza
McKennan, Eliza Ann, xvii
McKitrick, Mr., 143n
McLean, Mrs. James L., 537, 539n
McMain, James W., 17
McMillan, Colonel James W., 106, 108,
    110, 112, 124, 228n
Macon, Miss., 585
McPhaul, Mary Elizabeth, 424–25,
    448, 544

McPherson, W. D., 165n
McRae, 37, 43n, 49n, 50, 66, 195,
    227, 240
Madding, Dr. Robert F., 339
Madisonville, La., 455, 466n, 467,
    474–76, 480, 484, 495
Magnolia Mound plantation, 212n
Magruder, General John B., 509
Magruder, William H. N., 143n
Malvina (slave), xxv, 343, 372, 386, 414,
    417, 420, 543
Manassas, 66
Mandeville, La., 474, 477
Margret (slave), 17, 33, 173n, 233, 250,
    316, 439
Marston, Abigail, 244
Marston, Henry, xxn, 74n, 243, 248, 269,
    313, 455, 456
Martin, Dr. Amzi, 364–65
Mary (Brunot servant), 93
Mather, Anna, xviiin
Mather, George, xviiin
Matta, Andrew, 214
Matta, Minna, 214, 307
Maury, William L., 581–82
Maxey, General S. B., 318n, 430n
Mayes (Mays), Private Hugh, 496
Maynadier, Sallie, 34
Maynadier, Captain William, 34n
Merrimac, 196
Miller, Lieutenant Colonel H. H., 467n
Miller, John C., 308, 337–38, 453
Milliken, Samuel, 282–83, 292
Mills, Robert, 222n
Miltenberger, Alphonse, 471n, 476n
Miltenberger, Ernest, 471n, 497–98
Miltenberger, James, 471n, 497–98
Mississippi (Confederate), 50n, 66
Mississippi (Union), 441, 442
Mitchell, Mr., 98
Mitchell, Dr. William S., 601, 610
Mitchell, Mrs. William S., 602
Mobile, Ala., 157, 158, 286, 449

Moise, E. Warren, 144

Monitor, 196n

Montgomery, Mrs., 92

Moore, Edward E., 269n

Moore, Mary E., 252

Moore, Thomas Overton, 144

Morfit, Dr. Charles M., 49

Morgan, Ann (aunt). *See* Barker, Ann Morgan

Morgan, Aurore Hortense (Bena), 177, 227, 374n

Morgan, Beatrice Ford (Sister) (sister-in-law), 24, 53–54, 55, 219–20, 261, 488, 495, 500, 503, 548, 570, 582–83, 584, 585, 593, 605

Morgan, Caroline Hicky (aunt), 17, 177n, 226n, 332n, 372n

Morgan, Charlotte (niece), 14, 443, 500, 582, 593–95, 605

Morgan, Eliza Ann (sister). *See* LaNoue, Eliza Ann Morgan

Morgan, George Mather (brother), xx, xxii, 19, 22, 50, 77, 85, 86, 92, 113, 134, 152, 161, 179, 230–31, 234, 249, 254, 258, 266, 279, 280, 281, 314n, 341–42, 362, 415, 450, 457, 491, 509, 585, 609–11; described, 39; death of, 597–602, 603n, 604

Morgan, Gibbes (brother). *See* Morgan, Thomas Gibbes Morgan, Jr.

Morgan, Gloria. *See* Vanderbilt, Gloria Morgan

Morgan, Harry (brother). *See* Morgan, Henry Waller Fowler

Morgan, Harry Hays (nephew), xli, 489, 549

Morgan, Helen Trenholm (sister-in-law), xxxi, xxxiv, 316, 324, 604

Morgan, Henry Gibbes, 332–33, 335–37, 340, 612

Morgan, Henry Gibbes, Jr., xlin

Morgan, Henry Waller Fowler (Harry, Hal) (brother), xv-xvi, xxviii, 7n, 22, 24, 25–26, 33–34, 38–40, 42, 43–47, 59–60, 85, 87, 108, 115, 132, 134, 139, 149, 152, 180, 212–13, 215, 217, 234, 254–55, 260, 279, 281, 288, 316, 331, 372, 384, 404, 433, 435, 455, 469, 489–90, 514, 515–16, 547, 550, 585–86, 589–90, 598; death of, xv, 5–11, 53–55; described, 38

Morgan, Hicky (nephew), 489, 500, 549–50

Morgan, Howell (nephew), xxxiv, 505n, 507

Morgan, James B. (uncle), 599

Morgan, James Morris (Jimmy) (brother), xixn, xx, xxxi, xxxii-xxxiii, xxxiv, xxxivn, xxxv, xlin, 7n, 10, 13–16, 17n, 18, 37, 38, 39, 48, 49–50, 54, 56, 66, 77, 78, 85–86, 88, 92, 134, 149, 158, 161, 166–67, 179, 195, 226–27, 234, 249, 254, 266, 279–80, 284, 315–16, 324, 341–42, 351, 362, 370, 421–23, 435, 442, 509, 518n, 572n, 581–82, 585, 603–4, 607; described, 37, 39

Morgan, Colonel John Hunt, 239

Morgan, Lavinia (niece), 14, 500, 605

Morgan, Lavinia (sister). *See* Drum, Lavinia Morgan

Morgan, Lydia Carter (sister-in-law), 7n, 8, 10, 19, 21, 23, 30, 35, 36, 42n, 44, 45, 46, 56, 57, 102, 125, 133–34, 147, 158, 179, 234, 240, 255, 268, 278n, 279–82, 286, 292, 294, 297, 305, 306–7, 310, 316, 321, 348, 355, 390–91, 393, 406, 415, 427, 437, 442, 453, 493, 505, 526, 543, 581, 597, 600

Morgan, Mary, 177, 372n

Morgan, Miriam (niece), 516, 608

Morgan, Miriam Antoinette (sister), xixn, xx, xxi, xxxii, xxxiv, xl, 6, 9, 10, 12–13, 15–22, 23–26, 28, 30–32, 36, 40, 43, 45, 47, 48, 50, 55, 65, 67, 69, 70–71, 79, 86–115 passim, 124–38 passim, 140, 149–50, 154, 158–59, 161–79 passim,

Morgan, Miriam Antoinette (*cont'd*)
185, 209, 604–5, 609–10, 611; at
Westover, 189, 190, 194–95, 200–201,
202; at Linwood, 211–454 passim; in
Clinton, 242–64 passim; on journey to
New Orleans, 460–86 passim; in New
Orleans, 487–603 passim
Morgan, Morris (uncle), xvii, 9n
Morgan, Morris, Jr., 268
Morgan, Nellie (niece), 14, 500, 605
Morgan, Philip Hicky (brother), xx, xxii,
xxxin, 5, 13, 14, 19–22, 24n, 25, 46, 54–
55, 85, 104, 122, 162, 239, 245, 261,
288, 297, 331, 442, 450, 474, 487–502
passim, 509, 511, 515–31 passim, 541,
547–48, 551n, 568, 570, 572n, 576,
581, 582–83, 584–85, 598–99, 602,
606; described, 37; Sarah's defense of,
409–11, 562–63
Morgan, Mrs. Sarah, 539n
Morgan, Sarah Hunt Fowler (mother),
xvii–xviii, xx, xxi–xxii, xl, 5–8, 10, 12–
13, 15–16, 18, 22, 30, 33, 46, 50, 55, 65,
87–109 passim, 124, 127, 129, 145, 153,
157, 158, 166, 170–71, 177, 184, 215,
225, 227, 232–36, 239–41, 242, 284,
301, 371, 384, 397, 401, 409, 457–58; at
Westover, 185, 190, 194, 198, 203, 204–
5, 207, 209–11; in Clinton, 253–66
passim, 300, 310, 315, 316, 319, 324,
346, 359, 411, 422, 425, 429, 431, 441,
442, 449–50; on journey to New
Orleans, 461–63, 470, 473, 474, 479–
81, 483, 485–88; in New Orleans,
491–92, 500–501, 508, 516, 519–20,
528, 550–51, 554, 564, 570, 573, 577,
584–85, 590–91, 600–603, 605, 610
Morgan, Sarah Ida Fowler (diarist): birth
of, xix; attitude toward secession, xix-
xx, 74, 259; feminism of, xxiii-xxiv,
xxxvi-xxxviii, 81–84, 154–56, 175, 290,
545–46, 568–69, 579–80; attitude
toward men, xxiii-xxiv, 59–63, 166, 175,

182, 284, 290, 412, 532, 544–46, 548,
561, 568–69; education of, xxiv, 136–
37, 290; attitude toward blacks,
xxv-xxvi, 72, 91, 138, 213, 215, 250,
330–31, 436, 481; attitude toward
slavery, xxv-xxvi, 130–31; views on
dueling, xxviii, xxxii-xxxiii; importance
of diary to, xxviii, 51, 116–17, 121, 142–
43, 184, 215–16, 397, 436, 494, 532–33;
marriage of, xxxv; postwar newspaper
writing, xxxvi-xxxviii, 82n, 175n, 546n;
years in Paris, xl-xli; death of, xli;
attitude toward marriage, 60, 63, 80–
82, 175, 284, 458–60, 548, 550;
criticized by Baton Rouge citizens, 69–
73, 109–10, 113–14, 115, 177–78, 280;
attitude toward women, 73–74, 77, 80–
84, 121–24, 142, 175, 545–46, 569,
579–80; views on motherhood, 80–83;
attitude toward newspapers, 108, 143,
151, 162; visits pillaged Morgan home,
237–41; injured at Port Hudson, 333–
37; arrives in New Orleans, 482; takes
oath of allegiance, 485–86, 507–9
Morgan, Thelma. *See* Furness, Lady
Morgan, Thomas Gibbes, Jr. (brother),
xvii, xx, xxii, xxxiv, 7n, 8, 9, 19, 30, 40,
42n, 55, 59–60, 77, 85, 134, 147, 151,
159, 161, 168, 179, 180, 186, 233, 244n,
249, 254, 266, 278n, 279–99 passim,
308, 310, 314, 318–19, 323, 326n, 330,
333, 338, 347, 350–51, 355–57, 360,
361, 372, 375, 382, 388, 401, 415, 418,
421, 425, 427–29, 435, 439, 443, 449,
460, 491, 509, 520, 529, 580–81, 585,
610; described, 37–38; wounded, 292;
returns to Linwood, 292–93; death of,
597–600, 603n, 604
Morgan, Thomas Gibbes, Sr. (father), xvi,
xvii-xviii, xix-xx, 19n, 25, 30–33, 45–46,
54–57, 74n, 79, 80, 85, 114, 115, 116,
132, 147–48, 152, 212–13, 216–17, 221,
233, 237n, 239, 273, 288, 289, 331,

384, 401–2, 435, 451, 455, 481; illness
and death of, 11–22
Morgan, Thomas Gibbes III (nephew),
425, 448
Morrison, Captain Charles E., 285–86,
287–88, 295, 308–9
Morse, Mr., 354
Morse, Mrs., 355
Mud, Miss, 262
Murfreesboro, Tenn., 481

Nancy (slave), 137, 173n
Napoleon III, 471n
Nash, William H., 331n
Natchez, Miss., 277
Natchitoches, La., 144n
Neafus, George, 456
Netterville, Elizabeth, 248
New Orleans, xv, xviii, xix, xxii, xxxi,
xxxii, xxxiv, 64, 78n, 99n, 122, 143n,
164, 482, 490, 492n, 509n, 513, 525,
537, 606n; defeat of Confederate
defense forces at, 48, 50, 65–66; Union
occupation of, 48n; Confederate
withdrawal from, 52n; Morgans arrive
in, 482; newspapers in, 493n; mourns
death of Lincoln, 607–8
New Orleans, Jackson & Great Northern
Railroad, 53, 99n, 461
New Orleans *Daily Picayune,* 522n, 608n
New Orleans *Era,* 515, 517, 520n
New Orleans *True Delta,* 493
Newcomb, Lalla, 592
Newport, Robert Y., 220
Newport, Simpson W., 220n, 441
Newspapers: Sarah's criticism of, 108,
143, 162; in occupied New
Orleans, 493n
Newton, John, 121n
Nolan, Dr. John T., 27n, 177, 189, 190n,
191, 197, 206, 210–11, 261, 277
Nolan, Mary Elizabeth (Lilly), 190, 194,
198, 205, 210, 213

Nolan, Philadelphia (Phillie). *See*
McDowell, Philadelphia Nolan
Nolan, Virginia (Ginnie), 189, 190, 194,
199, 203, 204, 205–6, 207, 209,
210, 283
Norfolk, Va., 50, 77, 92, 229

Okolona, Miss., 224
Oliphant, Margaret, 408n
Olympe, Boisse, 503
Oneida, 206n
Opelousas, La., xxi, 144n, 258, 491n

Packwood, Captain George H., 455
Paine, Colonel Halbert E., 143n, 202n,
208n, 228n, 250n
Palmer, Captain James S., 63n
Palmerston, Lord, 151
Paris, France: Sarah's life in, xl–xli
Patrick, Robert, 286n, 353n
Peirce, Ada, 518–19, 522, 523, 526, 528,
537–38, 547, 552, 554, 556, 557, 561,
565–66, 570, 571, 587, 601
Peirce, Clementine Hyle, 556
Peirce, Levi, 518n, 556n
Peirce, Marie, 518n, 522, 524, 526, 537,
547, 548, 549, 552, 556, 557, 559, 570,
571, 587
Pemberton, General John C., 474, 475
Perkins, Miss, 470
Perkins, Dr. Jehu, 227
Perry, Admiral Matthew, 441n
Phillips, Mrs. Caroline, 95
Phillips, Philip, 153n
Phillips, Mrs. Philip, 153
Phillips, William D., 95n, 193
Phisse (slave), 340
Pike, William S., 23n, 123n, 165
Pinckney, Dr. Charles E., 52n
Pinkney, Theodore (The, Fedo), 52, 53n,
126, 179n, 247n, 251, 261, 265, 267,
505–7

Pinkney, William Elder (Will), 30–32, 52–53, 65, 75, 124–26, 128–29, 149, 165, 179n, 196, 200, 201, 211, 220–21, 226, 237, 245–46, 247n, 350, 401–3, 404, 426, 428, 429, 450, 505–6

Pinkney, Mrs. William Elder, 52–53, 402, 404

Piper, Jacob, 201

Plaquemine, La., 166, 257n

Pollock, George, Jr., 476n

Pollock, James, 476n

Ponchatoula, La., 262, 276, 447, 452, 460–61, 464, 469, 474, 479, 500

Pope, General John, 249, 277

Port Hudson, La., xxi, xxii, 52, 256, 262, 263, 265–66, 269n, 271, 274, 277, 286n, 303, 308n, 311, 318, 324, 325n, 327, 344, 345, 368, 375n, 411, 429, 430, 436n, 437, 439, 441, 451, 492n, 493, 504–5, 509n, 520n, 537, 540n, 541, 542, 544n, 595; siege of, xxi, 52n, 504–5; fortification of by Confederates, 52n; surrender of, 52n, 515, 517–18; Sarah's visits to, 274, 287–88, 333–38; Banks's advance on, 436–38; Union fleet's attempt to pass, 439–41

Port Republic, Va., 161n

Porter, Commodore William D., 193n, 277n

Postlethwaite, Mrs. J. C., 605

Postlewaithe, Jane, 605

Powell, Littleton M., 305, 365

Powell, Mordecai, 305

Powers, Hiram, 225n

Price, Almedia, 501–3, 510

Price, George R., 501n, 510

Price, Maud, 501n

Price, May, 501n

Prisons, military: Fort Warren, 66; Fort Jackson, 110n, 143, 144, 145, 146, 152; in New Orleans, 518, 520, 522, 523–24; Johnson's Island, 579, 581, 598, 599–600

Prisoners, 110, 114, 579; released from penitentiary at Baton Rouge, 228; brought to New Orleans from Port Hudson, 518–19, 520–24; at Johnson's Island, 581, 598–600

Prudent, Emile, 377

Purnell, Dr. George W., 220, 387n

Purnell, Mary, 220, 387

Randall, Dale B. J., xli

Raymond, Miss., 280n, 328n

Read, Lieutenant Charles W., 195–96, 198

Reeks, Austin John, xxxv

Renshaw, Henry, 27n

Renshaw, Medora, 27–28

Resolute, 157n

Richmond, 67n, 585

Richmond, Va., xxii, 50, 77n, 92, 107, 111n, 160, 161, 166, 266, 606

Riordan, B. R., xxxv

Ripley, Dwight, 235n

Ripley, Eliza McHatton, 44n, 165n, 183n, 235n

Ripley, Sarah, 259, 385, 387, 391, 456, 503n

Roberts, Mr., 143n

Roberts, Lieutenant Josiah, 110n

Roberts, Stephen, 110n

Robertson, James I., Jr., 325n

Robleaux, M., 372

Roland, Madame, 130

Ronaldson, Luther R., 211

Rose (slave), 42, 42n, 137, 150, 173n

Ross, Captain T. A., 360

Ruggles, General Daniel, 87n, 162, 166

Ryan, Mrs., 481

Ryan, Private James, 481, 483

St. Francisville, La., 223n

St. Martin, Alex, 231–32

St. Martin, William, 229–32

Salisbury, Private Henry, 495, 496n
Sambola, Anthony, 220
Scales, Midshipman Dabney M., 198, 200, 274, 290
Schuppert, Dr. Moritz, 417–18
Sciota, 59n
Scott, Colonel John S., 160n
Searle, Sir Francis, 495, 498
Secession, xv, xix, 36, 74, 410
Secession Convention, xv, 36
Seward, William H., 606–7
Sheppers, Louis, 167n
Shields, Lieutenant Colonel Thomas, 218
Shiloh, Battle of, xx, 40, 41, 53n, 441n, 502
Ship Island, 110n, 152–53
Shreveport, La., xxi, 144n
Siegling, General Rudolph, xxxix
Simonton, Colonel John M., 462
Slavery, xix, 330–31
Smith, Mr., 288
Smith, General Edmund Kirby, 258
Smith, Ida, 348
Smith, General Martin L., 325n
Smith, William, 522n
Smith, William Henry, 270n
Southworth, E.D.E.N., 270
Sparks, James H., 7, 35, 39–40, 43, 46, 113, 279, 308, 589
Sparks, William H., 44
Spratley, Major James W., 413, 417, 431–32, 522, 525, 542
Stanton, Edwin M., 143n, 145n
State House, xv, xviii, xix, xx, 9, 32, 67, 68, 106, 193, 225n, 228, 385, 513; burning of, 382
Steedman, Colonel I. G. W., 314, 334, 339, 389, 399–400, 406, 426–28, 431–33, 435, 439n, 441, 445, 449, 504, 515n, 519, 537, 552–57, 560–62, 566–69, 575–76, 597, 599; during imprisonment in New Orleans, 520–22, 523–24, 525–28, 529–32, 539–42, 544–

45; postwar meeting with Sarah, 532n, 545n
Steedman, Reuben, 339
Steedman, Captain Seth D., 389, 521, 539–40, 600
Stephens, Lieutenant Henry K., 198
Stith, James H., xviin, 19n, 30n, 124n, 385
Stith, Mattie Castleton, 19, 30, 104–5, 107, 124, 148, 177, 244–45, 278, 280–81, 385
Stone, Jane, 378–80, 381–82
Stone, Dr. John Wilmer, 378n
Stone, Midshipman S. G., 149
Stone, Dr. Warren, 450, 489
Sugar: manufacture of, 326, 328, 330–31
Sugar Planter (West Baton Rouge), 143n
Sumter, 196n
Szymanski, Colonel Ignatius, 474

Talbott, Midshipman Daniel B., 195, 197, 198, 201, 211, 274
Taylor, General Richard, 491n, 509n
Taylor, Zachary, xviiin
Tchefuncta River, 466, 472, 475, 477, 516
Tiche (slave), xxv, 17, 33, 88–89, 91, 95, 112, 114, 115, 129, 132, 173n, 181, 191, 212, 241, 243, 250, 279, 439, 463, 474–75, 477–78, 481
Todd, Captain John W., 608–9
Trenholm, George A., xxxin, 315–16, 604
Trenholm, Helen. *See* Morgan, Helen Trenholm
Trezevant, Fanny Davidson, 92, 254n, 279
Trezevant, James H., 36, 40, 41–42, 92n, 306
Tunnard, Mr., 105, 107, 171, 185
Tunnard, Alexander, 105n
Tunnard, William F., 105n
Tupelo, Miss., 104n
Turner, Miss, 202

Ullmann, General Daniel, 492n

Van Dorn, General Earl, 138, 154
Van Ingen, Private J. S., 373–74
Vanderbilt, 581n
Vanderbilt, Gloria, xlin
Vanderbilt, Gloria Morgan, 489n
Vanderbilt, Reginald C., 489n
Vicksburg, Miss., xxi, 49n, 50, 75, 111,
    124, 128, 149, 165, 169, 181n, 195n,
    196, 198n, 266n, 277, 324, 385n, 438,
    504, 514–15, 517–18
Virginia, 196n

Waller, William G., 16, 55, 102, 181,
    236, 250
Walsh, Henry, 9, 226, 254
Walter, Fanny, 190n
Walter, Mrs. Leocadie, 190n, 204–5, 208
Walter, Margaret, 190, 203, 204, 205
Warley, Lieutenant Alexander F., 66
Watson, George Washington, 203–6
Watson, William, 143n, 307n
Watt, John W., 570
West, Captain Edward, 278
Westover plantation, 185–86, 189
Wheat, Captain J. T., 40
Whitaker, Mrs. Rebecca, 259n
White Sulphur Springs, xxxv, xxxviii

Whiteman, 206
Wilcox, Mr., 591
Williams, Anna, 171
Williams, J. M., 94n, 171n, 213n
Williams, General Thomas, xxi, 99, 105,
    106–7, 108, 109, 114, 123n, 143, 153n,
    165n, 172n, 177, 181n, 202n, 206, 216,
    235n, 236; death of, xxi, 192–94, 201
Wilson (slave), 330
Wilson, Edmund, xxvi
Wilson, Major T. Friend, 451, 522
Wilson, Colonel William, 68, 76
Winona, 59n
Wissahickon, 67n
Withers, Colonel William T., 228
Wolfe, Henry L., 167n
Wolff, John L., 167n
Woods, Dr. A. V., 11–16, 43, 44, 45, 222,
    373, 397, 403–4, 407, 611
Woodward, C. Vann, xxvi
Wool, General John E., 276
Worley, Caleb, 251n, 271n, 297
Worley, Esther, 251n, 271n, 275, 287,
    300, 309, 325, 352, 354, 363, 454
Worley, Fred, 271, 348
Worthington, Lieutenant W. M., 469,
    475, 480
Wyatt-Brown, Bertram, xvi, xviin